*The Great
Republic*

The Great Republic

Nineteenth and
Early Twentieth-Century
America, 1820–1920

FOURTH EDITION

Bernard Bailyn
Harvard University

Robert Dallek
*University of California,
Los Angeles*

David Brion Davis
Yale University

David Herbert Donald
Harvard University

John L. Thomas
Brown University

Gordon S. Wood
Brown University

D. C. HEATH AND COMPANY
LEXINGTON, MASSACHUSETTS TORONTO

Address editorial correspondence to:

D. C. Heath
125 Spring Street
Lexington, MA 02173

SPECIAL NOTE

*T*HIS version of *The Great Republic* has been prepared for the use of readers who desire a one-volume history of the United States from 1820 to 1920. It encompasses Parts Three to Five of the fourth edition of the work and thus includes the complete text of all the chapters by David Brion Davis, David Herbert Donald, and John Thomas as they appear in the two-volume complete version.

For the convenience of readers, the Publisher's Foreword and the Introduction also appear exactly as in the complete version. The present volume, however, has been repaginated and provided with its own index.

PUBLISHER'S FOREWORD

$\int$INCE it was first published in 1977 *The Great Republic* has held an honored place in the small company of truly distinguished and pathbreaking textbooks in American history. The work's authoritative scholarship, interpretive richness, and elegant style have been widely recognized and admired, not only among teachers of United States history courses but among historians in general. As Bernard Bailyn recently stated, "Every historian—however technical—has an obligation to reach out to a broad public because the purpose of the whole effort is to make a culture aware of its origins and development." D. C. Heath is proud to be the publisher of this work in which these distinguished historians have set out to reach that wider public.

Those familiar with earlier editions will find all the original qualities still here: a supple literary style; sufficient detail to provide supporting evidence and memorable examples; special attention to the colonial- and Revolutionary-era origins of the American experience; a dedication to tracing the subtle interconnections of social, economic, and cultural strands with the history of public events; and a consistent commitment to explaining the importance of ideas— whether formally articulated or unspoken—in the shaping of history. But over the years *The Great Republic* has been refined in response to classroom experience and the evolution of historical scholarship, and we believe that this fourth edition is the finest version yet. Throughout the book, of course, the authors have drawn upon recent research to keep the interpretation up-to-date. For example, contemporary historians' fruitful work on the history of native Americans has enriched this account of our history. In the antebellum chapters, previous limitations of space have been slightly relaxed, allowing for more contemporary quotations and anecdotes that render the analysis less abstract, and the role of the 1857 depression in shaping the decade's disastrous political crisis receives more attention. The treatment of Reconstruction has been reorganized for greater clarity and to eliminate overlapping coverage of post–Civil War economic and political issues at the end of Part Four and the beginning of Part Five. Chapters 22 and 23 have been thoroughly rewritten, not only to achieve a more concentrated focus on Gilded Age economic and political topics, but also for greater interpretive clarity. And Part Six, which traces American history since 1920, has been expanded and rewritten. Readers will now find its central thread—the reshaping of progressivism into modern liberalism in the New Deal era, the liberal triumph in the 1960s, and the subsequent crisis of liberal ideas and policies—much more clearly described.

An even more dramatic change in the fourth edition is the book's format. As a publisher, D. C. Heath is acutely aware of the rapidly rising cost of producing elaborate full-color textbooks. Clearly, such a format has pedagogical as well as aesthetic justifications. But many instructors object to the higher price that their students must inevitably pay for a full-color textbook. We believe that *The Great Republic* will have a particularly strong appeal to those history teachers for whom the sacrifice of color illustrations is worth a substantial reduction in the net cost of the book. With this edition we have striven for a clean, elegant appearance, well illustrated with crisply reproduced black-and-white photographs chosen for their quality as visual documents. At the same time we have retained color where it is most necessary—in the book's broad array of maps.

Instructors should also welcome another feature of the fourth edition: the extensive set of supplements that they can add to the textbook, mostly at little or no cost. Neal Stout of the University of Vermont has written a stimulating student's guide to the study of history, *Getting the Most Out of Your U.S. History Course,* that is available free of charge to every student who purchases a new copy of either volume. A challenging workbook in historical geography, *Surveying the Land* by Robert Grant of Framingham State University, is also available to student readers at their instructor's request. So are two documentary anthologies that focus on American regional history: *Document Sets for the South in U.S. History* by Richard Purday of North Georgia College and *Document Sets for Texas and the Southwest in U.S. History* by J'Nell L. Pate of Collin County Community College. The *Study Guide* that accompanies *The Great Republic,* revised for this edition by Patrick Reagan of Tennessee Technological University, offers students a wealth of practical aids. Instructors may also order for their students' use a menu-driven computerized version of the *Study Guide,* available for Macintosh, IBM, and IBM-compatible computers.

For instructors' use, Heath also makes available an *Instructor's Guide and Test Item File,* revised for this edition by Herbert Lasky of Eastern Illinois University, offering a great many classroom-tested suggestions for teaching the survey course with *The Great Republic,* as well as over a thousand questions for quizzes and examinations. These questions are also available on disk—for IBM computers in both 3½- and 5¼-inch formats, and for the Macintosh computer. All the book's maps are reproduced on acetate transparencies. Ivan Steen of the State University of New York, Albany, has created for Heath a cassette tape of recordings of speeches, songs, and other aural documents from American history, which many instructors will find an important and intriguing supplement to their lectures.

For further information about these supplements and to arrange to receive them, instructors should contact their D. C. Heath campus or telemarketing representative, or telephone D. C. Heath toll-free at 1-800-235-3565.

Publisher and authors alike owe a deep debt of gratitude to the historians who reviewed the book, in whole or in part, specifically: **Carl Abbott,** Portland State University; **Guy Alchon,** University of Delaware; **Charles Alexander,** Ohio University; **David Bernstein,** California State University, Long Beach; **Iver Bernstein,** Washington University; **W. Roger Biles,** Oklahoma State University; **Bernard Burke,** Portland State University; **David Burner,** State University of New York, Stony Brook; **Paul Bushnell,** Illinois Wesleyan University; **Dorothy Brown,** Georgetown University; **David Colburn,** University of Florida; **John Milton**

Cooper, University of Wisconsin, Madison; **David Danbom,** North Dakota State University; **Michael Ebner,** Lake Forest College; **Leon Fink,** University of North Carolina, Chapel Hill; **Larry Gerber,** Auburn University; **David Hammack,** Case Western University; **Michael W. Homel,** East Michigan University; **Bruce Kuklick,** University of Pennsylvania; **Allan Lichtman,** American University; **Norman Markowitz,** Rutgers University; **Alan Matusow,** Rice University; **George McJimsey,** Iowa State University; **Anne McLaurin,** Louisiana State University, Shreveport; **Samuel T. McSeveney,** Vanderbilt University; **Thomas Mega,** University of St. Thomas; **Keith Olson,** University of Maryland, College Park; **Richard Pohlenberg,** Cornell University; **Carroll Pursell,** Case Western Reserve University; **James Rawley,** University of Nebraska, Lincoln; **Patrick Reagan,** Tennessee Technological University; **Leo Ribuffo,** George Washington University; **Judith Riddle,** Jefferson College; **Donald Rogers,** University of Hartford; **Nick Salvatore,** Cornell University; **Robert D. Schulzinger,** University of Colorado, Boulder; **June Sochen,** Northeast Illinois University; **Robert Thomas,** University of Washington; **Charles Tull,** Indiana University, South Bend; **Jules Tygiel,** San Francisco State University; and **William Wagnon,** Washburn University.

Many members of D. C. Heath's staff assisted ably in producing this edition. Special thanks are due to Andrea Cava and Martha Wetherill for long hours of painstaking work as production editors, to Henry Rachlin for design, to Martha Friedman and Martha Shethar for photo research, to Charles Dutton for overseeing the manufacturing process, and to Irene Cinelli for expertly producing the supplements.

James Miller
Senior Editor, History

INTRODUCTION

*T*HIS book is a history of the American people, from the earliest European settlements in the New World to the present. We call our book "The Great Republic," adopting a phrase that Winston Churchill used to describe the United States. No one can doubt the greatness of the American Republic if it is measured by the size of our national domain, the vastness of our economic productivity, or the stability of our governmental institutions. Less certain has been its greatness in the realm of culture, in the uses of power, and in the distribution of social justice. Our purpose has been to present a balanced story of American development—a story of great achievement, of enormous material success, and of soaring idealism, but also one of conflict, of turbulent factionalism, and of injustice, rootlessness, and grinding disorder.

Three general themes unify the six sections of this book. The first is the development of free political institutions in America. Understanding the United States today requires knowledge of conditions in the colonial period that made popular self-government at first possible, then likely, and in the end necessary. In the American Revolution the longings of provincial Britons for a total reformation of political culture were implemented in American political institutions. During the first half of the nineteenth century, democratic institutions and practices expanded to the limits of the continent, and they received their crucial testing in the American Civil War. By the twentieth century, urbanization and industrialization profoundly changed American society, but our democracy survived all of these changes, as well as depressions, international crises, and world wars. To understand why today, in the last decade of the twentieth century, no significant groups of Americans question our free institutions requires an understanding of how these institutions evolved from eighteenth-century republicanism to modern mass democracy.

Our second theme is the tension that has always existed in America between the interests of groups with special goals and needs and those of the society as a whole. From the beginning the New World, with its abundant resources, stimulated ambitions among the shrewd, the enterprising, and the energetic that often conflicted with the shared needs of the entire populace. The enormous expanse of the country and the admixture of peoples from every quarter of the world encouraged social fragmentation and fostered cultural diversity. But from colonial times to the present, there have been countervailing forces working for social stability and cultural homogeneity.

The Founding Fathers of the Republic were aware that there would be no automatic harmonizing of regional, economic, and social interests, and they worried that minorities might become subject to the tyranny of majorities. At the same time, they feared a centralized government powerful enough to impose order on these conflicting and local interests and active enough to defend the weak against the powerful. In the national and state constitutions they devised a mechanism for the mediation of struggles and for the protection of human rights. In the years since, the balance between the general welfare and the welfare of regions, states, and economic and social groups has often been precarious, and our book shows how, from time to time, that balance has tipped, sometimes in the direction of social order and stability, sometimes in favor of minority interests and individual rights. Much of our story deals with successive attempts, never fully satisfactory, to reconcile the needs of the whole country with the interests of the parts.

Our third theme reflects our recognition that the history of the United States has always been part of a larger history. Except for the native Americans, who had developed a complex and diverse indigenous civilization, the early settlers in America were all immigrants who brought with them the beliefs, values, and cultural legacy of the European and African societies in which they had been born. Naturally, then, developments in America have been closely and inextricably related to those abroad. We believe that the American Revolution, for all of its distinctiveness, needs to be viewed as one in a series of great democratic revolutions that swept the Western world. We think the leveling of social distinctions and the democratization of political life in Jacksonian America are closely related to similar contemporary movements in Europe. And we have stressed that the urbanization, mechanization, and bureaucratization of the United States by the end of the nineteenth century paralleled, copied, and influenced like transformations in the other modernizing nations.

By the twentieth century the connections between developments in the United States and those in the world at large became even closer, and the final sections of our book trace the emergence of the United States as a world power. We have told the story of our involvement in two devastating world wars, in addition to other, smaller conflicts all over the globe, from Korea to Vietnam to the Persian Gulf. We have shown how, in recent decades, the president of the United States has become the most influential political leader in the world, how variations in the American economy have affected the well-being of all other nations, and how, for better or worse, American popular culture has reached a global audience. At the same time, we have emphasized that changes in other parts of the world have profoundly affected American political life, economic growth, and social organization. In short, we have written an American history that is part of world history.

In presenting these three themes, the authors have started from a shared view of the nature of history. We all believe that history is a mode of understanding, not merely a collection of information about the past. Our obligation is not simply to describe what happened, but to explain it, to make clear why things developed as they did. We share, too, an aversion to any deterministic interpretation of history. At certain times economic and demographic forces are dominant, but they are themselves shaped by cultural forces. Great political events are sometimes triggered by economic drives, but at other times they are responses to ideologies.

We do not believe, then, that the course of American history was predetermined. The present condition of our national life has to be explained historically, stage by stage. In the pages that follow, we present both a narrative and an analysis of how the United States has come to be what it is today—a great power, but still a Great Republic, where freedom and equality are dreams that can become realities.

B. B.   D. H. D.
R. D.   J. L. T.
D. B. D.   G. S. W.

CONTENTS

PART THREE
Nationalizing the Republic, 1877–1920   353
John L. Thomas
Introduction   354

MAPS AND CHARTS

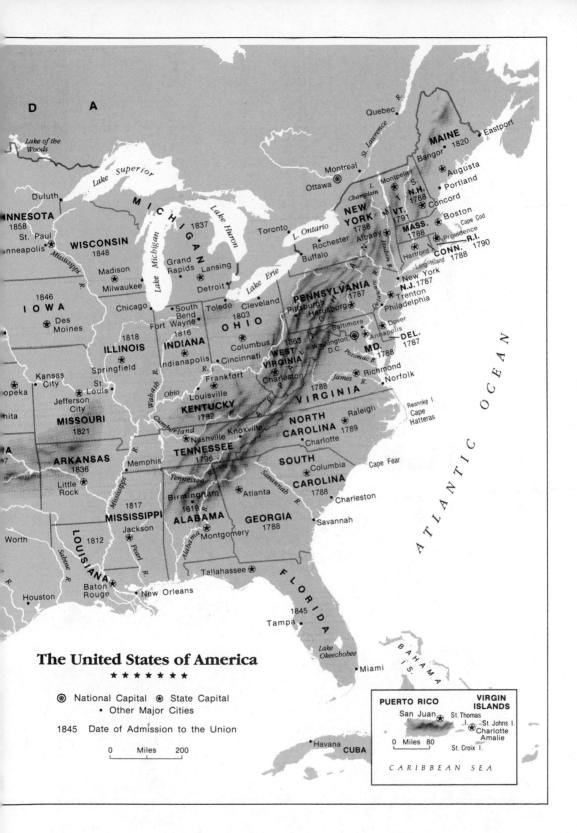

The United States of America

★ ★ ★ ★ ★ ★ ★ ★

◉ National Capital ⊛ State Capital
• Other Major Cities

1845 Date of Admission to the Union

0 ⊢———————⊣ 200
Miles

D A

Lake of the
Woods

Duluth

MINNESOTA
1858

St. Paul
Minneapolis

Mississippi R.

1846

IOWA

Des Moines

Lake Superior

M I C H I G A N

WISCONSIN
1848

Madison

Milwaukee

Lake Michigan

1837

Lake Huron

Grand
Rapids   Lansing

Detroit

Kansas
City

Topeka

Jefferson
City

Wichita

MISSOURI
1821

St.
Louis

Springfield

ILLINOIS

1818

Chicago

South
Bend
Fort Wayne

INDIANA
1816

Indianapolis

Cincinnati

Wabash R.

Ohio R.

Frankfort

KENTUCKY
1792

Louisville

Cumberland R.

Nashville

Memphis

TENNESSEE
1796

Tennessee R.

ARKANSAS
1836

Little
Rock

Mississippi R.

1817

MISSISSIPPI

Jackson

Pearl R.

Birmingham
1819

ALABAMA

Montgomery

Alabama R.

Fort
Worth

Houston

LOUISIANA
1812

Sabine R.

Baton
Rouge

New Orleans

R.

Toledo

Cleveland

OHIO
1803

Columbus

WEST
VIRGINIA
1863

Charleston

Knoxville

Charlotte

NORTH
CAROLINA
1789

SOUTH
CAROLINA
1788

Columbia

Charleston

GEORGIA
1788

Atlanta

Savannah R.

Savannah

Tallahassee

F L O R I D A
1845

Tampa

Lake
Okeechobee

Miami

Quebec

St. Lawrence R.

Montreal

Ottawa ◉

Toronto

L. Ontario

Rochester

Buffalo

Pittsburgh

PENNSYLVANIA
1787

Harrisburg

MAINE
1820

Bangor

Augusta

Portland

Concord

Boston

Providence

Hartford

Eastport

L. Champlain

Montpelier

N.H.
1788

VT.
1791

MASS.
1788

CONN.
1788

R.I.
1790

Cape Cod

NEW
YORK
1788

Albany

Hudson R.

Long Island

New York

N.J. 1787

Trenton

Philadelphia

Dover

DEL.
1787

Delaware R.

Baltimore

Annapolis

Washington,
D.C.

MD.
1788

Potomac R.

Richmond

Norfolk

VIRGINIA
1788

James R.

Raleigh

Reannke I.
Cape
Hatteras

Cape Fear

Lake Erie

A T L A N T I C   O C E A N

BAHAMA IS.

Havana

CUBA

CARIBBEAN SEA

PUERTO RICO

San Juan

VIRGIN
ISLANDS

St. Thomas
I.

St. Johns I.

Charlotte
Amalie

St. Croix I.

0 ⊢—————⊣ 80
Miles

PART ONE

Expanding the
Republic
1820–1860

David Brion Davis

$\mathcal{T}$HE END of the American Enlightenment and of the Revolutionary period also marked the end of attempts to model American society on European blueprints. By the 1820s it was becoming clear that the American people would quickly leap across restraints and limits of every kind. They were expansive, self-assertive, and extravagantly optimistic, and they believed that they had a God-given right to pursue happiness. In a nation of supposedly infinite promise, there could be no permanent barriers to the people's aspirations toward wealth and self-improvement.

This absence of barriers, of distinctions of rank, and of prescribed identities was what the famous French social critic Alexis de Tocqueville meant by "the general equality of condition among the people." When he visited the United States in 1831, nothing struck Tocqueville more forcibly than this leveling of ancient and inherited distinctions of rank. He took it to be "the fundamental fact" about American society; all other facts seemed "to be derived" from it. Tocqueville was aware of the economic and racial inequalities of American society. Indeed, he suggested that precisely the lack of traditional restraints, such as those associated with a landed aristocracy, opened the way for racial oppression and for a new kind of aristocracy created by business and manufacturing. A racial minority, such as the African Americans, seemed more vulnerable in a society where all white males were eager to assert their own equality.

All societies require a system of rules, restraints, and limits. In a traditional, premodern society, such as the European feudal regime to which Tocqueville looked back with some nostalgia, there was a certain stability to the territorial boundaries of a kingdom, an estate, or a people. Similarly, few people in such a traditional society questioned the customary rules that defined social rank, the rights and duties of lords and peasants, the inheritance of land, the limits of political power and economic enterprise, and the expectations appropriate for each individual. Men and women knew what they had been born to, what place they had been assigned by fate. There was a close relation between the narrow boundaries of the physical environment and the social boundaries that political, legal, and religious institutions imposed.

The United States, as Tocqueville repeatedly emphasized, had thus far managed to avoid anarchy while greatly expanding most people's possibilities of life. From the time of the first colonial settlements, Americans had evolved institutions that had ensured a degree of order and stability in social life, protecting the public good from the worst excesses of acquisitive self-interest. This protection of the public good had been the preeminent goal of republican political culture. By the early nineteenth century, however, there was a growing faith that the public good would best be served by allowing maximum freedom to the individual pursuit of self-interest.

In the period 1820–60 this drive for individual self-betterment led to an unprecedented economic and territorial expansion, to the migration of millions of Europeans to America, and to the settlement of millions of Americans in the new states and territories of the West. Much of the nation's foreign policy was devoted to extending territorial boundaries and to preventing European attempts to impose future barriers to American influence and expansion in the Western Hemisphere. Federal land policy encouraged rapid settlement of the West. Both national and state governments committed a large share of public resources to the construction of roads, canals, and railroads to overcome the barriers of mountains and increasing distance. Government at all levels actively sought to stimulate growth and economic opportunity. Much of the political ideology of the period was directed against forces and institutions, such as the Second Bank of the United States, that could be portrayed as restricting individual opportunity.

But for many thoughtful Americans, reformers as well as conservatives, there was a danger that these expansive energies would erode all respect for order, balance, and community purpose. The fear arose that the competitive spirit would lead to a fragmented society ruled by the principle "every man for himself and the devil take the hindmost." Some worried that the American people would become enslaved to money, success, and material gratification, and that the centrifugal forces of expansion would cause the nation to fly apart.

Most of the proposed remedies to social problems centered on the critical need to shape and reform individual character. Rather than looking to constitutional reforms or governmental programs, most Americans sought social change through the moral reformation of individuals. They believed that if self-interest could be enlightened by a sense of social responsibility, the nation could be saved from the dehumanizing effects of commercialism and competitive strife. This improvement of the individual was the great goal of the public schools, the religious revivals, and most of the new reform movements. It was a mission that gave a new importance and an educational role to mothers and to the middle-class home. In one sense these efforts at shaping character embodied a nostalgic desire to restore a lost sense of community and united purpose. But the crusades for moral improvement also served to modernize society, for they encouraged predictable and responsible behavior and moreover aimed at giving moral legitimacy to a market-oriented society—that is, to a society governed by the standards of economic exchange, of supply and demand.

The issue of black slavery—the South's "peculiar institution"—finally dramatized the conflict between self-interest and the ideal of a righteous society, a society that could think of itself as "under God." And it was the westward expansion of black slavery that ultimately became the testing ground for defining and challenging limits—the territorial limits of slavery, the limits of federal power, and the limits of popular sovereignty and self-determination. For most of the period, these matters remained ambiguous. This ambiguity allowed the North and South to expand together and resolve periodic conflicts by compromise.

By the 1850s, however, southern leaders were insisting that the equal rights of slaveholders would be subverted unless the federal government guaranteed the protection of slave property in the common territories. Northern leaders, eventually including many moderates who had always favored compromise, drew a firm line against imposing slavery on a territory against the wishes of the majority of settlers. To paraphrase the twentieth-century poet Robert Frost, the territorial question came down to what Americans were willing to wall in or wall out. In one form or another, Americans had to face the question of whether, in a free society, any limits could be imposed on the total domination of one person over another.

1

Population Growth and Economic Expansion

$\approx$

O UNDERSTAND the American experience during the four decades preceding the Civil War, one must grasp the dimensions of demographic and economic change that occurred during this period. Other nations have undergone periods of rapid growth and industrialization, accompanied by painful cultural adjustment and social conflict. In general, however, this modernizing experience has occurred in long-settled communities with traditions, customs, and class interests that served simultaneously as barriers to change and stabilizers of society. What distinguished American history in the period 1820–60 was that a modern market economy emerged in conjunction with the rapid settlement of "virgin land" and the unprecedented expansion of the western frontier.

There were few barriers to this double process, and the American people were determined to overcome what barriers there were. The American economy showed a remarkable freedom in the flow of goods, people, and capital in response to market forces. The ease with which resources were shifted from region to region and from agriculture to commerce or industry accounted for much of the economic growth in the early and mid-nineteenth century. No laws restricted the influx of European and Asian laborers. The Constitution ruled out any taxes on American exports. Thanks largely to southern pressure, the federal government gradually lowered protective tariffs on imports. The federal government's sale and donation of immense tracts of public land were intended to encourage individual enterprise in a free and unregulated market. Political stability, even in the rapidly created new states, helped to guarantee the security of private property and the legal enforcement of contracts. The states themselves actively promoted economic growth, but no other society had imposed so few fiscal, political, religious, and social restraints on the marketplace. No other society had been so confident that market forces constituted the "invisible hand" that kept the competitive economy in balance. No other society had become so

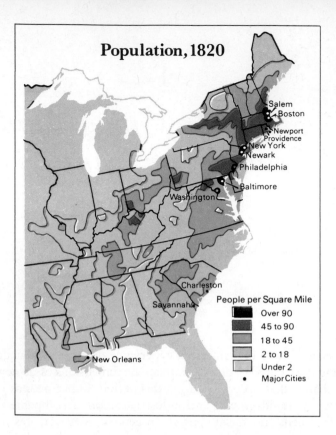

Population, 1820

Salem
Boston
Newport
Providence
New York
Newark
Philadelphia
Baltimore
Washington
Charleston
Savannah
New Orleans

People per Square Mile
Over 90
45 to 90
18 to 45
2 to 18
Under 2
• Major Cities

committed to the goals of maximizing individual profits by increasing productivity and lowering costs.

The result of this extraordinary freedom from limitations, along with the availability of land and the somewhat lagging availability of labor and capital, was extremely rapid economic growth. As perceived and experienced by living human beings, however, this growth was both liberating and extremely disruptive. "While trade is destined to free and employ the masses," Henry W. Bellows pointed out in 1845, "it is also destined to destroy for the time much of the beauty and happiness of every land. . . . We are free. . . . But the excitement, the commercial activity, the restlessness, to which this state of affairs has given birth, is far from being a desirable or a natural condition." Commercial expansion destroyed family self-sufficiency, pride in craftsmanship, and personal and family ties that unified residential communities with local economic markets. "We learn to live within ourselves," Bellows lamented, "we grow unsocial, unfraternal in feeling; and the sensibility, the affection, the cordiality, the putting forth of graces of a warm and virtuous heart, die or disuse . . . the domestic and social virtues languish."

Although the growth of national markets broadened the range of individual choice for businessmen, there was little choice for native Americans, slaves, unskilled laborers, landless farmers, and domestic servants: in short, for all those who were excluded by force or circumstance from the benefits of the market.

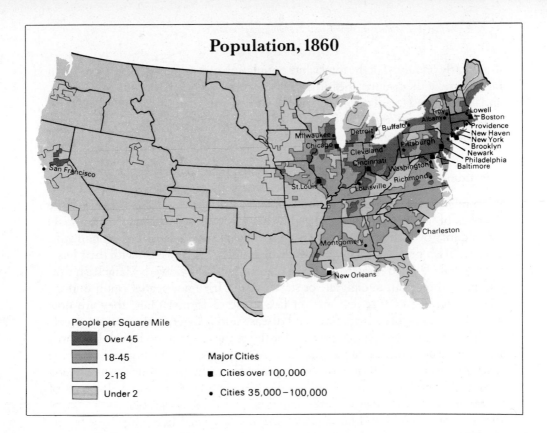

Population, 1860

People per Square Mile

- Over 45
- 18–45
- 2–18
- Under 2

Major Cities

- ■ Cities over 100,000
- • Cities 35,000–100,000

Cities labeled on map: San Francisco, Milwaukee, Chicago, Detroit, Buffalo, Cleveland, Cincinnati, Pittsburgh, St. Louis, Louisville, Washington, Richmond, Troy, Albany, Lowell, Boston, Providence, New Haven, New York, Brooklyn, Newark, Philadelphia, Baltimore, Charleston, Montgomery, New Orleans

Despite a generally rising standard of living, Americans in the pre–Civil War decades witnessed growing economic inequalities. Moreover, the nation's triumphs in economic and territorial expansion depended on two forms of outright racial exploitation: the forcible removal of the Indian people from rich lands east of the Great Plains; and the forced labor of black slaves who produced invaluable exports, mainly cotton, that helped finance America's economic growth.

Population Growth, Immigration, and Urbanization

From 1820 to 1860, America's population maintained the extraordinary rate of growth that had characterized the colonial and post-Revolutionary periods. The population increased by an average of 35 percent every decade, and the total population continued to double every twenty-five years. The United States sustained this high rate of growth until the 1860s. During the nineteenth century no European nation achieved a growth rate one-half as high as America's for even two decades.

America's population growth cannot be attributed to any single, consistent cause. Before the mid-1840s most of the population growth resulted from the remarkable fertility—the rate of reproduction—of the American people, reinforced by a relatively low rate of infant mortality. Like many countries in modern Africa and South America, the United States literally swarmed with children. In

1830 nearly one-third of the total white population was under the age of ten. Yet in most parts of the country the birthrate had actually begun to decline before 1810, and it continued to fall throughout the century. By the 1840s it was only the influx of European immigrants, who accounted for one-quarter of the total population increase in that decade, that maintained the previous rate of national growth.

The Immigrants   Immigration was partly the result of economic distress in Europe. Few Europeans would have left for America if population growth in their homelands had not pressed hard on available supplies of land, food, and jobs, and if they had not been displaced and made expendable by technological change in a capitalist, industrializing economy. In 1845 the Irish potato crop—which provided most ordinary Irish with their basic food supply—failed disastrously. Five years of famine followed. Many Irish thus had little choice but to emigrate or starve. As an Irish newspaper put it in 1847: "The emigrants of this year are not like those of former ones; they are now actually running away from fever and disease and hunger, with money scarcely sufficient to pay passage for and food for the voyage." And the British landlords who controlled Ireland helped to subsidize emigration in the hope of reducing taxes that were being levied for the support of workhouses, which were spilling over with starving laborers who had been evicted from the land. In parts of Germany and Scandinavia, governments encouraged emigration as a way of draining off unemployed farmers and artisans, who had been displaced by the modernization of agriculture and by competition from imported machine-made goods.

But the most important stimulus to immigration was the promise of jobs in the United States. Immigration soared during America's years of greatest prosperity, and it lagged during America's years of economic recession. Mass emigration from Europe was a direct response to the sudden demand in America for labor in construction and manufacturing, and to the supposedly limitless opportunity for landownership in the West. American promoters, representing shipping firms, labor contractors, manufacturers, and even the governments of western states, enticed Europeans with glowing accounts of the United States. More persuasive were the reports of fellow villagers or family members who had already crossed the Atlantic. "A poor man in Ireland could not do better than come here," one immigrant wrote to his father, "for it is the truth of a good country." Another recent Irish immigrant reported to his sister in 1841: "It would give me great pleasure to think that you Come here, for i think you would do verry well in this Country. . . . And my sister Bridget do what she can to come here. Let my sister Ellen know that she would get five shillings to six for making one dress here." In the 1830s, when northwestern Europe became aware of America's economic boom, of the North's shortage of labor, and of the opening of vast tracts of farmland in the West, the number of immigrants rose to nearly 600,000—approximately a fourfold increase over the previous decade. In the 1840s the number soared to about 1.5 million, and in the 1850s to about 2.8 million.

Emigration Agent's Office
By the 1840s the expansion of transatlantic commerce had greatly reduced the westbound steerage fare from Europe to America. Nevertheless, many emigrants, such as the Irish portrayed here, had to depend on loans, charitable gifts, or funds sent from relatives in America.

The swelling stream, although it originated almost entirely from north-western Europe, was anything but homogeneous. It included illiterate peasants from Germany and Ireland; highly skilled artisans from England, Germany, Belgium, and Switzerland; political refugees escaping the repression that followed the abortive European revolutions of 1830 and 1848; and Jews and other victims of religious discrimination. The Germans amounted to about 1.3 million immigrants, and many had sufficient funds to purchase farms in the West or at least to make their way to thriving German communities in Cincinnati, St. Louis, and Milwaukee. The Irish, numbering some 1.7 million, had few skills and often arrived penniless, traveling in the holds of westbound ships that had carried American lumber, grain, cotton, and other bulk products to Europe.

Cast off by Britain as an unwanted population, the Irish peasants were in effect dumped in the northeastern port cities or sometimes in Canada, from which they migrated southward. Many Irish immigrants grew so discouraged by the "overstocked" labor market that they returned to Ireland. Others gradually found employment in heavy construction work, in foundries and factories, and in domestic service. But for a while they swelled enormously the ranks of the recipients of public and private welfare.

Before the Civil War the proportion of foreign-born in the population as a whole never rose above 15 percent, but in Boston and New York City by the 1850s the figure had climbed to more than 50 percent. Over half the foreign-born lived in Ohio, Pennsylvania, and New York. This concentration of immigrants greatly accelerated the growth of cities in the Northeast and of the towns and villages along the Great Lakes and in the Ohio and Mississippi river valleys.

Urban Growth and Population Mobility   In 1860 four out of five Americans still lived in rural environments—that is, on farms or in settlements of less than 2,500. Nevertheless, by 1850 more than half the populations of Massachusetts and Rhode Island lived in urban centers; the United States as a whole did not become so urbanized until the 1920s. By 1860 eight American cities (three of them west of the Appalachian Mountains) had more than 150,000 inhabitants, a population that was exceeded at the time by only seven cities in industrial England. Although America could boast no metropolis equivalent to London, in 1860 the combined populations of Manhattan and Brooklyn exceeded 1 million. New York City, endowed with a superior harbor and with the Hudson River, which provided deep-water navigation into the interior, had won a further competitive advantage over other East Coast cities when in 1818 its merchants established the first regular scheduled sailings to Europe. Seven years later the Erie Canal opened cheap access to the Great Lakes and to the markets of the West. The success with which New Yorkers consolidated commercial capital and expanded transport routes led one observer to assert: "The great city of New York wields more of the destinies of this great nation than five times the population of any other portion of the country." Many immigrants, after crossing the Atlantic, simply settled where they landed. Philip H. Bagenal, an English traveler, noted that newcomers "blocked up the channels of immigration at the entrance, and remain like the sand which lies at the bar of a river mouth." Immigrants arrived and stayed in New York because it was America's great seaport and commercial center, a crucible of risk and opportunity.

Overall, the declining birthrate resulted in a slightly higher average age for the American population, but the influx of immigrants greatly enlarged the number of northeasterners between the ages of twenty and thirty. In 1850 more than 70 percent of the American people were still under thirty, a figure that takes on greater meaning when compared with the 63 percent for England and the 52 percent for France. Before the Civil War the Americans remained an extraordinarily youthful people, a circumstance that helps to account for their restlessness, their venturesomeness, and their impatience with boundaries of any kind.

Alexis de Tocqueville echoed the amazement of many Europeans at the "strange unrest" of a people who could be seen "continually to change their track for fear of missing the shortest cut to happiness":

> In the United States a man builds a house in which to spend his old age, and he sells it before the roof is on . . . he brings a field into tillage and leaves other men to gather the crops; he embraces a profession and gives it up; he settles in a place, which he soon afterwards leaves to carry his changeable longings elsewhere . . . and if at the end of a year of unremitting labor he finds he has a few days' vacation, his eager curiosity whirls him over the vast extent of the United States, and he will travel fifteen hundred miles in a few days to shake off his

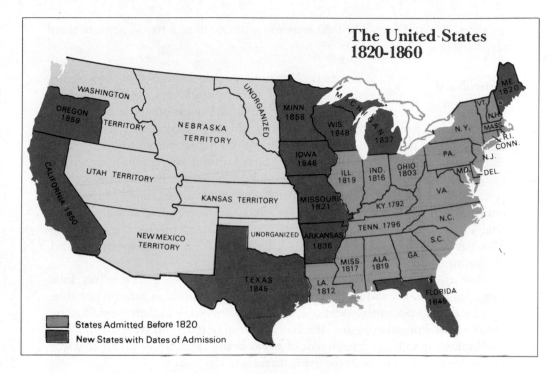

The United States
1820-1860

States Admitted Before 1820
New States with Dates of Admission

happiness. Death at length overtakes him, but it is before he is weary of his bootless chase of that complete felicity which forever escapes him.

This sense of limitless possibility helps explain the feverish westward rush of population. By 1860 the settled area of the United States was five times what it had been in 1790, and nearly half the people lived beyond the 1790 boundaries of settlement. As late as 1820 many Americans had thought it would take at least a century to settle the vast territory west of the Mississippi River. In 1860 the United States had firmly established its present continental boundaries, except for Alaska. No other nation had populated so much new territory in so short a time or had absorbed so many immigrants. No other had combined rapid urbanization with the dramatic expansion of an agricultural frontier and a transportation network.

Agriculture

Before the Civil War the majority of American families made their livings by supplying the primary human needs for food and clothing. Agriculture dominated the economy and provided the commodities for most of the nation's domestic and foreign trade. Even in towns and cities, families customarily kept a vegetable garden and perhaps a pig, a cow, and chickens. Many of the most seasoned urbanites could at least remember the smell of a barnyard from their childhoods.

Agricultural Expansion

The period 1820–60 was distinguished by two trends that might at first seem contradictory. On the one hand, the quickening pace of urbanization and industrialization brought a decisive shift toward nonagricultural employment. This shift had actually begun in the late eighteenth century, but it had started to slow before 1820, when approximately 71 percent of the labor force was gainfully employed in agriculture. By 1850, however, the proportion of farmers had fallen to 55 percent. This was the most rapid structural change in the economy during the entire nineteenth century. On the other hand, the same period saw a phenomenal expansion of agriculture into the "virgin lands" of the West and the Old Southwest, accompanied by revolutionary changes in transportation and marketing.

But these two trends were actually intimately related. The urban East provided the capital and markets that made the agricultural expansion possible. The food and fiber of the West and Old Southwest were indispensable for the industries and urban growth of the East. Western farming, fur trapping, mining, and lumbering were the spearheads of an expansive capitalist economy that was increasingly integrated with the great markets of the world.

A nation of farmers is almost by definition a nation at an early stage of economic development. "Despite the increasing availability of threshing, harvesting and reaping machines," the historian Jonathan Prude has noted, "many New England farmers continued to cling to familiar methods of cultivation, like the time-consuming hill method of planting Indian corn." Nevertheless, in nineteenth-century America, agriculture did not suggest a conservative way of life limited by the entrenched customs of a feudalistic past. "Let our farmers study their true interests," an agricultural reform journal advised: "Let them not stand while others are getting ahead. Let them be up and doing something to supply the wants of the towns and cities in their vicinity; and not the necessities only, but the tastes also. Let them raise flowers, even, if it will pay a profit. Why not?" Farming increasingly took on the characteristics of a speculative business.

The very isolation of individual farms, posted like sentries along lonely country roads, indicated that Americans placed efficiency above the community solidarity that was characteristic of tight-knit European peasant villages. The individual American farm family, practically imprisoned near the fields it worked and usually owned, had proved to be the most effective unit of production.

Four central conditions shaped America's unprecedented expansion of cultivated land. First, public policy continued to favor rapid settlement of the immense public domain, amounting to a billion acres if one includes the territorial acquisitions of the 1840s. There was no opposing interest in conserving natural resources and future revenue. Second, despite population growth, agricultural labor remained scarce and expensive, especially in frontier regions. Most

A Plank Road Contrasted with Mud
Wagons laden with lumber and hay speed along on the high and dry plank road, while the woman driving the team to the left struggles with the traveler's traditional nightmare: mud. Although improved roads made it easier for farmers to carry produce to local urban markets, they could not compete with canals and railroads in longer distance trade.

farm owners had to rely on an occasional hired hand to supplement the labor of their own families or of tenant families. In the South the price of slaves continued to rise. Third, the dispersion of settlement made farmers heavily dependent, for many decades, on navigable rivers and waterways for transportation. Fourth, the real-estate mentality of earlier periods burgeoned into a national mania as the westward movement and the mushrooming of towns brought spectacular rises in land values. Great land companies and private investors, representing eastern and European capital, purchased virtual empires of western land and then used every possible device to promote rapid settlement. Even the small farmers saw that it was more agreeable to make money by speculating in land than by removing stumps or plowing up the resistant blue-stem grass of the prairies. When Harriet Martineau, a famous British writer and popular economist, visited frontier Chicago in 1837, she exclaimed over the wild speculation in building lots: "I never saw a busier place than Chicago was at the time of our arrival. The streets were crowded with land speculators, hurrying from one sale to another.... [It] seemed as if some prevalent mania infected the whole people.... As the gentlemen of our party walked the streets, store-keepers hailed them from their doors, with offers of farms, and all manner of land-lots, advising them to speculate before the price of land rose higher."

From one point of view the pioneering outlook was progressive. There can be no doubt that Americans who moved were inventive, hardy, and willing to take risks. Often pushing forward ahead of roads and organized government, the frontier farmers engaged in a struggle by trial and error to succeed in the face of unfamiliar climate, insects, soil conditions, and drainage. In time they experimented with different crops, livestock, and transportation routes, searching for the commodity and market that would bring a predictable cash return. Although the federal government supplied little direct information to farmers, it continued Jefferson's tradition of promoting land surveys and sending expeditions into land west of the Mississippi River to collect information on flora and fauna, geology, watersheds, and Indians. This enterprising spirit, evident in both public and private endeavors, led to the discovery and exploitation of undreamed-of resources, confirming Tocqueville's judgment that "Nature herself favors the cause of the [American] people."

But the quest for immediate returns also led to a ruthless stripping of natural resources. In the absence of national legislation and national power, the timber, grasses, and minerals of the public domain invited a headlong scramble by the pioneers to cut trees, graze their cattle, and dig for ore. The government actually bought gold and silver that miners took from public property. European visitors were astonished at the American conviction that forests were a hostile element to be destroyed without regard for need. Trees, like the buffalo and beaver of the West, seemed so plentiful that few Americans could foresee a time of diminishing supply.

The soil itself, the most valuable of all resources, fared no better. Americans generally lacked the incentives and patience to conserve the soil by using fertilizers and by carefully rotating crops. They tended to look on land as a temporary and expendable resource that should be mined as rapidly as possible. This attitude, which was especially prevalent in the South and the West, reflected the common need to produce the most profitable single crop—wheat, corn, rice, tobacco, or cotton—in order to pay for land that had been purchased on credit. As one historical geographer has concluded, American farmers "earned well their reputation as 'soil killers'" as they speculated in land and pushed cultivation ever westward.

The entrepreneurial character of American agriculture owed much to the way new lands were originally settled. It is difficult for Americans of the late twentieth century to grasp the significance of the fact that before the Civil War the chief business of the federal government was the management and disposal of public land. Seeking revenue as well as rapid settlement, the government hastily surveyed tracts of western land and sold them to the highest bidder at public auction; the remainder was offered at the minimum price of $1.25 per acre. Because there was no limit on how many acres an individual or company might buy, investors eagerly bought blocks of thousands of acres. The great peaks of speculation coincided with the expansion of bank credit in the early 1830s and the mid-1850s. The profitable resale of western land depended on promoting settlement.

Speculators and Squatters

Speculators had always helped to shape the character of American agriculture. The great theme of American settlement was the continuing contest of will between absentee owners and the squatters who first developed the land and who often had some partial claim to it. Although squatters frequently sold their own claims to the succeeding waves of immigrants, they tended to picture wealthier speculators as greedy vampires. Yet the large speculators played a key role in financing the rapid settlement of the public lands. Pooling private capital, they lent money to squatters, often at illegally high interest rates, to finance the purchase of tools, livestock, and supplies. They extended credit for buying farms. They pressured local and national governments to subsidize canals and railroads. This speculation often involved considerable risk; the returns on investment depended on the speculators' ability to predict business conditions accurately and on how fast settlement took place.

Squatters for their part yearned for economic independence. They successfully agitated for state "occupancy laws" favoring the claims of actual settlers and guaranteeing them compensation, if evicted, for their cabins, fences, outbuildings, and other improvements. Squatters also pressed for a lowered minimum in the amount of public land that could be purchased—a restriction that by 1832 fell to forty acres. Above all, squatters called on the federal government to sanction squatting, formally allowing settlers to clear and cultivate tracts of public land prior to purchase. This policy of "preemption," which was developed in limited acts in the 1830s and finally established in a general law of 1841, gave squatters the right to settle land and then purchase as much as 160 acres at the minimum price in advance of public sale.

In practice the federal land system was a compromise between the interests of farmers and those of speculators. Government measures did nothing to curb speculators, who were in fact favored by the requirement, beginning in 1820, of full cash payment for public land. Speculators were also favored by lavish government donations of public land to military veterans, railroad companies, and state governments, as well as by the eventual pricing, at as little as 12.5 cents an acre, of land that had long been unsold. Federal land policy allowed speculators to amass great private fortunes by acquiring valuable tracts of the public domain. Yet the wide dispersion of freehold farms gave a grain of substance to the myth that any American could become an owner of property and an independent producer for the capitalist market.

Demand for Better Transportation

Access to growing markets was the overriding concern of the commercial farmer. Yet the craze during the early nineteenth century for building turnpikes, bridges, and plank roads failed to reduce significantly the cost of long-distance freight. The teams of horses that hauled wagons of freight over the nation's turnpikes averaged no better than two miles an hour. Not until canals began to link together other inland waterways could northern farmers think of concentrating on the production of corn and wheat for distant markets.

Steamboat on the Hudson
*After Robert Fulton's first steamboat sailed the Hudson River in 1807, as pictured above,
Americans quickly took advantage of their unparalleled system of navigable rivers. The
steamboat revolutionized transport, especially in the Mississippi valley and southern states.*

The Erie Canal, which was completed in 1825, united Northeast and West by
providing a continuous waterway from Lake Erie to the Atlantic. It was by far the
longest canal in the world, and it dramatically lowered shipping costs. In 1817 it
had cost 19.2 cents per mile to ship a ton of freight overland from Buffalo to New
York City. By the late 1850s the cost per mile, via the canal, had dropped to 0.81
cents. New York State had directed and financed this enormous undertaking, and
it soon reaped spectacular rewards. Foreign capital quickly flowed into the
country to meet the demand of other state and municipal governments, setting
off a canal-building mania that soon linked Pittsburgh with Philadelphia, and the
Ohio River with the Great Lakes. The high cost of building this network of
waterways, undertaken for the most part by the states themselves, severely
strained the credit of Ohio, Pennsylvania, and Indiana. But by sharply lowering
the costs of transport, the most successful canals had an enormous effect on
northern agriculture and industry.

By the mid-1830s the basic pattern of internal transportation began to shift
away from the traditional routes that had led from the Ohio and upper
Mississippi valleys to New Orleans and ocean shipment via the Gulf of Mexico.
Ohio Valley farmers would continue to ship grain and pork down the Mississippi
by flatboat. The richest markets, however, lay east of the Great Lakes, and for a
time the richest commercial agriculture developed in regions accessible by canal
to Lake Erie. By 1840 Rochester, New York, had become the leading flour-milling
center in the country. The marketing of grain became more efficient as brokers
and other middlemen began to arrange for storage, transport, sale, and credit.

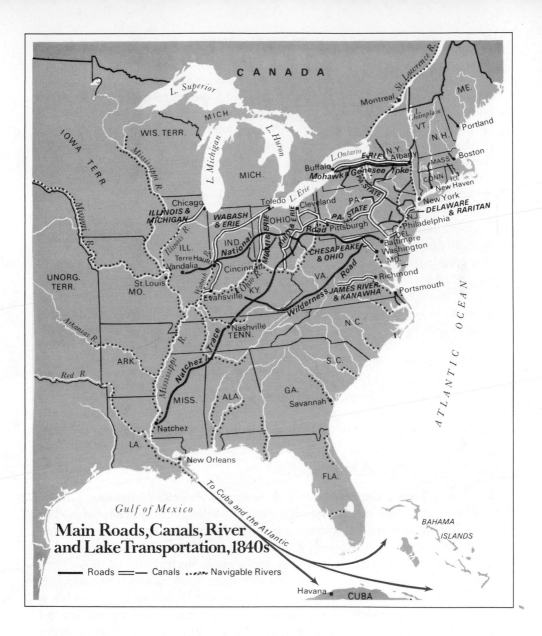

Main Roads, Canals, River and Lake Transportation, 1840s

Roads ═══ Canals ⋯⋯ Navigable Rivers

This transformation preceded the East–West railroad connections of the early 1850s.

The Commercialization of Agriculture

In both North and South, the expansion and commercialization of agriculture provided the impetus for the economy's accelerated growth and modernization. During the 1840s the United States began to export an increasing proportion of its agricultural output, partly in response to poor harvests in Europe and to Britain's repeal of its Corn Laws, which had excluded American and other foreign grain, even during the worst of the Irish famine. This new outflow of wheat and other foodstuffs helped pay for America's imports of manufactured products and the immense interest charges on foreign investment in American land, cotton, and railroads. Much of America's economic expansion depended on the country's ability to attract such investment from Europe. By diverting produce from domestic markets, agricultural exports also had the effect of sharply raising the price of domestic farm products. While this encouraged the further expansion of cash crops, the soaring price of food between 1848 and 1855 brought great hardship to nonagricultural workers in the Northeast and Midwest.

Continuing improvements in transportation enabled agricultural regions to specialize in the search for competitive advantages in response to the pressures of an increasingly national market. In the Midwest, north of the Ohio River, farmers began to buy trademarked tools and machines from authorized distributors. Steel plows, invented in the 1830s but widely accepted only in the 1850s, made it possible to break the tough sod and cultivate the rich but sticky soil of the prairies. Mechanical reapers had also been invented in the 1830s, but only in the 1850s did Cyrus McCormick's Chicago factory begin large-scale production and employ modern techniques of advertising and promotion. As the Midwest proved its superiority in producing wheat and other grains, along with wool, corn, pork, and beef, farmers in the East found it increasingly difficult to compete with their western counterparts. Instead eastern farmers began to specialize in the production of hay for horses and perishable foodstuffs for urban markets.

Industrialization and Railroads

There is still much controversy over the stages of America's economic growth. The best recent evidence suggests that a pattern of long-term accelerated growth in per-capita real income (income measured by purchasing power) preceded significant industrialization and probably originated in the 1820s or earlier from the interaction between urbanization and western agriculture. In those years manufacturing still mostly meant that goods were made by hand in households and in small shops or mills. Blacksmiths, coopers (barrel makers), cobblers, curriers (leather workers), hatters, tailors, weavers—these and other artisans and apprentices worked in central shops, mills, and stores, or traveled through the more sparsely settled countryside. Yet the independent artisans' world began to disintegrate in the 1820s as merchant capitalists expanded and reorganized markets and gradually gained control of the means of production.

Manufacturing   As had happened in England, cotton textiles became the leading industrial innovation. Although Britain tried to guard industrial know-how by strictly banning the export of cotton technology, the New Englander Francis Cabot Lowell memorized the design of textile machinery he saw in Lancashire. After returning to Waltham, Massachusetts, during the War of 1812, Lowell helped form the Boston Manufactur-

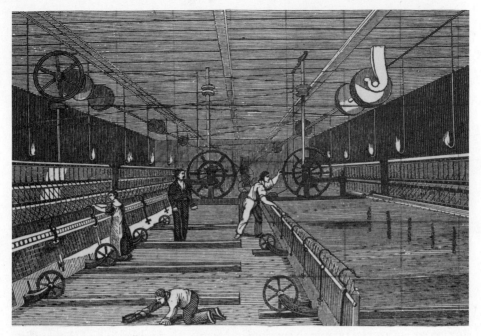

Mule Spinning in Lowell
The spinning of thread or yarn, traditionally done at home on a spinning wheel, became almost wholly mechanized when gigantic power-driven machines called mules not only drew and twisted fiber into thread or yarn but wound it for future use on a cylindrical quill or tube. In this view of a textile mill in Lowell, Massachusetts, the two workers, sweeper, and supervisor seem dwarfed by the machines.

ing Company and succeeded in constructing spinning machinery and an improved power loom. This technological triumph enabled Lowell and his associates to build a textile mill at Waltham in which spinning and weaving were all integrated under a single roof. Aided somewhat by protective tariffs, a group of wealthy Boston merchants pooled their capital and in the 1820s extended large-scale factory production to the new manufacturing centers like Lowell (named after Francis Cabot) and Chicopee, in Massachusetts. This so-called Waltham system of centralized factories owed much to the investment capital of New England merchants, who turned to manufacturing when the War of 1812 had curtailed international trade. It exploited the latest British technology, such as the power loom, and it continued to draw upon the expertise of immigrant British artisans.

If their products were to compete successfully with imported British textiles, New England manufacturers had to lower the cost and increase the efficiency of labor. American manufacturers had traditionally cut costs by employing children or families including children, who increased the labor force without increasing wages. Despite attempts to romanticize this kind of family employment, a young Connecticut worker voiced a common protest that "manufacturing breeds lords and Aristocrats, Poor men and slaves....I am for Agriculture....I cannot bear the idea, that I, or my children,...should be shut up 16 or 18 hours every day all our life like Slaves and that too for a bare subsistence!" It soon became apparent that children could not handle the frequent breakdowns of the new machinery or conform to the routine that was necessary for increased labor productivity.

By the late 1840s immigrants had begun to ease the general shortage of cheap factory labor. But for a few decades the Boston merchants relied on the unique expedient of employing adult young women, who were attracted to the factories by the provision of chaperoned dormitories and various cultural and educational amenities. Amazed by the interest of these "factory girls" in intellectual self-improvement, a visiting Harvard professor exclaimed: "I have never seen any-where so assiduous note-taking. No, not even in a college class, as in that assembly of young women, laboring for their subsistence." The merchant-manufacturers desired, no doubt sincerely, to avoid the moral degradation that had been a black mark on the British factory system. As economy-minded entrepreneurs, they also hoped to control their employees' leisure time, preventing the binges and self-proclaimed holidays that had always led to irregular work habits and absenteeism among preindustrial people. New England farm girls could also be hired for less than half the wages of male factory hands because they saw their employment as a temporary stage of independence between childhood and marriage and because the factory represented for them virtually the only possible liberation from the farm. As one young woman expressed her newfound sense of economic independence in a letter sent home to her sister on a New Hampshire farm: "Since I have wrote you, another pay day has come around. I earned 14 dollars and a half, nine and a half beside my board....I like it as well as ever and Sarah don't I feel independent of everyone! The thought that I am living on no one is a happy one indeed to me."

From 1815 to 1833 the cotton textile industry increased average annual output at the phenomenal rate of 16 percent. Slackening demand soon reduced the annual rate of growth to about 5 percent, but textile producers, including wool and carpet manufacturers, continued to pioneer in mechanization, in efficiency, and in the use of steam power.

New England also gave birth to the so-called American system of manufac-turing. This innovation depended on the imaginative adaptation of a machine-tool technology that had first been developed in England. Unlike the British, however, American manufacturers could not draw on a plentiful supply of highly skilled craftsmen with many years of training in an established craft tradition. Therefore American manufacturers encouraged the perfection of light machine tools that not only eliminated many hand operations but also allowed ordinary mechanics to measure within one-thousandth of an inch and to mill or cut metal with great precision. At the British Crystal Palace exhibition of 1851—a great international show of industrial techniques and products—American machinery astonished European experts. In 1854 one of the British commissions that had

The Working Woman
The woman pictured above is tending a power loom, weaving cloth from machine-spun thread.
She typifies the industrial work force that led New England through the first stage of the
industrial revolution.

been sent to study American achievements exclaimed over "the extraordinary ingenuity displayed in many of their labour-saving machines, where automatic action so completely supplies the place of the more abundant hand labour of older manufacturing countries."

The British investigators understood the significance for the future of such a seemingly ordinary device as a machine that produced 180 ladies' hairpins every minute. As early as 1853 an exuberant writer for the *United States Review* could predict that within a half-century machines would liberate Americans from the burdens of work: "Machinery will perform all work—automata will direct them. The only tasks of the human race will be to make love, study, and be happy."

But in 1860 American industry was still at an early stage of transition. There were sharp contrasts in the degree of industrialization with respect to different products and different regions. For example, despite an impressive expansion of output, the American iron industry was not nearly as successful as the cotton industry in adopting and improving the latest British technology. The continued use of small blast furnaces that used charcoal to produce malleable iron has been explained by the cheapness and availability of wood for charcoal, by the absence of bituminous coal east of the Allegheny Mountains, by the belated discovery and use of anthracite coal, and by the particular needs of local blacksmiths. Whatever the reasons, and American iron producers increasingly blamed political opponents of protective tariffs, American industry in the 1850s depended heavily on imported British wrought iron and railroad rails, and it lagged far behind Britain in exploiting coal, iron, and steam.

In the West manufacturing often reverted to preindustrial methods that had almost disappeared in the East. But even in the Northeast many goods were produced not in factories but by merchants who still relied on the "putting-out" system—that is, distributing raw materials to laborers who often owned their own tools and worked at home. Other merchant capitalists hired laborers essentially as instruments of production, for the workers had no share in the ownership of tools and machines, in managerial decisions, in the risks of marketing, or in the industrial product.

In 1860 American manufacturing still depended largely on water power, not steam. The typical firm employed a handful of workers, was unincorporated, and engaged in the small-scale processing of raw materials. Few industries processed the products of other industries. The nation's largest industries included some that were thoroughly mechanized, such as the production of cotton goods, flour, and meal. Some, however, were only partly mechanized, such as the manufacture of boots and shoes. And some were characterized by premodern technology and low labor productivity, such as lumbering and the making of men's clothing.

Railroad Building   The great railroad boom of the late 1840s and 1850s dramatized the growing links between industry and agriculture. Although the nation's railroads equaled the canals in mileage as early as 1840, canal barges and river steamboats were usually less expensive than railroads and continued to carry a significant proportion of freight throughout the antebellum period, the years before the Civil War. But by providing speedy access to isolated farms and distant markets, railroads extended the risks and promises of a commercial society and also opened the interior to port cities like Baltimore, Boston, and Charleston, which lacked major inland waterways.

While the smoke and roar of steam trains evoked thoughts of progress and prosperity, the locomotive also became a symbol of the monstrous forces of industry invading the serenity of rural America. In the summer of 1844, for example, the writer Nathaniel Hawthorne recorded a sudden disruption as he tried to commune with nature in a grove of woods known as "Sleepy Hollow": "But hark! There is the whistle of the locomotive—the long shriek, harsh, above all other harshness. . . . It tells a story of busy men, citizens, from the hot street, men of business; in short, of all unquietness; and no wonder that it gives such a startling shriek, since it brings the noisy world into the midst of our slumbering peace."

The development of railway networks was long delayed by primitive technology, a high incidence of breakdowns and accidents, and construction costs

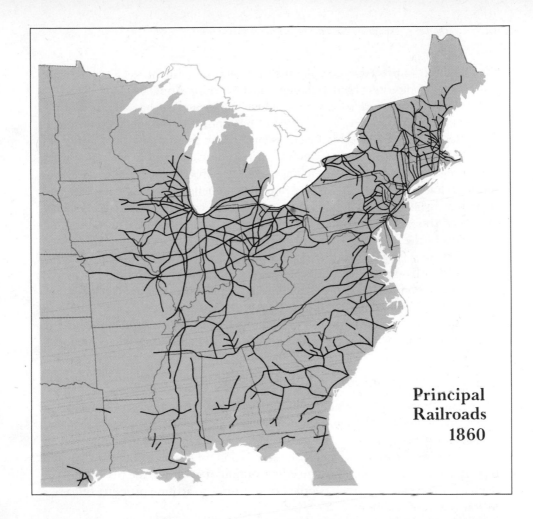

Principal
Railroads
1860

The First Steam Railroad Passenger Train in America.

Dawn of the Railroad Age
In 1831, five years after the Mohawk and Hudson Railroad Company received its charter, an English engineer piloted two carloads of passengers from Albany to Schenectady, New York. Within the next twenty years railroads had linked the Northeast to the Midwest, immensely lowering the cost of shipping farm produce and manufactured goods, and profoundly influencing every aspect of American society and culture.

that required unprecedented amounts of capital investment. As early as 1828, Baltimore promotors began building the first trans-Appalachian railroad to compete with New York's Erie Canal, which threatened to channel much of the western trade toward New York City. But not until 1853 did this Baltimore and Ohio Railroad reach the Ohio River. As late as 1860 there were still hundreds of small, independent lines with different widths of track. Nevertheless, by the early 1850s construction engineers were improving rails, roadbeds, bridges, and locomotives. Railroad corporations had amassed immense reserves of capital, and their managers were learning how to administer complex bureaucracies that employed thousands of workers and required instant interstate communication by means of the recently perfected electric telegraph. By 1854 tracks extended from New York City to the Mississippi River, and by 1860 to the Missouri River at St. Joseph, Missouri. This burst of western railroad construction led to the beginning of consolidation into main lines that further cemented economic ties between the West and the Northeast. By 1860 railroads had become the nation's first billion-dollar industry, spawning the first giant corporations and linking cash-crop farming with the production of iron, coal, lumber, and machine tools.

Population Distribution and Opportunity

There can be no doubt that the nation's overall economic growth brought impressive gains in income and standard of living. By 1860 the United States was well ahead of western Europe in per capita income; even the South, which lagged behind the Northeast, was richer than most nations of Europe. But historians still have much to learn about the actual distribution of wealth in the pre–Civil War decades, to say nothing of the people's opportunity to acquire property or to rise in status and occupation.

Discussions of America's economic opportunities generally omit three groups: the Indians; the black slaves; and the free blacks in both North and South, whose small economic gains in various skilled trades and service industries were severely damaged by competition from white immigrants. Even excluding these oppressed minorities, one finds many indications that economic inequality increased substantially from 1820 to 1860.

The Rich Grow Richer, 1820–1860 According to the best recent estimates, by 1860 the upper 5 percent of families owned over half the nation's wealth. The disparity was far greater in parts of the South, where the wealth of the average slaveholder was growing far more rapidly than that of the average nonslaveholder. The typical slaveholder was not only more than five times as wealthy as the average Northerner, but more than ten times as wealthy as the average nonslaveholding southern farmer. Even in the farming country of the eastern North Central states, where there was greater economic equality, the upper 10 percent of landholders owned nearly 40 percent of the taxable wealth. The national centers of inequality, however, were the growing urban regions from Boston to New Orleans. Although much statistical research remains to be done, it is clear that between 1820 and 1860 the big cities led the nation toward the increasing domination of the very rich. By 1860, according to one estimate, Philadelphia's richest 1 percent of the population owned half the city's wealth; the lower 80 percent of the city's population had to be content with 3 percent of the wealth. A relatively modest estimate concluded that the richest 5 percent of American families in 1860 received between 25 percent and 35 percent of the national income. Although these figures indicate an inequality far greater than that estimated for modern America, they are roughly comparable to the inequalities in northern Europe in the late nineteenth century.

This conclusion would not be so startling if America's pre–Civil War decades had not once been described and almost universally accepted as "the age of the common man." American politicians and journalists of the era eagerly expanded on the theme of "equality of condition," supposedly confirmed by the observations of Alexis de Tocqueville and other European visitors. On closer inspection, however, it is clear that Tocqueville and others claimed only that American fortunes were "scanty" compared with fortunes in Europe; that in America "most of the rich men were formerly poor"; and that in America "any man's son may become the equal of any other man's son." In other words, American inequalities were thought to be temporary and to enhance the incentives of a race to success in which all were free to compete.

This belief in America's unique capacity for avoiding permanent inequalities was especially reassuring by 1850, when European industrialism had produced undeniable evidence of misery, class conflict, and seething revolution. By that date American leaders could not hide their alarm over similar contrasts of wealth and extreme poverty in their own country, particularly when the urban poor congregated in slums beyond the reach of traditional religious and social discipline. Yet affluent Americans persuaded themselves that the poor were free to climb the ladder of success. They also firmly believed that the wealthiest citizens were, in the words of the powerful Kentucky senator Henry Clay, "enterprising self-made men, who have whatever wealth they possess by patient and diligent labor."

In truth, however, the fortunes of the John Jacob Astor family and of other leading American families compared favorably with the fortunes of the richest Europeans. Notwithstanding a few astonishing examples of rags-to-riches achievement, the great majority of America's rich and successful men had benefited from inherited wealth, an affluent childhood, or a prestigious family tradition. Between 1820 and 1860 there was a marked persistence of family wealth. In effect, the rich grew richer. In the cities, at least, they constituted an elite that became increasingly segregated by exclusive clubs, high social life, intermarriage, foreign travel, and business alliances.

At the other end of the spectrum was the mass of unskilled day laborers, who took what temporary jobs they could find and whose wages, even if regular, could not possibly support a family unless supplemented by the income of wives and children. No one knows the size of this unskilled, propertyless population, which drifted in and out of mill towns, flocked to the construction sites of canals and railroads, or gravitated to urban slums. In the 1840s and 1850s the largest cities attracted the chronic failures and castoffs who had no other place to turn. In 1849 New York City's first chief of police warned of "a deplorable and growing evil" in the city, "the constantly increasing number of vagrants, idle and vicious children of both sexes, who infest our public thoroughfares." The poor jammed themselves into the attics and dank, windowless basements of Boston's Half Moon Place, where as many as one hundred people might share the same overflowing privy; or into New York's notorious Old Brewery, a foul tenement that supposedly housed over a thousand beggars, pickpockets, whores, robbers, alcoholics, and starving children. Boston investigators described one such dwelling as "a perfect hive of human beings, without comforts and mostly without common necessaries; in many cases, huddled together like brutes, without regard to sex, or age, or sense of decency." In contrast with the society of mid-nineteenth-century England, the relatively unstructured society of America provided very few public agencies that could begin to enforce minimal standards of health, welfare, and safety.

Urban poverty was immensely aggravated by the arrival of so many immigrants that no conceivable public works program, even if nineteenth-century America had thought in such "New Deal" terms, could have provided the poor with adequate housing, sanitation, and safe water. More immigrants poured into the United States in the ten years between 1841 and 1851 than in the entire previous history of two and a half centuries. From 1848 to 1850 German immigrants ignited a raging cholera epidemic in New York and from New Orleans up the Mississippi and Ohio rivers. Cholera was compounded by new risks of typhus, typhoid, tuberculosis, and other diseases. Although the northern states had become by the late eighteenth century the healthiest region on earth, life expectancy fell 25 percent by 1850. In New York and Philadelphia life expectancy at birth plummeted to age twenty-four.

Social Mobility　　The extremes of wealth and poverty tell little about the amount of upward movement from one class to another. The available evidence indicates that the odds were heavily against an unskilled laborer's acquiring a higher occupational status. The overwhelming majority of unskilled workers remained unskilled workers. It is true that in the 1850s many of the sons of unskilled workers were moving into semiskilled factory jobs. But this generational advance was almost always limited to the next rung on the ladder. It was extremely rare for the children of manual workers, even skilled manual workers, to rise to the level of clerical, managerial, or professional employment.

Despite growing signs of semipermanent boundaries between occupational groups in the pre–Civil War decades, there were remarkably few expressions of class conflict or class interest. The rarity of such expressions is underscored by the temporary radicalism of lone figures like Orestes A. Brownson, who in 1840 published an eloquent analysis of the plight of the working classes. "Our business is to emancipate the proletaries," Brownson proclaimed, "as the past has emancipated the slaves. This is our work. There must be no class of our fellow men doomed to toil through life as mere workmen at wages." In 1844 Brownson converted to Roman Catholicism and thenceforth became a leading conservative theorist and defender of the church. Historians have sometimes been misled by the labor rhetoric of the Jacksonian period, a time when the rich felt it necessary to prove their humble origins and when politicians and even successful entrepreneurs proudly claimed to be "workingmen."

The labor leaders of the era were typically artisan proprietors and small businessmen who were intent on fixing prices and reducing the hazards of interregional competition. This is not to deny the importance of British artisans who, displaced by the British factory system, had migrated to the United States. These men, who reinforced the preindustrial craft traditions in America, were schooled in the techniques of secret organization and industrial warfare. Nor can one deny the courage of union organizers who faced conspiracy trials in the 1820s and 1830s, who saw their gains wiped out by the depression of 1837–42, and who finally formed city federations of craft unions and national trade unions in the 1850s. Yet the great strikes for higher wages and for the ten-hour day were staged by skilled printers, typographers, hatters, tailors, and other artisans. Employers, who were mostly supported by the courts and who benefited from fresh supplies of cheap immigrant labor, had little difficulty in breaking strikes. Although the Massachusetts Supreme Court led the way, in the case *Commonwealth* v. *Hunt* (1842), in ruling that trade unions were not in themselves conspiracies in restraint of trade, in 1860 only 0.1 percent of the American labor force was organized.

Even by the 1840s America's relative freedom from class consciousness and class conflict evoked considerable comment. According to Karl Marx and other European observers, the explanation could be found in the fresh lands of the American frontier, which provided an outlet for surplus population. In America, George Henry Evans's National Reform Association referred to the West as a "safety valve" that could and should provide an escape for workers whose opportunities were limited in the East. Evans contended in the 1840s that the nation owned enough land in the West to guarantee every family a farm. In the 1850s Horace Greeley, editor of the enormously influential *New York Tribune,* popularized the Republican party's slogan, "Vote yourself a farm." More than a generation later, the historian Frederick Jackson Turner and his followers developed a detailed theory that pictured the frontier as both a safety valve for the pressures of the industrializing East and a constant source of new opportunity.

The "safety-valve" theory, in its simplest and crudest form, has been thoroughly demolished. The eastern laborer, earning a dollar a day or less, could not afford to travel to the frontier and borrow funds for a farm and tools, even if he possessed the skills for western farming. The evidence shows that western land sales lagged in hard times, when a safety valve would be most needed, and

"Go Westward, Young Man!"
The lure of upward mobility and improving one's condition led thousands of young people, such as this young Vermont man depicted above, to abandon rural regions in the northeast and strike out for a supposedly better life in the west.

increased when prosperity drove up the prices of wheat and cotton. Except for a few cooperative settlement associations and a few hundred wage earners sent by antislavery groups to settle Kansas in the 1850s, there are no records to show that industrial workers were transformed into frontier farmers.

On the other hand, the westward surge of millions of Americans intensified and dramatized the central fact of American life: physical mobility. Wages in the Northeast might well have been lower if the farmers, shopkeepers, artisans, and small businessmen who did go West had stayed put. Some of these aspiring adventurers might have been forced to seek factory employment. Some might have become America's counterparts of Europe's labor organizers. Ironically, since young males predominated in the migration away from industrial New England, an increasing number of women there had no prospect for marriage and thus became part of a permanent industrial labor force. These women found themselves living permanently on the low wages from jobs they had taken while awaiting marriage.

Intense geographical mobility reinforced the myth of America's boundlessness, of its infinite promise. By 1850 one-quarter of the entire population born in New England states had moved to other states. The South Atlantic states experienced a no less striking westward drain of whites and of black slaves. In each decade the northern cities, towns, and factories witnessed an extraordinary inflow and outflow of population. Although few of these mobile Americans had a chance to acquire farms, they moved because they had hopes of finding life better somewhere else. And the hope may have been more significant than the reality they found. The reality was often grim for unskilled laborers, but the factories and towns they left behind had no need to worry about their accumulating grievances. The more fortunate and competitive movers could not doubt that Illinois was preferable to Ohio, or that New York City offered more opportunities than the rocky hillsides of Vermont.

It was obvious that the economic condition of most white Americans, except for the floating population of impoverished laborers, was improving. Even the lowliest Irish laborers in a factory town like Newburyport, Massachusetts, found that they could accumulate more property if they stuck to their jobs for a decade or longer. To maintain a savings account or eventually to buy a house required discipline, frugality, and multiple incomes; for some, additional incomes came at the expense of family members' education and leisure time. The Irish put a greater premium on home ownership than on education or occupational achievement. The Jews, on the other hand, tended to make every sacrifice for their family's education. Particularly for the families of manual workers, the gains were extremely limited. But these gains engendered pride in achieving what others had not achieved, and they were sufficient to prevent even a permanent working class from becoming a permanent and propertyless proletariat.

The incessant turnover of population and the lack of physical roots also gave force to the ideology of an open and boundless society—an ideology that was repeatedly stressed in newspaper articles, sermons, and political speeches. Who could tell what had become of all one's former neighbors and fellow workers? No doubt, some had hit it rich. The mystery of everyone's past made it believable that most men's positions had been won according to talent and performance—that in America, where the only limits were individual will and ability, most men got what they were worth. If in time a manual worker could finally boast of a savings account of $300, of owning the roof over his head, or of a son who had moved up to the next rung on the ladder, why should he doubt the common claim, "This is a country of self-made men," where most of the rich had once been poor?

The Cost of Expansion: The Indians

The rapid expansion of agriculture, North and South, depended initially on the displacement of the native population. The white Americans, determined to go where they pleased and to seize any chance for quick profit, regarded the millions of acres of western land as a well-deserved inheritance that should be exploited as quickly as possible. But in 1820 the prairies and forests east of the Mississippi River still contained approximately 125,000 native Americans. Although millions of acres had been cleared of Indian occupancy rights in accordance with Anglo-

American law, the physical presence of the Indians blocked the way to government sale of much public land that could lead to increased revenues, to profits from land speculation, and to the creation of private farms and plantations.

The Indians, hopelessly outnumbered by an invader with superior technology, had little room to maneuver. Although they had long sought trade and alliances with whites, native Americans had learned that advancing white settlements undermined tribal culture and destroyed the fish and game on which their economy depended. The Indians had little understanding of the whites' conceptions of private property and competitive individualism. But the whites were just as blind to the diversity and complexity of Indian cultures, to the native Americans' traditions of mutual obligation and communal ownership of land, and to the peculiarly advanced position of Indian women (Iroquois women, for example, played a crucial role in political and economic decisions). These cultural barriers made it easier for whites to think of Indians in terms of negative stereotypes as deceitful and blood-thirsty savages or as a weak and "childlike" race doomed to extinction. Even the more humane and well-meaning Christian missionary groups considered the destruction of Indian culture before the white advance as "the natural course of things." "There is no place on earth to which they can migrate, and live in the savage and hunter state," reported the Congregationalist Board of Commissioners for Foreign Missions in its 1824 address to Congress. "The Indian tribes must, therefore, be *progressively civilized* or *successively perish.*" In fact, the Indian response to white advances was complex, ranging from skillful warfare and stubborn negotiation to resigned submission in the face of treachery and superior force.

The native Americans had proved to be the major losers in the War of 1812. By ending the long conflict between Western settlers and European empires, this war had removed the Indians' last hope of finding white allies who could slow the advance of white Americans. The decisive victories of William Henry Harrison over the Shawnees in the Old Northwest, and of Andrew Jackson over the Creeks in the Old Southwest, had also shattered the hope of a union between northern and southern Indian confederations. These triumphs opened the way for the whites' exploitation of tribal divisions and for their abandonment of what Jackson termed "the farce of treating with Indian tribes" as units. Jackson thought that all Indians should be required as individuals to submit to the laws of the states, like everyone else, or to migrate beyond the Mississippi River, where they could progress toward civilization at their own pace.

Federal Indian Policy   The land-hungry frontiersmen faced controls on their actions in the form of a federal Indian policy that had evolved from imperial, colonial, and post-Revolutionary precedents. This makeshift policy rested on four premises that in time became increasingly contradictory.

First, in line with European legal concepts, the federal government continued to acknowledge that the Indian tribes were in some sense independent nations that had acquired rights of possession by prior occupancy of the land, even though they lacked many of the usual characteristics of sovereign countries. The federal government's continuing efforts to negotiate treaties, to purchase land, and to mark off territorial boundaries demonstrated that legitimate settlement by whites required at least symbolic consent from the native Americans. The same European model allowed the United States to punish "aggressor" tribes by demanding the cession of land as a legal compensation for the damages of war.

The second premise, a product of New World experience, was that Indian "occupancy" must inevitably give way to white settlement. White Americans, like the heirs of a dying relative, had an eventual right—an "expectancy," to use Jefferson's phrase—to the property that native Americans held. In theory this claim did not interfere with the existing property rights of Indians. It simply gave the American government an exclusive right to purchase Indian lands, thereby blocking any future imperial designs by European powers.

In practice, however, this doctrine led to the third premise—that of supreme federal authority over Indian affairs. Knowing the dangers of alliances between hostile Indians and foreign nations, the federal government had from the beginning assumed powers that would have been unthinkable in any other domestic sphere. It subjected all trade with the native Americans to federal licensing and regulation. It invalidated the sale or transfer of Indian lands, even to a state, unless made in accordance with a federal treaty. It guaranteed that the native Americans would be protected from white advances on lands that they had not ceded to the federal government. But unfortunately no federal administration had the will or military power to protect Indian rights while supervising the fair acquisition of land by whites. In a government that was increasingly inclined to listen to the voice of the people, the native Americans had no voice of their own.

The fourth premise, which Jefferson had stated and which gained momentum after the War of 1812, was that Indian culture, which whites called savagery, could not permanently coexist with American civilization. President James Monroe expressed the common conviction in a letter of 1817 to Andrew Jackson: "The hunter or savage state requires a greater extent of territory to sustain it, than is compatible with the progress and just claims of civilized life, and must yield to it." The government actively promoted schools, agriculture, and various "useful arts" among the native Americans, hoping to convert supposed nomadic hunters into settled farmers. This hope was nourished by the progress of the more populous southern tribes, particularly the Cherokees, whose achievements in agriculture, in developing a written alphabet, and in adopting white technology seemed to meet the American tests of capability. But the government also pressured the Cherokees into ceding tracts of valuable eastern land in exchange for lands west of the Mississippi River. By 1824 it was becoming clear that the five southern confederations—Cherokees, Creeks, Choctaws, Chickasaws, and Seminoles—could not survive even as temporary enclaves without federal protection against white exploiters. The southern tribes occupied western Georgia and North Carolina, as well as major portions of Tennessee, Florida, Alabama, and Mississippi. Thus their lands covered the heart of the future Cotton Kingdom. In

1825 President Monroe officially proposed that these and all other remaining tribes be persuaded to move west of the Mississippi River, a plan that Jefferson and others had long regarded as the only way of saving America's original inhabitants from ultimate extinction.

Conflict of Federal and State Laws   In Georgia white speculators, squatters, and gold miners had no desire to see civilized Indians living on choice land, and the fact that it was ancestral Indian land made little difference. In 1828, when the Cherokees adopted a constitution and claimed sovereign jurisdiction over their own territory, Georgia declared them to be mere tenants on state land, subject to the state's laws and authority. In 1832, in the case of *Worcester* v. *Georgia,* Chief Justice John Marshall ruled against the state. Georgia, he said, had no right to extend state laws to the Cherokees or their territory. "The several Indian nations," he maintained, were "distinct political communities, having territorial boundaries, within which their authority is exclusive, and having a right to all lands within those boundaries, which is not only acknowledged, but guaranteed by the United States." But President Jackson, who had already withdrawn the federal troops that had earlier been sent to protect Cherokee land from intrusion, had no intention of enforcing the Supreme Court's decision.

Jackson firmly believed that the native Americans should be subject to state law and to the forces of a free-market economy, in which individuals bought and sold commodities according to the laws of supply and demand. To deal with tribes as privileged corporate groups, he thought, was simply to reinforce the power of corrupt chiefs and cunning half-breeds, who prevented tribesmen from following their own best interest. Jackson had no doubt that the vast majority of Indians, when liberated from tribal tyranny, would willingly emigrate to the West. The civilized few would be free to cultivate modest tracts of land and would become responsible citizens of state and nation.

Jackson's denial of federal protection provided the needed incentives for a supposedly voluntary migration. Following Georgia's lead, other southern states harassed native Americans with laws that few tribesmen could comprehend. White traders and lawyers descended like locusts on Indian lands, destroying tribal unity and authority. In 1830 Congress supported Jackson's policy by voting funds that would enable the president to negotiate treaties for the removal of all the Indian tribes then living east of the Mississippi River. The government still considered it necessary to purchase title to Indian land and to grant allotments of land to individual tribal leaders who could prove a legitimate claim. Federal officials even sought to protect native Americans by supervising private contracts for the sale of land. The majority of Indians, however, had no concept of land as a measurable and salable commodity. A few of the more experienced Chickasaws and other tribesmen secured good prices for rich cotton land, but white speculators, who swiftly cornered between 80 and 90 percent of southern allotments, reaped windfall profits.

"Trail of Tears"
In this painting by Robert Lindneux, the dispossessed Cherokee are depicted in their forced exodus to Oklahoma, struggling to transport the few belongings they can carry to a bleak and unfamiliar homeland.

The government thus furthered its goal of removal by dispossessing the native Americans of their land. Victims of wholesale fraud, trickery, and intimidation, the great mass of southern Indians had no choice but to follow the so-called Trail of Tears to the vacant territory of what is today Oklahoma. Subjected to disease, starvation, and winter cold, thousands died along the way. Military force gave a cutting edge to removal deadlines: in 1838 federal troops herded 15,000 Cherokees into detention camps. "They are dying like flies," various witnesses reported. As one Cherokee recalled many years later: "Long time we travel on way to new land. People feel bad when they leave old Nation. Women cry and make sad wails. Children cry and many men cry, and all look sad like when friends die, but they say nothing and just put heads down and keep on towards West. Many days pass and people die very much." Meanwhile Indians north of the Ohio River had earlier been demoralized as whites had cut down the supply of game, negotiated treaties with factions of certain tribes that had accepted more of white civilization, and ensnared primitive societies with unfamiliar mechanisms of debt and credit. In 1832 the government crushed the resistance of Sac and Fox Indians in Illinois and Wisconsin, and in 1835 it launched a long and costly war against the Seminoles in Florida. By 1844, except for a few remaining pockets mainly in the backcountry of New York, Michigan, and Florida, removal had been accomplished.

In his Farewell Address of March 4, 1837, Jackson applauded this brutal policy of Indian removal as a great humanitarian achievement that had also happily removed the main block to America's economic growth:

> While the safety and comfort of our own citizens have been greatly promoted by their removal, the philanthropist will rejoice that the remnant of that ill-fated race has been at length placed beyond the reach of injury or oppression, and that paternal care of the General Government will hereafter watch over them and protect them.

The Beginning of Indian Reservations Ten years later, however, the government had recognized the impossibility of a "permanent Indian barrier" west of the Mississippi River. Having defeated all Indian attempts to resist the pressure of westward white migration, the government now began moving toward a policy of fencing native Americans within specified "reservations" and opening the otherwise boundless territory of the great West to wagon trains, cavalry, miners, farmers, surveyors, and railroad builders. Even in the 1820s a few perceptive Indian chieftains had foreseen that western lands would be no more invulnerable than the lands in the East. This conclusion was soon confirmed by the destruction of tribal game reserves and by the purchase of remaining Indian lands in Missouri and Iowa. The Anglo-Saxon settlers in Texas, who won independence from Mexico in 1836, asserted the unprecedented claim that Indians had no right whatever to possession of the land. Texas reaffirmed this doctrine after being annexed as a state in 1845, and even demanded that some 25,000 Apaches and other tribesmen be removed or face extermination. Years of border warfare finally led in 1854 to the Texans' acceptance of Indian reservations under federal jurisdiction. But the federal government found that it could not protect Texas tribes from being slaughtered by marauding whites and therefore authorized their removal to the territory north of the Red River, in what later became Oklahoma.

Meanwhile, between 1846 and 1860 government policy began to settle the fate of the strong western tribes that had previously been free to roam prairies and intermountain grasslands without concern for the conflicting claims of white nations. The American invasion and occupation of New Mexico in the Mexican War led to brutal punitive expeditions against the Navajo. In 1851 Congress passed the critically important Indian Appropriations Act, which was designed to consolidate western tribes on agricultural reservations, thereby lessening the danger to the tens of thousands of emigrants streaming toward California and Oregon and also to the proposed transcontinental railroad.

The degradation reached its climax in the 1850s in California, where federal restraints on white aggression disappeared. Whites molested the Diggers and other primitive native Americans, shooting the males for sport and enslaving the women and children. Farther east, the Apaches and powerful Plains tribes offered occasional and sometimes spectacular resistance. The famed encounters

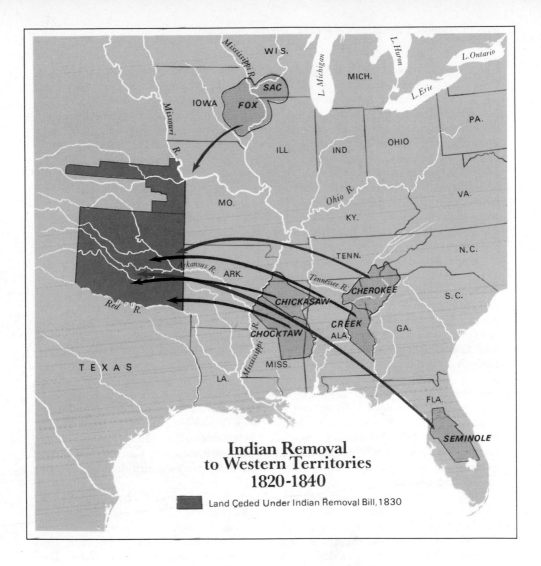

Indian Removal
to Western Territories
1820-1840

Land Ceded Under Indian Removal Bill, 1830

between Indians and the United States Cavalry came after the Civil War. But even by 1860 the western tribes had been demoralized, their economy had been fatally weakened when buffalo and other game became depleted, and increasing numbers of native Americans had been herded into compounds with boundaries that moved only inward.

SUGGESTED READINGS

For informative surveys and syntheses, often with detailed bibliographies, see George Danger-field, *The Awakening of American Nationalism, 1815–1828* (1965); Robert H. Wiebe, *The Opening of American Society: From the Adoption of the Constitution to the Eve of Disunion* (1984); Charles G. Sellers, *The Market Revolution, 1815–1848* (1992); Edward Pessen, *Jacksonian America: Society, Personality, and Politics,* rev. ed. (1978); Steven Hahn and Jonathan

Prude, eds., *The Countryside in the Age of Capitalist Transformation* (1985), and Russel B. Nye, *Society and Culture in America, 1830–1860* (1974). Lawrence A. Cremin, *American Education: The National Experience, 1783–1876* (1980), is a sweeping study not only of formal education, but of the transmission of knowledge in a democratic society. Many interpreters of the period draw heavily on Alexis de Tocqueville's classic work *Democracy in America,* of which there are many editions. Daniel I. Boorstin's *The Americans: The National Experience* (1965) emphasizes America's uniqueness, although more recent work has reversed this trend. The period is illuminated in different ways by Yehoshua Arieli, *Individualism and Nationalism in American Ideology* (1964); Rowland Berthoff, *An Unsettled People: Social Order and Disorder in American History* (1971); and Fred Somkin, *Unquiet Eagle: Memory and Desire in the Idea of American Freedom, 1815–1860* (1967). An anthology of primary source material, accompanied by extensive commentary, is David B. Davis, ed., *Antebellum American Culture: An Interpretive Anthology* (1979).

Population growth is analyzed by J. Potter, "The Growth of Population in America, 1700–1860," in *Population and History . . . ,* eds. D. V. Glass and D. E. C. Eversley (1965); and Richard A. Easterlin, *Population, Labor Force and Long Swings in Economic Growth: The American Experience* (1968). Maldwyn A. Jones, *American Immigration* (1960), is a useful introduction to the subject; it should be supplemented by Marcus L. Hansen, *The Atlantic Migration, 1607–1860* (1940); Oscar Handlin, *Boston's Immigrants* (1959); Robert Ernst, *Immigrant Life in New York City, 1825–1863* (1949); Kathleen N. Conzen, *Immigrant Milwaukee, 1836–1860* (1977); Kerby A. Miller, *Emigrants and Exiles: Ireland and the Irish Exodus to North America* (1985); and Carl Wittke, *The Irish in America* (1956). For urbanization and urban problems, see Sam Bass Warner, Jr., *The Urban Wilderness* (1972); Elizabeth Blackmar, *Manhattan for Rent, 1785–1850* (1989); Thomas Bender, *Toward an Urban Vision: Ideas and Institutions in Nineteenth-Century America* (1975); Richard C. Wade, *The Urban Frontier* (1964); and Paul Boyer, *Urban Masses and Moral Order in America, 1820–1920* (1978). Anthony F. C. Wallace, *Rockdale: The Growth of an American Village in the Early Industrial Revolution* (1978), is an imaginative but controversial interpretation of the way industrialization affected the entire life and culture of an American community.

For overviews of antebellum economic growth, see Thomas C. Cochran, *Frontiers of Change: Early Industrialism in America* (1981); W. Elliot Brownlee, *Dynamics of Ascent* (1974), and Stuart Bruchey, *Growth of the Modern American Economy* (1975). For a fascinating discussion of the economic thought of the pre–Civil War period, see Joseph Dorfman, *The Economic Mind in American Civilization,* vol. 2 (3 vols., 1946–49). Douglass C. North, *The Economic Growth of the United States, 1790–1860* (1961), stresses the importance of international trade. For the international impact of textile technology, see David J. Jeremy, *Trans-Atlantic Industrial Revolution: The Diffusion of Textile Technology Between Britain and America, 1790–1830* (1981). Peter Temin, *The Jacksonian Economy* (1969), challenges many of the traditional beliefs of historians. The best treatment of early American science is Robert V. Bruce, *The Launching of Modern American Science, 1846–1876* (1987).

Ray A. Billington, *Westward Expansion* (1974), presents an excellent survey of the history of the American West as well as a comprehensive bibliography. For the magic symbolism of California, see Kevin Starr, *Americans and the California Dream, 1850–1915* (1973). The fullest histories of agriculture are Percy W. Bidwell and John I. Falconer, *History of Agriculture in the Northern United States, 1620–1860* (1925), and Lewis C. Gray, *History of Agriculture in the Southern United States to 1860* (2 vols., 1933). A briefer and outstanding survey is Paul W. Gates, *The Farmer's Age: Agriculture, 1815–1860* (1960), which can be supplemented by Clarence H. Danhof, *Change in Agriculture in the Northern United States, 1820–1870* (1969).

The classic study of transportation is George R. Taylor, *The Transportation Revolution, 1815–1860* (1951). A monumental work, confined to New England, is Edward Kirkland, *Men,*

Cities, and Transportation (2 vols., 1948). For canals, see Harry N. Scheiber, *Ohio Canal Era* (1969), and R. E. Shaw, *Erie Water West* (1966).

For railroads, see Albert Fishlow, *American Railroads and the Transformation of the Ante-Bellum Economy* (1965); John F. Stover, *Iron Road to the West: American Railroads in the 1850s* (1978); Alfred D. Chandler, Jr., ed., *The Nation's First Big Business* (1965); and Thomas C. Cochran, *Railroad Leaders, 1845–1890* (1953). Christopher T. Baer, *Canals and Railroads of the Mid-Atlantic States, 1800–1860* (1981), is especially valuable for its detailed maps and tables. The organization and management of railroad corporations is masterfully analyzed in Alfred D. Chandler, Jr., *The Visible Hand: The Managerial Revolution in American Business* (1977). The role of government is treated in Carter Goodrich, *Government Promotion of American Canals and Railroads, 1800–1890* (1960); Louis Hartz, *Economic Policy and Democratic Thought* (1954); and Oscar Handlin and Mary F. Handlin, *Commonwealth: A Study of the Role of Government in the American Economy* (1969).

The best works on maritime trade are Robert G. Albion, *The Rise of New York Port* (1939), and Samuel E. Morison, *Maritime History of Massachusetts, 1789–1860* (1921). For the clipper ships, see C. C. Cutler, *Greyhounds of the Sea* (1930), and A. H. Clark, *The Clipper Ship Era* (1910). L. H. Battistini, *The Rise of American Influence in Asia and the Pacific* (1960), treats an important aspect of America's commercial expansion.

On manufacturing, Victor S. Clark, *History of Manufactures in the United States, 1607–1860* (3 vols., 1929), remains indispensable. Thomas C. Cochran, *Frontiers of Change: Early Industrialism in America* (1981), synthesizes the results of recent research and casts new light on the factors leading to rapid industrialization in Pennsylvania and New York. For New England's pioneers in modernization, see Robert F. Dalzell, Jr., *Enterprising Elite: The Boston Associates and the World They Made* (1987). The impact of industrialization on a rural and small-town culture is treated in Jonathan Prude, *The Coming of Industrial Order: Town and Factory Life in Rural Massachusetts, 1810–1860* (1983). The best specialized studies are Peter Temin, *Iron and Steel in Nineteenth Century America* (1964); Caroline F. Ware, *The Early New England Cotton Manufacture* (1931); Arthur H. Cole, *The American Wool Manufacture* (2 vols., 1926); and Otto Mayr and Robert C. Post, eds., *Yankee Enterprise: The Rise of the American System of Manufactures* (1981). Siegfried Giedion, *Mechanization Takes Command* (1948), contains a fascinating account of American technological innovation. A brilliant study of the significance of the new technology is Merritt R. Smith, *Harpers Ferry Armory and the New Technology: The Challenge of Change* (1977). H. I. Habakkuk, *American and British Technology in the Nineteenth Century* (1962), places American invention in a larger context, as does Carroll W. Pursell, Jr., *Early Stationary Steam Engines in America: A Study in the Migration of Technology* (1969). For a comprehensive reference work, see Melvin Kranzberg and Carroll W. Pursell, Jr., eds., *Technology in Western Civilization* (2 vols., 1967). The ideological impact of technology is imaginatively treated in John F. Kasson, *Civilizing the Machine: Technology and Republican Values in America, 1776–1900* (1976).

A pioneering study of social and economic mobility is Stephan Thernstrom, *Poverty and Progress* (1964). For disparities in the distribution of wealth and income, see Edward Pessen, *Riches, Class, and Power Before the Civil War* (1973), and Lee Soltow, "Economic Inequality in the United States in the Period from 1790 to 1860," *Journal of Economic History,* 31 (December 1971), 822–39. The discovery of poverty is analyzed in Robert H. Bremner, *From the Depths* (1956), and Raymond A. Mohl, *Poverty in New York, 1783–1825* (1971). On working-class culture and ideology, the best guides are Alan Dawley, *Class and Community: The Industrial Revolution in Lynn* (1977); Christine Stansell, *City of Women: Sex and Class in New York, 1789–1860* (1986); Paul G. Faler, *Mechanics and Manufacturers in the Early Industrial Revolution: Lynn, Massachusetts, 1780–1860* (1981); Bruce Laurie, *Working People of Philadelphia, 1800–1850* (1980); Bruce Laurie, *Artisans into Workers: Labor in Nineteenth-Century America* (1989); Herbert G.

Gutman, *Work, Culture, and Society in Industrializing America* (1976); Howard M. Gitelman, *Workingmen of Waltham* (1974); Peter R. Knights, *The Plain People of Boston* (1971); and Norman Ware, *The Industrial Worker, 1840–1860* (1959). For labor movements and protests, see David Montgomery, *Workers' Control in America: Studies in the History of Work, Technology, and Labor Struggles* (1979); Sean Wilentz, *Chants Democratic: New York City and the Rise of the American Working Class, 1788–1850* (1984); Joseph Rayback, *A History of American Labor* (1966); and Walter Hugins, *Jacksonian Democracy and the Working Class* (1960). For a richly informative analysis of women's experience in the most famous New England mill town, see Thomas Dublin, *Women at Work: The Transformation of Work and Community in Lowell, Massachusetts, 1826–1860* (1979). Two good studies of the ideology of the self-made man—Irvin G. Wyllie, *The Self-Made Man in America* (1954), and John G. Cawelti, *Apostles of the Self-Made Man* (1965)—should be supplemented by Daniel T. Rodgers, *The Work Ethic in Industrial America, 1850–1920* (1978). Although dealing with a later period, Richard Weiss, *The American Myth of Success* (1969), also sheds light on the earlier history of the subject.

A good introduction to Indian removal is Wilcomb E. Washburn, *The Indian in America* (1975). Francis P. Prucha, *American Indian Policy in the Formative Years* (1962), is sympathetic to government policymakers. Ronald N. Satz, *American Indian Policy in the Jacksonian Era* (1975), provides an informative account of the subsequent period. The most comprehensive studies of the so-called civilized tribes are William G. McLoughlin, *Cherokee Renascence in the New Republic* (1986) and Charles Hudson, *The Southeastern Indians* (1976); for the Far West, see Sherburne F. Cook, *The Conflict Between the California Indian and White Civilization* (1976). An outstanding work that corrects the mythology regarding the relation between the native Americans and western pioneers is John Unruh, *The Plains Across: The Overland Emigrants and the Trans-Mississippi West* (1979). There are three valuable related works in intellectual history: Roy H. Pearce, *The Savages of America* (1965); Richard Slotkin, *Regeneration Through Violence: The Mythology of the American Frontier, 1600–1860* (1973); and Roderick Nash, *Wilderness in the American Mind* (1967).

2

Shaping the American Character

Reform, Protest, Dissent, Artistic Creativity

⟨⟩

*T*HE DESIRE to transform character lay at the heart of American reform in the mid-nineteenth century. In line with republican tradition, reformers rejoiced that the nation was free from kings and nobles, from aristocratic institutions, and from status and roles defined at birth, with the flagrant exception of black slavery. Like other Americans, reformers were cheered by the absence or removal of traditional barriers to human progress. But in pursuing the good life that had supposedly been made accessible by the sacrifices of the Founders, Americans had somehow created a society of astounding moral and physical contrasts—a society of luxury and of squalor, of spiritual uplift and of degradation, of freedom and of bondage. In the eyes of dissenters and reformers, it often seemed that America was ruled only by the principles of ruthless self-interest and power.

During the pre–Civil War decades, political and religious leaders repeatedly warned that the fate of free institutions, both in the United States and in the rest of the world, depended on the moral and intellectual character of the American people. If the American people betrayed their high mission, the very idea of popular self-government would be discredited for centuries to come. Religious beliefs continued to differ about humanity's sinfulness or inherent capacity for love and social harmony. But Americans of various outlooks agreed that human nature was much like clay that can be molded to any shape before it hardens. And the American people were still at a highly plastic stage of development.

This conviction could be inspiring. In 1823, for example, Charles Jared Ingersoll, a Philadelphia lawyer and former congressman, delivered an influential *Discourse Concerning the Influence of America on the Mind.* Ingersoll was confident that the average American, as a result of the free and republican environment, stood far above the average European in both intelligence and virtue. He promised that American achievements in the arts and sciences would soon show

39

the world the full potentialities of human nature when it was not crippled by despotism and aristocratic privilege.

But a capacity for infinite improvement might also be a capacity for infinite corruption. Even the optimists tended to worry over the growing inadequacy of local religious and social institutions in the face of America's sensational expansion. The need to shape or change individual character gave a new social importance to educators, religious revivalists, popular essayists, phrenologists, and other promoters of self-improvement.

The spirit of reform and dissent was centered in the Northeast, and particularly in New England. During the years before the Civil War, this region spawned numerous crusades to regenerate the social order—to substitute love, harmony, and cooperation for what a leading religious reformer, William Ellery Channing, termed the "jarring interests and passions, invasions of rights, resistance of authority, violence, force" that were deforming the entire society. Whether these movements were religious or secular, most of them sought to bring American culture into harmony with a "higher law"—"the moral government of God"—as a means of preventing anarchy. Although reformers differed in their specific objectives, they shared a common desire to channel spiritual aspirations into the secular world of power.

The character of the reform movement of the pre–Civil War period was unique. Throughout history religious reformers had sent out missionaries to convert heathens and had sought to provide the world with models of saintly life, including dietary discipline and selfless commitment. But they had never created the kind of highly professional reform organizations that began to spring up in both Britain and America in the early nineteenth century.* These organizations were devoted to various goals—to building model penitentiaries, to persuading people to abstain from alcoholic drinks, and above all to abolishing slavery. The objectives were uncompromising, and the systematic techniques for mobilizing public opinion and exerting pressure on public officials were altogether novel.

Nevertheless these reform movements usually embodied a nostalgia for a supposedly simpler and more harmonious past. Members of the movements believed that the evils they combated had multiplied because of an alarming disintegration of family authority, of community cohesiveness, and of traditional morality. The various programs, therefore, had a dual objective for change and improvement. On the one hand, they attacked institutions, lifestyles, and traditional social roles that seemed to limit individual opportunity and to block the path of progress. On the other hand, they attempted to restore and revitalize the sense of purity, simplicity, and community that had been lost in the headlong pursuit of modernity and material improvement.

---

* Although Britain was still ruled by a monarch, a landed aristocracy, and an established church, a popular political culture had begun to emerge alongside vocal and dynamic minorities of religious dissent; consequently, there were strong similarities and lines of influence between reformers in Britain and the United States. See pp. 436–37.

"We Must Educate or Perish"

Shaping character, whether by school, church, prison, or asylum, seemed to be the only means of ensuring moral stability in an expansive and increasingly individualistic society. Lyman Beecher—best known today as the father of the novelist Harriet Beecher Stowe but in his own day the most prominent Protestant minister in the North—viewed the rapid settlement of the West with a mixture of exhilaration and alarm. By 1835 the states west of the Appalachian Mountains had grown so rapidly that he could predict a population of 100 million by 1900, "a day which some of our children may live to see." The West, Beecher believed, was a "young empire of mind, and power, and wealth, and free institutions." It contained the potential for nothing less than "the emancipation of the world." Beecher had no doubts about the West's material progress. The danger was "that our intelligence and virtue will falter and fall back into a dark minded, vicious populace—a poor, uneducated reckless mass of infuriated animalism." Beecher was aroused particularly by the supposed threat of Catholic immigrants, whom he pictured as the agents of foreign despots intent on subverting republican institutions. For Beecher, the hands-off policy of laissez-faire liberalism had erased the old republican concern for the common good. He therefore urged an immediate crusade to evangelize and educate the West: "For population will not wait, and commerce will not cast anchor, and manufacturers will not shut off the steam nor shut down the gate, and agriculture, pushed by millions of free men on their fertile soil, will not withhold her corrupting abundance. We must educate! We must educate! or we must perish by our own prosperity."

The State of Education Educational reformers had some reason for alarm. Even Massachusetts, which in 1837 established the nation's first state board of education, suffered from broken-down school buildings, untrained and incompetent teachers, and dependence on unequal and unpredictable local funding. The one-room country schoolhouse, often idealized in later years, not only was dirty, drafty, and overheated in winter, but was commonly packed with children of all ages—some old and rowdy enough to inflict beatings on male teachers and to prompt some women teachers to hide a pistol in a desk drawer. The soaring growth of eastern cities made middle-class citizens suddenly aware of begging street urchins, teenage prostitutes, gangs of juvenile delinquents, and vagrant children, who, like Mark Twain's Huckleberry Finn, had little desire to be "civilized."

Until the second quarter of the nineteenth century, the education of Americans was informal, unsystematic, and dependent on parental initiative and ability to pay. Even so, compared with most Europeans, white American males had always enjoyed a high rate of literacy, especially in New England. During the 1790s a surprising number of artisans and skilled laborers had sent their children to the "common pay schools" in New York City, where children of rich and poor backgrounds mingled. By the early nineteenth century, illiteracy was rapidly disappearing among white females. Boys and girls frequently attended the same schools, despite prejudices against gender integration. Some free schools expected parents to pay a small fee, and most tax-supported schools were intended only for the children of the very poor. Aside from school attendance, apprenticeship long served as a noteworthy means of education, providing the vocational skills that could not be learned in any school. Not until the mid-nineteenth century—and in the South not until after the Civil War—did education become increasingly confined to specialized institutions segregated from the mainstreams of adult social life.

Working-Class Demands
Middle-class religious reformers were not alone in demanding educational reform. In 1828 the organized mechanics and journeymen of Philadelphia, most of whom were skilled artisans and craftsmen who had served their apprenticeship, began to protest. As in other northeastern cities, these workers were angered by low wages, by the substitution of temporary child "apprentices" for skilled adult laborers, and by the erosion of the traditional craft system that had allowed apprentices and journeymen to rise within a given trade. The Philadelphia Working Men's party pressed for a broad range of economic and social reforms. One of these was for better educational opportunities. "The original element of despotism," proclaimed a party committee in 1829, "is a monopoly of talent, which consigns the multitude to comparative ignorance, and secures the balance of knowledge on the side of the rich and the rulers."

The demand for free tax-supported schools became a rallying cry for the workingmen's parties and associations that sprang up in New York, Boston, and dozens of small towns throughout the country. A group of New York workers expressed the typical rhetoric when they asked in 1830 "if many of the monopolists and aristocrats of our city would not consider it disgraceful to their noble children to have them placed in our public schools by the side of poor yet industrious mechanics." Although many of the leaders of these groups were not manual laborers, the short-lived workingmen's movement reflected an authentic desire for equal educational opportunity on the part of skilled laborers whose economic and social condition had begun to deteriorate.

For most workingmen economic grievances soon took precedence over education. The economic growth of the pre–Civil War decades called for more and more unskilled laborers, but not for a significant increase in the number of skilled and nonmanual workers who might benefit materially from an education beyond the "three Rs." In New York City, where the proportion of nonmanual and professional jobs changed very little from 1796 to 1855, many working-class parents questioned whether they should sacrifice family income in order to educate children for jobs that did not exist.

As early as 1832 the New York Public School Society pointed out: "The labouring classes of society will, to a great extent, withhold their children from school, the moment they arrive at an age that renders their services in the least available in contributing to the support of the family." Later evidence indicated that children under fifteen earned as much as 20 percent of the income of working-class families in Newburyport, Massachusetts. For such families compulsory attendance laws often threatened an unbearable drop in already subsistence level income. Not surprisingly, 40 percent of Newburyport's laborers admitted to the census takers in 1850 that their school-age children had not been enrolled in any school during the previous year. And many children who were enrolled could not attend regularly.

Moreover, by the 1840s the working class in the Northeast was becoming increasingly Roman Catholic. Although the public schools were theoretically secular—in New York and elsewhere, denominational schools had been deprived of public funding—the values and teachings of the schools were unmistakably Protestant. Most Americans of the mid-nineteenth century still thought that Americanism meant Protestantism. Protestant clergymen played a critical role on school committees and in school reform. They saw nothing sectarian about public school teachers' reading aloud from the King James Bible or teaching that the sixteenth-century Protestant Reformation had represented a liberation from Catholic despotism. Bishop John Hughes and other Catholic leaders saw the matter differently. In 1840 New York Catholics launched a political offensive against the Protestant monopoly of public education. As a result of this conflict, the Catholic church decided to construct its own separate system of schools, a costly program that took many decades to complete.

For many immigrants, Catholics, and working-class parents, the Protestant school reformers threatened to impose a uniform set of values on all segments of American society—a flagrant instance of violating minority rights. Resistance also arose from local authorities who feared any centralizing interference from a state board of education. Many conservatives insisted that parents should pay for education, if they could afford it, just as they would pay for any other service or commodity. Others, brought up on the tradition of church schools, feared that the teaching of moral values would be dangerously undermined if guided only by a vaguely Protestant and nondenominational spirit.

Educational Reformers

These obstacles to the expansion of public education were finally overcome by reformers like Horace Mann, who as the chief officer of the Massachusetts Board of Education from 1837 to 1848 became the nation's leading champion of public schools. Mann was a severe, humorless puritan who denounced intemperance, profanity, and ballet dancing along with ignorance, violence, and black slavery. Having personally struggled with the terrors of his New England Calvinist heritage, he had finally concluded that children were capable of infinite improvement and goodness. As a kind of secular minister, still intent on saving souls, he insisted that there must have been a time in the childhood of the worst criminal when, "ere he was irrecoverably lost, ere he plunged into the abyss of infamy and guilt, he might have been recalled." Mann offended traditional Christians by winning the fight in Massachusetts against specific religious instruction in the public schools. He outraged conservatives by asserting that private property is not an absolute right but rather a trusteeship for society and future generations. Trained as a lawyer, he decided as a young man that "the next generation" should be his clients. In pleading the cause of generations to come, he held that school taxes were not a "confiscation" from the rich, but rather a collection of the debt the rich owed to society.

Reformers placed a stupendous moral burden on the public schools. Horace Mann proclaimed the common school to be "the greatest discovery ever made by man." "Other social organizations are curative and remedial," he said; "this is a preventive and antidote." This characteristic argument suggests that the schools were to be a defense against undesirable change, preserving the cherished values of a simpler, more homogeneous America. Educators spoke of the frenzied pace of American life, of the diminishing influence of church and home. They held that the school should thus serve as a substitute for both church and home, preventing American democracy from degenerating into what Mann called "the spectacle of gladiatorial contests." The school, representing the highest instincts of society, could alone be counted on for cultivating decency, cooperation, and a respect for others. Women, reformers believed, were best suited as teachers because they exemplified the noncombative and noncompetitive instincts. Because they could also be employed for lower wages than men, women teachers soon predominated in New England's elementary schools.

The character traits most esteemed by educational reformers were precisely those alleged to bring material success in a competitive and market-oriented society: punctuality, cheerful obedience, honesty, responsibility, perseverance, and foresightedness. Public schools seemed to promise opportunity by providing the means of acquiring these traits. In the words of one school committee, the children "entered the race, aware that the prize was equally before all, and attainable only by personal exertion." The famed McGuffey's "Eclectic" series of readers, which after 1836 became the basic reading textbooks in countless schoolrooms and of which well over 100 million copies were eventually sold, taught young students that no possession was more important for getting on in the world than reputation—"a good name." On the other hand, the readers held out little hope of rags-to-riches success. When the good little poor boy sees other children "riding on pretty horses, or in coaches, or walking with ladies and gentlemen, and having on very fine clothes, he does not envy them, nor wish to be like them." For he has been taught "that it is God who makes some poor, and others rich; that the rich have many troubles which we know nothing of; and that the poor, if they are but good, may be very happy."

From a present-day viewpoint the educational reformers were often insensitive to the needs of non-Protestants, non-Christians, nonwhites, and women. Throughout the North, except in a few scattered communities, the public schools excluded black children. Many localities made no provision for blacks to be educated. Other towns and cities, including New York and Boston, distributed a small portion of public funds to segregated and highly inferior schools for blacks. By 1850 blacks constituted no more than 1.5 percent of Boston's population, but to achieve local desegregation still required a prolonged struggle on the part of militant blacks and white abolitionists. In 1855 Massachusetts became the single state in which no applicant to a public school could be excluded on account of "race, color or religious opinions." In marked contrast to the public schools, Oberlin, Harvard, Bowdoin, Dartmouth, and some other private colleges opened their doors to a few black students. In 1837 Oberlin also became America's first coeducational college. In general, however, American women had no opportunities for higher education except in female seminaries and, by the 1850s, a few western state universities.

By the 1850s Massachusetts had acquired all the essentials of a modern educational system: special "normal schools" for the training of female teachers; the placement of pupils in grades according to age and ability; standardized procedures for advancement from one grade to another; uniform textbooks; and a bureaucracy extending from the board of education down to superintendents, principals, and teachers. Although Massachusetts led the nation, by the 1850s it was possible for a New York City male child to proceed from an "infant school" to a college degree without paying tuition. Educational reformers, many of them originally New Englanders, had helped to create state-supported and state-supervised school systems from Pennsylvania to the new states of the Upper Mississippi Valley. In the 1850s the same cause made some headway in the South, particularly in Virginia and North Carolina.

Whatever prejudices and blind spots the public school movement may have had, it aroused the enthusiasm of hundreds of idealistic men and women who devoted time and energy to the cause. Northern legislators committed an impressive proportion of public spending to the education of succeeding generations. Particularly in the 1850s the movement trained a young generation of teachers inspired with missionary zeal. After the Civil War they would descend on the devastated South, equipped with an ideology for "reconstruction." Above all, the movement reinforced the American faith that social problems could be solved by individual enterprise, a diffusion of knowledge, and a reconstruction of moral character.

The Evangelical Age

Americans continued to look on the church, no less than on the public school, as a decisive instrument for shaping the national character. As in the post-Revolutionary period, religion became more widely accepted and democratic the more it achieved independence from the government. (In 1833 Massachusetts became the last state to give up an established church.) Despite the officially secular stance of American governments, evangelical Protestantism became increasingly identified with patriotism, democracy, and America's mission in the world. And despite the continuing division and competition among religious denominations, Americans increasingly appealed to religion as the only force in American life that could preserve a sense of community and united purpose.

Religious Revivals   Between 1820 and 1860 religious revivalism became a powerful organizing and nationalizing force that reached into all parts of American life and all corners of the vast nation—the South as well as the North, the cities as well as the western frontier. Church membership figures can be misleading since many people who regularly attended church could not meet the religious or financial obligations that were required for formal membership. But it has been estimated that by 1835 as many as three out of four adult Americans maintained some nominal relationship to a church. Most foreign observers agreed with Tocqueville that by the 1830s there was no country in the world in which the Christian religion retained "a greater influence over the souls of men."

For the majority of adults, evangelical Protestantism provided a common language and a common frame of reference. It explained not only the nature and ultimate destiny of human beings, but also the meaning of democracy and of American nationality. In the words of a non–church member, a young self-made man and future president of the United States, Andrew Johnson, "Man can become more and more endowed with divinity; and as he does he becomes more godlike in his character and capable of governing himself." Like millions of other Americans, Johnson believed that Christianity and political democracy were together elevating and purifying the people, working toward the day when it could be proclaimed: "The millennial morning has dawned and the time has come when the lion and the lamb shall lie down together, when the glad tidings shall be proclaimed . . . of man's political and religious redemption, and there is 'on earth, peace, good will toward men.'"

In some ways this evangelical vision transcended boundaries of class and section. Although it is possible to think of America as undergoing a single Great Revival during the six decades preceding the Civil War, the revival's social significance differed according to time and place. Some socioeconomic groups were more susceptible to religious enthusiasm than others. Some personality types were likely to view revivalists as self-righteous zealots who threatened to remove all fun from life. Others were likely to seize the chance to profess faith in Christ crucified, to announce repentance for their sins, to experience the liberation of rebirth, and as the popular hymn put it, to "stand up, stand up for Jesus!" For many Americans religion provided the key to social identity. It was not that people flocked to churches to meet the right kind of people, although some no doubt did. It was rather that the "right" kind of religion, as defined by employers, slaveholders, and other wielders of power, was often considered to bestow the "right" kind of character.

Religious revivalism depended on sensitivity to the community's norms and vital interests. In the South leaders of various denominations discovered that any open criticism of slavery could threaten the very survival of a church. The Baptist and Methodist churches thus gradually retreated from their cautious antislavery views of the late eighteenth century, which had supposedly bred discontent if not rebellion among black slaves. By the 1830s the most influential southern churches had begun to deny that there was any moral contradiction between slavery and Christianity. They also insisted that Christianity, rightly understood, posed no danger to "the peculiar institution."*

Civilizing the West   Revivalism also served as a socializing force in the nonslaveholding West, but the context and consequences were different. Easterners tended to think of the West as both lawless and sinful. From the lumber camps of Wisconsin to the mining camps of California, easterners' image of westerners was essentially the same: rough, dirty men who swore, gambled, got drunk, frequented houses of prostitution, and relished savage eye-gouging, knife-slashing fights. Although the stereotypes were exaggerated, there was no doubt that frontier communities strained nineteenth-century notions of decency and civilization.

The challenge of the West could not be met simply by building churches where none had existed before. When Theron Baldwin, a member of a Yale missionary group, arrived in Illinois in 1830, he was horrified by the ignorance of the settlers. Even in Vandalia, then the state's capital, Baldwin discovered that most of the pupils in his Sunday school class were illiterate. Nor could he find a literate adult in more than half the families he visited in the region. Religion, Baldwin concluded, could make no headway without education and an institutional rebuilding of society. Appealing for funds from the East, he expressed the New England ideal: "We wish to see the school house and church go up side by side and the land filled with Christian teachers as well as preachers." He added, significantly, that young men could come there "and in a short time get enough by teaching to purchase a farm that would ever after fill their barns with plenty and their hands with good things." Baldwin himself worked to secure from the legislature a charter for the first three colleges in the state. As a result of the labors of Baldwin and other young missionaries, the Old Northwest became dotted with academies, seminaries, and small denominational colleges.

Easterners who still thought of churches as fixed institutions within an ordered society did not understand that religious revivals were an effective instrument for shaping and controlling character. The frank emotionalism and homespun informality of the western and southern revivals disguised the fact that even the camp meetings were soon stabilized by rules, regulations, and the most careful advance planning. And camp meetings were by no means the most important tools of the revivals. The power of the revival movement flowed from the dynamic balance between popular participation and the control of leaders. According to the evangelical message, every man and woman, no matter how humble or trapped in sin, had the capacity to say "Yes!" to Christ's offer of salvation—to reject what was called "cannot-ism," and along with it an

_____

*For the impact of Christianity on the slaves' culture and on plantation life, as well as among the free blacks, see chapter 14, pp. 467–68.

Where Character Ultimately Leads
This fanciful diagram of values and human destiny dramatizes the connections between religion and education, and between behavior and one's ultimate fate. "The College" is significantly close to the path of virtues that lead to heaven. But out of the schoolhouse, with its disobedience to parents and teachers, come those who move from fighting and profanity to the "House of Sin," gambling, intemperance, cheating, and on to prison, the gallows, and hell. Such imagery was designed to impress—and frighten—young minds.

unsatisfying identity. Even for the poor and uneducated, consent opened the way for participation and decision making.

Peter Cartwright, for example, grew up in one of the most violent and lawless regions of Kentucky. His brother was hanged for murder, and his sister was said to have "led a life of debauchery." At the age of sixteen, Cartwright repented his sins at a Methodist camp meeting; at seventeen he became an "exhorter"; at eighteen, a traveling preacher; at twenty-one, a deacon; and at twenty-three, a presiding elder of the church. Each upward step required a trial period, followed by an examination of his conduct, ability, and purity of doctrine. The Methodists showed particular skill in devising a system that encouraged widespread participation and upward mobility in the church's organizational structure. But all the evangelical churches displayed the great American gift for organization. Revivals, they believed, could not take place by waiting for God to stir human hearts. Revivals required planning, efficient techniques, and coordinated effort. The need was not for educated theologians, but for professional promoters.

Christianity and the Social Order

Although revivalism was an organizing and socializing movement, it was also by definition selective. The people most likely to be converted were those who had had some Christian upbringing or those who were already disturbed by excessive drinking, gambling, fighting, disorder, and irresponsibility. Conversion itself reinforced crucial social distinctions. For one part of the community, religion became more than a matter of going to church on Sunday. The obligations of a new religious life required sobriety and responsibility from friends, family, employees, and business associates. The weekly "class meetings" and "love feasts" provided fellowship and helped to prevent backsliding. No doubt the solidarity of the converted individuals brought order and discipline to the community at large. But if the evangelicals always insisted that every man and woman could say "Yes!" there were always those who said "No!" The congregations that loved to hear their preachers "pouring hot shot into Satan's ranks" knew that Satan's ranks were concentrated on the other side of the tracks.

Religious revivals could accentuate social distinctions by forging an alliance among the more ambitious, self-disciplined, and future-oriented members of a community. In the fall of 1830, for example, the leaders of Rochester, New York, invited Charles Grandison Finney to save that booming town from sin. By far the most commanding and influential evangelist of the pre–Civil War period, Finney was a tall, athletic spellbinder, a former lawyer who had undergone a dramatic religious conversion in 1823. Although he lacked formal seminary training, Finney had been ordained as a Presbyterian minister and in 1825 had begun a series of highly unusual and spectacular revivals along the route of the newly constructed Erie Canal.

In 1831 Finney's triumphs in Rochester stunned Christian America. Communities from Ohio to Massachusetts appealed to him to save their collective souls. Finney's converts in Rochester were largely housewives, manufacturers, merchants, lawyers, shopkeepers, master artisans, and skilled journeymen. He appealed to people who had profited from the commercial revolution initiated by the building of the Erie Canal but who had become deeply disturbed by the immense influx of young transient laborers looking for work. Rochester's leaders had no control over the behavior of these youths. Significantly, during Rochester's revival years church membership declined among the hotel proprietors and tavern keepers who catered to the floating population of young males traveling the Erie Canal. Rochester's Protestant churches, interpreting the revival as a sweeping popular mandate, launched a crusade to purge the city of its dens of vice and unholy amusement. They also offered a "free church"—free of pew rents and other financial obligations—to the workers on the canal. Increasingly Rochester became divided between a Christian minority dedicated to education and upward advancement and an essentially nonpolitical, free-floating majority of disoriented and unskilled young men.

Philadelphia differed from Rochester in important respects, but there too religious revivals eventually redefined the boundaries of respectable and "modern" behavior. Unlike Rochester, which grew by 512 percent in the 1820s, Philadelphia was not a new boom town. An old city by American standards, Philadelphia was relatively resistant to religious enthusiasm. Revivalism had little appeal to the wealthy Quakers and conservative Presbyterian clergymen who dominated the city's religious life. Evangelical morality was even less appealing to

Philadelphia's workingmen, who preserved and cherished a traditional artisan, preindustrial culture. Largely because of irregular and undeveloped transportation to interior markets, Philadelphia workers suffered periodic layoffs. This forced leisure allowed them to enjoy traveling circuses, cockfights, drinking and gambling at the local taverns, and above all the boisterous comradeship of volunteer fire companies. Until 1837 neither the revival nor the closely related temperance movement made much headway among Philadelphia's manual workers. The people who reformed their drinking habits and who joined the reform-minded wing of the Presbyterian church were the professional and business groups who were ushering in the new industrial order. But in 1837 the financial panic and subsequent depression began to undermine the traditional habits and culture of the working class. Waves of religious revivalism, often Methodist in character, reached working-class neighborhoods. A new and more powerful temperance movement developed spontaneously from the ranks of master craftsmen, journeymen, shopkeepers, and the most ambitious unskilled laborers. In Philadelphia, as in Rochester, the decision to abstain from all alcohol was the key symbol of a new morality and of a new commitment to self-improvement. By the 1840s the evangelical workingmen could contrast their own sobriety and self-discipline with the moral laxity of mounting numbers of Irish immigrants. Not surprisingly, the revivalism that bolstered the self-respect of blue-collar native workers and their wives also contributed to passionate anti-Catholicism and to old-stock prejudice against a population that seemed to threaten the newly won dignity of manual labor.

Revivalism and Economic Prosperity   Revivals appeared to be the only hopeful counterforce against rampant individualism, self-serving politics, and corrupting luxury. As Finney put it, "the great political and other worldly excitements" of the time distracted attention from the interests of the soul. He held, accordingly, that these excitements could "only be counteracted by religious excitements." Only revivals could prevent the United States from sliding into the decay and collapse of ancient Greece and Rome. Only revivals could prepare the nation "to lead the way," in Lyman Beecher's phrase, "in the moral and political emancipation of the world."

Revivalism was fed by the moral doubts that inevitably accompanied rapid economic growth, the disruption of older modes of work and responsibility, the sudden accumulation of wealth, and the appearance of new class differences. Revivalist preachers denounced atheism far less than "Mammonism," the greedy pursuit of riches. They voiced repeated concern over the frantic pace of American life, the disintegration of family and community, and the worship of material success.

But revivalism seldom led to saintly withdrawal or to spiritualistic contemplation. Evangelical religion was above all activist, pragmatic, and oriented toward measurable results. The fame of Finney and the other great exhorters depended on the body count, or soul count, of converts. Finney proclaimed: "The results justify my methods—a motto that could as well have come from

John Jacob Astor or other entrepreneurs in more worldly spheres. Finney confidently predicted: "If the church will do her duty, the millennium may come in this country in three years." He knew, however, that a millennium would require no revivals, and that as a revivalist, although dedicated to virtue, he needed sin as much as a soldier needs war.

There was a close relation between the revivals and America's expansive economy. The exuberant materialism of American life furnished revivalists with continuing targets for attack and with vivid signs of community strife and moral shortcoming. Without moral crises there would be no cause for national rededication, and calls for rededication have long been America's way of responding to social change. But on another level the revivalists had merged their cause with America's secular destiny. They had repeatedly warned that without religion, American democracy would speedily dissolve into "a common field of unbridled appetite and lust." Yet instead of dissolving, the nation continued to prosper, expand, and reveal new marvels. Sometimes clergymen hailed the achievements as signs of national virtue and divine favor. More important, as a reflection of their increasing respect for efficient methods and material results, they applauded technological improvements as the instruments that God had provided for saving the world.

The telegraph, railroad, and steamship all quickened the way for spreading the gospel around the world, and thus they could be interpreted as signs of the coming millennium. But America's technology and rapid westward expansion could be justified only if Americans took the burdens of a missionary nation seriously. Samuel Fisher, the president of Hamilton College in upstate New York, elaborated on this message in an address to the American Board of Commissioners for Foreign Missions:

> Material activity, quickened and guided by moral principle, is absolutely essential to the development of a strong and manly character. . . . The product of this devotion to material interests is capital diffused through the masses; and capital is one of the means God uses to convert the world.

The diffusion of capital through the masses seemed to falter in 1857, when a financial crash brought a severe depression and unprecedented unemployment among factory workers. Economic insecurity formed the backdrop of what many took to be "the event of the century," the great urban revival of late 1857 and 1858. What distinguished this event from earlier religious revivals was the absence of revivalists. In Philadelphia and New York thousands of clerks and businessmen began to unite spontaneously for midday prayer. The New York *Herald* and the New York *Tribune* devoted special issues to the remarkable events—wealthy stockbrokers praying and singing next to messenger boys; revivals in the public high schools; joint services by Methodists, Episcopalians, Presbyterians, Baptists, and even the traditionally antirevivalist Unitarians. The spirit rapidly spread to manufacturing towns throughout the Northeast. Unscheduled and unconventional religious meetings sprang up in small towns and rural areas from Indiana to

Quebec. "It would seem," wrote one enthusiast, "that the mighty crash was just what was wanted...to startle men from their golden dreams." Americans had become too overbearing, too self-confident, too complacent in their success. Yet if God had shown his displeasure, as countless interpreters maintained, he had also chosen means that underscored America's promise. He had punished Americans with economic loss, which even the hardest head among the business community could understand.

The great revival of 1858 gave a new sense of unity to northerners, who had become increasingly divided by class and religious conflict, to say nothing of the issue of slavery. It also signified the maturity of an urban, industrial Protestantism that was committed to material progress and self-improvement. For good or for ill, the revivals reinvigorated America's official ideal of *Novus Ordo Seclorurm*—a New Order for the World—the phrase today stamped on every dollar bill, conveying the message that a new social order is to exist, that Americans carry the high burden of helping to create a better world.

The Cult of Self-Improvement

What made public schools and religious revivals seem so indispensable by the 1830s was the relative absence of authoritative institutions that could define social roles, rules of conduct, and models of character. There was no standing army, for example, that could train a military class or enforce unpopular public policy. The abolition of public support for established churches gave semiliterate evangelists the same official status as college-trained theologians. Some states guaranteed any citizen, regardless of training, the right to practice law in any court. Americans showed less and less respect for any intellectual elite, religious or secular, or for any group of self-perpetuating masters who claimed to preserve and monopolize a body of knowledge that the public at large could not understand.

Not only had American law rejected European notions of privileged social orders, but as time went on the courts swept away most of the legal barriers that had restrained individuals from entering into certain kinds of risky or unfair agreements. In other words, the law assumed that all society was a marketplace of competitive exchange in which each individual calculated the probable risks of a given choice of action. As a result of this new burden of individual freedom and responsibility, Americans began to place enormous importance on acquiring effective skills and up-to-date knowledge. Continuous self-improvement became the great ideal of the age.

Lyceums and Learning   To Americans of the late twentieth century, there is nothing novel about fads, cults, and nostrums that promise the solution to life's problems. But in the 1830s and 1840s the cult of self-improvement was unprecedented in both the boldness and the variety of its appeals. Some conservatives expressed alarm over the credulity of public opinion, assuming that fads and quackery posed a threat to public order. But in general the people desired not the restructuring of society, but self-knowledge and self-advancement. In the 1820s numerous respectable societies and institutes for adult education and "mutual improvement" began to spread from England to the United States. Tens of thousands of adults, first in New England and then in the Old Northwest, grew accustomed to attending lectures, concerts, and various cultural events at lyceums (public halls). Lyceum lectures covered a vast range of subjects, but in the early years of the movement they tended to concentrate on "useful knowledge" associated with moral improvement and popular science.

Americans generally equated the advance of science with the advance of human liberty, a linkage that was part of the heritage of the European Enlightenment. They believed that everyone could benefit from the scientific method, that the marvels and secrets of nature were open to all. But what most impressed and fascinated American audiences were lectures and books on the applications of science, demonstrating the ingenious ways that human beings could master nature. As early as 1829, Jacob Bigelow's *Elements of Technology* not only helped to popularize a new word, but gave impetus to the general public's growing inclination to see invention as the key to national progress. Excitement over the uses of technology and steam power was matched by a new curiosity about the human mind, which had shown that it could unlock nature's secrets.

Mind Control and Phrenology

The gap between public ignorance and the achievements of science could be bridged if someone invented the supreme technology, a technology for controlling the human mind. The quest for this power united many of the popular cults and fads. Mesmerists, for example, claimed to have discovered the laws of magnetic attraction and repulsion that governed relations between people. Spiritualists convinced hundreds of thousands that they had found techniques and apparatus for communicating with the dead and probing the laws of the occult. Even the manuals on self-improvement and character building, directed mainly at the young, presumed definitive knowledge of the mechanics of the brain. The Reverend John Todd's *Student's Manual* (1835), which sold by the hundreds of thousands, maintained that mental power depends on a strict conservation of bodily and especially sexual energies. Todd's thesis, repeated by countless physicians and other experts, was that masturbation and sexual excess posed the gravest threats to sanity, social order, and individual achievement. Self-improvement thus required the rigorous avoidance of unwholesome thoughts and tempting situations.

The most ambitious and institutionalized science of the mind, however, was phrenology, the invention of Franz Joseph Gall, a Viennese physician. Phrenology identified the supposed physical location in the brain of a large assortment of human "faculties," such as firmness, benevolence, acquisitiveness, destructiveness, and platonic love. Phrenologists claimed that they could precisely measure character from the form and shape of a head. Americans first responded to phrenology as a promising medical breakthrough. Gall's leading disciple, Johann Gaspar Spurzheim, became the first spreader of the cause. On a visit to

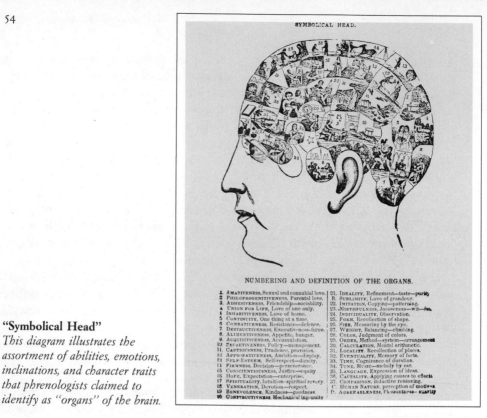

NUMBERING AND DEFINITION OF THE ORGANS.

1. AMATIVENESS, Sexual and connubial love.	21. IDEALITY, Refinement—taste—purity.
2. PHILOPROGENITIVENESS, Parental love.	B. SUBLIMITY, Love of grandeur.
3. ADHESIVENESS, Friendship—sociability.	22. IMITATION, Copying—patterning.
A. UNION FOR LIFE, Love of one only.	23. MIRTHFULNESS, Jocoseness—wit—fun.
4. INHABITIVENESS, Love of home.	24. INDIVIDUALITY, Observation.
5. CONTINUITY, One thing at a time.	25. FORM, Recollection of shape.
6. COMBATIVENESS, Resistance—defence.	26. SIZE, Measuring by the eye.
7. DESTRUCTIVENESS, Executiveness—force.	27. WEIGHT, Balancing—climbing.
8. ALIMENTIVENESS, Appetite, hunger.	28. COLOR, Judgment of colors.
9. ACQUISITIVENESS, Accumulation.	29. ORDER, Method—system—arrangement
10. SECRETIVENESS, Policy—management.	30. CALCULATION, Mental arithmetic.
11. CAUTIOUSNESS, Prudence, provision.	31. LOCALITY, Recollection of places.
12. APPROBATIVENESS, Ambition—display.	32. EVENTUALITY, Memory of facts.
13. SELF-ESTEEM, Self-respect—dignity.	33. TIME, Cognizance of duration.
14. FIRMNESS, Decision—perseverance.	34. TUNE, Music—melody by ear.
15. CONSCIENTIOUSNESS, Justice—equity	35. LANGUAGE, Expression of ideas.
16. HOPE, Expectation—enterprise.	36. CAUSALITY, Applying causes to effects
17. SPIRITUALITY, Intuition—spiritual revery.	37. COMPARISON, inductive reasoning.
18. VENERATION, Devotion—respect.	C. HUMAN NATURE, perception of motives
19. BENEVOLENCE, Kindness—goodness.	D. AGREEABLENESS, Pleasantness—suavity
20. CONSTRUCTIVENESS, Mechanical ingenuity	

"Symbolical Head"
This diagram illustrates the assortment of abilities, emotions, inclinations, and character traits that phrenologists claimed to identify as "organs" of the brain.

America in 1832, he was ushered around as a celebrity by New England dignitaries, including Supreme Court Justice Joseph Story and the Yale chemist Benjamin Silliman. For a time phrenology enjoyed intellectual prestige through the support of Horace Mann, the famous Unitarian preacher William Ellery Channing, and a number of business leaders, among them Abbott Lawrence. As usual, however, the American public displayed far more interest in practical application than in theory. Two skillful promoters, Orson and Lorenzo Fowler, helped to convert phrenology into a major business enterprise. In the cities audiences of thousands paid fees for lengthy lectures expounding the new science. Thousands more flocked to salons to have their characters analyzed. Traveling lecturers and mail-order courses enlightened the countryside. By the mid-1850s the *American Phrenological Journal* had a circulation of more than 50,000.

In many ways phrenology perfectly suited the needs of a population that was devoted to technique and uncertain of its own character. In an expansive and socially disruptive economy, phrenology provided a new set of guidelines that reduced the fear of risk. For example employers, who could no longer rely on long-term apprenticeships, on personal knowledge of an employee's family, or even on a worker's reputation in the community, could request a phrenological examination. Young men who dreamed of many careers but could decide on none welcomed a science that would measure their talents and capabilities. The great message of phrenology was individual adjustment. In a world of confusing and changing expectations, it furnished boundaries and specific identities. It told the individual which traits to cultivate and which to restrain. Criminologists not only found a physical explanation for deviant behavior, but also discovered a new hope for preventing crime by identifying potential criminals and by teaching convicts to control their overdeveloped antisocial faculties. Although Americans gradually came to realize that the results of phrenology could not substantiate its high promise, they had expressed an ardent desire—which would continue to our own time—for a popular science of human behavior.

Emerson Ralph Waldo Emerson came closer than anyone else to being America's "official" philosopher of the nineteenth century. Like phrenology, Emerson's essays and lyceum lectures offered something for everyone and thus nourished hope for reducing friction and creating social harmony. There is no way of knowing how much influence Emerson actually had on American thought and culture, but he certainly helped to stimulate the great literary renaissance of the 1850s. For decades to come his writings were a source of inspiration for reformers, businessmen, and countless ordinary folk. It can be argued that Emerson's worship of power and of self-improvement provide the spiritual backdrop for the entire progressive era of the early twentieth century.

Yet Emerson's thought escapes all attempts at classification or categorization. His words awakened reformers, but he wrote the most penetrating critiques of reform of his generation. Although homespun and down-to-earth, at the same time he was among the most abstract American thinkers. An ardent champion of cultural independence, he defined the mission of native artists and writers, yet he exploited his knowledge of the newest currents of German and English thought. He was the leading figure in a group that introduced to America German idealist philosophy, usually referred to by the awkward term *Transcendentalism,* taken from the work of the great German philosopher of the late eighteenth century, Immanuel Kant. But Emerson advocated an extreme form of individualism and never felt comfortable as a member of any association. His brief, pointed sayings on self-reliance were later quoted by anarchists and yet were framed on the walls of the nation's business leaders.

Emerson's spongelike capacity to absorb ideas and the common attitudes of his time, as well as his empathy for all sides and commitment to none, had much in common with America's greatest weaknesses and strengths. To various audiences he proclaimed that "who so would be a man, must be a nonconformist." To the youth of America he delivered the reassuring thought: "We but half express ourselves, and are ashamed of the divine idea which each of us represents. Trust thyself: every heart vibrates to that iron string." He criticized Americans for their single-minded pursuit of wealth and fame, for their obsession

Ralph Waldo Emerson
(1803–82)

with material things. But the point of this protest against materialism and conformity—which became clearer as both Emerson and his audiences grew older—was the need for a continuing reshaping and reinvigoration of the American character.

To Emerson the great peril that threatened the American people was not injustice, but a fragmentation of soul: "The reason why the world lacks unity and lies broken and in heaps, is because man is disunited with himself." The essential problem, then, was one of reconstituting character, of recovering a sense of the whole. By self-reliance Emerson really meant a detachment from society in order to achieve the sense of wholeness that flowed from unity with God—or, as Emerson put it, "the Oversoul." This notion that every "private man" possesses infinite and godlike capacities was an inspiring ideal, perfectly suited to the fantasies and aspirations of many Americans. At times, however, this doctrine meant that Emerson had no standard beyond power and success: "Power is, in nature, the essential measure of right."

Dissent: The Mormons as a Test Case

The history of the Mormons is seldom included in discussions of American dissent and reform. Yet Mormonism was not only America's first truly native religion; it began as a radical expression of dissent. This dissent was so extreme that Mormons found that they could survive only by building their own refuge in the remote deserts of the Far West. Because the early history of Mormonism exemplifies so many of the aspirations and difficulties of other dissenters—who also wished to live in their own ways in accordance with a higher moral law, free from the religious and political contaminations of their time—the Mormon experience can serve as an introduction, or a "test case." Essentially, the Mormons tested the outermost limits of permissible dissent, as well as the ability of any minority group or subculture to withstand the pressures of American secular society.

Joseph Smith, Founder

In 1830 Joseph Smith, Jr., published the Book of Mormon in Palmyra, New York. He said that the work was a translation of mysterious golden plates containing the history of an ancient Christian civilization in the New World. It portrayed the American Indians as the degenerate but saveable descendants of an ancient Hebrew tribe, and it foresaw a new American prophet who would discover the lost history and reestablish Christ's pure Kingdom in the New World. Smith in 1830 was an athletic, friendly, cheerful, intensely imaginative man of twenty-four, who claimed he had long had religious visions and revelations. He was the son of one of America's many families of drifters, debtors, and habitual losers, whose poverty worsened as they drew closer to the belts of commercial prosperity. Smith had been born in the hills of Vermont, and his parents had migrated to that caldron of progress and poverty—of religious revivalism and new social movements—in upstate New York that was soon to be known as the Burned-Over District. Shortly after the publication of the Book of Mormon, Smith organized the Church of Christ, which in 1834 would be renamed the Church of Jesus Christ of Latter-day Saints.

Faced at the outset with religious persecution, Smith knew that the saints must ultimately move westward and build their city of God at some divinely appointed spot near the Indian tribes they were commissioned to convert. As he was told to do in his revelations, he dispatched missionaries to scout out the Missouri frontier. In 1831 a few Mormons established an outpost near Independence, Missouri, which Smith designated as the site of the New Jerusalem, and which was then the eastern end of the Santa Fe Trail. During the same year, Smith and his New York followers migrated to Kirtland, Ohio, where Mormon missionaries had converted an entire community.

Persecution of the Mormons

By 1839 the Mormons had met defeat in both Ohio and Missouri and were fleeing to a refuge of swampy Illinois farmland that Smith had bought along the eastern shore of the Mississippi River. In Ohio the Mormons had experimented with communal ownership of property and with an illegal wildcat banking venture that had brought disaster during the Panic of 1837. In Missouri proslavery mobs, hostile to any group of nonslaveholding Yankees and inflamed by reports that Mormons intended to bring free blacks into the state, had destroyed the settlements around Independence. A series of armed encounters, beginning with an attempt to bar

Mormons from voting, led to outright warfare and to Governor L. W. Boggs's proclamation that the Mormons had to be treated as enemies—that they "had to be exterminated, or driven from the state." At Haun's Mill a band of Missourians massacred nineteen Mormon men and boys. Smith himself was convicted of treason and sentenced to be shot. But he managed to escape, and in Illinois some 12,000 to 15,000 Mormons finally built their model city of Nauvoo, which the legislature incorporated in 1840 as a virtually independent city-state. The Mormons' political power derived from the decisive weight they could throw in state elections that were fairly evenly balanced between Whigs and Democrats. Beginning in 1840 their numbers grew as the result not only of missionary work in the East, but also of the immigration of thousands who had been converted to Mormonism in the manufacturing districts of England. The English converts' route to the American Zion was eased by the church's highly efficient planning authority, which took care of the details of travel.

By the early 1840s visitors to Nauvoo marveled at the city's broad streets, carefully laid out in neat squares, and at the steam sawmills and flour mill, the factories, hotel, and schools. Although the Nauvoo temple, supported by thirty gigantic pillars and walls of hewn stone, was not yet complete, it promised to be, in the words of the poet John Greenleaf Whittier, "the most splendid and imposing architectural monument in the new world." Dressed in the uniform of a lieutenant general, Smith commanded the Nauvoo legion of 2,000 troops. In 1843 he dictated the official revelation, which he never made public, justifying the practice of plural marriage, or polygamy. The next year he established the secret Council of Fifty, a secular authority independent of the church, and gave it the mission of building a world government that would prepare the way for Christ's Kingdom.

But Smith felt the American world closing in on him and his fellow Mormons. Sensing that the surrounding society would not long tolerate Mormon power and that dissident Mormons were rebelling against his institution of plural marriage and his being secretly crowned king, Smith unsuccessfully tried to persuade the new Republic of Texas to sponsor an independent Mormon colony along the contested border with Mexico. While also sending secret diplomatic missions to Russia and France, he tried to influence the established order through normal political channels. But neither the federal government nor the 1844 presidential candidates would defend the Mormons' claims against Missouri outlaws who had seized thousands of Mormon farms and buildings. As a gesture of protest, Smith finally announced his own candidacy for the highest office in the land. But well before the election, he ordered the destruction of a printing press that had been set up by Mormon dissidents, who had declared: "We will not acknowledge any man as king or lawgiver to the church." Illinois then charged Smith with treason and locked him and his brother in the Carthage jail. On June 27, 1844, a "mob" made up of a state militia group including many prominent non-Mormon citizens stormed the jail and killed them both.

To the Mormons the Prophet's martyrdom brought shock, division, and a struggle over what kind of religion Mormonism should become. It also tem-

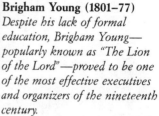

Brigham Young (1801–77)
*Despite his lack of formal
education, Brigham Young—
popularly known as "The Lion
of the Lord"—proved to be one
of the most effective executives
and organizers of the nineteenth
century.*

porarily appeased the aggression of anti-Mormons and gave Smith's followers time to plan an exodus. Brigham Young, like Smith, a man of humble Vermont origin, soon emerged as the leader of the Mormon majority and as one of the nineteenth century's greatest organizers. Although dissenting factions trekked off to northern Michigan, Texas, Pennsylvania, and parts of the Midwest, Young received indispensable support from the elite Quorum of the Twelve Apostles and the Council of Fifty. He succeeded in preserving order and morale while considering and rejecting possible refuges in British and Mexican territory. Before the end of 1845 the Mormon leadership had decided to send an advance company of 1,500 men to the valley of the Great Salt Lake, then still part of Mexico. As a result of mounting persecution and harassment, the Mormons soon concentrated their energies on evacuating Nauvoo, on selling property at tremendous sacrifice, and on setting up refugee camps stretching from eastern Iowa to Winter Quarters, a temporary destination in eastern Nebraska. The last refugees crossed the Mississippi River at gunpoint, leaving Nauvoo a ghost town. During the summer of 1846 some 12,000 Mormons were on the road; 3,700 wagon teams stretched out across the prairies of Iowa.

In the summer of 1847, Brigham Young led an advance party of picked men across the barren wastes of Nebraska and Wyoming to the Great Salt Lake Valley of Utah. In September a second band of 2,000 weary Mormons found a home in the new Zion. During the same year the American defeat of Mexico brought Utah

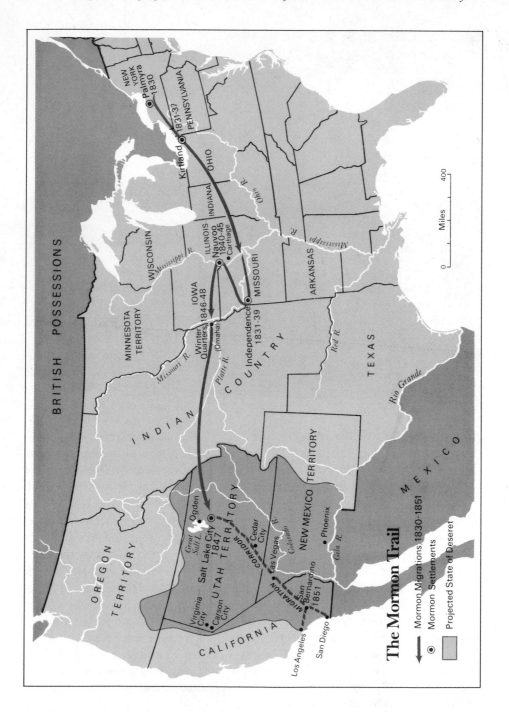

The Mormon Trail

within the boundaries of the United States. The Mormons had contributed a battalion of five hundred men who had marched with the American army across New Mexico to southern California, and whose pay had helped to finance the migration to Utah. Yet by 1848 the Mormons occupied an inland mountain fortress, a thousand miles beyond the Kansas frontier, and seemed at last to be the masters of their own destiny. When federal judges and other officials arrived in the territory, they found that the Mormons had held a census, adopted a constitution, elected Young governor, and established what they called the State of Deseret, complete with its own currency and army. The religiously run government was responsible for the remarkably rapid and orderly settlement of the valley, for the collective labor and central economic planning that brought irrigation to the dry but fertile land, and for the coordinated expansion that in ten years established ninety-six colonies, extending in a corridor from Salt Lake City to San Diego.

Ten years before the time when South Carolina defied federal authority by firing on Fort Sumter and thus beginning the Civil War, federal officials fled from Utah, denouncing Young's government as a church-state fundamentally disloyal to the United States. Although the Mormons claimed to be loyal to the Constitution and acknowledged their status as an American territory, they intended to pay little attention to the authorities who had been sent from Washington. When Young publicly proclaimed the sacred doctrine of polygamy, which Mormon leaders had privately practiced for more than a decade, he presented a ready-made issue to outraged reformers, ministers, and politicians. President Buchanan felt the need for appeasing this popular clamor and of forcibly establishing federal authority in Utah. In 1857 he dispatched a regular army force of 2,500 men to impose federal law on the Mormons. In an irony of history, they were led by Albert Sidney Johnston, who would soon be a Confederate general resisting an invasion by the United States.

Fortunately for the Mormons, winter storms trapped the expedition in the Rocky Mountains, allowing time for behind-the-scenes negotiations. Governor Young proclaimed martial law and threatened to burn Salt Lake City to the ground and "to utterly lay waste" the land if Utah were invaded. States' rights Democrats had little enthusiasm for setting precedents that might be turned against southern slavery, and although Buchanan had sworn that he would "put down the Mormon rebellion," he decided early in 1858 to proclaim a "pardon" to the inhabitants of Utah if they would obey United States laws and cooperate with federal officials. To prove their strength, however, the Mormons evacuated Salt Lake City. Johnston's army entered a deserted city, greeted only by squads of tough police, "glowering from beneath their hat-brims, with clubs in their hands, and pistols ready slung at their belts." The later withdrawal of federal troops concluded the so-called Mormon War, which brought no change in the actual government of Utah. When Buchanan's successor, Abraham Lincoln, was asked what he proposed to do about the Mormons, he answered, "I propose to let them alone." Lincoln, of course, had other problems on his hands.

No story in American history is more incredible. From the outset Mormonism embodied the longings and hopes of people who had not shared in the growing prosperity and social modernization of the early nineteenth century. After listening to a Mormon service in Massachusetts, the poet Whittier observed that "they speak a language of hope and promise to weak, weary hearts, tossed and troubled, who have wandered from sect to sect, seeking in vain for the primal manifestation of the divine power." The new church recruited most of its members from the more remote and isolated parts of New England; from the sparsely populated southern districts of New York and the adjacent parts of northern Pennsylvania; from the rural backcountry of the Upper South and frontier Midwest; and eventually from both rural and manufacturing districts of Wales, Lancashire (in northern England), and Scandinavia. Few of these converts were well-to-do, well educated, or well established in settled communities. They were mainly small farmers who had been displaced by commercial agriculture, and footloose tradesmen and artisans who had been bypassed by expanding markets. All were people already uprooted and highly mobile, long engaged in a search for communal and religious security.

The Meaning of Mormon Dissent

Because the Mormon search for authority took religious form, it is easy to miss its radical challenge to American secular values and institutions. Against a pluralistic, permissive, and individualistic society, the Mormons pitted a higher authority that rested on a rock of unswerving certainty and conviction. Their institutions, based on divine authority, cast doubt on the legitimacy of popular sovereignty, secular law, and established government. The claim that divine revelation sanctioned such a practice as polygamy challenged the basic premises of secular law and morality. And according to their enemies, the Mormons' communal economy subverted private property, encouraged wholesale theft, and excluded non-Mormon enterprise from Utah. Far worse, the Mormons had shown little Christian patience in response to persecution. If like the earliest Christians they had looked for strength from the blood of their martyrs, they had also promised retaliation, or "blood atonement," to their enemies.

But the Mormons were not revolutionaries. Despite many points of dissent, Mormonism had much in common with the developing culture of pre–Civil War America. No other American denomination so fully incorporated the so-called Protestant ethic of work, or the rule of abstaining from tobacco and all alcoholic drinks as a symbol of their own self-discipline and modernizing values. In many respects the Mormons' ideal of a religious state was an extreme version of the ideal of Lyman Beecher, the New England revivalist reformer, and of countless other evangelists who insisted that rampant democracy must be guided by a higher moral force.

In sum, Mormonism was both a radical protest against the values of an individualistic, competitive, uprooting, and disinheriting world, and a way of achieving solidarity and authority that enabled its members to adjust to that world. During the pre–Civil War decades no other movement—with the exception of the movement among southerners to defend black slavery—posed so serious a challenge to the ideology of the industrializing, urbanizing, and modernizing North. The Mormons probed the outermost limits of tolerance, the violent limits where dissent verged on treason, and finally established their own fragile refuge beyond—but soon within—America's geographical frontiers. Unlike southerners, they escaped the major confrontation of civil war. But their unique success required a prolonged accommodation with and ultimate surrender to the civilization against which the South finally waged civil war.

The Benevolent Empire

Like the founders of Mormonism, the reformers of the early nineteenth century were responding to the breakdown of social rules and moral authority associated with a traditional society. To restore "the moral government of God" was the supreme goal of the so-called Benevolent Empire—an informal coalition of home and foreign missionary societies, the American Tract Society, the American Sunday School Union, the American Society for the Promotion of Temperance, the American Colonization Society, the Prison Discipline Society, and the General Union for Promoting the Observance of the Christian Sabbath. Even William Lloyd Garrison, who later came to symbolize radical abolitionism and a defiance of church and state, began his career in the 1820s as a lowly but ardent champion of these seemingly conservative reform organizations. Like many ministers and wealthy humanitarians, young Garrison deplored the rising "mobocracy," the "lawless multitude" who enjoyed liquor, violence, profanity, sexual vice, and vulgar entertainment. American social reform originated in the crusade to purify public morals and find new means, such as the asylum and penitentiary, for instilling habits of regularity, sobriety, obedience, and responsibility.

The Reform of Society

Ideals of purification and the exclusion of undesirables dominated the activities of the Benevolent Empire. Having already provided for the abolition of slavery in the northern states, many antislavery reformers wanted to send the free blacks back to Africa, an idea that gained increasing support during the early nineteenth century, especially among missionary groups who assumed that American blacks would help to Christianize the land of their ancestors. Drunkards were to be banished from the sight of respectable society. Criminals and deviants of various kinds were to be walled off in prisons and asylums, where "their stubborn spirits are subdued, and their depraved hearts softened, by mental suffering," as some New York reformers put it in 1822. When deviants were institutionalized, they could neither disturb nor contaminate a society that needed to concentrate on business and on moral virtue. Some enthusiastic prison reformers even argued that society itself should be modeled on "the regularity, and temperance, and sobriety of a good prison."

Unlike the Mormons, these reformers aspired to lead and transform the dominant secular society. Although they sought to gather together like-minded promoters of virtue, they originally gave no thought to withdrawing from a sinful society in order to practice virtue. Most of the leaders of the Benevolent Empire were men of economic and educational attainment. They could think of themselves, under "normal" circumstances, as the natural leaders of their communities. They tended to idealize the New England heritage of ordered and homogeneous communities governed by educated ministers and political leaders. Above all, they looked increasingly to Britain for models of "practical Christianity" and organized reform.

Organized humanitarianism had a long history in Britain, but during the Napoleonic wars (1798–1815) it grew dramatically. A vast campaign was undertaken in Britain to reform public morals, to Christianize the world, and to unite rich and poor by an affectionate bond of humanitarianism that would replace the traditional deference to the upper classes, which had begun to decay even in England. The British and Foreign Bible Society, founded in 1804, became the model for nonsectarian organizations committed to the ideal of "Christian unity." The Bible Society also became a pioneer in highly specialized organization as it acquired women's auxiliaries, skilled professional agents, and teams of "visitors" assigned to specific towns, districts, and streets to collect funds, interview poor families, and distribute Bibles. This kind of systematic division of labor was soon adopted by hundreds of British societies and was eventually copied by the Mormons to organize their community in Utah.

British societies were formed to promote Christianity among the Jews, observance of the Christian Sabbath, universal peace, and the abolition of slavery. There were societies to suppress immorality, antireligious publications, juvenile delinquency, and cruelty to animals; societies to aid the poverty-stricken blind, the industrious poor, orphans of soldiers and sailors, and "Poor, Infirm, Aged Widows, and Single Women, of Good Character, Who Have Seen Better Days." The English, who seem to have outdone the Americans as a nation of joiners, even launched the Society for Returning Young Women to Their Friends in the Country.

By the 1820s Britain appeared suddenly to have moved into the forefront of humanitarianism. The evangelical reformers won particular prestige by taking the lead in the successful campaign to abolish the African slave trade. Most Americans, however, remembered the British invasions of the United States during the War of 1812 and continued to think of England as a nation of tyranny and political corruption. Thus they remained suspicious of any alleged humanitarian change of heart in Britain. But the New England clergy welcomed news of England's moral transformation. Confronted by the collapse of Federalist political power, by the growing political force of public opinion, and by irresistible demands for the separation of church and state, many New England clergymen adopted the organizational apparatus of British benevolence as a means of securing control of American culture. With the aid of allies from the other parts of the Northeast, these New England ministers and reformers succeeded in capturing and Americanizing the British evangelical spirit and in institutionalizing it in New York City, Philadelphia, and regions stretching west to Illinois.

From about 1810 to 1830 the Benevolent Empire developed gradually as local societies for the reformation of morals enlarged their objectives through various interstate and interlocking personal networks. A remarkable number of the original promoters of benevolent societies were students or recent graduates of Andover Theological Seminary in Massachusetts, founded by Congregationalists in 1809 in opposition to Harvard's drift toward the liberal, rationalistic creed of Unitarianism. Andover was a seedbed for missionary work in Asia, Africa, and the American West. Many of the seminary's alumni took up such secular causes as black colonization, prison reform, and the suppression of intemperance. Louis Dwight, for example, who traveled the country as an agent for the American Bible Society, was so shocked by the squalor and disorder of jails that he became a leading crusader for the penitentiary system of total silence, close surveillance, and solitary confinement at night used in the Auburn, New York, prison. This Auburn system, Dwight maintained, "would greatly promote order, seriousness, and purity in large families, male and female boarding schools, and colleges."

These Andover reformers worked closely with serious-minded young ministers and laymen who had attended Yale or Princeton, as well as with rich and pious businessmen like Edward C. Delavan, Gerrit Smith, and the Tappan brothers. Delavan, a former wine merchant and Albany real estate magnate, contributed a fortune to the temperance cause. The reform movements nourished by the Benevolent Empire moved in radical as well as conservative directions. Gerrit Smith, a land baron in upstate New York, promoted innumerable reforms ranging from Sunday schools, penitentiaries, and temperance to radical abolitionism, women's rights, and world peace. Arthur and Lewis Tappan, who were wealthy importers and retail merchants in New York City, contributed money and leadership to a whole galaxy of local and national reform societies, especially those devoted to the abolition of slavery.

The Sabbatarian Movement

The movement to enforce the Christian Sabbath reveals some of the basic concerns of the Benevolent Empire, as well as the obstacles that prevented the emergence of a much-hoped-for "Christian party in politics." In 1810 Congress had passed a law requiring the mail to flow seven days a week, in order to meet the critical business demands for faster communication. Sunday mail service immediately drew fire from Lyman Beecher and other New Englanders, and subsequently it provoked national debate. For devout Christians the Sabbath evoked memories of a less hurried, agrarian past. Even merchants, although wrapped up in their own success and totally involved in worldly pursuits, found the silent Sabbath a reassuring symbol of spiritual goals that justified the previous six days of earthly cares and ambition.

It is significant that Sabbatarian reform originated in the boom town of Rochester, not in the long-settled urban areas along the coast. Rochester's established ministers had come from New England and New Jersey, where a quiet

Sabbath had been enforced by custom and law. But the Erie Canal passed directly under the windows of Rochester's First Presbyterian Church, and the rowdy boatmen made no effort to lower their voices during the hours of Sunday prayer. In 1828 the town's leading ministers, real estate magnates, and entrepreneurs enlisted Lyman Beecher and Lewis Tappan in a national crusade to persuade Congress to enforce the laws of God. Although unsuccessful, the movement was historically important because it polarized "serious Christians" against the multitude; because it prepared the way for collaboration between wealthy New York humanitarians and social activists, inspired by the revivals of Charles Grandison Finney; and because it marked the transition between merely distributing Bibles and resorting to direct political and economic action. It should also be emphasized that Rochester lay at the heart of the Burned-Over District and that the Sabbatarian movement coincided with the Anti-Masonic crusade,* Finney's revivals, the perfection and extension of the Auburn penitentiary system, and the birth of Mormonism.

Although the various causes taken up by the Benevolent Empire appear conservative when compared with later abolitionism, feminism, and perfectionism, they too challenged vested interests and provoked immediate and furious resistance. The Sabbatarian movement, for example, threatened loss to owners of boat lines, ferries, taverns, theaters, and stores, much as the temperance movement threatened not only brewers, distillers, and distributors, but also thousands of grocers and storekeepers whose customers expected a free pick-me-up as a sign of hospitality. Like the more militant temperance reformers, the Sabbatarians urged true Christians to boycott offending proprietors. Between Buffalo and Albany they also established their own six-days-a-week Pioneer Stage Line, a counterpart of the special temperance hotels and of the abolitionist shops that sold only produce made by free labor. These "anti"-institutions, which were almost uniformly unsuccessful, were intended to be sanctuaries—virtuous, disciplined environments set off from a chaotic and corrupting society—and models for the world to imitate. But like other reformers, the Sabbatarians were also committed to an imperial mission. Setting a precedent for later abolitionists, they organized a great petition campaign to persuade Congress to stop the Sunday mails. Like the abolitionists, they warned that unless Congress acknowledged a "higher law," the nation had little chance for survival:

> If this nation fails in her vast experiment, the world's last hope expires; and without the moral energies of the Sabbath it will fail. You might as well put out the sun, and think to enlighten the world with tapers...as to extinguish the moral illumination of the Sabbath, and break this glorious mainspring of the moral government of God.

---

*For Anti-Masonry, see chapter 15, pp. 514, 516.

But as the Mormons later discovered, many Americans were suspicious of people who claimed to stand for the moral government of God. By 1831 the Benevolent Empire had failed in its most daring and secular missionary efforts to regenerate society. Lyman Beecher had early defined the supreme goal of the missionary and benevolent societies: to produce "a sameness of views, and feelings, interests, which would lay the foundation of our empire upon a rock." But this purpose smashed against the rocklike resistance of people who refused to be homogenized, especially under Yankee direction. In response to the Sabbatarians' petitions, Congress agreed with a Kentucky senator who drafted a report stating that the national legislature was not "a proper tribunal to determine the laws of God." The colonization movement—the movement to send free blacks to Africa—did much to unite northern urban blacks in opposition to the idea. These blacks angrily affirmed that they would not accept a foreign refuge as a substitute for justice: "We will never separate ourselves voluntarily from the slave population of this country. Let not a purpose be assisted which will stay the cause of the entire abolition of slavery." Ironically, resistance to the Benevolent Empire also appeared in the South and Southwest, where an antimission movement appealed to so-called Hard-Shell Baptists and rural Methodists. These groups found no biblical support for benevolent societies and bitterly resisted any attempts to bring religious instruction to the blacks. Further, as one Baptist declared, "our backwoods folks" simply could not understand the pretentious talk of the "young men come from the eastern schools."

The Benevolent Empire solved no social problems. It received no credit for legislative triumphs of the magnitude of Britain's abolition of the slave trade (1807) and gradual emancipation of West Indian slaves (1833). By 1837, moreover, internal conflicts had shattered all hope of a united front among evangelical reformers. Growing divisions over slavery simply intensified suspicions and grievances that had long been festering on every level. Rivalry between religious groups weakened the supposedly nondenominational societies that northern Presbyterians and Congregationalists had always controlled. In 1837, when the Presbyterian church separated into conservative Old School and liberal New School camps, the economic depression also sharply reduced humanitarian gifts and thus further weakened the various organizations of the Benevolent Empire. The major Protestant churches, however, continued much of the work under denominational auspices.

Waging the War   It can be argued that the true revolution in American reform began in the 1820s with the militancy, the dedication, the towering expectations, and the phenomenal organization of the nonsectarian, evangelical societies. It began, that is, when an agent of the Sunday School Union, addressing the well-to-do members of the Bible Society, repeated the British motto: "Not by exactions from the opulent but by the contributions from all"; it began when the organizer of foreign missions called for a "vast body like a host prepared for war"; it began when the benevolent societies developed the techniques of modern fund-raising campaigns. The real revolution began with the mass production of literally millions of moralistic tracts, priced cheaply enough to undersell all commercial publications and marketed by discounts and other techniques that were far ahead of commercial practice. By 1830, in short, the evangelicals had devised all the apparatus needed for a massive conquest of American culture.

Although the conquest had ethnic, class, and geographical boundaries, few invading armies or political revolutions have had such a far-reaching effect on an entire society as the Benevolent Empire did. In 1834 the Temperance Society estimated that it had more than 1.25 million members; in 1836 the American Tract Society alone sold more than 3 million publications. In 1843, in response to the depression that had filled New York City's streets with thousands of beggars and vagrants, the New York Association for Improving the Condition of the Poor imitated the earlier models and sent teams of agents to gather information district by district and to distribute food, fuel, and clothing. The needy recipients could not help but be influenced, one way or another, by the association's links with the temperance movement, its conviction that poverty was a problem of individual morality, and its commitment to making the poor "respectable." If the reformers harbored little sympathy for sinners who refused to be saved, their ideology rested on a belief in human perfectibility, strongly laced with hopes for an American millennium.

The reformers' confidence in human perfectibility inspired a multitude of efforts, especially in the 1840s, to liberate individuals from all coercive forces and institutions. Perfectionism—the belief that people are capable of unlimited moral improvement—took both religious and secular forms. Suddenly, new things seemed possible, new ways of thinking and acting seemed worth trying. The nation had never before witnessed such frothy experimentation, such gusty defiance of traditional wisdom, or such faith in spontaneous love and harmony. Some reformers won fame for their success in emancipating individual victims of deafness, blindness, and insanity. Samuel Gridley Howe, best known for his pioneering work with the blind and deaf-blind, expressed the growing view that even criminals were "thrown upon society as a sacred charge." "Society," Howe said, "is false to its trust, if it neglects any means of reformation." Prison reformers tried, with little success, to transform penitentiaries into communities of rehabilitation and to persuade society of the need for parole, indeterminate sentences, and sympathetic care for discharged convicts. Nativists, who were alarmed by the increasing number of Catholic immigrants, publicized cases of Catholic women who had escaped from supposedly tyrannical and immoral nunneries, and demanded laws that would liberate Catholic laymen from the control of their priests.

Temperance　　　The temperance movement, a direct outgrowth of the Benevolent Empire, illustrates this mixture of humanitarianism, intolerance, progressivism, and self-righteousness. Although sometimes portrayed as religious cranks and killjoys, the temperance reformers were

Temperance
The worst evil of alcohol, according to temperance reformers, was its destruction of family harmony and the sanctity of the home. Innumerable storybooks and illustrations pictured a husband and father inflamed by spiritous liquor, attacking his helpless wife and children.

responding to a genuine social problem. During the early 1800s, per capita consumption of hard liquor far exceeded even the highest twentieth-century levels. Alcohol abuse undoubtedly contributed to family discord and child abuse, to public disorder, and to lowered productivity and rising social costs. By the mid-1830s various groups of urban artisans and northern free blacks endorsed temperance as a prerequisite for self-improvement. At the same time, middle-class champions of total abstinence became embroiled in bitter disputes over biblical approval or disapproval of drinking wine.

In 1840 the movement took a new direction when groups of reformed alcoholics began organizing "Washingtonian Societies," which appealed to working-class people and to members of subcultures that had not been reached by the traditional temperance organizations. At society meetings former drunkards told rapt audiences what hell was really like, sometimes reenacting the agonies of the delirium tremens that their excessive drinking had induced. Old-guard temperance leaders tried to use and patronize the Washingtonians, much as some white abolitionists tried to use and patronize fugitive slaves. But the middle-class societies never felt comfortable with the former victims of intemperance or with the boisterous showmanship that induced thousands of disreputable looking people to pledge themselves, at least temporarily, to total abstinence.

Faith in "moral suasion"—individual conversion to abstinence—disintegrated in the face of hundreds of thousands of German and Irish immigrants who had little taste for Yankee moralism. The celebrated "Maine law" of 1851, which outlawed the manufacture and sale of alcoholic beverages, marked the maturing of a new campaign for legal coercion in the form of statewide prohibition. On both local and state levels, bitter political conflicts erupted over the passage, repeal, and enforcement of prohibition laws. For temperance reformers of the 1850s, it was no longer safe to rely on the individual's mastery of temptation. The crucial act of will was now to be made by the state, which would attempt to remove the temptation. In less than thirty years, one of the supreme goals of the Benevolent Empire had been handed over to the realm of political power. Faith in moral influence and liberation had yielded to what the *American Temperance Magazine* hailed as the only force that drunkards could comprehend—"the instrumentality of the law."

Feminism and Perfectionism

By the second quarter of the nineteenth century, a broad protest movement, with strong religious undercurrents, was unfolding against forms of oppression and inequality that had long been accepted as inevitable. A major—and bitterly controversial—part of this protest movement attacked slavery.* But by the 1830s abolitionism had become intertwined with attacks against the traditional subordination of women. The founders of the feminist movement, like the male abolitionists, had mostly served apprenticeships in the moral-reform and temperance societies of the Benevolent Empire. Hundreds of female benevolent societies provided women with invaluable experience in fund-raising, organization, and public speaking. As women increasingly defied traditional restraints on engaging in public activities, they increasingly demanded equal educational and employment opportunities.

Women were not only deprived of higher education, barred from the professions, and denied the right to vote. Upon marriage, most women also surrendered any legal right to their own earnings and property. Harriet Robinson, who began working in a Massachusetts textile mill at age eleven and who in 1836 participated in one of the first women's strikes against wage cutting, recalled that many workers were "fugitives" from oppressive husbands and had thus assumed false names in order to prevent their husbands from legally seizing their wages. These conditions evoked a mounting protest from writers like Catharine Beecher, a daughter of Lyman Beecher and sister of Harriet Beecher Stowe. While conceding that women should not infringe on the "male sphere" of business and politics, Catharine Beecher exposed the oppression of mill girls, fought for improved female education, and attempted to enlist thousands of American women as teachers in a great crusade "to secure a proper education to the vast multitude of neglected American children all over our land." This

---

*For abolitionism, see chapter 14, pp. 472–83.

Making Fun of Feminists' Complaints
A favorite tactic of antifeminists was to spoof the reversal of gender roles. If rights were equalized, this cartoon suggests, men could expect to find themselves washing clothes, sewing, and tending babies while women ventured out into the world in carriages driven by other women.

agitation focused attention on women's collective interests, problems, and responsibilities, and thus contributed to a new feminist consciousness.

Female Abolitionists Abolitionism provided female reformers with an egalitarian ethic and with a public forum for attacking entrenched injustice. From the outset the radical abolitionist movement led by William Lloyd Garrison attracted a group of exceptionally talented writers such as Maria Weston Chapman, Lydia Maria Child, Abby Kelley, and Lucretia Mott. Among Garrison's most important converts were Sarah and Angelina Grimké, two outspoken sisters who had abandoned their father's South Carolina plantation and had then been converted to Quakerism and abolitionism in Philadelphia. Because they could speak of southern slavery from personal experience, the Grimkés had a striking effect on New England audiences. In 1837 they boldly lectured to mixed audiences of men and women, an offense that outraged ministers and conservative reformers who believed that women should move within a precisely limited "sphere." The Grimkés attacked the hypocrisy of conservative abolitionists who scoffed at the biblical justifications for slavery advanced in the South but who then invoked the Bible when defending female subservience. The Garrisonians convinced the Grimkés that the Christian "principles of peace" were at the root of all reform; the Grimkés helped to convince the Garrisonians that the same principles applied to the "domestic slavery" of women to men.

Sarah Grimké was especially penetrating when she criticized the way most American girls were trained and conditioned to accept a separate sphere, or what later historians have termed "the cult of domesticity":

> During the early part of my life, my lot was cast among the butterflies of the fashionable world; and of this class of women, I am constrained to say, both from experience and observation, that their education is miserably deficient; that they are taught to regard marriage as the one thing needful, the only avenue to distinction; hence to attract the notice and win the attentions of men, by their external charms, is the chief business of fashionable girls. They seldom think that men will be allured by intellectual acquirements, because they find, that where any mental superiority exists, a woman is generally shunned and regarded as stepping out of her "appropriate sphere," which, in their view, is to dress, to dance, and to set out to the best possible advantage her person. . . .
>
> There is another and much more numerous class in this country, who are withdrawn by education or circumstances from the circle of fashionable amusements, but who are brought up with the dangerous and absurd idea, that marriage is a kind of preferment; and that to be able to keep their husband's house, and render his situation comfortable, is the end of her being. . . . For this purpose more than for any other, I verily believe the majority of girls are trained. . . .

In 1840 the issue of women's participation in abolitionist conventions caused a final split in the national abolitionist organization, the American Anti-Slavery Society. The more conservative faction, led by Arthur and Lewis Tappan, abandoned the society to the Garrisonian radicals. Female abolitionists increasingly stressed the parallels between their own powerlessness and the legal status of slaves. At Seneca Falls, New York, in 1848, Elizabeth Cady Stanton and Lucretia Mott finally organized the first convention in history devoted to women's rights. The convention's Declaration of Sentiments, modeled on the Declaration of Independence, proclaimed that "the history of mankind is a history of repeated injuries and usurpations on the part of man toward woman, having in direct object the establishment of an absolute tyranny over her." Among the list of specific grievances Stanton insisted on mentioning the exclusion of woman from "her inalienable right to the elective franchise."

Despite this demand for political rights, the National Women's Rights conventions of the 1850s devoted the greatest attention to legal and economic disabilities and to challenging ministers' insistence that the Bible placed the "weaker sex" in a subordinate "sphere." "Leave woman," Lucy Stone, a radical feminist leader, demanded, "to find her own sphere."

Although abolitionism provided the feminists with a sympathetic audience and with ready-made channels of communication, the relationship was also limiting in the sense that women's rights were always subordinate to the seemingly more urgent cause of slave emancipation. This dependence is evident even in the rhetoric of the radical feminists who compared the prevailing system

Lucy Stone (1818–93)
After rebelling as a girl against the subordination of her sex, Lucy Stone taught school and finally earned her way through Oberlin College. A radical abolitionist and lecturer on women's rights, she chose to keep her maiden name after she married Henry B. Blackwell, a businessman who fully supported her feminist views. Lucy Stone continued to fight for women's suffrage during and after the Civil War.

of marriage to a private plantation in which every woman was a slave breeder and a slave in the eyes of her husband.

Communitarianism   The quest for social equality led some reformers including abolitionists to join experimental communities where they could escape from the coercions and frustrations of competitive labor and of the private, isolated family. Some of these communities were inspired by secular social theories. In the 1820s, for example, the socialist experiment at New Harmony, Indiana, was based on the doctrines of Robert Owen, a wealthy Scottish industrialist turned radical humanitarian. In the 1840s a wide scattering of projects drew on the theories of Charles Fourier, a French social philosopher. The most successful communities, however, were those of religious sects like the Rappites and Shakers or those disciplined by the authority of extraordinary leaders such as John Humphrey Noyes.

Noyes had studied theology at Andover and Yale. He was a perfectionist who believed that the millennium had already begun and that the time had arrived for "renouncing all allegiance to the government of the United States, and asserting the title of Jesus Christ to the throne of the world." Garrison's rejection of all coercive government owed much to the influence of Noyes, who had proclaimed that "as the doctrine of temperance is total abstinence from alcoholic drinks, and the doctrine of antislavery is immediate abolition of human bondage, so the doctrine of perfectionism is the immediate and total cessation from sin." For Noyes and his followers there was no point in attacking a single sin like slavery when all Americans were enslaved by the bonds of private property and monogamous marriage, both of which imprisoned the human spirit behind walls of sinful possessiveness. At Putney, Vermont, and then at Oneida, New York, Noyes and his growing group of disciples developed a cohesive community based on a nonexclusive form of plural marriage, the collective ownership of property, and the discipline of "mutual criticism." The Oneida experiment, which flourished from 1847 to 1879, posed a radical alternative to the economic, sexual, and educational practices of the surrounding society.

The Tensions of Democratic Art

The continuing democratization of American culture produced a profound uneasiness about the artistic standards and precedents of European culture. On the one hand, American writers and artists felt the need to proclaim their independence from Europe and to create a genuinely native art, stripped of aristocratic associations. On the other hand, by the 1820s it was becoming clear that political independence did not guarantee cultural independence and that republican institutions would not automatically give birth to the Great American Masterwork. Improved transportation, coupled with a prolonged period of peace in Europe after the end of the Napoleonic wars in 1815, made it easier for Americans to cross the Atlantic in search of inspiration and training.

Even the more ardent cultural nationalists viewed Europe with awe and fascination. Often shocked by European contrasts between elegance and squalor, they were also dazzled by the great cathedrals, castles, spacious parks, monumental public buildings, museums, and villas. From Washington Irving's *Alhambra* (1832) to Nathaniel Hawthorne's *Marble Faun* (1860), American writers expressed their enchantment with castles and ruins, with places that had been steeped in centuries of history. Whatever its evils, Europe teemed with associations that fed the imagination. It was the continent of mystery, of beauty, of romance—in short, of culture. For many American artists it was also at least a temporary refuge from the materialism, vulgarity, and hurried pace of life they found in the United States. It is significant that Washington Irving was living in England when he created the classic American tales "Rip Van Winkle" and "The Legend of Sleepy Hollow" (1819–20). James Fenimore Cooper was living in Paris when he wrote *The Prairie* (1827). Horatio Greenough, America's first professional sculptor and a champion of democratic artistic theory, completed his gigantic, half-draped statue of George Washington—a statue that had been commissioned by the United States government—in his studio in Florence.

It would be a mistake, however, to think of American art of the period as slavishly imitative. Although Americans tended to express native subject matter in conventional artistic forms, they became increasingly skilled and sophisticated in their mastery of the forms. The choice of native material also affected the total character of a work. For example, space, nature, and the wilderness took on new qualities as Thomas Cole, Asher B. Durand, and other painters of the Hudson River School sought to idealize the American landscape. Cooper's five "Leatherstocking Tales"—*The Pioneers* (1823), *The Last of the Mohicans* (1826), *The Prairie* (1827), *The Pathfinder* (1840), and *The Deerslayer* (1841)—were far more than American versions of Sir Walter Scott's "Waverley novels." Like William Gilmore

Horatio Greenough's Washington

Horatio Greenough catered to popular neoclassical taste when he depicted the nation's first president in a Roman toga, seated in a pose resembling Zeus as carved by the great Greek sculptor Phidias. Commissioned by Congress, this gigantic statue was originally intended for the Capitol's rotunda, but when the lighting failed, Congress had it moved to the eastern front of the Capitol, where it became the butt of numerous jokes. Undiscouraged, Greenough wrote in a letter of 1847: "When…the true sculptors of America shall have filled the metropolis with beauty and grandeur, will it not be worth $30,000 [the staggering cost of his sculpture] to be able to point to the figure and say: 'There was the first struggle of our infant art'?"

Simms's tales of the southern frontier and backcountry, they gave imaginative expression to a distinctively American experience with Indians, violence, the law, and the meaning of social bonds in a wilderness setting. The popular New England poets and men-of-letters chose homey, everyday subjects that disguised both their literary skill and learnedness. Thus Henry Wadsworth Longfellow, a translator of Dante and a master of meter, celebrated the village blacksmith. John Greenleaf Whittier sang of the barefoot boy. And the highly cultivated James Russell Lowell delivered political satire in the homespun Yankee dialect of an imaginary Hosea Biglow.

Art as Product By the 1820s it was becoming clear that art in America would have to be marketed like any other commodity, and that the ideal of the dabbling gentleman amateur would have to give way to the reality of the professional who wrote, carved, or painted for a living. Federal, state, and local governments did award a few commissions for patriotic and historical subjects, but political squabbles over art (including the seminudity of Greenough's Washington) dampened artists' desire for government patronage. The need to compete for middle-class customers and audiences helps to explain the dominant patriotic, lesson-teaching, and sentimental themes of popular American culture.

Thomas Cole's *The Voyage of Life, Childhood*
In 1839 and 1849 Thomas Cole, America's leading landscape painter, depicted the four stages of human life, "Childhood," "Youth," "Manhood," and "Old Age," as parts of a "Voyage" in a small boat set against a melodramatic landscape of cliffs, peaks, and stormy or radiant skies. In "Childhood," pictured here, a smiling angel guards a baby cushioned in a bed of flowers. "The rosy light of the morning," Cole wrote, "the luxuriant flowers and plants, are emblems of the joyousness of early life." Cole associated life's stages both with the earth's seasons and with the course of a nation's history.

Art as Character Shaper

A self-consciously democratic art, as opposed to the remnants of folk art that it began to replace, had to justify itself by serving such an essentially nonartistic need as the shaping of character. Before the Civil War both literature and the so-called fine arts claimed to perform educational, quasi-religious functions. They provided models to imitate, they trained and refined the emotions, and they taught that sin is always punished and virtue rewarded. Art promoted patriotism by glorifying the American Revolution and deifying George Washington. It defined idealized sex roles by identifying the American male as the man of action and the conqueror of nature—hunter, trapper, scout, mountain man, seafaring adventurer—while at the same time associating the American female with confinement in a home and with refinement of emotions—physical frailty, periods of melancholy, and a sensitivity expressed by sudden blushing, paleness, tears, and fainting. Above all, art furnished models of speech, manners, courtship, friendship, and grief that helped establish standards of middle-class respectability.

A few writers achieved the imaginative independence to interpret character and sensibility in new ways. Edgar Allan Poe, who strove for commercial success while remaining committed to the ideal of art as an independent craft, gave a dark coloring to the stock themes of sentimental poetry and fiction. In a different way

Henry David Thoreau (1817–62)
Although Thoreau published only two books in his own lifetime, including the classic Walden: or, Life in the Woods *(1854), he came to be regarded in the twentieth century as one of the greatest writers America has produced.*

Nathaniel Hawthorne subtly went beyond the conventions of sentimental moralism in *The Scarlet Letter* (1850), *The House of the Seven Gables* (1851), and *The Blithedale Romance* (1852). This period of creativity, later termed the American Renaissance, included Walt Whitman's *Leaves of Grass* (1855), which not only celebrated the boundless potentialities of American experience but took joy in defying the conventional limits of poetic language. Herman Melville's *Moby-Dick* (1851), one of the world's great novels, also fused native subject matter with new and distinctively American artistic forms. Henry David Thoreau's *Walden* (1854) stated a goal that could be applied to many of the best works of the period. Thoreau had nothing but contempt for the conventional efforts to shape character in the interest of social conformity. But his decision to live by himself on Walden Pond was an experiment in self-improvement. The goal of his experiment, and of the art it produced, was to break free from the distractions and artificialities that disguised "the essential facts of life"—"to drive life into a corner, and reduce it to its lowest terms." "For most men, it appears to me," he said, "are in a strange uncertainty about it, whether it is of the devil or of God."

Suggested Readings

An excellent collection of source material on children can be found in the first volume of Robert H. Bremner, ed., *Children and Youth in America: A Documentary History* (1970–71). Two important studies of the history of juvenile delinquency are Joseph M. Hawes, *Children in Urban Society* (1971), and Robert M. Mennel, *Thorns and Thistles* (1973).

Lawrence A. Cremin, *American Education: The National Experience, 1783–1876* (1980), is the most comprehensive account of American education in antebellum America. Michael Katz, *The Irony of Early School Reform* (1968), sharply challenges the self-congratulatory tradition of educational history. Three important studies, also critical but more balanced, are Carl F. Kaestle, *Pillars of the Republic: Common Schools and American Society, 1780–1860* (1983); Carl Kaestle, *The Evolution of an Urban School System: New York City, 1750–1850* (1973); and Stanley K. Schultz, *The Culture Factory: Boston Public Schools, 1789–1860* (1973). Rush Welter, *Popular Education and Democratic Thought in America* (1962), presents a more traditional approach, and so does the excellent biography by Jonathan Messerli, *Horace Mann* (1972). Among the special studies of note are Bernard Wishy, *The Child and the Republic: The Dawn of Modern American Child Nurture* (1968); Marianna C. Brown, *The Sunday School Movement in America* (1961); Ruth Elson, *Guardians of Tradition: American Schoolbooks of the Nineteenth Century* (1964); Vincent P. Lannie, *Public Money and Parochial Education* (1968); and Merle Curti, *The Social Ideas of American Educators* (1935). The best introduction to higher education is Frederick Rudolph, *The American College and University* (1962), which can be supplemented by Theodore R. Crane, ed., *The Colleges and the Public, 1767–1862* (1963), and by Richard Hofstadter and Wilson Smith, *American Higher Education: A Documentary History* (2 vols. 1961). For the origins of women's higher education, see Barbara Miller Solomon, *In the Company of Educated Women: A History of Women and Higher Education in America* (1985).

The most imaginative treatment of revivalism is the first section of Perry Miller, *The Life of the Mind in America* (1965). William G. McLoughlin, Jr., *Modern Revivalism* (1959), gives a more detailed and systematic account of individual revivalists, and more recently McLoughlin has written a stimulating interpretive essay, *Revivals, Awakenings, and Reform: An Essay on Religion and Social Change in America, 1607–1977* (1978). A recent biography of the king of early revivalists is Keith J. Hardman, *Charles Grandison Finney, 1792–1875: Revivalist and Reformer* (1987). Two bold and sweeping reinterpretations of nineteenth-century religion are John Butler, *Awash in a Sea of Faith: Christianizing the American People* (1990), and Nathan O. Hatch, *The Democratization of American Christianity* (1989). Charles A. Johnson, *The Frontier Camp Meeting* (1955), is the standard history of the subject. The wider social impact of revivalism in New York State is brilliantly traced in Whitney R. Cross, *The Burned-Over District* (1950), but this must now be supplemented by Paul E. Johnson's *A Shopkeeper's Millennium: Society and Revivals in Rochester, New York, 1815–1837* (1978) and Mary P. Ryan's indispensable *Cradle of the Middle Class: The Family in Oneida County, New York, 1790–1865* (1981). No less insightful for an understanding of religion, politics, regional variation, and reform is Randolph A. Roth, *The Democratic Dilemma: Religion, Reform, and the Social Order in the Connecticut River Valley of Vermont, 1791–1850* (1987).

The fullest general history of American religion is Sydney E. Ahlstrom, *A Religious History of the American People* (1972), which should be supplemented on special topics by Charles H. Lippy and Peter W. Williams, eds., *Encyclopedia of the American Religious Experience* (3 vols., 1988). A provocative study analyzing the cultural alliance between Protestant ministers and middle-class women is Ann Douglas, *The Feminization of American Culture* (1977). A different and no less valuable perspective is provided by Lori D. Ginzberg, *Women and the Work of Benevolence: Morality, Politics, and Class in the Nineteenth-Century United States* (1990). Among the special studies of unusual interest are Henri Desroche, *The American Shakers from Neo-Christianity to Pre-Socialism* (1971); Nathan Glazer, *American Judaism* (1957); Daniel W. Howe, *The Unitarian Conscience* (1970); Martin Marty, *The Infidel: Freethought in American Religion* (1961); William G. McLoughlin, Jr., *The Meaning of Henry Ward Beecher* (1970); Theodore Maynard, *The Story of American Catholicism* (1960); Ernest L. Tuveson, *Redeemer Nation: The Idea of America's Millennial Role* (1968); D. H. Meyer, *The Instructed Conscience: The Shaping of the American National Ethic* (1972); T. D. Bozeman, *Protestants in an Age of Science: The Baconian Ideal and Antebellum American Religious Thought* (1977); Colleen McDannell, *The Christian Home in Victorian America, 1840–1900* (1986), and Winton U. Solberg, *Redeem the Time: The Puritan Sabbath in Early America* (1977).

Perry Miller, *Life of the Mind in America* (1965), contains a brilliant analysis of legal thought in America. A masterly interpretive work is James W. Hurst, *Law and Social Order in the United States* (1977), which should be contrasted with the challenging and highly innovative work by Morton I. Horwitz, *The Transformation of American Law, 1780–1860* (1977). An important aspect of constitutional development is traced in Bernard Schwartz, *From Confederation to Nation: The American Constitution, 1835–1877* (1973). Leonard W. Levy, *The Law of the Commonwealth and Chief Justice Shaw* (1957), is an outstanding study of a leading jurist. The standard biographies of Marshall and Taney are Albert I. Beveridge, *The Life of John Marshall* (4 vols., 1916–19), and Carl B. Swisher, *Roger B. Taney* (1936).

On science, the last section of Perry Miller's *Life of the Mind* contains important insights. The best general works are Robert V. Bruce, *The Launching of Modern American Science, 1846–1876* (1987) and George Daniels, *American Science in the Age of Jackson* (1968). For medicine, see Richard H. Shryock, *Medicine and Society in America* (1960), and Martin Kaufman, *Homeopathy in America: The Rise and Fall of a Medical Heresy* (1971). Among the best biographies of individual scientists are Edward Lurie, *Agassiz: A Life of Science in America* (1960), and Frances Williams, *Matthew Fontaine Maury* (1963).

John D. Davies, *Phrenology: Fad and Science* (1955), is highly informative. Carl Bode treats the popularization of knowledge in *The American Lyceum* (1956), and reveals popular taste and culture in *The Anatomy of American Popular Culture* (1959). Stephen Nissenbaum, *Sex, Diet, and Debility in Jacksonian America: Sylvester Graham and Health Reform* (1980), is a fascinating study of a popular but neglected aspect of self-improvement. Lewis O. Saum, *The Popular Mood of Pre–Civil War America* (1980), disputes the belief that most Americans were dedicated to progress and self-improvement. Various aspects of self-improvement and changing views of gender roles are examined in Steven Mintz, *A Prison of Expectations: The Family in Victorian Culture* (1983); James C. Whorton, *Crusaders for Fitness: The History of American Health Reformers* (1982); and Carroll Smith-Rosenberg, *Disorderly Conduct: Visions of Gender in Victorian America* (1985).

The most illuminating studies of Emerson's thought are Joel Porte, *Representative Man: Ralph Waldo Emerson in His Time* (1979), and Stephen Whicher, *Freedom and Fate: An Inner Life of Ralph Waldo Emerson* (1953). Anne C. Rose, *Transcendentalism as a Social Movement, 1830–1850* (1981), succeeds in rooting Transcendentalism in the concrete needs and aspirations of New England society. Perry Miller, ed., *The Transcendentalists* (1950), is a difficult but magnificent anthology. Walter Harding's *Thoreau: Man of Concord* (1960), and Joseph W. Krutch, *Henry David Thoreau* (1948), can be supplemented with profit by Robert D. Richardson, Jr., *Henry Thoreau: A Life of the Mind* (1986) and Richard Lebeaux, *Young Man Thoreau* (1977). F. O. Matthiessen, *American Renaissance* (1941), is a brilliant and unsurpassed study of Emerson, Thoreau, Hawthorne, Melville, and Whitman. For connections between such major writers and the penny press, trial reports, and sensational fiction, see David S. Reynolds, *Beneath the American Renaissance: The Subversive Imagination in the Age of Emerson and Melville* (1988). For the theme of masculinity, see David Leverenz, *Manhood and the American Renaissance* (1989).

Whitney R. Cross, *The Burned-Over District* (1950), analyzes the origins of secular reform as well as of Mormonism and other religious movements. Leonard J. Arrington and Davis Bitton, *The Mormon Experience: A History of the Latter-day Saints* (1979), Jan Shipps, *Mormonism: The Story of a New Religious Tradition* (1985), and Klaus I. Hansen, *Mormonism and the American Experience* (1981), are the best introductions to Mormonism. Fawn M. Brodie, *No Man Knows My History: The Life of Joseph Smith* (1945), Leonard J. Arrington, *Brigham Young: American Moses* (1985), and Linda K. Newell and Valeen T. Avery, *Mormon Enigma: Emma Hale Smith, Prophet's Wife, "Elect Lady," Polygamy's Foe* (1984), are readable and extremely valuable biographies. Klaus I. Hansen, *Quest for Empire* (1967), is a valuable account of the Mormons' efforts to prepare for a worldly Kingdom of God. Some of the best specialized studies are D. Michael Quinn, *Early Mormonism and the Magic World View* (1986); Lawrence Foster, *Religion and Sexuality: Three American Communal Experiments of the Nineteenth Century* (1981); and Robert B. Flanders, *Nauvoo: Kingdom on the Mississippi* (1965). A dramatic and authoritative narrative of the westward migration is Wallace Stegner, *The Gathering of Zion: The Story of the Mormon Trail* (1964). Leonard I. Arrington's two works *Great Basin Kingdom* (1958) and *Building the City of God: Community and Cooperation Among the Mormons* (1976) are masterly accounts of the Mormon settlement of Utah. Norman F. Furniss, *The Mormon Conflict, 1850–1859* (1960), covers the so-called Mormon War.

There are no satisfactory general works on the relation between religion and secular reform, although much can be learned from the previously cited books by Randolph Roth, Mary P. Ryan, Lori D. Ginzberg, Paul E. Johnson, and Whitney R. Cross. Important aspects of the subject are examined in Carroll Smith-Rosenberg, *Religion and the Rise of the American City: The New York Mission Movement* (1971); Charles I. Foster, *An Errand of Mercy: The Evangelical United Front* (1960); Nancy A. Hewitt, *Women's Activism and Social Change* (1984); Clifford S. Griffin, *Their Brothers' Keepers: Moral Stewardship in the United States* (1960); and Timothy L. Smith, *Revivalism and Social Reform* (1957). The temperance movement, a critical link between evangelical religion and secular reform, is well described in Ian R. Tyrrell, *Sobering Up: From Temperance to Prohibition in Antebellum America* (1979). See also Barbara Leslie Epstein, *The Politics of Domesticity: Women, Evangelism, and Temperance in Nineteenth-Century America* (1981). For American drinking habits, see W. I. Rorabaugh, *The Alcoholic Republic: An American Tradition* (1979).

An original work that is indispensable for understanding the changing status of women and the origins of feminism is Nancy F. Cott, *The Bonds of Womanhood: "Woman's Sphere" in New England, 1780–1835* (1977), which should be supplemented by Barbara I. Berg, *The Remembered Gate: Origins of American Feminism—The Woman and the City, 1800–1860* (1978), and Keith M. Melder, *Beginnings of Sisterhood: The American Woman's Rights Movement, 1800–1850* (1977). William Leach, *True Love and Perfect Union: The Feminist Reform of Sex and Society* (1980), is an original and provocative study of feminism and women's position in antebellum and postbellum society. A helpful overall survey of both family history and women's changing aspirations is Carl N. Degler, *At Odds: Women and the Family in America from the Revolution to the Present* (1980). Other useful works are Ellen C. DuBois, *Feminism and Suffrage: The Emergence of an Independent Women's Movement in America, 1848–1869* (1978); W. L. O'Neill, *Everyone Was Brave: The Rise and Fall of Feminism in America* (1970); and Page Smith, *Daughters of the Promised Land* (1970). For individual biographies, see Elisabeth Griffith, *In Her Own Right: The Life of Elizabeth Cady Stanton* (1984); Otelia Cromwell, *Lucretia Mott* (1971); Celia Morris Eckhardt, *Fanny Wright: Rebel in America* (1984); and Gerda Lerner, *The Grimké Sisters from South Carolina: Rebels Against Slavery* (1967). For the changes in state laws relating to women's ownership of property and other legal rights, see Peggy A. Rabkin, *The Legal Foundations of Female Emancipation* (1980).

David S. Rothman, *The Discovery of the Asylum* (1971), is a brilliant interpretation of reformatory institutions. The most imaginative study of early prisons is W. David Lewis, *From Newgate to Dannemora: The Rise of the Penitentiary in New York* (1965). Blake McKelvey, *American Prisons* (1936), is a more comprehensive reference. On the insane, the best guides are Ellen Dwyer, *Homes for the Mad: Life Inside Two Nineteenth-Century Asylums* (1987); Helen E. Marshall, *Dorothea Dix: Forgotten Samaritan* (1937); and Gerald N. Grob, *Mental Institutions in America: Social Policy to 1875* (1973). For the reformer who did most for the deaf and blind, see Harold Schwartz, *Samuel Gridley Howe* (1956).

The classic work on the peace movement is Merle Curti, *The American Peace Crusade, 1815–1860* (1929), which should be supplemented by Peter Brock, *Pacifism in the United States: From the Colonial Era to the First World War* (1968).

On communitarian settlements, the best general works are Mark Holloway, *Heavens on Earth* (1951), and the relevant chapters in Lawrence Foster, *Religion and Sexuality: The Shakers, the Mormons, and the Oneida Community* (1984), and Donald D. Egbert and Stow Persons, *Socialism and American Life* (2 vols., 1952). The communitarian phase inspired by Robert Owen is masterfully covered by I. F. C. Harrison, *Quest for the New Moral World: Robert Owen and the Owenites in Britain and America* (1969). For the New Harmony experiment, see also William Wilson, *The Angel and the Serpent* (1964), and Arthur Bestor, *Backwoods Utopias: The Sectarian and Owenite Phases of Communitarian Socialism in America, 1663–1829,* 2d enl. ed. (1970). The best introduction to the Oneida community is Maren L. Carden, *Oneida: Utopian Community to Modern Corporation* (1969). For Noyes himself, see Robert D. Thomas, *The Man Who Would Be Perfect: John Humphrey Noyes and the Utopian Impulse* (1977). Three other studies of unusual importance are Lawrence Veysey, ed., *The Perfectionists: Radical Social Thought in the North, 1815–1860* (1973); Michael Fellman, *The Unbounded Frame: Freedom and Community in Nineteenth-Century Utopianism* (1973); and William H. Pease, *Black Utopia: Negro Communal Experiments in America* (1963).

Of the numerous studies of important literary figures, the following have special value for the historian: Richard Chase, *The American Novel and Its Tradition* (1957); Joel Porte, *The Romance in America: Studies in Cooper, Poe, Hawthorne, Melville, and James* (1969); A. N. Kaul, *The American Vision: Actual and Ideal Society in Nineteenth-Century Fiction* (1963); R. W. B. Lewis, *The American Adam: Innocence, Tragedy and Tradition in the Nineteenth Century* (1955); and David Levin, *History as Romantic Art* (1959). For Whitman, see Gay Allen, *The Solitary Singer* (1967). An informative introduction to Poe is Edward Wagenknecht, *Edgar Allan Poe: The Man Behind the Legend* (1963). Newton Arvin has written two fine literary biographies: *Herman Melville* (1950), and *Longfellow: His Life and Work* (1963). For Hawthorne, see Edward Wagenknecht, *Nathaniel Hawthorne: Man and Writer* (1961).

Van Wyck Brooks, *The Flowering of New England, 1815–1865* (1936), is still highly readable and informative. On the South, the best guide is Jay B. Hubbell, *The South in American Literature, 1607–1900* (1954). Henry Nash Smith, *Virgin Land: The American West as Symbol and Myth* (1950), is a brilliant study of the imaginative portrayal of the West. The early publishing industry is analyzed in William Charvat, *Literary Publishing in America, 1790–1850* (1959). For popular literature, see Mary Kelly, *Private Woman, Public Stage: Literary Domesticity in Nineteenth-Century America* (1984); Herbert R. Brown, *The Sentimental Novel in America, 1798–1860* (1940); and Frank L. Mott, *Golden Multitudes: The Story of Best Sellers in the United States* (1947). Mott, *American Journalism* (1962), is the standard source on newspapers. The first volume of Mott's monumental *A History of American Magazines* (5 vols., 1957) is a mine of information. For folk songs, see Alan Lomax, *The Folk Song in North America* (1969).

Oliver W. Larkin, *Art and Life in America* (1949), is a comprehensive study of the early history of art and architecture. On painting it should be supplemented by Barbara Novak's superb study, *Nature and Culture: American Landscape and Painting, 1825–1875* (1980), as well as by David C. Huntington, *Art and the Excited Spirit: America in the Romantic Period* (1972), and James T. Flexner, *That Wilder Image: The Painting of America's Native School from Thomas Cole to Winslow Homer* (1962). Neil Harris, *The Artist in American Society: The Formative Years, 1790–1860* (1966), is a sensitive study of art as a profession. Arthur H. Quinn, *American Drama* (2 vols., 1955), is a comprehensive introduction to the theater. A more imaginative work is David Grimstead, *Melodrama Unveiled* (1968). On architecture, see Roger G. Kennedy, *Greek Revival America* (1989) and Wayne Andrews, *Architecture in America* (1960). The best guides to early American music are Gilbert Chase, *America's Music* (1955); H. Wiley Hitchcock, *Music in the United States* (1969); and Dena I. Epstein, *Sinful Tunes and Spirituals: Black Folk Music Through the Civil War* (1977).

3

The Peculiar Institution

⌐

$\mathcal{H}$ISTORIANS still debate the importance of similarities and differences between the antebellum North and South. Was the South simply a variant form of American society and culture, or was it becoming a separate and indigestible nation within a nation? Clearly the two regions shared much in common: the American Revolutionary heritage; a commitment to constitutional government and to English laws and judicial procedure; a loyalty to national political parties and a growing acceptance of universal suffrage for white males; a widespread hunger for evangelical religion combined with an insistence on the separation of church and state. The typical southerner, like the typical northerner, was a small farmer who tried to achieve both relative self-sufficiency and a steady income from marketable cash crops. Nor was the South distinctive in its dedication to white supremacy. As slavery gradually disappeared in the North during the first decades of the nineteenth century, antiblack racism became more intense. Free blacks were barred from schools, colleges, churches, and public accommodations. Excluded from all but the most menial jobs, they were also deprived of the most elemental civil rights. But racism did not necessarily mean an approval of human slavery. As the North moved rapidly toward an urban and industrial economy, northerners celebrated the virtues and benefits of free labor, which they hailed as the keystone of free institutions. Having earlier assumed that slavery was a "relic of barbarism" that the forces of social and economic progress would gradually destroy, they looked on the South with dismay as black slavery became the basis for a vigorous, expanding economy and as southerners took the lead in the rush for western land.

Rise of the Cotton Kingdom

From 1820 on, southerners benefited from three advantages unavailable in the North. First, the climate and soil of large parts of the South were ideally suited to growing cotton, the indispensable raw material for the industrial revolution, which was well under way in Great Britain and was already beginning in New

Eli Whitney's First Cotton Gin
When Eli Whitney, the brilliant Yankee inventor, applied in 1793 for a patent on his first cotton gin, American cotton production was limited to high-quality "sea-island" cotton grown only on the coast of South Carolina and Georgia. Whitney's invention, which was soon improved and enlarged, efficiently separated the hard seeds from the lint of short-staple cotton, which could be cultivated inland on wide belts of land extending from Georgia and South Carolina to Texas. Since this technological breakthrough coincided with a soaring demand for cotton in the industrializing regions of Europe and New England, it became the foundation for the South's famous "Cotton Kingdom."

England. The perfection of the cotton gin and screw press, devices for extracting cotton from the plant and compressing it into bales, gave southerners benefits of technological innovation that northerners did not begin to approximate until the late 1850s. Second, the rapid improvement and wide use of steamboats opened the way to upriver navigation of the Mississippi and of the rich network of other southern rivers, thereby lowering transportation costs even more dramatically than the northern canals did. Third and most important, southern agriculture could exploit the forced labor of black slaves, whose numbers increased from 1.5 million in 1820 to nearly 4 million in 1860. A self-reproducing labor force had long distinguished the South from other slave societies in the New World. These included Brazil and Cuba, which until the mid-nineteenth century remained dependent on the continuing importation of slaves from Africa. The unprece- dented natural increase of the slave population in the South enabled white southerners to clear and settle the vast Cotton Kingdom, extending from Georgia to Louisiana, Arkansas, and eventually eastern Texas.

Scholars still dispute important questions relating to the economics of slavery. But one must begin by emphasizing the shortage of white labor as a crucial condition affecting both northern and southern agriculture. All American farmers wanted the independence and relative security of owning their own land. Since land was generally accessible, especially in the West, it was difficult for farmers to hire nonfamily labor in order to expand production, specialize, and take advantage of a rising demand for cash crops, such as wheat, cotton, and corn.

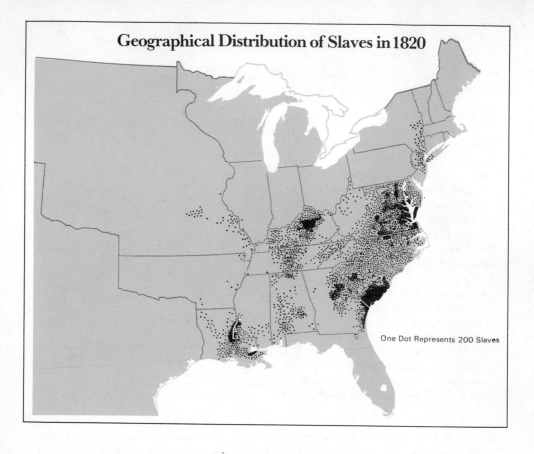

Geographical Distribution of Slaves in 1820

One Dot Represents 200 Slaves

In the North this labor shortage led to improved transportation, labor-saving machinery, and promotional schemes to attract immigrants. Between 1820 and 1860, for example, these three developments wholly transformed the New England labor market for the textile industry. Labor shortages were so severe in the early part of this period that factory owners and supervisors had to scramble for recruits just to keep the mills in operation. As railroad and highway networks expanded, however, local labor markets became more regional. As mills drew employees from the entire Northeast, immigrants from Ireland and Canada further expanded the potential labor supply. Moreover, the gradual mechanization of previously hand-powered processes, such as those in weaving, drove many outworkers from their farms or shops into the mills. By the 1850s, then, owners and supervisors of New England's textile mills virtually ceased to complain that they were "short of hands." Throughout this period the situation was entirely different in the South, where black slaves provided a highly mobile and flexible supply of labor. Large planters and speculators could quickly transport an army of involuntary workers to clear rich western land or could sell slaves to meet the labor demands of expanding areas. Even prospering family farmers could buy or rent a few slaves to increase their output of cotton or other cash crops. The flexibility of the system also enabled planters to allocate needed labor to raising

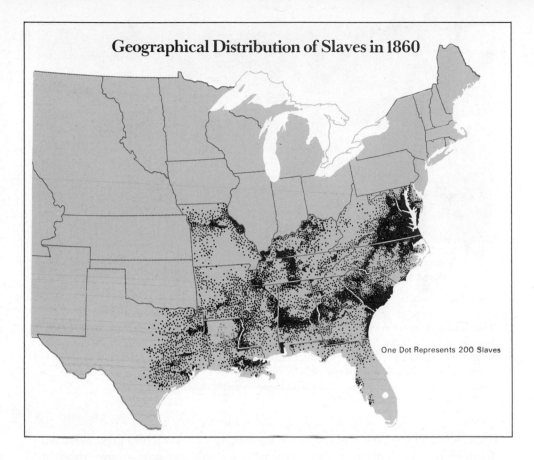

Geographical Distribution of Slaves in 1860

One Dot Represents 200 Slaves

livestock and growing foodstuffs for domestic consumption. And when market conditions improved, slaveholders could increase the proportion of work time devoted to cotton or other cash crops.

These various advantages also meant that slaves became the major form of southern wealth, and slaveholding became the means to prosperity. Except for the bustling port of New Orleans, great urban centers failed to appear, and internal markets declined. European immigrants, having no wish to compete with slave labor, generally shunned the region. Investment flowed mainly into the purchase of slaves, whose soaring price reflected an apparently limitless demand. The large planters, who profited from the efficiency of mobilizing small armies of slaves in specialized working groups or "gangs," soon ranked among America's richest men. In 1860, indeed, two-thirds of the richest Americans—men with estates of $100,000 or more—lived in the South.

There can be no doubt that investment in slaves brought a considerable return, or that the slave economy grew rapidly throughout the pre–Civil War decades. Yet essentially the system depended on the world's demand for cotton as it entered the age of industrialization, led by the British textile industry. At times the South's production of cotton exceeded international demand, and cotton prices fell sharply in the economic depressions known as the Panics of 1819 and

Sugar Manufacture

For over two hundred years sugar was the preeminent commodity produced by slaves in the West Indies; Europe's demand for sugar was the driving force behind most of the slave trade between Africa and the New World. In the United States, however, sugar production developed relatively late and was confined to southern Louisiana and a few other regions with a suitable climate. Slave labor was applied not only to the cultivation of sugarcane but also to the stages of manufacture needed to extract and refine sugar, molasses, and related products.

1837. But until the Civil War the world market for cotton textiles grew at such a phenomenal rate that both southern planters and British manufacturers thought only of infinite expansion. By 1840 the South grew more than 60 percent of the world's cotton; during the pre–Civil War boom more than three-fourths of the South's cotton was exported abroad. Much of it went to Britain, amounting to more than 70 percent of that country's cotton imports. In addition the South shipped cotton to the rising industries of continental Europe, including Russia. Throughout the antebellum period cotton accounted for over half the value of all American exports, and thus it paid for the major share of the nation's imports. A stimulant to northern industry, cotton also contributed to the growth of New York City as a distributing and exporting center that drew income from commissions, freight charges, interest, insurance, and other services connected with the marketing of America's number-one commodity.

Neither American sellers nor British buyers felt comfortable about their dependence on a single source of prosperity. British manufacturers searched unsuccessfully for alternative sources of high-grade cotton. Although the South continued to export large quantities of rice, tobacco, and other cash crops, southern business conventions unsuccessfully called for a more balanced economy. In Louisiana wealthy sugar growers expanded production by using new technology for the processing of cane. Plantation owners effectively applied slave labor to cultivating hemp, corn, and grain; to mining and lumbering; to building canals and railroads; and even to manufacturing textiles, iron, and other industrial products. Yet the South's economic growth and prosperity depended ultimately on foreign markets.

No other American region contained so many farmers who merely subsisted on their own produce; yet in no other region had agriculture become so speculative and commercial—for small cotton farmers who could not afford slaves, as well as for the planter elite. A typical farmer cultivating sixty-five acres in the Georgia Upcountry, for example, might devote most of his soil to growing corn, wheat, oats, fruit, and vegetables to cover his own family's subsistence needs and give over only an acre or two to cash crops like cotton intended for sale in the market. In such settlements, "habits of mutuality" among neighbors and kin, rather than competition in the marketplace, governed social relations. Yet by the 1850s an increasing number of voices arose, even in the Georgia Upcountry, imploring farmers to speculate in cash crops "to extend the cotton planting area . . . until every foot of land throughout the cotton growing region shall be brought into cultivation." Like some of the later Third World regions where involuntary labor produced raw materials for industrial nations, the South was intimately connected with industrial capitalism and yet cut off from its liberalizing and diversifying influences.

The Slave Masters   In theory the southern slaveholder possessed all the power of any owner of chattel property. This power was limited only by state laws (which were generally unenforceable) that protected slaves from murder and mutilation; that set minimal standards for food, clothing, and shelter; and that prohibited masters from teaching slaves to read or allowing them to carry firearms or roam about the countryside. These slave codes acknowledged that bondsmen were human beings who were capable of plotting, stealing, fleeing, or rebelling, and who were likely to be a less "troublesome property" if well cared for under a program of strict discipline. Yet the laws also insisted that the slave was a piece of property that could be sold, traded, rented, mortgaged, and inherited. They did not recognize the interests and institutions of the slave community, or the slave's right to marry, to hold property, or to testify in court.

In practice it proved impossible to treat human beings as no more than possessions or as the mere instruments of an owner's will. Most masters were primarily motivated by the desire for profit. They wanted to maximize their slaves' productivity while protecting the value of their capital investment, a value that kept rising with the generally escalating trend in slave prices. Accordingly, it made sense to provide a material standard of living that would promote good health and a natural increase in the size of slave families, and thus increase capital gains. It also made sense to keep the slaves' morale as high as possible and to encourage them to do willingly and even cheerfully the work they would be forced to do in the last resort. Convinced of the moral legitimacy of the system, most slaveowners sincerely believed that their own best interests were identical with their slaves' best interests. "The master should never establish any regulation among his slaves," cautioned *DeBow's Review,* "until he is fully convinced of its

Slave Cabins in Georgia
*Because the material conditions of slave life depended on the wealth, self-interest, and good
will of individual owners, slave housing ranged from relatively comfortable cabins to
overcrowded shanties whose occupants had little protection from the elements. Southern
apologists had some grounds for claiming that American slaves were better housed and fed
than were the laboring classes of Europe. Most abolitionists wisely insisted that the moral evil
of slavery had nothing to do with the material standard of life.*

propriety and equity. . . . The negro should feel that his master is his lawgiver and
judge; and yet is his protector and friend, but so far above him, as never to be
approached save with in the most respectful manner." Masters therefore sought
to convince the slaves of the essential justice of slavery, and they expected
gratitude for their acts of kindness, indulgence, and generosity, and even for their
restraint in inflicting physical punishment.

　　But slaves were not passive, agreeable puppets who could be manipulated at
will. As human beings they had one overriding objective: self-preservation at a
minimal cost of degradation and of loss of self-respect. To avoid punishment and
win rewards, they carried out their owners' demands with varying degrees of
thoroughness. But black slaves became cunningly expert at testing their masters'
will. They learned how to mock while seeming to flatter; how to lighten unending
work with moments of spontaneity, song, intimacy, and relaxation; how to exploit
the whites' dependence on black field drivers and household servants; and how to
play on the conflicts between their masters and white overseers. In short, they
learned through constant experiment and struggle how to preserve a core of

dignity and self-respect. Sarah Gayle, the young wife of an Alabama governor, recorded in her diary the frustrations she felt over the "insubordination" of a slave named Hampton:

> I never saw such a negro in all my life before—he did not even pretend to regard a command of mine, and treated me, and what I said, with the utmost contempt. He has often laughed in my face and told me that I was the only mistress he ever failed to please, on my saying he should try another soon [a threat to sell Hampton], he said he could not be worsted, and was willing to go.

Although slavery "worked" as an economic system, its fundamental conflict of interests created a highly unstable and violent society. The great sugar planters in Louisiana and cotton growers in the delta country of Mississippi, often employing more than one hundred slaves on a productive unit, tried to merge Christian paternalism with a kind of welfare capitalism. They provided professional medical care, offered monetary rewards for extra productivity, and granted a week or more of Christmas vacation. Yet these same plantations were essentially ruled by terror.

Even the most humane and kindly masters knew that only the threat of violence could force gangs of field hands to work from dawn to dusk "with the discipline," as one contemporary observer put it, "of a regular trained army." Frequent public floggings reminded every slave of the penalty for inefficient labor, disorderly conduct, or refusal to accept the authority of a superior. Bennet H. Barrow, a particularly harsh Louisiana slaveowner, maintained discipline by ordering occasional mass whippings of all his field hands, by chaining offenders or ducking them under water, and even by shooting a black who was about to run away. Barrow also distributed generous monetary bonuses to his slaves and bought them Christmas presents in New Orleans. The South could point to far gentler masters who seldom inflicted physical punishment. Slaves understood, however, that even the mildest of whites could become cruel despots when faced with the deception or ingratitude of people who, regardless of pretenses to the contrary, were kept down by force.

Masters also uneasily sensed that circumstances might transform a loyal and devoted slave into a vengeful enemy. It is true that white southerners could congratulate themselves on the infrequency of serious slave uprisings, especially when the South was compared with Brazil and most of the Caribbean. Yet in the French colony of Saint Domingue (Santo Domingo), which at one time had enjoyed at least as secure a history as the American South, the greatest of all slave revolts had begun in 1791 and had led to the creation of the black republic of Haiti, after the mobilized slaves had defeated the best armies of Spain, England, and France. And indeed the South had no immunity from slave revolts. In 1822 South Carolinians hanged thirty-five blacks after uncovering Denmark Vesey's plot for a full-scale uprising, a plot that involved some of Charleston's most trusted household servants. Nine years later Nat Turner led some seventy slaves on a bloody rampage through Southampton County, Virginia. To the outside

Identifying Marks of Ownership

Illustrations of slave branding were usually of British origin and referred to the West Indies, where Africans had long been systematically branded after disembarking from the slave ships. In the early nineteenth century, southern states tried to prohibit branding (although not until 1833 in South Carolina), but some advertisements for runaway slaves continued to refer to brands, which were sometimes inflicted as a punishment. Abolitionists exploited the theme, along with the slaves' semi-nudity, as a way of dramatizing the excesses of slaveholder power.

world southerners presented a brave facade of self-confidence, and individual masters reassured themselves that their own slaves were happy and loyal. But rumors of arson, poisoning, and suppressed revolts continued to flourish. Alarmists frequently warned that outside agitators were secretly sowing discontent among the slaves. This widespread fantasy at least hinted at the truth: not only did slavery have little approval in the outside world, but the institution ultimately depended on the sheer weight of superior force.

The difficulties in generalizing about the slave's world are compounded by the geographic, climatic, and cultural diversities of the "South"—a region in which mountain highlands, pine forests, and swampy lowlands are all frequently encountered within a few hundred miles of one another.

Almost half of the southern slaveholders owned fewer than five slaves; 72 percent owned fewer than ten. The typical master could thus devote close personal attention to his human property. Many small farmers worked side by side with their slaves, an arrangement that might have been far more humiliating for the slaves than working in a field gang under black "drivers." From the slave's viewpoint, much depended on an owner's character, on the norms of a given locality, on the accidents of sale, and on the relative difficulty of harvesting cotton, rice, tobacco, or sugar.

Slave experiences covered a wide range—from remarkable physical comfort and a lack of restraint to the most savage and unrelieved exploitation. But to dwell on contrasting examples of physical treatment is to risk losing sight of the central horror of human bondage. As the Quaker John Woolman pointed out in the eighteenth century, no human is saintly enough to be entrusted with total power over another. The slave was an inviting target for the hidden anger, passion, frustration, and revenge from which no human is exempt. A slave's work, leisure, movement, and daily fate depended on the will of another person.

Moreover, despite the numerical predominance of small slaveholders, most southern slaves were concentrated on large farms and plantations. Over half belonged to owners who held twenty or more slaves; one-quarter belonged to productive units of more than fifty slaves. In the South slave ownership was the primary road to wealth, and the most successful masters cornered an increasing share of the growing but limited human capital. Therefore most slaves experienced fairly standardized patterns of plantation life.

Life on the Plantation

By sunrise black drivers herded gangs of men and women into the fields. Slave women, including pregnant women and nursing mothers, were subjected to heavy field labor. Even small children served as water carriers or began to learn the lighter tasks of field work. Slaves too old for field work took care of small children and also worked in the stables, gardens, and kitchens. This full employment of all available hands was one of the economies of the system that increased the total output from a planter's capital investment. Nevertheless slaves often succeeded in maintaining their own work rhythm and in helping to define the amount of labor a planter could reasonably expect. Bursts of intense effort required during cotton picking, corn shucking, or the eighteen-hours-a-day sugar harvest were followed by periods of festivity and relaxation. Even in relatively slack seasons, however, there were cattle to be tended, fences to be repaired, forests to be cleared, and food crops to be planted.

Black slaves were saved from becoming mere robots in the field by the strength of their own community and evolving culture. There has long been controversy over the degree to which African cultural patterns were able to survive in North America. In contrast to Brazil, where continuing slave importations sustained for blacks a living bond with African cultures, the South had a black population in which the vast majority were removed by several generations from an African-born ancestor. Some research has uncovered striking examples of African influence in the southern slaves' oral traditions, folklore, songs, dances, language, sculpture, religion, and kinship patterns. The question at issue is not the purity or even the persistence of distinct African forms. In the New World all imported cultures underwent blending, adaptation, and combination with other elements. The point is that slaves, at least on the larger plantations,

A Slave Family
Although slave marriages were not recognized or protected in any way by state law, slaves observed their own traditions of courtship, marriage ceremony, naming children after ancestors or relatives, and burying deceased family members. This 1862 photograph of a slave family on a Beaufort, South Carolina plantation shows that generational continuity could sometimes be maintained despite the threat of separate sale of family members. Note the absence, however, of a single young adult male.

created their own African-American culture, which helped to preserve the most crucial areas of life and thought from white domination. Within such a culture, sustained by strong community ties, slaves were able to maintain a sense of apartness, of pride, and of independent identity. Plantations with more than fifty slaves contained an average of fewer than two adult white males, a fact that dramatizes the relative weakness of white surveillance and the reliance on a hierarchy of black managers, artisans, and mechanics.

African kinship patterns seem to have been the main vehicle for the maintenance of cultural identity. As in West Africa, children were frequently named for grandparents, who were revered even in memory. Kinship patterns survived even the breakup of families, although mother-headed families and family fragmentation were far commoner on plantations with fewer than fifteen slaves. On larger plantations black strangers often took on the functions and responsibilities of grandparents, uncles, and aunts. Many younger slaves were cared for and protected by "aunts" and "uncles" who were not blood kin. These older teachers and guardians passed on knowledge of the time when their ancestors had not been slaves, before the fateful crossing of the sea. This historical awareness inspired hope in a future time of deliverance—a deliverance that slaves associated with the Jews' biblical flight from Egypt, with the sweet land of Canaan, and with the Day of Jubilee. In the words of one spiritual:

> *Dear Lord, dear Lord, when slavery'll cease*
> *Then we poor souls will have our peace;—*
> *There's a better day a-coming,*
> *Will you go along with me?*
> *There's a better day a-coming,*
> *Go sound the jubilee!*

Historians have recently recognized how important the slave family was as a refuge from the dehumanizing effects of being treated as chattel property. The strength of family bonds is suggested by the thousands of slaves who ran away from their owners in search of family members separated through sale. The myth of weak family attachments is also countered by the swarms of freedmen who roamed the South at the end of the Civil War in search of their spouses, parents, or children, and by the eager desire of freedmen to legalize their marriages.

Nevertheless the slave family was a highly vulnerable institution. Although many slaveowners had moral scruples against separating husbands from wives or small children from their mothers, even the strongest scruples frequently gave way in times of economic need. The forced sale of individual slaves in order to pay a deceased owner's debts further increased the chances of family breakups. In some parts of the South, it was common for a slave to be married to another slave on a neighboring or even distant plantation, an arrangement that left visitation at the discretion of the two owners. At best, slave marriage was a precarious bond, unprotected by law and vulnerable to the will of whites.

In sexual relations there was a similar gap between moral scruples and actual practice. White planter society officially condemned miscegenation—interracial sexual unions—and tended to blame lower-class whites for fathering mulatto children. Yet there is abundant evidence that many slaveowners, sons of slaveowners, and overseers took black mistresses or sexually exploited the wives and daughters of slave families. This abuse of power was not as universal as northern abolitionists claimed, but it was common enough to humiliate black women, to instill rage in black men, and to arouse shame and bitterness in white women. No one conveyed this message more poignantly than Sarah Grimké, the abolitionist daughter of a wealthy South Carolina slaveholding family:

[T]he virtue of female slaves is wholly at the mercy of irresponsible tyrants, and women are bought and sold in our slave markets, to gratify the brutal lust of those who bear the name of Christians. In our slave States, if amid all her degradation, and ignorance, a woman desires to preserve her virtue unsullied, she is either bribed or whipped into compliance, or if she dares resist her

Auctioning Slaves
Nothing revealed the basic inhumanity of slavery more than the slave auction, an institution that was allowed even in the nation's capital. Because state laws defined them as chattel property, slaves were openly traded and sold on the market. Even the most sheltered or privileged slave could face the auction block as the result of an owner's indebtedness or the settlement of his estate. On such occasions mothers were sold separately from their children, husbands were separated from wives, human beings were examined, probed, and bid for like cattle.

seducer, her life by the laws of some of the slave States may be, and has actually been sacrificed to the fury of disappointed passion. . . .

Nor does the colored woman suffer alone: the moral purity of the white woman is deeply contaminated. In the daily habit of seeing the virtue of her enslaved sister sacrificed without hesitancy or remorse, she looks upon the crimes of seduction and illicit intercourse without horror, and although not personally involved in the guilt, she loses that value for innocence in her own, as well as the other sex, which is one of the strongest safeguards to virtue.

The larger slave communities provided some stability and continuity for the thousands of blacks who were sold and shipped to new environments. On the larger plantations one could find conjurers whose alleged magic powers were thought to ward off sickness, soften a master's heart, or hasten the success of a

An African Church in Cincinnati
In northern cities like Cincinnati, Ohio, blacks created and patronized their own African churches for two reasons: in white churches they were treated as inferiors and often forced to sit in a balcony or in special pews; in their own churches they could give uninhibited expression to a blend of African and Christian traditions that formed the core of African-American culture. Black churches became centers of antislavery activism and trained a large proportion of the leaders of the free black community.

courtship. There were black preachers who mixed Christianity with elements of West African religion and folklore. In the slave quarters particular prestige was attached to those who excelled at the traditional memorizing of songs, riddles, folktales, superstitions, and herb cures—who were carriers, in short, of African-American culture. These forms of oral communication allowed free play to the imagination, enabling slaves to comment on the pathos, humor, absurdity, sorrow, and warmth of the scenes they experienced. Together with the ceremonial rituals, especially at weddings and funerals, the oral traditions preserved a sanctuary of human dignity that enabled slaves to survive the humiliations, debasement, and self-contempt that were inseparable from human bondage.

As a result of the evangelical revivals,* southern planters increasingly promoted the religious conversion of their slaves. Even by the first decades of the nineteenth century, a growing number of churchmen and planters had argued

---

*On nineteenth-century revivalism in the South, see chapter 13, pp. 418–19.

that religious instruction would make slaves more obedient, industrious, and faithful. The ideal Christian master would treat his slaves with charity and understanding. The ideal Christian slave would humbly accept his assigned position in this world, knowing that his patience and faithfulness would be rewarded in heaven. Servitude, in short, could be softened, humanized, and perfected by Christianity. The reality of slavery fell short of the ideal, as indicated, for example, by the ghastly infant mortality and malnutrition of slave children. Religion may have induced many masters to take a sincere interest in their slaves' welfare, but it could not eliminate the cruelty and injustice inherent in the system.

No white preachers could entirely purge Christianity of overtones that tended to oppose slavery. Nor could whites prevent black preachers from converting Christianity into a source of self-respect, dignity, and faith in eventual deliverance—the longed-for Day of Jubilee. In both North and South free blacks responded to growing racial discrimination by forming what they called African churches, usually Baptist or Methodist. And despite the efforts by whites to control every aspect of their slaves' religion, the slaves created their own folk religion and shaped it to their needs and interests. As one ex-slave from Texas recalled, "The whites preached to the niggers and the niggers preached to theyselves."

The South as a "Slave Society"

By the 1830s black slavery had come to dominate all aspects of southern society. Old-fashioned defenses of slavery as an unfortunate although necessary evil were beginning to give way to aggressive self-justification. Ironically, as the South became increasingly isolated from the free-labor ideology of the Western world, the expansion of cotton cultivation helped assure southern leaders that slavery was indispensable to northern and British industry, which promoted the idealization of free labor. Accordingly, slaveholders regarded their critics as ungrateful hypocrites who would bite the hand that fed them.

The meaning of the phrase *slave society* is best illustrated by the West Indian colonies of the eighteenth and early nineteenth centuries. There black slaves typically made up 90 percent or more of an island's population. Political and social life was wholly dominated by large plantation owners, their managers and agents, and the merchants who lived off the system. There was almost no dissent over the question of black slavery.

Parts of the South almost approximated this model: the swampy lowcountry of South Carolina and the adjoining Sea Islands; the fertile Black Belt, extending from Georgia to Mississippi; the delta counties of Mississippi and the sugar parishes (counties) of Louisiana. But unlike the small and isolated West Indian islands, the sprawling South was in no way a solid and uniform society. In 1860, out of a white population of some 8 million, roughly 10,000 families belonged to the planter "aristocracy." Fewer than 3,000 families owned over one hundred slaves. Barely one out of four white southerners owned a slave or belonged to a

Florida "Crackers"
The term "cracker" referred originally to frontier outlaws and "great boasters" and braggarts, but in the nineteenth century it was applied to southern backwoodsmen and "poor whites" in general. This Florida family, guarding their palm-frond hut, lived in a subsistence-level economy that was far removed from the great market-oriented plantations.

family that did. There were extensive regions of eastern Tennessee and western Virginia where blacks, slave or free, were a rarity. Slavery had declined sharply in most of the Upper South—most dramatically of all in Delaware, where fewer than 2,000 slaves remained by 1860. Nor could most of the nonslaveholding majority be classed as hillbillies and poor whites. In addition to artisans, factory workers, and professionals, there were millions of small farmers in the South who worked their own land or who grazed herds of cattle, pigs, and horses in the forests and open range of the public domain.

Nevertheless, except for a few isolated pockets, the South did become a slave society dominated politically and ideologically by a plantation-owning elite. Throughout the pre–Civil War period, slaveholding remained the most widespread and obvious road to wealth and status. By 1860 millions of nonslaveholders believed that any serious threat to slavery was sufficient justification for southern independence; many of them, especially in the Southwest, had reasonable hopes of acquiring land and becoming planters even though the cost of buying slaves was soaring. Others, such as the yeoman farmers of the Georgia Upcountry, recognized that black slavery served their own interests by limiting their participation in market wage relations. "It is a well-known fact in the South," reported the Atlanta *Daily Intelligencer* in 1856, "that it is to preserve their own independence that non-slaveholding voters of the South have ever been staunch supporters of slavery." And small farmers often depended on a neighboring slaveowner's cotton gin or political patronage—and knew that in turn he depended for security on their services as armed patrols that searched the countryside for any unauthorized movement of blacks.

Dominance of the Planter Class   The planter class could also draw on a rich tradition of political leadership. In the South—but not in the North—the eighteenth-century connection between wealth and personal political power had endured. Political leadership sprang directly from the ownership of slaves, which was supposed to provide leisure, a concern for public order, and a certain paternalistic self-assurance in exercising authority. The southern planter elite demonstrated skill in commanding the loyalty of nonslaveholding whites and also in disciplining dissent within the white population. The southern code of honor also sanctioned an open resort to violence. According to South Carolina's chief apologist for dueling, such formalized combat "will be persisted in as long as man's independence, and a lofty personal pride in all that dignifies and ennobles the human character, shall continue to exist." By the 1830s numerous southern abolitionists and southerners with simply a strong distaste for slavery had emigrated to the North or West after abandoning hope of challenging the entrenched idea that black slavery was a necessary evil that should be discussed as little as possible. They left behind them a plantation-owning elite that was solidified in its defense of slavery and militantly intolerant of dissent.

Southern white unity centered on race. Southern society was dedicated to the ideal of equality of opportunity as long as the ideal applied only to whites. It was also a region that depended economically on a system of labor exploitation that was difficult to square with republican and liberty-loving principles. Racial doctrine—the supposed innate inferiority of blacks—became the primary instrument for justifying the persistence of slavery, for rallying the support of nonslaveholding whites, and for defining the limits of dissent. In 1837 Chancellor William Harper of South Carolina summed up the prevailing dogma: "That the African negro is an inferior variety of the human race, is, I think, now generally admitted, and his distinguishing characteristics are such as peculiarly mark him out for the situation which he occupies among us."

Southern Free Blacks   The key to racial policy was the status of free blacks. Before the nineteenth century this status had been ambiguous, and the number of free blacks was insignificant. By 1810, however, as a result of the emancipations that had accompanied and followed the Revolution, there were 100,000 free blacks and mulattoes in the southern states. This group, the fastest-growing element in the southern population, was beginning to acquire property, to found "African" churches and schools, and to assert its independence, especially in the Upper South. In response, white legislators tightened restrictions on private acts of freeing slaves in an effort to curb the growth of an unwanted population. A rash of new laws, similar to the later Black Codes of Reconstruction,* reduced free blacks almost to the status of slaves without masters. The new laws regulated their freedom of movement, forbade them to associate with slaves, subjected them to surveillance and discipline by whites, denied them the legal right to testify in court against whites, required them to work at approved jobs, and threatened them with penal labor if not actual reenslavement. Ironically, in parts of the Deep South free blacks continued to benefit from a more flexible status because there were fewer of them in the population than elsewhere in the South and they could serve as valued intermediaries between a white minority and a slave majority, as in the West Indies. Racial discrimination was worse in the Upper South, precisely because slavery was economically less secure in that region.

Decline of Antislavery in the South

From the time of the Revolution, a cautious, genteel distaste for slavery had been fashionable among the planters of the Upper South. This Jeffersonian tradition persisted even after the more militant abolitionists had been driven from the region and after Methodist and Baptist leaders had backtracked on various resolutions encouraging gradual emancipation. The desire to find some way of ridding the South of its "burden" or "curse," as the Jeffersonian reformers called it, was kept alive by some of the sons of affluent plantation owners who went to the North or to Europe to study.

The hope of removing the South's burden also won support from a few broad-minded plantation owners, mostly Whigs,† who were troubled by the economic decline of eastern Virginia and Maryland, and by the continuing loss of population to the Southwest. In 1832 the belief that slavery was "ruinous to the whites" received unexpected support in the Virginia legislature from non-slaveholders who lived west of the Blue Ridge Mountains and who had various motives for challenging the political control of tidewater planters. But in the end their arguments, advanced in a notable legislative debate of 1832 in response to Nat Turner's revolt,‡ demonstrated the power of racism. Even the non-slaveholding dissenters acknowledged that bondage had benefits for blacks and that its destructive effects on white society could be ended only by gradually freeing and deporting the entire black population. The antislavery delegates failed even to carry a resolution that would have branded slavery as an evil to be dealt with at some future time.

---

*For the Black Codes, see chapter 20, pp. 674, 684.

†For southern Whigs, see chapter 15, pp. 509–16.

‡For Nat Turner's revolt, see pp. 461, 473.

The Proslavery Argument

By the early 1840s—less than a decade later—such a public debate would have been inconceivable in any southern state. By then regional loyalty, intensified by sectional conflict, required that southerners believe slavery to be a "positive good." The proslavery argument ranged from appeals to ancient Greek and Roman precedents to elaborate biblical interpretations designed to prove that slavery had never been contrary to the laws of God. Drawing on the romantic and chivalric literary fashions of the time, southern writers represented the plantation as a feudal manor blessed with human warmth, mutual duties, knightly virtues, and loyalty to blood and soil.

The most striking part of the proslavery ideology was its indictment of liberalism and capitalism—its well-documented charge that the prevailing rule in so-called free societies, as George Fitzhugh put it, was "every man for himself, and the devil take the hindmost." In his *Sociology for the South* (1854) and *Cannibals All!* (1857), Fitzhugh sharply criticized the philosophic premises of an individualistic, egalitarian society. He also examined the destructive historical consequences of dissolving the social and psychological networks that had once given humanity a sense of place and purpose. Fitzhugh, the most rigorous and consistent proslavery theorist, presented the master-slave relation as the only alternative to a world in which unlimited self-interest had subjected propertyless workers to the impersonal exploitation of "wage-slavery." He was consistent enough to renounce *racial* justifications for actual slavery and to propose that the benefits of the institution he boasted of be extended to white workers. But these arguments, however interesting theoretically, only showed how far Fitzhugh had moved from social reality. Racism lay at the heart of the South's unity. The enslavement of whites was unthinkable, and in the 1850s the South even rejected extremist proposals for expelling or reenslaving a quarter of a million free blacks. Fitzhugh's theories did more to expose the moral dilemmas of free society than to illuminate the actual complexities and contradictions of the South.

It is true that moral doubts persisted, especially in the Upper South. But after the 1830s these doubts were more than counterbalanced by the conviction that emancipation in any form would be a disaster, for blacks as well as for whites. Southerners channeled their moral concern into dedicated efforts to reform, improve, and defend what they called the peculiar institution. It was almost universally accepted that to own slaves meant to have a sense of duty and a burden—a duty and a burden that defined the moral superiority of the South. This duty and burden was respected by nonslaveholding southerners, who were prepared to defend it with their lives. That, perhaps, was the ultimate meaning of a "slave society."

Radical Abolitionism

Black slavery was the first issue to expose the limitations of the Benevolent Empire. Even by 1830 there was a striking gap between the public optimism of the evangelical humanitarians and their whispered despair concerning black slavery.

Harsh realities made the gap increasingly noticeable. Despite the fact that federal law prohibited slave imports from Africa, the natural increase of the American slave population exceeded all earlier expectations. The number of slaves in the United States increased from approximately 1.5 million in 1820 to more than 2 million in 1830. This figure represented almost one-sixth of the total United States population and more than twice the number of slaves in the British and French West Indies. The number of free blacks grew during the 1820s from about 234,000 to 320,000.

The Failure of Black Colonization

In 1830 the American Colonization Society transported a total of only 259 free blacks to Liberia, the West African colony that the society had established as a refuge for American blacks. Yet most reformers still regarded colonization as the only solution: "We must save the Negro," as one missionary put it, "or the Negro will ruin us." Racial prejudice was pervasive in the Benevolent Empire, and it was by no means unknown among later radical abolitionists. But the new and significant fact was the rising tide of virulent racism among the working classes of the North. Prejudiced as they may have been, many leaders of the colonization movement were sincere opponents of slavery who abhorred the growing racism of the northern masses and who saw black emigration as the only realistic means for preventing racial war in the North and for inducing southern masters to free their slaves.

A series of events reinforced the realization that white America could not solve its racial problem by shipping a few hundred free blacks each year to Liberia. In 1829 David Walker, a Boston black who belonged to the Massachusetts General Colored Association, published his revolutionary *Appeal to the Colored Citizens of the World,* which justified slave rebellion and warned white Americans that if justice were delayed blacks would win their liberty "by the crushing arm of power." The pamphlet created an uproar, and copies smuggled by sailors soon appeared among blacks in the Deep South. Then in 1831 Nat Turner, a trusted Virginia slave, led the bloodiest slave revolt the South had yet experienced. At the end of the same year a far larger uprising rocked the British colony of Jamaica. In Britain mass demonstrations continued to demand the immediate and unconditional emancipation of West Indian slaves. When Parliament responded in 1833 with generous monetary compensation to slaveowners to cover part of the financial loss of emancipation, and with an apprenticeship plan to prepare slaves for freedom, a few Americans concluded that effective political action of any kind required a mammoth mobilization of public opinion.

The Ethical Basis of Abolitionism

To the young abolitionists who began to appear in the early 1830s, black slavery was the great national sin. The fusion of American religious revivalism with the influence of the British antislavery movement was symbolized by Theodore Dwight Weld, the son of a Connecticut minister. Weld was a convert and close associate of the famous evangelist Charles Grandison Finney in upstate New York. Weld's closest friend and religious model was Charles Stuart, a visiting British reformer who worked with Finney's disciples in the Burned-Over District and then in 1829 returned to England to throw himself into the battle for slave emancipation. After being urged by Stuart to take up the cause in America, Weld shifted from temperance and educational reforms to abolitionism, becoming one of the most fearless and powerful lecturers in the area from Ohio to Vermont. Early in 1833 he wrote a letter to William Lloyd Garrison, whom he knew only by reputation. In it he illuminated the meaning of slavery as sin:

> That no condition of birth, no shade of color, no mere misfortune of circumstances, can annul the birth-right charter, which God has bequeathed to every being upon whom he has stamped his own image, by making him a free moral agent, and that he who robs his fellow man of this tramples upon right, subverts justice, outrages humanity, unsettles the foundations of human safety, and sacrilegiously assumes the prerogatives of God; and further, tho' he who retains by force, and refuses to surrender that which was originally obtained by violence or fraud is joint partner in the original sin, becomes its apologist and makes it the business of every moment to perpetuate it afresh, however he may lull his conscience by the vain plea of expediency or necessity.

Weld's statement sums up a moral command that sprang from three fundamental convictions. He believed that all men and women have the ability to do what is right and therefore are morally accountable for their actions; that the intolerable social evils are those that degrade the image of God in human beings, stunting or corrupting people's capacities for self-control and self-respect; and that the goal of all reform is to free individuals from being manipulated like physical objects. As one follower of William Lloyd Garrison put it, the goal of abolitionism was "the redemption of man from the dominion of man."

The fact that Weld and other abolitionists were almost wholly concerned with ideals was both their greatest strength and their greatest weakness. America was supposedly a nation of doers, of practical builders, framers, drafters, organizers, and technicians. The overriding question, in abolitionist eyes, was whether the nation would continue to accommodate itself to a social system that was based on sheer violence. To propose rational plans or to get embroiled in debates over the precise means and timing of emancipation would only give slavery's defenders an advantage. What the times required, therefore, was "an original motive power" that would shock and awaken public opinion, create a new moral perspective, and require legislators to work out the details, however imperfectly, of practical emancipation. In 1831 William Lloyd Garrison admitted: "Urge immediate abolition as earnestly as we may, it will alas! be gradual abolition in the end. We have never said that slavery would be overthrown by a single blow; that it ought to be we shall always contend."

William Lloyd Garrison (1805–79)
Raised by an indigent mother abandoned by his alcoholic father, Garrison began his career as a printer and a conservative supporter of the Benevolent Empire before moving on to become the most famous and controversial American abolitionist. Courageous and supremely confident of the rectitude of his own moral views, Garrison owed much of his prominence to the anger and outrage he provoked among slaveholders, northern clergymen, ordinary citizens, and even other abolitionists and reformers. As an agitator determined to expose the sins of slavery, racism, and all forms of coercive authority, Garrison continues to arouse controversy among historians.

The Abolitionists On one level the abolitionists realistically saw that the nation had reached a dead end on slavery. Instead of gradually withering away, as earlier optimists had hoped, the evil had grown and had won increasing acceptance among the nation's political leaders and most powerful institutions. Therefore the abolitionists took on the unpopular role of agitators, of courageous critics who stood outside the popular refuges of delusion, hypocrisy, and rationalization. In 1830 Garrison went to jail for writing libelous attacks against a New England merchant who was shipping slaves from Baltimore to New Orleans. After his fine was paid and his release was secured by the wealthy supporter of reform groups, Arthur Tappan, Garrison in 1831 founded his newspaper *The Liberator* in Boston. In the first issue he hurled out his famous pledge: "I will be as harsh as truth, and as uncompromising as justice. . . . I am in earnest—I will not equivocate—I will not excuse—I will not retreat a single inch—AND I WILL BE HEARD."

Although *The Liberator* had an extremely small circulation and derived most of its support from black subscribers in the Northeast, Garrison succeeded in being heard. In the South especially, newspaper editors seized the chance to reprint specimens of New England's radicalism, accompanied by their own furious rebuttals. Even before the end of 1831, mere months after *The Liberator* first appeared, the Georgia legislature proposed a reward of $5,000 for anyone who would kidnap Garrison and bring him south for trial. Garrison also championed the free blacks' grievances against the Colonization Society, which he had once supported, and mounted a blistering attack against the whole concept of colonization. He pointed out that the hope for colonization confirmed and reinforced white racial prejudice and that racial prejudice was the main barrier the abolitionists faced in the North. Largely as a result of Garrison's early and independent leadership, the American Anti-Slavery Society, founded in 1833, committed itself to at least a vague legal equality of whites and blacks, and totally rejected colonization.

Even though they had practically declared war against the values, institutions, and power structure of Jacksonian America, the abolitionists continued to think of their reform societies as simple extensions of the Benevolent Empire. They assumed that they could quickly win support from churches and ministers—that they could persuade the pious, influential, and respectable community leaders that racial prejudice was as harmful as intemperance. Then, after mobilizing righteous opinion in the North, they could shame the South into repentance. Abolitionists did not think of themselves as provokers of violence and disunion. Rather, it was slavery that had brought increasing violence and threats of disunion. A national commitment to emancipation, they believed, would ensure harmony and national union.

Like the wealthy British supporters of humanitarian causes (including antislavery), Arthur Tappan and his brother Lewis moved from various benevolent causes to that of immediate emancipation. By 1833 humanitarians in Great Britain had won the support of the established order, as well as of middle-class public opinion. But in America, precisely because the Tappans had wealth and prestige, they were viciously attacked for encouraging Garrison and other radicals and for betraying the common interests that had allowed leaders in different sections to do business with one another. Mass rallies in the South pledged as much as $50,000 for the delivery of Arthur Tappan's body, dead or alive. In New York City, business leaders vainly pleaded with the Tappan brothers, whose lives were being repeatedly threatened by 1834, to give up their radical activities. In that year prominent New Yorkers cheered on a mob of butcherboys and day laborers who smashed up Lewis Tappan's house and burned the furnishings. Only the unexpected arrival of troops prevented an armed assault on the Tappans' store.

Antiabolitionists played on popular suspicions of England, charging that men like George Thompson, an English friend of Garrison, had been sent "to foment discord among our people, array brother against brother...to excite treasonable opposition to our government...to excite our slave population to rise and butcher their masters; to render the South a desert, and the country at large the scene of fraternal war." Abolitionists continually invoked the ideals of the Declaration of Independence and portrayed themselves as fulfilling the Revolution's promise. But their enemies styled themselves as minutemen defending American liberties. The mob riots of the Revolutionary periods appeared to legitimize the antiabolitionist riots that spread across the North in the 1830s. For the most part this mob violence was carefully planned, organized, and directed toward specific goals, such as the destruction of abolitionist printing presses and the intimidation of free blacks. The leaders were "gentlemen of property and standing"—prominent lawyers, bankers, merchants, doctors, and local political leaders of both the Democratic and Whig parties. In most towns and cities the white abolitionists and free blacks received little protection from the forces of law and order. The colonizationists, already weakened by financial difficulties and internal division, took the lead in accusing the abolitionists of being "amalgamationists" who would not stop short of encouraging black men to woo the daughters of white America.

Abolitionism and Freedom of Speech This racist bugaboo brought the northern crowds into the streets and also lay behind the abolitionists' most dramatic break with the Benevolent Empire. Lane Theological Seminary in Cincinnati was meant to be one of the empire's crowning achievements—a beachhead of benevolence on the Ohio River, a staging ground for the missionary conquest of the West. Arthur Tappan paid the salary of the president of the seminary, Lyman Beecher. He also paid the way for Theodore Weld, then thirty-one, to study there. Early in 1834 Weld conducted at Lane an eighteen-day soul-searching revival on the question of slavery. After converting many students and nonstudents to the doctrine of immediate emancipation, Weld led his band into the slums where the black residents of Cincinnati lived. There they set up libraries, conducted evening classes, and fraternized with the city's "untouchable" caste, the blacks. In Weld's view educational institutions had a duty to train minds for the new "era of disposable power and practical accomplishment."

But to the Tappans' dismay, Lane's board of trustees voted to silence Weld and the other antislavery leaders, and Lyman Beecher—who was still a supporter of colonization—went along with the decision.

Various leaders of American higher education agreed that antislavery agitation endangered the fundamental purposes of American colleges. In response, almost all the Lane students walked out of the seminary with Weld. Some ended up in Arthur Tappan's newly financed college, Oberlin. But many joined Weld as traveling agents for the American Anti-Slavery Society, of which Arthur Tappan was president, braving showers of rotten eggs and stones in order to address the American people.

As a product of the Benevolent Empire, abolitionism drew on and perfected techniques of mass communication that gave the nation its first taste of modern "public relations." By 1835 the new steam printing press and other technological improvements had reduced the cost and increased the volume of mass publication. In 1834 the Anti-Slavery Society distributed 122,000 pieces of literature; in 1835 the figure rose to 1.1 million. President Jackson and various national and local authorities expressed alarm over this attempt to apply the methods of the Bible Society and Tract Society to a revolutionary purpose—a purpose that threatened one of the nation's chief capital investments as well as a national system for racial

The Killing of an Abolitionist
A woodcut illustration of the anti-abolitionist mob attacking the printing office of Elijah P. Lovejoy in Alton, Illinois on November 7, 1837. Lovejoy's death dramatized the issue of free speech and public repression.

control. But although the government encouraged the destruction of abolitionist mail, it could do nothing about the traveling abolitionist lecturers in the North, the "antislavery bazaars" held to raise funds and distribute literature, the auxiliary societies for ladies and children, or the flood of propaganda in the forms of medals, emblems, posters, bandannas, chocolate wrappers, songs, and children's readers.

The rapid growth of abolitionist societies, coupled with violent efforts to suppress them, led to sharp divisions of opinion over abolitionist principles and tactics. One turning point was the celebrated martyrdom in 1837 of Elijah P. Lovejoy, a New England abolitionist who, like the Mormons, had been driven out of Missouri and had established a refuge in Illinois. While trying to defend a new printing press from an antiabolitionist mob, Lovejoy was shot and killed. His violent death dramatized the issue of civil liberties and won new support for the abolitionists; and it also forced abolitionists to debate the proper response to violence, since Lovejoy and his men had used arms in self-defense.

Nonresistance   Garrison, who had nearly been lynched in 1835 by a Boston mob, had become convinced that violence was a disease infecting the entire body of American society. He came to believe that whenever the nation faced any issue of fundamental morality, such as the treatment of Indians, blacks, or dissenters, it resorted to the principle that might

106

makes right. The only Christian response, Garrison maintained, was to renounce all coercion and adhere to the perfectionist ideal of absolute nonresistance. If abolitionists tried to oppose power with power, as Lovejoy had done, they were certain to be crushed. They would also dilute their moral argument, since the essence of slavery was the forcible dominion of man over man. In 1838 Garrison and his followers formed the New England Non-Resistance Society. This group condemned every kind of coercion—not only defensive war and capital punishment, but lawsuits, prisons, and insane asylums, unless designed solely for "cure and restoration."

Thus there began to emerge in New England abolitionism a radical repudiation of all limits imposed on the individual by the threat of force. Black slavery and racial oppression were merely extreme manifestations of an evil embodied in the male-dominated family, the criminal law, and the police power of the state. By 1843 Garrison concluded that the majority rule was simply the rule of superior power, with no protection for human rights. The Union, he asserted, had always been a compact for the preservation of slavery, and the Constitution was therefore "a covenant with death, and an agreement with Hell." The Garrisonians demanded withdrawal from corrupt churches and from all connection with the corrupt government. They refused to vote or engage in any political activities. Calling for disunion with the South, they also crossed the threshold of symbolic treason and declared themselves enemies of the Republic.

In interesting ways the Garrisonians' rhetoric paralleled the rhetoric of the Mormons. "The governments of the world," Garrison announced in 1837, "are all anti-Christ." Yet by 1845 he also cast off the Old Testament, arguing that God could never have approved of slavery and violence. Instead of moving beyond the geographic frontiers to establish the Kingdom of God, as the Mormons had done, Garrison defended his own fortress of moral independence within a hostile society.

Political Antislavery: From the Liberty Party to Free Soil

By the 1840s, however, most abolitionists expressed new hopes for transforming the dominant society by means of the political process. There were various indications of this growing involvement in political action. During the late 1830s thousands of antislavery petitions poured into Congress as a popular challenge to the "gag rule," which prevented congressional discussions of slavery.* Former president John Quincy Adams, then a Whig congressman from Massachusetts, used every parliamentary trick to defend the petitioners' rights. Antislavery Whigs like congressmen Joshua Giddings and Salmon P. Chase, both of Ohio, capitalized on their constituencies' resentment of the "gag rule" and other sectional compromises that sacrificed moral principle. Liberal Democrats, such as senators Thomas Morris of Ohio and John P. Hale of New Hampshire, voiced growing dissatisfaction with their party, which professed

---

*For the "gag rule," see chapter 15, pp. 503–04.

to attack economic privilege while serving the interests of wealthy slaveowners. And after 1842, when the Supreme Court ruled that the Fugitive Slave Law of 1793 applied solely to the federal government's responsibility in helping to recover fugitives, five northern states enacted "personal liberty laws" prohibiting state officials from assisting in the recapture of runaway slaves.

For the most part, political abolitionists hoped to pursue their goals by promoting antislavery candidates and by bringing well-organized public pressure on the two major parties to prohibit the interstate slave trade, to abolish slavery in the District of Columbia, and to prevent any further expansion of slavery in western states and territories—the only antislavery measures that the Constitution seemed to allow. In 1839, however, Alvan Stewart, a lawyer and president of the New York State Anti-Slavery Society, drew most of the non-Garrisonian abolitionists into a temporary third party. It was hoped that this Liberty party, which ran James G. Birney for president in 1840, would win a balance of power in closely contested regions of the North and would thus free Whigs and Democrats from the stranglehold of what abolitionists called the Slave Power—an alleged conspiratorial alliance of southern slaveowners and their northern supporters.* By 1855 the judicious Charles Francis Adams could confidently assert that the Slave Power, consisting of "three hundred and fifty thousand men, spreading over a large territorial surface, commanding the political resources of fifteen states, was also in undisputed possession of all the official strongholds in the general government."

The Libertymen blamed the Slave Power for the economic depression that had begun in 1837, for the undermining of civil liberties, and for most of the other ills that the nation had suffered. Although Birney captured only a small fraction of the potential antislavery vote in the elections of 1840 and 1844, the Liberty party succeeded in popularizing the belief in a Slave Power conspiracy. By offering voters an abolitionist alternative to even moderately antislavery Whigs and Democrats, the Libertymen also stimulated figures like Giddings, Chase, and Hale to make a bolder appeal for antislavery votes.

By 1848 the more extreme political abolitionists had come to the conclusion that the Constitution gave Congress both the power and the duty to abolish slavery in the southern states. But in that year most abolitionists looked to the more moderate, broadly coalitionist Free-Soil party, which promised only to remove all federal sanctions for slavery by abolishing the institution in the District of Columbia, by excluding it from the territories, and by employing all other constitutional means to deprive it of national support.

The Free-Soil platform of 1848, unlike the platform of the Liberty party, ignored the legal discriminations that free blacks suffered. Many of the dissident northern Democrats who helped form the party had consistently opposed black

---

*The politics of the 1840s, in which debate over the expansion of slavery played a central role, is discussed more fully in chapter 16.

suffrage and had exploited white racist prejudice. And indeed abolitionism in general became more acceptable in the North by accommodating itself to white racism. Many blacks increasingly resented the attention given to such other interests of white reformers as women's rights, nonresistance, and communitarian experiments, to say nothing of the hypocrisy of many reformers regarding racial equality in the North. They also resented the patronizing attitudes of white abolitionists who might defend abstract ideals of equality while in practice treating blacks as inferiors who had to be led.

Black Abolitionists From the outset black abolitionists had worked closely with the antislavery societies in New England and New York. Beginning with Frederick Douglass's celebrated escape from slavery in 1838 and his enlistment as a lecturer for Garrison's Massachusetts Anti-Slavery Society in 1841, fugitive slaves performed the indispensable task of translating the abolitionists' abstract images into concrete human experience. The lectures and printed narratives of Douglass, William Wells Brown, Ellen Craft, Henry Bibb, Solomon Northup, and other escaped slaves did much to undermine whatever belief there was in the North that slaves were kindly treated and contented with their lot. The wit and articulate militancy of black abolitionists like Henry Highland Garnet, James McCune Smith, Sarah Parker Remond, and Charles Lenox Remond, coupled with the towering dignity of Douglass, also helped to shake confidence in the popular stereotypes of black inferiority.

Yet black abolitionists faced barriers and physical dangers that made the difficulties of white abolitionists seem like child's play. When Douglass and Garrison traveled together on lecture tours, it was Douglass who experienced constant insult, humiliation, and harassment. Black vigilance committees could help a small number of fugitives find their way to relative security in Canada— and blacks were the main conductors on the so-called Underground Railroad— but except in Massachusetts black abolitionists had little leverage for loosening the rocklike discriminatory laws. Instead white abolitionists kept pressuring blacks to keep a low profile, to act the part assigned to them by white directors (who presumably knew the tastes of an all-white audience), and to do nothing that might spoil the show.

In the 1840s black leaders gradually cast off the yoke that had bound them to a white man's cause, and tried to assert their own leadership. In 1843, at the Convention of the Free People of Color held at Buffalo, Garnet openly called for a slave rebellion, arguing that it was a sin to submit voluntarily to human bondage. Douglass adhered to his own version of nonresistance until 1847, when he broke with Garrison over the idea of founding a black abolitionist newspaper, *The North Star.* In the same year Garrison sadly reported that Charles Lenox Remond had proclaimed that "the slaves were bound, by their love of justice, to RISE AT ONCE, en masse, and THROW OFF THEIR FETTERS."

But speeches were one thing, action another. Black abolitionists had always looked to voting—a right few blacks possessed—as the most promising route to

Frederick Douglass (1818–95)
*The greatest black leader of the
nineteenth century, Frederick
Douglass was born into slavery
in Maryland (he never knew his
birth date), and as a house
servant learned to read and
write. In 1838 he escaped to the
North, and in 1841 he began to
lecture for the Massachusetts
Anti-Slavery Society. After
publishing his masterful*
Narrative of the Life of
Frederick Douglass, *he lectured
widely in Britain. Returning to
the United States in 1847, he
edited his own newspaper,* The
North Star. *An eloquent and
prolific reformer, Douglass fought
for women's rights as well as
racial equality.*

power. For the most part, therefore, they supported the Liberty party in 1840 and
1844, and the Free-Soil party in 1848. The drift of antislavery politics, however,
was away from black civil rights in the North and emancipation in the southern
states. Rather, the drift was now toward walling off of the western territories—a
walling off, in all probability, of free blacks as well as slaves. It is not surprising
that by 1854 Martin Delaney and a few other black leaders were talking of a
separate black nation, or that blacks who had proudly defended their American
heritage and right to American citizenship were beginning to reconsider voluntary colonization in Africa or Haiti.

By 1854, however, many northern whites had also concluded that the Slave
Power had seized control of America's Manifest Destiny, thereby appropriating
and nullifying the entire evangelical and millennial mission.* Moreover, the
Fugitive Slave Law of 1850, requiring federal agents to recover fugitive slaves
from their sanctuaries in the North, directly challenged the North's integrity and
its new self-image as an asylum of liberty. The arrival of federal "kidnappers" and
the spectacle of blacks being seized in the streets invited demonstrations of
defiance and civil disobedience. Increasing numbers of former moderates echoed
Garrison's rhetoric of disunion, and an increasing number of former nonresis-
tants called for a slave uprising or predicted that the streets of Boston might "yet
run with blood." Wendell Phillips, a Boston aristocrat and the most powerful of
all abolitionist orators, rejoiced "that every five minutes gave birth to a black
baby," for in its infant wail he recognized the voice that should "yet shout the war

---

*For Manifest Destiny, see chapter 16; for the contest over admitting Kansas as a slave state, chapter 17.

cry of insurrection; its baby hand would one day hold the dagger which should reach the master's heart."

In the 1850s northern abolitionists finally concluded that if the Slave Power were not crushed by rebellion or expelled from the Union, it would cross every legal and constitutional barrier and destroy the physical ability of northerners to act in accordance with the moral ability that had been the main legacy of religious revivals. The western territories were thus the crucial testing ground that would determine whether America would stand for something more than selfish interest, exploitation, and rule by brutal power. All the aspirations of the Benevolent Empire, of evangelical reformers, and of perfectionists of every kind could be channeled into a single and vast crusade to keep the territories free, to confine and seal off the Slave Power, and thus to open the way for an expansion of righteous liberty and opportunity that would surpass all worldly limits.

Suggested Readings

The best general guides to sectional conflict and the coming of the Civil War are David M. Potter, *The Impending Crisis, 1848–1861* (completed and edited by Don E. Fehrenbacher, 1976), and James M. McPherson, *Battle Cry of Freedom: The Civil War Era* (1988). Allan Nevins, *Ordeal of the Union* (2 vols., 1947), is a highly readable and informative survey of the same subject. William W. Freehling, *The Road to Disunion: Secessionists at Bay, 1776–1854* (1990), contains many valuable insights. A short and imaginative reinterpretation is James Oakes, *Slavery and Freedom: An Interpretation of the Old South* (1990).

A comprehensive picture of the South as a slave society can be found in Clement Eaton's *A History of the Old South: The Emergence of a Reluctant Nation* (1975) and *Freedom of Thought in the Old South* (1940). The growth of sectional feeling is outlined in more detail in Charles S. Sydnor, *The Development of Southern Sectionalism, 1819–1848* (1948); Richard E. Ellis, *The Union at Risk: Jacksonian Democracy, States' Rights and the Nullification Crisis* (1987); Alison Goodyear Freehling, *Drift Toward Dissolution: The Virginia Slavery Debate of 1831–1832* (1982); Drew Gilpin Faust, *The Creation of Confederate Nationalism: Ideology and Identity in the Civil War South* (1988); and Avery O. Craven, *The Growth of Southern Nationalism, 1848–1861* (1953). Carl N. Degler, *The Other South: Southern Dissenters in the Nineteenth Century* (1974), traces the decline of antislavery protest. H. Shelton Smith, *In His Image, But . . .* (1972), is a fine study of the growing racism in the southern churches. Two valuable studies of non-slaveholding southern whites are Steven Hahn, *The Roots of Southern Populism: Yeoman Farmers and the Transformation of the Georgia Upcountry, 1850–1890* (1983), and J. William Harris, *Plain Folk and Gentry in a Slave Society: White Liberty and Black Slavery in Augusta's Hinterlands* (1985). For the story of a remarkable slaveholding black family in South Carolina, see Michael P. Johnson and James L. Roark, *Black Masters: A Free Family of Color in the Old South* (1984). A penetrating study of the mythology of the Old South, often northern in origin, is William R. Taylor, *Cavalier and Yankee* (1961). C. Vann Woodward's essays in *The Burden of Southern History* (1960) and *American Counterpoint* (1971) are indispensable for understanding the South. The mind of the planter class is brilliantly illuminated by two accounts contemporary with the period: C. Vann Woodward, ed., *Mary Chesnut's Civil War* (1981), and Robert M. Myers, ed., *The Children of Pride: A True Story of Georgia and the Civil War* (1972). James Oakes, *The Ruling Race: A History of American Slaveholders* (1982), is a provocative interpretation of slaveholders as calculating capitalists. George M. Fredrickson, *White Supremacy: A Com-*

parative Study in American and South African History (1981), brilliantly compares the development of slavery and racism in the United States and South Africa. A lucid analysis of slavery, race, and class in a crucial border state, which sheds light on broader sectional divergence, is Barbara Jeanne Fields, *Slavery and Freedom on the Middle Ground: Maryland During the Nineteenth Century* (1985).

Eugene D. Genovese, *Roll, Jordan, Roll* (1974), is a monumental study of black slavery in the South. It is beautifully complemented, with respect to black and white women, by Elizabeth Fox-Genovese, *Within the Plantation Household: Black and White Women of the Old South* (1988). The most comprehensive study of the economics of slavery, which includes discussions of slave culture, antislavery, and the political and social conditions that led to a victorious antislavery coalition, is Robert William Fogel, *Without Consent or Contract: The Rise and Fall of American Slavery* (1989). A different and no less valuable perspective on the southern economy can be found in Gavin Wright, *The Political Economy of the Cotton South: Households, Markets, and Wealth in the Nineteenth Century* (1978). An excellent survey of the more traditional literature on this subject is Harold D. Woodman, ed., *Slavery and the Southern Economy* (1966). For the use of slaves in nonagricultural employment, see Robert S. Starobin, *Industrial Slavery in the Old South* (1970). Gang labor in the fields depended on black supervisors, a subject well treated by William L. Van Deburg, *The Slave Drivers: Black Agricultural Labor Supervisors in the Antebellum South* (1988). Herbert G. Gutman, *The Black Family in Slavery and Freedom, 1750–1925* (1976), is a pioneering work on a fundamental aspect of slave culture. For black women, the student should also consult Jacqueline Jones, *Labor of Love, Labor of Sorrow: Black Women, Work, and the Family from Slavery to the Present* (1985), and Deborah Gray White, *Ar'n't I a Woman? Female Slaves in the Plantation South* (1985). A model study of free women in a key Virginia town is Suzanne Lebsock, *Free Women of Petersburg: Status and Culture in a Southern Town, 1784–1860* (1984). For an illuminating discussion of the slaves' society, based mainly on slave narratives, see John W. Blassingame, *The Slave Community* (rev. ed., 1979). Two rich collections of source material are Willie Lee Rose, ed., *A Documentary History of Slavery in North America* (1976), and John W. Blassingame, ed., *Slave Testimony* (1977). As an overall survey of slavery as an institution, Kenneth Stampp's *The Peculiar Institution* (1956) has not been superseded. Willie Lee Rose, *Slavery and Freedom* (1982), is a collection of essays that combine wide-ranging interests with insightful wisdom. David B. Davis, *Slavery and Human Progress* (1984), places southern slavery and emancipation within a context of world history from antiquity to modern times.

The synthesis of African and Christian religious forms is carefully studied in Albert J. Raboteau, *Slave Religion: The "Invisible Institution" in the Antebellum South* (1978). A rich and comprehensive study of black folklore and culture is Lawrence W. Levine, *Black Culture and Black Consciousness: Afro-American Folk Thought from Slavery to Freedom* (1977). The origins in slave culture of black national consciousness are traced in Sterling Stuckey, *Slave Culture: Nationalist Theory and the Foundations of Black America* (1987).

The standard work on proslavery thought is William S. Jenkins, *Pro-Slavery Thought in the Old South* (1935), which should be supplemented by Harvey Wish, *George Fitzhugh* (1943); Drew Gilpin Faust, *A Sacred Circle: The Dilemma of the Intellectual in the Old South, 1840–1860* (1977); and Drew Gilpin Faust, *James Henry Hammond and the Old South: A Design for Mastery* (1982). A fresh and highly original reinterpretation of southern society and culture is Bertram Wyatt-Brown, *Southern Honor: Ethics and Behavior in the Old South* (1982). For the evangelical revival in the South, see Anne C. Loveland, *Southern Evangelicals and the Social Order, 1800–1860* (1980). Ira Berlin, *Slaves Without Masters* (1975), is a superb analysis of free blacks in the South. John H. Franklin, *From Slavery to Freedom* (1974), is the best introduction to African-American history. George M. Fredrickson, *The Black Image in the White Mind: The Debate on Afro-American Character and Destiny, 1817–1914* (1971), is a brilliant study of racism in

America. More specialized works of importance are Eugene H. Berwanger, *The Frontier Against Slavery: Western Anti-Negro Prejudice and the Slavery Extension Controversy* (1967), and William Stanton, *The Leopard's Spots: Scientific Attitudes Toward Race in America, 1815–1859* (1960).

The literature on abolitionism is voluminous. The historical precedents and background are covered in David B. Davis, *The Problem of Slavery in Western Culture* (1966), and *The Problem of Slavery in the Age of Revolution, 1770–1823* (1975). The best brief account of later abolitionism is James B. Stewart, *Holy Warriors: The Abolitionists and American Slavery* (1976), which should be supplemented by Ronald G. Walters's more interpretive study, *The Antislavery Appeal: American Abolitionism After 1830* (1976). An innovative study of the motivations and inner dynamics of abolitionism is Lawrence J. Friedman, *Gregarious Saints: Self and Community in American Abolitionism, 1830–1870* (1982). Gilbert H. Barnes, *The Anti-Slavery Impulse* (1933), is a dramatic and readable study, emphasizing the role of Theodore Weld and the Lane Seminary rebels. For an opposing and brilliantly argued view, see Aileen S. Kraditor, *Means and Ends in American Abolitionism: Garrison and His Critics on Strategy and Tactics* (1967). A similarly powerful and creative work is Lewis Perry, *Radical Abolitionism: Anarchy and the Government of God in Antislavery Thought* (1973). Robert H. Abzug, *Passionate Liberator: Theodore Dwight Weld and the Dilemma of Reform* (1980), is a probing biography of one of the most fascinating abolitionists. Other informative biographies include Bertram Wyatt-Brown, *Lewis Tappan and the Evangelical War against Slavery* (1969); Betty Fladeland, *James Gillespie Birney: Slaveholder to Abolitionist* (1955); John L. Thomas, *The Liberator: William Lloyd Garrison* (1963); Gerda Lerner, *The Grimké Sisters from South Carolina: Rebels Against Slavery* (1967); David Donald, *Charles Sumner and the Coming of the Civil War* (1960); and Hugh Davis, *Joshua Leavitt: Evangelical Abolitionist* (1990). The connection between antislavery and feminism is imaginatively explored by Jean Fagan Yellin, *Women and Sisters: The Antislavery Feminists in American Culture* (1989). Provocative approaches can be found in Lewis Perry and Michael Fellman, eds., *Antislavery Reconsidered: New Perspectives on the Abolitionists* (1979). Leonard L. Richards, *"Gentlemen of Property and Standing": Anti-Abolition Mobs in Jacksonian America* (1970), keenly analyzes antiabolition violence. Concerning civil liberties, see Russel B. Nye, *Fettered Freedom: Civil Liberties and the Slavery Controversy* (1963), and Thomas O. Morris, *Free Men All: The Personal Liberty Laws of the North, 1780–1861* (1974). Abolitionists' disillusion with the compromising stand taken by America's churches is set forth insightfully in John R. McKivigan, *The War against Proslavery Religion: Abolitionism and the Northern Churches, 1830–1865* (1984). For the conflict between conscience and "positive law" as judges struggled with issues related to slavery, see the brilliant study by Robert M. Cover, *Justice Accused: Antislavery and the Judicial Process* (1975).

For the politics of antislavery, see Richard H. Sewell, *Ballots for Freedom* (1976). For slavery and theories of constitutional law, see William M. Wiecek, *The Sources of Antislavery Constitutionalism in America, 1760–1848* (1977). Benjamin Quarles, *Black Abolitionists* (1969), is a pioneering study of a subject long neglected by historians. For the important role played by black American abolitionists who toured and lectured in Britain, see R. J. M. Blackett, *Building an Antislavery Wall: Black Americans in the Atlantic Abolitionist Movement, 1830–1860* (1983). The dilemma of black abolitionists is also illuminated by Jane H. Pease and William H. Pease, *They Who Would Be Free: Blacks' Search for Freedom, 1830–1861* (1974). For Frederick Douglass, the preeminent black leader of the nineteenth century, the best biography is William McFeely, *Frederick Douglass* (1991).

4

Politics
Cohesion and Division
1820–1840

⌒

$\mathcal{T}$HE GENERATION of Americans who came to maturity in the early nineteenth century carried a unique burden. As "children of the Founding Fathers," they could not achieve immortal fame by winning independence from British tyranny. Instead their assigned mission was vigilant preservation—the preservation of what the famous lawyer Rufus Choate called the "beautiful house of our fathers" against divisive ambition, corruption, sectional jealousy, and arbitrary power.

For a time it seemed that Liberty and Union could be preserved by patriotic rhetoric honoring hallowed figures like Thomas Jefferson and John Adams (who both died on July 4, 1826, exactly fifty years after the adoption of the Declaration of Independence), and by the election of presidents from the so-called Virginia Dynasty. The last in that succession, James Monroe, still appeared in public dressed in his Revolutionary War uniform. After the War of 1812, the collapse of the Federalist party fostered the illusion of an Era of Good Feelings in which a single national party would guarantee republican simplicity, order, and self-restraint. In his second inaugural address in 1821, President Monroe invoked the image of harmony. The American people, he affirmed, constituted "one great family with a common interest." Four years later President John Quincy Adams, also a Republican, voiced similar sentiments and happily observed that "the baneful weed of party strife" had been uprooted. Most Americans still associated political parties with the self-serving, aristocratic factions that had dominated British politics. In a republican nation, as in a republican family, no room could be allowed for selfish alliances representing separate interests.

This ideal of family unity was, however, far removed from social and economic realities. In chapter 12 we have already considered the revolutionary expansion and triumph of a market economy in the decades following the War of 1812. The sudden burgeoning of cities and towns, the construction of vast new transportation networks, the rise of manufacturing and the influx of tens of thousands of immigrants, the collapse of local markets and traditional patterns of self-sufficiency, the alarming growth in economic inequalities—all these transformations signaled an abrupt departure from the world of the Founders. Precisely because Americans were so fearful of betraying their Revolutionary and republican heritage, politicians often disguised innovation behind rhetorical appeals to preserve or return to the genuine spirit of the Founders.

This mythology of *continuity* obscured the sheer novelty of the two-party political system that emerged from the turmoil of the 1820s, a decade characterized by increasing sectional tension, class conflict, and democratization of politics. Between 1819 and 1821 Congress faced the most dangerous crisis it had yet experienced when northern and southern representatives deadlocked over the admission of Missouri as a new slave state. Simultaneously, the financial panic of 1819, followed by a severe depression, aroused widespread hostility toward banking corporations and other groups that had used political influence to gain economic privilege. Economic recovery and expansion only intensified demands for equality of opportunity, as various competing classes, localities, and social groups became increasingly aware of the unequal effects of government policies concerning tariffs, banking and currency, and public land sales. By the mid-1820s it was becoming painfully clear that widening opportunities for some Americans meant narrowing opportunities for others. Ironically, the post-Revolutionary generation finally found a way of containing the many factions that had arisen by institutionalizing division in the form of political parties.

In the national election of 1824 candidates still represented factions of a single Republican (or Democratic Republican) party. By 1828 a new Democratic party had emerged under the leadership of Andrew Jackson; their opponents, whom the Democrats tried to identify with the old, discredited Federalists, were first called National Republicans and then in the early 1830s adopted the name Whigs. The Democrats and their National Republican or Whig opponents were national coalitions of sectional, class, economic, ethnic, and religious interests, held together by compromise and cooperation. To maximize votes, politicians had to find ways of arousing apathetic citizens on more than immediate local issues. The basic political style that emerged in antebellum America—in the South and West as well as in the North—centered on the portrayal of some self-serving, privileged interest that had secretly consolidated power and had begun to shut off from others equal access to the rewards of national growth. In an era of relative security from foreign dangers, politicians continued to portray their opponents as heirs of the British and Tories who were seeking to undermine American liberties and betray the heritage of the Founders. From the early 1830s to the early 1850s, the two-party system helped preserve national cohesion. The Democrats and Whigs survived as national coalitions as long as they drew significant support from *both* the slaveholding and nonslaveholding states. But when black slavery, the institution that most flagrantly subverted liberty and opportunity, was seriously questioned in a national forum, the unifying force of the parties was destroyed.

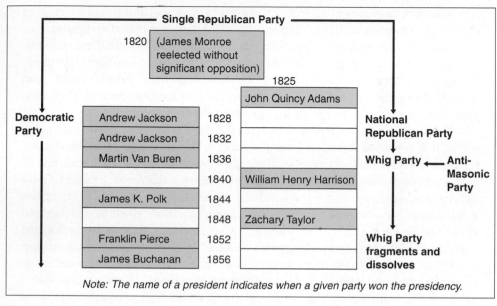

The Two-Party System

"A Fire Bell in the Night": The Missouri Compromise

From the time of the Continental Congress, American leaders had recognized that a serious dispute over slavery could jeopardize their bold experiment in self-government. Beginning with the Constitutional Convention, the entire structure of national politics had been designed to prevent any faction from directly threatening southern slaveholders and thereby subverting common national interests. It is therefore not surprising that before 1819 slavery never became a central issue in national politics. But it was an issue that sat like an unactivated bomb in the minds of the foremost political leaders.

The agreement to keep the bomb unactivated rested on two unwritten understandings: that the North would recognize the property rights of southern slaveholders, and that the South would recognize slavery as an evil that should be discouraged and eventually abolished whenever it became safe and practicable to do so. Changing circumstances, including the shifting balance of sectional power, forced repeated challenges to these understandings. The challenges took the form of clashes in Congress, during which representatives from the Lower South threatened to dissolve the Union and even hinted at the possibility of civil war. On each occasion the resulting compromise strongly favored the South. This political process demonstrated the Americans' remarkable ability to make pragmatic adjustments in the interest of national stability. Yet these successful compromises depended on the dangerous assumption that southern threats of disunion would always be met by northern concessions.

The militancy of the Lower South's congressional leaders was based on a realistic estimate of the future. For a time the North could afford to make concessions because slavery seemed to endanger no vital northern interests. But after 1815 humanitarian causes had increasing appeal in the North, and more and more northerners expressed moral and patriotic misgivings over the westward expansion of slavery. Sooner or later, as southerners like John Randolph predicted, these northern antislavery sentiments would become strong enough to create new sectional parties. Even by 1820, as a result of rapid population growth in the North, the major slaveholding states held only 42 percent of the seats in the House of Representatives. Only the Senate could provide a firm defense against potential northern encroachments, and the key to the Senate was new slave states. In the Senate, following the admission of Mississippi and Alabama (1817, 1819), eleven slave states balanced eleven free states.

Sectional Conflict The Missouri crisis erupted in February 1819, when the House was considering a bill that would enable the people of Missouri to draft a constitution and be admitted as a slave state. Slaves constituted nearly one-sixth of the territory's population. James Tallmadge, Jr., a New York Jeffersonian Republican, offered an amendment that prohibited the further introduction of slaves into Missouri and provided for the emancipation, at age twenty-five, of all children of slaves born after Missouri's admission as a state. During the prolonged and often violent debate, Senator Jonathan Roberts of Pennsylvania urged his colleagues not to admit Missouri "with her features marred as if the fingers of Lucifer had been drawn across them." Nathaniel Macon of North Carolina responded that restricting slavery necessarily implies eventual emancipation and even racial equality: "Are you willing to have black members of Congress? . . . There is no place for free blacks in the United States." The House approved Tallmadge's amendment by an ominously sectional vote. The Senate, after equally violent debates, passed a Missouri statehood bill without any restrictions on slavery. The issue seemed hopelessly deadlocked.

Virginia now took the lead in militancy, trying to arouse a generally apathetic South to a common peril. "This momentous question," Jefferson announced from Monticello, where he had retired, "like a fire bell in the night, awakened and filled me with terror." Along with Madison and other Virginia statesmen, Jefferson was convinced that the attempt to exclude slavery from Missouri was part of a Federalist conspiracy to create a sectional party and destroy the Union.

The Missouri crisis was aggravated by a sense that understandings had been broken, veils torn off, and true and threatening motives exposed. The congressional debates rekindled the most divisive issues that supposedly had been settled in the Constitutional Convention, and thus raised the hypothetical question of disunion. This reenactment of 1787 was underscored by the prominence in the congressional debates of two of the Constitutional Convention's surviving antagonists—Charles Pinckney of South Carolina, who now insisted that Congress had no power to exclude slavery from even the unsettled territories; and Rufus King of New York, the alleged leader of the Federalist conspiracy, who now announced that any laws upholding slavery were "absolutely void, because [they are] contrary to the law of nature, which is the law of God."

It was a new generation of northerners, however, who had to reaffirm or reject the kind of compromises over slavery that had created the original Union. Like the Founders, the northern majority in Congress could do nothing about slavery in the existing states. But there had been an understood national policy, these northerners believed, enshrined in the Northwest Ordinance, committing the government to restrict slavery in every feasible way. This understanding had seemingly been confirmed by southern statements that slavery was an evil inherited from the past. The North had accepted the original slave states' expectations that migrating slaveholders would not be barred from bringing their most valuable property—their slaves—into the territories south of the Ohio River and east of the Mississippi River. But Missouri occupied the same latitudes as Illinois, Indiana, and Ohio (as well as Kentucky and Virginia). To allow slavery to become legally entrenched in Missouri might thus encourage its spread throughout the entire West, harming free labor and industry. Southerners had long argued, however illogically, that if slavery were diffused over a large geographical area, it would weaken as an institution, and the likelihood of slave uprisings would diminish. In 1820 Daniel Raymond, a prominent northern political economist, gave the obvious reply: "Diffusion is about as effectual a remedy for slavery as it would be for the smallpox, or the plague."

Southerners were particularly alarmed by the argument of some northern congressmen that the constitutional guarantee to every state of "a republican form of government" meant that Missouri could not be admitted as a slave state. The argument implied that Virginia and other southern states fell short of having "a republican form of government" and therefore would not be admissible to a new Union. If this argument prevailed, the southern states would be reduced to a second-class status. If they accepted the northern definition of a republican form of government, they had no choice but to take steps toward abolishing slavery or to face, like colonies, the punitive measures of an imperial authority.

The Terms of Compromise

Henry Clay, the Speaker of the House of Representatives, exerted all the powers of his office and of his magnetic personality in order finally to achieve a compromise. A small minority of northern congressmen agreed to drop the antislavery provision for Missouri, while a small minority of southerners agreed that slavery should be excluded from the remaining and unsettled portions of the Louisiana Purchase north of latitude 36°30′, the same latitude as the southern border of Missouri. In effect, this measure limited any further expansion of slavery within the Louisiana Purchase to Arkansas and what would later become Oklahoma. Given the sectional balance of power, the swing vote favoring these concessions was sufficient to carry the compromise. The way was now opened for admitting Maine as a free state, since the Senate had refused to accept Maine's statehood until the House had abandoned efforts to restrict slavery in Missouri.

The press and legislatures of the North generally interpreted the Missouri Compromise as a victory for the South. A new hope arose that public pressure

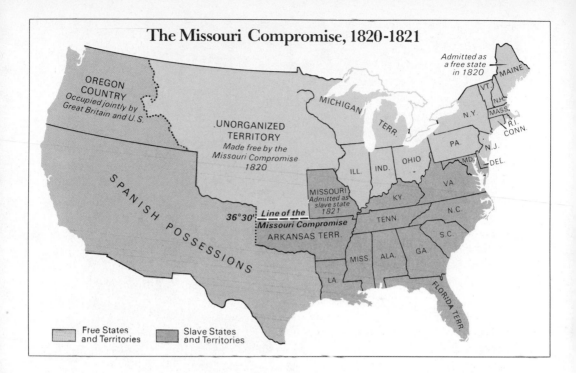

The Missouri Compromise, 1820-1821

OREGON COUNTRY
Occupied jointly by Great Britain and U.S.

SPANISH POSSESSIONS

UNORGANIZED TERRITORY
Made free by the Missouri Compromise 1820

MICHIGAN TERR.

MAINE — Admitted as a free state in 1820

VT.
N.H.
N.Y.
MASS.
R.I.
CONN.
PA.
N.J.
OHIO
MD.
DEL.

ILL. IND.

MISSOURI
Admitted as slave state 1821

VA.
KY.

36°30' — Line of the Missouri Compromise

ARKANSAS TERR.

TENN.

N.C.

S.C.

MISS ALA. GA.

LA.

FLORIDA TERR.

Free States and Territories

Slave States and Territories

could force Missouri to adopt a constitution providing for gradual emancipation. But the defiant Missourians drafted a constitution that prohibited the state legislature from emancipating slaves without the consent of their owners and that barred free blacks and mulattoes from entering the state. Since free blacks had been recognized as citizens by some of the eastern states, this second provision violated the constitutional guarantee that "the citizens of each State shall be entitled to all privileges and immunities of citizens in the several States." Northern congressmen now stood firm in rejecting the Missouri constitution and, in effect, the entire compromise. Eventually, in 1821, Clay's skillful manipulation of committees produced a second compromise prohibiting Missouri from discriminating against the citizens of other states—an abstract resolution that still left citizenship undefined. The country applauded Clay for saving the Union.

But the Union would never be the same. In southern eyes the uninhibited debates on slavery had opened a Pandora's box of dangers. The free blacks of Washington had packed the galleries of the House and had listened intently to antislavery speeches. In 1822, during the trial of the conspirators associated with Denmark Vesey, the free black leader of a planned racial insurrection in South Carolina, a Charleston slave testified that Vesey had shown him an antislavery speech delivered by Rufus King, "the black man's friend." The link between the Missouri debates and a sizable slave conspiracy stunned South Carolina, confirming its worst fears. The cumulative effect was twofold: to unite all whites in the suppression of dangerous discussion, and to strengthen the hand of states' rights extremists and of the defenders of slavery as a positive good.

Henry Clay (1777–1782)
Henry Clay's campaign posters stressed national economic growth and public welfare, goals to be directly fostered by protective tariffs and a national bank.

The End of Republican Unity

The Missouri crisis alerted politicians to the perils of sectional division. The North's unexpected outrage over the admission of a new slave state convinced many southerners that they needed to cultivate rising northern leaders. One such leader was Martin Van Buren, whose faction of young "Bucktails" had captured control of the New York Republican party by 1820. Van Buren, whose shrewdness, ambition, and personal charm made up for his lack of family prestige and connections, viewed the clamor over slavery as evidence of a dangerous breakdown in party loyalty. New national organizations were needed that could prevent sectional conflict. Party distinctions, he said, were infinitely safer than geographical ones. If party distinctions were suppressed, their place would inevitably be taken by "geographical differences founded on local instincts or what is worse, prejudices between free and slaveholding states."

The Van Buren faction also stated a new conception of political parties as agencies of the people. When the Bucktails were attacked by their opponents as the Albany Regency, a label suggesting the oppressive British regency of the Prince of Wales (1811–20) that had governed in place of the insane George III, Van Buren's faction replied with a strong defense of political parties—a defense that later Democrats and Whigs would echo. In America, Van Buren's followers claimed, political parties drew their power from the people instead of from kings or aristocratic cliques; therefore the American people could safely extend their loyalty to parties. American parties, far from being self-serving, required a selfless submission to the will of the organization. This respect for party discipline was later summed up by a prominent Whig who declared that he "would vote for a dog, if he was the candidate of my party." In theory, the excesses of one party would inevitably be exposed by the other party, and public opinion would decide between them. Responsiveness to the people would thus be ensured as each party strove to win the largest possible mandate from the people.

Van Buren's appeal for disciplined national parties came at the right moment. As early as 1821 it was evident that the Virginia Dynasty of presidents would end in 1825 with Monroe's second term. The Republicans, no longer confronted by Federalist opponents, were splitting into personal and sectional factions. One group responded to the vibrant nationalism of Henry Clay's so-called American System—a policy for direct government encouragement of economic expansion by such means as protective tariffs, a national bank, and federal aid for internal improvements. But other "Old Republicans," including Van Buren, viewed government intervention in the economy in terms of the old "country opposition" ideology—as a revival of the kinds of alliances between political power and special privilege that had corrupted Britain. By the early 1820s many Americans, especially in the South and West, had ample grounds for fearing that a northeastern business elite would gain economic control of the nation's banks and system of credit.

The Election of 1824   Monroe's second administration was dominated by political maneuvering to determine who would be his successor. Three of the leading contenders—William H. Crawford, John Quincy Adams, and John C. Calhoun—were nationally distinguished members of Monroe's cabinet. A Georgian born in Virginia, Crawford was secretary of the treasury during several administrations and had won prestige as America's minister to France during the War of 1812. He was an advocate of states' rights and limited federal power, was supported by the aged Thomas Jefferson and other influential Virginians, and would be heavily favored in any congressional party caucus. Van Buren led the Crawford forces in Congress. But the skeleton congressional caucus that nominated Crawford carried little weight, and an incapacitating illness further diminished his chances.

The other leading candidates bypassed the established procedure of nomination by congressional party caucus and sought support from state legislatures. Three of the remaining aspirants were closely associated with the economic nationalism that had alienated the Old Republicans. John Quincy Adams, the secretary of state and the nation's most experienced diplomat, could easily expect solid support from his native New England but would always be aloof from the rough-and-tumble campaigning of the South and West. John C. Calhoun, the secretary of war, had little support outside his own state, South Carolina. A graduate of Yale and a product of America's first small law school, Calhoun was one of the few political leaders of his time who could be described as an intellectual. He withdrew from the presidential race before the election, assuming that his almost certain choice as vice-president would help him win the highest office in 1828. Henry Clay, the popular "Harry of the West," had won national prestige as a parliamentarian and engineer of compromise in the House of Representatives.

The fifth candidate, Andrew Jackson, entered the contest unexpectedly and at a later stage. Unlike the other candidates, he had taken no clear stand on the controversial issues of the day, and his brief terms in the House and Senate had been undistinguished. Jackson's national fame arose from his victory over the British at the Battle of New Orleans in the War of 1812, as well as from his unswerving efforts to clear the West of Indians, thus promising unlimited opportunities for white Americans. But "Old Hickory," as Jackson was widely known, was a good bit more than a military hero and an Indian fighter. Born on the Carolina frontier and orphaned at age fourteen, Jackson had studied law and had finally emigrated to Nashville, Tennessee, where he became attached by marriage and business connections to the local network of leading families. Far from remaining aloof from the rising market economy, he prospered as an attorney, land speculator, and planter, and became the master of more than one hundred slaves. The Tennessee leaders who originally promoted Jackson for the presidency did not take his candidacy seriously, hoping only to use his popularity as a military hero for their own local purposes. But in 1823 Jackson's backers were astonished when the movement caught fire in Pennsylvania and other states. Old Hickory turned out to be an astute politician who perfectly gauged the national temper and who, once launched on the road to the presidency, skillfully managed his own campaign.

Jackson won a plurality of both the popular and the electoral votes in the election of 1824, and therefore he could legitimately claim to be the choice of the people. But because no candidate had won an electoral majority, the responsibility of electing a president fell to the House of Representatives. It had been expected that if no candidate should win the electoral majority, the House would elect Clay. But despite his appeal in Kentucky and other western states, Clay had run fourth in electoral votes and was therefore excluded by the Twelfth Amendment from further consideration. Clay threw his decisive support behind Adams, who was elected president and who soon appointed Clay secretary of state. This so-called corrupt bargain deeply embittered Calhoun, who, although he became vice-president, was already beginning to defect from his former colleagues' economic nationalism. It also infuriated Jackson, who almost immediately launched a campaign to unseat Adams in 1828.

J. Q. Adams (1767–1848)
John Quincy Adams personified the intellectual as statesman. A man of learning and of wide diplomatic experience, he was more at home in the courts and capitals of Europe than in the caucuses and public forums of American politics.

John Quincy Adams as President

This final collapse of Republican unity proved to be a disaster for Adams's presidency. Adams inaugurated his administration by proposing a sweeping program of federal support for internal improvements, science, education, and the arts. "The great object of the institution of civil government," Adams told Congress, "is the improvement of the condition of those who are parties to the social compact.... Roads and canals, by multiplying and facilitating the communications and intercourse between distant regions and multitudes of men, are among the most important means of improvement. But moral, political, intellectual improvement are duties assigned by the author of Our Existence to social no less than to individual man." Adams hoped that Congress would subsidize western explorations and an astronomical observatory. He soon discovered, however, that he lacked the mandate and the power for even the simple tasks of government. One of the most intelligent and farseeing presidents, Adams was also one of the least successful, in part because he had no taste for the kind of political maneuvering needed to build a base of support. Unfairly accused of being a monarchist with an arrogant contempt for the people, he had the misfortune of inheriting the presidency when it had fallen into decay. His own inexperience with the realities of American political life helped to make him the unmourned victim, in 1828, of the first modern presidential contest.

Jackson's Rise to Power

Andrew Jackson, the leader of the rising Democratic coalition, precisely fitted the need for a popular national political leader. His stately bearing and natural dignity befitted one of "nature's noblemen," someone who had risen to greatness without benefit of family connections, formal education, or subservience to any faction. Jackson's promoters spread the romantic mythology and stimulated voter activism by every conceivable means: ballads, placards, barbecues, liberty pole raisings, local committees, and militia companies marching in torchlit parades. In contrast to the office-grubbing politicians and to the coldly dignified, highly cultivated John Quincy Adams, here was a frontiersman, a truly self-made man, a soldier of iron will who personified the will of the people, a man without disguises or pretension who moved decisively in the light of simple moral truths. The Jackson image, in short, was an image of reassuring stability in the face of bewildering social and economic change.

Jackson also fitted the need for a leader who understood the new meaning of party politics. Against the Adams-Clay alliance, he molded a coalition that included among other groups the followers of Calhoun (who became his running mate in 1828), Virginia's Old Republicans, influential westerners who had become disillusioned with Clay, former Federalists who had lost office in New Jersey, and Van Buren's powerful Albany Regency. This new Democratic party appealed to many urban workers and immigrants, to frontier expansionists and Indian haters, to many southern planters, and to various northeastern editors, bankers, and manufacturers who built local Democratic machines as the means of gaining or preserving power.

The "Tariff of Abominations"
Looking ahead to the election of 1828, Jackson's state organizers bypassed the local ruling gentry and concentrated for the first time on mobilizing the necessary popular vote to capture the full electoral vote of critical states. Because the new coalition contained Pennsylvanians who clamored for higher tariffs and South Carolinians who detested tariffs, keeping unity required delicate manipulation. In 1828 Jackson's leaders in Congress helped to pass the so-called Tariff of Abominations, an opportunistic bill that made arbitrary concessions to various groups that were demanding protection against foreign competition. These leaders assumed that southern support for Jackson was secure, that the new duties on raw materials would win votes from northern and western protectionists, and that the most objectionable provisions could be blamed on the Adams administration. The subsequent outrage in the South suggested that Jackson as president could no longer get by with vague statements favoring a "judicious" tariff. Yet southerners knew that a Jackson-Calhoun alliance was far more promising than the economic nationalism of Adams and Clay, who were now known as National Republicans.

The Election of 1828

ELECTORAL POPULAR
Jackson (Dem.) 178 647,286
Adams (Nat. Rep.) 83 508,064
5 6 Divided

The Election of 1828 In a general sense the election of 1828 affirmed the people's rejection of policies that seemed to encourage special privileges for the business classes as a result of the government's direct involvement in the market economy. Yet the Jacksonian Democrats, for all their talk of liberty and equality, never questioned the privilege of owning slaves and counting three-fifths of the slave population for purposes of representation. In the South, Jackson's 200,000 supporters, accounting for 73 percent of that section's vote, gave him 105 electoral votes; in the North, where he won only slightly more than half the popular vote, his 400,000 supporters gave him only 73 electoral votes. The election also proved the effectiveness of campaign organization and of the promotional techniques that Jackson's managers, particularly Van Buren, had perfected.

Once in power the Democrats soon adopted two instruments that solidified popular support for party rule. The first was a system of patronage, called the spoils system, that continued practices begun during previous administrations and tried to give them legitimacy. Jackson ardently defended the theory that most

Jackson Poster, 1828
In the presidential campaign of 1828 Jackson's strength and firmness were symbolized by the hickory tree. The nation's most revered military hero, Jackson promised to preserve the ideals of the Founding Fathers.

public offices required no special abilities or experience, that they should frequently rotate among loyal deserving party workers, and that party rule should prevent the establishment of a permanent and parasitic class of civil servants. In fact, however, Jackson actually removed no more than one-fifth of the surviving federal officeholders.

The second mechanism was the national party convention. This, like various other Jacksonian measures, had earlier been initiated by anti-Jackson forces. As an alternative to nomination by legislative caucus, the "convention" suggested by its very name a return to fundamental law—to the direct voice of the people assembled in a constitution-making body. Although party conventions could do no more than frame partisan platforms and nominate partisan candidates, they pretended to represent the true interests of the people. In theory, since they drew representatives from a broad spectrum of society, they were more democratic than legislative caucuses. In practice, they were more subject to manipulation by political machines. But like the partisan spoils system, the party convention symbolized the central appeal of Jackson's party. It promised to break the rigid crust of privilege and eliminate all institutional barriers to individual opportunity. It also provided the assurance of solidarity with a party headed by a man of the people, a man who magnified the idealized self-image of millions of Americans.

Certain principles and aspirations distinguished the Jacksonian Democrats from their National Republican (and later Whig) opponents. Jackson had long given voice to the West's demand for territorial expansion as a way to ensure economic opportunity. As the first westerner elected to the presidency, he symbolized a geographical shift of political power. Of course, not all westerners

Andrew Jackson (1767–1845)
Sixty-two years old when he became president, Andrew Jackson was one of the strongest and most vigorous chief executives in American history. Despite his dedication to states' rights, he expanded the power of the presidency and affirmed the supremacy of the federal union.

supported Jackson. Those who understood that western economic expansion depended on access to eastern markets and on investment capital from the East and Europe favored federal aid for internal improvements, a program that Henry Clay sponsored. But although Jackson vetoed the Maysville Road Bill (which would have authorized funds to build a road in Kentucky), suggesting that federal support for internal improvements was unconstitutional, he did not lose the majority of western voters. Many westerners had come to view federally supported internal improvements as sources of waste and corruption. Others learned that, despite Jackson's pronouncements, federal support for roads and canals continued to pour in from a Congress that was less concerned with constitutional theory than with constituents' needs. On the whole, the West cheered for Jackson because it had come to see itself as the home of the values that Jackson fought for: a rural society of independent farmers, committed to individual enterprise and local self-determination.

To say that Jacksonian Democrats were advocates of minimal government and laissez-faire policies is accurate but insufficient.* They knew that on the local

---

*Laissez-faire means the government's refusal to intervene in economic matters beyond the minimum needed to maintain peace and property rights.

and state levels, economic opportunity hinged on political power. And Jackson was the most forceful and aggressive president since Washington. During the preceding administrations the chief executive's powers had been siphoned off by cabinet rivals and a jealous Congress. With the aid of party discipline, Jackson soon exerted his dominance over Congress by an unprecedented use of vetoes and pocket vetoes (the refusal to sign a bill during the last ten days of a congressional session). Except for Van Buren, whom he chose as secretary of state, Jackson treated his cabinet in the manner of the army's commander in chief. Unlike his predecessors, Jackson escaped the coercion of disloyal and powerful cabinet members by relying on a group of informal advisers, the so-called Kitchen Cabinet, who could be trusted or dismissed at will.

The Threat of National Division: Tariffs, Nullification, and the Gag Rule

Protective Tariffs   Tariffs and fiscal policy were obvious testing grounds for defining the federal government's role in national economic life. The economy was still more regional than national, and the national government had few functions. The critical issues of the day therefore grew out of the commitment to protective tariffs and a national bank that had resulted from the War of 1812. The Middle Atlantic states, which were the most vulnerable to competition from European manufactured goods, had long been the political stronghold of protectionism. During the 1820s, as New England's economy became increasingly dependent on the production of wool and on textile manufacturing, Daniel Webster and other New England leaders abandoned their traditional defense of free trade and portrayed protective tariffs as the key to economic growth and individual opportunity. Simultaneously, however, the Lower South became increasingly hostile to tariffs that threatened to raise the price of manufactured goods and to curtail foreign markets for rice and cotton exports. For a time the Democrats successfully arranged compromises among the various interests and regions that were represented in the party. But in 1832 Congress passed a tariff bill that was unresponsive to the demands of the Lower South. South Carolina thereupon defied federal authority and sought to arouse the rest of the slaveholding South to the dangers of being victimized economically by the federal government. The tariff, South Carolina's state legislature charged, was essentially "intended for the protection of domestic manufactures, and the giving of bounties to classes and individuals engaged in particular employments, at the expense and to the injury and oppression of other classes and individuals," namely, the agricultural producers of the South. South Carolinians believed that acceptance of this dependence would reduce their state to the status of a colony and deprive it of any effective protection against antislavery ideas. "[W]e will not submit to the application of force, on the part of the Federal Government," the legislature warned, "to reduce this State to obedience." Such an attempt at coercion, it announced, would be considered "inconsistent with the longer continuance of South Carolina in the Union."

South Carolina's sudden threat of disunion severely tested the American political system, and it involved issues that went far beyond the protective tariff. In no other state had a planter elite succeeded so well in commanding the allegiance of small farmers, both slaveholding and nonslaveholding, and in preventing the development of an effective two-party system. Despite continuing conflicts between the coastal and upcountry regions, there were few checks on states' rights extremists who were able to exploit fears of a slave uprising and anger over persisting agricultural depression, high consumer prices, and sagging prices for rice and cotton in foreign markets.

Moreover, of all the southern states South Carolina had the closest historical, geographical, and cultural ties with the British West Indies. Like those British colonies, South Carolina had a dense concentration of slaves, and its merchants and plantation owners had continued to import African slaves until 1808, when the Atlantic slave trade was forbidden by federal law. South Carolinians were acutely aware that in Britain a seemingly harmless movement to end the slave trade had been transformed, by 1823, into a crusade for slave emancipation. And they knew that the West Indians, although still a powerful faction in Parliament, had found no way of countering commercial policies that had hastened their economic decline. The lesson was clear. The West Indian colonies had once been far richer and more valued than Canada or New England. But at Christmas 1831 a massive slave revolt had broken out in Jamaica. By 1832 the West Indians' representatives in England were beginning to accept the inevitability of slave emancipation even though they were convinced this would lead to certain economic ruin.

Theory of Nullification   South Carolina's leaders believed that their state could escape a similar fate only by reasserting state sovereignty and insisting on the strict limitation of national power. The tariff issue made an ideal testing ground for the defense of slavery without risking the explosive effects of debating the morality of slaveholding. Because the power to tax and regulate trade could also be used to undermine slavery, the two questions had been linked in the Constitutional Convention of 1787 and in the Missouri debates. Conversely, a state's power to nullify a tariff would be a guarantee not only against economic exploitation but also against direct or indirect interference with slavery. Calhoun anonymously wrote the South Carolina *Exposition* on behalf of that state, refining the theoretical arguments that were being put forward by South Carolina's most militant leaders. According to Calhoun, in any dispute between federal and state interests the ultimate appeal must be directed to a state convention—the same body that had originally enabled the state to ratify the Constitution. Otherwise, a national majority, controlling the federal courts as well as Congress, would have unlimited power. The tyranny of the majority could be curbed only if each state retained the

John C. Calhoun (1782–1850)
*Although Calhoun never realized
his lifelong ambition to become
president, he served in the House
of Representatives, in the Senate,
as secretary of war, secretary of
state, and vice-president of the
United States. An ardent
nationalist in his youth, he
became the foremost defender of
southern slavery and states'
rights.*

right to either accept or nullify, within its own jurisdiction, the national majority's decisions. Calhoun carefully distinguished nullification from secession. He looked for means by which states might exercise an authentic, although limited, sovereignty while remaining within the Union.

The nullification controversy was complicated by the shifting pressures of state, sectional, and national politics. Calhoun, the vice-president, hoped to succeed Jackson as president, and many South Carolinians still believed they could achieve their goals through the Democratic party. Calhoun did not disclose his authorship of the *Exposition* until 1831, when he had split with Jackson over various personal and political issues. When Jackson purged Calhoun's followers from his cabinet and administration, Van Buren became in effect the president's chosen successor and the nation's vice-president during Jackson's second term. Nevertheless Calhoun continued to aspire to the presidency. He believed that nullification would be a means of satisfying South Carolina's "fire-eater" extremists and of establishing the Union on a more secure basis, while still preserving his own national following.

By 1832, however, South Carolina had become increasingly isolated from the rest of the South and had also failed to unite the West against an alleged northeastern conspiracy to discourage western settlement. Although many southerners detested protective tariffs and maintained that states had a right to secede from the Union, southern legislatures turned a stony face to nullification. As a result there was no regional convention of southern delegates that might have moderated South Carolina's suicidal course by reinforcing the hand of the South

Carolina unionists who risked their lives and reputations in a violent and losing struggle with the extremists. In the fall of 1832 South Carolina held a state convention that directly challenged federal authority by making it unlawful after February 1, 1833, to collect tariff duties within the state.

South Carolina chose the wrong president to test. Andrew Jackson was a wealthy slaveholder, but he was also a shrewd politician. Although his maturing views on tariffs and internal improvements were close to those of the South Carolina elite, he had fought for the military supremacy of the United States, crushing British and Indian armies; he had hanged English meddlers in Spanish Florida; and he had ordered the execution of an unruly teen-age soldier. He was probably the toughest of America's presidents. When South Carolina nullified the tariff of 1832, the old general privately threatened to lead an invasion of the state and have Calhoun hanged. In a public proclamation to the people of South Carolina, Jackson warned: "To say that any state may at pleasure secede from the Union is to say that the United States are not a nation, because it would be a solecism to contend that any part of a nation might dissolve its connection with the other parts, to their injury or ruin, without committing any offense. ...Disunion by armed force is *treason.*" Jackson sent reinforcements to the federal forts in Charleston harbor but publicly sought to avoid armed conflict by relying on civilian revenue agents to enforce the law and by warning that armed resistance would be punished as treason.

As in 1820, the crisis ended in a compromise that failed to resolve fundamental conflicts of interest and ideology. In an attempt to head off civil war, Henry Clay, assisted by Calhoun, secured the passage of a compromise bill that would gradually reduce tariff duties over a period of nine years. But this measure was accompanied by a "force bill," reaffirming the president's authority to use the army and navy, when necessary, to enforce federal laws. South Carolina's fire-eaters continued to call for armed resistance; the governor himself recruited a volunteer army. Early in 1833, however, the state convention repealed its earlier nullification of the tariff and, to save face, nullified the force bill. Jackson ignored this defiant gesture. He had already branded as unlawful and unconstitutional the claim that any state could annul the laws of the United States. In effect he had told rebellious states that secession was their only escape, and that secession would be met with armed force.

"Gag Rules" The compromise did not relieve South Carolina's suspicions and anxieties. The nullification controversy had failed to provide the assurance of constitutional safeguards against a hostile national majority. Southern extremists demanded ironclad guarantees that would permanently bar the abolitionists' "incendiary publications" from the mails and prevent Congress from receiving petitions calling for the abolition of slavery in the District of Columbia. In actuality, the Democratic party fulfilled these objectives in a less formal way. The Jackson and Van Buren administrations, dependent on the large Democratic vote in the South, encouraged federal postmasters to stop abolitionist literature at its point of origin. Despite continuing protest from northern Whigs, northern Democrats also provided southern congressmen of both parties with enough votes to maintain "gag rules" from 1836 to 1844, a procedure that automatically tabled abolitionist petitions in Congress and helped prevent explosive debates on the subject of slavery. Many northerners were outraged by these infringements on civil and political liberties. But South Carolinians were also dissatisfied with pragmatic mechanisms for security that depended on the continuing support of the national Democratic party. Without further constitutional protections, they feared that a shift in northern opinion might induce Congress to withdraw all federal sanction and protection of slavery.

The Bank War, the Panic of 1837, and Political Realignments

The Bank War   Meanwhile, President Jackson had extended his national popularity by declaring "war" on the Second Bank of the United States (BUS). Jackson had long harbored a mistrust of banks in general, especially of the BUS. Van Buren, Senator Thomas Hart Benton of Missouri, Amos Kendall of the Kitchen Cabinet, and other key presidential advisers shared these sentiments. To understand their "hard-money" position, it is important to realize that the national government issued no "paper money" like that in circulation today. Payment for goods and services might be in gold or silver coin (specie) or, more likely, in paper notes issued by private commercial banks. The value of this paper currency fluctuated greatly, which meant that wages or other payments might suddenly decline in purchasing power. The hard-money Democrats realized that large commercial transactions could not be carried on with specie. But they believed that the common people, including small businessmen as well as farmers and wage earners, should not be burdened with the risk of being cheated by a speculative currency. They also knew that a policy favoring the greater circulation of gold and silver coin, which seemed magically endowed with some fixed and "natural" value, would win votes for the party.

To a large degree, however, the nation's reserves and transfers of gold and silver were controlled by the BUS. The BUS performed many of the functions of a truly national bank. Its own notes could be exchanged for specie, and they were accepted by the government as legal payment for all debts to the United States. The BUS had large capital reserves, and it limited the issue of its own highly stable notes. It was therefore a creditor to the hundreds of state-chartered banks throughout the country. It also served as a clearinghouse and regulatory agency for their money, refusing to accept notes that were not backed by sufficient reserves of specie. By promoting monetary stability, the BUS helped to improve the public reputation of banks in general and eased the difficulties of long-distance transfers of goods and credit. Moreover, it mobilized a national reserve of capital on which other banks could draw. Consequently, most state banks favored congressional renewal of the BUS charter, which was scheduled to expire in 1836.

Opponents of the bank feared the concentration of so much economic power in a few hands and worried that the federal government had practically no control over the bank, although the government provided one-fifth of the bank's capital. The bank's critics complained that, even under the expert management of the bank's president, Nicholas Biddle, this partly public institution was far more oriented to the interests of its private investors than to the interests of the general public. Senator Daniel Webster, the main lobbyist for rechartering the BUS, not only was the director of the Boston branch but also relied heavily on Biddle for private loans and fees for legal and political services. To Jackson the BUS had become a "monster institution," unconstitutionally diverting public funds for private profit. The central issue, then, was how far the government should subsidize and become allied with private business interests in order to promote the regulated growth of a national market economy.

The famous "Bank War" erupted into open conflict in 1832, when Webster and Clay launched a legislative offensive, partly to prevent Jackson's reelection. They knew that they could win support from many Democrats for the passage of a bill rechartering the BUS. Therefore they were confident that the president could not veto the measure without fatally damaging his chances for reelection in the fall. But Jackson took up their challenge. In a masterful veto message he spelled out the principles that would be the basis for "Jacksonian democracy" and for populist politics in the decades to come. Jackson denounced the BUS as a privileged monopoly. He vowed to take a stand "against all new grants of monopolies and exclusive privileges, against any prostitution of our Government to the advancement of the few at the expense of the many." Jackson in no way favored equalizing wealth or otherwise removing distinctions derived from "natural and just advantages." He insisted that "equality of talents, of education, or of wealth cannot be produced by human institutions." But he believed that government should provide "equal protection, and, as heaven does its rains, shower its favors alike on the high and the low, the rich and the poor." The BUS, he declared, represented a flagrant example of government subsidy to the privileged—of laws that made "the rich richer and the potent more powerful." Jackson also warned of the dangerous provisions that allowed foreigners to buy BUS stock and thus to acquire influence over American policy. In defiance of the Supreme Court's decision in *McCulloch* v. *Maryland* (1819), the president argued that the BUS was unconstitutional.

Webster and other conservative leaders immediately cried that the president was trying "to stir up the poor against the rich." But the election of 1832 decisively vindicated Jackson's political shrewdness and bold leadership. Old Hickory would have won a sweeping victory even if the opposition votes had not been divided between Henry Clay, the National Republican candidate, and William Wirt, the reluctant leader of the Anti-Masons, a party based on the widespread fear that free institutions were endangered by the secret society of Freemasons.

Having been reelected, Jackson was confident that the supporters of the BUS could never override his veto. He vowed to pull out the fangs of the "monster institution" by removing all of the deposits placed in the bank by the federal government.

Many of the president's advisers opposed this aggressive and arguably illegal policy, since the BUS already seemed doomed. Jackson had to rid himself of two secretaries of the treasury before he found in Roger B. Taney a secretary who would carry out his will. The removal policy also raised new problems. According to Jackson's plan, federal funds would be dispersed among chosen state-chartered banks that were soon dubbed "pet" banks. For the policy to succeed, Jackson had to persuade the banking community that decentralization would not bring economic disaster. On the other hand, the BUS's president, Nicholas Biddle, needed to produce a minor financial panic to underscore the powerful role of the BUS in maintaining financial stability. Biddle could not exert his full financial powers, however, without adding to popular hostility to the bank. In the winter of 1832–33 Biddle instituted a tight-money policy, but the limitation on credit was not serious enough to shake Jackson's resolution. Jackson also gained political leverage through his careful choice of pet banks to which federal funds were to be transferred. Many bankers who had earlier hoped to keep clear of the political struggle were eager to receive interest-free federal funds that would enable them to expand their loans and other commercial operations. Jackson's victory was fairly complete by the spring of 1834. Two years later, when the charter of the BUS terminated, the United States was left without a central banking agency of any kind.

Jackson's Hard-Money Policy

Like many triumphs, the destruction of the BUS caught the victors in a web of problems. The Democrats claimed that by slaying the "monster," they had purged the nation of a moral evil. Yet the deposit of federal funds in pet banks encouraged the expansion of credit, and in the mid-1830s the nation reeled from the intoxication of a speculative boom. As the volume of bank notes soared, it became so easy to purchase federal land on credit that the value of land sales jumped nearly tenfold in four years. The General Land Office made so many sales in this period that the phrase "doing a land office business" became synonymous with reaping huge profits from speculation. The federal surplus grew—an unimaginable phenomenon for twentieth-century generations, who have known only federal deficits and mounting public debts. Some of the more obstinate Jacksonian advisers even bemoaned this surplus because there seemed to be no place to put the funds that would not corrupt the Republic. Whatever the administration did invited trouble. On the one hand, if it distributed funds to the states, it would feed the speculative boom by encouraging further construction of roads and canals and other kinds of "improvements." On the other hand, if it kept the funds in the pet banks, these banks clearly had to be regulated by the federal government: otherwise they too might feed inflation by issuing vast quantities of paper money based on the new reserves of federal funds they had received.

Slowly Jackson and his successor, Van Buren, who was elected in 1836, moved toward a policy of hard money. They tried to reduce or eliminate the circulation of small-denomination bank notes and to set a minimal requirement for the pet banks' specie reserves. In 1836 Jackson also issued an executive order, the so-called Specie Circular, requiring payment in specie for purchase of public land. The specie circular represented a direct federal effort to curb speculation and thus to control economic fluctuations. This controversial measure was a sign of the growing dominance of the antibank and hard-money factions in the Democratic party. The subsequent nomination and election of Van Buren strengthened the hand of those Democrats who found hostility to all banks politically effective.

The Panic of 1837   In 1837 a banking panic brought an abrupt end to the speculative boom. By 1839 a severe depression had developed that persisted to the mid-1840s. This painful downturn in investment, prices, and employment was primarily the product of a business cycle still tied to agriculture (mainly cotton) and related to British demand, British investment, and the international flow of silver. In many respects the American economy still resembled the economy of a colony or underdeveloped nation dependent on

Jackson over the Cliff
An anti-Democratic cartoon portrays Thomas Hart Benton—the Democratic senator from Missouri who favored gold and silver coinage to paper money and who led the fight in the Senate to "expunge" the Bank of the United States—encouraging Jackson to pursue the "Gold Humbug" even though this policy leads to disaster. Van Buren, meanwhile, has decided "to deviate a little." A "shin plaster" was a contemptuous term for small-denomination currency issued during the depression of 1837 when banks were suspending specie payment.

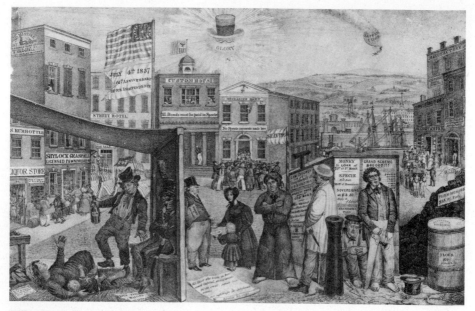

"The Times"

This complex cartoon portrays the allegedly disastrous results of the Democratic rule: the government's hard money policy leads to a run on the bank, which has suspended specie payments; the custom house is deserted; debtors are herded into the sheriff's office; beggars and unemployed artisans crowd the streets; scenes of drunkenness are linked with the unruliness of immigrants and Locofoco radicals.

foreign investment and on raw material exports. Hence the American economy was vulnerable to sudden contractions of British credit coupled with temporary drops in the British demand for cotton.

As bankruptcies multiplied, the business community blamed the widespread suffering on Jacksonian fiscal policies. These policies, they charged, had first fueled reckless expansion by destroying the BUS and then had suddenly limited credit by requiring specie for the purchase of public land. But as bankers and businessmen deserted the Democratic party, the dominant hard-money, laissez-faire faction argued that the economic collapse proved the folly of government partnership with even pet banks.

After three years of bitter Democratic-Whig struggle, President Van Buren finally achieved a "divorce of bank and state" with the passage of the Independent Treasury Act (1840). But this measure probably prolonged the depression. It locked federal funds into "independent" subtreasuries of the United States government that were insulated from the banking community, thereby depriving the banking system of reserves that might have encouraged loans and aided economic recovery.

**The Democrats'
Legacy**

The ambiguity of the Democrats' program can be illuminated by pointing to two inconsistencies. First, their economic policies did little to aid the groups of farmers and artisans whom the Democrats claimed to represent. The political attacks on privilege may have strengthened an abstract commitment to equality, embodied in a new democratic ideology that built on older republican traditions. Yet the Democrats' ultimate beneficiaries were southern planters who were aided by Indian removal, lowered tariffs, and the suppression of antislavery literature and petitions. Moreover, the policy of economic laissez-faire seemed to offer the South assurances that the federal government would not interfere with the interstate movement of slave labor. By 1838 Calhoun and his followers returned to the Democratic party, which they had earlier left in protest against Jackson's authoritarian style. As it turned out, Calhoun's return paved the way for southern domination of the Democratic party in the two decades to come.

Second, the nation's banking system continued to grow into an integrated system, and the nation's economy continued to grow with serene disregard for the fluctuation of power between the Democrats and Whigs. Jackson's and Van Buren's attempts to withdraw the government from what they saw as a corrupting economy had little effect on the general trends of economic development.

Whigs and the Two-Party System

The Democrats controlled the White House for most of the thirty years following Jackson's 1828 victory. Between 1828 and 1856 their presidential nominees defeated every opposition candidate except William Henry Harrison in 1840 and Zachary Taylor in 1848, both of whom died in office. John Tyler, the vice-president who succeeded Harrison only a month after the latter's inauguration, soon returned to his original Virginia Democratic loyalties and principles. Millard Fillmore, Zachary Taylor's successor, was a genial but colorless Whig party hack who had begun his political career as an Anti-Mason and ended it by running for president in 1856 on the nativist and anti-Catholic "Know-Nothing" (or American) party ticket.

But the Democrats' dominance of the presidency is deceptive. By the late 1830s Whigs could match Democratic strength in most parts of the country. Although the South has commonly been pictured as a preserve for states' rights Democrats, Whigs predominated as the South's representatives in three out of five Congresses elected between 1832 and 1842. Whig strength was particularly evident on local, county, and state levels.

The viability of the two-party system depended essentially on vigorous local conflict—on the ability of a second party to challenge incumbents by convincing voters that a genuine alternative was available. To maintain party loyalties, leaders tried to exploit or manufacture conflicts, to dramatize party differences, and to be responsive enough to public demands to convince voters that their grievances

"King Andrew the First"
The Whig image of Jackson as an autocratic king, brandishing the veto and trampling the Constitution under foot.

could be resolved through the ballot. The Whigs, like the Democrats, claimed to represent the interests of the *excluded* people against a privileged and self-serving "power." In 1844 the Whig journalist Calvin Colton characterized the Jackson administration as a "ONE MAN POWER" where "the long-established, simple, and democratic habits of the people, social and political, were superseded by the dictation of a Chief, and by the aristocratic assumptions of his menials." Since no incumbent party could possibly avoid patronage, the game of two-party politics consisted of proving that the incumbents were partial to their friends and thus insincere in claiming to serve the common good. In effect, both parties were torn between a desire to battle for the special interests of their permanent followers and a need to advocate bland, lofty goals that would attract the widest possible national following. From the mid-1830s to the early 1850s both Democrats and Whigs were remarkably successful in cultivating partisan loyalty: once voters had acquired a party identity, they persisted over the years in voting for Whig or Democratic candidates; state legislators and congressmen generally exhibited the same party loyalty in roll-call votes on divisive measures.

Webster, Clay, and Calhoun

Like the Democrats, the Whigs were a wholly new coalition. They were not, as the Democrats charged, simply Federalists in disguise—the Democrats themselves recruited an impressive number of ex-Federalist leaders. In Congress the Whigs first began to emerge in a legislative rebellion against Jackson's so-called Executive Usurpation. During the summer of 1832, Jackson's veto of the bill rechartering the BUS led to the temporary coalition of three of the most formidable senators in American history. All longed for the presidency. By 1832 they had won fame as godlike deliverers of majestic oratory that dazzled aspiring young men.

Daniel Webster, "a steam engine in trousers" in the words of the Englishman Sydney Smith, struck the keynote when he attacked "King Andrew" as a reincarnation of the French monarch Louis XIV, who had declared, "I am the State." A man of humble New Hampshire origins and aristocratic Boston tastes, Webster had risen in the legal profession by emulating and paying deference to New England's commercial elite. Many years after Webster's death, Henry Cabot Lodge voiced the common conclusion that his "moral character was not equal to his intellectual force." Webster was a heavy drinker, given to extravagant living and continual debt. His rich, booming voice and commanding physical presence could never quite convey the moral sincerity that most northeastern Whigs expected of their leaders. Yet Webster upheld their traditional mistrust of divisive parties and their traditional ideal of government by "disinterested gentlemen." He succeeded in blending this conservative tradition with a celebration of material and moral progress. As the agent of commercial and manufacturing interests in Massachusetts, he was flexible enough to shift his style of argument from the forums of the Supreme Court and the Senate to the stump of popular politics. Always, however, he pleaded for the natural harmony of interests that, he claimed, the Democratic party threatened to undermine.

Henry Clay joined Webster's assaults on Jackson's alleged despotism. He considered himself a Jeffersonian Republican and the leader of the National Republicans, the label originally applied to Jackson's opponents. Clay's program, which he called the American System, was designed to maximize federal support for industry, economic growth, and national self-sufficiency. He was a Kentuckian born in Virginia, and he had also risen from humble origin. Like Webster, he was notorious for extravagant living, although Clay's self-indulgence took the typically southern forms of gambling, dueling, and horse racing. A slaveowner and brilliant courtroom lawyer, Clay assumed two contradictory political roles. He competed with Jackson as a western man of the people, a coonskin man of nature. But Clay had also helped to negotiate the Treaty of Ghent, which had ended the War of 1812; he had been John Quincy Adams's secretary of state; and he had represented the western business and commercial interests that demanded federal aid for internal improvements. One of the greatest political manipulators in nineteenth-century America, Clay had unequaled talents in caucuses, committee rooms, and all-night boardinghouse negotiations.

John C. Calhoun was the most unpredictable of the three anti-Jackson leaders. Calhoun had originally been a militant nationalist, but in the 1820s he had become a militant defender of slavery and states' rights. He had been Jackson's nominal ally until personal conflicts had provoked a fatal split. Despite Calhoun's dramatic turnabouts, contemporaries admired the clarity and logical force of his arguments and respected his earlier distinguished service as secretary of war. But Calhoun's role in the nullification controversy made him a dangerous ally in the developing Whig coalition. Most southern Whig leaders shared the economic and nationalist views of the northern Whigs; Calhoun did not.

Whig Philosophy   The Whig outlook on the world was almost too diffuse to be termed an ideology. Like the Democrats, Whigs dreamed of a glorious future for America as the greatest nation the world had ever seen, and they found confirmation of that dream in the measurable growth of the country's population, wealth, and power. Far more than the Democrats, they associated the "spirit of improvement" with concrete technological and social inventions, which would allow "conservatism and progress," as Millard Fillmore put it, "to blend their harmonious action." They assumed that steam power, the telegraph, railroads, banks, corporations, prisons, factories, asylums, and public schools all contributed to an advancing civilization and to an increasing equality of opportunity. For individuals and the nation alike, Whigs advocated saving from income, capital accumulation, budgetary planning, and fiscal responsibility. Whigs opposed aggressive territorial expansion as a cure-all for economic problems. As the Whig newspaper editor Horace Greely observed in 1851: "Opposed to the instinct of boundless acquisition stands that of Internal Improvement. A nation cannot simultaneously devote its energies to the absorption of others' territories and the improvement of its own. In a state of war, not law only is silent, but the pioneer's axe, the canal digger's mattlock, and the house-builder's trowel also." Whigs insisted that America's expansion and power should be harnessed to social objectives and stabilized by publicly acknowledged moral boundaries. Alarmed by the excesses of uncontrolled individualism, they expressed continuing and sometimes hysterical concern over the loss of community—over what they saw as demagogues who won support by inciting the poor against the rich, children against parents, wives against husbands, and geographic section against geographic section.

Whigs thought of themselves as conservatives, and they often invoked European theories that stressed the organic unity of society and the necessity of balancing human rights with social duties. Yet the Whig ideal of government was essentially optimistic and progressive. In 1825, long before the Whig party began to take shape, John Quincy Adams advanced the central Whig idea that the Constitution had given the central government both the duty and the necessary powers to promote "the progressive improvement of the condition of the governed."

The Whig party began to appear on a popular level by 1834. At that time it was essentially a loose coalition of state and local groups opposed to Jacksonian

Democrats. Because they were reluctant to allow the Jacksonians a monopoly of the popular label "democrat," the anti-Jacksonians sometimes called themselves Democratic Whigs. The final acceptance of the term *Whig* was significant. Superficially the label suggested an identity with the British "country-opposition" that had allegedly defended the British constitution against the despotism of the pro-Catholic Stuart kings in the late seventeenth century and against the encroachments of George III in the eighteenth century. This imagery linked "King Andrew" with the various arbitrary and despotic European monarchs. These parallels may seem farfetched, but the very act of drawing parallels with Europe contained a deeper significance. Unlike the Democrats, the Whigs tended to deny the uniqueness of the American experience and to place less faith in political institutions than in economic and cultural progress. They also tended to look on Britain, despite its monarchical and aristocratic institutions, as a model of economic and cultural progress. The most thoughtful Whig spokesmen considered America less a revolutionary departure from the rest of the world than a testing ground for progressive forces that were universal and that depended essentially on moral character.

The Whig Constituency
In all parts of the country, Whigs attracted a broad cross section of the electorate. This cross section was often weighted in favor of the wealthy, the privileged, and the aspiring. But it also included the victims of overt discrimination. In the North this constituency included most of the free blacks; British and German Protestant immigrants; manual laborers sympathetic with their employers' interests; business-oriented farmers; educators, reformers, and professional people; well-to-do merchants, bankers, and manufacturers; and active members of the Presbyterian, Unitarian, and Congregationalist churches. In the South the party had particular appeal to urban merchants, editors, bankers, and those farmers and planters who associated progress with expanding commerce, capital accumulation, railroads, and economic partnership with the North.

During their initial stages of organization the Whigs faced three formidable problems. First, in the populous northern states like New York, Pennsylvania, and Massachusetts they had to find strategies for uniting the economic interests of the National Republicans with the moral and cultural aspirations of various groups alienated by the incumbent Democrats. Second, they had to get rid of the elitist stigma that had been fastened first on John Quincy Adams and then on the defenders of the BUS. Thus they had to prove somehow that they were better democrats than the Democrats. Finally, they had to find delicate maneuvers for bypassing senatorial prima donnas like Webster and Clay and selecting less controversial presidential candidates who could appeal to the nation without arousing dissension and jealousy among the various state party organizations.

The way these problems were met is well illustrated by the career of Thurlow Weed of New York, who became the model of the nineteenth-century political boss and manipulator. A self-made man, Weed first acquired a voice in New York politics as editor of the *Rochester Telegraph* and a bitter foe of Van Buren's Albany

Regency. In 1827 Weed and his young protégé William H. Seward took up the cause of Anti-Masonry as a means of embarrassing the ruling Van Buren machine. In western New York Anti-Masonry had suddenly become a kind of religious crusade after the abduction and probable murder of William Morgan, a former Freemason who wanted to disclose the secrets of the fraternal society. The crusade expressed widespread popular resentment against the Masonic fraternity, which knit many of the wealthier and more powerful urban leaders of the state into a secret brotherhood that was pledged to mutual aid and support. Weed and Seward succeeded in portraying the Van Buren regime as the agent of Freemasonry—a "monster institution"—intent on suppressing legal investigation and prosecution of the alleged murder and on disguising statewide links between Masonic political influence and economic privilege. This antielitist rhetoric helped to counteract the Democrats' claims of being the true champions of the people against the unpopular Adams administration in Washington. By 1830 Anti-Masons had captured approximately one-half the popular vote in New York State. When the movement showed increasing signs of strength in other northern states, Weed and other strategists worked to absorb the National Republicans into a new anti-Jackson coalition.

Although the Anti-Masons organized the first national political convention in American history, Weed began to sense that the movement could be no more than a springboard for a successful national party. Weed launched his powerful *Albany Evening Journal* as an Anti-Masonic newspaper, but he increasingly downplayed Masonry and combined blistering attacks on the Albany Regency with the advocacy of various social reforms. To his political cronies and businessmen backers, Weed kept insisting that the Jacksonians could never be beaten so long as they continued to convince the people that they alone represented "the principle of democracy...the poor against the rich." By 1834 Weed had abandoned Anti-Masonry and had succeeded in organizing a New York Whig coalition.

In 1836 the Whigs tried to broaden their appeal by nominating various regional candidates for president, including Daniel Webster of Massachusetts and Hugh White of Tennessee. But it was Weed's candidate, William Henry Harrison of Ohio, who won the most electoral votes (by running three strong regional candidates, the Whigs hoped to deprive Van Buren of an electoral majority and thus let the outcome be decided, as in 1824, in the House of Representatives). Harrison, or "Old Tippecanoe," famous for his military defeat of the Shawnee Indians at Tippecanoe in 1811, appealed to many former Anti-Masons and won strong support in the South as well as in New York, Ohio, and Pennsylvania.

After years of patient organizing, wire-pulling, and passing out cigars, Weed finally came into his own in 1838 when he succeeded in getting William Seward elected governor of New York. As the master of patronage, the official state printer, and the "dictator" of the New York machine, Weed was now in a position to challenge his old archrival Van Buren, who claimed to be the president of the common people.

Whig Campaign Tactics in 1840
*One of the political gimmicks used by the Harrison and Tyler campaign to attract public
attention was to parade behind a huge ball as enthusiasts rolled it from one city to another.
This particular procession moved across the entire state of Ohio and part of Kentucky.*

The Election of 1840 In 1840 Weed played a key role in blocking the Whigs'
nomination of Clay and in opening the way for Har-
rison. Weed's young follower, Horace Greeley, edited the Whigs' most influential
newspaper, *The Log Cabin,* which set the pace for the campaign by attacking
President Van Buren as an affected dandy who had transformed the White House
into a palace of effeminate luxury. Greeley and others portrayed Harrison as a
frontiersman of simple tastes. His symbols were a barrel of cider (whether hard or
soft depended on the locality) and a log cabin with a welcoming coonskin at the
door. Because Harrison was popularly known as "Old Tippecanoe" from his
victory in 1811 over Tecumseh's Indian confederacy in the Northwest, Whigs
adopted the triumphant campaign slogan, "Tippecanoe and Tyler too!" Harrison's victory seemed to show that Weed and fellow strategists had overcome the
Whigs' political liabilities. They could rival the Democrats in populistic appeals,
in carnival-style hucksterism, and, above all, in grassroots organization.

Nevertheless the Whigs never found a magnetic national leader who, like
Jackson for the Democrats, could become a unifying symbol for their party.
Harrison died of pneumonia a month after his inauguration. John Tyler, the vice-
president who succeeded him after some debate over Tyler's constitutional
status, soon betrayed the economic principles of the party. In 1844 the Whigs
nominated Clay, but he went down to defeat for the third time. Thereafter the
Whigs returned to the tested expedient of nominating apolitical military
heroes--Zachary Taylor in 1848 and Winfield Scott in 1852.

The Whigs' difficulties went beyond the weaknesses of their presidential
candidates. Despite their political pragmatism and impressive party discipline,

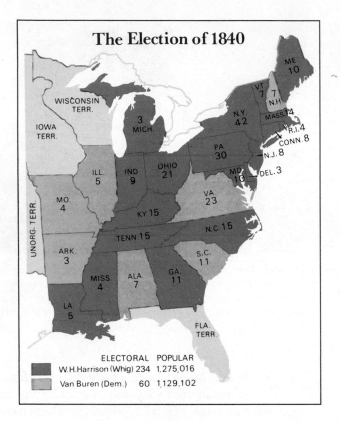

The Election of 1840

ME. 10
VT. 7 7 N.H.
WISCONSIN TERR.
N.Y 42
MASS.14
IOWA TERR.
3 MICH.
R.I.4
CONN. 8
PA. 30
N.J. 8
ILL. 5
IND 9
OHIO 21
MD. 10 DEL. 3
MO. 4
VA. 23
KY. 15
N.C. 15
TENN. 15
ARK. 3
S.C. 11
MISS. 4
ALA. 7
GA. 11
LA. 5
FLA. TERR.
UNORG. TERR.

	ELECTORAL	POPULAR
W.H.Harrison (Whig)	234	1,275,016
Van Buren (Dem.)	60	1,129,102

the Whigs contained a militant, reform-minded element that resented the compromises necessary for a national party. Anti-Masonry had been one of the early expressions of such reformist and issue-oriented politics, and many of the Anti-Masons who had joined the Whigs had never been comfortable with the opportunism of the Weed school of leaders, who placed victory above principle. In addition to the Anti-Masons, the Whig party became the uneasy home for people who wanted laws enforcing a stricter Sabbath, laws prohibiting the sale of alcohol, laws barring slavery from the territories and abolishing slavery in the District of Columbia, and laws prolonging the time before an immigrant could be naturalized or allowed to vote. These causes were nourished by the spread of Protestant religious revivals in the North. They had little appeal among southern Whigs and hardheaded supporters of Clay's American System.

Limitations of the Two-Party System   Nevertheless, although a national party's strength depended on a continuing sensitivity to the needs of its constituent groups, it also served as a disciplining and educational force, imposing definite limits to individual, local, and regional self-assertion. The political issues of the 1840s tended to reinforce such party loyalty.

The majority of state legislators voted a strict Whig or Democratic line even when a different position might have harmonized better with local or personal interests. Whig or Democratic nerve centers were established at the grassroots level through the appointment of loyal party men to positions in local land offices, post offices, and customhouses. Until the early 1850s, when voters became disillusioned with traditional alternatives and when the Whig party began to fall apart, the two-party system worked as a powerful cohesive force in American society. Unfortunately, this political stability depended on the illusion of constant and sharply defined differences between two parties—parties that were intended to represent the interests of white Americans alone. The existence of national parties succeeded in moderating sectional conflict, but it did so at the cost of suppressing alternatives to the expansion of slavery and of stifling national debate over America's most dangerous conflict of interest.

Jacksonian Democracy

The limitations of the two-party system should not obscure the extraordinary fact that a functioning democracy had emerged in the United States. While historians continue to ponder and debate the contradictions of the so-called Age of Jackson, particularly the simultaneous expansion of slavery and democracy, one needs to recognize the utter novelty of popular sovereignty in action. The United States was the first nation in the world in which the great majority of free adult males not only possessed the vote but also cast their ballots (some 78 percent of adult white males voted in the election of 1840, and this level of turnout persisted until the Civil War). In contrast to the republicanism of the Federalist and Jeffersonian periods, the political system did not promote "natural aristocrats" who could supposedly preserve the public good. On the contrary, politicians deferred frankly and unashamedly to the people—or to interest groups among the people—and a revered leader like Jackson became charismatic precisely because he was thought to embody the wisdom of the common man.

What amazed Alexis de Tocqueville and other European observers, who were sensitive to the seething, volcanic upheavals of Europe, was the realization that America's "great social revolution" had almost "reached its natural limits... in a simple, easy fashion, or rather one might say that that country sees the results of the democratic revolution taking place among us [i.e. in Europe], without experiencing the revolution itself." In America, where the ideal of equality had never been pitted against an entrenched aristocracy, there had been no mass exterminations, no coups d'état, no secret police, no repressive armies or controlling bureaucracy. Conservatives might complain that farmers, artisans, and even women no longer knew their "place," that society had become so "leveled" that distinctions of rank had lost all meaning. As cheap newspapers and protest movements proliferated, no institution, tradition, or class remained invulnerable from attack. Despite widening disparities in wealth, America's political culture became profoundly antielitist and suspicious of privilege.

Democracy, as Tocqueville came to understand, had as much to do with a state of mind, with expectations of the future, as with political institutions:

> When citizens are classified by rank, profession, or birth, and when all are obliged to follow the career which chance has opened before them, everyone thinks that he can see the ultimate limits of human endeavor quite close in front of him, and no one attempts to fight against an inevitable fate. It is not that aristocratic peoples absolutely deny man's capacity to improve himself, but they do not think it unlimited....
>
> But when castes disappear and classes are brought together, when men are jumbled together and habits, customs, and laws are changing, when new facts impinge and new truths are discovered, when old conceptions vanish and new ones take their place, then the human mind imagines the possibility of an ideal but always fugitive perfection.

Writing a new preface to his *Democracy in America* in 1848, when revolutions convulsed most of Europe, Tocqueville cautioned against turning to America "in order slavishly to copy the institutions she has fashioned for herself." But "where else," he asked, "can we find greater cause of hope or more valuable lessons?"

Chronology

1820 Missouri Compromise. Maine admitted as twenty-third state. Reelection of James Monroe without opposition symbolizes "Era of Good Feelings."	**1828** John C. Calhoun's anonymous South Carolina Exposition and Protest. Congress passes "Tariff of Abominations." Election of Andrew Jackson as president brings triumphant victory to new Democratic party.
1821 Henry Clay effects "Second Missouri Compromise." Missouri admitted as twenty-fourth state.	**1830** Jackson vetoes Maysville Road Bill. Anti-Masonic party holds first national party convention.
1822 Denmark Vesey's conspiracy to lead massive slave uprising in South Carolina exposed.	**1832** Beginning of Jackson's "war" against Second Bank of the United States (BUS). Special convention in South Carolina nullifies new protective tariff. Jackson reelected president.
1824 John Quincy Adams elected president by House of Representatives after failure of any candidate to win electoral majority.	
1827 Thurlow Weed takes up cause of Anti-Masonry.	**1833** Congress provides for a gradual lowering of tariffs but passes Force Bill authorizing Jackson to

	enforce federal law in South Carolina.		to widespread bankruptcies and default of several states.
1836	Jackson's "specie circular." Martin Van Buren elected president.	1840	Congress passes Van Buren's Independent Treasury Act. William H. Harrison elected president; Whigs in power.
1837	Financial panic brings many bank failures and suspension of specie payment.	1841	John Tyler becomes president upon Harrison's death.
1839	A major depression begins, leading	1844	James K. Polk elected president.

SUGGESTED READINGS

Arthur M. Schlesinger, Jr., *The Age of Jackson* (1945), should be used with caution but is still an indispensable introduction to political democratization. The best recent syntheses and reinterpretations are Edward Pessen, *Jacksonian America: Society, Personality, and Politics* (rev. ed., 1978); Robert H. Wiebe, *The Opening of American Society: From the Constitution to the Eve of Disunion* (1984); Charles G. Sellers, *The Market Revolution, 1815–1848* (1992); and Harry L. Watson, *Liberty and Power: The Politics of Jacksonian America* (1990).

Other studies that illuminate various aspects of democratization, including rent wars and local rebellions, are Shaw Livermore, Jr., *The Twilight of Federalism* (1962); Chilton Williamson, *American Suffrage: From Property to Democracy* (1960); Henry Christman, *Tin Horns and Calico: A Decisive Episode in the Emergence of Democracy* (1945); David M. Ludlum, *Social Ferment in Vermont* (1939); Marvin E. Gettleman, *The Dorr Rebellion* (1973); and John Ashworth, *"Agrarians" and "Aristocrats": Party Political Ideology in the United States, 1837–1846* (1983).

Lee Benson, *The Concept of Jacksonian Democracy: New York as a Test Case* (1961), challenges the traditional historical categories of liberalism and conservatism. Richard P. McCormick, *The Second American Party System: Party Formation in the Jacksonian Era* (1966), also deemphasizes political issues and ideology. These pioneering works should be supplemented by Richard Hofstadter, *The Idea of a Party System* (1969); Ronald P. Formisano, *The Birth of Mass Political Parties: Michigan, 1827–1861* (1971); Formisano, *The Transformation of Political Culture: Massachusetts Parties, 1790s–1840s* (1983); Joel Silbey, ed., *Transformation of American Politics, 1840–1860* (1967); Jean H. Baker, *Affairs of Party: The Political Culture of Northern Democrats in the Mid-Nineteenth Century* (1983); Douglas T. Miller, *Jacksonian Aristocracy: Class and Democracy in New York, 1830–1860* (1967); and Michael F. Holt, "The Antimasonic and Know-Nothing Parties," and Holt, "The Democratic Party," in *History of U.S. Political Parties,* ed. Arthur M. Schlesinger, Jr., vol. 1 (*1789–1860: From Factions to Parties*) (4 vols., 1973). For fascinating studies of the Anti-Masonic party, see William Preston Vaughn, *The Antimasonic Party in the United States, 1826–1843* (1983), and Paul Goodman, *Towards a Christian Republic: Antimasonry and the Great Transition in New England, 1826–1836* (1988). Michael F. Holt, *The Political Crisis of the 1850s* (1978), points to important connections between political ideology and the working of the party system.

For the election of 1828, see Robert V. Remini, *The Election of Andrew Jackson* (1963). Two imaginative studies of Jacksonian ideology are Marvin Meyers, *The Jacksonian Persuasion* (1957), and John W. Ward, *Andrew Jackson: Symbol for an Age* (1955). For the most comprehensive biography of Jackson, see Robert V. Remini, *Andrew Jackson and the Course of American Empire, 1767–1821* (1977); *Andrew Jackson and the Course of American Freedom, 1822–1832* (1981); and *Andrew Jackson and the Course of American Democracy, 1833–1845* (1984). Jackson's presidency is also ably covered by Richard B. Latner, *The Presidency of Andrew Jackson: White House Politics, 1829–1837* (1979). John Niven, *Martin Van Buren and the Romantic Age of American Politics* (1983), and Donald B. Cole, *Martin Van Buren and the American Political System* (1984), bring out the central importance of a much underrated political leader. Informative essays on all the presidential elections can be found in Arthur M. Schlesinger, Jr., ed., *History of American Presidential Elections, 1789–1968,* vol. 1 (4 vols., 1971). See also Richard P. McCormick, *The Presidential Game: The Origins of American Presidential Politics* (1982), and Lawrence Frederick Kohl, *The Politics of Individualism: Parties and the American Character in the Jacksonian Era* (1988).

The standard work on the tariff issue is Frank W. Taussig, *The Tariff History of the United States* (1931). The best introduction to the banking controversy is Robert V. Remini, *Andrew Jackson and the Bank War* (1967). The main authorities on the history of banking are Bray Hammond, *Banks and Politics in America from the Revolution to the Civil War* (1957); J. Van Fenstermaker, *The Development of American Commercial Banking 1782–1837* (1965); and Fritz Redlich, *The Molding of American Banking* (2 vols., 1947–51). Thomas P. Govan, *Nicholas Biddle* (1959), presents a strong defense of the president of the Bank of the United States. The wider political ramifications of the controversy are examined in William G. Shade, *Banks or No Banks: The Money Question in Western Politics* (1972), and John M. McFaul, *The Politics of Jacksonian Finance* (1972).

On the Missouri crisis of 1820, Glover Moore, *The Missouri Controversy* (1953), is still the most thorough and convincing account. William W. Freehling, *Prelude to Civil War* (1966), presents a masterful interpretation of South Carolina's growing militancy and of the nullification and gag-rule controversies. For the general question of sectionalism, see William J. Cooper, *The South and the Politics of Slavery, 1528–1856* (1978). The most penetrating and informative study of politics in a southern state is J. Mills Thornton III, *Politics and Power in a Slave Society: Alabama, 1800–1860* (1978).

There is still no adequate history of the Whig party and its antecedents, but Daniel W. Howe, *The Political Culture of the American Whigs* (1980), brilliantly illuminates the Whig ideology. See also Lynn L. Marshall, "The Strange Stillbirth of the Whig Party," *American Historical Review,* 62 (January 1967), 445–68; and Thomas H. O'Connor, *Lords of the Loom: The Cotton Whigs and the Coming of the Civil War* (1968). Political history is always enriched by the biographies of influential figures. The transition from the era of the Founders is imaginatively analyzed in Drew R. McCoy, *The Last of the Fathers: James Madison and the Republican Legacy* (1989). A fine study of Jackson's three towering opponents is Merrill D. Peterson, *The Great Triumvirate: Webster, Clay, and Calhoun* (1987). For Calhoun, see also John Niven, *John C. Calhoun and the Price of Union: A Biography* (1988). An older and more comprehensive biography is Charles M. Wiltse, *John C. Calhoun: Nationalist, 1782–1828* (1944), *Nullifier, 1829–1839* (1949), and *Sectionalist, 1840–1850* (1951). For Henry Clay, see Clement Eaton, *Henry Clay and the Art of American Politics* (1957); for Webster, see Irving H. Bartlett, *Daniel Webster* (1978), and Robert F. Dalzell, Jr., *Daniel Webster and the Trial of American Nationalism, 1843–1852* (1973).

Other fine biographies that shed much light on the political history of this period include Martin Duberman, *Charles Francis Adams, 1807–1886* (1961); Samuel F. Bemis, *John Quincy Adams and the Foundations of American Foreign Policy* (1949) and *John Quincy Adams and the Union* (1956); William Nisbet Chambers, *Old Bullion Benton: Senator from the New West* (1956); William E. Smith, *The Francis Preston Blair Family in Politics* (2 vols., 1933); Harry

Ammon, *James Monroe: The Quest for National Identity* (1971); Charles G. Sellers, Jr., *James K. Polk: Jacksonian, 1795–1843* (1957) and *Continentalist, 1843–1846* (1966); Robert Dawidoff, *The Education of John Randolph* (1979); Glyndon G. Van Deusen, *William Henry Seward* (1967); K. Jack Bauer, *Zachary Taylor: Soldier, Planter, Statesman of the Old Southwest* (1985); Frederick J. Blue, *Salmon P. Chase: A Life in Politics* (1986); David H. Donald, *Charles Sumner and the Coming of the Civil War* (1960); Carl B. Swisher, *Roger B. Taney* (1935); Holman Hamilton, *Zachary Taylor* (1951); William Y. Thompson, *Robert Toombs of Georgia* (1966); James P. Shenton, *Robert John Walker: A Politician from Jackson to Lincoln* (1961); Glyndon G. Van Deusen, *Thurlow Weed: Wizard of the Lobby* (1947); and John W. DuBose, *The Life and Times of William Lowndes Yancey* (2 vols., 1892). Richard Hofstadter, *The American Political Tradition* (1948), provides brilliant sketches of a number of pre–Civil War leaders.

5

Expansion and New Boundaries

⟨~⟩

$\mathcal{T}$HE 1840S marked the beginning of a new era. In the North recovery from a long depression was accompanied by rapid urban growth, the extension of machine production and of the factory system, the influx of hundreds of thousands of immigrants, and the construction of vast railway networks linking western farms with eastern markets. In the South the remarkable profitability of cotton and sugar plantations confirmed a whole region's unapologetic commitment to slave labor. The moral discomforts that had troubled Jefferson's generation of southerners had finally given way to a proud and self-conscious identity as a "progressive slave society." This sectional confidence was bolstered not only by the world's demand for cotton but also by the American annexation of Texas. The resulting Mexican War, which extended America's boundaries to the Pacific, led some southern leaders to dream of a vast tropical empire based on the slave labor of an "inferior race." These spectacular fulfillments of trends and aspirations that had been developing since the War of 1812 posed grave challenges to governmental policy and to the nation's sense of its own character.

There were other dark shadows in this overall picture of growth and economic integration. In the mid-1850s investment and industrial production both underwent a slowdown, which culminated in the financial panic of 1857. For the first time the business cycle seemed to be primarily geared to the fluctuations of *nonagricultural* forces in the domestic economy, among them speculative investment in railroads. Significantly, the South suffered little from the essentially industrial depression of the late 1850s. Southern leaders could not refrain from gloating over the economic vulnerability of northern industry and the insecurities of "wage slavery." Northern leaders angrily accused the South of contributing to the depression by defeating northern moves for protective tariffs and free homesteading in the West. Slave-grown cotton remained an important contributor to the North's industrial growth. But many northerners perceived the South as a holdover of colonial dependency—a dependency on British markets that blocked the way to national self-sufficiency.

Foreign Dangers, American Expansion, and the Monroe Doctrine

America's foreign policy had always presupposed the national government's commitment to protect and support the South's "peculiar institution." However, the nation's foreign policy reflected many other interests and motives, and protecting slavery was not explicitly acknowledged as a vital objective until 1844. The overriding objective in the early nineteenth century, as in the post-Revolutionary period, was to prevent Britain or France from acquiring a foothold in the increasingly vulnerable Spanish territories of North America. But those territories, including Cuba, East and West Florida, and Texas, were a threat mainly to the slaveholding South. The War of 1812 made clear that possession of the Floridas was essential for the security of the entire Lower South. From bases in supposedly neutral Spanish Florida, the British had incited Indian raids, had encouraged slave desertions, and had originally planned to launch an invasion to cut off New Orleans from the rest of the United States. The revolution of 1791–1804 in the French colony of Saint Domingue (which became the Republic of Haiti) had also shown that war could ignite a massive slave uprising and totally destroy a slaveholding society.

Decline of New World Slavery One of the consequences of the Napoleonic wars at the beginning of the nineteenth century was the fatal weakening of slaveholding regimes in most parts of the New World. Not only did France lose Haiti, the most valuable sugar colony in the world, but Napoleon's seizure of Spain opened the way for independence movements in the immense Spanish territories from Mexico to Chile. The prolonged wars of liberation undermined the institution of slavery and committed the future Spanish-American republics to programs of gradual emancipation. After the British abolished the slave trade in their own colonies at the beginning of the nineteenth century, they embarked on a long-term policy of suppressing the slave trade of other nations. By 1823, when little remained of the former Spanish, Portuguese, and French New World empires, slavery was a declining institution except in Brazil, Cuba (still a Spanish colony), and the United States.

This wider context of New World slavery dramatizes a momentous irony of American foreign policy from the time of Jefferson's presidency to the Civil War. The extension of what Jefferson called an "empire for liberty" was also the extension of an empire for slavery and thus a counterweight to the forces that threatened to erode slavery throughout the hemisphere. Jefferson himself initiated the policy of trying to isolate Haiti economically and diplomatically in order to end the spread of black revolution. In 1820, in the midst of the Missouri crisis and in response to Spain's delay in ratifying the Transcontinental Treaty of 1819, ceding East Florida, Jefferson privately assured President Monroe that the United States could soon acquire not only East Florida but also Cuba and Texas. Cuba was at the time becoming the world's greatest producer of slave-grown sugar, and Jefferson confidently predicted that Texas would be the richest state in the Union, partly because it would produce more sugar than the country could consume.

There is no reason to think that American statesmen consciously plotted to create a vast empire for slavery—at least until the 1840s. From the annexation of Florida in 1821 to the annexation of Texas in 1845, the United States acquired no new territory that could upset the balance between free states and slave states achieved by the Missouri Compromise. The Old Southwest contained immense tracts of uncleared and uncultivated land, and many southerners feared that reckless expansion would lead to excessive production, which would lower the price of cotton and other cash crops.

Slavery and Territorial Expansion   The connections between slavery and national expansion were more indirect. They involved two basic and continuing assumptions that governed foreign policy. The first assumption was that territorial expansion was the only means of protecting and extending the principles of the American Revolution in a generally hostile world. "The larger our association," Jefferson had predicted, "the less will it be shaken by local passions." According to this nationalist view, Americans could deal with domestic imperfections once the nation had achieved sufficient power to be secure. Thus ardent nationalists like John Quincy Adams felt that personal misgivings over slavery had to give way to the need for a united front against the monarchical despots of Europe. During the Missouri crisis the antislavery forces could never overcome the unfair charge that they were serving Britain's interests by fomenting sectional discord and blocking the westward expansion of the United States.

The second assumption, held with passionate conviction by every president from Jefferson to Polk, was that Great Britain was America's "natural enemy." These presidents saw Britain as a kingdom ruled by selfish interest, filled with a deep-rooted hatred for everything America represented, and committed to the humiliation and subjugation of its former colonies. Anglophobia had much to do with the swift death of the Federalist party. This hatred of England was nourished by contemptuous anti-American essays in British periodicals and by unflattering descriptions by English travelers that were widely reprinted in the United States. According to Mrs. Frances Trollope's *Domestic Manners of the Americans,* published in 1832, "the theory of equality may be very daintily discussed by English gentlemen in a London dining room . . . but it will be found less palatable when it presents itself in the shape of a hard greasy paw, and is claimed in accents that breathe less of freedom than of onions and whiskey. Strong, indeed, must be the love of equality in an English breast, if it can survive a tour through the Union." Many Americans blamed Britain for the economic depressions of 1819 and 1837.

Irish immigrants regarded the English as their hereditary enemies. No American politician could risk even the suspicion of being an unintentional agent of British interests. It was thus an unhappy coincidence that British interests veered increasingly toward antislavery—which some American leaders interpreted, not without some reason, as a cloak for new forms of economic and ideological imperialism.

The American takeover of Florida established precedents for the future and also coincided with the dramatic southwestward expansion of cotton and slavery. As early as 1786 Jefferson had warned against pressing "too soon on the Spaniards." For the time being, he believed, it was best that East and West Florida be in Spanish hands. He feared, however, that the Spanish were "too feeble to hold them [the Floridas] till our population can be sufficiently advanced to gain it [the Floridas] from them piece by piece." By 1810 there were enough American settlers in the Baton Rouge district of West Florida to stage an armed rebellion against Spanish rule. President Madison, claiming that West Florida was part of the Louisiana Purchase, promptly annexed the section of the Gulf coast extending eastward to the Perdido River. To prevent any possible transfer of West Florida to Great Britain, Congress sanctioned Madison's annexation. But it balked at plans to seize East Florida during the War of 1812.

The Transcontinental Treaty of 1819 Negotiations with Spain after the War of 1812 involved not only Florida but also the entire western boundary of the United States. Spain had never recognized the validity of Napoleon's sale of Louisiana, a sale prohibited by the treaty that had earlier transferred the territory from Spain to France. Luis de Onís, the Spanish minister to the United States, tried to limit American claims to the narrowest strip possible west of the Mississippi River. But as the negotiations dragged on, the South American wars of independence increasingly undermined Spain's position. Secretary of State John Quincy Adams proved to be a tough and skillful bargainer, and in 1818 Andrew Jackson, then the American military commander in the South, immensely strengthened Adams's hand. Without official authorization Jackson invaded East Florida, captured the main Spanish ports, deposed the governor, and hanged two English troublemakers. The excuse was that Florida had become a refuge for fugitive slaves and a base for Seminole Indian raids on American settlements.

Thus Onís was faced with the temporary seizure of his main bargaining card, and he feared that the United States would begin aiding the rebellious Spanish colonies. He therefore agreed to the Transcontinental Treaty of 1819, which ceded the Floridas to the United States in return for American acknowledgment that Texas was not part of the Louisiana Purchase—a questionable claim that the Americans had already put forward. In fact, Onís had been desperate enough to give up most of Texas. But as President Monroe assured General Jackson, "We ought to be content with Florida, for the present, and until the public opinion . . . [in the Northeast] shall be reconciled to any further change."

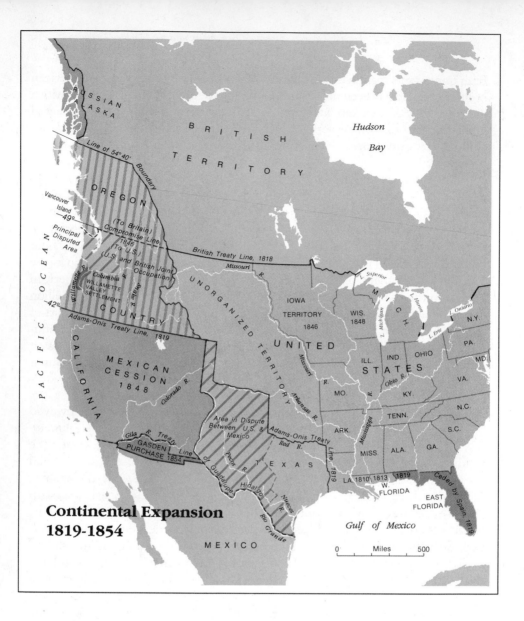

Continental Expansion 1819–1854

For Adams the Transcontinental Treaty (also known as the Adams-Onís Treaty), which was ratified in 1821, was "a great epoch [turning point] in our history." Not only did it transfer the Floridas to the United States, but it extended American territorial claims to the Pacific Ocean. The rather weak Spanish claims to the Pacific Northwest were ceded to the United States. Spain also agreed to an international boundary that extended northward from the Sabine River (which divided Louisiana from Texas) to the Red River, westward along the Red and Arkansas rivers to the Rocky Mountains, and then along the forty-second parallel to the Pacific.

At the time the Transcontinental Treaty was being negotiated, Spain was reasserting its control in Mexico, which had revolted for the first time in 1808–15.

But the revival of Spanish rule proved temporary. In 1820 a revolution in Spain itself permitted the Mexicans to declare their independence once again. By 1822 the burden of defending the boundaries that had been established by the Transcontinental Treaty had fallen on an independent but weak and war-torn Mexico.

Events Leading to the Monroe Doctrine The collapse of the Spanish Empire led directly to the Monroe Doctrine. By 1823 it was clear that Spain could never force its rebellious colonies to return to their former status. Moreover, Britain and the United States had a common interest in preventing the autocratic monarchies of continental Europe from intervening in Latin America in Spain's behalf. Under pressure from the Russian tsar, France was about to invade Spain to put down its revolution, which aimed at establishing a constitutional monarchy. It was known that the French foreign minister had grandiose schemes for imposing on Latin America the kind of reactionary monarchical government that predominated in continental Europe. Although Great Britain was not willing to risk war, it was strongly opposed to French intervention in Spain. And while not a promoter of independent republics, the British government had no intention of allowing the continental powers' anti-revolutionary zeal to interfere with Britain's growing commercial dominance in the former Spanish Empire. George Canning, the British foreign minister, there-fore proposed a joint Anglo-American declaration that would assert that neither Britain nor the United States had designs on former Spanish territory, and would warn other nations against intervention.

The British offer presented the Monroe administration with a serious dilemma. The United States was the only nation that had begun to recognize the independent republics of Spanish America, but only Britain had the power to deter France and Spain from trying to reconquer them. Moreover, Russia— which was leading the reactionary crusades in Europe and which already occupied Alaska—in 1821 claimed a monopoly over the North Pacific. Russian traders were becoming more active in the Oregon country, a region that Britain and the United States had agreed to occupy jointly at least until 1828. Accepting the British offer of a joint declaration would have the drawback of temporarily preventing the American annexation of Cuba. Despite this disadvantage, the idea appealed to the elder statesmen Jefferson and Madison, as well as to Monroe and most of his cabinet.

But the question of accepting the British offer was complicated by the forthcoming presidential election of 1824. The nationalist, anti-English vote was much on the minds of the leading candidates. Secretary of State John Quincy Adams was already being portrayed by his rivals as a former Federalist and as secretly pro-British. Despite his proved nationalism and loyal service to Republican administrations, Adams was vulnerable to these charges because of his New England and Federalist background. He was also the only candidate who was not a slaveowner. He knew that as secretary of state he would bear the largest share of political liability resulting from any Anglo-American alliance. He had long gone out of his way to publicize his resistance to British pressure for an anti-slave-trade treaty. Therefore Adams now insisted on a unilateral American declaration against European intervention in the New World, much as he insisted on a unilateral policy against the slave trade. It would be more candid and dignified, Adams pointed out, to declare the United States' principles directly to Russia and France than "to come in as a cock-boat in the wake of the British man-of-war."

Adams's arguments prevailed. Monroe sent to Congress a message, largely written by Adams, setting forth what has become known as the Monroe Doctrine. By stating that America would not intervene in the "internal concerns" of European states, Monroe in effect repudiated the popular clamor in the United States for aiding the various revolutionary struggles against despotism in Europe, including the Greek war for independence from Turkey. But America's warning to Europe against its future colonization of the New World extended to Britain as well as to Russia and France. And the Monroe Doctrine in no way prevented America's own expansion in the New World.

For some time the Monroe Doctrine had little practical consequence, except perhaps in proving Adams to be a nationalist and thus in helping him to win the presidency. Regardless of American pronouncements, it was British naval power that ensured the independence of Spanish America. Yet by rejecting an Anglo-American alliance, the Monroe administration also set a precedent for opposing any foreign attempts to limit the expansion of slavery. No doubt Monroe was thinking only of monarchical institutions when he warned that the United States would consider as dangerous to America's peace and safety any attempt by Europeans to extend "their system" to the Western Hemisphere. By the 1830s, however, antislavery was an integral part of the British "system," and many southerners regarded the expansion of slavery as vital to America's "peace and safety."

Annexation of Texas   The Texas issue eventually tested this point and led to a proslavery reformulation of the Monroe Doctrine. For abolitionists in both Britain and the United States, it was not inevitable that Texas should become a slave state. In 1829 Mexico had abolished slavery in all its provinces (including California), and it provided loopholes only for the stubborn Anglo-American settlers in Texas. By 1830 the Mexican government had become alarmed by the growing autonomy of the Anglo-American settlements in Texas, by the intrigue accompanying the United States government's secret efforts to purchase Texas, and by the Jacksonian press's agitation for annexation. Consequently, in 1830 the Mexican government tried to prohibit the further immigration of Anglo-Americans and the further importation of slaves. It also sought to promote European settlements in Texas, which would be a buffer against encroachments from the United States. Since black slavery had only begun to take root in Texas, British reformers were beginning to look on the province as a promising site for cultivating cotton with free labor. Benjamin Lundy, an Amer-

The Fall of the Alamo
After the Anglo-Texans declared their independence on March 2, 1836, General Santa Anna led a large army into the province and on March 6 wiped out a small garrison of Americans, including David Crockett, at the Alamo mission in San Antonio. The martyrdom of these heroes did much to inflame anti-Mexican sentiment in the United States.

ican Quaker abolitionist, even tried in the early 1830s to establish a refuge in Texas for free blacks from the United States.

But during his travels in Texas, Lundy found evidence of growing proslavery sentiment and of various plots to throw off Mexican rule and annex Texas to the United States. The Mexican government was in fact capable of neither governing the Anglo-Texans nor satisfying their needs. In 1836, after President Antonio López de Santa Anna had abolished Mexico's federal constitution and had imposed centralized rule, the Texans proclaimed their independence. Their new constitution, modeled on the United States Constitution, specifically legalized black slavery. Meanwhile Santa Anna's army had wiped out a small band of Texas rebels at San Antonio's Alamo Mission, and cries for revenge resounded in the American press. A great influx of volunteers from the officially neutral United States went to the aid of the Texans. Led by General Sam Houston, Texan forces crushed the Mexican army at San Jacinto and captured Santa Anna. Soon thereafter the Texans voted overwhelmingly to join the United States.

As late as 1835 President Jackson had tried to buy not only Texas but all the Mexican territory stretching northwestward to the Pacific. His main object was to secure "within our limits the whole bay of St. Francisco." By then Americans had long been engaged in trade along the Santa Fe trail, and settlers were beginning to arrive by sea in sparsely populated California. After the Texan revolution, however, Jackson knew that a premature attempt at annexation would in all likelihood bring on a war with Mexico, which refused to acknowledge Texan independence. It would also arouse the fury of the Northeast and lead to a

Sam Houston (1793–1863)
Leader of the badly outnumbered Texans whose spectacular victory at San Jacinto in 1836 secured Texas's independence from Mexico, Houston went on to become president of the new republic, then senator from the new state. In 1861 as governor, Houston's stand against Texas's secession from the Union forced him out of office.

sectional division within the Democratic party in the election year of 1836. But Jackson knew that California was important to the whaling and maritime interests of the Northeast. New England whalers and cargo ships had begun to make portions of the Pacific an American preserve. Jackson therefore secretly advised the Texans to bide their time and to establish a claim to California, "to paralyze the opposition of the North and East to Annexation." He assumed that this opposition would fade as soon as northerners concluded that annexing Texas would lead to the acquisition of California.

The passage of time, however, encouraged the hopes of American and British opponents of slavery. Jackson's Democratic successor, Martin Van Buren, was too dependent on northeastern support to risk taking a role himself in agitating the public with the question of annexation. John Quincy Adams's eloquent speeches in the House of Representatives, in which he served for seventeen years after he retired as president, popularized the view that the southern Slave Power had engineered the Texas Revolution and the drive for annexation. In 1838 Adams carried on a three-week filibuster, presented hundreds of antislavery petitions, and finally defeated a move to annex Texas by joint resolution. The rebuffed Texan leaders withdrew their formal proposal for annexation and began to think seriously of building an independent empire. As time went on, they looked to Britain and France for financial support and for diplomatic aid in ending the dangerous state of war with Mexico.

The spring and summer of 1843 marked a decisive turn of events. John Tyler, who had been elected as Harrison's vice-president in 1840 and had then become president after Harrison's death, had been disowned by the Whig party. He was therefore courting southern Democrats and searching for an issue that would win him reelection. Daniel Webster, the last of his Whig cabinet members, finally resigned as secretary of state after negotiating with Britain the Webster-Ashburton Treaty, which settled disputed borders with Canada and provided for cooperative measures in suppressing the Atlantic slave trade. The treaty was immediately attacked by Democrats for betraying American interests. Through Calhoun's influence, Webster was replaced by Abel P. Upshur, a Virginian who had defended slavery as a "positive good." For the first time, an entire administration was in the hands of ardent proslavery southerners who saw territorial expansion as the key to southern security.

Britain and Texas   Although British leaders did not want to antagonize the South, on which Britain depended for cotton, they were sensitive to one abolitionist argument. An independent Texas might begin importing slaves from Africa, thereby adding to Britain's difficulties in suppressing the Atlantic slave trade. The British had evidence that American officials in Cuba were conniving with slave smugglers and that American ships participated in the illegal slave trade to Cuba. Texas might open another rich market for the same interests. Therefore, when Britain offered Texas a treaty of recognition and trade, it included a secret agreement to outlaw the slave trade. Otherwise, under close questioning from a delegation of abolitionists, Foreign Secretary Lord Aberdeen conceded only two points: first, that in serving as mediator between Texas and Mexico, Britain hoped that any peace agreement would include a commitment to slave emancipation; and second, that as everyone knew, the British public and government hoped for the abolition of slavery throughout the world.

These words caused anger and alarm in Washington. The Tyler administration was convinced that West Indian emancipation had proved to be an economic and social disaster. According to the prevailing southern theory, the British were now determined to undermine slavery in other nations in order to improve the competitive advantage of their own colonies, including India. But southerners never comprehended the depth of antislavery sentiment among the British middle class. Having subsidized West Indian emancipation by paying £20 million in compensation to former slaveowners, British taxpayers wanted assurance that Britain's short-term sacrifices would not lead to the expansion of plantation slavery in neighboring regions of the Caribbean and the Gulf of Mexico.

Regardless of the truth, however, southerners had long been inclined to believe that British antislavery was part of a long-term diplomatic plot to seal off and contain the United States within an arc of British influence extending from Cuba and Texas to California, Oregon, and Canada. In 1843 this conviction was seemingly confirmed by the exaggerated reports of Duff Green, President Tyler's secret agent in Britain and France and a friend of Calhoun. According to Green, the British government was about to guarantee interest on a loan to Texas on the condition that Texans abolish slavery. The plan would make Texas a British satellite and a place of refuge, like Canada, for fugitive slaves from the United States. Green claimed that, by erecting a barrier of freedom across the southwestern flank of the slaveholding states, the British could effectively join northern abolitionists in destroying both slavery and the federal Union.

Like many myths, this elaborate fantasy rested on a thin foundation of truth. It interpreted every event as part of a master plan, and it justified national desires that were otherwise difficult to justify. It furnished the pretext for the grand strategy that would govern American expansionist policy for the next five years. In response to an appeal for advice from Secretary of State Upshur, Calhoun in 1843 secretly spelled out the steps for implementing this policy. He called for private assurances to Texas that as soon as a propaganda campaign had been launched to soften northern opposition, the administration would secure annexation. In order to win support from the land-hungry farmers of the Old Northwest, Calhoun also suggested linking Texas annexation with the assertion of American claims to Oregon. As a preliminary step in carrying out this plan, he wanted to demand a formal explanation from Britain for policies that threatened "the safety of the Union and the very existence of the South."

Calhoun himself soon had the power to begin implementing this grand design. Early in 1844 Upshur was killed in an accident, and Calhoun succeeded him as secretary of state. Soon afterward a Whig newspaper revealed that the administration had been engaged for months in secret negotiations with Texas and that Tyler was about to sign an annexation treaty. In response to a growing northern uproar, Calhoun seized on and made public the British government's private statement that Britain "desires, and is constantly exerting herself to procure, the general abolition of slavery throughout the world." By skillfully distorting and publicizing the British diplomatic notes, Calhoun tried to identify the antiannexation cause with a British plot to destroy the Union. He lectured the British on the blessings of black slavery, employing faulty statistics from the census of 1840 to argue that emancipation in the North had produced black insanity, crime, suicide, and degeneracy. He also informed Mexico that because of the British conspiracy to subvert southern slavery, the United States was forced to annex Texas in self-defense.

The Expansionist Issue and the Election of 1844

This open defense of slavery by an American secretary of state marked the beginning of a sectional conflict over slavery and expansionism that severely tested the party system. President Tyler's defection from the Whigs, in addition to Calhoun's presidential ambitions and independence from party discipline, complicated the political maneuvering that set the stage for the 1844 campaign. With an eye to northern votes, both Henry Clay and Martin Van Buren, the leading Whig and Democratic contenders, felt compelled by April 1844 to express their opposition to the immediate annexation of Texas.

James K. Polk (1795–1849)
As Speaker of the House of Representatives, Polk served President Andrew Jackson as a loyal lieutenant. In 1844 Jackson, as the retired elder statesman of the Democratic party, supported Polk's candidacy for president after Martin Van Buren had taken a public stand against annexing Texas. As a young "dark horse" in the race, Polk defeated the veteran Van Buren for the Democratic nomination. Polk's election as president helped the outgoing Tyler administration to secure Texas's annexation and led directly to the Mexican War and to the acquisition of Oregon as well as California and the southwest.

In the Senate the Missouri Democrat Thomas Hart Benton led the attack against the trickery of Tyler and Calhoun. Seven other Democratic senators, all northerners, joined the Whigs in decisively rejecting the annexation treaty. Yet the Whig opposition to expansion encouraged the Democratic party to close ranks and rally behind patriotic demands for the "reannexation of Texas" and the "reoccupation of Oregon." (These demands assumed that Texas had been part of the Louisiana Purchase and that Britain had never had legitimate claims to the region south of 54°40′, the border of Russian Alaska.) The issue of expansion diverted attention from the Democrats' internal disputes over banking and fiscal policy, and it also enabled a southern-dominated coalition to defeat Van Buren and nominate James K. Polk, a Jacksonian expansionist from Tennessee, as the Democratic candidate for the 1844 election.

As Calhoun had predicted, the Oregon question became an ideal means for exploiting national Anglophobia and winning northern support for national expansion. For decades the British Hudson's Bay Company had ruled the region north of the Columbia River, although the United States had strong claims to the Columbia itself and to the territory extending southward to latitude 42°. New England ships had long frequented the entire Pacific Northwest in search of sea otter furs for the China trade, and since the 1820s American trappers had developed a thriving trade in beaver and other furs within the region west of the Rockies. As American traders challenged the political and judicial authority of the powerful Hudson's Bay Company, it became more difficult to resolve conflicting Anglo-American claims. Moreover, in 1827, when the two nations had

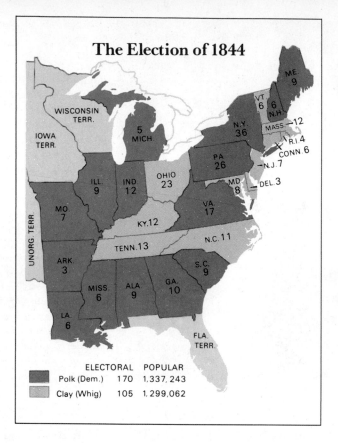

The Election of 1844

	ELECTORAL	POPULAR
Polk (Dem.)	170	1,337,243
Clay (Whig)	105	1,299,062

renewed a "joint occupation" agreement that simply deferred any settlement of national boundaries, no one could foresee the future appeal of Oregon's fertile Willamette Valley to farmers in the Old Northwest. American missionaries working with the Indians sent back glowing reports of the rich farmland in the Willamette Valley, and these helped spread the "Oregon fever" of the 1840s. Thousands of families risked the perils of overland travel to the Pacific. In 1843 the first of the great overland wagon migrations along the Oregon Trail took place, and the resulting claims to "All Oregon" including what later became Washington state, Idaho, and southern British Columbia, acted as a political balance wheel for the annexation of Texas.

In the 1844 election, as in other elections of the time, voter preference depended less on issues than on ethnic, religious, and party loyalty. And so, concerned about the crucial swing vote, Clay, the Whig candidate, retreated from his earlier stand against Texas annexation. His last-minute gestures for southern support persuaded thousands of northern Whigs to vote for James G. Birney, the Liberty party candidate, who stood firm against annexation. More popular votes were actually cast against Polk than for him. Although Polk barely won the election, he would certainly have lost it if Birney's 15,000 votes in New York State had gone to Clay.

Nevertheless the incumbent President Tyler and the triumphant Democrats interpreted the election as a mandate for the immediate annexation of Texas. The

Democrats in Congress united in championing the new expansionism, allowing the outgoing Tyler administration to secure annexation by joint resolution of both houses of Congress. After a tense period of international intrigue, the Republic of Texas rejected offers of peace from Mexico and mediation from Britain. In December 1845, having bypassed territorial status, Texas entered the Union as a new slave state.

The Mexican War and Manifest Destiny

The admission of Texas coincided with President Polk's aggressive reformulation of the Monroe Doctrine. In his annual message of December 2, 1845, Polk warned that henceforth the United States would not tolerate any kind of European interferences designed to limit the spread of the American form of government or the right of any peoples of North America "to decide their own destiny." By this Polk meant the right to be annexed to the United States. In the case of Texas, whose boundaries were still extremely controversial, annexation meant a federal commitment to the restoration of slavery in a region in which it had earlier been outlawed by Mexico. Only the future could determine the fate of Cuba, California, and Oregon—provinces that Polk very much had in mind. And the future too would determine precisely how the people would "decide their own destiny," an ideal soon to be known as "popular sovereignty."

Oregon and California

President Polk's warnings about European interference were directed mainly at Britain. He emphasized that the danger of British economic or political interference, even apart from physical colonization, justified an indefinite expansion of America's boundaries. He also rejected further negotiation with Britain over the Oregon question and asked Congress to give notice of the termination of the 1827 joint occupation agreement. The dismayed British government ignored the belligerent rhetoric, but it commissioned new steam warships and ordered a naval force to the northeast Pacific.

Although Polk hoped to force British concessions regarding Oregon, his primary objective was California, a Mexican province that contained no more than 10,000 white, mostly Hispanic inhabitants. In 1845 a British consul correctly observed that California was at the mercy of whoever might choose to take possession of it. Polk feared that the British might seize the province as compensation for money owed by Mexico. Months before Polk's December message, the government had ordered the commodore of the American Pacific Squadron to take San Francisco and other ports if he could "ascertain with certainty" that Mexico had declared war against the United States.

Polk's secretary of state, James Buchanan, also sent secret instructions to Thomas Larkin, the American consul at Monterey, California, telling him to foil British plots and to foment, as cautiously as possible, a spirit of rebellion among the Spanish Californians. Finally, only days after Polk's belligerent message, America's dashing "Pathfinder," Captain John C. Frémont, arrived in California

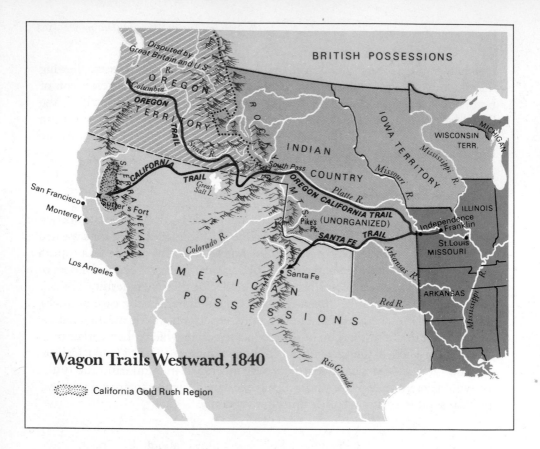

Wagon Trails Westward, 1840

California Gold Rush Region

at the head of a "scientific expedition" of heavily armed engineers. Frémont had been exploring the Mexican West without permission from Mexico, and he would soon defy the Mexican authorities in California and encourage the small population of Anglo-American settlers in an uprising, supposedly in their own self-defense.

Slidell's Mission   December 1845 also marked the arrival in Mexico City of Polk's secret minister, John Slidell, who had orders to win Mexican acceptance of the Rio Grande River as the new border with the United States, as well as to purchase as much of New Mexico and California as possible. His instructions emphasized the determination of the United States to prevent California from becoming a British or French colony, and authorized Slidell to extend to Mexico as much as $25 million for the territories desired. The Americans also offered to assume the debts owed by Mexico to American citizens.

The Mexican government had previously been willing to settle the Texas dispute. But one of Mexico's numerous revolutions was about to erupt, and the unstable government could not dare recognize an American envoy who made such sweeping demands—demands that had already been leaked to the American press. Mexican nationalists considered Texas a "stolen province," and they especially resented the wholly unfounded claim that Texas extended to the Rio Grande. In 1816 Spain had designated the Nueces River, 130 miles north and east of the Rio Grande, as the boundary between the provinces of Tamaulipas and Texas; this was the boundary that appeared on American and European maps. In 1836, however, when the Texans had captured the Mexican president, Santa Anna, he had been forced to agree to the Rio Grande boundary as a condition for his release. The Mexican government had promptly rejected this extortionary agreement. By the end of 1845, Mexican nationalists hoped for European support and were eager for a war of revenge against American imperialists.

War with Mexico   On learning of Slidell's failure, the Polk administration was also eager for war but wanted a pretext that would justify seizing California. In January 1846 the president ordered General Zachary Taylor, who had been poised for the move, to march to the Rio Grande. Without opposition, American ships blockaded that river and Taylor took up a position across the Rio Grande from the Mexican town of Matamoros, toward which he aimed his cannons. By early May, however, Washington had heard no news of hostilities, and the impatient president and cabinet decided that Mexico's unpaid debts and the rebuff to Slidell were sufficient grounds for war. Then, just as Polk had drafted a war message to Congress, news arrived of a minor skirmish between Mexican and American patrols. Polk could now indignantly inform Congress that war already existed. He said, "Notwithstanding all our efforts to avoid it [war] exists by the act of Mexico herself. [Mexico] has passed the boundary of the United States, has invaded our territory and shed American blood upon the American soil."

By any objective interpretation, Americans had crossed the Mexican boundary and had shed Mexican blood on Mexican soil. American expansionists, however, believed that the protests from Europe simply confirmed that the growth of the United States was a blow to political and religious tyranny. It was America's mission, expansionists assumed, to liberate the peoples of California, Mexico, Cuba, Central America, and even Canada, allowing them to share in the blessings of republican government, religious freedom, and modern technology. In 1845 an influential Democratic editor had coined the electric phrase "Manifest Destiny," at the same time denouncing the policy of other nations of "hampering our power, limiting our greatness and checking the fulfillment of our manifest destiny to overspread the continent allotted by Providence for the free development of our yearly multiplying millions."

But the crusade to prevent Europe from imposing a "balance of power" in North America strained the fragile balance on which the Union had always depended—the balance of power between North and South. In the Northeast and particularly in New England, the Mexican War provoked thunderous outrage. It was denounced from press and pulpit as a war of brutal aggression, plotted by the Slave Power to extend slavery and secure permanent control over the free states. The Massachusetts legislature went so far as to proclaim the president's war-inciting acts unconstitutional. The war remained unpopular with

Major Campaigns of the Mexican War

the great majority of Whig leaders, even in the South, who objected to Polk's devious tactics and to the way in which Congress had been stampeded into a declaration of war in order to "rescue" Zachary Taylor's army, which had falsely been said to be endangered. Typical of Whig opposition to the war were Representative Abraham Lincoln's "spot resolutions," which incisively questioned whether the spot at which hostilities had commenced was really, as Polk claimed, on *"our own soil."* Lincoln described Polk's justifications for war as "half insane mumbling" and declared that "the blood of Abel is crying to heaven against him."

Settlement of the Oregon Controversy

By June 1846, a month after the war had begun, even the prowar western Democrats were angered when Polk allowed the Senate to assume full responsibility for approving a treaty that gave to Britain Vancouver Island and all of the Oregon country north of the forty-ninth parallel. As the western expansionists rightly suspected, southerners had never been enthusiastic about adding probable free states in the Pacific Northwest, and Polk had no wish to risk war with Britain when he was intent on dismembering Mexico.

Yet the nation as a whole supported the war. Remembering that opposition to the War of 1812 had split and destroyed the Federalist party, Whigs in Congress dutifully voted for military appropriations and congratulated themselves on the fact that the army's two leading generals, Zachary Taylor and Winfield Scott, were also Whigs. Taylor was the first to win glory. Within a few months, and with few American casualties, he defeated Mexican armies much larger than his own, crossed the Rio Grande, and captured the strategic town of Monterrey, thereby commanding northeastern Mexico. According to Democratic critics, he then settled down to prepare for the presidential campaign of 1848, which he won. In February 1847, however, Taylor crushed another Mexican army more than three times the size of his own in the battle of Buena Vista. The Mexican army was led by Santa Anna, who had earlier been exiled from Mexico. Polk had allowed Santa Anna to enter Mexico from Cuba because he believed that this self-styled "Napoleon of the West" would persuade Mexico to sue for peace.

By early 1847 Polk's professed objectives had been achieved. Mexico's defense of California collapsed so suddenly that the only serious conflict stemmed from the rival and uncoordinated American onslaughts: Consul Larkin's

The Way They Go to California
The discovery of gold in California followed closely on the heels of the American conquest of this Mexican territory. Would-be prospectors were so eager to rush to California from all parts of the country that cartoonists made much sport of imaginary air vehicles supplementing the overcrowded ships bound for Central America or the Pacific.

efforts to mobilize the dissatisfied Spanish Californians; Frémont's leadership of the Anglo-American settlers; the American navy's capture of the port towns; and the arrival of an overland force, led by Colonel Stephen W. Kearny, which conquered New Mexico on the way to San Diego.

But the war was far from over. What the Mexicans lacked in leadership and modern armament, they made up for in national pride and determination. The United States could hardly claim an efficient military machine, but the army sparkled with talent. The roster of young officers read like a gallery of later Union and Confederate heroes: Lee, Grant, Sherman, Meade, McClellan, Beauregard, Stonewall Jackson, and even Jefferson Davis. For Europeans, whose memories of Napoleonic battles had receded into more than thirty years of romantic haze, the American military triumphs were stupendous. The Manchester *Guardian* wrote that the American victories were without parallel, "except in that of Alexander the Great through Persia, Hannibal from Spain to the gates of Rome, or Napoleon over the Alps into Italy." Instead of one Napoleon, America had them "by the dozen."

Treaty of Guadalupe Hidalgo The events that astonished even hostile Europeans began with General Scott's invasion of central Mexico in March 1847. In the United States Americans were becoming increasingly divided over the meaning of Manifest Destiny. As the American army pushed toward Mexico City, "our Destiny higher an' higher kep' mountin'," in the caustic words of the New England poet James Russell Lowell. By September, after winning a series of hotly contested battles, American troops had captured Mexico City and were resting in the halls of the Montezumas. The Mexicans still refused to surrender. Some southerners believed that slavery could be extended at least into the northern states of Mexico; some antislavery northerners believed that Mexico would be a force for freedom, and therefore they favored annexing the whole country. In general, however, the Democratic leaders—Polk, Buchanan, Lewis Cass, Stephen Douglas, Sam Houston, Jefferson Davis—demanded and expected to get no less than a third of the country south and west of the Rio Grande. They were therefore outraged when Nicholas Trist, America's negotiator whom Polk had angrily ordered to return from Mexico, proceeded to conclude the unauthorized Treaty of Guadalupe Hidalgo. Instead of capitalizing on America's conquests, Trist settled for the same terms that Slidell had been prepared to offer before the war: the United States was to pay Mexico $15 million and assume up to $3.25 million in Mexican debts to American citizens. In return the United States obtained California, New Mexico, and the Rio Grande boundary for Texas, a vast territory containing about 75,000 Spanish-speaking people who had no say about falling under United States rule. Polk would have liked to reject the treaty for being too favorable to Mexico, but he feared that further war and prolonged negotiations would split the already divided Democratic party in an election year. Alarmed by the growing antiwar and Free-Soil movement among northern Democrats, he reluctantly submitted

"The Occupation of the Capital of Mexico by the American Army," by P. S. Daval
Americans enter the historic square, or Zocalo, of Mexico City, March 1847.

PLUCKED:
OR,
THE MEXICAN EAGLE BEFORE THE WAR!   THE MEXICAN EAGLE AFTER THE WAR!

The Triumph of the American Eagle
This cartoon displays the sense of triumphant pride most Americans felt over Mexico's humiliating defeat in 1848.

the treaty to the Senate, which approved it in March 1848. Although the results of the war disappointed the more ardent United States expansionists, the conquests left a legacy of bitterness in Mexico, which continued to view its northern neighbor as a hypocritical aggressor.

Attempts to Acquire Cuba President Polk also had other cards up his sleeve. In 1848 the Democratic expansionists launched an intensive propaganda campaign to annex the Yucatán Peninsula, a rebellious province that had seceded from Mexico and whose white inhabitants were in danger of being exterminated by hostile Indians. Polk feared British intervention and realized that the American army in Mexico was virtually unemployed, and thus he invited Congress to act. But enthusiasm waned when news arrived that the Yucatán racial crisis had subsided.

Polk was actually far more interested in acquiring Cuba. Like the Yucatán Peninsula, Cuba guarded access to the Gulf of Mexico. Its traditional strategic importance would be increased by any future canal connecting the Gulf of Mexico with the Pacific—something that was already much discussed. Britain, being on the verge of war with Spain in 1848, might at any time gain control of Cuba. Many of Cuba's sugar growers, resenting Britain's increasing interference with their slave-labor system and fearing the continuing spread of emancipation in the West Indies, believed that annexation to the United States was their only guarantee of remaining a prosperous slave society.

The Polk administration knew, however, that the North would not approve the use of military force to acquire more than one-third of a million additional black slaves. Polk's only alternative was to try, with the utmost caution and secrecy, to persuade Spain that $100 million was a good price for a colony that was about to rebel or to be lost to Britain. But Spain greatly prized the only rich remnant of its once-great empire and contemptuously rejected the bungled overtures of Polk's minister. The prospects for annexing Cuba were further dashed when Lewis Cass, the Democratic presidential candidate who favored the purchase of Cuba and the annexation of Yucatán, was defeated in the fall of 1848 by the nonexpansionist Zachary Taylor.

Southern hopes for acquiring Cuba now turned to encouraging a Cuban revolution against Spain. Groups of Cuban emigrés, aided by American expansionists, planned a series of filibustering invasions to liberate the Cuban people. By 1850, however, the anxieties of Cuban planters had subsided and their desire to be taken over by the United States had faded. In 1851, in an episode that strangely anticipated the Bay of Pigs disaster of 1961, Cubans captured the entire expedition of Narcisco López, a southern hero, and executed him and fifty of his American followers.

Schemes for further expansion revived under the Democratic administration of Franklin Pierce (1853–57). Members of Pierce's cabinet gave encouragement to John A. Quitman, a filibuster from Mississippi who spent years waiting for the opportune moment to lead a gigantic invasion of Cuba. The invasion never took place, and in 1854 President Pierce warned that the government would prosecute Americans who violated the laws ensuring the nation's neutrality in foreign conflicts. Yet in 1856 Pierce's administration accorded diplomatic recognition to a regime established in Nicaragua by another American filibuster, William Walker. Walker, a native of Tennessee, had earlier led an invasion of Lower California (part of Mexico), where he had unsuccessfully proclaimed an independent republic. Having won acquittal for this violation of America's neutrality laws, Walker became involved in a revolution in Nicaragua. In 1856, aided by a small army of American volunteers, he emerged as president of the Central American nation.

Because Nicaragua occupied a strategic location as a transit point between the Atlantic and Pacific oceans, it became the site of intense Anglo-American rivalry. In the Clayton-Bulwer Treaty of 1850, both nations agreed not to take over any territory in Central America and to ensure that any future interoceanic canal would be unfortified and open to vessels of all countries. But the Clayton-Bulwer Treaty was extremely unpopular, especially in the South, and Walker appealed to American Anglophobia to win support for his dream of a Caribbean empire. He also reestablished slavery in Nicaragua but was soon driven out of the country by the armed forces of neighboring Central American nations that were supported by powerful American shipping interests.

Except for some ardent expansionists in the South, Americans were cooling toward proposals for further territorial acquisitions. In 1854 the Senate almost defeated a treaty that provided for the purchase from Mexico of a parcel of land south of the Gila River in what is now southern New Mexico and Arizona. The land was considered essential for building a railroad that would connect the southeastern states with southern California. But although James Gadsden, Pierce's negotiator with Mexico, had originally sought to obtain the northern part of five Mexican provinces and all of Lower California, the Senate insisted on cutting 9,000 square miles from the modest segment of desert that Mexico had been willing to sell.

In 1854 the expansionist intrigues of Pierce's administration culminated in the secret meetings of America's ministers to Spain, France, and Great Britain, who drafted a long memorandum to the State Department justifying the forcible seizure of Cuba if the island could not be purchased from Spain. Labeled the Ostend Manifesto, the secret memorandum was leaked to the American public at a moment of explosive sectional conflict. It confirmed many northerners' belief that the Slave Power would continue to expand unless checked by political might. One of the authors of the manifesto was James Buchanan, the minister to Britain. In 1856 Buchanan became the Democratic presidential candidate, and his platform openly called for annexing Cuba. By this time, however, the heated controversy over legalizing slavery in Kansas had diverted attention from further national expansion.

CHRONOLOGY

1819	Transcontinental (Adams-Onís) Treaty. Spain renounces claims to the Floridas and Pacific Northwest; United States renounces claims to Texas.	**1845**	Texas enters Union as slave state. Polk gives aggressive reformulation to Monroe Doctrine. John Slidell's unsuccessful mission to Mexico to negotiate purchase of New Mexico and California.
1823	President issues Monroe Doctrine.	**1846**	Beginning of Mexican War. General Zachary Taylor invades Mexico from the north. Treaty with Britain divides Oregon Territory along forty-ninth parallel.
1829	Mexico abolishes slavery.		
1836	Texas proclaims its independence from Mexico. Martin Van Buren elected president.		
1838	John Quincy Adams's filibuster defeats move to annex Texas.	**1847**	General Winfield Scott captures Vera Cruz and Mexico City.
1841	John Tyler becomes president on death of Harrison.	**1848**	Treaty of Guadalupe Hidalgo ends Mexican War and establishes Rio Grande as border. Secret attempts to purchase Cuba from Spain. Zachary Taylor elected president.
1842	Webster-Ashburton Treaty settles disputed U.S.–Canada boundary; provides for extradition of fugitives.		
1843	"Oregon Fever"; first overland caravans to Oregon.	**1854**	Ostend Manifesto favors U.S. purchase or annexation of Cuba. Railroads link New York City with the Mississippi River.
1844	Senate rejects Calhoun's Texas annexation treaty. James K. Polk elected president.	**1857**	Financial panic and depression.

SUGGESTED READINGS

Ray A. Billington and Martin Ridge, *Westward Expansion* (1982), covers every aspect of America's westward expansion and contains an encyclopedic bibliography. Albert K. Weinberg, *Manifest Destiny* (1935), is a fascinating study in intellectual history, but it should be supplemented by Edward M. Burns, *The American Idea of Mission: Concepts of National Purpose and Destiny* (1957). For American expansionism and Manifest Destiny, see Thomas R. Hietala, *Manifest Design: Anxious Aggrandizement in Late Jacksonian America* (1985), and Reginald Horsman, *Race and Manifest Destiny: The Origins of American Racial Anglo-Saxonism* (1981). In three outstanding revisionist studies, Frederick W. Merk reemphasizes the importance of slavery and the fear of British encroachments on the West: *Manifest Destiny and Mission in American History: A Reinterpretation* (1963); *The Monroe Doctrine and American Expansionism 1843–1849* (1966); and *Slavery and the Annexation of Texas* (1972). For a detailed treatment of western diplomatic history, see D. M. Fletcher, *The Diplomacy of Annexation: Texas, Oregon and the Mexican War* (1973).

The fullest history of the origins of the Monroe Doctrine is Dexter Perkins, *The Monroe Doctrine, 1823–1826* (1927). Ernest R. May, *The Making of the Monroe Doctrine* (1975), stresses the importance of domestic politics preceding the presidential election of 1824. For the European background, see E. H. Tatum, Jr., *The United States and Europe, 1815–1823* (1936), and C. C. Griffin, *The United States and the Disruption of the Spanish Empire* (1937). For a general introduction to American foreign policy, see Lloyd C. Gardner et al., *Creation of the American Empire* (1973); for a more traditional view, see Samuel F. Bemis, *A Diplomatic History of the United States* (1965). The standard work on Asia is A. Whitney Griswold, *The Far Eastern Policy of the United States* (1938).

On Texas two of the standard works are by William C. Binkley: *The Texas Revolution* (1952) and *The Expansionist Movement in Texas, 1836–1850* (1925). Much can still be learned from the older, nationalistic studies: J. H. Smith, *The Annexation of Texas* (1911), and E. C. Barker, *Mexico and Texas, 1821–1835* (1928). For a meticulous portrayal of the Mexican point of view, see Gene M. Brack, *Mexico Views Manifest Destiny, 1821–1846* (1976).

The best study of the American settlement of Oregon is Malcolm Clark, Jr., *Eden Seekers: The Settlement of Oregon, 1812–1862* (1981). Fredrick W. Merk has written several superb essays on the Anglo-American diplomacy regarding Oregon: *Albert Gallatin and the Oregon Problem* (1950), and *The Oregon Question: Essays in Anglo-American Diplomacy and Politics* (1967). For general histories of the Northwest, see Norman A. Graebner, *Empire on the Pacific* (1955); Oscar O. Winther, *The Great Northwest* (1947); and Earl Pomeroy, *The Pacific Slope: A History* (1965).

By far the best account of the overland emigration to the Far West is John D. Unruh, Jr., *The Plains Across: The Overland Emigrants and the Trans-Mississippi West, 1840–1860* (1979). For the experience of women and the division of sex roles, see John Mack Faragher, *Women and Men on the Overland Trail* (1979); Sandra L. Myres, *Westering Women and the Frontier Experience, 1800–1915* (1982); and Julie Roy Jeffrey, *Frontier Women: The Trans-Mississippi West, 1840–1860* (1979). Two outstanding studies of the earlier, midwestern frontier are John Mack Faragher, *Sugar Creek: Life on the Illinois Prairie* (1986), and Malcolm J. Rohrbough, *The Trans-Appalachian Frontier: Peoples, Societies, and Institutions, 1775–1850* (1978). The fascinating story of government exploration of the West is described with admirable care in William H. Goetzmann, *Army Exploration in the American West, 1803–1863* (1959). Gloria G. Cline, *Exploring the Great Basin* (1963), is also an invaluable study. For the all-important fur trade, see David J. Wishart, *The Fur Trade of the American West, 1817–1840* (1979), which can be supplemented by H. M. Chittenden, *The American Fur Trade of the Far West* (3 vols., 1935). Although sometimes scorned by professional historians, Bernard DeVoto's *Across the Wide Missouri* (1947), which deals with the Mountain Men and the fur trade, and DeVoto's *The Year of Decision, 1846* (1943), which considers the political, social, and cultural events surrounding America's war with Mexico, are exciting, readable, and basically accurate accounts of the early West.

J. H. Smith, *The War with Mexico* (2 vols., 1919), is still useful as a comprehensive source of information, but students should turn first to Robert W. Johannsen, *To the Halls of the Montezumas: The Mexican War in the American Imagination* (1985). The best recent account of the military campaigns is K. Jack Bauer, *The Mexican War, 1846–1848* (1974). Gene M. Brack, *Mexico Views Manifest Destiny* (1976), deserves special mention for its insight into the Mexican motives for war. For the conquest of California, see Neal Harlow, *California Conquered: The Annexation of a Mexican Province, 1846–1850* (1982). For an understanding of the Mexican provinces before American annexation, see David J. Weber, *The Mexican Frontier, 1821–1846:*

The American Southwest Under Mexico (1982). John H. Schroeder, *Mr. Polk's War: American Opposition and Dissent, 1846–1848* (1973), is an excellent study of antiwar sentiment. Much relevant information on these years of decision can also be found in Paul H. Bergeron, *The Presidency of James K. Polk* (1987), which presents a more moderate portrayal of Polk than does Charles G. Sellers's standard biography, *James K. Polk: Continentalist, 1843–1846,* vol. 2 (1966). See also William R. Brock, *Parties and Political Conscience: American Dilemmas, 1840–1850* (1979). For American involvement in Cuba and Central America, see William O. Scroggs, *Filibusters and Financiers: The Story of William Walker and His Associates* (1916), and Robert E. May, *The Southern Dream of a Caribbean Empire, 1854–1861* (1973).

6

Compromise and Conflict

❧

ON THE surface the two-party system resolved the dangerous sectional conflicts that had been unleashed by the annexation of Texas, the Mexican War, and the acquisition of a new continental empire. By the early 1850s cohesion and compromise seemed to have triumphed over division. Middle-class Americans were more prosperous than they ever had been before, and for the most part they were able to ignore or rationalize evidence of continuing injustice and exploitation. Public interest in further empire building faded, despite attempts by Democratic leaders to revive the people's enthusiasm. There was sufficient challenge, it seemed, in settling a continent, constructing more miles of railroad track in the 1850s than could be found in the rest of the world combined, and extending American commerce. In 1854, for example, Commodore Matthew Perry used diplomatic tact and a display of naval power to help break down the Japanese government's already crumbling resistance to Western trade and influence. In view of such global as well as domestic opportunities, political realists believed that the North did not desire to interfere with slavery in the South. In the eyes of moderates, there was no reason for the North to fear that slavery would expand beyond its "natural limits" in Missouri, Arkansas, and Texas.

There were hazards, however, in this triumph of moderation. The stormy passions that culminated in the Compromise of 1850 gave way to political apathy and disenchantment. Voters complained that Whigs and Democrats had the same self-serving lust for office, mouthed the same stale rhetoric on such stale issues as banks and tariffs, and were equally unresponsive to public needs and fears. For reasons that varied in each state and locality, significant numbers of voters abandoned their former party allegiance. One consequence of this broad realignment was the rapid disintegration of the Whigs, especially in the South. By 1855 the anti-Catholic Know-Nothing party had replaced the Whigs as the dominant alternative to the Democrats in the Northeast. In all sections of the country, the weakening of balanced national parties opened the way for new and more extreme appeals to resist the encroachments of some supposedly anti-republican "power."

The American fear of unchecked power and special privilege was deeply rooted in the colonial and Revolutionary past. The fear acquired new dimensions, however, as the restraints of local customs and traditions gave way to individual enterprise and unrestrained capitalism. For a time the party system had succeeded in channeling and moderating public alarm over the rise of various "powers," such as the Freemasons, the "Monster Bank," the "Money Power," Jackson's "monarchical" presidency, and the alleged British conspiracy to block American expansion. In each case, alarmist rhetoric was ultimately balanced by the political realities of a two-party system. By the mid-1850s, however, the national Whig party had collapsed and the controversy over slavery in the territories began to distract attention from anti-Catholic nativism. At this ominous juncture, the Americans' fear of unchecked power became grounded in the concrete conflict of interests between free and slave societies.

Like a magnetic field, black slavery polarized opposing clusters of values, interests, and aspirations. "Are you for Freedom, or are you for Slavery?" Senator Charles Sumner asked a crowd at Boston's Faneuil Hall: "Are you for God, or are you for the Devil?" Echoing the theme that there could be no peace between slavery and democracy, Theodore Parker, Boston's famous Unitarian minister, affirmed that "the idea which allows Slavery in South Carolina will establish it also in New England." Southerners believed that any withdrawal of federal sanction and protection for slavery would expose private property to the tyranny of a national majority, undermine the equal sovereignty of the states, and lead America in the direction of European "wage-slavery" and class warfare—to say nothing of race mixing and black revolt.

By the mid-1850s a growing number of northerners had become convinced that black slavery, by supporting "idle planters" and by associating work with servility, undermined the dignity of labor. As an alternative to the whips and chains of the South, the North offered an idealized vision of prosperity and progress without exploitation—a vision of industrious farmers and proud artisans, of schoolhouses, churches, town meetings, and self-made men. The vast territories of the West, unfenced and held in common by the American people, would thus become the critical testing ground for two competing versions of the American dream.

Free Soil and the Challenge of California

Once the United States had acquired the vast Mexican territories from Texas to California, national decisions had to be made. All the constitutional issues and the political and moral arguments of the Missouri crisis of 1819–21 were revived. Would the South be able to maintain its balance of power in the Senate? What was the precise nature of congressional power over territories and the creation of

Poster for a Free Soil Rally

new states? Would the government limit the future expansion of slavery? Would it adopt a policy of noninterference? Or would it perhaps openly sanction slavery by recognizing black slaves as a form of property entitled to federal protection in the western territories?

The Wilmot Proviso It was predictable that a move would be made in Congress to prohibit slavery in the territories acquired during the Mexican War; similar moves had been made since 1784 concerning the trans-Appalachian West, Mississippi, Louisiana, Arkansas, and Missouri. In 1846 the motion came from David Wilmot, a Pennsylvania Democrat who disavowed any sympathy for the southern slaves and who wished to exclude free blacks as well as slaves from the new western territories. The Wilmot Proviso, a proposed amendment to an appropriation bill, was extraordinarily significant because it was used to challenge what protesters called "Mr. Polk's War" and all that it meant. The legislatures of fourteen free states eventually endorsed the proviso's principle of barring slavery from any territories obtained from Mexico. The House of Representatives several times approved the measure, which antislavery members continued to offer, but enough northern senators ignored the instructions of their states to bring defeat in the Senate.

From 1847 to 1850 this sectional insistence that the territories ceded by Mexico remain "free soil" challenged Whig and Democratic party unity. "There can be no compromise between right and wrong," proclaimed Joshua R. Giddings, the antislavery Whig congressman from Ohio. Many southern Whigs denounced any proposal for excluding slavery from the territories as a direct violation of southern rights and of state equality. "The North is insolent and unyielding," declared Georgia Whig Alexander Stephens. "My southern blood...is up and...I am prepared to fight at all hazards and to the last extremity in vindication of our honor and our rights." The more extreme Calhounites tried to erode national party loyalties by uniting all southerners in defense of sectional rights and in opposition to any candidate who failed to oppose the Wilmot Proviso. In the North in the election of 1848, both Whigs and Democrats suffered losses to the new Free-Soil party, which endorsed the Wilmot Proviso and which nominated Martin Van Buren for president. So-called Conscience Whigs, centered in Massachusetts, refused to vote for Zachary Taylor, the former general and Louisiana slaveholder nominated by the Whigs. The Conscience Whigs claimed that moral protest against the further expansion of slavery should take precedence over the material and political advantages of a united Whig party. Free-Soil Democrats were led by the so-called New York Barnburners, politicians who had been angered when the Democrats rejected Van Buren in favor of Polk in 1844 and who then had been further alienated when Polk's administration had favored rival Democratic factions in distributing patronage.

But this upsurge of sectional politics proved to be temporary and quite unsuccessful in undermining the two-party system. Both the Whig and the Democratic parties evaded official commitment on the territorial issue and unashamedly made contradictory appeals to northern and southern voters. In the election of 1848, Van Buren received only 14 percent of the popular vote in the North and won no electoral votes for his Free-Soil party. Taylor carried even Massachusetts, where the Whig defections seemed most threatening; Whigs actually gained strength in the South. As a result of this defeat, Van Buren and most of his Free-Soil Democratic followers returned to the national Democratic party that now shared common interests in opposing a new Whig administration. The Conscience Whigs mostly returned to their uneasy alliance with the so-called Cotton Whigs, led by such powerful New England textile manufacturers as Abbott Lawrence and Nathan Appleton, who desired a continuation of their profitable trade relations with the cotton-producing South. And early in 1849 it became clear that the Calhounites had little hope of winning support for a new southern rights coalition. The nation's voters appeared to have subdued sectionalism's threat to federal union.

The survival of national parties did nothing, however, to resolve the territorial issue or to break the congressional deadlock over the Wilmot Proviso. Northern Democrats had favored either extending the Missouri Compromise line of 36°30′ to the Pacific or leaving the question of slavery to territorial legislatures without congressional interference. The latter alternative was known as popular sovereignty. President Taylor, on the other hand, tried to prevent further sectional confrontations by urging California and New Mexico to draft constitutions and to apply for immediate statehood. This strategy would have avoided congressional action either sanctioning or banning slavery. Both Taylor and his southern opponents recognized that the inhabitants of the Far West, if

California Gold Diggers

Gold mining was an arduous and usually unsuccessful enterprise that was both exhausting and disheartening to many of the migrants who streamed to California from Australia, Europe, and Latin America as well as from the eastern states. Nevertheless, there was always the hope of striking pay dirt and becoming rich almost overnight.

allowed to organize state governments, would almost certainly vote to exclude black slavery (and perhaps free blacks as well). These settlers, most of whom had lived in the intensely racist states of the Old Northwest, cared little about the fate of the slaves in the South, but they feared the competition of slave labor in a "land of promise" that was supposedly reserved for aspiring whites.

Suddenly antiblack feeling became acute in California. Gold was discovered in the American River in 1848, and the great gold rush of 1849 brought tens of thousands of settlers who resented the prolongation of ineffective military government and who clamored for instant statehood. It also brought a small number of southern masters and slaves—and of free black prospectors who, according to hostile whites, were "proverbially lucky." White miners considered it unfair to compete with slave labor, and they also considered it degrading "to swing a pick side by side with the Negro," whether free or slave. Fear and hatred of blacks, particularly in the mining regions, led the California constitutional convention of 1849 to copy the sections of the newly written Iowa constitution that prohibited slavery.

In Oregon, which was organized as a separate territory south of the Columbia River, the fusion of racism with antislavery was even more clear-cut. Although few blacks had arrived in the region by 1844, the provisional government followed the models of the Old Northwest and ordered the removal of both slaves and free blacks. The South succeeded in delaying Oregon's elevation to territorial status until 1848, and as late as 1857 there was a strong drive to legalize slavery in the Oregon Territory. After heated public debate, a referendum decisively rejected slavery but approved even more decisively the constitutional exclusion of free black settlers—a measure that Congress accepted as part of the state's constitution.

By 1849, however, southerners tended to interpret even these dubious forms of antislavery as abolitionism in disguise. Most southern leaders, whether Whig or Democrat, had moved from a defensive policy of censorship and gag rules to an aggressive hostility to any barrier, however theoretical, to the expansion and legitimation of slavery. They feared that enactment of the Wilmot Proviso would swing the full weight of the federal government against the institution of slavery, which it had always protected. By 1849 Free-Soil and antislavery congressmen had already linked the Wilmot Proviso with demands for abolishing slavery in the District of Columbia, which, like the territories, was subject to federal legislation. The new personal liberty laws of the northern states also raised the prospect that the North would become as secure a refuge for runaway slaves as British Canada, to which a small number of blacks had successfully escaped.

Indeed, for a growing number of southern diehards, the Northeast was by the late 1840s becoming a perfect replica of the British enemy. Britain, these southerners believed, had first exploited its own slave colonies, then ruined them under the influence of misguided humanitarianism, and finally used antislavery as a mask of righteousness in assuming commercial and ideological domination of the world. According to a typical proslavery editorial printed in a Democratic newspaper in 1860, the West Indian blacks freed by the British had "degenerated into a barbarism not much in advance of their race in Africa.... It is altogether useless to say that the negro has a right to liberty, when it can be conclusively demonstrated that he is physically unadapted for it.... The British experiment of emancipation... in the West Indies... proves it beyond a doubt." Furthermore, the Northeast, like England, was attracting millions of immigrant wage earners, was developing vast urban centers, and was gaining mastery over the mysterious sources of credit and investment capital. Unless Dixie made its stand, it would therefore share the fate of the exploited, debt-ridden, and ravaged West Indies. If the South were deprived of land and labor for expansion, its boundaries pushed back from the west and the Gulf of Mexico as well as from the north, it would then be subjected by a tyrannical government to slave emancipation and race mixing.

The Crisis of 1850

The Taylor administration faced a succession of problems that exposed irreconcilable divisions within the Whig party. Zachary Taylor was a recent convert to the Whig party (previously, he had never even voted); he had run for president as a military hero and as a man "above party." As president he aggravated the mistrust of the so-called Old Whigs when, seeking to broaden the administration's national support, he bypassed party faithfuls in distributing patronage. Taylor also seemed to betray traditional Whig principles when he tried to build a broad coalition that could compete with the Democrats, who were gaining enormous strength from the votes of recent immigrants.

The preceding administration, that of the Democrat Polk, had reestablished the Independent Treasury, reaffirming the Democrats' opposition to any alliance between government and banks.* It had also enacted the Walker Tariff, which had drastically reduced the duties the Whigs had established in 1842. To the dismay of Old Whigs, Taylor balked at proposals to repeal both these Democratic measures, and he advocated compromises that would avoid unnecessary conflict. Simultaneously, southern Whigs, who had thought they could trust a Louisiana planter, were shocked to discover that Taylor had no objection to admitting California as a free state. In fact Taylor even dumbfounded his powerful Georgia backer Robert Toombs by saying that if Congress saw fit to pass the Wilmot Proviso, "I will not veto it."

When the Thirty-first Congress convened in December 1849, there was a prolonged and ominous conflict over electing the Speaker of the House. It soon became clear that Taylor's program for immediately admitting California and New Mexico as states would receive no support from southern Whigs or even from such party chieftains as Clay, Webster, and Seward. Even one new free state would break the balance of fifteen free states and fifteen slave states represented in the Senate. Tensions were heightened by the knowledge that all northern legislatures, with one exception, had instructed their senators to insist on the Wilmot Proviso in any agreement concerning the territories. Also, a growing number of southern legislatures were appointing delegates to attend a convention at Nashville in June 1850 to consider potentially revolutionary measures for the defense of southern rights.

Clay's Resolutions
In January 1850 the aging Henry Clay temporarily recovered leadership of the Whig party by offering the Senate a series of compromise resolutions. An adept and skillful bargainer, Clay had been credited with saving the Union in 1820 and 1832, at the time of the Missouri and nullification crises, and he now sought a permanent solution to sectional strife. As an alternative to the Wilmot Proviso and to the popular southern plan that would extend the Missouri Compromise line to the Pacific, Clay favored admitting California as a free state, in accordance with the clear wishes of its settlers. He proposed that no restrictions on slavery be imposed in the rest of the vast territory that had been acquired from Mexico (New Mexico and Utah territories included most of present-day Colorado, Arizona, and Nevada). Clay also attempted to resolve the critical Texas issue. Texas claimed a

---

*For the Independent Treasury, see chapter 15, p. 508.

182

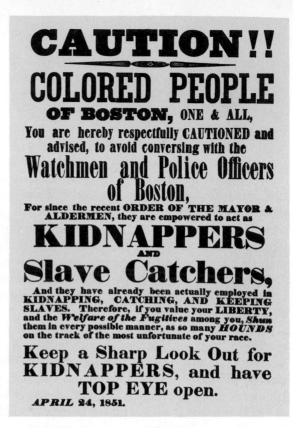

Countering the Fugitive Slave Law
This abolitionist broadside dramatizes the ways in which the Fugitive Slave Law impinged upon the lives of the people of Boston while also warning the black population about the danger of being kidnapped by conniving public officials and shipped off to the South as a slave.

western boundary that included more than half of the present state of New Mexico and parts of Oklahoma and Colorado. As a result there was an imminent danger of border conflict between the armed forces of Texas and the United States, a conflict that could easily escalate into civil war. Further, when Texas had become an American state it had lost its former customs revenue, which was a matter of considerable concern to the influential holders of Texas bonds. To resolve these problems, Clay proposed that the United States government assume the Texas debt—which promised windfall profits to Texas bondholders as compensation for Texas's acceptance of New Mexico's territorial claims.

In a gesture to northern feelings, Clay recommended that Congress prohibit professional slave trading in the District of Columbia, to rid the national capital of the moral eyesore of slave pens and public auctions. But he also urged that Congress ease southern fears of abolitionists' intentions by formally denying that it had authority to interfere with the interstate slave trade and by promising that slavery would never be abolished in the District of Columbia without the consent of its citizens, as well as the consent of neighboring Maryland. Finally, in this so-called Omnibus Bill, Clay proposed that Congress adopt a fugitive-slave law that would severely punish anyone who obstructed slaveholders' efforts to recover runaway slaves in any part of the United States.

The Compromise of 1850

The ensuing congressional struggle to achieve the so-called Compromise of 1850 took place on two distinct levels. On the loftier level the Senate became a public forum for some of the most famous and eloquent speeches in American history—speeches that clarified conflicting principles, conflicting political philosophies, and conflicting visions of America's heritage, mission, and destiny. Calhoun, so ill and so near death that he had to listen as a colleague read his farewell address to the nation, argued that a tyrannical northern majority had gradually excluded southerners from 1.25 million square miles of territory. No further compromises could save the South from a continuing loss of power or prevent the day when a hostile and increasingly centralized government would carry out the demands of the abolitionists. The Union, he declared, might be saved if the North agreed to open all the territories to slaveholders and to restore, by constitutional amendment, an equal and permanent balance of sectional power. Otherwise self-preservation would require the South to separate—and to fight if the North refused to accept secession in peace.

Daniel Webster, in his famous reply on March 7, 1850, insisted: "There can be no such thing as a peaceable secession." Recoiling in horror from the prospect of disunion and civil war, he pleaded for compromise and for a charitable spirit toward the South. He agreed with southern complaints against the abolitionists and supported Clay's demand for an effective fugitive-slave law. The territorial issue, he claimed, should be no cause for further discord. Convinced that slave labor could never be profitable in the western territories, Webster saw no need for a further legal exclusion that could only antagonize the South.

On March 11 the growing antislavery audience in the Senate found a spokesman in William H. Seward, the New York Whig leader who had helped engineer Taylor's candidacy but who now refused to support the president's plan. Seward, whom Webster described as "subtle and unscrupulous" and dedicated "to the one idea of making himself president," gave political force to the traditional abolitionist doctrine concerning the territories: "There is a higher law than the Constitution, which regulates our authority over the domain... the common heritage of mankind."

These and other great speeches raised momentous issues, but it is unlikely that they changed many votes. The second level of struggle involved political infighting that ranged from bribes and lobbying by speculators in Texas bonds to patient and tireless work by committees of experts faithful to American political procedures and to the technicalities of constitutional law. Apart from the moderating influence of powerful banking and business interests, which stood to gain by national unity, four circumstances contributed to the final congressional approval of the Compromise of 1850.

First, despite signs of an ominous sectional division of parties, Stephen Douglas rallied a core of Democrats, particularly from the Old Northwest and border states, who could counteract the combined pressures of southern and northern extremists. Second, Douglas's drive to win southern support for a

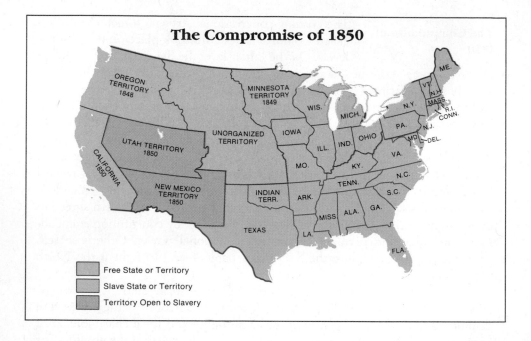

railroad connecting Chicago with the Gulf of Mexico (soon known as the Illinois Central Railroad) demonstrated the rewards that could be gained through sectional cooperation. Third, under Douglas's leadership the Senate wisely abandoned the Omnibus Bill that combined most of the compromise in one package. This move allowed both houses of Congress to form sectional alliances that were just barely strong enough to carry each measure—the North overcoming southern resistance to the admission of California as a free state and the abolition of the slave trade in the District of Columbia; the South, thanks to many northern abstentions, having its way in enacting the new Fugitive Slave Law. Finally, President Taylor, who had shown no sympathy for the compromise, died suddenly in July. Millard Fillmore, his successor, was close to Webster and Clay and threw the full weight of his administration behind the compromise. Fillmore also skillfully defused the explosive crisis over the Texas–New Mexico boundary. In September 1850 much of the nation sank back in relief, assuming that the adoption of Clay's and Douglas's proposals marked the end of serious sectional conflict.

Thus the Compromise of 1850 was made up of the following points: (1) the admission of California as a free state; (2) the organization of the rest of the Mexican cession into two territories, New Mexico and Utah, without a federal restriction on slavery; (3) the adjustment of the Texas–New Mexico boundary; (4) the award of $10 million to Texas as compensation for the land yielded to New Mexico; (5) the prohibition of the slave trade but not of slavery itself in the District of Columbia; and (6) a stringent fugitive-slave law. This complex con-

Blacks Resist the Fugitive Slave Law
When Edward Gorsuch and his son tried to recover four escaped slaves at Christiana,
Pennsylvania, in September 1851, they provoked a battle with a community of blacks who had
given shelter to the fugitives. The blacks killed Gorsuch and wounded his son. Some thirty
blacks and whites, including two Quakers who had refused to join a posse to round up the
blacks, were arrested and charged with treason against the United States. After a trial that
attracted national attention, the jury acquitted all of the defendants.

gressional agreement created an illusion of peace, but there was no real consensus
on any of the critical issues. In the District of Columbia, trading and selling of
slaves continued, although not as openly as before. Blacks, and particularly
Indians, continued to be held as slaves on the supposedly free soil of California.
The Fugitive Slave Law, which deprived accused blacks of a jury trial and of the
right to testify in their own defense, dramatized the agonizing consequences of
enforcing a national compromise for which the North had little taste.*

One of the northern responses to this law was the serial publication in 1851 of
Harriet Beecher Stowe's *Uncle Tom's Cabin,* a novel that soon reached millions in
book form and in stage presentations. Mrs. Stowe's popular classic, today often
underrated as a literary work, interpreted the moral and psychological evils of
slavery in terms that were perfectly attuned to the culture of northern evangelical
Protestantism, especially to its belief in the sanctity of the family. *Uncle Tom's
Cabin* vividly demonstrated the ability of slavery to destroy or corrupt the family
unit. And it encouraged every reader who sympathized with the fictional
fugitives, in their terrible ordeal of escape, to share the guilt of a compromise that
gave national sanction to slave catchers.

---

*For northern reactions to the Fugitive Slave Law, see chapter 14, p. 482.

Harriet Beecher Stowe (1811–96)
The daughter of Lyman Beecher, Harriet Beecher Stowe suddenly became not only the most famous member of an illustrious family, but also the world's most admired and hated woman. Bitterly attacked in the South, she was lionized in England and soon became an international literary celebrity.

Popular Sovereignty   It was on the territorial issue that the Compromise of 1850 seeded the worst storm clouds of the future. The compromise was deliberately ambiguous concerning the territories. Congress appeared to reaffirm its authority to prohibit slavery in the territories, for it delegated this authority to the legislatures of Utah and New Mexico, subject to the possible veto of a federally appointed governor or of Congress itself. To appease the South, however, Congress publicly expressed doubts about the constitutionality of this authority, which could be determined only by the Supreme Court. In effect Congress invited slaveholders to challenge the constitutionality of any restrictions that territorial governments might make on their property rights before the state governments had been established. Most southerners reluctantly accepted "popular sovereignty" because it at least left the doors open to slavery. Northern moderates—called "doughfaces" by their antislavery enemies—were convinced that popular sovereignty would ultimately guarantee free states but would avoid a congressional showdown that would lead to the South's secession.

To pragmatists like Daniel Webster and Stephen Douglas, it seemed inconceivable that national policy of any kind could reverse the dominant western pattern of free-labor settlement. Cultivating cotton was too profitable and the value of slaves too great to encourage risky experiments in the semiarid West. It is true that in 1852 Utah legally recognized slavery and that in 1857 New Mexico adopted a slave code. Yet neither territory acquired more than a handful of black slaves. Southerners, long accustomed to the security of slave patrols and local law enforcement agencies, were fearful of taking valuable human property into a region where courts might invoke the old Mexican law prohibiting slavery and where legislatures might at any time be swayed by the convictions of the free-soil and antiblack majority. Moderates like Douglas claimed that the Compromise of

1850 was a "final settlement," but in fact it narrowed the area of future acceptable compromise. The belief grew in the South that disunion would be the inevitable—and the only honorable response to any further northern threats.

Destabilizing the Two-Party System

Despite the occasional appearance of parties oriented to special issues, American political history has been dominated by a two-party system inclined toward compromise and addressed to a wide range of local and national interests. The more historians have learned about American political behavior, the more they have marveled over the unique events of the early and mid-1850s: the destabilization of the traditional party system, the sudden collapse of the Whig party, and the unlikely rise to power of a sectional third party, the Republicans. Imagine the surprise people would feel today if in the space of six years the Democrats or Republicans were to disappear and be replaced by an "extremist" regional party that actually succeeded in electing a president! The political transformation of the mid-1850s is all the more significant since it opened the way for the election of Abraham Lincoln, the secession of the southern states, and the Civil War.

Immigration and Nativism

It is important to recall that the Whig and Democratic parties both claimed to defend republican traditions against various kinds of privilege or threatening "powers," and also relied on state and local issues for their high voter turnouts. The period from 1844 to 1860 was characterized by vigorous economic growth that evaporated many of the concerns that had risen to the fore after the Panic of 1819 and the depression of 1837–43. Many voters grew bored with debates over banking, fiscal policy, tariffs, and internal improvements. What did shock many native-born Americans between 1845 and 1854 was the largest influx of immigrants, as a percentage of the nation's total population, in all American history. The nearly 3 million immigrants who arrived in those brief years equaled the total 1850 population of nine of the North's sixteen states! Although it is easy in retrospect to take pride in America's heritage as a nation of immigrants and a haven for the oppressed, one should not underestimate the physical disruption and revolutionary cultural impact produced by the disembarkation of armies of foreigners, many of them destitute, who differed in religion, customs, language, and ethnic values from most native-born Americans.

Because the immigrants, although usually of peasant origin, tended to congregate in the larger cities of New York, Massachusetts, Pennsylvania, and Ohio, nativists predictably blamed them for overcrowded tenements, the collapse of sanitary facilities, and an escalation of street crime and violence. The most explosive conflicts, however, arose from the fact that the great majority of the Irish and many of the German newcomers were Roman Catholics. Anti-Catholicism had been deeply embedded in colonial America, and the religious revivals of the 1820s and 1830s had cultivated the belief that the survival of republican government depended on the liberating and unifying force of Protestantism.

Protestant revivalists had repeatedly attacked any cohesive group, such as the Freemasons or the Mormon or Catholic churches, that supposedly put institutional loyalty above individual moral choice. Prominent northern clergymen, mostly Whigs, had saturated the country with lurid and often hysterical anti-Catholic propaganda. Their actions had contributed to mob violence and church burning, which culminated in a bloody Philadelphia riot in 1844. On one occasion, however, a group of nativists actually protected a Catholic church against a rival mob.

Fortunately, bigotry was partly counterbalanced by the political self-interest of the two-party system. Even a prejudiced politician understood that immigrants cast votes, at least after the five years' wait required for naturalized citizenship. While the Irish in particular flocked to the Democratic banner, Whig leaders like Governor William H. Seward of New York knew that their own political fortunes depended on capturing part of the immigrant and Catholic vote. Seward offended many of his fellow Whigs by advocating public support for Catholic schools. Until 1853 the need to attract at least some immigrant voters in closely contested elections kept nativism from acquiring a political focus.

Even by 1850, however, it was becoming clear that the hundreds of thousands of newcomers, with their divergent values and lifestyles, threatened the Whig dream of an ordered, morally progressive, and homogeneous society—what one nativist congressman referred to as "a unity of character and custom." And Catholic leaders, among them Archbishop John Hughes of New York, made no apologies for their own mobilization of political power or for their own vision of a Catholic America. As Hughes launched a counteroffensive against tax support for public schools, which he considered seedbeds of Protestant indoctrination, the nativists warned that immigrant voters slavishly obeyed the orders of their priests who, as agents of European despotism, sought to undermine America's republican institutions. The fact that the Catholic church had opposed the European revolutionary movements of 1848—and supported the subsequent restoration of repressive government in France, Austria-Hungary, and the Italian and German states—reinforced many Americans' fear of antirepublican subversion. Paradoxically, nativists concluded that America's very commitment to freedom of speech and representative institutions had made it that much easier for an authoritarian church to subvert those institutions: "[T]his Church," a prominent nativist wrote in 1856, "relying on the 'profligacy of our politicians,' has freely declared its intentions (being an alien), to substitute the mitre for our liberty cap, and blend the crozier with the stars and stripes! and to subvert 'the very Citadel of Republican strength in the free education of youth and the consequent independence of mind.'"

The "Hidden Depression" An economic crisis, which is only beginning to be understood by historians, greatly reinforced the popular appeal of nativism, especially to urban craftsmen, tradesmen, and petty merchants. Although the period 1848–55 has generally been interpreted as a time of prosperity, especially for farmers and planters, it brought acute distress to millions of northern manual workers. For nonfarm workers, who made up approximately one-fourth of the North's electorate, real wages—that is, wages adjusted for the cost of living—plummeted. Skilled workers of various kinds were replaced by casual day laborers; in the Midwest as well as Northeast, layoffs multiplied in the iron, construction, and lumber industries. This so-called hidden depression was partly the result of unprecedented immigration and a rapidly expanding labor force, which put downward pressure on wages and, because of the shortage of housing, upward pressure on rents. Simultaneously, food prices soared as American merchants exported grains and other foodstuffs to meet European demand.

While the disastrous hardships of native-born workers were the result of complex shifts in national and international markets, which also encouraged the massive westward flow of immigrant workers, it was easy to scapegoat the immigrants themselves as the source of all evil, as the corrupters of a once pure and prosperous America. Employers helped this process along by recruiting immigrant workers as strikebreakers. The early 1850s witnessed the rapid growth of trade unions and the outbreak of numerous strikes. Yet when faced with hungry mouths to feed, foreign-born workers were generally willing to take the place of strikers, at much lower pay. And by 1860 some 69 percent of New York City's labor force was foreign-born.

As early as the mid-1840s nativist workers in Philadelphia and New York City had begun organizing various secret fraternal orders to advance their own interests. Although hostile toward the temporizing and elite leadership of the Whig and Democratic parties, groups like the Order of United Americans were less concerned with politics than with providing mutual aid, insurance, and other kinds of assistance to native-born workers. Secrecy was in part a shield against the legal actions taken to prevent workers from unionizing or "conspiring" to present a united front to employers. Increasingly angered by the way politicians of both parties catered to the immigrant vote, the Order of United Americans mounted a drive in 1851 to defend New York's public schools against politicians who accepted the position of the Catholic church. The nativists also merged traditional working-class demands—such as an end to imprisonment for debt—with appeals for more police control of public drunkenness, prostitution, and rioting, all of which they associated with immigrants. As "the Know Nothing fever" reached "epidemic" proportions, as one Pennsylvanian reported, the nativists proclaimed that "Americans must rule America; and to this end native-born citizens should be selected for all State, Federal and municipal offices of government employment, in preference to all others."

The Election of 1852 The election of 1852 was the last "normal" election, preceding the disintegration of the two-party system. And the contest revealed the strains of trying to mitigate or conceal the nativist and sectional controversies. Despite the moderating efforts of most politicians, the "ethnocultural" issues raised by immigrants and nativists overlapped and competed for public attention with the sectional hostility engendered by the debates and decisions of 1850.

In 1852 the Whigs were still seriously divided over the Compromise of 1850. In deference to southern demands, the party's 1852 platform endorsed this essentially Democratic "final settlement" of the slavery issue. Southern Whigs, however, were infuriated by the party's refusal to renominate Fillmore, whom many northerners saw as a puppet of the Slave Power. Winfield Scott, the military hero whom the Whigs finally nominated for president, showed signs of becoming a Seward protégé, like Zachary Taylor. Because southerners no longer trusted northern Whigs as reliable allies in the defense of slavery, the party suffered a devastating defection of southern voters in the election of 1852. The Whig party was already beginning to die in the South. In the North, simultaneously, a distinctive Whig identity became blurred. The Whig platform was very similar to the Democratic platform, which led to widespread cynicism and apathy. Moreover, northern Whigs made clumsy and unsuccessful attempts to compete with the Democrats for the votes of immigrant Catholics. This strategy alienated the growing number of Whig nativists—as well as many native-born Democrats of Protestant background—who believed that the professional politicians' hunger for votes had betrayed America's heritage of republicanism, Protestantism, and independence from foreign influence, including that of the Catholic pope.

On a superficial level, the decisive victory in 1852 of Franklin Pierce (pronounced "Purse"), a bland northern Democrat from New Hampshire, could be interpreted as confirmation of a national desire for compromise and mediocrity. Pierce was the kind of president who appeared to agree with all factions and with the arguments of anyone who happened to have his ear. On a deeper level, however, the results of state and local elections in 1852 showed that voters felt that the existing parties were unresponsive to the people's needs. Anti-Catholic nativism suddenly became the way of asserting previously vague grievances. The Order of United Americans took over a small organization called the Order of the Star-Spangled Banner and enlarged it into an effective political machine. In the state elections of 1853 Whigs were challenged and badly damaged in various parts of the North by independent tickets that went by various names. Democrats and especially Whigs suffered from the militancy of the temperance movement, whose leaders, associating Catholic immigrants with an alcohol-loving culture, demanded state prohibition laws like the one enacted in Maine in 1851.

The Know-Nothing Upsurge

The remarkable upsurge of political nativism, manifested in 1854 by the Know-Nothing or American party, indicated a widespread popular hostility toward the traditional Democrats and Whigs. The name Know-Nothing came from the fact that party members, when asked by outsiders about the party's organization, were supposed to say they "knew nothing." The Order of the Star-Spangled Banner, which was the nucleus of the Know-Nothing party, remained an obscure secret society until the local spring elections of 1854, when entire tickets of secret Know-Nothing candidates were swept into office by write-in votes. Local digni-

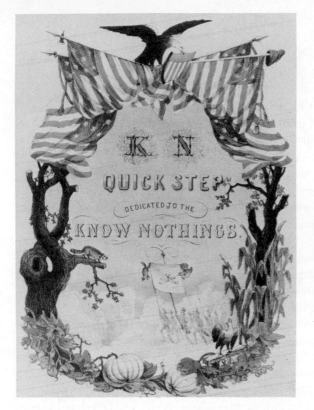

Singing with the Know-Nothings
The nativist Know-Nothings publicized their cause with popular songs such as this "Quick Step," which appealed to patriotism with an image of marching Minute Men preparing to fight alien forces.

taries of the traditional parties, often confident that they were unopposed, found themselves thrown out of office by men they had never heard of. In Massachusetts the Know-Nothings won 63 percent of the popular vote. In the congressional election of 1854 seventy or more Know-Nothings were sent to the House of Representatives, where for a time they held the balance of power.

By 1855 the Know-Nothings, now officially called the American party, had captured control of most of New England and had established roots in every state of the Union. They had become the dominant party opposing the Democrats in New York, Pennsylvania, California, and the border states. They had also made striking inroads in Virginia, North Carolina, Georgia, Kentucky, and Texas. Ironically, while northern Know-Nothings often merged nativism with antislavery, attacking the Catholic church as a proslavery institution, southern nativists pictured immigrants themselves as potential abolitionists and pointed out that immigrants, by avoiding the slaveholding states, were increasing the political power of the tyrannical North. In the South and in the border states, people also hoped that the Know-Nothing movement would distract attention from abolitionism and finally end the "needless" sectional disputes over slavery.

As we have seen, nativism had special appeal for artisans and manual workers who associated immigrants with a new and threatening America—an America of increasing urban poverty, of factories and railroads, and of rising prices and abruptly changing markets. The Know-Nothing movement began to subside after 1855, when the number of immigrants arriving in the country had declined and improved economic conditions had lessened the fear of competition for jobs. Nevertheless in two years the Know-Nothings had replaced the Whigs as a national political force. And in much of the Northeast the Know-Nothings had defeated or prevented the spread of the new Republican party, which had been founded in 1854 to prevent the extension of slavery into the western territories. In 1855 it appeared that the Know-Nothings, rather than the Republicans, would become the dominant national party challenging the Democrats.

In 1856 Millard Fillmore ran as the candidate of the combined American (Know-Nothing) and Whig parties and received nearly 44 percent of the popular vote in the slaveholding states. Nativism was weaker in the Old Northwest, where there was a greater tolerance of immigrants. Yet there the Republican party capitalized on a similar disenchantment with the old parties, often at the expense of the Democrats. Moreover, in 1854 the Democrats had suffered irretrievable losses throughout the North; in that section their representation in Congress had fallen from ninety-one seats to twenty-five. These sudden defections to the Know-Nothing and Republican parties meant that, henceforth, northern Democrats would have little leverage within their restructured national party, which became increasingly southern-dominated.

The Know-Nothing movement is significant because it helped to destroy the existing party system. Once in power, the Know-Nothings failed to restrict immigration or to lengthen the traditional five years' residence required for naturalized citizenship. Like other parties, the short-lived American party proved to be vulnerable to political ambition and compromise. But before being absorbed by the Republicans, the Know-Nothings brought about a massive shift in voter alignments, undermined national party discipline, and hastened the total disappearance of the Whigs. The importance of this ominous development cannot be exaggerated. When the discipline of the party system was swept away, sectional conflict could no longer be suppressed or safely contained.

The Confrontation over Kansas

From 1854 to 1856 northern politics displayed a dramatic shift in the perception of adversaries: the southern Slave Power, in its lawless attempts to seize the virgin lands of Kansas, replaced Roman Catholic immigrants as the primary threat to republican institutions and the promise of American life. Yet for a time it appeared that Know-Nothings had the upper hand over their Republican rivals. They were better organized and were the dominant power in most of the northern states. It was not until June 1855 that a national council of the Know-Nothings divided along sectional lines over the controversial Kansas-Nebraska Act of 1854. And it was the continuing storm over Kansas that enabled the Republicans to smother or absorb the nativists and become the major political force in the North.

The Kansas-Nebraska Act

Stephen Douglas, the northern Democratic leader, had long been interested in the organization and settlement of the Nebraska Territory—the vaguely defined region west and northwest of Missouri and Iowa. This immense portion of the Louisiana Purchase had been reserved for Indians, and there were few white settlers in the region. As a senator from Illinois, Douglas had a frank interest in the transcontinental railroad routes, which, he expected, would make Chicago the hub of mid-America. He was also an ardent patriot and expansionist, convinced that America should free the world from despotism. He thought the only serious obstacle to this mission was England, which, Douglas believed, had instigated the subversive activities of the American abolitionists, who in turn had provoked the militancy of the southern extremists. These southerners had then blocked the organization of the territories north of the Missouri Compromise line of 36°30'.

By 1854, when Douglas was chairman of the Senate Committee on Territories, he had concluded that the Missouri Compromise must be modified to overcome southern fears. This course of action, he thought, was the only way to open the Nebraska country to settlement, to bind the nation together with transcontinental railroads and telegraph, to fulfill the American mission of driving Great Britain from the continent, and to reunite the fractured Democratic party under his own leadership. He therefore drafted a bill that applied to Nebraska the popular sovereignty provision that Congress had already applied to Utah and New Mexico under the terms of the Compromise of 1850. This unexpected move destroyed nearly four years of relative sectional peace.

At first Douglas tried to play down the contradiction between popular sovereignty and the slavery prohibition of 1820, which applied to all the Louisiana Purchase territory north of the present state of Oklahoma. In 1850 Congress had left it to the courts to resolve any conflicts between popular sovereignty and the unrepealed Mexican law prohibiting slavery in Utah and New Mexico. Douglas hoped to bypass the Missouri Compromise in the same way. But William Seward and other antislavery Whigs plotted to make the Nebraska bill as objectionable as possible. At the same time, a powerful group of southern senators, the disciples of Calhoun, conspired to make repeal of the Missouri Compromise a test of Democratic party loyalty.

After a series of caucuses Douglas recognized that the Nebraska bill would not pass unless southerners were assured that *all* territories would be legally open to slaveholders. Aided by his southerner allies, Douglas helped to persuade President Pierce to throw administration support behind a new proposal that would declare the Missouri Compromise "inoperative and void" because it was "inconsistent with the principles of nonintervention by Congress with slavery in the States and Territories, as recognized by the legislation of 1850." This new bill would also provide for the organization of two separate territories, Kansas and Nebraska. By simply affirming that the rights of territorial governments were "subject only to the Constitution of the United States," Douglas's new bill evaded the critical question of whether popular sovereignty included the right to exclude

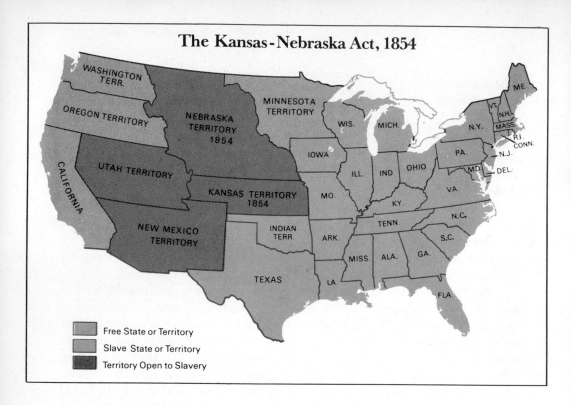

The Kansas-Nebraska Act, 1854

Free State or Territory
Slave State or Territory
Territory Open to Slavery

slavery before a state was constituted. In this form the Kansas-Nebraska bill of 1854 won almost unanimous support from southern Whigs and Democrats and from enough northern Democrats to pass both houses of Congress.

Southern leaders, no less than Stephen Douglas, were astonished by the outrage that exploded across the North. Opponents interpreted the bill as the violation of a "sacred compact," the Missouri Compromise, and as a shameless surrender to the Slave Power. The legislatures of five northern states passed resolutions condemning the Kansas-Nebraska Act. Thousands of northern workingmen, who had traditionally been hostile to abolitionists, condemned the attempt to repeal "the Missouri Compromise, in order to introduce Slavery into *our* free territory of Nebraska and Kansas." These rallies of laborers, who had once looked to the Democratic party for land reform, called the Kansas-Nebraska Act "a crime, a breach of plighted faith," and "a violation not only of our just rights but of the rights of man." When Douglas was traveling by train, he saw so many figures of himself hanging from trees and burned in effigy that he joked, "I could travel from Boston to Chicago by the light of my own effigy." According to the law's defenders, the cries of betrayal were sheer hypocrisy, for antislavery northerners themselves had rejected the principle of the Missouri Compromise by refusing to extend the compromise line to the Pacific coast. Yet the breach of faith, however interpreted, led to a rapid dissolution of other shared understandings and political restraints. For the first time, the two sections became sharply polarized, and antislavery and proslavery moderates began to perceive each other as more dangerous than the extremists.

Rise of the Republican Party What most alarmed proslavery moderates was the sudden appearance of a new and wholly sectional party, which they scornfully termed the "Black Republicans." In the eyes of its enemies, this party professed moderation but tried to use the goal of excluding slavery from the territories as a means of capturing control of the federal government. Even moderate southerners believed that, instead of being satisfied that California was free and that the number of free states was bound to increase, the self-styled Republicans (who had resurrected Jefferson's old party label) were intent on humiliating the South and on reducing the slaveholding states to colonial status.

The Republicans actually represented a coalition of various groups of Free-Soilers, antislavery Democrats, Conscience Whigs, and nativists who shared a common fear of Slave Power aggression, symbolized by the move to legitimize slavery in Kansas. While most Republican leaders disavowed any ties with the abolitionists, they popularized the abolitionist portrait of the South as a land in which the absolute personal power of slaveholders had nourished tyrannical behavior, arrogance, drunken indolence, sexual depravity, and a contempt for wholesome labor. Republican newspapers, such as Horace Greeley's influential New York *Tribune,* dwelled particularly on the economic liabilities of the slave system, stressing that it was the Slave Power and not immigrants who actually threatened the living standard of northern workers. Slave labor, according to Republican dogma, was not only inefficient and nonproductive, but degraded the very meaning of manual work. "Enslave a man," Greeley explained, "and you destroy his ambition, his enterprise, his capacity. In the constitution of human nature, the desire of bettering one's condition is the mainspring of effort." Slavery also diverted capital from investments that would benefit the entire nation; it stunted the growth of southern markets, to say nothing of cities and internal improvements. The evils of slavery therefore reached into the pocketbook of every northerner. To allow the westward expansion of such a cancerous system would destroy the hopes and values on which America had been built.

By the mid-1850s southerners were keenly aware of the growing contrast between their own rural economy and the economy of the urbanizing Northeast. The great cotton boom of the 1850s seemed to prove that even unparalleled southern prosperity could not narrow the gap in wealth. Picturing themselves as the nation's true producers of wealth, slaveholders blamed northern middlemen—epitomized by Wall Street bankers and merchants—for siphoning off their just rewards. The new Republican party represented the final and fatal spearhead of a conspiracy that allied abolitionists, renegade Democrats, and the remnants of powerful Whig combines, such as the Seward and Weed machine of New York. The earlier Liberty and Free-Soil parties had never had a chance of success. But in 1856 the Republicans, hardly two years after their appearance, carried eleven of the sixteen free states. Colonel John C. Frémont, the Republican presidential candidate, amassed an astonishing popular vote and would have defeated James Buchanan, the Democratic candidate, if he had carried Pennsylvania and Illinois.

The Crisis over Kansas

Even for antislavery moderates, the events in Kansas following passage of the Kansas-Nebraska Act seemed to prove that compromise had only encouraged proslavery conspirators to take over the western territories. In 1854 and 1855 some 1,700 proslavery Missourians had crossed the Kansas border in order to cast fraudulent votes, intimidate election judges, and ensure that "popular sovereignty" would exclude any fair debate on the desirability of slavery. The Republicans believed that unless drastic countermeasures were taken, America's free white workers would be deprived of the land and opportunity that was their birthright. By failing to provide definite legal measures for excluding slavery from the territories, Congress had guaranteed that the issue would be decided by numerical and physical force.

The crisis over Kansas was actually the result of complex rivalries and aspirations. The government opened the territory to settlement before Indian treaties had been ratified and before Indian tribes—many of them recently moved to Kansas from the East—had been dispossessed and pushed onto reservations. In 1854 thousands of white settlers began the scramble for Kansas land, searching for the best town sites and the most likely railroad routes of the future. Even without the slavery issue Kansas would have been the scene of a speculative mania and a shameless defrauding of the Indians.

But the passions that were generated by slavery swept aside the last fragile restraints, including the frontier's customary rules against jumping (disregarding) prior land claims. According to Missouri's fiery ex-senator David R. Atchison, a free Kansas would inevitably lead to the end of slavery in Missouri: "We are playing for a mighty stake; if we win we carry slavery to the Pacific Ocean; if we fail we lose Missouri, Arkansas, and Texas and all the territories; the game must be played boldly." Atchison thus helped to organize bands of so-called Border Ruffians to harass settlers from the free states. On the opposite side, opponents of slavery organized a New England Emigrant Aid Company with the purpose of colonizing Kansas with free-state settlers. Although Stephen Douglas referred to the Emigrant Aid Society as "that vast moneyed corporation," the movement was in fact poorly financed, and it succeeded in transporting barely 1,000 settlers to Kansas. But the movement's sensational promotion fed the fantasies of Missourians and southerners that eastern capitalists were recruiting armies of abolitionists and equipping them with Sharps rifles. "We will before six months rolls round," promised Atchison, "have the Devil to play in Kansas and this State [Missouri], we are organizing to meet their organization, we will be compelled to shoot, burn & hang, but the thing will soon be over. We intend to 'Mormanise' the abolitionists."

The acts of terrorism reached a climax in May 1856, both in Kansas and on the floor of the United States Senate. Antislavery newspapers declared that a civil war had actually begun in Kansas when a large proslavery force sacked the free-state town of Lawrence. "The War Actually Begun," ran a headline in the New York *Tribune:* "Triumph of the Border Ruffians—Lawrence in Ruins—Several

"Border Ruffians" Heading for Kansas
A group of armed proslavery Missourians on their way to cast ballots in Kansas.

Persons Slaughtered—Freedom Bloodily Subdued." Although free-state migrants greatly outnumbered the settlers from Missouri and other slave states, the federal government sanctioned only the proslavery government that had been elected by fraud. On May 21 a federal marshal led a large body of armed men into Lawrence for the purpose of arresting members of the antislavery government who had been charged with high treason. After the arrests had peacefully been made and the marshal had disbanded his posse, a zealous sheriff took unauthorized command of the group, which proceeded to bombard and burn the hotel that sheltered the Emigrant Aid Society, destroy the presses of two antislavery newspapers, and destroy other buildings in the town.

The revenge for such proslavery outrages was even more savage. Even fervid southern alarmists had not imagined anything as brutal as John Brown's retaliatory massacre at Pottawatomie Creek. Brown, a fanatical ne'er-do-well with an abolitionist background and abolitionist connections, thought of himself as an agent of God's vengeance. He led four of his sons and two followers in a night attack on an unprotected settlement, brutally executing five men and boys who were vaguely associated with the proslavery party.

Even in the nation's capitol, all pretense of civility collapsed. Speakers became inflamed, personal, malicious, even before news arrived of the proslavery attack on Lawrence. Senator Charles Sumner of Massachusetts, after denouncing

Violence in the United States Senate
Note that in this depiction of Preston Brooks attacking Senator Charles Sumner on the Senate floor, some southern senators are laughing or protecting Brooks from interference after Sumner has fallen away from his desk.

"the crime against Kansas" and "the rape of a virgin territory, compelling it to the hateful embrace of slavery," delivered studied insults to the elderly Andrew Butler, a senator from South Carolina. On the Senate floor Butler's cousin, Preston Brooks, a young congressman from South Carolina, later savagely attacked the seated Sumner with a cane, leaving him unconscious, bleeding profusely, and seriously injured. This triumph of "Bully" Brooks won applause from much of the South—indeed, Brooks was deluged with souvenir canes and invited to celebratory dinners. For many northerners, Sumner's Senate seat, which remained empty for more than three years during his prolonged recovery, was a silent warning that southerners could not be trusted to respect any codes, agreements, or sets of rules. Nothing could have been more favorable for the Republican party. "The outrage upon Sumner & the occurrences in Kansas," Abraham Lincoln wrote to Senator Lyman Trumbull, "have helped us vastly."

"Occurrences in Kansas" continued to aid Republican aspirations in the North. By 1857 there could be no doubt that the overwhelming majority of Kansas settlers opposed admitting the territory as a slave state. Like the white settlers in California and Oregon, they wanted to exclude free blacks along with slaves. For most Kansans these were minor matters compared to other issues, among them squatter rights, rival railroad routes, the disposal of Indian lands, and the desirability of free homesteads. What made slavery an explosive question in Kansas—and what made Kansas a detonating fuse for the nation—was the federal government's effort to bypass the people's will.

The Pierce and Buchanan administrations made a series of miscalculations. In the first tumultuous stage of settlement, as we have seen, the Pierce administration had legally recognized a proslavery territorial legislature established by wholesale fraud. Many moderates hoped that the flagrant acts of this provisional legislature—such as making it a felony to question the right to hold slaves in Kansas—would soon be repealed by a more representative body. But the free-state settlers chose to boycott the elections that the "legal" proslavery government authorized and to establish their own extralegal government and constitution.

The Lecompton Constitution
In 1857 the Buchanan administration was thus committed to support the outcome of an official election of delegates to a constitutional convention in Lecompton, Kansas, in preparation for Kansas statehood, even though only one eligible voter in twelve had gone to the polls. By then southerners had become convinced that the security of the slave system hinged on making Kansas a slave state. Buchanan had become equally convinced that the survival of the Democratic party hinged on appeasing the South—in 1856, 119 of his 174 electoral votes had come from slave states. In Kansas there were no moderating influences on the proslavery convention that drafted the so-called Lecompton constitution. In Washington the declining power of the northern Democrats gave a similarly unrestrained hand to the southern Democrats who dominated Buchanan's administration.

Stephen Douglas considered the vote in Kansas on the proslavery Lecompton constitution a total subversion of popular sovereignty. Instead of being allowed to accept or reject the constitution as a whole, voters were asked only to approve the article guaranteeing for the future the right of slave property. If the article were rejected, the Lecompton constitution would still protect the legal status of the slaves already in the territory. Although the free-state majority again protested by abstaining from voting, Buchanan used the powers of his office to pressure Congress into admitting Kansas as a slave state. This policy caused a bitter break with Douglas, who denounced Buchanan's attempt to "force this constitution down the throats of the people of Kansas, in opposition to their wishes." In 1858, as in 1854, Congress became the scene of a violent sectional struggle. But this time Douglas led the antiadministration forces. Buchanan stood firm, sacrificing much of his remaining Democratic support in the North. In the end, in 1858, the Buchanan administration suffered a crushing defeat when advocates of Kansas's admission as a free state forced a popular vote in Kansas on the *whole* of the Lecompton constitution. The territory's electorate rejected the constitution by a vote of nearly 10 to 1, although at the cost of indefinitely postponing statehood. (Kansas ultimately became a free state in 1861.)

Dred Scott and the Lincoln-Douglas Debates

By the stormy 1850s the largest Protestant churches had divided along sectional lines; the Whig party had collapsed. The Democratic party had survived, but the Lecompton struggle helped to split it fatally. Although the Democratic party had given the South disproportionate access to national power, this access depended on winning the support of northern allies. As the number of such allies began to dwindle, they were partly replaced by southern Whigs. Thus as the Democratic party became more southern in character, there were fewer restraints on attempts to test the party loyalty of northern Democrats and to adopt an openly proslavery program. The Lecompton constitution was actually the second such critical test imposed on northern Democrats. The first test was the *Dred Scott* decision.

The *Dred Scott* Decision

The southerners who dominated the Supreme Court decided to use the *Dred Scott* case as a way to resolve critical issues that Congress had long evaded. From the time that the Court had received the case, late in 1854, to the Court's long-delayed decision in 1857, the primary issue was whether Congress had the constitutional right to prohibit slavery in any territory or to delegate such a right to territorial governments, as implied by Stephen Douglas's formula of "popular sovereignty." In the recently disputed territories of New Mexico, Utah, and Kansas, no judicial cases involving the exclusion of slavery had yet arisen.

There had been many previous suits for freedom by slaves who had lived with their masters as temporary residents of free states. Even southern courts had sometimes granted freedom to such slaves, but the decisions had depended on complex technical issues that mostly involved state law. What distinguished *Dred Scott,* a Missouri slave who sued the state for his freedom, was that he and his master, an army surgeon, had lived together for several years not only in the free state of Illinois, but also in a part of the Wisconsin Territory where slavery had been federally prohibited by the Missouri Compromise. Despite this clear violation of federal law, Scott's initial trials in Missouri courts were confined to narrower issues.

In 1854 technical complications allowed Scott's lawyers to transfer his suit for freedom to the United States Circuit Court for the District of Missouri. This first federal trial raised a preliminary question that courts had never resolved and that affected the enforcement of the Fugitive Slave Law of 1850. Were any black persons citizens to the extent of being qualified by the Constitution to bring suit in a federal court? After years of debate and postponement in the United States Supreme Court, this jurisdictional question enabled Chief Justice Roger Taney (pronounced "Tawney") to link Scott's individual claim with momentous constitutional issues. For if blacks were not citizens entitled to constitutional rights and privileges, Dred Scott would be subject only to the laws of Missouri, and blacks seized under the Fugitive Slave Law of 1850 would have no recourse to federal courts. Moreover, the Dred Scott case involved a second question of enormous significance. The Court had to decide whether Congress had exceeded its powers in 1820 when it had outlawed slavery in the Louisiana Purchase north of 36°30'. If so, Dred Scott was still a slave and therefore could not bring suit in federal court.

By the end of 1856 the *Dred Scott* case had received widespread national publicity, with newspapers summarizing the opposing arguments that were delivered before the Court. Although informed observers anxiously awaited a verdict that might have explosive political consequences, they generally expected the Court to deny its jurisdiction on narrow technical grounds, thus confirming the judgment of lower courts that Scott was still a slave. When the decision was finally announced, in 1857, seven of the justices rejected Scott's claim to freedom, but all nine wrote separate opinions. There is still controversy over what parts of the "Opinion of the Court," written by Chief Justice Taney, represented the opinion of a majority of the justices.

Taney's opinion stated three sweeping conclusions. First, Taney held that at the time the Constitution of the United States had been adopted, blacks had "for more than a century been regarded as beings of an inferior order . . . so far inferior that they had no rights which the white man was bound to respect; and that the negro might justly and lawfully be reduced to slavery for his benefit." Taney further contended that neither the Declaration of Independence nor the Constitution had been intended to apply to blacks—whether slave or free. Even if free blacks in certain states had later been granted citizenship, Taney said, they were not citizens "within the meaning of the Constitution of the United States." They were not entitled to the rights and privileges of a citizen in any other state, nor could they sue in a federal court.

After thus denying the Supreme Court's jurisdiction over Dred Scott, the second major conclusion of Taney's decision dealt with the substantive issues. As for Scott's residence in Illinois, the Court had already recognized the principle that the status of a slave taken to a free state should be determined by the laws of the slave state to which he had returned. On Scott's residence in the federal territory north of 36°30′, Taney ruled that the Missouri Compromise had been unconstitutional. Congress, he declared, had no more power to take away a citizen's property in a federal territory than it did in a state.

Finally, having argued that slaves could not be differentiated from other forms of property protected by the Fifth Amendment, Taney stated his third major conclusion. Congress, he ruled, could not give a territorial government powers that exceeded those of the federal government: "It could confer no power on any local Government, established by its authority, to violate the provisions of the Constitution." This judgment struck directly at Douglas's interpretation of popular sovereignty, and it upheld the extreme southern view that the people of a territory could not legally discriminate against slave property until they acquired the sovereignty of statehood.

Reaction to the Decision

Both the South and President Buchanan were jubilant. Despite vigorous dissenting opinions from justices John McLean and Benjamin R. Curtis, the highest court in the land had ruled that excluding slavery from the territories—the goal that had brought the Republican party into existence—was unconstitutional. Republican newspapers, among them the New York *Tribune,* scornfully replied that the decision was "entitled to just as much moral weight as would be the judgment of a majority of those congregated in any Washington bar-room." Stephen Douglas, the leading contender for the Democratic presidential nomination in 1860, remained silent for many weeks. He wholly agreed with the denial of black citizenship and took credit for the congressional repeal of the Missouri

Compromise. Yet his relations with Buchanan and the South were already strained, and he knew that his future career hinged on finding a way to reconcile the southern version of limited popular sovereignty, embodied in the *Dred Scott* decision, with his own constituents' demand for genuine self-determination.

Douglas finally presented his response to the *Dred Scott* decision in an important speech at the Illinois statehouse in May 1857. He argued that the constitutional right to take slaves into a territory was a worthless right unless it was sustained, protected, and enforced by "police regulations and local legislation." By contrasting an empty legal right with the necessary public support to enforce such a right, Douglas denied any meaningful contradiction between the *Dred Scott* decision and his own principle of popular sovereignty.

Two weeks later Abraham Lincoln gave his reply to Douglas from the same forum. Terming the *Dred Scott* decision erroneous, Lincoln reminded his audience that the Supreme Court had frequently reversed its own decisions, and he promised that "we shall do what we can to have it to over-rule this."

Elected to Congress as a Whig in 1846, Lincoln had suffered politically from his opposition to the Mexican War. But since 1854, when he had attacked the Kansas-Nebraska Act, he had been making a new career by pursuing Douglas. Lincoln was a self-educated Kentuckian, shaped by the Indiana and Illinois frontier. In moral and cultural outlook, however, he was not far from the stereotyped New Englander. He abstained from alcohol, revered the idea of self-improvement, dreamed of America's technological and moral progress, and condemned slavery as a moral and political evil. He told a Chicago audience in 1858, "I have always hated slavery I think as much as any Abolitionist. . . . I have always hated it, but I have always been quiet about it until this new era of the introduction of the Nebraska Bill began. I always believed that everybody was against it, and that it was in course of ultimate extinction."

The Kansas-Nebraska Act taught Lincoln that men like Douglas did not care whether slavery was "voted *down* or voted *up.*" It also allowed him to exercise his magnificent talents as a debater and stump speaker—talents that had already distinguished him as a frontier lawyer, a state legislator, and an attorney and lobbyist for the Illinois Central Railroad and other corporations. Lincoln's humor, his homespun sayings, and his unaffected self-assurance all diverted attention from his extraordinary ability to grasp the central point of a controversy and to compress an argument into its clearest and most striking form. In 1856, after a period of watchful waiting, Lincoln played an important part in the belated organization of the Illinois Republican party. Two years later the Republican state convention unanimously nominated him to run for Douglas's Senate seat.

The Lincoln-Douglas contest was unprecedented in both form and substance. At the time senators were elected by state legislatures,* and no party

---

*Only after 1913, with the adoption of the Seventeenth Amendment, did the direct popular election of senators begin.

convention had ever nominated a candidate. In an acceptance speech on June 16, 1858, Lincoln concisely and eloquently stated the arguments he would present directly to the people, appealing for a Republican legislature that would then be committed to elect him to the Senate. Since Douglas had unexpectedly rejected the proslavery Lecompton constitution and had joined the Republicans in fighting it, Lincoln needed to persuade the electorate that Douglas's own crusade for popular sovereignty had rekindled the agitation over slavery and led directly to the *Dred Scott* decision and the Lecompton constitution. According to Lincoln, Douglas's moral indifference to slavery disqualified him as a leader who could stand firm against the Slave Power. For Lincoln was wholly convinced that the conflict over slavery would continue until a crisis had been reached and passed. As he said in his famous "House Divided" speech of 1858:

> "A house divided against itself cannot stand."
> I believe this government cannot endure, permanently half *slave* and half *free.*
> I do not expect the Union to be *dissolved*—I do not expect the house to *fall*—but I *do* expect it will cease to be divided.
> It will become *all* one thing, or *all* the other.
> Either the *opponents* of slavery, will arrest the further spread of it, and place it where the public mind shall rest in the belief that it is in course of ultimate extinction; or its *advocates* will push it forward, till it shall become alike lawful in *all* the States, *old* as well as *new—North* as well as *South.*
> Have we no *tendency* to the latter condition?

The "House Divided" speech signified a turning point in American political history. Lincoln stated that expediency and a moral neutrality toward slavery had undermined the Founders' expectation that slavery was "in course of ultimate extinction." If the North continued to make compromises and failed to defend a boundary of clear principle, the South was certain to dictate "a second Dred Scott decision," depriving every state of the power to discriminate against slave property. In Lincoln's view, Douglas's Kansas-Nebraska Act had been part of a master plan or conspiracy, which Lincoln compared to "a piece of *machinery*" that had been designed to legalize slavery, step by step, throughout the United States. In asserting that "the people were to be left 'perfectly free' subject only to the Constitution, Douglas had provided "an exactly fitted *niche,* for the Dred Scott decision to afterwards come in, and declare the perfect freedom of the people, to be just no freedom at all."

Lincoln was not an abolitionist. He was convinced that prohibiting the further spread of slavery would be sufficient to condemn it to "ultimate extinction," a belief shared by many southern leaders. Yet he insisted on a public policy aimed at that goal—a public policy similar to that of Great Britain in the 1820s or, in Lincoln's eyes, to that of the Founders. For Lincoln, rejecting popular sovereignty was the same as rejecting the moral indifference exemplified by Douglas; and this was the first step toward national redemption.

A Lincoln-Douglas Debate
As Lincoln stands and gestures before an Illinois crowd, Douglas sits quietly to the left of Lincoln, next to his water glass.

The Lincoln-Douglas Debates

Douglas seemed to be the nation's most likely choice for president in 1860. His struggle with Lincoln for reelection to the Senate in 1858 therefore commanded national attention. Making full use of newly constructed railroads, the two candidates traveled nearly 10,000 miles in four months. They crisscrossed Illinois, their tireless voices intermingling with the sounds of bands, parades, fireworks, cannons, and cheering crowds. Each community tried to outdo its rivals in pageantry and in winning the greatest turnout from the countryside. Lincoln and Douglas agreed to participate in seven face-to-face debates, which are rightly regarded as classics in the history of campaign oratory. Douglas tried to make the most of his experience as a seasoned national leader (at forty-five he was four years younger than Lincoln) and to portray his opponent as a dangerous radical. According to Douglas, Lincoln's "House Divided" speech showed a determination to impose the moral judgments of one section on the other. Lincoln's doctrines threatened to destroy the Union and to extinguish the world's last hope for freedom. Douglas also exploited his listeners' racial prejudice, drawing laughter from his sarcastic refusal to question "Mr. Lincoln's conscientious belief that the negro was made his equal, and hence his brother."

Lincoln searched for ways to counteract the image of a revolutionary. Always insisting on the moral and political wrong of slavery, he repeatedly acknowledged that the federal government could not interfere with slavery in the existing states. He opposed repeal of the Fugitive Slave Law. He wholly rejected the idea of "perfect social and political equality with the negro." He did maintain, however, that blacks were as much entitled as whites to "all the natural rights enumerated

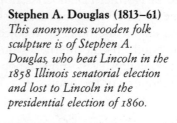

Stephen A. Douglas (1813–61)
*This anonymous wooden folk
sculpture is of Stephen A.
Douglas, who beat Lincoln in the
1858 Illinois senatorial election
and lost to Lincoln in the
presidential election of 1860.*

in the Declaration of Independence, the right to life, liberty, and the pursuit of happiness." If the black was "perhaps" not equal in moral or intellectual qualities, "in the right to eat the bread, without leave of anybody else, which his own hand earns, *he is my equal and the equal of judge Douglas, and the equal of every living man.* [Great applause.]"

The election in Illinois was extremely close. The Republicans did not win enough seats in the legislature to send Lincoln to the Senate, but the campaign immediately elevated him to national prominence. Lincoln had expressed and defended a Republican antislavery ideology that combined fixed purpose with a respect for constitutional restraints. Lincoln had also magnified the gap that separated the Republicans from Douglas and other anti-Lecompton Democrats. He had further isolated Douglas from proslavery southern Democrats who were already embittered by Douglas's "treachery" with regard to the Lecompton constitution. They were then outraged by Douglas's response to Lincoln in the debate at Freeport, Illinois, where Douglas had maintained that regardless of what the Supreme Court might decide about the constitutionality of slavery in a territory, the people had the "lawful means to introduce it or exclude it" as they pleased. Repeating his familiar point that slavery could not exist "a day or an hour

anywhere" unless it was supported by local police regulations, Douglas emphasized that the "unfriendly legislation" of a territorial government could effectively prevent slavery from being introduced. As Lincoln quipped, this was to say,
"A thing may be lawfully driven from a place where it has a lawful right to stay."

In 1859 the breach between Douglas and the South could no longer be
contained. The people of Kansas ratified a new constitution prohibiting slavery,
thereby giving bite to Douglas's so-called Freeport Doctrine. In the Senate, where
Douglas had been ousted from his chairmanship of the Committee on Territories,
he led the fight against the southern demand for a federal slave code protecting
slave property in all the territories. During a tour of the South, Douglas became
alarmed by the growing movement, led by young proslavery "fire-eaters," to
revive and legalize the African slave trade. Looking ahead to the Democratic
convention of 1860, Douglas issued what amounted to an ultimatum about the
party platform. Northern Democrats, he insisted, would not allow the party to be
used as a means for reviving the African slave trade, securing a federal slave code,
or pursuing any of the other new objectives of southern extremists. Douglas
warned the South that northerners would not retreat from defending genuine
popular sovereignty, even though popular sovereignty was clearly running
against the interests of the South.

The Ultimate Failure of Compromise

By 1860 a multitude of previously separate fears, aspirations, and factional
interests had become polarized into opposing visions of America's heritage and
destiny. Traditional systems of trust and reciprocity had collapsed.

John Brown's Raid   John Brown, who had warred against slavery in Kansas,
was a key symbol in this polarization. Since 1857 Brown
had been held in high esteem by the most eminent New England reformers and
literary figures. Backed financially by a secret group of abolitionists, Brown also
cultivated close ties with free black communities in the North. On the night of
October 16, 1859, he and some twenty heavily armed white and black followers
seized part of the federal arsenal at Harpers Ferry, Virginia (now West Virginia).
Brown hoped to begin the destruction of slavery by igniting a slave revolt and
creating in the South a free-soil refuge for fugitives. After resisting federal troops
for two days, Brown surrendered; he was tried for conspiracy, treason, and
murder, and was hanged.

During his trial Brown claimed to have acted under the "higher law" of the
New Testament. He insisted that "if I had done what I have for the white men, or
the rich, no man would have blamed me." For Brown the higher law was not a
philosophical abstraction but a moral command to shed blood and die in the
cause of freedom. In the eyes of armchair reformers and intellectuals, Brown's
courage to act on his principles made him not only a revered martyr but also a
symbol of all that America lacked. Democratic editors and politicians, however,

John Brown (1800–59)
Leader of the Pottawatomie massacre in 1856 and the raid on the Harpers Ferry arsenal in 1859, Brown has often been portrayed as a fanatical and probably insane abolitionist who believed that God had ordained him to destroy slavery. Yet no other white man won such respect from the free black community. Ralph Waldo Emerson, speaking for many Northern intellectuals, called Brown "a pure idealist of artless goodness."

saw Brown's criminal violence as the direct result of the irresponsible preaching of William H. Seward and other so-called Black Republicans. The Democratic New York *Herald* reprinted Seward's speech on the "irrepressible conflict between slave and free states" alongside news accounts from Harpers Ferry. Many southerners came to the stunned realization that Brown's raid could not be dismissed as the folly of a madman, since it had revealed the secret will of much of the North. A Virginia senator concluded that Brown's "invasion" had been condemned in the North "only because it failed." In the words of Jefferson Davis, a Mississippi senator who had been Pierce's secretary of war, the Republican party had been "organized on the basis of making war" against the South.

Ironically, both the Republicans and the southern extremists agreed that slavery must expand under national sanction if it were to survive. They also agreed that if the *Dred Scott* decision was valid, the government had an obligation to protect slave property in all the territories. This denial of any middle ground made it logical for southern fire-eaters to argue that a revived African slave trade would allow more whites to own slaves and would thus help to "democratize" the institution. Above all, both the Republicans and the southern extremists rejected popular sovereignty as Douglas had defined it. For southerners the Constitution prohibited either Congress or a territorial legislature from depriving a settler of his slave property. For the Republicans the Constitution gave Congress both the duty and the power to prevent the spread of an institution that deprived human beings of their inalienable right to freedom.

Because these positions were irreconcilable, the northern Democrats held the only keys to possible compromise in the presidential election of 1860. But like the Republicans, the Douglas Democrats had drawn their own firm limits against further concessions to southern extremists. Early in 1860 Jefferson Davis challenged those limits by persuading the Senate Democratic caucus to adopt a set of resolutions committing the federal government to protect slavery in the territories. For Davis and other southern leaders, a federal slave code was the logical extension of the *Dred Scott* decision. They also agreed that the forthcoming Democratic platform must uphold the principle of federal protection of slave property. The Douglas Democrats knew that such a principle of guaranteed protection would completely undercut their reliance on legislation "unfriendly" to slavery in a territory and that such a plank would guarantee their defeat in the North.

Division of the Democratic Party In April 1860 the fateful Democratic national convention met at Charleston. When a majority of the convention refused to adopt a platform similar in principle to Davis's Senate resolutions, the delegates from eight southern states withdrew, many of them assuming that this disunionist gesture would force the Douglas faction to compromise. Douglas held firm to his principle of popular sovereignty, and as a result he could not muster the two-thirds majority that was needed for nomination. In a surprise move the northern Democrats then agreed to adjourn the convention and to reconvene six weeks later in Baltimore.

At Baltimore the Democratic party finally destroyed itself as a national force. Delegates from the Lower South again seceded, and this time they adopted an extreme proslavery platform and nominated Vice-President John C. Breckinridge of Kentucky for the presidency. The northern remnants of the party remained loyal to popular sovereignty, however it might be modified in practice by the *Dred Scott* decision, and nominated Douglas.

Meanwhile the division of the Democrats at Charleston had given the Republicans greater flexibility in nominating a candidate. In 1858 Douglas had portrayed Lincoln as a flaming abolitionist, and the South had accepted the image. To the North, however, Lincoln appeared more moderate and less controversial than the better-known Senator Seward of New York. Unlike Seward, Lincoln was not popularly associated with the higher-law doctrines that had led to Harpers Ferry. Although Lincoln disapproved of Know-Nothing nativism, he was more discreet than Seward and thus stood less chance of losing the nativist vote in Pennsylvania and other critical states. If some northerners regarded him as a crude buffoon from the prairies, he appealed to many other northerners as the tall rail-splitter of humble origins, a man of the people, an egalitarian. Lincoln had made few enemies and was associated with few issues, but he had given general endorsement to the proposed Homestead Act, protective tariffs, and a

Campaign Poster
The Republican candidates for president and vice-president in 1860.

transcontinental railroad—all programs that were popular in the North and West and that had been blocked in Congress by the South. In May, at the Republicans' boisterous convention in Chicago, Lincoln finally overcame Seward's early lead and received the nomination.

The presidential campaign of 1860 was filled with the noisy hucksterism and carnival atmosphere that had been standard since 1840. The Republicans tended to discount the warnings of serious crisis, and they contemptuously dismissed southern threats of secession as empty bluff. The Breckinridge Democrats tried to play down these threats and to profess their loyalty to the Constitution and the Union. Yet various groups of moderates realized that both the Constitution and the Union were in jeopardy. This was the message of the new Constitutional Union party, which was led largely by former Whigs and which won many supporters in the Upper South. And this was the message that Stephen Douglas repeated bravely and incessantly—in the South as well as in the North—in the first nationwide speaking campaign by a presidential candidate.

The Election of 1860　In November the national popular vote was divided among four candidates, and Lincoln received only 40 percent of the national total. Yet he received 180 electoral votes—57 more than the combined total of his three opponents. He carried every free state except New Jersey, and he won 4 of New Jersey's 7 electoral votes. In ten of the slave states, however, he failed to get a single popular vote. Breckinridge, the southern Democrat, captured all the states of the Lower South as well as Delaware,

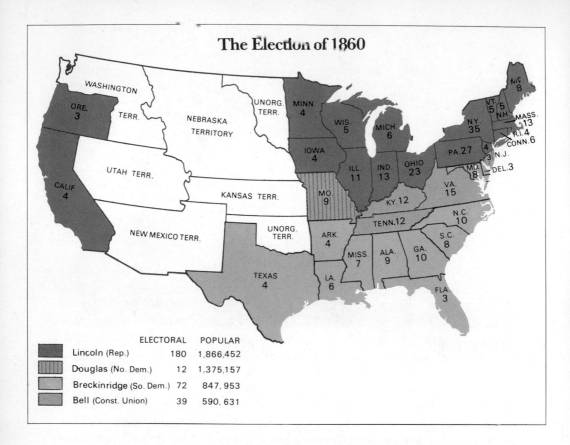

The Election of 1860

	ELECTORAL	POPULAR
Lincoln (Rep.)	180	1,866,452
Douglas (No. Dem.)	12	1,375,157
Breckinridge (So. Dem.)	72	847,953
Bell (Const. Union)	39	590,631

Maryland, Arkansas, and North Carolina. John Bell, the leader of the once-powerful Whig party in Tennessee and the candidate of the Constitutional Union party, carried Tennessee, Kentucky, and Virginia. Although Douglas received approximately 525,000 more popular votes than Breckinridge, and trailed Lincoln by only 491,000, he won a mere 12 electoral votes (9 from Missouri and 3 from New Jersey). In many respects it was not really a national election. In the North it was essentially a contest between Lincoln and Douglas; in the South, between Breckinridge and Bell.

For the South the worst fears and predictions of forty years had come true. The United States had never had an administration that was openly hostile to black slavery. Lincoln's reassurances regarding the constitutional protection of slavery in the existing states could not mitigate the crucial facts. The election had proved that the North was populous enough to bestow national power on a minority party that had no support in the South. The Republican party was committed to free-labor ideology and to the proposition that slavery was morally wrong. Slaveholders would have to take Lincoln's professions of restraint on good faith. If he or his successors should become more militant, they could not be checked by a balance of political power. A dominant sectional party would control federal patronage, the postal service and military posts, and the appointment of federal judges and other officeholders. Considerations of this kind strengthened the hand of secessionists. On December 20, 1860, South Carolina crossed the threshold that had been so closely approached during the nullification crisis. A special convention repealed the state's ratification of the Constitution and withdrew South Carolina from the Union. Unlike Jackson when faced with similar defiance, President Buchanan maintained that the federal government could do nothing to prevent the move.

Unionists mounted stiffer resistance to secession in other states of the Lower South. The chief controversies, however, involved timing—whether to follow the stampede of the fire-eating militants or to wait until Lincoln had shown his true colors. By February 1, 1861, the militants had triumphed in Mississippi, Florida, Alabama, Georgia, Louisiana, and Texas. Inevitably the shock produced reflex actions toward the traditional saving compromise. Senator John Crittenden of Kentucky initiated the first of such moves two days before South Carolina officially seceded. Although Crittenden's proposed amendments to the Constitution were defined as moderate, they matched the most extravagant southern demands of a few years before. Even so, the leaders of the Lower South knew that no "compromise" would be secure unless the Republican party miraculously cast off its antislavery principles. Most Republicans could not publicly approve Crittenden's "unamendable" amendment that would have guaranteed the permanent security of slavery. Nor could they return to the old Democratic proposal for extending the Missouri Compromise line to the Pacific. The 1850s had shown that federal commitment to establishing and protecting slavery south of that line would only encourage southern ambitions in the Caribbean and Latin America. As Lincoln confidentially warned William Kellogg, his spokesman in Congress: "Entertain no proposition for a compromise in regard to the *extension* of slavery. The instant you do, they have us under again; all our labor is lost, and sooner or later must be done over.... The tug has to come and better now than later."

By 1860 the North and South had moved beyond the reach of compromise. The United States had originally emerged from an act of secession—from a final rejection of compromise with Britain. Even after independence had been won, Americans continued to perceive Britain as a conspiratorial power that threatened to hold back the nation's expansive energies. But despite this threat, America had continued to prosper and expand. The period from 1820 to 1860 witnessed a continuing extension of limits, an overleaping of boundaries of every kind. History seemed to confirm the people's wish for total self-determination. The American people, like the American individual, seemed to be free from the burdens of their past and free to shape their own character. The one problem that their ingenuity could not resolve was black slavery, which the Founders had seen as an unwanted legacy of British greed. Ironically, the South increasingly came to regard black slavery as the necessary base on which freedom must rest. For the North a commitment to slavery's ultimate extinction was the test of freedom. Each section detected a fatal change in the other—a betrayal of the principles and mission of the Founders. Each section feared that the other had become transformed into a despotic and conspiratorial "power" very similar to the original British enemy. And both sections shared a heritage of standing firm against despotism.

It was not accidental that the greatest American novel of the period, Herman Melville's *Moby-Dick* (1851), tells of the destruction that inevitably flows from denying all limits, rules, and boundaries. The novel concerns Captain Ahab's relentless and stubborn pursuit of a great white whale, a "nameless, inscrutable, unearthly thing" that becomes a symbol for all the opposing, unknown forces of life. Ahab, who commands a crew containing most of the races and types of humanity, thinks that he can become the master of his own fate. Ignoring a series of warnings and portents, he is incapable of admitting that he might be wrong or that there might be forces beyond his control.

Melville's novel is full of rich and universal meaning concerning the heroic yet impossible quest to know the unknowable. Since Americans of the 1850s believed that God would ensure the triumph of democracy in the world, they could not accept Melville's brooding skepticism. Nevertheless there was a lesson for pre–Civil War America in this tale of a highly rational but half-crazed captain—a captain who becomes so obsessed with his mission that he finally throws his navigation instruments overboard so that he can steer only toward the visible spout of the whale. Captain Ahab seeks liberation in an unswerving pursuit and conquest of limits. In the end he dooms himself and his ship to destruction.

CHRONOLOGY

1846 Wilmot Proviso fuses question of slavery's expansion with consequences of Mexican War.
Walker tariff, adopted for revenue only, eliminates principle of protection.

1848 Gold discovered on American River in California.
Van Buren, running for president on Free-Soil ticket, receives 10 percent of popular vote.
Zachary Taylor elected president.

1850 In Congress, violent sectional debate culminates in Compromise of 1850.
Fugitive Slave Law requires federal agents to recover escaped slaves from sanctuaries in the North.
Taylor's death makes Millard Fillmore president.

1851 Herman Melville's *Moby-Dick.*

1852 Franklin Pierce elected president.
Harriet Beecher Stowe's *Uncle Tom's Cabin.*

1853 Upsurge of political nativism, the Know-Nothings.

1854 Spectacular Know-Nothing election victories.
Collapse of Whigs.
New Republican party emerges.
Commodore Perry opens Japan to American trade.
Kansas-Nebraska Act rekindles sectional controversy over slavery.

1856 John Brown's murderous raid at Pottawatomie Creek.
James Buchanan elected president.

1857 *Dred Scott* decision.
In Kansas, proslavery Lecompton constitution ratified as free-state men refuse to vote.

1858	Lincoln-Douglas debates.		Abraham Lincoln elected president.
1859	John Brown's raid on Harpers Ferry.		South Carolina secedes from the Union.
1860	Democratic party, deadlocked at Charleston convention, finally divides along sectional lines at Baltimore.	**1861**	Mississippi, Florida, Alabama, Georgia, Louisiana, and Texas secede.

SUGGESTED READINGS

David M. Potter, *The Impending Crisis, 1848–1861* (1976), continues to be an excellent guide to the topics discussed in the present chapter. But see also James M. McPherson, *Battle Cry of Freedom: The Civil War Era* (1988); William J. Cooper, *The South and the Politics of Slavery 1828–1865* (1978); Cooper, *Liberty and Slavery: Southern Politics to 1860* (1983); and other general survey or interpretive works cited at the end of chapters 12, 15, and 16. The titles on the causes of the Civil War, listed at the end of chapter 18, are also highly relevant.

On California, the best general guide is Andrew F. Rolle, *California: A History* (1969). For the California gold rush and western mining in general, see Rodman W. Paul, *California Gold: The Beginnings of Mining in the Far West* (1947), and Paul, *Mining Frontiers of the Far West, 1848–1880* (1963). Kevin Starr, *Americans and the California Dream, 1850–1915* (1973), presents brilliant vignettes of early California history. For the experiences of blacks in California, see Rudolph M. Lapp, *Blacks in Gold Rush California* (1977). Chinese immigration and anti-Chinese sentiment is admirably treated in Alexander Saxton, *The Indispensable Enemy: Labor and the Anti-Chinese Movement in California* (1975).

Holman Hamilton, *Prologue to Conflict* (1964), is the most detailed and accurate account of the Compromise of 1850. For the preceding presidential election, see Joseph G. Rayback, *Free Soil: The Election of 1848* (1970). Stanley W. Campbell, *The Slave Catchers: Enforcement of the Fugitive Slave Law, 1840–1860* (1968), traces the consequences of the most unpopular provision of the Compromise of 1850. Stephen Douglas's motives for introducing the Kansas-Nebraska Act are judiciously weighed in Robert W. Johannsen, *Stephen A. Douglas* (1973). This definitive biography is also an excellent source on the later Kansas controversy and the Lincoln-Douglas debates. The tangled local conflicts over land and railroad sites are illuminated in Paul W. Gates, *Fifty Million Acres: Conflicts over Kansas Land Policy, 1854–1890* (1954), and James C. Malin, *The Nebraska Question, 1852–1854* (1953). For Harriet Beecher Stowe's world-famous response to the Kansas controversy, see Philip van Doren Stern, *Uncle Tom's Cabin, an Annotated Edition* (1964), and Charles H. Foster, *The Rungless Ladder: Harriet Beecher Stowe and New England Puritanism* (1956).

The political realignment of the 1850s has been reinterpreted in Michael F. Holt, *The Political Crisis of the 1850s* (1978), and also in Joel H. Silbey, *The Partisan Imperative: The Dynamics of American Politics Before the Civil War* (1985). The appalling political corruption of the 1850s is exposed in Mark W. Summers, *The Plundering Generation: Corruption and the Crisis of the Union, 1849–1861* (1987). Robert William Fogel, *Without Consent or Contract: The Rise and Fall of American Slavery* (1989), presents a challenging thesis regarding the effects of immigration on the living standard of native workers and the links between nativism and an antislavery coalition. Ray Billington, *The Protestant Crusade, 1800–1860* (1938), provides an outstanding overview of anti-Catholic nativism. The best studies of political nativism are Michael F. Holt, "The Politics of Impatience: The Origins of Know-Nothingism," *Journal of*

American History, 60 (September 1973), and Holt, *Forging a Majority: The Formation of the Republican Party in Pittsburgh* (1969).

A recent and monumental work that explains the unique conditions that gave rise to the Republican party is William E. Gienapp, *The Origins of the Republican Party, 1852–1856* (1987). See also Hans L. Trefousse, *The Radical Republicans* (1969). Eric Foner, *Free Soil, Free Labor Free Men: The Ideology of the Republican Party Before the Civil War* (1970), is a penetrating study of the Republicans' thought and values. For the Democratic party, see the classic work by Roy F. Nichols, *The Disruption of American Democracy* (1948), and Jean H. Baker, *Affairs of Party: The Political Culture of Northern Democrats in the Mid-Nineteenth Century* (1983). The definitive study of the *Dred Scott* decision is Don E. Fehrenbacher, *The Dred Scott Case: Its Significance in American Law and Politics* (1978). Paul Finkelman, *An Imperfect Union: Slavery, Federalism and Comity* (1981), examines the problem of slaveholders who took their slaves into free states and shows that Lincoln had grounds for fearing a "second Dred Scott decision."

John Brown, a man of violence, has been the subject of violently conflicting interpretations. For traditional and hostile views, see James C. Malin, *John Brown and the Legend of Fifty-Six* (1942), and the brilliant essay by C. Vann Woodward in *The Burden of Southern History* (1960). More sympathetic evaluations can be found in Stephen B. Oates, *To Purge the Land with Blood: A Biography of John Brown* (1970); Benjamin Quarles, *Allies for Freedom: Blacks and John Brown* (1974); and Louis Ruchames, ed., *John Brown: The Making of a Revolutionary* (1969).

Robert W. Johannsen's biography of Douglas, listed above, treats the Lincoln-Douglas debates, and a penetrating analysis can be found in Don E. Fehrenbacher, *Prelude to Greatness: Lincoln in the 1850s* (1962). The debates themselves are presented in an authoritative edition by Paul M. Angle, ed., *Created Equal? The Complete Lincoln-Douglas Debates of 1858* (1958). Harry V. Jaffa, *Crisis of the House Divided: An Interpretation of the Issues in the Lincoln-Douglas Debates* (1959), gives the brilliant, far-reaching, and somewhat eccentric interpretation of a conservative political philosopher.

Most of the biographical studies of Lincoln listed at the end of chapter 18 are relevant here. Fehrenbacher's *Prelude to Greatness* is important, and mention should be made of James G. Randall, *Lincoln, the Liberal Statesman* (1947); Benjamin Quarles, *Lincoln and the Negro* (1962); and, above all, Allan Nevins, *The Emergence of Lincoln* (2 vols., 1950).

The climactic impasse between North and South is imaginatively presented in three major and very different studies: Kenneth M. Stampp, *America in 1857: A Nation on the Brink* (1990); Roy F. Nichols, *The Disruption of American Democracy* (1948); and David M. Potter, *Lincoln and His Party in the Secession Crisis* (1942). Avery O. Craven, *The Coming of the Civil War* (1942), stresses the importance of propaganda and irrationality. For the hopes and fears of contemporaries, see J. Jeffrey Auer, ed., *Antislavery and Disunion, 1858–1861: Studies in the Rhetoric of Compromise and Conflict* (1963). No one has yet written a wholly satisfactory account of the secessionist movements in the South. For conflicting interpretations, see William L. Barney, *The Secessionist Impulse: Alabama and Mississippi* (1974); Daniel W. Crofts, *Reluctant Confederates: Upper South Unionists in the Secession Crisis* (1989); Steven A. Channing, *Crisis in Fear: Secession in South Carolina* (1970); Charles B. Dew, "Who Won the Secession Election in Louisiana?" *Journal of Southern History,* 36 (February 1970), 18–32; Dwight L. Dumond, *The Secession Movement, 1860–1861* (1931); William J. Evitts, *A Matter of Allegiances: Maryland from 1850 to 1861* (1974); and R. A. Wooster, *The Secession Conventions of the South* (1962).

Two works that describe the northern response to secession are Kenneth M. Stampp, *And the War Came: The North and the Secession Crisis, 1860–61* (1950), and Howard C. Perkins, ed., *Northern Editorials on Secession* (2 vols., 1942). For the election of 1860, see Elting Morison, "Election of 1860," in *History of American Presidential Elections, 1789–1968,* ed. Arthur M. Schlesinger, Jr., vol. 2, 1097–1122 (4 vols., 1971). On the futile gestures for compromise, see Albert J. Kirwan, *John J. Crittenden: The Struggle for the Union* (1962), and Robert G. Gunderson, *Old Gentlemen's Convention: The Washington Peace Conference of 1861* (1961).

PART TWO

Uniting the Republic

1860–1877

David Herbert Donald

$\mathcal{T}$HESE [Northern] people hate us, annoy us, and would have us assassinated by our slaves if they dared," a Southern leader wrote when he learned that a "Black Republican," Abraham Lincoln, would certainly be elected president in 1860. "They are a *different* people from us, whether better or worse and *there is no love* between us. Why then continue together?" The sectional contests of the previous decades suggested that Americans had become members of two distinct—and conflicting—nationalities. By 1860 Northerners and Southerners appeared not to speak the same language, not to share the same moral code, and not to obey the same law. Compromise could no longer patch together a union between two peoples so fundamentally different. "I do not see how a barbarous and a civilized community can constitute one state," Ralph Waldo Emerson gravely concluded, and many Northerners concurred with him. "The North and the South are heterogeneous and are better apart," agreed the *New Orleans Bee.*

On first thought, the four-year civil war that broke out in 1861 seems powerfully to confirm the view that the Union and the Confederacy were two distinct nations. Yet the conduct of the war suggests that Northerners and Southerners were not so different as their political and intellectual leaders had maintained. At the beginning of the conflict, both governments tried in much the same ways to mobilize their poorly organized societies for battle. As the war progressed, both Union and Confederacy adopted similar diplomatic, military, and economic policies. By the end of the war, both governments were committed to abolishing slavery, the one institution that had most clearly divided the sections in 1860.

The Reconstruction era, which followed the Civil War, gives further evidence that the inhabitants of the North and the South were—as they had always been—part of the same nationality. There were relatively few, and only limited, social experiments or political innovations during Reconstruction. Shared beliefs in limited government, in economic laissez-faire, and in the superiority of the white race blocked drastic change. Meanwhile common economic interests and national political parties pulled the sections back into a common pattern of cooperation.

In the backward glance of history, then, the Civil War takes on a significance different from its meaning to contemporaries and participants. In retrospect it is clear that it was less a conflict between two separate nations than a struggle within the American nation to define a boundary between the centralizing and nationalizing tendencies in American life and the opposing tendencies toward localism, parochialism, and fragmentation.

7

Stalemate

1861–1862

$\approx$

$\mathcal{D}$URING the first two years of the Civil War, as the Union and the Confederacy grappled with each other inconclusively, it seemed that two distinct and incompatible nations had emerged from the American soil. Certainly the aims announced by their leaders were totally inconsistent. President Abraham Lincoln announced that the United States would "constitutionally defend, and maintain itself"; the territorial integrity of the nation must not be violated. For the Confederate States, President Jefferson Davis proclaimed that his country's "career of independence" must be "inflexibly pursued." As the rival governments raised and equipped armies, attempted to finance a huge war, and sought diplomatic recognition and economic assistance abroad, the people of the two sides increasingly thought of each other as enemy nations: Yankees and Rebels. It is easy to understand why Lord John Russell, the British foreign minister, concluded: "I do not see how the United States can be cobbled together again by any compromise. . . . I suppose the break-up of the Union is now inevitable."

A shrewder observer might have noted that the Union and the Confederate governments faced similar wartime problems and tried to solve them with the same wartime solutions. Northerners and Southerners on the battlefields found each other to be not two alien peoples, but kindred peoples. That identity made the conflict truly a brothers' war.

The Rival Governments

The government of the Confederate States was in most respects a duplicate of the United States government from which the Southern states had just withdrawn. Delegates of the six states of the Lower South (South Carolina, Georgia, Alabama, Mississippi, Florida, and Louisiana) met in Montgomery, Alabama, in early February 1861 and promptly drafted a Confederate Constitution; delegates from Texas, which had seceded on February 1, arrived late. The new charter largely followed the wording of the one drawn up in Philadelphia in 1787. To be sure, the Confederate Constitution recognized the "sovereign and independent character" of the constituent states, but it also announced that these states were forming "a permanent federal government," and it listed most of the same restrictions on state action that had been included in the United States Constitution. Unlike that document the Confederate charter used no euphemism about persons "held to Service or Labour" but instead recognized explicitly "the right of property in negro slaves." Otherwise the two documents were substantially and intentionally identical. As the secessionist Benjamin H. Hill of Georgia explained, "We hugged that [United States] Constitution to our bosom and carried it with us."

Inaugurating the Presidents

For president of the new republic, the Montgomery convention chose Jefferson Davis of Mississippi, who had ardently defended Southern rights in the United States Senate but who had only reluctantly come to advocate secession.* If the crowds that thronged the streets of Montgomery on February 18, 1861, hoped to hear a stirring inaugural from the new Southern head of state, they were disappointed. Stepping forward on the portico of the Alabama statehouse, Davis gave a long, legalistic review of the acts of Northern aggression that had led to the formation of the new government. He pledged to use force, if necessary, to "maintain...the position which we have assumed among the nations of the earth." But he spoke in a tone more melancholy than martial. He saw himself as the leader of a conservative movement. "We have labored to preserve the Government of our fathers in its spirit," he insisted.

Just two weeks later, from the portico of the yet unfinished Capitol in Washington, another conservative took his inaugural oath. The capital city was thronged, as Nathaniel Hawthorne wrote, with "office-seekers, wire-pullers, inventors, artists, poets, prosers (including editors, army correspondents, attaches of foreign journals, and long-winded talkers), clerks, diplomatists, mail contractors, [and] railway directors." On public buildings along the route of the inaugural procession, sharpshooters were strategically placed, to prevent any pro-Southern interruption of the proceedings. Abraham Lincoln's inaugural address was similar in tone to Davis's. Lincoln vowed that the Union would be preserved and gave a low-keyed version of the previous sectional quarrels. He explained his

---

*The Montgomery convention drew up a provisional constitution of the Confederacy, established itself as the new republic's provisional legislature, and named Jefferson Davis the provisional president. It also drew up a permanent constitution, which was submitted to the states for ratification. Regular elections were held in the fall of 1861 both for members of the Confederate Congress and for president. Reelected without opposition, Davis was formally inaugurated as the first and only regular president of the Confederate States on February 22, 1862.

Jefferson Davis (1808–89)
"The hour and the man have met!" proclaimed William L. Yancey, presenting Jefferson Davis to the admiring throngs at Montgomery in February 1861. Intelligent, experienced, and incorruptible, the Senator from Mississippi seemed the ideal president for the new Confederacy.

personal view on slavery, but he also pledged that he contemplated "no invasion—no using of force" against the seceded states. In a warning softened by sadness, he reminded his listeners of the oath he had just taken to preserve, protect, and defend the government of the United States, and he entreated his Southern fellow citizens to pause before they assailed it. "In *your* hands, my dissatisfied fellow-countrymen," he concluded, "and not in *mine,* is the momentous issue of civil war."

Organizing the Two Administrations

In the weeks immediately following the two inaugurations, the central problem confronting both Davis and Lincoln was how to form viable governments. In Davis's Confederacy everything had to be started afresh. Even the most routine legal and governmental matters could not be taken for granted. For example, until the Confederate Congress passed an act that addressed the matter, it was not certain whether the laws of the United States enacted before 1861, and the decisions of the United States courts, were binding in the seceded states. The new nation had to choose a flag—although some purists objected, claiming that the Confederacy, which represented the true American spirit, ought to retain the Stars and Stripes and let the Union look for a new banner.

In selecting his cabinet advisers, President Davis theoretically had a free hand, but his range of choice was severely limited. No man of doubtful loyalty to the new government could be permitted a place in the cabinet. Thus no Southern Unionist in the tradition of Henry Clay, John J. Crittenden, and John Bell was invited. On the other hand, because Davis wanted the world to see that the Confederacy was governed by sober, responsible men, he excluded all the most conspicuous Southern fire-eaters. Then, too, he had to achieve some balance between former Whigs and former Democrats, and he felt obliged to secure a wide geographical spread by appointing one member of his original cabinet from each of the seven Confederate states except Mississippi, which he himself represented. Davis's cabinet thus consisted neither of his personal friends nor of the outstanding political leaders of the South, except for Secretary of State Robert Toombs, a Georgian who served only briefly.

Such a cabinet might have sufficed in a country where administrative procedures and routines were firmly rooted. Instead in the Confederacy there was everywhere a lack of preparation, a lack of resources for running a government. Typical was the Confederate Treasury Department, which initially consisted of one unswept room in a Montgomery bank, "without furniture of any kind; empty... of desks, tables, chairs or other appliances for the conduct of business." The secretary of the treasury had to pay for the first rickety furniture out of his own pocket.

Disorganization and improvisation also characterized Lincoln's government in Washington. The Union had the advantage of owning the Capitol, the White House, and the permanent records of the United States government, and it had a recognized flag and a postal system. But in other respects it was thoroughly demoralized. Lincoln's administration had no clear mandate from the people, for the president had received less than 40 percent of the popular vote in the 1860 election. The Union had an army of only 14,657 men, and every day army and navy officers announced that they were defecting to the South. Its treasury was empty. Some of the most experienced clerks in the Washington offices were leaving to join the Confederacy, and many who remained were of suspect loyalty. The confusion was compounded by the presence in the capital of hundreds of office seekers, party workers who had helped elect the first Republican administration and, under the spoils system, expected to oust Democratic incumbents. Accompanied by their representatives or senators and bearing huge rolls of letters of recommendation, the office seekers besieged Lincoln in the White House. Wryly the president compared himself to an innkeeper whose clients demanded that he rent rooms in one wing of his hotel while he was trying to put out a fire in the other.

Not one member of the Lincoln administration had previously held a responsible position in the executive branch of the national government. Many, including the president himself, had no administrative experience of any sort. Like Davis, Lincoln made no attempt to form a coalition government. His cabinet included no leaders of the Douglas wing of the Democratic party or of the Constitutional Union party. Nor, after a few unsuccessful efforts, did he name Unionists from the South. Instead all members of his cabinet were Republicans. That fact, however, scarcely gave his government unity, for several of Lincoln's cabinet appointees had themselves been candidates for the Republican nomina-

Abraham Lincoln (1809–65)
"Probably," wrote Walt Whitman, "the reader has seen physiognomies...that, behind their homeliness or even ugliness, held superior points so subtle, yet so palpable, making the real life of their faces almost as impossible to depict as a wild perfume or fruit taste...such was Lincoln's face—the peculiar color, the lines of it, the eyes, mouth, expression. Of technical beauty it had nothing—but to the eye of a great artist it furnished a rare study, a feast, and fascination."

tion in 1860 and were rivals of Lincoln and of each other. The most conspicuous member was the wily and devious secretary of state, William H. Seward, a man who spoke extravagantly but acted cautiously. Seward felt that he had a duty to save the nation through compromise and conciliation despite its bumbling, inexperienced president. Seward's principal opponent in the cabinet was Secretary of the Treasury Salmon P. Chase, pompous and self-righteous, who had an equally condescending view of Lincoln's talents and who lusted to become the next president. The other members, with whom Lincoln had only limited personal acquaintance, were appointed because they were supposed to have political influence or to represent key states.

Winning the Border States

Desperately needing time to get organized, these two shaky rival administrations immediately confronted a problem and a crisis, which were intimately interrelated. The problem concerned the future of the eight remaining slave states, which had not yet seceded. Although these states were tied to the Deep South by blood and sentiment and feared abolitionist attacks on their "peculiar institution" of slavery, they refused to rush out of the Union. In January 1861 Virginia had elected a convention to consider secession, but it dillydallied and did nothing. In February North Carolinians and Tennesseans voted against holding secession conventions. When the Arkansas and Missouri conventions met in March, they voted not to secede. Up to April 1861, Kentucky, Maryland, and Delaware held neither elections nor conventions. But the loyalty of all these states to the Union clearly depended on the policy Lincoln's government adopted toward the Confederacy.

Crisis over Fort Sumter   The Fort Sumter crisis was the first test of that policy. It concerned the fate of the United States installations in the seceded states that still remained under the control of Washington. At Fort Pickens in Pensacola Bay, an uneasy truce held between the Union troops in the garrison and the Confederate forces on the Florida mainland. The real trouble spot was Fort Sumter, in the harbor of Charleston, South Carolina. Its garrison, which consisted of about seventy Union soldiers and nine officers under the command of Major Robert Anderson, was no serious military threat to the Confederacy, but its presence at Charleston, the very center of secession, was intolerable to Southern pride. Confederates insisted that President Davis demonstrate his devotion to the Southern cause by forcing Anderson and his men out immediately. Many Northerners, who had despairingly watched as fort after fort was turned over to the Confederates during the final months of the Buchanan administration, likewise saw Sumter as a test of the strength and will of the Lincoln administration.

Despite these pressures powerful voices in both governments urged compromise or at least delay. All but two members of Lincoln's cabinet initially thought that Sumter should be evacuated. Davis's secretary of state was equally opposed to hasty action. When the Confederate cabinet discussed attacking Fort Sumter, Toombs solemnly warned: "The firing upon that fort will inaugurate a civil war greater than any the world has yet seen."

But Anderson's situation made some action necessary. When Charleston authorities prohibited further sale of food to the troops in the fort, the garrison faced starvation. On March 5, the day after he was inaugurated, Lincoln learned that Anderson and his men could hold out no longer than April 15 unless they were resupplied. Since Lincoln had just pledged that he would "hold, occupy, and possess" all places and property belonging to the government, he promptly directed his secretary of the navy to outfit an expedition to bring provisions to Fort Sumter. At the same time, recognizing how dangerously explosive the Charleston situation was, he explored alternatives. One possibility was to reinforce Fort Pickens, in the relatively calm area of Florida. Doing so would allow Lincoln to demonstrate his firmness of purpose, even if he had to withdraw Anderson from the Charleston harbor. But the naval expedition sent to Florida miscarried, the Union commander at Pickens misunderstood his orders, and the planned reinforcement could not be completed in time for Lincoln to know about it before Anderson's deadline for surrender. Another possibility was to consent to a peaceable withdrawal from Fort Sumter in return for assurances that the still-undecided border states would remain in the Union. "If you will guarantee to me the State of Virginia, I shall remove the troops," Lincoln confidentially promised a prominent Virginia Unionist. "A State for a fort is no bad business." But the Virginians delayed, and a rainstorm kept a delegation of Unionists from reaching Washington; Lincoln received no firm pledge. Seeing no other possible course, he let the expedition bearing food and supplies sail for Sumter.

President Davis understood that Lincoln was not committing an act of aggression in merely supplying Fort Sumter. Indeed, he predicted that for political reasons the United States government would avoid making an attack so long as the hope remained of retaining the border states. But the Confederate president's hand was forced, too. Hotheaded Governor Francis Pickens and other South Carolina extremists, impatient with Davis's caution, prepared to attack the fort. Rather than let Confederate policy be set by a state governor, Davis ordered General P. G. T. Beauregard, in command of the Confederate forces at Charleston, to demand the surrender of Fort Sumter. Anderson responded that he would soon be starved out, but he failed to promise to withdraw by a definite date. Beauregard's officers felt they had no alternative but to take the fort by force. At 4:30 A.M. on April 12, firing began. Outside the harbor the relief expedition Lincoln had sent watched impotently while Confederates bombarded the fort. After thirty-four hours, with his ammunition nearly exhausted, Anderson had to surrender.

Lincoln promptly called for 75,000 volunteer soldiers to put down the "insurrection" in the South. On May 6 the Confederate Congress countered by formally declaring that a state of war existed. The American Civil War had begun.

Both at the time and later there was controversy about the responsibility for beginning the conflict. Critics claimed that, by sending the expedition to resupply Fort Sumter, Lincoln deliberately tricked the Confederates into firing the first shot. Indeed, some months after the event, Lincoln himself told a friend that his plan for sending supplies to Major Anderson had "succeeded." "They attacked Sumter," he explained; "it fell, and thus, did more service than it otherwise could." That statement clearly reveals Lincoln's wish that if hostilities began the Confederacy should bear the blame for initiating them, but it does little to prove that Lincoln wanted war. It is well to remember that the Confederates took the initiative at Sumter. It was Charleston authorities who cut off Anderson's food supply; it was Confederate authorities who decided that, although the fort offered no military threat, Anderson must surrender; and it was the Southerners who fired the first shot. Writing privately to the Confederate commander at Fort Pickens, President Davis had acknowledged that there would be a psychological advantage if the Southerners waited for the Union government to make the initial attack. But, he added, "When we are ready to relieve our territory and jurisdiction of the presence of a foreign garrison that advantage is overbalanced by other considerations." These other considerations impelled Davis to demand Fort Sumter's surrender.

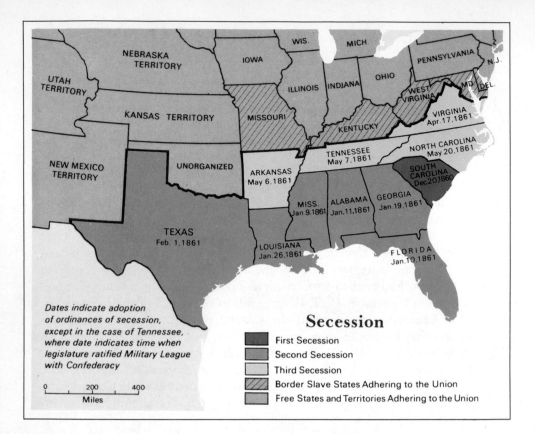

Dates indicate adoption
of ordinances of secession,
except in the case of Tennessee,
where date indicates time when
legislature ratified Military League
with Confederacy

0   200   400
|_____|_____|
        Miles

Secession

First Secession
Second Secession
Third Secession
Border Slave States Adhering to the Union
Free States and Territories Adhering to the Union

**Decisions in the
Border States**

Initially, the Confederacy, not the Union, benefited from the attack on Fort Sumter. The slave states still in the Union now had to make a choice of allegiances, and for a time it seemed that all would join the Confederacy. Virginia governor John Letcher spurned Lincoln's call for troops as a bid "to inaugurate civil war," and on April 17 the state convention hastily passed a secession ordinance. Technically secession was subject to popular ratification. But in fact the convention's action immediately linked to the Confederacy the most populous and influential state of the Upper South, with its long tradition of leadership, its vast natural resources, and its large Tredegar Iron Works.

Other border states acted only a little less quickly. On May 6 the Arkansas convention voted, with only five members dissenting, to withdraw from the Union. When Lincoln's call for troops reached Governor Isham Harris of Tennessee, he replied haughtily, "In such an unholy crusade no gallant son of Tennessee will ever draw his sword," and he began private negotiations with Confederate officials. On May 7 the Tennessee state legislature ratified the arrangements Harris had already made and voted to secede. On May 20 the North Carolina convention, under pressure from pro-Confederate newspapers to withdraw from the "vile, rotten, infidelic, puritanic, negro-worshipping, negro-stealing, negro-equality...Yankee-Union," unanimously adopted a secession ordinance.

Far to the west, the Confederacy scored another victory in the Indian Territory (later to become the state of Oklahoma). Confederate Commissioner Albert Pike had little success with the Plains Indians there, but he won over most of the Five Civilized Nations, many of whom were slaveowners. The Confederacy agreed to pay all annuities that the United States government had previously provided, and it allowed these tribes—the Choctaws, Chickasaws, Creeks, Seminoles, and Cherokees—to send delegates to the Confederate Congress. In return these tribes promised to supply troops for the Confederate army. Most of the tribes loyally supported the Southern effort throughout the war, and the Cherokee chief, Brigadier General Stand Watie, did not formally surrender until a month after the war was over. A rival faction among the Cherokees, headed by Chief John Ross, as well as most of the Plains Indians favored the Union cause.

Elsewhere along the border, the Confederacy fared less well. Delaware, although it was a slave state with sentimental ties to the South, never really contemplated secession. In Maryland, a bitterly divided state, the decision was much more painful. On April 19 a pro-Confederate mob in Baltimore fired on a Massachusetts regiment en route to Washington, and communications were then cut between the Union capital and the rest of the country. For a time it seemed highly probable that Maryland would secede. But Lincoln arranged for further shipments of Union troops to bypass Baltimore until passions could cool. By May Baltimore was back under Union control, and the mayor, along with nineteen members of the state legislature, was unceremoniously arrested and jailed without trial. In the 1861 fall elections, Maryland chose an uncompromising Unionist as governor, and thereafter there was no further question of secession.

In Missouri the Union cause was managed with less skill. Although the pro-Southern governor denounced Lincoln's call for troops as "illegal, unconstitutional, revolutionary, inhuman, [and] diabolical," public opinion was so evenly divided that secession probably would not have occurred except for the Union commander Nathaniel Lyon, who started hostilities by overrunning an encampment of prosecessionist militia near St. Louis. Confederate sympathizers rallied to protect them, and for two days there was bloody street fighting in the city. Open warfare followed. Union forces controlled the area around St. Louis; secessionists commanded by Sterling Price dominated most of the rest of the state. After General John C. Frémont became commander of the department of the West, with his headquarters in St. Louis, the territory under Union control was gradually extended. During the next three years, guerrilla warfare devastated the Missouri countryside as neighbor fought neighbor. The bitterness was further aggravated when free-soil men from Kansas, remembering how Missouri "border ruffians" had once tried to extend slavery into their territory, crossed the border to take revenge on secessionist sympathizers. In turn, Confederate gangs (the most notorious led by the horse thief and murderer William C. Quantrill) preyed on Missouri Unionists.

Far more adroit was Lincoln's handling of Kentucky—his native state, as well as Jefferson Davis's. As in Missouri, the governor was an outright secessionist, but strong Unionist sentiment prevented the calling of a state convention. Thus there was a stalemate, and Kentucky declared itself neutral in any conflict between the United States and the Confederacy. Between May and September 1861, both the Lincoln and the Davis governments claimed to accept this neutrality; but at the same time, each tried to strengthen the hands of its supporters in Kentucky. Finally, suspecting that Union forces were about to seize a position in Kentucky, the Confederates moved first and took Columbus. Federal troops then entered Paducah, and neutrality was dead. But these months of wavering had given Kentucky Unionists a chance to plan and organize, so that the state did not join the Confederacy like Tennessee or become a fierce battleground like Missouri. Lincoln himself played a large role in bringing about this outcome. He gave Kentucky affairs close attention and was careful to assure prominent Kentuckians privately that he "intended to make no attack, direct or indirect, upon the institution or property [meaning slavery] of any State."

Although most Virginians favored the Confederacy, the Union had loyal supporters in the western counties of the state. The people of these counties had long resented the domination of the state by the planters of the tidewater region and had little interest in slavery. When the Virginia convention voted for secession, a sizable minority of the delegates, mostly from these western counties, were opposed, and they went home vowing to keep their state in the Union. A series of exceedingly complex maneuvers followed, including the summoning of several more-or-less extralegal conventions and the creating of a new government for what was termed "reorganized" Virginia, rivaling the secessionist government at Richmond. This "reorganized" government then gave its permission—as required by the United States Constitution—for the counties west of the mountains to form a new and overwhelmingly Unionist state of West Virginia. Not until 1863, when all these steps were completed, was the new state admitted to the Union. Thus by that date there were no fewer than three state governments on Virginia soil: the pro-Confederate government at Richmond; the "reorganized" pro-Union government, which had few supporters and huddled under the protection of Northern guns at Alexandria; and the new Union government of West Virginia.

In summary, then, after Fort Sumter was fired on, the border states divided. Virginia, Arkansas, Tennessee, and North Carolina went with the Confederacy; Delaware, Maryland, Missouri, Kentucky, and, presently, West Virginia remained in the Union.

Importance of the Border States
It is impossible to exaggerate the importance that these decisions, made early in the conflict, had on the conduct of the Civil War. For the Confederacy it was essential that states from the Upper South join the secession. For all the brave talk at Montgomery, the Confederacy was not a viable nation so long as it consisted only of the seven states in the Deep South. The population of these seven states was only one-sixth that of the remaining states of the Union. In all the Gulf States

in 1861, there was not a single foundry to roll heavy iron plate or to cast cannon, nor a large powder works, nor indeed a single important factory. But when Virginia, North Carolina, Arkansas, and Tennessee joined the Confederacy, they almost doubled its population. What is more, they brought to the new nation the natural resources, the foundries and factories, and the skilled artisans that made it possible to rival the Union. To recognize the economic and psychological strength added by these states of the Upper South—and also to escape the sweltering summer heat of Montgomery—the Confederacy in May 1861 moved its capital from Montgomery to Richmond.

But if the states of the Upper South brought the Confederacy strength, they also limited its freedom of action. Richmond and Virginia became so important to the South that the Confederate government became obsessed with defending them—at the expense of neglecting the vital western theaters of military operations.

For Lincoln's government, too, the border states were vital. If Maryland had seceded, the capital at Washington would have been surrounded by enemy territory—cut off from the Union states of the North and the West. Confederate control of Kentucky would have imperiled river transportation along the Ohio, and the secession of Missouri would have endangered traffic on the Mississippi and disrupted communication with Kansas and the Pacific coast. Although Lincoln grieved over the secession of the states that joined the Confederacy, he could feel proud that by keeping four slave states in the Union he was preventing the Southern armies from recruiting from a population that was three-fifths as large as that of the original Confederacy.

So important were the border states for the Union that special pains had to be taken not to disturb their loyalty. In particular, Lincoln saw that there must be no premature action against slavery. European nations might fail to understand the nature of the American Civil War, and Northern abolitionists might denounce their president as "the slave-hound from Illinois," but Lincoln knew that to tamper with slavery would result in the loss of the border states, particularly Kentucky. "I think to lose Kentucky is nearly the same as to lose the whole game," he wrote to a friend. "Kentucky gone, we cannot hold Missouri, nor, as I think, Maryland. These all against us, and the job on our hands is too large for us. We would as well consent to separation at once, including the surrender of this capitol."

Raising the Armies

While Lincoln and Davis were moving in parallel fashion to win the support of the border states, ordinary folk in the North and South were rallying around their flags. On both sides the firing on Fort Sumter triggered a rush to enlist. "War! and volunteers are the only topics of conversation or thought," an Oberlin College student reported when the news reached Ohio. "The lessons today have been a mere form. I cannot study. I cannot sleep, I cannot work, and I don't know

**Private John Werth, Richmond Howitzer Battalion, C.S.A., and an Illinois
Volunteer of 1861**
*As soon as volunteers were sworn in and received their uniforms and equipment, most rushed
to photographers' studios to have pictures made for their loved ones.*

as I can write." An Arkansas youth recorded identical emotions: "So impatient
did I become for starting that I felt like a thousand pins were pricking me in every
part of the body and [I] started off a week in advance of my brothers."

**The Rush to
Volunteer**
Ordinarily a volunteer offered to enlist in one of the
regiments that was being raised in his community.
Wealthy citizens and prominent politicians usually took
the lead in recruiting these companies. Inevitably these regiments displayed a
wide variety of arms, ranging from rusty flintlocks to the latest sharpshooting
rifles. Often their uniforms bore distinctive insignia. (For example, a Louisiana
battalion recruited from the daredevil New Orleans roustabouts called themselves the Tigers, and their scarlet skullcaps bore mottoes like "Tiger on the
Leap" and "Tiger in Search of a Black Republican." Perhaps the most colorful—
and impractical—uniforms were those of the Northern Zouave regiments,

Recruiting Poster for Zouave
Regiment

dressed in imitation of the French troops in North Africa. (These soldiers,
wearing their red fezzes, scarlet baggy trousers, and blue sashes, were magnificent in military reviews, but when they had to wade across a stream, their baggy
garments ballooned around them and they floated down the current like so many
exotic waterlilies.) When a regiment's ranks were filled, there was invariably a
farewell ceremony, featuring rousing addresses, lengthy prayers, and the presentation of the regimental flag, often hand-sewn by patriotic wives and sweethearts
of the enlisted men. Then, loaded with hams, cakes, and sweetmeats provided by
fellow townsmen, the men went off to war.

**Wartime
Maladministration**
Neither the Union nor the Confederate War Department knew what to do with the flood of volunteers.
Leroy P. Walker, the first Confederate secretary of war,
had had no military training and no administrative experience. An amiable
Southern gentleman, fond of prolonged conversations with visitors and of writing rambling three-page business letters, Walker was wholly unable to cope with
the situation. Complaining that he lacked arms and equipment, he refused the
services of regiment after regiment. Perhaps 200,000 Confederate volunteers
were thus rejected in the first year of the war.

The Northern war office was equally chaotic. Simon Cameron, the secretary of war, had been forced on Lincoln as part of a political bargain. Cameron's main objective was to become the undisputed boss of Pennsylvania politics. There is no evidence that he used his cabinet position to line his own pockets, but he did employ his huge patronage to strengthen his faction of Pennsylvania Republicans. Lacking administrative talents, Cameron, like Walker, simply could not deal with the flood of volunteers, nor could he supervise the hundreds of contracts his office had to make for arms, ammunition, uniforms, horses, and dozens of other articles for the army. Haste, inefficiency, and corruption inevitably resulted. For example, in October 1861 General Frémont, desperately needing horses for his cavalry in Missouri, contracted to purchase 411 animals. Subsequent investigation proved that 350 of the horses supplied him were undersized, under- or overaged, ringboned, blind, spavined, and incurably unfit for service; 5 were dead. Unable to equip the Union volunteers as they rushed to defend the flag, Cameron thought it was his principal duty "to avoid receiving troops faster than the government can provide for them."

As the war wore on, the initial zeal for volunteering abated. Many of the men rejected by Walker and Cameron in the early months of the conflict were never available again. Soon even those whose services had been accepted began to exhibit less enthusiasm for the war. Most had expected the army to be like the peacetime militia, to which all able-bodied white men belonged; the monthly militia rallies had been the occasion for fun and frolic, punctuated by a little uneven military drill, a considerable amount of political oratory, and a great deal of drinking. Now they discovered that war was not a lark. Belonging to the army meant discipline, spit-and-polish cleaning of equipment, and hours of close-order drill. A soldier's life was one of endless monotony, interrupted occasionally by danger from enemy bullets and more frequently by diseases resulting from inadequate food and clothing, lack of vaccination, filthy drinking water, and open latrines. By the end of 1861, many Union volunteers were beginning to count the weeks until the end of their three-month term of enlistment. Confederate regiments, which had been enrolled for a year, were about ready to disband in the spring of 1862.

Reorganization and Conscription

Of necessity Lincoln and Davis moved almost simultaneously to strengthen their war departments in order to give more central direction to their armies. In January 1862, having persuaded Cameron to become American minister to Russia, Lincoln named a former Democrat, the brusque and imperious Edwin M. Stanton, to the War Department. Stanton quickly reorganized the department, regularized procedures for giving out war contracts, and investigated frauds. Standing behind an old-fashioned writing desk, looking like an irritable schoolmaster before a willful class, Stanton heard all War Department business in public. He curtly dismissed patronage seekers, even when congressmen accompanied them; contractors had to state their prices in loud, clear voices; and even a petitioner bearing a letter of introduction from the president might be abruptly shown to the door. Working incessantly, Stanton saw to it that the Union army became the best-supplied military force the world had ever seen.

It took a bit longer for Davis to find a war secretary to his liking. When Walker, to everyone's relief, resigned in September 1861, Davis replaced him briefly with Judah P. Benjamin and then, after Benjamin became the Confederate secretary of state, with George Wythe Randolph. Randolph did much to see that Robert E. Lee and Thomas J. ("Stonewall") Jackson had the necessary arms and supplies for their 1862 campaigns. But when Randolph and Davis disagreed over strategy, the secretary had to go, and in November 1862 he was succeeded by the sallow and cadaverous James A. Seddon. As one of his clerks remarked, Seddon looked like "an exhumed corpse after a month's interment." Nevertheless he was diligent and efficient. He also had the good sense to give solid support to subordinates of great ability. Perhaps the most competent of these was General Josiah Gorgas, head of the Confederate ordnance bureau. Thanks to Gorgas's efforts, the Confederacy, which in May 1861 had only about 20 cartridges for each musket or rifle, by 1862 had built powder plants capable of producing 20 million cartridges. This was enough ammunition to supply an army of 400,000 men for twelve months.

While both presidents were strengthening their war departments, they also moved, in 1862, to take a more active role in recruiting troops. Because the twelve-month period of enlistment of Confederate troops expired in the spring of 1862, Davis warned that the Southern army would be decimated just as Union forces were approaching Richmond. The Southern Congress felt uncomfortable in ignoring the principle of state sovereignty proclaimed in the Confederate Constitution. But on April 16, 1862, it passed a national conscription act, which made every able-bodied white male between the ages of eighteen and thirty-five subject to military service. This first conscription law in American history, however, exempted numerous groups from military service, ranging from druggists to Confederate government officials; and a subsequent law excused planters or overseers supervising twenty or more slaves. The Confederate conscription act was meant less to raise new troops than to encourage veterans to reenlist. The law provided that if the men stayed in the army, they could remain in their present regiments and elect new officers; but if they left, it threatened, they could be drafted and assigned to any unit that needed them.

Lincoln's government moved toward conscription a little more slowly. Volunteering all but stopped after the bloody campaigns in the summer of 1862,* and the army needed 300,000 new men. Union governors suggested to the president that a draft would stimulate volunteering, and on July 17 the United States Congress passed a loosely worded measure authorizing the president to set quotas of troops to be raised by each state and empowering him to use national

---

*For these military operations, see pp. 612–17.

force to draft them if state officials failed to meet their quotas. This first Union conscription law was intentionally a bogeyman that the governors used to encourage enlistments, and it brought in only a handful of men.

Financing the War

Hard as it was for the Union and Confederate governments to raise troops, it was even harder to supply and pay for them. Although the United States in 1860 was potentially one of the great industrial nations of the world, it was still primarily an agricultural country, with five out of six of its inhabitants living on farms. The factories that would be called on to supply vast armies were mostly small in scale. Some 239 companies manufactured firearms in 1860; their average invested capital was less than $11,000. Textile mills, especially for the manufacture of woolens, were larger, but ready-made clothing was still sewn in small shops. The country produced an abundance of foodstuffs, but there was no effective whole-sale marketing system for meat and grain. According to 1860 maps 30,000 miles of railroads crisscrossed the country, but most of these were short spans, each under its own corporate management. Often they were not connected to other lines at common terminals and had different rail gauges. Sending a boxcar from, say, Baltimore to St. Louis required diplomacy, improvisation, frequent transshipment, long delays, and a great deal of luck. Commercial transactions were impeded because the United States did not have a national bank; indeed, the country did not even have a national currency, for most of the circulating money consisted of bills issued by the numerous state banks, depreciating at various rates.

Problems of the Treasury Departments

Yet Union and Confederate leaders had somehow to mobilize this disorganized economy to support an enormous war effort. Both governments relied primarily on privately owned rather than government-operated factories to supply their armies. Necessity more than a theoretical preference for free enterprise lay behind this choice. If individual businessmen and corporations had little experience in the large-scale production of goods, the civil servants in Washington and Richmond had even less. Where it seemed useful, both governments supplemented the output of private industry with production from government-owned plants. While the Lincoln administration was purchasing firearms from Colt, Remington, and dozens of other manufacturers, it continued to rely on its own armories, especially the one at Springfield, Massachusetts, for some of its best weapons. The South was even more largely rural and agricultural than the North, and thus it had to be more active in establishing government-owned plants, the most successful of which was the huge powder factory at Augusta, Georgia. But both governments contracted with private individuals and corporations for most of the arms, clothing, and other equipment needed for the armies.

It was easier to contract for supplies than to pay for them. Both Union and Confederacy began the war with empty treasuries. When Secretary of the Treasury Chase took up his duties in Washington, he was horrified to discover that between April and June 1861 the expenses of the Union government would exceed its income by $17 million. Chase, who had built his reputation as an antislavery lawyer and politician, was inexperienced in financial matters, and he began casting about desperately for solutions.

But Chase's difficulties were nothing compared with those of his Confederate counterpart, Christopher G. Memminger, who had to make bricks without clay as well as without straw. Like Chase, Memminger had no extensive experience in financial matters, and his neat, systematic mind was troubled by the free and easy ways of government wartime expenses. He did what he could to bring order—by requiring Confederate Treasury employees to keep regular nine-to-five hours, by outlawing drinking on the job, and by insisting that his visitors curb their customary long-windedness and promptly state their business. These measures, however, did little to solve Confederate financial difficulties.

Sources of Revenue Neither secretary seriously thought of financing the war through levying taxes. For either the Union or the Confederacy to impose heavy taxation in 1861 might well have killed the citizens' ardor for war. Americans were not used to paying taxes to their national government. For thirty-five years before the war, there had been no federal excise duties. In 1860 the United States Treasury had no internal revenue division, no assessors, no inspectors, and no agents. Since tariffs were a more familiar method of raising revenues, both secretaries hoped for large customs receipts. But when the Republicans in the Union Congress passed the high protective Morrill Tariff in 1861 and raised rates even higher in 1862, they effectively killed that source of revenue. At the same time the Union blockade of the South reduced the amount and value of goods brought into Confederate ports and cut the Southern income from tariffs. In desperation the Union government in August 1861 resorted to a direct tax of $20 million, levied on each state in proportion to population; much of it was never collected. That same month, the Confederates imposed a "war tax" of 0.5 percent on taxable wealth. Davis's government, like Lincoln's, had to rely on the states to collect this tax, and most of them preferred issuing bonds or notes to levying duties on their people.

In neither country was borrowing a realistic possibility for financing the war. Americans of the 1860s were products of the Jacksonian era, with its suspicion of paper certificates of indebtedness. Thus Americans preferred to hoard rather than to invest their surplus funds. The rival Union and Confederate governments themselves shared this same suspicion of paper and this trust in hard money, or specie. In the North, Secretary Chase insisted that the banks of New York, Philadelphia, and Boston subscribe to a $150 million federal bond issue, but he was unwilling to take anything but gold or silver in payment. In December 1861 the resulting drain on bank reserves of precious metals, coupled with uncertainty over the course of the war, forced Northern banks to suspend payments in specie for the notes they had issued to the public in past years. Nor was Chase more successful in his early attempts to sell Union bonds directly to small investors. The Confederacy followed much the same course in its borrowing. An initial loan of $15 million was quickly subscribed to, with the result that Southern banks, including the strong institutions of New Orleans, were obliged to give up virtually all their precious metals to the new government. Consequently, they could no longer redeem their notes in gold or silver. Memminger's attempt to sell subsequent Confederate bonds directly to the Southern people ran into the difficulty that nobody had any precious metals. Urged by Vice-President Alexander H. Stephens and other Confederate orators, plantation owners in the fall of 1861 subscribed tobacco, rice, cotton, and other commodities to purchase bonds. But since the Union blockade cut off the market for these products, the Confederate government realized little from the loan.

Recourse to Paper Money   In consequence, by early 1862 both governments began to issue paper money, backed only by the promise that someday they would redeem the paper money in specie. Both treasury secretaries agreed to this policy reluctantly. Memminger, a prominent hard-money advocate before the war, had to resort to the printing presses in 1861. The Confederacy issued $100 million in paper money in August 1861, and the next year it printed millions of dollars more. Having denounced "an irredeemable paper currency, than which no more certainly fatal expedient for impoverishing the masses and discrediting the government of any country, can well be devised," Chase found it even more embarrassing than Memminger to resort to treasury notes. But in January 1862 he had no alternative. Declaring that an issue of paper money was now "indispensably necessary," he persuaded Congress to authorize the printing of $150 million in non-interest-bearing United States treasury notes (which were promptly dubbed "greenbacks" because of their color). Rarely does history provide such a tidy illustration of how huge impersonal forces overrule the preferences and will of individual statesmen.

Wartime Diplomacy

In diplomacy as in economic policy, the Union and the Confederacy moved along parallel paths during the first two years of the war. Neither Lincoln nor Davis had much knowledge of diplomacy or took an active role in the conduct of foreign policy. Both, however, had difficulties with their secretaries of state.

Seward, Lincoln's principal adviser, would ultimately rank as one of the greatest secretaries of state, but in the early stages of the Civil War he gave evidence of eccentricity, coupled with deep personal ambition. At the height of the Sumter crisis, he submitted to Lincoln a private memorandum complaining that the government as yet had no policy for dealing with secession, announcing his readiness to take over the president's function and shape a suitable policy, and suggesting that the administration's proper course was to "change the question before the public from one upon slavery...for a question upon union or disunion." This redefinition of the critical issue was to be accomplished by provoking a confrontation with foreign powers. If allowed, Seward would "seek explanations from Great Britain and Russia"—for what offenses he did not specify; he "would demand explanations from Spain and France, categorically, at once," presumably over their threatened intervention in the affairs of Santo Domingo and Mexico; and if Spain and France did not respond forthwith, he would urge a declaration of war against these powers. Lincoln, to his enduring credit, quietly filed away this memorandum, refrained from dismissing a secretary who planned to bring on a world war, and allowed Seward time to come to his senses.

Despite Lincoln's efforts to keep the matter quiet, word of Seward's aggressive inclinations leaked out in conversations at Washington dinner tables, and diplomats at the capital soon had a pretty good idea of what was in the secretary's mind. Perhaps awareness of Seward's hair-trigger temper did something to make European governments more cautious in their relations with the United States and less eager to recognize the Confederacy.

Davis too had trouble with his state department. Robert Toombs, the first Confederate secretary of state, was as ambitious and overbearing as he was able. Deciding that the path to glory lay on the battlefield rather than in the cabinet, Toombs soon resigned to take a commission in the Southern army. His successor, R. M. T. Hunter, was equally ambitious, and—perhaps with an eye on the 1868 Confederate presidential election—he too promptly resigned, to become senator from Virginia. In March 1862 Davis finally found his man in Judah P. Benjamin, who had already been Confederate attorney general and secretary of war. Serving until the end of the war, Benjamin cleverly reflected the changing moods of his chief, but he was not an innovator in foreign policy. In the words of a critical Northerner who visited Richmond during the war, Benjamin had a "keen, shrewd, ready intellect, but not the stamina to originate, or even to execute, any great good, or great wickedness."

Union and Confederate diplomatic appointments abroad were a rather mixed lot. Perhaps Lincoln lacked tact in appointing the German-born Carl Schurz as minister to conservative, monarchical Spain, for Schurz was considered a "red republican" because of his participation in the German revolution in 1848. But Davis also showed a total failure to understand British antislavery sentiment by sending William L. Yancey, the most notorious Southern fire-eater, as first Confederate commissioner to Great Britain. On the positive side, the Union minister to Great Britain, Charles Francis Adams, exhibited the patience and restraint that were required in his difficult assignment. The dignity of this son of President John Quincy Adams and grandson of President John Adams made him a match even for the aristocratic British foreign minister, Lord John Russell. Of the Confederate emissaries abroad, John Slidell of Louisiana probably proved the ablest. The wily, adroit, and unscrupulous Slidell was perfectly at home in the court of Napoleon III, Napoleon Bonaparte's nephew, who had reestablished the imperial regime in France and was eager to spread French influence in the world.

European Neutrality Much to the disappointment of Americans on both sides, the European powers' attitudes toward the Civil War were not primarily shaped by the actions of American ministers, secretaries of state, or even presidents. Nor, during 1861 and 1862, were they shaped by appeals to economic self-interest. Southerners firmly believed that cotton was king and expected that pressure from British and French textile manufacturers would compel Great Britain and France to recognize the Confederacy and to break the Union blockade. But European manufacturers had an ample stockpile of cotton, purchased before the outbreak of hostilities, and therefore they were not much affected by the cutoff of Southern cotton in 1861. By 1862 cotton mills in both Britain and France were suffering, but Union and Confederate orders for European arms, ammunition, and other equipment counterbalanced these losses. There was great hardship among the workers in the cotton mills, especially in the Lancashire district of England, where unemployment was high. But these work-ers' complaints were relatively ineffectual because Britain still did not allow the workers to vote.

Northerners were equally disappointed by the attitudes of the European governments. Knowing the strength of the antislavery movement abroad, par-ticularly in Great Britain and France, they expected the European powers to condemn the slaveholding Confederacy. Their hope was unrealistic because, during the early years of the war, the Union government took no decisive steps toward emancipation. Indeed, Lincoln pledged that he would not interfere with slavery where it existed, Seward called the abolitionists and "the most extreme advocates of African slavery" equally dangerous to the Union, and Union gener-als helped Southern masters reclaim their runaway slaves. Confused by the mixed signals, European opponents of slavery could do little to influence the attitudes of their governments toward the war in America.

Northerners and Southerners alike failed to understand that the policy of European states toward the Civil War would be determined largely by considera-tions of national self-interest. An uneasy balance of power prevailed in Europe, and no nation was eager to upset it by unilateral intervention in the American conflict. But joint action by the European powers was always difficult because of mutual suspicion, and in the 1860s it was virtually impossible because of the nature of the British government. The British prime minister, Lord Palmerston, who was nearly eighty years old, headed a shaky coalition government that was certain to fall if it undertook any decisive action. With the British government thus immobilized, Russia favoring the Union cause, and Prussia and Austria mostly indifferent to the conflict, the ambitious Napoleon III found his inclina-tions to meddle in favor of the Confederacy effectively curbed.

As a result European nations announced their neutrality early in the war. Queen Victoria's proclamation of May 13, 1861, was typical in recognizing that a state of war existed between the United States and "the states styling themselves the Confederate States of America" and in declaring neutrality. None of the European proclamations recognized the Confederacy as a nation—that is, no one declared that it was a legitimate, independent power, entitled to send ambassadors and ministers abroad and to receive those from other nations, to enter into treaties with other powers, or, in general, to be treated just like any other sovereign state. But the proclamations did recognize the Confederates as belligerents. That acknowledgment meant that the Southerners were not to be considered simply a group of riotous or rebellious individuals, but as participants in a systematic, organized effort to set up their own independent government. Under international law, recognition as a belligerent entitled the Confederacy to send out privateers without their being considered pirate ships. Acknowledgment that a state of war existed in America also meant that the Union government could not declare Southern ports closed to foreign ships. To exclude foreign shipping, the North would have to maintain an effective blockade of the Confederacy. Initially, therefore, these European proclamations of neutrality and recognition of Southern belligerency seemed a great Confederate success. In fact, however, they were both necessary and warranted by international law—and, despite Seward's rantings, they were truly impartial.

The Trent Affair   In November 1861 the rash action of a Union naval officer threatened to upset this neutrality. Union Captain Charles Wilkes learned that President Davis was replacing the temporary commissioners whom he had sent to France and Britain with permanent envoys, John Slidell and James M. Mason. Wilkes decided to capture these diplomats en route. Off the shore of Cuba on November 8, 1861, his warship stopped the British merchant ship *Trent,* Union officers boarded and searched the vessel, and Mason and Slidell were unceremoniously removed, transferred to a Union ship, and sent to Boston for imprisonment. Wilkes's action was a clear violation of international law. When news of the incident reached Europe, hostility toward the Union government flared up. "You may stand for this," Prime Minister Palmerston told his cabinet, "but damned if I will!" The British foreign minister, Russell, drafted a stiff letter demanding the immediate release of the envoys. It was clear that the Lincoln government faced a major crisis if it held its prisoners. After conferring with cabinet members and senators, the president decided on Christmas Day to release the Southern envoys. He would fight only one war at a time.

Even with the firm intention of remaining neutral, European powers found their patience tested as the American war stretched on without apparent chance of ending. International relations were disturbed, commerce was disrupted, textile manufacturing was suffering, and neither North nor South seemed able to achieve its goal. Increasingly, support built up in both France and Britain for offering mediation to the combatants, and such an offer inevitably involved recognition of the Confederacy as an independent nation. In September 1862

COTTON IN THE STOCKS.

M. Mercier :—" HOW MUCH LONGER IS THIS TO LAST? OR ARE YOU WAITING UNTIL WE INTERFERE?"

"Cotton in the Stocks"
The Union blockade sealed off Southern exports of cotton and helped produce severe hardships in the textile-producing regions of Great Britain and France. This 1862 cartoon shows the French minister to Washington, Henri Mercier, threatening Uncle Sam with European intervention if the blockade is not lifted.

Palmerston and Russell agreed to explore a mediation plan involving France and Russia as well as Great Britain, but pro-Union members of the British cabinet, among them the Duke of Argyll and George Cornewall Lewis, replied with strong arguments against mediation. Faced with dissension within his unstable coalition and given no encouragement by Russia, Palmerston by October 1862 had changed his mind and concluded that the European states must continue to be lookers-on until the war took a more decided turn.

Battles and Leaders

But on the battlefields in 1861 and 1862, there were no decided turns. Engagement followed engagement, campaign followed campaign, and neither side could achieve a decisive victory. The stalemate was baffling to both Northern and Southern armchair strategists, who had been sure that the war would be short and decisive and would end in an overwhelming victory for their own side.

Confederate war planners counted among their assets the fact that some of the best graduates of West Point led their armies and that President Davis himself had military training and experience. They believed that Southern men had more fighting spirit than Northerners, and they were probably correct in thinking that Southerners had more experience in handling firearms and were better horsemen. They knew that the Confederacy would generally act on the defensive and assumed that the offensive Union army would have to be at least three times as large as the Southern army. Since Southern forces could operate on interior lines, they could move more quickly and easily than Union forces, which would have to travel longer distances. While recognizing the superiority of the Northern navy, Southerners knew that the Confederacy had 3,500 miles of coastline, with innumerable hidden harbors and waterways through which shipping could escape. When Confederate strategists added to all these assets the fact that Southern soldiers were fighting on their home ground, where they knew every road and byway, they saw no reason to doubt ultimate victory.

But an equally good case could be made for the inevitability of a Union victory. The population of the Union in 1860 was about 20.7 million; that of the Confederacy, only 9.1 million. Moreover, 3.5 million of the inhabitants of the South were blacks—mostly slaves, who, it was presumed, would not be used in the Confederate armies. Along with this superiority in manpower, the North had vastly more economic strength than the Confederacy. The total value of all manufactured products in all eleven Confederate states was less than one-fourth that of New York alone. The iron furnaces, forges, and rolling mills in the United States were heavily concentrated in the North. The North in 1860 built fourteen out of every fifteen railroad locomotives manufactured in the United States. Northern superiority in transportation would more than compensate for Southern interior lines, as only 30 percent of the total rail mileage of the United States ran through the states forming the Confederacy. The Union navy, which experienced few defections to the South, was incomparably superior. And the blockade that President Lincoln announced at the outbreak of hostilities would cut off, or at least drastically reduce, Southern imports from Europe. When Northern planners added to the advantages of their side the possession of an established government, the recognition of foreign powers, and the enormous enthusiasm of the people for maintaining the Union, they could not doubt that victory would be sure and swift.

Jomini's Game Plan In fact these assets substantially canceled each other during the first two years of the war and produced not victory, but deadlock. As the armies engaged in complex maneuvers and in indecisive battles, Union and Confederate commanders largely employed the same strategic plans, for most had learned the art of war from the same teachers. In fifty-five of the sixty biggest battles of the war, the generals on both sides had been educated at West Point, and in the remaining five, a West Pointer led one of the opposing armies. At the military academy they had studied the theories of the French historian and strategist Baron Henri Jomini. Some had read Jomini's works in the original French or in translation; more, doubtless, had absorbed his ideas from the abridgment and interpretation of his work, *Elementary Treatise on Advance-Guard, Outpost, and Detachment of Service of Troops* (1847), written by Dennis Hart Mahan, who for a generation taught at the academy and greatly influenced his students.

Jomini's military theories constituted a complex body of doctrine, subject to many differing interpretations. But as his theories were understood by American commanders, they stressed the importance of the conquest of territory and emphasized that the seizure of the enemy's capital was, "ordinarily, the objective point" of an invading army. Jomini had pictured a battle situation in which two armies were drawn up in opposing lines, one offensive and the other defensive, and he had even prepared a set of twelve diagrams showing the possible orders of battle. In all twelve, a major determinant of victory was the concentration of force—the bringing to bear of a powerful, united force on the enemy's weakest point. Warfare was thus something like an elaborate game of chess, an art that only professional soldiers could fully master.

Most of the military operations during the first two years of the Civil War can best be understood as a kind of elaborate illustration of Jomini's theories, slightly modified to fit the American terrain. The first big battle of the war occurred on July 21, 1861, when Union General Irwin McDowell, under much pressure from Northern newspapers and much badgered by exuberant politicians in Congress, reluctantly pushed his poorly organized army into Virginia. He expected to encounter the Confederates, under General Beauregard, near Centreville. Numerous sightseers from Washington followed the Union forces, expecting to witness a spectacular victory. In the ensuing battle of Bull Run (or Manassas), both armies tried to apply the same battle plan from Jomini's treatise: each attempted a main attack on the enemy left flank, to be followed by a secondary thrust at his center and right wings. If completely executed, the two plans would have had the amusing result of leaving each army in the opponent's original place. But the Confederates also followed another of Jomini's principles, that of concentration of force. By using the railroad, they rushed General Joseph E. Johnston's troops from the Shenandoah Valley to join Beauregard's main force. The Union troops fought bravely and initially seemed to be carrying the day, but after Johnston's men were in position, the Union army was thrown back and then routed. Weary and disorganized, Northern troops limped back to the Potomac and safety. Panic among the onlookers heightened the confusion. The Confederates were almost equally demoralized by their victory and were unable to pursue. The South thus lost its easiest opportunity to follow Jomini's maxim and seize the enemy's capital.

After this initial engagement it was clear that both armies needed reorganization and training before either could attempt further campaigns. Despite growing impatience for action, there was little significant military engagement during the rest of 1861 except for minor encounters in Kentucky and Missouri. During this period General George Brinton McClellan, who was credited with some overrated small successes in western Virginia, was summoned to Washington to bring order to the Union army. With enormous dash and enthusiasm, the young commander began to whip the Northern regiments into fighting shape. He insisted on careful drill and inspection; he demanded the best of food and equipment for his men; and he refused to move forward until his army was thoroughly prepared.

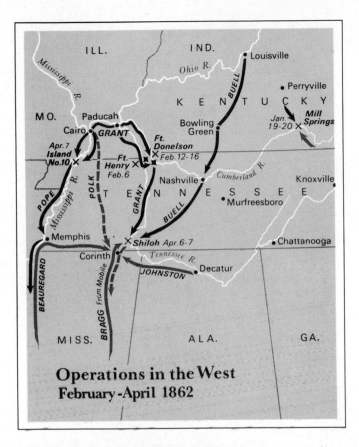

**Operations in the West
February-April 1862**

The War in the West, 1862

By early 1862 Union armies were ready to advance, not only in the East, but in all the theaters of war. Taking advantage of numerical superiority, Union commanders concentrated on a series of weak spots in the Confederate defenses, just as Jomini had directed. In January General George H. Thomas defeated a Confederate force at Mill Springs, Kentucky, and made a significant break in the Southern defense line west of the Appalachian Mountains. The next month General Ulysses S. Grant made an even more important breach in that line. In collaboration with the Union gunboats on the Tennessee and Cumberland rivers, Grant captured Fort Henry and Fort Donelson, requiring the Confederate army in the latter fort to accept his terms of unconditional surrender.

The Southerners now had to abandon Tennessee. Union armies under Grant and Don Carlos Buell pushed rapidly after them until stopped at the battle of Shiloh (April 6–7). General Henry Wager Halleck, the Union commander for the entire western theater, was dissatisfied with Grant's generalship and took personal charge of the army after Shiloh. Halleck was a dedicated disciple of Jomini (whose works he had translated) and concentrated his force for a push on Corinth, Mississippi, in order to break the important rail connection that linked Memphis and the western portion of the Confederacy with the East.

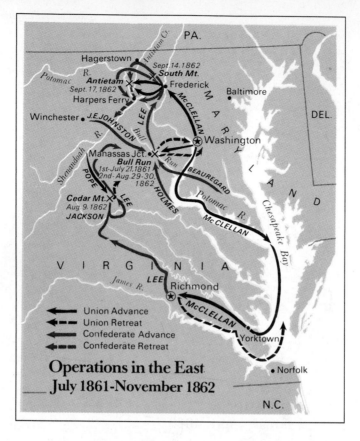

Union Advance
Union Retreat
Confederate Advance
Confederate Retreat

**Operations in the East
July 1861–November 1862**

The Peninsula Campaign

A Union advance in the eastern theater promised to be equally successful. After long delays McClellan began his offensive against Richmond. Instead of attacking overland from the north, he transported his troops to Fort Monroe, on the peninsula between the York and James rivers. McClellan complained bitterly because Lincoln violated the principle of concentration and held back 40,000 troops to defend Washington. Nevertheless McClellan prepared to follow Jomini's advice and seize the Confederate capital.

At this point in the gigantic, synchronized Union offensive, designed to crush the Confederacy, everything began to go wrong. The difficulties stemmed in part from human inadequacies. Although good theoreticians and able administrators, Halleck and McClellan were indecisive fighters. Halleck took nearly two months to creep from Shiloh to Corinth, stopping to fortify his position every night. By the time he reached his destination, the Southern army had moved south with all its provisions. Equally cautious was McClellan's advance on the peninsula, where he allowed 16,000 Confederate soldiers under General John B. Magruder to hold up his magnificent army of 112,000 until the Confederates could bring reinforcements to Richmond. The trouble was partly that these Union campaigns required the coordinated movement of forces larger than any seen before on the American continent, directed by commanding officers who had never led anything larger than a regiment. But the Union failed chiefly because able Confederate generals had read the same books on strategy as the Union commanders and knew how to fight the same kind of battles.

While McClellan slowly edged his way up the peninsula, the Confederate commander, Joseph E. Johnston, who had rushed in with reinforcements, kept close watch until the Union general unwisely allowed his forces to be divided by the flooded Chickahominy River. Applying Jomini's principle of concentration on the enemy's weakest spot, Johnston on May 31–June 1 fell upon the exposed Union wing in battles at Fair Oaks (or Seven Pines), which narrowly failed of being a Confederate triumph. When Johnston was wounded in this engagement, President Davis chose Robert E. Lee to replace him.

Lee quickly revealed his military genius by showing that he knew when to follow Jomini's principles and when to ignore them. Remembering from his days at West Point how slow McClellan was, Lee allowed "Stonewall" Jackson to take 18,000 men from the main army for a daring campaign through the Shenandoah Valley. Jackson defeated and demoralized the Union forces in the Shenandoah and so threatened Washington that Lincoln withheld reinforcements that he had promised McClellan. After Jackson had accomplished this objective, Lee reverted to the principle of concentration and ordered Jackson promptly to rejoin the main army before Richmond. The combined Confederate force fell upon McClellan's exposed right flank at Mechanicsville. Lee failed to crush McClellan; but in a series of engagements known as the Seven Days (June 25–July 1), he forced the Union armies to beat a slow, hard-fought retreat to the banks of the James River, where it lay under the protection of Northern gunboats. Lee had saved Richmond.

The Confederate Counteroffensive

As the Union advances ground to a halt by midsummer 1862, the Confederates planned a grand offensive of their own. In the West two Southern armies under generals Braxton Bragg and Edmund Kirby-Smith swept through eastern Tennessee in August; by September they were operating in Kentucky, where they were in a position to cut the supply line for Buell's army in Tennessee. The early phases of their offensive were brilliantly successful, but the campaign as a whole was fruitless because of a lack of coordination between the two Southern armies and because of Bragg's indecisiveness. After a bloody battle at Perryville (October 8), the Confederate forces withdrew toward Chattanooga, followed by the Union army at a respectful distance.

The more daring part of the Confederate offensive was in the East. While McClellan's army was slowly being withdrawn from the peninsula, Lee turned quickly on the Union forces in central Virginia under the braggart general John Pope. Concentrating his entire strength on this segment of the Union army, Lee scored a brilliant Confederate victory in the second battle of Bull Run (August 29–30) and was now free to push into the North. He crossed the Potomac into

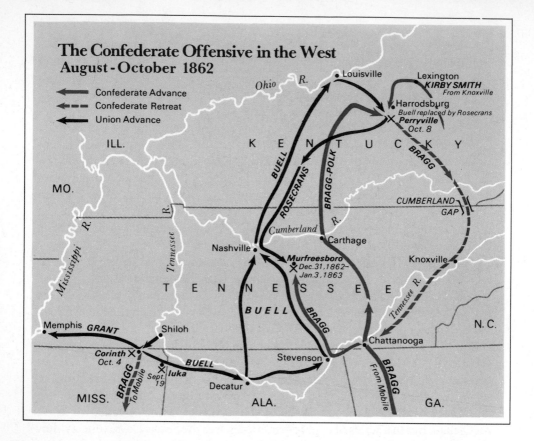

The Confederate Offensive in the West
August - October 1862

Confederate Advance
Confederate Retreat
Union Advance

Ohio R.
Louisville
Lexington
KIRBY SMITH
From Knoxville
Harrodsburg
Buell replaced by Rosecrans
Perryville
Oct. 8

ILL.
KENTUCKY

MO.
BUELL
ROSECRANS
BRAGG-POLK
BRAGG
CUMBERLAND GAP

Mississippi R.
Tennessee R.
Cumberland R.
Cumberland
Carthage
Nashville
Knoxville
Murfreesboro
Dec. 31, 1862 – Jan. 3, 1863

T E N N E S S E E
Tennessee R.
N.C.

Memphis **GRANT**
Shiloh
BUELL
BRAGG
Chattanooga
Corinth X
Oct. 4
BRAGG
To Mobile
X **Iuka**
Sept. 19
BUELL
Decatur
Stevenson
From Mobile
BRAGG
From Mobile

MISS.
ALA.
GA.

Maryland, where he hoped to supply his ragged army and to rally the inhabitants of that state to the Confederate cause.

Lee's invasion of Maryland ended with the battle of Antietam (September 17), an indecisive engagement whose very inconclusiveness clearly demonstrated the impossibility of ever ending the war as long as it was fought by the conventional rules. McClellan, once again the Union commander, moved slowly to catch up with Lee's army because he wanted to concentrate all his forces for an attack. Lee in turn waited in a defensive position behind Antietam Creek at Sharpsburg, Maryland, because he too needed to concentrate his troops, a portion of whom had been sent on a successful expedition to capture Harpers Ferry. When McClellan was finally ready to take the offensive, he followed one of Jomini's battle plans precisely, and Lee defended his position by the same rules. The result was the bloodiest day of the Civil War. In areas of the battlefield like the cornfield, the Dunker church, the Bloody Lane, and Burnside's bridge, men fell as in a slaughterhouse. By the end of the day there were more than 25,000 casualties, with at least 5,000 dead. The next day an eyewitness noted "the most appalling sights upon the battlefield...the ground strewn with the bodies of the dead and the dying...the cries and groans of the wounded...the piles of dead men, in attitudes which show the writhing agony in which they died—faces

A Union Hospital
The superintendent of the Union nursing corps was Dorothea L. Dix, who had led a movement to improve the lot of the mentally ill. To counteract the general impression that nurses were women of low moral character, she insisted that appointees had to be plain looking and over thirty years old.

distorted ... begrimed and covered with clotted blood, arms and legs torn from the body or the body itself torn asunder."

Quietly Lee slipped back into Virginia, and McClellan did not pursue him. The Confederate offensive was over, and with it ended an era. If Jomini's strategy could lead only to stalemate, it was time for both Union and Confederacy to experiment with new ways of waging war.

CHRONOLOGY

1861 Secession of remaining states of Deep South (Texas, Louisiana, Mississippi, Alabama, Georgia, and Florida).
Jefferson Davis begins term as president of the Confederate States of America.

Abraham Lincoln inaugurated as president of the United States of America.
Firing on Fort Sumter precipitates war.
Secession of border slave states (Virginia, North Carolina, Tennessee, and Arkansas).

1861 Union army routed at first battle of
Bull Run (Manassas).
McClellan heads Union forces.
Trent affair threatens to change
European neutrality.

1862 Both Union and Confederacy
adopt paper money.
Union general U. S. Grant captures
Fort Henry and Fort Donelson.
Grant's advance checked at Shiloh.
Battle of the ironclads: *Virginia
(Merrimack)* vs. *Monitor.*
McClellan's peninsula campaign

brings Union army to outskirts
of Richmond, the Confederate
capital.
Robert E. Lee becomes com-
mander of Army of Northern
Virginia.
Confederate victory at second
battle of Bull Run.
Bloody battle between Lee and
McClellan at Antietam.
Confederate invasion of Kentucky.
Lincoln issues preliminary
Emancipation Proclamation.
Confederate victory at
Fredricksburg.

SUGGESTED READINGS

An excellent guide to the extensive literature on the causes of Civil War is Thomas J. Pressly, *Americans Interpret Their Civil War* (1954).

James M. McPherson, *Battle Cry of Freedom* (1988), is the best narrative history of the Civil War. Other useful one-volume accounts are Peter J. Parish, *The American Civil War* (1975); J. G. Randall and David Herbert Donald, *The Civil War and Reconstruction* (1969); and James M. McPherson, *Ordeal by Fire* (1982). The most complete modern account is Allan Nevins, *The War for the Union* (4 vols., 1959–71). Shelby Foote, *The Civil War* (3 vols., 1958–74), is a spirited narrative, written on a grand scale.

There are several excellent reference works: Mark M. Boatner III, *The Civil War Diction-ary* (1988); Patricia L. Faust, ed., *Historical Times Illustrated Encyclopedia of the Civil War* (1986); and Steward Sifakis, *Who Was Who in the Civil War* (1988).

On the Sumter crisis, see David M. Potter, *Lincoln and His Party in the Secession Crisis* (1942); Kenneth M. Stampp, *And the War Came* (1950); and Richard N. Current, *Lincoln and the First Shot* (1963). Daniel W. Crofts, *Reluctant Confederates* (1989), explores the plight of the border states.

The best history of the Confederacy is Emory M. Thomas, *The Confederate Nation, 1861–1865* (1979). The fullest life of the Confederate president is Hudson Strode, *Jefferson Davis* (3 vols., 1955–64). Rembert W. Patrick, *Jefferson Davis and His Cabinet* (1944), is revealing on Confederate administration. Three Confederate diaries are invaluable: *Mary Chestnut's Civil War,* ed. by C. Vann Woodward (1981); John B. Jones, *A Rebel War Clerk's Diary* (2 vols., 1866); and Robert G. H. Kean, *Inside the Confederate Government,* ed. by Edward Younger (1955).

The most recent biography of Abraham Lincoln is Stephen B. Oates, *With Malice Toward None* (1977). Benjamin P. Thomas, *Abraham Lincoln* (1952), has long remained standard. The fullest and most flavorful of the biographies is Carl Sandburg, *Abraham Lincoln: The War Years* (4 vols., 1939). The most scholarly and critical is J. G. Randall and Richard N. Current, *Lincoln the President* (4 vols., 1945–55). A brilliant psychoanalytical interpretation is Charles B. Strozier, *Lincoln's Quest for Union* (1982). Mark E. Neely, Jr., *The Abraham Lincoln Encyclopedia* (1982), is exceptionally useful. The diaries of three of Lincoln's cabinet officers are indispensable: Howard K. Beale, ed., *The Diary of Edward Bates* (1933); David Donald, ed., *Inside Lincoln's*

Cabinet [Salmon P. Chase] (1954); and Howard K. Beale and Alan W. Brownsword, eds., *Diary of Gideon Welles* (3 vols., 1960).

The standard work on Anglo-American relations remains Ephraim D. Adams, *Great Britain and the American Civil War* (2 vols., 1925). Frank L. Owsley, *King Cotton Diplomacy* (1959), David P. Crook, *The North, the South, and the Powers* (1974), and Brian Jenkins, *Britain & the War for the Union* (2 vols., 1974–80), are valuable. See also Glyndon G. Van Deusen, *William Henry Seward* (1967); Martin B. Duberman, *Charles Francis Adams* (1961); and David Donald, *Charles Sumner and the Rights of Man* (1970). Franco-American relations are admirably covered in Lynn M. Chase and Warren F. Spencer, *The United States and France: Civil War Diplomacy* (1970), and Daniel B. Carroll, *Henri Mercier and the American Civil War* (1971).

On social and economic conditions, see Paul W. Gates, *Agriculture and the Civil War* (1965), and Mary E. Massey, *Bonnet Brigades: American Women and the Civil War* (1966). Developments on the Southern home front are sketched in Charles W. Ramsdell, *Behind the Lines in the Southern Confederacy* (1944), and Bell I. Wiley, *The Plain People of the Confederacy* (1943). Emerson D. Fite, *Social and Industrial Conditions in the North During the Civil War* (1910), remains the best survey. For the continuing debate on the effect of the war on American economic growth, see Ralph Andreano, ed., *The Economic Impact of the American Civil War* (1961), and David T. Gilchrist and W. David Lewis, eds., *Economic Change in the Civil War Era* (1965).

Studies dealing with other aspects of the war years are listed at the end of the following chapter.

8

Experimentation

1862–1865

⤙

AT THE outset of the Civil War, both President Lincoln and President Davis assumed that the conflict would be a limited and relatively brief one, waged in conventional fashion by armies in the field and having little impact on the economic, social, and intellectual life of their sections. The events of 1861–62 proved these expectations utterly wrong. It slowly became clear that to carry on the war, Americans in both North and South had to break with tradition and experiment broadly. They had to try new forms of government action, new modes of social and economic cooperation, and new patterns of thought.

Because the Union was ultimately victorious, it would be easy to conclude that Northerners were more willing to experiment, and better able to mobilize all their resources, for what has been called the first modern war. But such a judgment makes the historian the camp follower of the victorious army. The record shows instead that both the Confederacy and the Union attempted innovations that were daringly original for the time. It also shows that both sides resorted to much the same kinds of experimentation during the final years of the war.

Evolution of a Command System

The bloody and indecisive campaigns of 1861 and 1862 made innovators out of both Union and Confederate soldiers. Experience under fire convinced them not to follow Jomini's tactics. The French writer had conceived of a tactical situation in which infantrymen, drawn up in close, parallel lines, blazed away at each other with muskets that could be loaded perhaps twice a minute and that had an effective range of one hundred yards. But Civil War soldiers were equipped with rifles that not only were more quickly loaded, but had an effective range of about eight hundred yards. In Jomini's day the offensive force had the great advantage: rushing forward with bayonets fixed, charging troops could break the defenders' line before they had time to reload. But in the Civil War the advancing force was exposed to accurate fire during the last half-mile of its approach. In consequence, nine out of ten infantry assaults failed, and the Civil War soldier had little use for his bayonet—except perhaps as a spit on which to cook meat.

Soldiers on both sides rapidly learned how to make defensive positions even stronger. At the beginning of the war, most military men were scornful of breastworks and entrenchments, arguing that they pinned down a defending force and made it more vulnerable to a charge. When Lee, on assuming command of the Army of Northern Virginia in 1862, ordered his men to construct earthworks facing McClellan's advancing troops, Confederate soldiers bitterly complained and called their new general the King of Spades. But when they saw how entrenchments saved lives, they changed their tune. Lee became to the Confederate common soldier "Marse Robert," the general who looked after his men's welfare. What Confederate generals started, Union commanders imitated. By the end of 1862, both armies dug in wherever they halted. Using spades and canteens, forks and sticks, soldiers pushed up improvised earthworks and strengthened them with fence rails and fallen logs.

Experience also quietly killed off Jomini's view that warfare was restricted to professionals. In the early days of the conflict, commanders believed that warfare should not do harm to civilians or their property. When McClellan's army pushed up the peninsula, the general posted guards to keep his soldiers from raiding Confederate farmers' cornfields. Similarly, Halleck permitted slaveowners to search his camp in order to reclaim their runaway slaves. By the end of 1862, such practices had vanished. Soldiers joyfully foraged through civilians' watermelon patches, cornfields, and chicken roosts while their officers ostentatiously turned their backs. Northern generals exhibited a growing reluctance to permit the recapture of fugitive slaves who had fled to the Union lines. As early as May 1861 General Benjamin F. Butler at Fort Monroe, Virginia, refused to return three such fugitives on the grounds that they were contraband of war. "Contrabands" became a code name for escaped slaves, and in 1862 the United States Congress showed what it thought of Jomini's notion of limited warfare by prohibiting military officers from returning runaways.

Lincoln Takes Command

The deadlock of 1861–62 also brought about a transformation of the command systems of both the Union and the Confederate armies. Because the Union lost so many battles during the first two years of the conflict, Lincoln was forced to experiment. His initial venture came in mid-1862. Since he distrusted McClellan's capacity to keep an eye on the overall progress of the war while also leading a campaign to capture Richmond, Lincoln brought in Halleck from the West to serve as his military adviser, and gave him the grand title of general in chief. The position was not a viable one, for it placed Halleck in conflict with the other

Reburial of the Dead
After each major Civil War battle, in order to prevent the spread of disease, the dead had to be hastily buried, often in mass graves. Months later, soldiers had the gruesome task of excavating these graves, trying to sort and identify the remains, and giving them a proper burial.

generals, especially McClellan. It also often put him at odds with Secretary of War Stanton and exposed him to what he called the "political Hell" of pressure from congressmen. In addition Halleck's slowness, his indecisiveness, and his rigid adherence to Jomini's principles made him hostile to all innovation, and Lincoln soon concluded that he was of little more use than a clerk.

Seeing no alternative, Lincoln then tried to direct military operations himself. In the eastern theater he replaced McClellan, after his failure to follow up his partial success at Antietam, with the incompetent Ambrose E. Burnside. Burnside led the Army of the Potomac into the battle of Fredericksburg on December 13, 1862, one of the most disastrous—and surely the least necessary—Union defeats of the war. The appointment of "Fighting Joe" Hooker, a boastful egotist who was fond of the bottle, to replace Burnside brought no better luck to the Union cause. The battle of Chancellorsville (May 1–4, 1863) was still another Confederate triumph—but a victory won at a great price, for "Stonewall" Jackson was accidentally fired on by his own Southern soldiers and was mortally wounded.

Still trying to direct military operations himself, Lincoln watched anxiously as Lee in the midsummer of 1863 began his second invasion of the North, this time pushing into Pennsylvania. When Hooker appeared unable or unwilling to

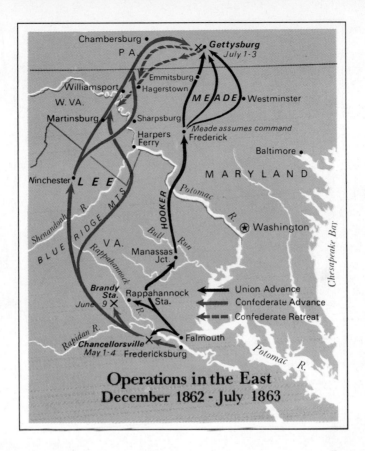

Operations in the East
December 1862 - July 1863

pursue the Confederates, Lincoln replaced him with the shy, scholarly George Gordon Meade, who assumed command of the army only three days before the climactic battle of Gettysburg (July 1–3, 1863). Rushing all available forces to that Pennsylvania town, Meade succeeded in turning back the invaders. At last the Army of the Potomac had won a victory—but Meade failed to pursue, and Lee's army recrossed the Potomac to safety. "We had them within our grasp," Lincoln lamented. "We had only to stretch forth our hands and they were ours. And nothing I could say or do could make the Army move."

Lincoln was no more successful in trying to direct the trans-Appalachian theater of war. After the battle of Perryville in October 1862, it was clear that Don Carlos Buell must be replaced, and the president chose W. S. Rosecrans. Lincoln urged him to push on to Chattanooga, the rail hub of the Confederacy, but en route Rosecrans encountered Bragg's army in the bloody and indecisive battle of Murfreesboro (December 30, 1862–January 2, 1863). Although Rosecrans claimed victory, his army was so badly mauled that he could not advance for another six months. Finally, in June 1863 he maneuvered the Confederates out of Chattanooga, but in pursuing Bragg's army he received a smashing defeat at Chickamauga (September 19–20). Only the rocklike determination of General George H. Thomas prevented the reverse from becoming a rout, and Rosecrans's

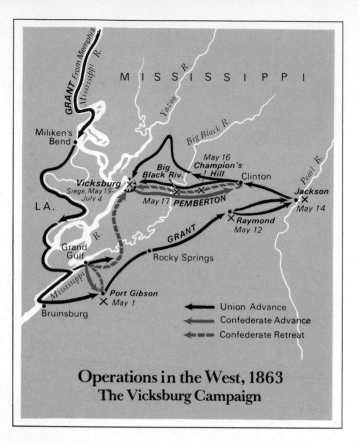

Operations in the West, 1863
The Vicksburg Campaign

army limped back into Chattanooga. Disoriented by defeat, Rosecrans, as Lincoln said, behaved "like a duck hit on the head" and allowed Bragg to besiege the city.

Farther west, Lincoln's personal direction of the Union armies proved equally ineffectual. Here the major objective was Vicksburg, the last major city on the Mississippi River still in Confederate hands; when it fell, the eastern part of the Confederacy would be severed from the trans-Mississippi region.

Grant's Success at Vicksburg

Grant commanded the Union forces in this area after Halleck went to Washington, and William Tecumseh Sherman was his ablest lieutenant. After a frontal assault on the almost impregnable bluffs of Vicksburg failed to drive out the Confederates, commanded by General John C. Pemberton, Grant devised a bold new strategy without aid from Washington. Using the navy's gunboats and transports to run his ammunition and supplies down the Mississippi River past the Vicksburg batteries, Grant marched his army to a point on the west bank south of the city, staged a rapid amphibious crossing, and—before the Confederates could recover from their surprise—pushed rapidly inland. To Lincoln's dismay he thus abandoned his base of supplies, announcing that he planned to live on the countryside. First he struck at Jackson, the capital of Mississippi, to drive back the small Confederate force that General Joseph E. Johnston had collected there. Then he turned on Pemberton's army and forced it into Vicksburg. After two ill-advised assaults, the Union army settled down to besiege the city, while from the river the Union gunboats kept up a constant bombardment. As civilians in the city took to caves for safety, and as starvation made mule meat a delicacy, Pemberton fought back as well as he could, but on July 4, 1863— the day after Gettysburg—he had to surrender his army and the city.

When the news reached Washington, Lincoln, who had distrusted Grant's strategy, wrote the general a handsome apology: "I now wish to make the personal acknowledgment that you were right, and I was wrong." The president was happy to be proved wrong, for Grant's success meant that he finally had a general who knew how to plan a campaign and fight it. Putting Grant in command of all the troops in the West, Lincoln directed him to relieve the army cooped up in Chattanooga. Quickly Grant and Sherman came to the rescue. They opened up a line of communication to the starving Union troops in Chattanooga, now commanded by Thomas instead of the inept Rosecrans, and brought in reinforcements. On November 23–25 the combined forces routed Bragg's encircling army and drove it back into Georgia.

Two New Systems of Command
This further victory gave Lincoln a solution to the problem of command, which had so long troubled him. Early the next year he brought Grant to Washington. Grant became a lieutenant general and was assigned to command all the armies of the United States. Initially, Washington observers thought the burden might be too much for this "short, round-shouldered man," whom they now saw for the first time. One observer reported that the new lieutenant general "had no gait, no station, no manner, rough, light-brown whiskers, a blue eye, and rather a scrubby look withal...rather the look of a man who did, or once did, take a little too much to drink." But appearances were deceiving, for in the next few days Grant set forth a broad strategy for winning the war. Taking advantage of Northern superiority in manpower, he planned a simultaneous advance of all Union armies, so that the Confederates must divide their forces or else leave their territory open to invasion. The idea of involving all the Northern forces at once made sense to Lincoln. "Oh, yes! I can see that," he exclaimed. "As we say out West, if a man can't skin he must hold a leg while somebody else does." Accepting Grant's plan, Lincoln created a modern command system for the United States army, with the president as commander in chief, Grant as general in chief, and Halleck as essentially a chief of staff, while Stanton as secretary of war ably supported all the others.

Meanwhile the Confederate command system was also evolving through experimentation. The tremendous victories won by Lee and the Army of Northern Virginia made it unnecessary constantly to change commanders in the East, but by 1863 it was evident that there must be a reorganization of Confederate commanders in the West. Davis instituted what was, in effect, a theater command system. Lee led the forces in Virginia, Joseph E. Johnston (now recovered from his wound) commanded the troops between the mountains and the Mississippi River, and Edmund Kirby-Smith was in charge of all troops in the vast trans-Mississippi region.

The new system was only partially successful. Kirby-Smith became a kind of supercommander of the trans-Mississippi theater (which was becoming increasingly isolated as Union forces captured point after point on the Mississippi) and did an effective job of recruiting and organizing the troops in his region. He stepped up trade with Mexico, so that impressive amounts of European munitions and supplies came in by way of Matamoros, Mexico. So strengthened, "Kirby-Smithdom," as it was popularly called, fared better than most of the rest of the South. But Kirby-Smith did little to make the vast resources of his command available to the government at Richmond.

In the central theater a strong Confederate command system failed to emerge. Johnston claimed that he did not know the extent and nature of his duties. Repeatedly he asked whether he was supposed to take field command of the widely scattered armies of Bragg (near Chattanooga) and of Pemberton (at Vicksburg), or was merely to serve as adviser to those generals. Knowing that both were protégés of President Davis, Johnston did not dare give a positive order to either. In consequence, he made only a feeble effort to replace the unpopular Bragg and diverted a few of his troops to support Pemberton. Johnston could not persuade Pemberton to leave Vicksburg while there was still time, and he watched in impotent impatience as the Confederate army there was cornered and starved into surrender.

In the eastern theater the brilliant successes of Lee and his lieutenants allowed the Army of Northern Virginia to operate essentially as it wished, without much regard for the needs of the Confederacy elsewhere. Lee, who had direct access to President Davis, resisted any attempt to weaken his force. In mid-1863, rather than attempt to relieve Vicksburg, Lee deliberately chose to invade the North again, in the vain hope that this course would relieve pressure on Confederate armies elsewhere. The result was the defeat at Gettysburg and the capture of Vicksburg.

Even so, by 1864 Lee was the only Confederate commander who retained the confidence of the country and of his troops. As Southern defeats became more numerous than victories, a strong demand welled up in the Confederate Congress for coordinated direction of all Southern armies, and men naturally looked to Lee. The general was, however, opposed to accepting these broader responsibilities and did all that he could to discourage the plan. When the Confederate Congress in January 1865 passed an act requiring the appointment of a commander in chief of all the armies, it had Lee in mind, and Davis named him. But Lee made it clear that he would continue to be essentially a theater commander, responsible only to Davis. Thus the Confederacy never developed a truly unified command system like the Union's.

The Naval War

Necessity compelled the Confederacy to take the lead in experimentation in naval warfare. Southerners were not a seagoing people and had no tradition of ship-building. Initially Secretary of the Navy Stephen R. Mallory had not a single ship at his command. He had to improvise, and he did so with imagination and remarkable success.

In the early months of the war, the long Southern coastline seemed to be at the mercy of the Union fleet, which could pick the most vulnerable points for attack. In November 1861 a Union naval force commanded by Flag Officer Samuel F. DuPont routed the weak Confederate defenders of Port Royal Sound, on the South Carolina coast, and Northern troops occupied Beaufort and the adjoining South Carolina Sea Islands. The victory gave the vessels in the Atlantic blockading fleet a much-needed fueling station and also brought freedom to the numerous slaves of the area. In February and March 1862 another Union expedition easily reduced Confederate positions on Roanoke Island and at New Bern, North Carolina, and enabled the Northern blockaders to keep a closer watch on Hatteras Sound. David G. Farragut's fleet in April 1862 helped capture New Orleans, the Confederacy's largest city.

By this time the Confederacy had greatly strengthened its coastal defenses, and further Union successes came slowly and at great cost. In April 1863 the Confederates repelled a vast Union armada, commanded by DuPont, that tried to capture Charleston. That stronghold of secession remained in Confederate hands until nearly the end of the war. Equally effective were the Confederate defenses of Wilmington, North Carolina, which became the main Southern port on the Atlantic through which supplies from Europe were imported. Not until January 1865 could Union troops capture Fort Fisher, the principal defense of Wilmington. The powerfully protected harbor of Mobile remained in Southern hands until August 1864, when the sixty-three-year-old Admiral Farragut, lashed in the rigging of his flagship so that he would not fall to his death if wounded, led his fleet past the defending Confederate forts to seize the last remaining major Southern port on the Gulf of Mexico.

Innovations in Naval Warfare To supplement the coastal batteries that protected these and other harbors, the Confederate navy experimented with new weapons. They used torpedoes extensively for the first time in warfare. These "infernal machines," constructed of kegs, barrels, and cans filled with explosives, were sometimes anchored at the entrance of Southern harbors. At other times they were turned loose to float with the tide toward attacking Union vessels, and on still other occasions they were propelled at the end of long poles by a small boats whose crews were willing to undertake the suicidal risk. Even more risky were the several Confederate experiments with submarines. The most successful of these novel vessels was the *H. L. Hunley,* propelled under water by a crank turned by its eight-man crew.

After four unsuccessful trials, in which all members of the crews were killed, the *Hunley* in February 1864 sank the Union warship *Housatonic* in Charleston harbor, but the submarine itself was lost in the resulting explosion.

Mallory quickly concluded that the Confederacy could never build as large a fleet as the Union, and early in the war he urged the construction of iron-armored ships, against which the wooden vessels of the North would stand no chance. Despite shortages of iron and a lack of rolling mills, the Confederacy developed a surprising number of these vessels. The most famous of the Confederate iron-clads was the *Virginia*, originally the United States warship *Merrimack*, which had been sunk when Union forces abandoned the Norfolk navy yard at the beginning of the war. Raised and repaired, the *Virginia* had its superstructure covered with four-inch iron plate and carried a cast-iron ram on its prow. On March 8, 1862, just as McClellan began his campaign on the peninsula, the *Virginia* emerged and began attacking the wooden vessels of the Union fleet at Hampton Roads. In the first day's action the ironclad destroyed two of the largest ships in the squadron and ran a third aground. Reappearing on the second day, the *Virginia* found its way barred by a curious Union vessel, the *Monitor,* which looked like a tin can on a raft. Belatedly contracted for by the slow-moving Union navy department, the *Monitor,* designed by John Ericsson, was a low-lying ironclad with a revolving gun turret. The battle between the *Virginia* and the *Monitor* ended in a draw, but the Confederate ship had to return to Norfolk to repair its defective engines. Two days later, when forced to abandon Norfolk, the Southerners ran the *Virginia* ashore and burned the vessel to prevent its capture. The South's most promising hope for breaking the blockade was lost.

Mallory was equally prompt in purchasing or commissioning conventional vessels for the Confederate navy. These ships were designed not to combat Union warships, but rather to harass the United States merchant marine. The most successful of these vessels was the CSS *Alabama,* built to Southern specifications at the Laird shipyards in Liverpool, England, and commanded by Raphael Semmes. Ranging over the Atlantic, Indian, and Pacific oceans, the *Alabama* between 1862 and 1864 hunted down and destroyed sixty-nine Union mer-chantmen, valued at more than $6 million. Not until nearly the end of the war could the Union navy corner and sink the raider. By this time, however, the *Alabama,* along with other Confederate cruisers, had virtually exterminated the United States carrying trade.

But however imaginative and innovative, Confederate navy officials could not keep pace with the growth of the Union navy under the slow but honest direction of Navy Secretary Gideon Welles. Drawing on the vast industrial resources of the North and on the experience of its seagoing population, Welles was able to build up the United States navy from its 42 active vessels in 1861, only 26 of which had steam power, to 671 ships in December 1864, of which 71 were ironclad. Navy personnel rose from 7,400 at the start of the war to 68,000 at its end. Superbly equipped and managed, the Union fleet maintained an ever-tightening blockade of the Southern coast. According to the best—but not wholly reliable—statistics, the Union fleet captured not more than one in ten blockade runners in 1861, and not more than one in eight in 1862. But by 1864 it caught one in three, and by 1865, every other one.

The Wartime Economy

Inevitably these huge military and naval operations put a heavy strain on the economic resources of the combatants. In the Confederacy one result was a sharp shift in the nature of Southern agriculture. When the outbreak of war cut off Northern markets and the blockade increasingly sealed off European outlets for cotton and tobacco, farmers—at the urging of the Confederate and state governments—turned to producing grain and other foodstuffs. Cotton production in the South dropped from 4 million bales in 1861 to 300,000 bales in 1864.

In the North, too, farmers began producing more grain. Partly because of inflation, the price of wheat rose from 65 cents a bushel in December 1860 to $2.26 a bushel in July 1864. Farmers, especially in the Middle West, saw a chance to make money. At first the labor shortage kept them from expanding their acreage, for many farmhands enlisted in the Union army at the outbreak of the war. But machines soon made up for the absent men. One of Cyrus Hall McCormick's reapers could replace from four to six farmhands, and McCormick sold 165,000 of his machines during the war.

Industry also grew in both the Union and the Confederacy. As the Union blockade cut off imports, Southern factories gained a virtual monopoly in that region, and military and civilian needs provided an insatiable market. It is hard to measure Southern industrial growth, both because there was no Confederate census and because inflation affected all prices, yet there are some indications that manufacturing could be very profitable. For example, the 1862 conscription acts exempted the owners of certain basic industries provided that their annual profits were no more than 75 percent. Under the astute management of Joseph Anderson, the Tredegar Iron Works at Richmond, the largest privately owned factory in the South and the primary source of Confederate cannon, made profits of 100 percent in 1861 and of 70 percent in 1862.

Northern manufacturing was equally profitable, especially when it produced items needed for the army. The demand for uniforms enabled woolen mills to pay 25 percent dividends by 1865, compared to the 9 percent dividends they had paid before the war. Moreover, the number of woolen mills more than doubled during the war. Investors were willing to pour money into industry more confidently than before because Congress raised tariffs to levels that virtually excluded competing European products. War demands made the mass production of ready-made clothing profitable, and the army's need for shoes speeded the introduction of Gordon McKay's machine for sewing soles to uppers. Simultaneously, in an unrelated development, the discovery of oil at Titusville, Pennsylvania, in 1859 led to a wartime boom in the new petroleum industry.

Structural Changes in the Two Economies These changes had an important impact on the structure of the American economy. The increase in the number of factories encouraged entrepreneurship. In the North men like John D. Rockefeller and Andrew Carnegie, who started their fortunes during the war, continued to dominate the industrial scene after 1865. When the South began rebuilding its industry in the 1870s and 1880s, it looked for leadership to its wartime entrepreneurs and to the Confederate commanders who had experience in directing the labor of large numbers of men. The war also encouraged the growth of large, rather than small, factories. Obliged to contract for huge shipments, both the Union and the Confederate governments naturally turned to those manufacturing companies that were financially and physically able to handle them. The selective process was accelerated because larger firms could pay agents in Washington or Richmond who understood the requirements of the army and navy—as well as those of influential congressmen and bureaucrats.

Most important of all, the wartime experience changed attitudes toward the role of the national government in the economy. Since the destruction of the Second Bank of the United States in the Jacksonian era, the national government had done little to regulate or control the economy. But during the war both the Union and the Confederate governments took steps that affected every branch of economic life. In passing the Homestead Act of May 20, 1862, which offered any citizen 160 acres of the public domain after five years of continuous residence on the land, the Union Congress signaled its intention henceforth to give more attention to the nation's farmers—as it did in creating the federal Department of Agriculture that same year. The Morrill Act of 1862, designating vast tracts of the public domain to support agricultural (land-grant) colleges, was further evidence of the same purpose. Both Union and Confederate governments found it necessary to regulate transportation, especially railroads, during the war. Davis, despite his strict interpretation of the Confederate Constitution, urged his Congress to finance the construction of some missing links in the Southern rail system. Lincoln in July 1862 signed the Pacific Railroad Act, giving enormous tracts of the public land to support the construction of a transcontinental rail route.

In both the United States and the Confederate States, private citizens became aware, often for the first time, of the economic impact of their national governments. In the Confederacy, the Impressment Act of March 1863 authorized government agents to seize civilian food, horses, wagons, or other supplies if required for the army, and to set an arbitrary price for the confiscated goods. In the Union the creation of a new national banking system in 1863 (amended and strengthened in 1864) meant, among other things, that a uniform national currency began to replace the dozens of issues by local banks.* Citizens, paying

---

*In return for purchasing government bonds, banks chartered by the national government were allowed to issue national bank notes, which gradually replaced the state bank notes and local scrip hitherto in use. A tax placed on state bank notes in 1865 ensured that this national currency would have no competition in the future.

national taxes in national currency, grew accustomed to the idea that their national government would henceforth play a positive role in the economic life of the country.

Inflation and Its Consequences

During the desperate final years of the Civil War, the Union and Confederate treasury departments had to experiment with new ways to finance the war. Both imposed broad excise duties. The Internal Revenue Act, enacted by the Union Congress on July 1, 1862, has been fairly characterized as an attempt to tax everything. The act imposed duties on all sorts of manufactures, with a fresh duty levied each time the raw material underwent a new process. In a carriage, for example, the leather, the cloth, the wood, and the metal were each taxed; then the manufacturer was taxed for the process of putting them together; the dealer was taxed for selling the carriage; and the purchaser, having paid a sufficient price to cover all these duties, was taxed in addition for ownership. Heavy duties fell on luxuries like billiard tables and yachts, and taxes on professions and occupations covered, as Representative James G. Blaine said, "bankers and pawn brokers, lawyers and horse-dealers, physicians and confectioners, commercial brokers and peddlers." Ultimately these taxes brought in about 21 percent of the total wartime expenditures of the Union government.

The Confederacy moved more slowly, but on April 24, 1863, it too adopted a comprehensive tax measure. This included an income tax, occupational and license taxes ranging from $40 for bowling alleys to $500 for bankers, and what later generations would call an excess profits tax. A unique feature of the Confederate legislation was the tax-in-kind, which compelled producers of wheat, corn, oats, potatoes, sugar, cotton, tobacco, and other farm products to pay one-tenth of their crop each year to the government. A last, desperate attempt in March 1865 to tax all coin, bullion, and foreign exchange was made too late to have any effect. All told, the Confederacy raised only about 1 percent of its income from taxes.

The sale of bonds contributed little more to the Confederate treasury. Values were so uncertain in the wartime South that investors were afraid to tie up their money in such fixed investments, and doubts spread as to when and whether the Confederate government would even pay the interest on its obligations. In the Union, on the other hand, bonds became a major source of revenue. At first Treasury Secretary Chase could not sell bonds, even at a discount, but when he appointed his friend Jay Cooke, the Philadelphia banker who also had an office in Washington, as special agent of the Treasury Department, the story changed. Using high-pressure advertising, Cooke launched an extensive propaganda campaign that extolled the merits of the "five-twenties"—bonds bearing 6 percent interest, which could be paid off after five years and must be redeemed in twenty years. Cooke was so successful that between 600,000 and a million citizens were persuaded to invest in the public debt, and the entire loan of half a billion dollars was oversubscribed. But in 1864, as the war stretched on endlessly and victory appeared nowhere in sight, the market for bonds collapsed. Resigning for political reasons, Chase left office at an opportune moment to preserve his reputation as a financier, and Cooke went with him. Chase's successor, William Pitt Fessenden, could raise money only through short-term loans at an exorbitant rate of interest. Not until the very end of the war, when victory was obviously near, did the sale of Union bonds pick up, and Cooke, reappointed special agent, attracted many additional investors.

The Resort to Paper Money

Thus through necessity both governments continued to depend on paper money. The Union treasury, which had cautiously issued its first greenbacks in 1862, printed more and more during the rest of that year and during 1863 as well, until most of the $450 million authorized by Congress was in circulation. The value of these greenbacks gradually declined. A Union treasury note with a face value of one dollar was worth 99.86 cents in gold in 1862, but by 1864 it was worth only 62.66 cents, and by early 1865, 50.3 cents. In the Confederacy, where the printing presses never stopped, paper money had even less value. Perhaps $2 billion in unredeemable paper was issued in all. A Confederate treasury note for one dollar, worth 82.7 cents in gold in 1862, dropped to 29 cents in 1863 and to 1.7 cents in early 1865. In a desperate attempt to halt the slide, the Confederate Congress in February 1864 undertook a partial repudiation of these notes, but the confusing and complex legislation was badly administered and served further to undermine trust in the government and its money. Having lost the confidence of the country, Treasury Secretary Memminger resigned in the summer of 1864—at about the same time that Chase left the Union Treasury Department. Memminger's successor, the South Carolina banker and businessman George A. Trenholm, could devise no better solution for the Confederacy's financial woes than to urge citizens to donate to the government their money, jewels, gold and silver plate, and public securities.

The excessive amount of paper money was only one of many factors that produced runaway inflation in both the North and the South. With importations largely cut off (in the North by the high protective tariff and in the South by the Union blockade), with the productive labor force sharply reduced because of the number of men in military service, and with a huge portion of all goods required to supply the armies and navies, civilians had to expect shortages and high prices.

Profits and Deprivation

In both sections some people profited from the wartime economy. War contracts helped pull the Union economy out of a sharp depression, and higher prices spurred on manufacturers, who could now look for higher profits. The demand for grain, along with the Homestead Act, encouraged new settlers to begin farming, and the development of petroleum and other new industries made for quick fortunes. The wartime boom in the North had a hectic quality about it, and people spent their easily earned money quickly lest it be worth less in the future. Many of the new rich were extravagant and hedonistic. Angrily the *New York Independent* asked in June 1864:

> Who at the North would ever think of war, if he had not a friend in the army, or did not read the newspapers? Go into Broadway, and we will show you what is meant by the word "extravagance." Ask [A. T.] Stewart [the department-store owner] about the demand for camel's-hair shawls, and he will say "monstrous." Ask Tiffany what kinds of diamonds and pearls are called for. He will answer "the prodigious," "as near hen's-egg size as possible," "price no object." What kinds of carpetings are now wanted? None but "extra." ... And as for horses the medium-priced five-hundred-dollar kind are all out of the market. A good pair of "fast ones" ... will go for a thousand dollars sooner than a basket of strawberries will sell for four cents.

But not everyone in the North shared in this wartime prosperity. Wages lagged sadly behind prices, so that in real income a worker between 1861 and 1865 lost 35 percent of his earnings. Women, who composed one-fourth of the nation's manufacturing force in 1860, were especially hard hit. Soldiers could send their wives and mothers only a pittance for support, and as more and more women found it necessary to work, employers actually cut their wages. Even the United States government participated in this practice. At the Philadelphia armory, the government in 1861 paid a seamstress 17 cents for making a shirt; three years later, when prices were at their highest, it cut the wage to 15 cents. Meanwhile private contractors paid only 8 cents.

Suffering in the North was, however, relatively minor when compared to that in the South. To be sure, residents of some parts of the agricultural South who were never disturbed by Union troops had only minor shortages to complain of. As imported goods disappeared from the grocers' shelves, they resorted to sassafras tea and to "coffee" made of parched rye, okra seeds, corn, and even sweet potatoes, the grounds of which were said to be a remarkable cleaning agent for curtains and carpets. Because salt was in short supply, meat could not be preserved, and Southerners ate more chicken and fish. As clothing wore out, they increasingly turned to homespun, and velvet draperies and brocaded rugs found new uses as gowns and overcoats.

But the thousands of Southerners in the path of the armies had to think not just of shortages, but of survival. Hundreds of families fled before the invading Union armies, often attempting to take their slaves with them, but nowhere could these refugees find assurance of safety. Their lives took on a desperate, nightmarish quality, and merely existing from one day to the next was a struggle. There was never enough of anything, including food. Recalling those unhappy days, one writer declared that "the Confederacy was always hungry."

The greatest destitution appeared in towns and cities, where supplies had to be brought in over the rickety Southern railroad system. White-collar workers, especially those on fixed government salaries, were particularly hard hit. The famous diary of J. B. Jones, a clerk in the Confederate War Department at Richmond, is a melancholy record of shortages and high prices. In May 1864 he reported that beans in Richmond were selling for $3 a quart, meal for $125 a bushel, and flour for $400 a barrel. Richmond, he observed, was an astonishingly clean city since "no garbage or filth can accumulate." The citizens of the Confederate capital were obliged to be "such good scavengers" that there was "no need of buzzards."

Deprivation was the more painful because, as in the North, some made enormous profits from the war. The blockade runners, who preferred to bring in compact, expensive items like silks and jewels rather than bulky supplies for the army, often reaped fantastic profits. Speculators flourished. As early as the winter of 1862 the governor of Mississippi learned that the families of volunteers in his state were seriously suffering because of the lack of corn and salt, while rich planters held back their ample supply of both commodities, waiting for the inevitable rise in prices. Trading with the enemy was even more profitable. The practice was completely illegal but tacitly permitted by both Confederate and Union officials. Southern women and men who were initiated into the mysteries of the trade bought up as much cotton as they could find in their neighborhoods and took it to convenient exchange points like Memphis and Natchez to sell to the Yankees for coffee, clothing, and luxuries. Late in the war they accepted payment in United States greenbacks, which Southerners valued more than their own depreciated currency.

Conscription and Conflict

Along with economic grievances, the unfairness of conscription was the source of bitter complaints by Northerners and Southerners alike during the Civil War.

The Confederate conscription act of 1862 theoretically made all able-bodied white males between the ages of eighteen and thirty-five equally eligible for military service, but the Southern Congress promptly began exempting large categories of men. As men rushed to enter "bombproof" occupations and claim exemptions, the outcry against the Confederate conscription system grew louder. One of the strongest critics was Governor Joseph E. Brown of Georgia, who protested, "The conscription Act, at one fell swoop, strikes down the sovereignty of the States, tramples upon the constitutional rights and personal liberty of the citizens, and arms the President with imperial power." After attempting unsuc-cessfully to induce the Georgia supreme court to declare conscription uncon-stitutional, Brown proceeded to undermine the policy by naming his supporters to state jobs exempt from military service. According to some estimates he put 15,000 able-bodied Georgians into this exempt category; certainly he created 2,000 justices of the peace and 1,000 constables, none of whom had to serve in the army. Less prominent than Brown but equally potent were the critics who complained that conscription was class legislation that benefited the educated and the wealthy. They objected especially to the so-called "twenty-nigger" provision, which clearly favored plantation owners at the expense of farmers. "Never did a law meet with more universal odium than the exemption of slave owners," wrote Senator James Phelan of Mississippi to President Davis. "It has aroused a spirit of rebellion . . . and bodies of men have banded together to desert."

Despite intense criticism and dubious results, the Davis administration continued conscription, for it saw no other way to raise the needed number of men. Indeed, as the war progressed, the Confederacy was obliged to experiment with even more stringent legislation. In a new conscription act of February 17, 1864, the Confederate Congress declared that all white males between the ages of seventeen and fifty were subject to the draft, with the seventeen-year-old boys and the men above forty-five to serve as a reserve for local defense. As a concession to small planters, the act exempted one farmer or overseer for every plantation with fifteen slaves; but it abolished most other exemptions, on the theory that once skilled laborers were in the army, the government could detail them to the forges and factories where they were most needed. Total mobilization of manpower was, however, far beyond the competence of the shaky Confederate government, and in practice the industrial-detail system never worked. As the Confederacy scraped the bottom of the barrel, more and more white Southerners began thinking about the one group of able-bodied males who did not serve in the armies, the blacks.

In the North, too, conscription evoked bitter criticism. The first effective Northern draft act, passed by the Union Congress on March 3, 1863, was obviously unfair. The act declared that all able-bodied males between the ages of twenty and forty-five (except for certain high governmental officials and the only sons of widows and of infirm parents) were liable to military service. But it promptly contradicted itself by permitting those who could afford to do so to hire substitutes. In an effort to keep the price of substitutes down, it also permitted a man to purchase outright exemption from military service for $300.

As in the South, there was immediate and widespread hostility toward conscription. The system favored the wealthiest citizens and the most prosperous sections of the country. A well-to-do man like George Templeton Strong of New York, for example, did not dream of serving in the army; he paid $1,100 for a substitute, "a big 'Dutch' boy of twenty or thereabouts," who, as Strong remarked complacently, "looked as if he could do good service." Rich towns and counties raised bounty funds to encourage volunteering, so that none of their citizens would have to be drafted; and as the war went on, they offered higher and higher bounties. The volunteers they sought were by no means all local residents who needed a little financial inducement; many of them were professional bounty hunters, who went from place to place enlisting, receiving bounties, and promptly deserting. Perhaps the record for bounty jumping was held by one John O'Connor, who when arrested in March 1865 confessed to thirty-two such desertions.

Part of the outcry against conscription in the North stemmed from the unfairness of the quotas the president was authorized to announce for each state, presumably giving credit for the number of volunteers it had previously supplied.

The Democratic governor of New York, Horatio Seymour, engaged in angry correspondence with Lincoln and finally forced the president to admit that the quota assigned to New York was excessive. This and similar concessions, however, came too late to placate those who were threatened by the draft. In Wisconsin, Kentucky, and Pennsylvania, in Troy, Newark, and Albany, there was outright resistance to the enrolling officers, and in several instances federal troops had to be brought in to quell the uprisings. But none of these outbreaks was as large or ferocious as that in New York City, where the drawing of the first draftees' names triggered a three-day riot (July 13–15, 1863) by a mob of predominantly Irish workingmen. Turning first against the enrollment officers and the police, the rioters then exhibited their hostility toward the rich by plundering fine houses and rifling jewelry stores. The mob acted with hideous brutality toward blacks, whom the rioters feared as economic competitors and blamed for the war and hence for conscription. After sacking and looting a black orphan asylum, the rioters chased down any blacks unwary enough to appear on the streets and left those they could catch hanging from lampposts. The Union government had to rush in troops from the Gettysburg campaign to stop the rioting and disperse the mob.

Despite all resistance, Lincoln's government continued conscription because, as in the Confederacy, there seemed to be no other source of soldiers. Even so, the draft remained cumbersome and often ineffectual. In 1864, for example, 800,000 names were drawn, but so many were exempted because of health or occupation, and so many others hired substitutes or paid the commutation fee, that only 33,000 were actually inducted into the army. As conscription proved both unfair and ineffective, citizens in the North, like those in the South, began to think of the value of black soldiers.

Steps Toward Emancipation

Just as African Americans played a central role in causing the Civil War, so they played a major role in determining its outcome. At the beginning there was an unspoken agreement that the Civil War was to be a white man's fight, and both the Union and the Confederate governments in 1861 refused to accept black volunteers. In the Confederacy during the first two years of the war, virtually nobody questioned the correctness of this decision. After all, as Vice-President Alexander H. Stephens announced, slavery was "the real 'cornerstone'" on which the Confederate States had been erected, and few Southern whites could even contemplate the possibility of arming slaves or of freeing blacks who became soldiers.

In the Union, on the other hand, powerful voices from the beginning urged the emancipation of slaves and the enlistment of blacks. Frederick Douglass, the leading spokesman of blacks in the North, repeatedly insisted: "Teach the rebels and traitors that the price they are to pay for the attempt to abolish this Government must be the abolition of slavery." Abolitionists, white and black,

Black Teamsters near the Signal Tower at Bermuda Hundred, Virginia, 1864
Although there was opposition in both the Confederacy and the Union to the emancipation of slaves, neither side was reluctant to employ blacks in nonmilitary service. For both armies blacks served as teamsters, butchers, drovers, boatmen, bakers, shoemakers, and nurses. Nearly 200,000 blacks performed labor for the Union armies.

again and again instructed Lincoln that he could win the war only if he emancipated the slaves. Senator Charles Sumner of Massachusetts visited the White House almost daily in his efforts to persuade Lincoln that emancipation was the *"one way to safety,* clear as sunlight—pleasant as the paths of Peace."

This antislavery sentiment was so influential that several of the president's subordinates who fell into disfavor with the administration tried to appeal to it. But President Lincoln, aware of the dangerous complexity of the issue, patiently overruled each of these subordinates, declaring that emancipation was a question "which, under my responsibility, I reserve to myself."

Nonmilitary Employment of Blacks

Unwillingness to arm or emancipate the slaves did not signify any reluctance to employ blacks in nonmilitary service. Slaves were the backbone of the Confederate labor force. If blacks had not continued to cultivate and harvest the grain, the Confederacy could never have fielded so large an army. Equally important was the role played by blacks, slave and free, in the industrial production of the Confederacy. In the Tredegar Iron Works, for example, half the 2,400 employees were blacks; they included not merely unskilled workers, but puddlers, rollers, and machinists. Blacks also performed indispensable service for the quartermaster and commissary departments of the Confederacy, laboring as teamsters, butchers, drovers, boatmen, bakers, shoemakers, and blacksmiths; and they were nurses in many Confederate hospitals.

Contrabands Following the Union Army
Wherever Union armies advanced into the South, they attracted throngs of slaves who escaped from their masters and, packing their meager belongings on their backs or in rickety wagons, sought the protection of the federal soldiers.

So essential was black labor to the existence of the Confederacy that President Davis had to ensure that enough blacks were available for this service. From the beginning of the war, Confederate authorities sought to compel slaves to work on fortifications. Some states, notably Virginia, moved promptly to require owners to lease their slaves to the government when needed. But the Confederate government itself did not act until March 1863. At that time the Confederate Congress, despite much opposition from slaveowners, authorized the impressment of slaves, whose owners were to receive $30 a month. In February 1864 the Southern Congress permitted military authorities to impress more slaves, whether or not these officials had obtained the consent of the slaveowners.

Meanwhile the Union was also making full use of black labor. As slaves fled from their masters to the Union army, they were put to use as teamsters, cooks, nurses, carpenters, scouts, and day laborers. Perhaps half a million blacks crossed over to the Union lines, and nearly 200,000 of these performed labor for the army. Many of these "contrabands" brought with them valuable information about the location of Confederate troops and supplies. Occasionally some brought even more valuable assets. Robert Smalls and his brother, who were slaves in Charleston, South Carolina, in May 1862 daringly seized the Confederate side-wheel steamer *Planter,* navigated it out of the harbor ringed with Confederate guns, and delivered it to the blockading Union fleet.

Debate over Emancipation in the North

When the war seemed to have reached a stalemate, Northern sentiment grew more favorable to freeing and arming the slaves. Republican congressmen were ahead of the president on these questions. As early as August 1861 they had passed an act declaring that slaves who had supported the Confederate military were free. In March 1862 Congress forbade the Union army to return fugitive slaves. And on July 17, 1862, in a far-reaching confiscation act, Congress declared that slaves of all persons supporting the rebellion should be "forever free of their servitude, and not again [to be] held as slaves." These measures were, however, poorly drafted and not readily enforced, so that they had little practical consequence. But Congress's abolition of slavery in the District of Columbia on April 16, 1862, was more effective.

Powerful forces in the North, however, opposed emancipation. The border states, where slavery still prevailed, threatened to break away from the Union if emancipation became a Northern war aim. In the free states antiblack prejudice was rampant, and many feared that emancipation would result in a massive migration of blacks to the North, where they would compete with white laborers for jobs. Belief in black inferiority was general, and the experience of Union soldiers in the South often strengthened this stereotype, for the fugitive slaves who fled to their camps were for the most part illiterate, ragged, and dirty.

Lincoln hated slavery, but during the initial stages of the war he could move toward emancipation only in a roundabout way. In early 1862 he made an earnest, although ultimately unsuccessful, plea to the border states to devise plans of gradual, compensated emancipation, for which he promised federal financial assistance. At the same time, he took antiblack sentiment into account by favoring plans to settle freedmen (ex-slaves) in Central America and Haiti.

By the fall of 1862, however, Lincoln felt able to act decisively against slavery. In failing to adopt his program of gradual emancipation, the border states had lost their chance. Blacks showed little interest in his plans for colonization, which in any case were poorly thought out and could only lead to disaster. As casualties mounted, Northern soldiers came to think that it was time to enroll blacks in the army, although they did not necessarily shed their prejudices against blacks. But most influential in changing Lincoln's mind was his grim recognition that after eighteen months of combat, the war could not be ended by traditional means. "We...must change our tactics or lose the war," he concluded.

Waiting only for McClellan to end Lee's invasion at Antietam, Lincoln on September 22, 1862, issued a preliminary emancipation proclamation. This announced that unless the rebellious states returned to their allegiance, he would on January 1, 1863, declare "all persons held as slaves" in the territory controlled by the Confederates to be "then, thenceforward, and forever free." Since the president justified his action on the ground of military necessity, it was appropriate that the definitive Emancipation Proclamation, which was issued at the beginning of the new year, officially authorized the enrollment of black troops in the Union army.

Company E, 4th U.S. Colored Infantry, at Petersburg
General Benjamin F. Butler used black troops in his assault on Petersburg because, he said, "I knew that they would fight more desperately than any white troops, in order to prevent capture, because they knew . . . that if captured they would be returned into slavery."

The War Department promptly began to accept black recruits. These were not, to be sure, the first black soldiers to serve in the war, for without permission from Washington a few blacks had been enrolled in the Union forces on the Sea Islands of South Carolina, in Louisiana, and in Kansas. But large numbers of blacks now joined the army. They were enrolled in segregated regiments, nearly always with white officers, and they received less pay than did white soldiers. By the end of the war there were 178,895 black soldiers in the Union army—more than twice the number of soldiers in the Confederate army at Gettysburg.

At first most Union officials thought that black regiments would be useful only for garrison duty, but in such bitterly contested engagements as Fort Wagner and Port Hudson, Miliken's Bend and Nashville, they demonstrated how well they could and would fight. The battle record of these black troops did much to change popular Northern stereotypes of the black man.

The South Moves Toward Emancipation

Meanwhile, and much more slowly, sentiment was growing in the Confederacy for the military employment of blacks. Support for arming the slaves emerged first in those areas devastated by Northern armies. After Grant's successful Vicksburg campaign, the *Jackson Mississippian* boldly called for enrolling slaves in the Confederate army. Although other Mississippi and Alabama newspapers echoed the appeal for black recruits, the most powerful voice for arming the slaves was that of General Patrick R. Cleburne, who witnessed how easily the powerful Union army broke the thin Confederate line at Chattanooga. Seeing no other source of manpower, Cleburne and his aides addressed a long letter to General Joseph E. Johnston, who had succeeded Bragg as commander of the army of Tennessee, urging "that we immediately commence training a large reserve of the most courageous of our slaves, and further that we guarantee freedom within a reasonable time to every slave in the South who shall remain true to the Confederacy in this war."

So drastic a proposal was bound to rouse strong opposition. On learning of Cleburne's letter, President Davis ordered it suppressed. But the subject would not die. As Union armies moved closer to the Confederate heartland, Virginia editors also began to urge arming the blacks, and in October 1864 a meeting of Southern governors proposed "a change of policy on our part" as to the slaves. Finally, on November 7, 1864, President Davis put himself at the head of the movement in a deliberately obscure message to Congress. Urging further impressment of blacks for service with the army, Davis argued that the Confederate government should purchase the impressed slaves.

However ambiguously it was phrased, Davis's proposal clearly looked toward the end of slavery, and it at once encountered powerful resistance. Davis, said his enemies, proposed the confiscation of private property; he was subverting the Constitution. His plan would be a confession to the world of the South's weakness. It would deplete the labor force needed to feed the army. And most frightening of all, it would arm black men, who at best might desert to the Union armies and at worst might take up arms against their masters.

Despite all opposition, the Confederate government pushed ahead with the plan, for it had no other reservoir of manpower. In February 1865 the scheme received the backing of General Lee, who wrote that employing blacks as soldiers was "not only expedient but necessary" and announced plainly that "it would be neither just nor wise . . . to require them to serve as slaves." The next month, by a very close vote, the Confederate Congress passed an act calling for 300,000 more soldiers, irrespective of color. No provision was made to free blacks who enrolled, but the Confederate War Department in effect smuggled emancipation into the measure through the orders it issued for its enforcement. Promptly the recruiting of black troops began, and some black companies were raised in Richmond and other towns. By this time, however, it was too late even for such a revolutionary experiment, and none of the black Confederate soldiers ever saw military service.

Europe and the War

Although the Union and Confederate governments moved toward emancipating and arming the blacks because of military necessity, both recognized how profoundly their actions affected the continuing struggle for European recognition and support. Informed Americans were aware of the intensity of European antislavery sentiment. But so long as neither government took a bold stand against the South's peculiar institution, European antislavery leaders were puzzled and divided by the war. Lincoln's Emancipation Proclamation ended the confusion. European antislavery spokesmen recognized that the proclamation marked a new era. Within three months after the final Emancipation Proclamation was issued, fifty-six large public meetings were held in Great Britain to uphold the Northern cause.

Union diplomacy needed such popular support, for there was still a possibility of European intervention in the war. Although the gravest threat had passed in the fall of 1862, before the full effect of the Emancipation Proclamation could be sensed abroad, Emperor Napoleon III of France continued to contemplate the advantages that might come of meddling in American affairs. Napoleon hoped that the division of the United States would help him establish a puppet empire in Mexico under Archduke Maximilian of Austria. When Northern military fortunes were at their low point in February 1863, after the battle of Fredericksburg, Napoleon offered to mediate between the two belligerents. Shrewdly judging that Great Britain and Russia were not behind the French move, Secretary of State Seward spurned the offer.

The warships being built for the Confederacy in British shipyards were more dangerous to the Union cause than was Napoleon's clumsy diplomacy. Supplying either belligerent in war with armed ships was contrary both to international law and to British statutes, but a loophole in the law made it possible to sell unarmed vessels separately from the armaments that would convert them into men of war. In March 1862 the ship that became the CSS *Florida* sailed from a British shipyard, and in July of that year the more powerful *Alabama* set forth to begin its raids. Even as these raiders swept the Union merchant marine from the high seas, a more formidable Confederate naval threat—this time to the blockade itself— was being forged in the form of two enormous ironclad steam rams under construction at the Laird yards in Liverpool.

The British government wished to observe its neutrality laws, but the legal machinery was slow and cumbersome. When Union minister Charles Francis Adams called the attention of the foreign office to the rams, Lord Russell replied that he could not act to detain them unless there was convincing evidence of Confederate ownership. Adams and his aides rushed to secure proof that the vessels were intended for the Confederacy, but British law officers were unconvinced. Finally, in utter exasperation, Adams on September 5, 1863, sent Russell a final warning against permitting the ships to sail, adding: "It would be superfluous in me to point out to your Lordship that this is war." Fortunately, two days before receiving Adams's ultimatum, Russell had already decided to detain the rams, and the Confederates' final hope of breaking the blockade was lost.

With that crisis, the last serious threat of European involvement in the American war disappeared. So indifferent, or even hostile, to the Southern cause was the British cabinet that late in 1863 Confederate Secretary of State Judah P. Benjamin ordered James M. Mason, his envoy, to leave London on the grounds that "the Government of Her Majesty [Queen Victoria] . . . entertains no intention of receiving you as the accredited minister of this government."

President Davis was keenly aware of the influence that emancipation had exerted in uniting European opinion against the South, and he sought similarly to capitalize on the actions against slavery that the Confederate States took during the final months of the war. In January 1865 he sent Duncan F. Kenner, one of Louisiana's largest slaveholders, on a secret mission to Europe. Kenner was authorized to promise the emancipation of slaves in return for European recognition and aid to the Confederacy. The experiment came too late, for now it was evident that Northern victory was inevitable. Neither the French nor the British government expressed interest in Kenner's proposal.

Wartime Politics in the Confederacy

The military and diplomatic advantages resulting from emancipation were to a certain extent counterbalanced by its political disadvantages. In the Confederacy there had been from the beginning of the war a sizable disloyal element. Unionism was strong in the Upper South, in the mountain regions, and in some of the poorer hill counties. As the war went on, some of the Southern malcontents joined secret peace societies such as the Order of the Heroes, which had its following in the Carolinas and Virginia. Disloyalty extended into the ranks of the Confederate army, especially after conscription was initiated, and desertion was widespread. Some men left because their families needed them at home; some felt a greater loyalty to their states than to the Confederacy as a whole; but many were disillusioned with the whole idea of Southern independence. About one out of every nine soldiers who enlisted in the Confederate army deserted. Sometimes deserters formed guerrilla bands that preyed equally on Confederate and Union sympathizers. When halted by an enrollment officer and asked to show his pass to leave the army, a deserter would pat his gun defiantly and say, "This is my furlough."

Probably no action of the Davis administration could have won over these actively disloyal citizens, but the policies of the Confederate government alienated also a large number of entirely loyal Southerners. Some of these critics complained that President Davis was timid and tardy. He was sickly, neurasthenic, and indecisive, they said; he could not tolerate strong men around him and relied for advice on yes men; he did not know how to rouse the loyalty and passions of the Southern people; he lacked courage to put himself at the head of the Southern armies and lead the Confederacy to victory.

Many more Confederates were bitterly critical of their president for exactly the opposite reasons. Davis's plan to arm and free the slaves reinforced their conviction that he intended to undermine the principles on which the Confederacy had been founded. Conscription, they argued, had begun the subversion of state sovereignty, guaranteed by the Constitution. They found evidence of Davis's dictatorial ambitions in his requests that Congress suspend the writ of habeas corpus, so that disloyal persons could be arrested and imprisoned without trial. Congress grudgingly agreed to the suspension for three limited periods, but late in 1864 it rejected Davis's appeals for a further extension on the ground that it would be a dangerous assault on the Constitution. Although infringements on civil liberties were infrequent in the Confederacy, and no Southern newspaper was suppressed for publishing subversive editorials, the critics warned that Davis was reaching after imperial powers. Leading this group of Davis's critics was none other than the vice-president of the Confederate States, Alexander H. Stephens, who spent most of the final years of the war not in Richmond but in Georgia, stirring up agitation against the president's allegedly unconstitutional usurpation of power, and simultaneously complaining of Davis's "weakness and imbecility."

The congressional elections of 1863, held after Southerners had begun to realize the gravity of their defeats at Gettysburg and at Vicksburg, greatly strengthened the anti-Davis bloc. During the following year the president often could muster a majority in Congress only because of the consistent support of representatives from districts in the upper South overrun or threatened by advancing Northern armies. But by the desperate winter of 1864–65, not even this support could give Davis control of Congress. Now in a majority, the president's critics refused his request for control over the state militias and rejected his plea to end all exemptions from conscription. Even as Sherman's army advanced through the Carolinas,* Congress endlessly debated Davis's plan for arming the slaves. Over presidential opposition, it passed an act creating the position of general in chief, advising Davis to name Lee. Fearful of attacking the president directly, congressional critics began investigations of several of his cabinet officers, and they introduced resolutions declaring that the resignation of Secretary of State Benjamin, Davis's closest friend and most trusted adviser, would be "subservient of the public interest." Secretary of War James A. Seddon also came under fire, and when the Virginia delegation in Congress called for his resignation, he felt obliged to leave the cabinet. In January 1865, for the first and only time, the Confederate Congress overrode a presidential veto.

Wartime Politics in the North

Meanwhile, in the North, Abraham Lincoln and his government were subjected to the same kinds of criticism. Pro-Confederate sympathy was strongest in the states of the Upper South that remained in the Union, in those parts of the Old Northwest originally settled by Southerners, and in cities like New York, where the Irish immigrant population was bitterly hostile to blacks. Northerners joined secret societies, such as the Knights of the Golden Circle and the Order of American Knights, devoted to bringing about a negotiated peace, which inevitably would entail recognizing Confederate independence. Although most members of these secret "Copperhead" organizations intended nothing more subversive than replacing a Republican administration with a Democratic one, certain of the leaders were ready to accept the dissolution of the Union. Some idea of the

---

*For Sherman's advance in 1864–65, see below, pp. 649–50.

extent of unrest in the North can be gained from the figures on desertion: one out of every seven who enlisted in the Union armies deserted.

Much of the criticism of the Lincoln administration came from those who were entirely loyal to the Union but who deplored the measures the president took to save it. They complained bitterly when Lincoln, without waiting for congressional approval, suspended the writ of habeas corpus so that suspected subversives could be arrested without warning and imprisoned indefinitely. Although Chief Justice Roger B. Taney protested against the unconstitutionality of these arrests, Lincoln refused to heed his objections. Several thousand persons were thus arbitrarily imprisoned. Critics also complained when the Lincoln administration curbed the freedom of the press. Because of the publication of allegedly disloyal and inflammatory statements, the *Chicago Times,* and *New York World,* the *Philadelphia Evening Journal,* and many other newspapers were required to suspend publication for varying periods of time.

Lincoln's Emancipation Proclamation, followed by the arming of black soldiers, gave his critics further evidence of his ambition to become dictator and of his diabolical plan to change the purpose of the war. So unpopular was the policy of emancipation that Lincoln's preliminary proclamation, together with the inability of Union generals to win victories, seriously hurt his party in the congressional elections of 1862. In virtually every Northern state there was an increase in Democratic votes. The Republican majority in Congress was now paper-thin, and the administration kept that lead only because the army interfered in the Maryland, Kentucky, and Missouri elections. Just as Jefferson Davis's control of the Confederate Congress after 1863 depended on the votes of border state representatives, so Abraham Lincoln's majority in the Union Congress rested on the support of representatives from the same region.

Republican Criticism of Lincoln

If Democrats complained that Lincoln acted arbitrarily and too swiftly, critics within his own party held that he was too slow, too cautious, and too indecisive. His own attorney general, Edward Bates, felt that the president could cope with "neither great *principles* nor great *facts.*" Lincoln lacked "practical talent for his important place," concluded Senator Sumner, who thought that in his slowness to act and his indecisiveness the president resembled the bumbling French king Louis XVI more than any other ruler in history.

Dissatisfaction with Lincoln was so widespread that when Congress reassembled in December 1862, after the fiasco at Fredericksburg, the Senate Republican caucus tried to force the president to change his cabinet. Just as Davis's critics made Benjamin their target, so Republican senators blamed Secretary of State Seward for the weakness of the Lincoln administration and the poor handling of the war. By forcing Seward's resignation, these critics hoped to make Chase (who had fed them stories of Lincoln's incompetence) in effect premier. This maneuver distressed Lincoln deeply, and he thwarted it with great skill. He secured Seward's resignation and forced Chase also to offer his; then he declined both resignations by announcing that either one would leave the cabinet unbalanced. His cabinet remained intact, and the president remained responsible for Union policy.

Such sleight of hand was not enough to make dissent within Lincoln's own party disappear. Gradually two rival Republican factions emerged, the Conservatives, or Moderates, and the Radicals—whom their enemies called Jacobins, comparing them to the extremists of the French Revolution. The Conservatives were represented by Seward in the cabinet and by Senator James R. Doolittle of Wisconsin in Congress. They continued to think that the war could be won by conventional means and opposed such experiments as emancipation, the arming of slaves, and the confiscation of rebel property. The Radicals, on the other hand, represented by Chase in the cabinet and by Sumner and Thaddeus Stevens in Congress, were eager to try more drastic experiments. They demanded that the entire Southern social system be revolutionized, that Southern slaveholders be punished and, increasingly, that blacks be given not merely freedom, but civil and political equality as well.

Lincoln refused to align himself with either faction and tried to be even-handed in distributing federal patronage to both. He shared the Conservatives' desire for a speedy peace and a prompt reconciliation between the sections; but he recognized that in casting about for votes to carry through their plans, they would be "tempted to affiliate with those whose record is not clear," even persons infected "by the virus of secession." As for the Radicals, he conceded that "after all their faces are set Zionwards" but he objected to their "petulant and vicious fretfulness" and thought they were sometimes "almost *fiendish*" in attacking Republicans who disagreed with them. Because of his neutrality, the president gained the distrust and abuse of both factions.

The Election of 1864   The split within the Republican party was the more serious because the presidential election of 1864 was approaching. The Democrats had a handsome, glamorous candidate in General George B. McClellan, and they had a powerful set of issues. They could capitalize on war weariness. They made much of Lincoln's arbitrary use of executive power and the infringement of civil liberties. They objected to the unfairness of the draft. They showed how the Republican Congress had benefited the Northeast by enacting protective tariffs, handing out railroad subsidies, and creating a national banking system. The Democrats endlessly harped on the antiblack theme, charging that the Lincoln administration had changed the war for union into a war for emancipation. If Lincoln was reelected, they charged, Republicans were planning to amalgamate the black and white races. The word *miscegenation* (race mixing) made its first appearance in an 1864 campaign document.

Even in the face of such powerful opposition, the Republicans in the winter of 1863–64 divided sharply when Lincoln in December 1863 announced a plan for reconstructing the Southern states. The president promised amnesty to all Confederates except for a few high government officials. He also proposed to reestablish civilian government in the conquered areas of the South. If in any state 10 percent or more of those who had voted in 1860 would take an oath swearing future loyalty to the United States and pledging acceptance of emancipation, the president promised to recognize the legality of the government these voters set up. Fearing that his program would put the prewar leadership back in control of the South and would leave freedmen in peonage, the Radicals pushed the Wade-Davis bill through Congress. This bill required that more than half the number of 1860 voters in each Southern state swear allegiance and participate in drafting a new constitution before their state could be readmitted to the Union. This measure was passed at the end of the 1864 congressional session, and Lincoln killed it by refusing to sign it after Congress had adjourned. The Radicals were furious. Senator Benjamin F. Wade and Representative Henry Winter Davis, the sponsors of the vetoed bill, issued a public statement accusing the president of "usurpations" and claiming that he had committed a "studied outrage upon the legislative authority of the people."

Lincoln had control of the federal patronage and of the party machinery, and so he was readily renominated in June 1864 by the Republican national convention, which selected Andrew Johnson of Tennessee as his running mate. But the unanimity of the vote was only a facade. After an unsuccessful attempt to run Chase as a rival to Lincoln, some ultra-Radicals had already thrown their support to a third-party ticket headed by General Frémont, who had been hostile to the president since his removal from command in Missouri. Even after Lincoln had been renominated, other Radicals tried to persuade the party to pick a new candidate. As late as September 1864 a questionnaire sent to Republican governors, leading editors, and prominent congressmen drew a virtually unanimous response that if Lincoln could be persuaded to withdraw from the race, Republicans should name another standard-bearer. As Massachusetts Governor John A. Andrew expressed the general sentiment, Lincoln was "essentially lacking in the quality of leadership." So bleak was the outlook that a few weeks before the elections, the president himself conceded that McClellan was likely to win.

Northern Victory

Until the fall of 1864, then, the wartime history of the United States and of the Confederate States moved in parallel lines as each government improvised experiments that might lead to victory. But in the final months of the struggle, the course of the two rivals dramatically diverged. Increasing dissension and unrest marked Jefferson Davis's last winter in office, while Abraham Lincoln won triumphant reelection in November 1864. By April 1865 the Confederacy was dead, and a month later Davis was in irons, like a common criminal, at Fort Monroe, Virginia. The Union was victorious, and Lincoln, killed by the bullet of the mad assassin John Wilkes Booth, lived in memory as the nation's martyred president who had freed the slaves and saved the Union.

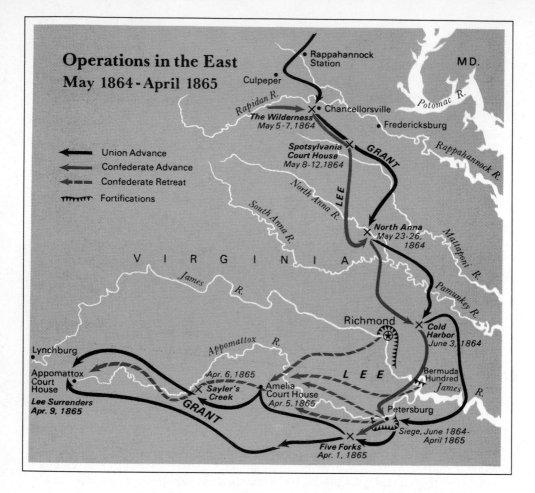

Operations in the East May 1864 – April 1865

- MD.
- Rappahannock Station
- Culpeper
- Rapidan R.
- Potomac R.
- The Wilderness *May 5-7, 1864*
- Chancellorsville
- Fredericksburg
- Rappahannock R.

Union Advance
Confederate Advance
Confederate Retreat
Fortifications

- Spotsylvania Court House *May 8-12, 1864*
- GRANT
- LEE
- North Anna R.
- South Anna R.
- Mattaponi R.
- North Anna *May 23-26, 1864*
- V I R G I N I A
- James R.
- Pamunkey R.
- Richmond
- Cold Harbor *June 3, 1864*
- Lynchburg
- Appomattox R.
- LEE
- Bermuda Hundred
- James R.
- Appomattox Court House
- Lee Surrenders *Apr. 9, 1865*
- Sayler's Creek *Apr. 6, 1865*
- Amelia Court House *Apr. 5, 1865*
- GRANT
- Petersburg
- Siege, June 1864 – April 1865
- Five Forks *Apr. 1, 1865*

Campaigns in the East, 1864–1865

The very different fates of the Lincoln and Davis administrations were decided, in large part, on the battlefield. When Grant became general in chief of the Union armies in 1864, he decided to make his headquarters not in Washington, but with the often-defeated Army of the Potomac. Working closely with Meade, the actual commander of that army, Grant developed a plan for pushing Lee back on the defenses of Richmond. Stopped in the bloody battle of the Wilderness (May 5–7), Grant did not retreat, as other Union commanders had done. Instead he pushed around Lee's right flank, attempting to get between him and the Confederate capital. Stopped again at Spotsylvania (May 8–12), Grant again did not retreat but sent word to Washington: "I propose to fight it out along this line if it takes all summer."

After a disastrous direct assault on the Confederate lines at Cold Harbor (June 3), Grant again skillfully maneuvered around Lee's right flank, crossed the James River, and joined Union troops already there under General Butler. He then began what became known as the "siege" of Petersburg and Richmond—incorrectly so, since the two cities were not fully surrounded and since supplies continued to come in from the South and West. But as Grant's lines constantly lengthened, he cut these access routes one by one. Pinned down before Richmond, Lee remembered "Stonewall" Jackson's brilliant diversionary campaign of 1862 and sent what men he could spare under Jubal A. Early into the Shenandoah Valley. Although Early achieved initial success and even pushed on to the outskirts of Washington, Grant did not loosen his grip on Richmond. Instead he sent brash, aggressive Philip H. Sheridan to the Shenandoah Valley, ordering him not merely to drive out the Confederates, but to devastate the countryside so that thereafter a crow flying over it would have to carry its own rations. Sheridan followed his orders explicitly, and Early's army was smashed. More than ever before, the fate of the Confederacy was tied to Richmond and to Lee's army.

Campaigns in the West, 1864–1865 Meanwhile, on May 7, 1864, Sherman had begun his slow march through northwestern Georgia, opposed by the wily Joseph E. Johnston, who made the Union troops pay for every foot they advanced. But as Sherman neared the railroad hub of Atlanta, President Davis—who had never trusted Johnston—removed the

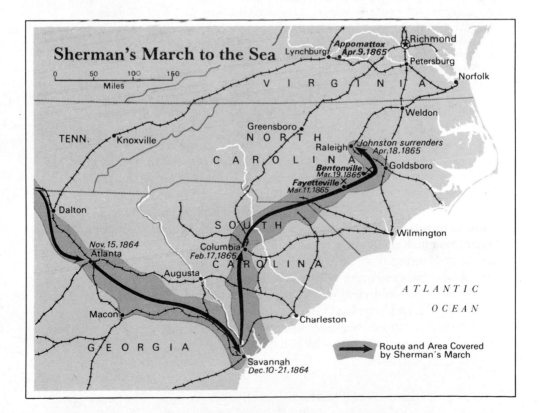

The Union Army Entering Richmond, April 9, 1865
Attempting to destroy military supplies as they withdrew from Richmond, Confederate authorities accidently started fires that devastated much of the center of the city. When Union troops entered, whites made a point of staying out of sight, but Richmond blacks joyfully welcomed the federal soldiers who brought them freedom.

general and put John B. Hood in command. In a series of attacks on the overwhelmingly superior Union forces (exactly the sort of engagement Johnston had so skillfully avoided), Hood was defeated. On September 2 Sherman occupied Atlanta. News of the victory reached the North just before the presidential election and made a farce of the Democratic platform's assertion that the war was a "failure."

Next, casually dispatching Thomas to fend off Hood and to hold Tennessee, Sherman turned his back on the smoking ruins of Atlanta and set out on a march toward Savannah and the sea, where he knew that a Union fleet was waiting with supplies.* Meeting only light resistance, Sherman's men cut a swath through central Georgia, destroying railroads, military supplies, and even many private houses. Sherman's objective was as much psychological as military. "I can make the march," he had promised Grant, "and make Georgia howl!"

Offering captured Savannah to Lincoln as a Christmas present, Sherman turned his army north, pushing aside the depleted Confederate forces that again

---

*Attempting to force Sherman back, Hood invaded Tennessee but was stopped in the battle of Franklin (November 30, 1864) and routed in the battle of Nashville (December 15–16).

"General Robert E. Lee Leaving the McLean House After the Surrender at Appomattox, 1865," by A.W. Waud

After accepting Grant's terms of surrender, Lee stepped out to the porch of the McLean House and signaled his orderly to bring up his horse. While the animal was being bridled, one of Grant's aides remembered, Lee "gazed sadly in the direction...where his army lay—now an army of prisoners. He thrice smote the palm of his left hand slowly with his right fist in an absent sort of way." Then he mounted, and Grant saluted him by raising his hat. "Lee raised his hat respectfully, and rode off at a slow trot to break the sad news to the brave fellows whom he had so long commanded."

were under the command of Johnston. His men took Columbia, South Carolina, which was burned either by intention or by accident, and drove on into North Carolina. Grant meanwhile clamped down ever tighter on Richmond. At last, on April 2, 1865, Lee found his position untenable. Warning President Davis and his government to flee, he tried to lead his ragged troops to join Johnston's dwindling force. Cut off by Grant, Lee had no alternative but to surrender, and on April 9 at Appomattox Court House he told his weary, hungry men to lay down their arms. On April 18 Johnston followed by surrendering to Sherman (although the final terms were not agreed on until April 26). When the news reached the trans-Mississippi region, Kirby-Smith surrendered in June. The war had lasted almost precisely four years.

The Union cause and the Lincoln administration were the beneficiaries of these victories. The critics of the government had been most vocal, their opposition most powerful, in the heartbreaking summer months of 1864, when Grant seemed to be getting nowhere in Virginia and Sherman appeared unable to bag his enemy in Georgia. Northern morale and support for the president mounted perceptibly at the news of Sherman's success at Atlanta and of Farragut's victory at Mobile Bay. Conversely, support for Davis's administration dwindled and critical voices became louder as Confederate reverse followed reverse. In a certain sense, then, victory begot victory, and defeat begot defeat.

Why the North Won the War   Yet this is circular reasoning and does not explain the final Union triumph after so many earlier Confederate successes. For a fuller understanding one must turn to the slow but steady mobilization of the North's infinitely superior economic resources and to the gradual erosion of those in the South. The effect of Northern economic and industrial superiority was not fully felt until after more than two years of war; it took time to award contracts, to expand factories, to recruit skilled laborers, and to deliver the products. But observers noted that by 1863 Lee's veterans invading Pennsylvania looked like a gaggle of "barefooted, ragged, lousy, [but] disciplined, desperate ruffians." These troops were so badly supplied and so poorly fed that their line of march was "traceable by the deposit of dysenteric stool the army leaves behind it." By 1863 the Union armies, on the other hand, were so completely equipped that their paraphernalia became a hindrance. When Northern soldiers advanced, they shucked off layers of great-coats, blankets, and other unnecessary supplies. By the end of the war, Union economic superiority was most evident in the Northern transportation system. Southern railroads by that time had worn out. In the Union, on the other hand, some 5,000 more miles of railroad were in operation in 1865 than at the start of the war—a figure that does not include the numerous military railroads operated in the South. Moreover, because they had to link up with the newly authorized Union Pacific Railroad, Northern lines had all converted to a standard rail gauge.

Supplies, however, do not fight wars, nor do trains; men do. From the start the North's overwhelming population advantage counted heavily against the Confederacy. That advantage increased during the conflict. In the course of the four years of war, more than 180,000 male immigrants of military age settled in the North, whereas there was virtually no immigration to the Confederacy. In addition the black population became another vast source of Union manpower. Confederates dared not tap this source until their cause was already lost.

But men, no matter how numerous, fight well only if ably led by their military commanders and inspired by their political leaders. It would be hard to argue that Northern generalship was superior to that of the South. While Grant has his admirers, most students of Civil War military history consider Robert E. Lee the greatest commander. Nor is it easy to maintain that the political leadership of the North was markedly superior. Later generations, recalling the eloquence of the Gettysburg Address and the mystical beauty of the second inaugural address, have found it difficult to remember that for most of his administration Lincoln was considered uninspiring and ineffectual. Had Lincoln been defeated for

A Dead Confederate Soldier at Fort Mahone, Near Petersburg, Virginia, April 2, 1865
In the final bloody battles of the war, the Confederacy lost men who could not be replaced. "Where is this to end?" asked General Josiah Gorgas. "No money in the Treasury—no food to feed Gen. Lee's army—no troops to oppose Gen. Sherman—what does it all mean…? Is the cause really hopeless?"

reelection in 1864, he would doubtless be rated as an honest but unsuccessful president. On the other hand, had the Southern states been able to win their independence, Jefferson Davis would undoubtedly rank as the George Washington of the Confederacy.

There were, of course, important differences between the two wartime presidents, but these were of less significance than the differences in the political systems in which they had to work. Like many more recently emerging nations, the Confederacy tried to present a facade of unity to the world. It was a one-party—or, more properly, a no-party—state. Southerners feared that party divisions would suggest that they were less than unanimous in seeking independence. The most careful analysis of the voting records of Confederate congressmen has been able to show, at most, only the beginnings of party lines. Small temporary factions rather than permanent political parties dominated the Confederate Congress. President Davis had many enemies, and they were constantly attacking him from all directions, like a swarm of bees. His friends were divided, and he could never rally them into a unified group. As with the Congress, so with the people. It is safe to guess that if at any point the voters of the Confederacy had been asked to endorse their president or to topple him, Davis would have received overwhelming support. But lacking political parties, Southerners had no way of making this sentiment felt.

In the Union, on the other hand, the two-party system remained active. The Democrats continued as a formidable, if not always united, force throughout the war. They came close to winning a majority in Congress in the 1862 elections; and even in 1864 McClellan received 45 percent of the popular vote—at a time when the strongest opponents of the Republican party were still out of the Union and, of course, not voting. Such a powerful opposition party compelled the Republican factions, however bitterly at odds with each other, to work together. Conservatives and Radicals might disagree over slavery, emancipation, and reconstruction, but they all agreed that any Republican administration was preferable to a Democratic one.

It was, then, the absence of political machinery in the South that weakened Davis's regime and rendered him unable fully to mobilize the material and spiritual resources of the Confederacy. And it was the much-maligned two-party system that allowed Lincoln, despite quarrelsome and impassioned attacks from fellow Republicans, to experiment boldly and to grow into an effective wartime leader.

CHRONOLOGY

1863 Lincoln issues final Emancipation Proclamation.
Confederates defeat Union army under Hooker at Chancellorsville.
Lee's invasion of the North checked by Union army under Meade at Gettysburg.
Grant captures Vicksburg.
Draft riots in the North.
Confederate army under Bragg defeats Union forces at Chickamauga.
Union victory at Chattanooga (Lookout Mountain and Missionary Ridge).
Lincoln offers lenient reconstruction program.

1864 Grant named Union general in chief.
Grant's direct advance on Richmond checked at the Wilderness, Spotsylvania, and Cold Harbor.

Grant moves south of James River to begin "siege" of Petersburg.
Sherman pushes back Confederates under Joseph E. Johnston and captures Atlanta.
Farragut captures Mobile.
Lincoln reelected president over Democrat McClellan.
Sherman marches from Atlanta to the sea.

1865 Sherman pushes northward through South Carolina and North Carolina.
Lee gives up Petersburg and Richmond, and Confederate government flees.
Lee surrenders at Appomattox.
Johnston surrenders to Sherman.
Kirby-Smith surrenders Confederate forces west of the Mississippi.
Lincoln assassinated; Andrew Johnson becomes president.

SUGGESTED READINGS

Most of the studies listed at the end of the previous chapter also relate to the topics discussed in this chapter.

The best general analysis of military operations is Herman Hattaway and Archer Jones, *How the North Won* (1983). On the Northern armies the most comprehensive work is Kenneth P. Williams's *Lincoln Finds a General* (5 vols., 1949–59). The most readable is Bruce Catton's trilogy on the Army of the Potomac: *Mr. Lincoln's Army* (1951); *Glory Road* (1952); and *A Stillness at Appomattox* (1953). Michael C. C. Adams, *Our Masters the Rebels* (1978), is a provocative interpretation. Among the best biographies of Union generals are Stephen W. Sears, *George B. McClellan: The Young Napoleon* (1988); William S. McFeely, *Grant* (1981); and Lloyd Lewis, *Sherman* (1932).

Grady McWhiney and Perry D. Jamison, *Attack and Die* (1982), is an interpretation of Confederate strategy. Douglas S. Freeman, *Lee's Lieutenants* (3 vols., 1942–44), examines Confederate commanders in the eastern theater, while Thomas Connelly, *Army of the Heartland* (2 vols., 1967–71), is an excellent account of those in the West. Among the most significant biographies of Confederate generals are Douglas S. Freeman, *R. E. Lee* (4 vols., 1934–35); Frank E. Vandiver, *Mighty Stonewall* (1957); Grady McWhiney, *Braxton Bragg and Confederate Defeat* (1969); and Richard M. McMurry, *John Bell Hood and the War for Southern Independence* (1982). Steven E. Woodworth, *Jefferson Davis and His Generals* (1990), analyzes the reasons for Confederate failure in the West, while Alan T. Nolan, *Lee Considered* (1991), offers a negative appraisal of the Confederacy's leading general.

Gerald F. Linderman, *Embattled Courage* (1987), shows how Union and Confederate soldiers found the realities of battle at odds with their expectations. Two books by Bell I. Wiley provide a fascinating social history of the common soldiers of the Civil War: *The Life of Johnny Reb* (1943) and *The Life of Billy Yank* (1952).

The best accounts of Civil War naval operations are Virgil C. Jones, *The Civil War at Sea* (3 vols., 1960–62), and Bern Anderson, *By Sea and by River* (1962). Rowena Reed, *Combined Operations in the Civil War* (1978), is an important study. See also John Niven's fine biography, *Gideon Welles: Lincoln's Secretary of the Navy* (1973). Stephen R. Wise, *Lifeline of the Confederacy* (1988), deals with blockade running.

The story of Confederate politics has to be pieced together from Wilfred B. Yearns, *The Confederate Congress* (1960); Thomas B. Alexander and Richard E. Beringer, *The Anatomy of the Confederate Congress* (1972); and Frank L. Owsley, *State Rights in the Confederacy* (1925). See also Paul D. Escott, *After Secession: Jefferson Davis and the Failure of Confederate Nationalism* (1978).

James A. Rawley, *The Politics of Union* (1974), is the best general study. There are several analyses of Republican factions and leadership: T. Harry Williams, *Lincoln and the Radicals* (1941); William B. Hesseltine, *Lincoln and the War Governors* (1948); Hans L. Trefousse, *The Radical Republicans* (1969); and Allan G. Bogue, *The Earnest Men: Republicans of the Civil War Senate* (1981). On the Democrats, see Joel H. Silbey, *A Respectable Minority* (1977), and Jean H. Baker, *Affairs of Party* (1983).

Benjamin Quarles, *The Negro in the Civil War* (1953), is comprehensive. James M. McPherson, ed., *The Negro's Civil War* (1965), is a valuable set of documents, skillfully interwoven. *Freedom: A Documentary History of Emancipation,* ed. by Ira Berlin and others (1982), is richly rewarding. Bell I. Wiley, *Southern Negroes, 1861–1865* (1938), is a standard account. The early chapters of Leon F. Litwack, *Been in the Storm So Long* (1979), superbly recapture slave life during the war. The authoritative account of Negro troops in the Union army is Dudley T. Cornish, *The Sable Arm* (1956), and Joseph T. Glatthaar, *Forged in Battle*

(1990) tells the dramatic story of black soldiers and their white officers. William S. McFeely, *Frederick Douglass* (1991), is a superior biography of the influential African-American leader.

For explanations of the collapse of the Confederacy, see Henry S. Commager, ed., *The Defeat of the Confederacy* (1964); David Donald, ed., *Why the North Won the Civil War* (1960); and Bell I. Wiley, *The Road to Appomattox* (1956).

9

Reconstruction

1865–1869

⌒

A HOUSE divided against itself cannot stand," Abraham Lincoln prophesied in 1858. The Civil War proved that the United States would stand, not as a loose confederation of sovereign states but as one nation, indivisible. Never again would there be talk of secession. The war also ended slavery, the most divisive institution in antebellum America. Weakened by the advances of the Union armies and undermined by Lincoln's Emancipation Proclamation, slavery received its deathblow in February 1865, when Congress adopted the Thirteenth Amendment, outlawing slavery and involuntary servitude. After three-fourths of the states had ratified it, the amendment became part of the Constitution in December 1865.

But the Civil War did not settle the terms and conditions on which the states, sections, races, and classes would live in the firmly united "house." Those problems formed the agenda of the Reconstruction era, one of the most complex and controversial periods in American history. During these postwar years some basic questions had to be answered. What, if any, punishment should be imposed on Southern whites who had supported the Confederate attempt to break up the Union? How were the recently emancipated slaves to be guaranteed their freedom, and what civil and political rights did freedmen have? When and on what conditions were the Southern states, so recently in rebellion, to be readmitted to the Union—that is, entitled to vote in national elections, to have senators and representatives seated in the United States Congress, and, in general, to become once more full-fledged, equal members of the United States?

The initial moves to answer these questions came from the president, whose powers had grown significantly during the war years. In December 1863 President Lincoln announced a generous program of amnesty to repentant rebels and inaugurated a plan for reorganizing loyal governments in the South when as few as 10 percent of the voters in 1860 were willing to support them. After Lincoln's assassination in April 1865, President Andrew Johnson, his successor, continued the process of Reconstruction under a similar plan. Johnson, like Lincoln, expected Southern whites to take the lead in establishing new state governments loyal to the Union. To begin the process, the president appointed a provisional governor for each of the former Confederate states (except those in which Lincoln had already initiated Reconstruction). Johnson directed these provisional governors to convene constitutional conventions, which were expected to adopt the Thirteenth Amendment ending slavery, to nullify or repeal the ordinances of secession, and to cancel state debts incurred for the prosecution of the war. By early 1866 each of the states that had once formed the Confederacy had completed most of these required steps, and the president viewed the process of Reconstruction as concluded. He recommended that the senators and representatives chosen by these reorganized governments promptly be given their rightful seats in Congress.

Presidential Reconstruction drew criticism from the outset. Having jealously watched executive power grow during the war, Congress was ready to reestablish its political equality with the presidency, and even to reassert its superior influence. Unlike President Lincoln, Andrew Johnson had no popular mandate. Johnson, a Tennessee Democrat and former slaveholder, was an inflexible and aggressive man who did not understand that politics is the art of compromise.

After an initial attempt to cooperate with the new president, Republican leaders in 1866 began to draw up their own plans for Reconstruction. The first congressional plan was embodied in the Fourteenth Amendment to the Constitution, which made it clear that blacks were citizens of the United States and tried to define the rights and privileges of American citizens. When the Southern states refused to ratify this amendment, congressional Republicans moved in 1867 to a tougher program of reorganizing the South by insisting that blacks be allowed to vote. Under this second plan of congressional Reconstruction, every Southern state (except for Tennessee, which had been readmitted to the Union in 1866) received a new constitution that guaranteed to men of all races equal protection of the laws. Between 1868 and 1871, all these states were readmitted to the Union. Republican governments, which depended heavily on black votes, controlled these states for a period ranging from a few months in the case of Virginia to nine years in the case of Louisiana.

Paths Not Taken

Contemporaries called this the period of Radical Reconstruction—or, very often, Black Reconstruction. It is easy to understand why many Americans viewed these changes as little short of revolutionary. No amendments had been added to the Constitution since 1804; but within the five years after the Civil War, three new and far-reaching amendments were adopted. The Thirteenth Amendment ended slavery, the Fourteenth Amendment defined the rights of citizens, and the Fifteenth Amendment (1870) prohibited discrimination in voting because of race or color. The national government, which so recently had tottered on the edge of defeat, was now more powerful than at any previous point in American history.

The Southern ruling class of whites, lately in charge of their own independent government, now had to ask for pardon. More than 3 million blacks, slaves only a few months earlier, were now free and entitled to the same privileges as all other citizens. Americans fairly gasped at the extent and the speed of the changes that had occurred in their society, and it is hardly surprising that most subsequent historians accepted this contemporary view of the Reconstruction era as one of turbulent disorder.

Without denying that real and important changes did occur during the Reconstruction period, it might help to put these changes into perspective by inventing a little counterfactual, or imaginary, history—a recital of conceivable historical scenarios that never in fact occurred. For example, it would be easy to imagine how the victorious North might have turned angrily on the defeated South. In 1865 Northerners had just finished four years of war that had cost the Union army more than 360,000 casualties. Americans of the Civil War era and subsequent generations had to pay at least $10 billion in taxes to destroy the Confederacy. Northerners had reason to believe, moreover, that their Confederate opponents had conducted the war with fiendish barbarity. Sober Union congressmen informed their constituents that the Confederates had employed "Indian savages" to scalp and mutilate the Union dead. Reliable Northern newspapers told how in April 1864 General Nathan Bedford Forrest and his Confederates overran the defenses of Fort Pillow, Tennessee, manned by a black regiment and, refusing to accept surrender, deliberately beat, shot, and burned their prisoners. The influential *Harper's Weekly Magazine* carried apparently authentic drawings of a goblet that a Southerner had made from a Yankee soldier's skull and of necklaces fashioned of Yankee teeth that Southern ladies wore. When Union armies liberated Northern prisoners from such hellholes as Andersonville, Georgia, pictures of these half-starved skeletons of men, clad in grimy tatters of their Union uniforms, convinced Northerners that Jefferson Davis's policy had been "to starve and freeze and kill off by inches the prisoners he dares not butcher out-right."

After the murder of President Lincoln by the Southern sympathizer John Wilkes Booth, an outraged North could easily have turned on the conquered Confederacy in vengeance. The victorious Northerners might have executed Jefferson Davis, Alexander H. Stephens, and a score of other leading Confederates and might have sent thousands more into permanent exile. The triumphant Union might have erased the boundaries of the Southern states and divided the whole region into new, conquered territories. Northerners might have enforced the confiscation acts already on the statute books and seized the plantations of rebels, for distribution to the freedmen.

But nothing so drastic happened. No Confederate was executed for "war crimes" except Major Henry Wirtz, commandant of the infamous Andersonville prison, who was hanged. A few Southern political leaders were imprisoned for their part in the "rebellion," but in most cases they were promptly released. To be sure, Jefferson Davis remained in prison for two years at Fort Monroe, and he was under indictment for treason until 1869, when all charges were dropped. His case was, however, as unusual as it was extreme. One reason for the long delay in bringing him to trial was the certainty that no jury, Northern or Southern, would render an impartial verdict. There was no general confiscation of the property of Confederates, and no dividing up of plantations.

Another scenario—this time featuring the Southern whites—is equally conceivable, but it too did not happen. For four years Confederate citizens had been subjected to a barrage of propaganda designed to prove that the enemy was little less than infernal in his purposes. Many believed the Southern editor who claimed that Lincoln's program was "Emancipation, Confiscation, Conflagration, and Extermination." According to the North Carolina educator Calvin H. Wiley, the North had "summoned to its aid every fierce and cruel and licentious passion of the human heart"; to defeat the Confederacy it was ready to use "the assassin's dagger, the midnight torch, . . . poison, famine and pestilence." Charges of this kind were easy to credit in the many Southern families that had relatives in Northern prison camps, such as the one at Elmira, New York, where 775 of 8,347 Confederate prisoners died within three months for lack of food, water, and medicine. The behavior of Union troops in the South, especially of Sherman's "bummers," members of raiding forces who plundered indiscriminately in Georgia and the Carolinas, gave Southerners every reason to fear the worst if the Confederate government failed.

It would therefore have been reasonable for Confederate armies in 1865, overwhelmed by Union numbers, to disband quietly, disappear into the countryside, and carry on guerrilla operations against the Northern invaders. Indeed, on the morning of the day when Lee surrendered at Appomattox, Confederate General E. P. Alexander advocated just such a plan. He argued that if Lee's soldiers took to the woods with their rifles, perhaps two-thirds of the Army of Northern Virginia could escape capture. "We would be like rabbits and partridges in the bushes," he claimed, "and they could not scatter to follow us." The history of more recent wars of national liberation suggests that Alexander's judgment was correct. At least his strategy would have given time for thousands of leading Southern politicians and planters, together with their families, to go safely into exile, as the loyalists did during the American Revolution.

But again, no such events occurred. A few Confederate leaders did leave the country. For example, General Jubal A. Early fled to Mexico and from there to Canada, where he tried to organize a migration of Southerners to New Zealand. But when he found that nobody wanted to follow him, Early returned to his home and his law practice in Virginia. A few hundred Confederates migrated to Mexico and to Brazil. But most followed the advice of General Lee and General Wade Hampton of South Carolina, who urged their fellow Southerners to "devote their whole energies to the restoration of law and order, the reestablishment of agriculture and commerce, the promotion of education and the rebuilding of our cities and dwellings which have been laid in ashes."

Still another counterfactual historical scenario comes readily to mind. Southern blacks, who for generations had been oppressed in slavery, now for the first time had disciplined leaders in the thousands of black soldiers who had served in the Union army. They also had weapons. The blacks could very easily have turned in revenge on their former masters. Seizing the plantations and other property of the whites, the freedmen might have made the former Confederacy a black nation. If the whites had dared to resist, the South might have been the scene of massacres as bloody as those in Haiti at the beginning of the nineteenth century, when Toussaint L'Ouverture drove the French from that island.

Many Southern whites feared, or even expected, that the Confederacy would become another Haiti. They were frightened by reports that blacks were joining the Union League, an organization that had originated in the North during the war to stimulate patriotism but during the Reconstruction era became the stronghold of the Republican party in the South. The secrecy imposed by the league on its members and its frequent nighttime meetings alarmed whites, and they readily believed reports that the blacks were collecting arms and ammunition for a general uprising. Fearfully, Southern whites read newspaper accounts of minor racial clashes. Indeed, whites were told, racial tension was so great that blacks "might break into open insurrection at any time."

But no such uprising occurred. Although the freedmen unquestionably hoped to obtain the lands of their former masters, they did not seize them. Indeed, black leaders consistently discouraged talk of extralegal confiscation of plantations. Nor did freedmen threaten the lives or the rights of whites. One of the earliest black political conventions held in Alabama urged a policy of "peace, friendship, and good will toward all men—especially toward our white fellow-citizens among whom our lot is cast." That tone was the dominant one throughout the Reconstruction period, and in many states blacks took the lead in repealing laws that disfranchised former Confederates or disqualified them from holding office.

The point of these three exercises in counterfactual history is, of course, not to argue that the Civil War brought no changes in American life. The preservation of the Union and the emancipation of the slaves were two consequences of tremendous importance. Instead, these exercises suggest that conventional accounts of the Reconstruction period as a second American Revolution are inadequate. During these postwar years there were swift and significant changes in Southern society, but the shared beliefs and institutions of the American people—North and South, black and white—set limits to these changes.

Constitutionalism as a Limit to Change

One set of ideas that sharply curbed experimentation and political innovation during the Reconstruction period can be labeled constitutionalism. It is hard for twentieth-century Americans to understand the reverence with which their nineteenth-century ancestors viewed the Constitution. Next to the flag, the Constitution was the most powerful symbol of American nationhood. Tested in the trial of civil war, the Constitution continued to command respect—almost veneration—during the Reconstruction era.

States' Rights   Among the most unchallenged provisions of the Constitution were those that separated the powers of state and national government. Although the national government greatly expanded its role during the war years, Americans still tended to think of it as performing only the specific functions delegated to it in the Constitution. These functions allowed the national government virtually no authority to act directly on individual citizens. For example, the national government could neither prevent nor punish crime; it had no control over public education; it could not outlaw discrimination against racial minorities; and it could not even intervene to maintain public order unless requested to do so by the state government. Virtually everybody agreed, therefore, that if any laws regulating social and economic life were required, they must be the work of state and local, not of national, government.

Consequently, nobody even contemplated the possibility that some federal agency might be needed to supervise the demobilization after Appomattox. Everybody simply assumed that after some 200,000 of the Union army volunteers bravely paraded down Pennsylvania Avenue on May 23–24, 1865, and received applause from President Johnson, the cabinet, the generals, and members of the diplomatic corps, the soldiers would disband and go back to their peaceful homes. This is precisely what they did. Of the more than one million volunteers in the Union army on May 1, 1865, two-thirds were mustered out by August, four-fifths by November. The United States government offered the demobilized soldiers no assistance in finding jobs, purchasing housing, or securing further education. It paid pensions to those injured in the war and to the families of those who had been killed, but assumed no further responsibility. Nor did anyone think of asking the national government to oversee the transition from a wartime economy to an era of peace. By the end of April 1865, without notice the various bureaus of the army and navy departments simply suspended requisitions and purchases, government arsenals slowed down their production, and surplus supplies were sold off.

Hardly anybody thought that the national government might play a role in rebuilding the warworn South. The devastation in the South was immense and ominous. The Confederate dead totaled more than a quarter of a million. In Mississippi, for example, one-third of the white men of military age had been killed or disabled for life. Most Southern cities were in ruins. Two-thirds of the Southern railroads were totally destroyed; the rest barely creaked along on worn-out rails with broken-down engines. But none of these problems was thought to be the concern of the United States government.

Ruins of Charleston
When the Confederate government evacuated Charleston on April 3, 1865, orders were given to burn supplies that might fall into the enemy's hands. There were heavy explosions as ironclads, armories, and arsenals were blown up. The next morning, as the fires spread, a mob of men and women, whites and blacks, began to plunder the city.

The national government's failure to come to the rescue was not caused by vindictiveness. To the contrary, Union officials often behaved with marked generosity toward Confederates. After Lee's hungry battalions surrendered at Appomattox, Grant's soldiers freely shared their rations with them. All over the South, federal military officials drew on the full Union army storehouses to feed the hungry. But the federal government did not go beyond these attempts to prevent starvation, and very few thought that it should. Not until the twentieth century did the United States make it a policy to pour vast sums of money into the rehabilitation of enemies it had defeated in war.

Rebuilding therefore had to be the work of the Southern state and local authorities, and this task imposed a heavy burden on their meager resources. In Mississippi one-fifth of the entire state revenue in 1866 was needed to provide artificial limbs for soldiers maimed in the war. The resources of the South were obviously inadequate for the larger tasks of physical restoration. Drawing on antebellum experience, Southern governments did the only thing they knew how to—namely, they lent the credit of the state to back up the bonds of private companies that promised to rebuild railroads and other necessary facilities. These companies were underfinanced, and the credit of the Southern states after Appomattox was questionable, to say the least. Therefore these bonds had to be sold at disadvantageous prices and at exorbitant rates of interest. In later years, when many of these companies defaulted on their obligations and southern state governments had to make good on their guarantees, these expenditures would be condemned as excessive and extravagant. Democrats blamed them on the Republican regimes established in the South after 1868. In fact, however, immediately after the war the need for physical restoration was so obvious and so pressing that nearly every government—whether controlled by Democrats or Republicans—underwrote corporations that promised to rebuild the region.

The Freedmen's Bureau

Even in dealing with the freedmen—the some 3 million slaves emancipated as a result of the war—the United States government tried to pursue a hands-off policy. In North and South alike, few influential leaders thought that it was the function of the national government to supervise the blacks' transition from slavery to freedom. Even abolitionists, genuinely devoted to the welfare of blacks, were so accustomed to thinking of the black man as "God's image in ebony"—in other words, a white man in a black skin—that they had no plans for assisting him after emancipation. In 1865 William Lloyd Garrison urged the American Anti-Slavery Society to disband because it had fulfilled its function, and he suspended the publication of *The Liberator.* Sharing the same point of view, the American Freedmen's Inquiry Commission, set up by the Union War Department in 1863, unanimously opposed further governmental actions to protect the blacks. "The negro does best when let alone," argued one member of the commission, Samuel Gridley Howe, noted both for his work with the deaf, dumb, and blind and for his hostility to slavery. "We must beware of all attempts to prolong his servitude, under pretext of taking care of him. The white man has tried taking care of the negro, by slavery, by apprenticeship, by colonization, and has failed disastrously in all; now let the negro try to take care of himself."

But the problem of caring for the freedmen could not be dismissed so easily. Wherever Union armies advanced into the South, they were "greeted by an irruption of negroes of all ages, complexions and sizes, men, women, boys and girls . . . waving hats and bonnets with the most ludicrous caperings and ejaculations of joy." "The poor delighted creatures thronged upon us," a Yankee soldier reported, and they insisted: "We'se gwin wid you all." "What shall be done with them?" commanders in the field plaintively wired Washington.

A Group of Freedmen in Richmond, Virginia, 1865
A central problem of Reconstruction years was the future of the freedmen. Nobody had made any plans for a smooth transition from slavery to freedom. Consequently, when emancipation came, as one former slave recalled, "We didn't know where to go. Momma and them didn't know where to go, you see, after freedom broke. Just like you turned something out, you know. They didn't know where to go."

The administration in Washington had no comprehensive answer. Initially it looked to private humanitarian organizations to rush food, clothing, and medicine to the thousands of blacks who thronged in unsanitary camps around the headquarters of each Union army. The New England Freedmen's Aid Society, the American Missionary Association, and the Philadelphia Society of Friends [Quakers] promptly responded, but it was soon clear that the problem was too great for private charity.

Gradually sentiment grew in the North for the creation of a general Emancipation Bureau in the federal government—only to conflict directly with the even stronger sentiment that the national government had limited powers. Out of this conflict emerged the Freedmen's Bureau Act of March 3, 1865. Congress established the Bureau of Refugees, Freedmen, and Abandoned Lands under the jurisdiction of the War Department. It entrusted to the new agency, for one year after the end of the war, "control of all subjects relating to refugees and freedmen." To head the new organization, Lincoln named Oliver O. Howard, a Union general with paternalistic views toward blacks.

At first glance, the Freedmen's Bureau seems to have been a notable exception to the rule that the national government should take only a minor, passive role in the restoration of the South. Howard had a vision of a compassionate network of "teachers, ministers, farmers, superintendents" working together to

The Freedmen's Union Industrial School, Richmond, Virginia
Freedmen were eager to learn, and both the old and the young flocked to schools sponsored by the Freedmen's Bureau. Most of these schools taught only reading, writing, and arithmetic, but this one, in Richmond, gave instruction in sewing, cooking, and other domestic skills.

aid and elevate the freedmen; and, under his enthusiastic impetus, the bureau appointed agents in each of the former Confederate states. The bureau's most urgent task was issuing food and clothing, mostly from surplus army stores, to destitute freedmen and other Southern refugees. This action unquestionably prevented mass starvation in the South. The bureau also took the initiative in getting work for freedmen. The bureau agents feared on the one hand that Southern landlords would attempt to exploit and underpay the freedmen, but they were also troubled by the widespread belief that blacks, once emancipated, would not work. The agents therefore brought laborers and landlords together and insisted that the workers sign labor contracts.

The bureau's most successful work was in the field of education. The slow work of educating the illiterate Southern blacks had already begun under the auspices of army chaplains and Northern benevolent societies before the creation of the bureau. Howard's bureau continued to cooperate with these agencies, providing housing for black schools, paying teachers, and helping to establish normal (teachers') schools and colleges for the training of black teachers. The freedmen enthusiastically welcomed all these educational efforts. During the day, black children learning the rudiments of language and arithmetic crowded into the classrooms; in the evenings, adults "fighting with their letters" flocked to the schools, learning to read so that they would not be "made ashamed" by their children. "The progress of the scholars is in all cases creditable and in some remarkable," reported one of the teachers condescendingly. "How richly God has endowed them, and how beautifully their natures would have expanded under a tender and gentle culture."

Even more innovative was the work of the bureau in allocating lands to the freedmen. During the war many plantations in the path of Union armies had been deserted by their owners, and army commanders like Grant arranged to have these lands cultivated by the blacks who flocked to their camps. The largest tract of such abandoned land was in the Sea Islands of South Carolina, which Union troops had overrun in the fall of 1861. Although speculators bought up large amounts of this land during the war, many black residents were able to secure small holdings. When General W. T. Sherman marched through South Carolina, he ordered that the Sea Islands and the abandoned plantations along the river-banks for thirty miles from the coast be reserved for black settlement and directed that the black settlers be given "possessory titles" to tracts of this land not larger than forty acres. The act creating the Freedmen's Bureau clearly contemplated the continuation of these policies, for it authorized the new bureau to lease confiscated lands to freedmen and to "loyal refugees." The bureau could also sell the land to these tenants and give them "such title thereto as the United States can convey."

But if the Freedmen's Bureau was an exception to the policy of limited federal involvement in the reconstruction process, it was at best a partial exception. Although the agency did extremely valuable work, it was a feeble protector of the freedmen. Authorized to recruit only a minimal staff, Howard had to rely heavily on Union army officers stationed in the South—at just the time when the Union army was being demobilized. Consequently, the bureau never had enough manpower to look after the rights of the freedmen; toward the end of its first year of operation, the bureau employed only 799 men, 424 of whom were soldiers on temporary assigned duty. Important as the work of the bureau was in black education, its chief function was to stimulate private humanitarian aid in this field. In providing land for the freedmen, the bureau was handicapped because it controlled only about 800,000 acres of arable land in the South, at best enough for perhaps one black family in forty. Moreover, Congress and the president repeatedly undercut its efforts to distribute land to the blacks. The very wording of the act creating the bureau suggested congressional uncertainty about who actually owned deserted and confiscated lands in the South. When President Johnson issued pardons to Southerners, he explicitly called for the "restoration of all rights of property." In October 1865 the president directed Howard to go in person to the Sea Islands to notify blacks there that they did not hold legal title to the land and to advise them "to make the best terms they could" with the white owners. When blacks bitterly resisted what they considered the bureau's betrayal, Union soldiers descended on the islands and forced blacks who would not sign labor contracts with the restored white owners to leave. Elsewhere in the South the record of the bureau was equally dismal.

In short, belief in the limited role to be played by the national government affected the rehabilitation of the freedmen, just as it did the physical restoration of the South and the demobilization in the North. The United States government was supposed to play the smallest possible part in all these matters, and its minimal activities were to be of the briefest duration.

It is certain that most whites in the North and in the South fully approved of these strict limitations on the activities of the national government. It is harder to determine what the masses of freedmen thought. On the one hand stands the protest of the Sea Island blacks when they learned they were about to be dispossessed: "Why, General Howard, why do you take away our lands? You take them from us who have always been true, always true to the Government! You give them to our all-time enemies! That is not right!" On the other is Frederick Douglass's reply to the question "What shall we do with the Negroes?" The greatest black spokesman of the era answered: "Do nothing with them; mind your business, and let them mind theirs. Your doing with them is their greatest misfortune. They have been undone by your doings, and all they now ask and really have need of at your hands, is just to let them alone."

Laissez-Faire as a Limit to Change

Along with the idea of limited government went the doctrine of laissez-faire ("let things alone"), which sharply limited what the government could do to solve the economic problems that arose after the Civil War. Except for a handful of Radical Republicans, such as Charles Sumner and Thaddeus Stevens, most congressmen, like most academic economists, were unquestioning believers in an American version of laissez-faire. Although they were willing to promote economic growth through protective tariffs and land grants to railroads, they abhorred government inspection, regulation, and control of economic activities. These matters, they thought, were ruled by the unchanging laws of economics. "You need not think it necessary to have Washington exercise a political providence over the country," William Graham Sumner, the brilliant professor of political and social science, told his students at Yale. "God has done that a great deal better by the laws of political economy."

Reverence for Private Property No violation of economic laws was considered worse than interference with the right of private property— the right of an individual or group to purchase, own, use, and dispose of property without any interference from governmental authorities. There was consequently never a chance that most congressmen would support Thaddeus Stevens's radical program to confiscate all Southern farms larger than two hundred acres and to divide the seized land into forty-acre tracts among the freedmen. "An attempt to justify the confiscation of Southern land under the pretense of doing justice to the freedmen," declared the *New York Times,* which spoke for educated Republicans, "strikes at the root of all property rights in both sections. It concerns Massachusetts quite as much as Mississippi."

Experts in the North held that the best program of Reconstruction was to allow the laws of economics to rule in the South with the least possible interference by the government. Obsessed by laissez-faire, Northern theorists failed to consider the physical devastation in the South caused by the war, and they did not recognize how feeble were the South's resources to rebuild its economy. Even excluding the loss of slave property, the total assessed property evaluation of the Southern states shrank by 43 percent between 1860 and 1865.

Southern Economic Adjustments

Northern experts also failed to take into account the psychological dimensions of economic readjustment in the South. For generations Southern whites had persuaded themselves that slavery was the natural condition of the black race, and they truly believed that their slaves were devoted to them. But as Union armies approached and slaves defected, these Southerners were compelled to recognize that they had been living in a world of misconceptions and deceits. So shattering was the idea that slaves were free that some Southern whites simply refused to accept it. Even after the Confederate surrender, some owners would not inform their slaves of their new status. A few plantation owners angrily announced that they were so disillusioned that they would never again have anything to do with blacks, and they sought, vainly, to persuade European immigrants and Chinese coolies to work their fields.

Even those whites who on the surface accepted emancipation betrayed the fact that, on a deeper emotional level, they still could only think of blacks as performing forced labor. "The general interest both of the white man and of the negroes requires that he should be kept as near to the condition of slavery as possible, and as far from the condition of the white man as is practicable," announced one prominent South Carolinian. "Negroes must be made to work, or else cotton and rice must cease to be raised for export." The contracts that in 1865 planters signed with their former slaves under pressure from the Freedmen's Bureau were further indications of the same attitude. Even the most generous of these contracts provided that blacks were "not to leave the premises during work hours without the consent of the Proprietor," that they would conduct "themselves faithfully, honestly and civilly," and that they would behave with perfect obedience" toward the landowner.

Nor did the advocates of laissez-faire take into account the blacks' difficulties in adjusting to their new status. *Freedom*—that word so often whispered in the slave quarters—went to the heads of some blacks. A few took quite literally the coming of what they called Jubilee, thinking that it would put the bottom rail on top. Nearly all blacks had an initial impulse to test their freedom, to make sure that it was real. Thus during the first months after the war there was much movement among southern blacks. "They are just like a swarm of bees," one observer noted, "all buzzing about and not knowing where to settle."

Much of this black mobility was, however, purposeful. Thousands of former slaves flocked to the Southern towns and cities where the Freedmen's Bureau was issuing rations, for they knew that food was unavailable on the plantations. Many blacks set out to find husbands, wives, or children from whom they had been forcibly separated during the slave days. A good many freedmen joined the general movement of the Southern population away from the coastal states, which had been devastated by war, and migrated to the southwestern frontier in Texas. Most blacks, however, did not move so far but remained in the immediate vicinity of the plantations where they had labored as slaves.

The freedmen's reluctance in 1865 to enter into labor contracts, either with their former masters or with other white landowners, was also generally misunderstood. Most blacks wanted to work—but they wanted to work on their own land. Freedmen knew that the United States government had divided up some abandoned plantations among former slaves, and many believed that on January 1, 1866—the anniversary of their freedom under Lincoln's Emancipation Proclamation—all would receive forty acres and a mule. With this prospect of having their own farms, they were unwilling to sign contracts to work on plantations owned by others.

Even when the hope of free land disappeared, freedmen resisted signing labor contracts because, as has been noted, so many white landowners expected to continue to treat them like slaves. The blacks were especially opposed to the idea of being again herded together in the plantation slave quarters, with their communal facilities for cooking and washing and infant care, and their lack of privacy. Emancipation did much to strengthen the black family. Families divided by slave sales could now be reunited. Marital arrangements between blacks, which had not been legally valid during slavery, could be regularized. Freedmen's Bureau officials performed thousands of marriage ceremonies, and some states passed general ordinances declaring that blacks who had been living together were legally man and wife and that their children were legitimate. This precious new security of family life was not something blacks were willing to jeopardize by returning to slave quarters. Before contracting to work on the plantations, they insisted on having separate cabins, scattered across the farm, each usually having its own patch for vegetables and perhaps a pen for hogs or a cow.

When these conditions were met, freedmen in the early months of 1866 entered into labor contracts, most of which followed the same general pattern. Rarely did these arrangements call for the payment of wages, for landowners were desperately short of cash and freedmen felt that a wage system gave landowners too much control over their labor. The most common system was sharecropping. Although there were many regional and individual variations, the system usually called for the dividing of the crop into three equal shares. One of these went to the landowner; another went to the laborer—usually black, although there were also many white sharecroppers in the South; and the third went to whichever party provided the seeds, fertilizer, mules, and farming equipment.

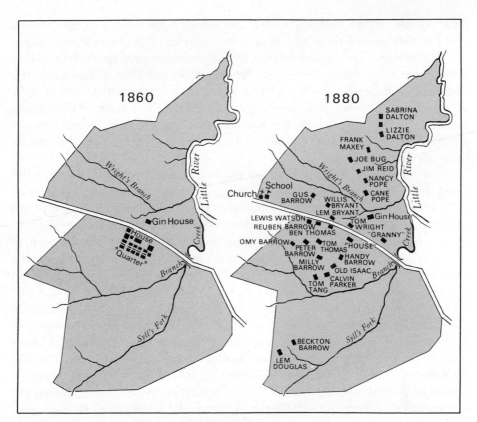

The Same Georgia Plantation in 1860 and 1880
Before the Civil War, slave quarters were located close together, all near the white master's house, so that he could impose order and prevent secret meetings of the blacks. After emancipation, freedmen insisted upon scattering out over the plantation, so that each family could have its own house and some privacy.

This system had several advantages for the landowner. At a time when money was scarce, he was not obliged to pay out cash to his employees until the crop was harvested. He retained general supervision over what was planted and how the crop was cultivated, and he felt he was more likely to secure a good harvest because the freedmen themselves stood to gain by a large yield. Blacks too found the sharecropping system suited to their needs. They had control over how their crops were planted and when they were cultivated and harvested. They could earn more money by working harder in the fields.

The "Breakup" of the Plantation System

To some observers the disappearance of the slave quarters and the resettling of families in individual, scattered cabins seemed to mark a revolution in the character of Southern agriculture. According to the United States census, the number of Southern landholdings doubled between 1860 and 1880, and their average size dropped from 365 acres to 157 acres. But these figures are misleading, because the census takers failed to ask farmers whether they owned their land or were sharecroppers. An examination of tax records, which show landownership, in the representative state of Louisiana helps correct the census distortion. Between 1860 and 1880 in Louisiana, the number of independently owned farms of less than one hundred acres actually dropped by 14 percent, while during the same period the number of plantations increased by 287 percent. By 1900 plantations of one hundred acres or more encompassed half the cultivated land in the state, and more than half the farmers were not proprietors.

If the postwar period did not see the breakup of large plantations, it did bring some significant changes in ownership and control of the land. Hard hit by debt, by rising taxes, and by increasing labor costs, many Southern planters had to sell their holdings, and Northern capital flowed into the region after the war. More tried to cling to their acres by going heavily into debt. Since the postwar Southern banking system was inadequate, the principal source of credit was the local merchant, who could supply both the landowner and his sharecroppers with clothing, shoes, some food, and other necessities to tide them over the lean months between the planting of the tobacco or cotton crop and its harvest. On each sale the merchant charged interest, to be paid when the crop was sold, and he also charged prices ranging from 40 percent to 110 percent higher for all goods sold on credit. It is hardly surprising that those landowners who could afford to do so set up their own stores and extended credit to their own sharecroppers— and quite soon they discovered they were making more profits from mercantile enterprises than from farming. Planters who could not make such arrangements frequently had to sell their lands to the neighborhood merchant. It is not accidental that in William Faulkner's twentieth-century series of novels that constitute a fictional saga of Southern history, the power of landowning families like the Compsons and the Sutpens diminished during the postwar years, while the Snopes family of storekeepers—hard-trading, penny-pinching, and utterly unscrupulous—emerged prosperous and successful.

It would be a mistake, however, to accept without reservation the novelist's hostile characterization of the Southern merchant. The storekeeper insisted on the crop-lien system, which required the farmer legally to pledge that the proceeds from his crop must go first to pay off his obligations to the merchant, because he knew that crops could fail throughout the South, as they did in both 1866 and 1867. And if the merchant urged farmers to forget about soil conservation, diversification, and experimentation with new crops, he did so because he realized that the only way to pay his own debts was to insist that his debtors raise cotton and tobacco, for which there was a ready cash market.

Thus merchants, landowners, and sharecroppers—white Southerners and black Southerners—became locked into an economic system that, at best, promised them little more than survival. At worst, it offered bankruptcy, sale of lands, and hurried nighttime migrations in an attempt to escape from a set of debts in one state but with little more than the hope of starting a new set in another.

By the 1880s, then, the South had become what it remained for the next half-century—the nation's economic backwater. In 1880 the per capita wealth of the South was $376, compared with per capita wealth outside the South of $1,086. Yet this impoverished region had to deal with some of the most difficult political and racial problems that have ever confronted Americans. In attacking these problems, Southerners, black and white, could expect no assistance from the government, because such intervention would violate the unchanging laws of laissez-faire economics.

Political Parties as a Limit to Change

The most influential institutions that blocked radical change during Reconstruction were the national political parties. The fact that both parties were conglomerates of different and often competing sectional and class interests meant that parties had to decide on their policies through compromise and concession. That process nearly always screened out extreme and drastic measures.

Nationally the Democratic party was torn by two conflicting interests during the postwar years. On the one hand, Democrats sought the immediate readmission of the Southern states under the governments President Johnson had set up. Controlled by whites hostile to the Republican party, these states would surely send Democrats to Congress and support Democratic candidates in a national election. Even during the 1850s the South had increasingly become a one-party region; now the goal of a solidly Democratic South appeared within reach. On the other hand, too-enthusiastic advocacy of the Southern cause could hurt Democrats in the North by reviving talk of disloyalty and the Copperhead movement during the war. To blunt such attacks, Democrats had no choice but to urge restraint on their colleagues in the former Confederacy.

Among Republicans, similar constraints dampened any ideas of taking vengeance on the South or of encouraging blacks to seize control of that region. From its beginnings the Republican party had been an uneasy alliance of antislavery men, former Whigs, dissatisfied Democrats, and Know-Nothings. The factional disputes that racked Lincoln's administration showed the weakness of the ties that bound these groups together. It was a bad omen for the party that Republicans disagreed most sharply over Lincoln's plan to reorganize the Southern state governments.

Presidential Reconstruction
During the first year after Lincoln's death, quarrels among Republicans were somewhat muted because practically all members of the party joined in opposing President Johnson's program of Reconstruction. Followed by only a handful of Conservative Republicans, including Secretary of State Seward and Navy Secretary Gideon Welles, Johnson began to work closely with the Democrats of the North and South. He announced that the Southern states had never been out of the Union, and he insisted that, under the provisional governments he had set up, they were entitled to be represented in Congress.

It is easy to understand why almost all Republicans—whether they belonged to the Radical or Moderate faction—rejected the president's argument. Members of both these wings of the party were outraged when the Southern elections of 1865, held at the president's direction, resulted in the choice of a Confederate brigadier-general as governor of Mississippi, and they were furious when the new Georgia legislature named Alexander H. Stephens, the vice-president of the Confederacy, to represent that state in the United States Senate.

Republicans had even more reason to fear these newly elected Southern officials because, although many of the Southerners had been Whigs before the war, they clearly contemplated allying themselves with the Democratic party. However much Republicans disagreed among themselves, they all agreed that their party had saved the Union. They believed, with Thaddeus Stevens, "that upon the continued ascendancy of that party depends the safety of this great nation." Now this ascendancy was threatened. The threat was the more serious because once the Southern states were readmitted to the Union they would receive increased representation in Congress. Before the Civil War, only three-fifths of the slave population of the South had been counted in apportioning representation in the House of Representatives; but now that the slaves were free men, all would be counted. In short, the Southern states, after having been defeated in the most costly war in the nation's history, would have about fifteen more representatives in Congress than they had before the war. And under the president's plan all Southern Congressmen unquestionably would be Democrats.

Republicans of all factions were equally troubled by the fear of what white Southerners, once restored to authority, would do to the freedmen. The laws that the Southern provisional legislatures adopted during the winter of 1865–66 gave reason for anxiety on this score. Not one of these governments considered treating black citizens just as they treated white citizens. Instead the legislatures adopted special laws, known as the Black Codes, to regulate the conduct of the freedmen. On the positive side, these laws recognized the freedmen's right to make civil contracts, to sue and be sued, and to acquire and hold most kinds of property. But with these rights went restrictions. The laws varied from state to state, but in general they specified that blacks might not purchase or carry firearms, that they might not assemble after sunset, and that those who were idle or unemployed should "be liable to imprisonment, and to hard labor, one or both, . . . not exceeding twelve months." The Mississippi code prevented blacks from renting or leasing "any lands or tenements except in incorporated cities or towns." That of South Carolina forbade blacks from practicing "the art, trade or business of an artisan, mechanic or shopkeeper, or any other trade, employment or business (besides that of husbandry, or that of a servant)." So clearly did these measures seem designed to keep the freedmen in quasi-slavery that the *Chicago Tribune* spoke for a united, outraged Republican party in denouncing the first of these Black Codes, that adopted by the Mississippi legislature: "We tell the white men of Mississippi that the men of the North will convert the state of Mississippi into a frogpond before they will allow any such laws to disgrace one foot of soil over which the flag of freedom waves."

The Fourteenth Amendment For these reasons, all Republicans were unwilling to recognize the regimes Johnson had set up in the South; when Congress reassembled in December 1865, they easily rallied to block seating of the Southern senators and representatives. All agreed to the creation of a special joint committee on Reconstruction to handle questions concerning the readmission of the Southern states and their further reorganization. In setting up this committee, congressional Republicans carefully balanced its membership with Radicals and Moderates. Its most conspicuous member was the Radical Stevens, but its powerful chairman was Senator William Pitt Fessenden, a Moderate.

Congressional Republicans found it easier to unite in opposing Johnson's plan of Reconstruction than to unite in devising one of their own. Congressional leaders recognized that it would take time to draft and adopt a constitutional amendment and then to have it ratified by the required number of states. Therefore, early in 1866 they agreed on interim legislation that would protect the freedmen. One bill extended and expanded the functions of the Freedmen's Bureau, and a second guaranteed minimal civil rights to all citizens. Contrary to expectations, Johnson vetoed both these measures. Refusing to recognize that these measures represented the wishes of both Moderate and Radical Republicans, the president claimed that they were the work of the Radicals, who wanted "to destroy our institutions and change the character of the Government." He vowed to fight these Northern enemies of the Union just as he had once fought Southern secessionists and traitors. The Republican majority in Congress was not able to override Johnson's veto of the Freedmen's Bureau bill (a later, less sweeping measure extended the life of that agency for two years), but it passed the Civil Rights Act of 1866 over his disapproval.

While relations between the president and the Republicans in Congress were deteriorating, the joint committee on Reconstruction continued to meet and consider various plans for reorganizing the South. With its evenly balanced membership, the committee dismissed the president's theory that the Southern states were already reconstructed and back in the Union, as well as Thaddeus Stevens's view that the Confederacy was conquered territory over which Congress could rule at its own discretion. It also rejected Charles Sumner's more elaborate argument that the Southern states had committed suicide when they seceded, so that their land and inhabitants now fell "under the exclusive jurisdiction of Congress." More acceptable to the majority of Republicans was the "grasp of war" theory advanced by Richard Henry Dana, Jr., the noted Massachusetts constitutional lawyer who was also the author of *Two Years Before the Mast.* Dana argued that the federal government should hold the defeated Confederacy in the grasp of war only for a brief and limited time, during which it must act swiftly to revive state governments in the region and promptly to restore the constitutional balance between national and state authority. Dana's theory was an essentially conservative one: it called for only a short period of federal domination and looked toward the speedy restoration of the Southern states on terms of absolute equality with the loyal states.

Finding in Dana's theory a constitutional source of power, the joint committee after much hard work produced the first comprehensive congressional plan of Reconstruction—the proposed Fourteenth Amendment to the Constitution, which Congress endorsed in June 1866 and submitted to the states for ratification. Some parts of the amendment were noncontroversial. All Republicans accepted its opening statement: "All persons born or naturalized in the United States, and subject to the jurisdiction thereof, are citizens of the United States and of the State wherein they reside." This provision was necessary in order to nullify the Supreme Court's decision in the *Dred Scott* case (1857), which had denied citizenship to African Americans. There was also no disagreement about the provision declaring the Confederate debt invalid.

All the other provisions of the amendment, however, represented a compromise between Radical and Moderate Republicans. For example, Radicals wanted to keep all Southerners who had voluntarily supported the Confederacy from voting until 1870. Indeed, the arch-Radical Stevens urged: "Not only to 1870 but 18,070, every rebel who shed the blood of loyal men should be prevented from exercising any power in this Government." Moderates favored a speedy restoration of all political rights to former Confederates. As a compromise, the Fourteenth Amendment excluded high-ranking Confederates from office, but it did not deny them the vote.

Similarly, the Fourteenth Amendment's provisions protecting the freedmen represented a compromise. Radicals like Sumner (who was considered too radical to be given a seat on the joint committee) wanted an outright declaration of the national government's right and duty to protect the civil liberties of the former slaves. But Moderates drew back in alarm from entrusting additional authority to Washington. The joint committee came up with a provision that granted no power to the national government but restricted that of the states: "No State shall make or enforce any law which shall abridge the privileges and immunities of citizens of the United States; nor shall any State deprive any person of life, liberty, or property, without due process of law; nor deny to any person within its jurisdiction the equal protection of the laws."

Finally, another compromise between Radicals and Moderates resulted in the amendment's provision concerning voting. Although Sumner and other Radicals called black suffrage "the essence, the great essential," of a proper Reconstruction policy, Conservatives refused to give the national government power to interfere with the state requirements for voting. The joint committee thereupon devised a complex and, as it proved, unworkable plan to persuade the Southern states voluntarily to enfranchise blacks, under threat of having their representation in Congress reduced if they refused.

The Fourteenth Amendment's feasibility as a program of Reconstruction was never tested because of the outbreak of political warfare between President Johnson and the Republican party, which had elected him vice-president in 1864. During the summer of 1866, Johnson and his friends tried to create a new political party, which would rally behind the president's policies the few Conservative

Republicans, the Northern Democrats, and the Southern whites. With the president's hearty approval, a National Union Convention held in Philadelphia in August stressed the theme of harmony among the sections. The entry into the convention hall of delegates from Massachusetts and South Carolina, arm in arm, seemed to symbolize the end of sectional strife. The president himself went on a "swing around the circle" of leading Northern cities, ostensibly on his way to dedicate a monument to the memory of another Democrat, Stephen A. Douglas. In his frequent public speeches Johnson defended the constitutionality of his own Reconstruction program and attacked Congress—and particularly the Radical Republicans—for attempting to subvert the Constitution. In a final effort to consolidate sentiment against Congress, he urged the Southern states not to ratify the proposed Fourteenth Amendment. With the exception of Tennessee, which was controlled by one of Johnson's bitterest personal and political enemies, all the former Confederate states rejected the congressional plan.

The Second Congressional Program of Reconstruction   When Congress reassembled in December 1866, the Republican majority therefore had to devise a second program of Reconstruction. Cheered by overwhelming victories in the fall congressional elections, Republicans felt even less inclined than previously to cooperate with the president, who had gone into political opposition, or to encourage the provisional regimes in the South, which had rejected their first program. Republican suspicion that Southern whites were fundamentally hostile toward the freedmen was strengthened by reports of a race riot in Memphis during May 1866, when a mob of whites joined in a two-day indiscriminate attack on blacks in that city. An even more serious affair occurred four months later in New Orleans, when a white mob, aided by the local police, attacked a black political gathering with what was described as "a cowardly ferocity unsurpassed in the annals of crime." In New Orleans, 45 or 50 blacks were killed, and 150 more were wounded.

Once again, however, the Republican majority in Congress found it easier to agree on what to oppose than on what to favor in the way of Reconstruction legislation. Stevens urged that the South be placed under military rule for a generation and that Southern plantations be sold to pay the national debt. Sumner wanted to deny the vote to large numbers of Southern whites, to require that blacks be given the right to vote, and to create racially integrated schools in the South. Moderate Republicans, on the other hand, were willing to retain the Fourteenth Amendment as the basic framework of congressional Reconstruction and to insist on little else except the ratification of the amendment by the Southern states.

The second congressional program of Reconstruction, embodied in the Military Reconstruction Act of March 2, 1867, represented a compromise between the demands of Radical and Moderate Republican factions. It divided

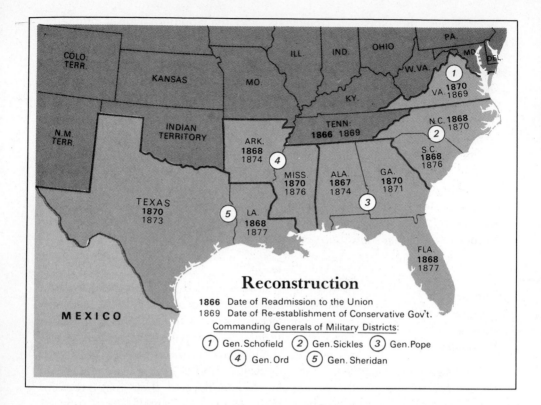

Reconstruction

1866 Date of Readmission to the Union
1869 Date of Re-establishment of Conservative Gov't.
Commanding Generals of Military Districts:

(1) Gen. Schofield (2) Gen. Sickles (3) Gen. Pope
(4) Gen. Ord (5) Gen. Sheridan

the ten former Confederate states that had not ratified the Fourteenth Amendment into five military districts. In each of these states there were to be new constitutional conventions, for which black men were allowed to vote. The task of these conventions was to draft new state constitutions that provided for black suffrage, and they were required to ratify the Fourteenth Amendment. When thus reorganized, the Southern states could apply to Congress for readmission to the Union.

It was easy to recognize the radical aspects of this measure, which Democrats pointed out during the congressional debates and President Johnson denounced in his unsuccessful veto of the act. In particular, the requirement of black suffrage, which Sumner sponsored, seemed to Radicals "a prodigious triumph."

In fact, however, most provisions of the Military Reconstruction Act were more acceptable to Moderate than to Radical Republicans. The measure did nothing to give land to the freedmen, to provide education at national expense, or to end racial segregation in the South. It did not erase the boundaries of the Southern states. It did not even sweep away the provisional governments Johnson had established there, although it did make them responsible to the commanders of the new military districts. So conservative was the act in all these respects that Sumner branded it as "horribly defective."

Intent on striking some kind of balance between the Radical and Conservative wings of the Republican party, the framers of the Military Reconstruction Act drafted the measure carelessly. As Sumner had predicted, the act
promptly proved to furnish "Reconstruction without machinery or motive
power." Having to choose between military rule and black suffrage, the Southern
provisional governments chose the former, correctly believing that army officers
generally sympathized with white supremacy. To get the Reconstruction process
under way, Congress therefore had to enact a supplementary law (March 23,
1867), requiring the federal commanders in the South to take the initiative, when
the local governments did not, in announcing elections, registering voters, and
convening constitutional conventions. During the summer of 1867, as the president, the attorney general, and Southern state officials tried by legalistic interpretations to delay the Reconstruction program, Congress had to pass two further
supplementary acts, explaining the "true intent and meaning" of the previous
legislation.

With these measures, the congressional Reconstruction legislation affecting
the South was substantially completed. Both the first and the second congressional plans of Reconstruction were compromises between the Radical and the
Moderate factions in the Republican party. The Radicals' insistence on change
was essential in securing the adoption of this legislation, but the Moderates
blocked all measures that would have revolutionized the social and economic
order in the South.

Impeachment   The same need to compromise between the factions of
                                   the Republican party dictated Congress's policy toward
the president during the Reconstruction years. Almost all Republicans were
suspicious of President Johnson and feared that he intended to turn the South
over to Confederate rule. Johnson's repeated veto messages, assailing carefully
balanced compromise legislation as the work of Radicals and attacking Congress
as an unconstitutional body because it refused to seat congressmen from all the
states, angered Republicans of both factions. Therefore, most Republicans
wanted to keep a close eye on the president and sought to curb executive powers
that had grown during the war. In 1867, fearing that Johnson would use his power
as commander in chief to subvert their Reconstruction legislation, Republican
factions joined to pass an army appropriations bill that required all military
orders to the army—including those of the president himself—to go through the
hands of General Grant. Suspecting that Johnson wanted to use the federal
patronage to build up a political machine of his own, they enacted at the same
time the Tenure of Office Act, which required the president to secure the Senate's
consent not merely when he appointed officials, but also when he removed them.

The Republicans in Congress were prepared to go this far in impressive
unanimity—but no farther. When Radical Republican James M. Ashley in January 1867 moved to impeach the president, he was permitted to conduct a half-
serious, half-comic investigation of Johnson's alleged involvement in Lincoln's

"Awkward Collision on the Grand Trunk Columbia Railroad"
This cartoon depicts presidential and congressional Reconstruction as two engines going in opposite directions on the same rails. Andrew Johnson, driver of the locomotive "President," says: "Look here! One of us has got to [go] back." But Thaddeus Stevens, driver of the locomotive "Congress," replies: "Well, it ain't going to be me that's going to do it, you bet!"

assassination, his purported sale of pardons, and other trumped-up charges. But when Ashley's motion reached the House floor, Moderate Republicans saw that it was soundly defeated.

A subsequent attempt at impeachment fared better, but it also revealed how the Radical and Moderate factions blocked each other. In August 1867, President Johnson suspended from office Secretary of War Edwin M. Stanton, who was collaborating closely with the Radicals in Congress. As required by the Tenure of Office Act, he asked the Senate to consent to the removal. When the Senate refused, the president removed Stanton anyway and ordered him to surrender his office. News of this seemingly open defiance of the law caused Republicans in the House of Representatives to rush through a resolution impeaching the president, without waiting for specific charges against him to be drawn up.

The trial of President Johnson (who was not present in court but was represented by his lawyers) was a test of strength not merely between Congress and the chief executive, but also between the Radical and the Moderate Republicans. Impeachment managers from the House of Representatives presented eleven charges against the president, mostly accusing him of violating the Tenure of Office Act but also censuring his repeated attacks on Congress. With fierce joy Radical Thaddeus Stevens, who was one of the managers, denounced the president: "Unfortunate man! thus surrounded, hampered, tangled in the meshes of his own wickedness—unfortunate, unhappy man, behold your doom!"

But Radical oratory could not persuade Moderate Republicans and Democrats to vote for conviction. They listened as Johnson's lawyers challenged the constitutionality of the Tenure of Office Act, showed that it had not been intended to apply to cabinet members, and proved that, in any case, it did not cover Stanton, who had been appointed by Lincoln, not Johnson. When the critical vote came, Moderate Republicans like Fessenden voted to acquit the president, and Johnson's Radical foes lacked one vote of the two-thirds majority required to convict him. Several other Republican Senators who for political expedience voted against the president were prepared to change their votes and favor acquittal if their ballots were needed.

Nothing more clearly shows how the institutional needs of a political party prevented drastic change than did this decision not to remove a president whom a majority in Congress hated and feared. The desire to maintain the unity of the national Republican party, despite frequent quarrels and endless bickering, overrode the wishes of individual congressmen. Throughout the Reconstruction period Moderate Republicans felt that they were constantly being rushed from one advanced position to another in order to placate the Radicals, who were never satisfied. More accurately, Radical Republicans perceived that the need to retain Moderate support prevented the adoption of any really revolutionary Reconstruction program.

Racism as a Limit to Change

A final set of beliefs that limited the nature of the changes imposed on, and accepted by, the South during the Reconstruction period can be labeled racism. In all parts of the country, white Americans looked with suspicion and fear on those whose skin was of a different color. For example, in California white hatred built up against the Chinese, who had begun coming to that state in great numbers after the discovery of gold and who were later imported by the thousands to help construct the Central Pacific Railroad. White workers resented the willingness of the Chinese to work long hours for "coolies" wages; they distrusted the unfamiliar dress, diet, and habits of the Chinese; and they disliked all these things more because the Chinese were a yellow-skinned people. Under the leadership of a newly arrived Irish immigrant, Dennis Kearney, white laborers organized a workingman's party with the slogan "The Chinese must go."

Anti-Chinese Agitation in San Francisco: A Meeting of the Workingman's Party on the Sand Lots
Racism in postwar America took many forms. In California its strongest manifestation was in the hostility toward the Chinese immigrants stirred up by Dennis Kearney's workingman's party.

The depression that gripped the nation in 1873* gave impetus to the anti-Chinese movement. Day after day thousands of the unemployed gathered in the San Francisco sandlots to hear Kearney's slashing attacks on the Chinese and on the wealthy corporations that employed them. In the summer of 1877, San Francisco hoodlums, inspired by Kearney, burned twenty-five Chinese laundries and destroyed dozens of Chinese homes. The movement had enough political strength to force both major parties in California to adopt anti-Chinese platforms, and California congressmen succeeded in persuading their colleagues to pass a bill limiting the number of Chinese who could be brought into the United States each year. Because the measure clearly conflicted with treaty arrangements with China, President Rutherford B. Hayes vetoed it, but he had his secretary of state initiate negotiations leading to a new treaty that permitted the restriction of immigration. Congress, in 1882, passed the Chinese Exclusion Act, which suspended all Chinese immigration for ten years and forbade the naturalization of Chinese already in the country.

---

*For the Panic of 1873, see chapter 21, p. 55.

Northern Views of the Black Race

If white Americans became so agitated over a small number of Chinese, who were unquestionably hard-working and thrifty and who belonged to one of the most ancient of civilizations, it is easy to see how whites could consider blacks an even greater danger. There were more than 3 million blacks in the United States, most of them recently emancipated from slavery. The exploits of black soldiers during the war—their very discipline and courage—proved that blacks could be formidable opponents. More than ever before, blacks seemed distinctive, alien, and menacing.

Most American intellectuals of the Civil War generation accepted black inferiority unquestioningly. Although a few reformers like Charles Sumner vigorously attacked this notion, a majority of philanthropic Northerners accepted the judgment of the distinguished Harvard scientist Louis Agassiz concerning blacks. He held that while whites during antiquity were developing high civilizations, "the negro race groped in barbarism and never originated a regular organization among themselves." Many adopted Agassiz's belief that blacks, once free, would inevitably die out in the United States. Others reached the same conclusion by studying Charles Darwin's recently published *Origin of Species* (1859), and they accepted the argument put forward by Darwin's admirers that in the inevitable struggle for survival "higher civilized races" must inevitably eliminate "an endless number of lower races." Consequently, the influential and tenderhearted Congregational minister Horace Bushnell could prophesy the approaching end of the black race in the United States with something approaching smugness. "Since we must all die," he asked rhetorically, "why should it grieve us, that a stock thousands of years behind, in the scale of culture, should die with few and still fewer children to succeed, till finally the whole succession remains in the more cultivated race?"

When even the leaders of Northern society held such views, it is hardly surprising that most whites in the region were openly antiblack. In state after state whites fiercely resisted efforts to extend the political and civil rights of blacks, partly because they feared that any improvement in the condition of blacks in the North would lead to a huge influx of blacks from the South. At the end of the Civil War only Maine, New Hampshire, Vermont, Massachusetts, and Rhode Island allowed blacks to have full voting rights; in New York only blacks who met certain property-holding qualifications could have the ballot. During the next three years in referenda held in Connecticut, Wisconsin, Kansas, Ohio, Michigan, and Missouri, constitutional amendments authorizing black suffrage were defeated, and in New York voters rejected a proposal to eliminate the property-holding qualifications for black voters. Only in Iowa, a state where there were very few blacks, did a black suffrage amendment carry in 1868, and that same year Minnesota adopted an ambiguously worded amendment. Thus at the end of the 1860s, most Northern states refused to give black men the ballot.

In words as well as in votes, the majority of Northerners made their deeply racist feelings evident. The Democratic press constantly cultivated the racial fears of its readers and regularly portrayed the Republicans as planning a "new era of miscegenation, amalgamation, and promiscuous intercourse between the races." From the White House, denouncing Republican attempts "to Africanize the [Southern] half of our country," President Andrew Johnson proclaimed: "In the progress of nations negroes have shown less capacity for self-government than any other race of people.... Whenever they have been left to their own devices they have shown an instant tendency to relapse into barbarism." Even Northern Republicans opposed to Johnson shared many of his racist views. Radical Senator Timothy O. Howe of Wisconsin declared that he regarded "the freedmen, in the main ... as so much animal life," and Senator Benjamin F. Wade of Ohio, whom the Radical Republicans would have elevated to the presidency had they removed Johnson, had both a genuine devotion to the principle of equal rights and an incurable dislike of blacks. Representative George W. Julian of Indiana, one of the few Northern congressmen who had no racial prejudice, bluntly told his colleagues in 1866: "The real trouble is that *we hate the negro.* It is not his ignorance that offends us, but his color.... Of this fact I entertain no doubt whatsoever."

Both personal preferences and the wishes of their constituents inhibited Northern Republicans from supporting measures that might have altered race relations. When Sumner sought to remove from the books federal laws that recognized slavery or to prohibit racial discrimination on public transportation in the District of Columbia, his colleagues replied: "God has made the negro inferior, and ... laws cannot make him equal." Such congressmen were hardly in a position to scold the South for racial discrimination or to insist on drastic social change in that region.

Southern Views of the Black Race

If racism limited the innovation that northerners were willing to propose during the Reconstruction period, it even more drastically reduced the amount of change that white southerners were prepared to accept. Racial bigotry runs through both the private correspondence and the public pronouncements of Southern whites during the postwar era. "Equality does not exist between blacks and whites," announced Alexander H. Stephens. "The one race is by nature inferior in many respects, physically and mentally, to the other. This should be received as a fixed invincible fact in all dealings with the subject." A North Carolina diarist agreed: "The Anglo-Saxon and the African can never be equal ... one or the other must fall." Or, as the Democratic party of Louisiana resolved in its 1865 platform: "We hold this to be a Government of white people, made and to be perpetuated for the exclusive benefit of the white race; and ... that people of African descent cannot be considered as citizens of the United States, and that there can, in no event, nor under any circumstances, be any equality between the white and other races." The Black Codes were the legal embodiment of these attitudes.

These racist views shaped the attitudes of most Southern whites toward the whole process of Reconstruction. White Southerners approved of President

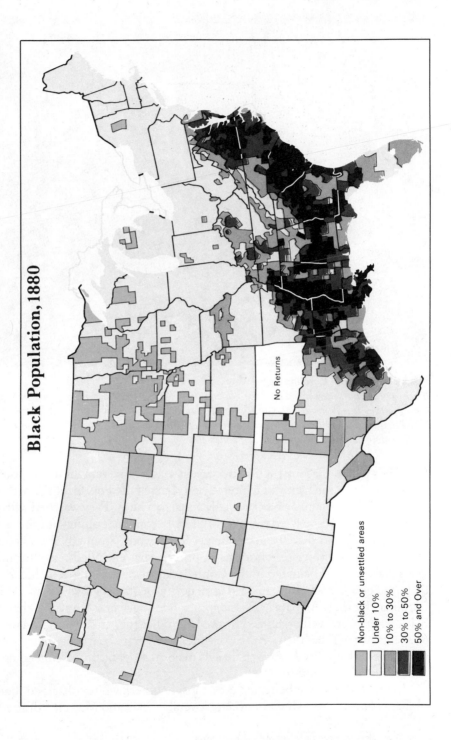

Black Population, 1880

No Returns

Non-black or unsettled areas
Under 10%
10% to 30%
30% to 50%
50% and Over

Blacks in the South Carolina Legislature
Blacks voted and were elected to office under the Radical Reconstruction program. In South Carolina they briefly formed a majority in the House of Representatives. Hostile observers noted that some black members engaged in idle chatter, read the newspapers, and put their feet on their desks while the legislature was conducting business.

Johnson's plan of Reconstruction because it placed government in the Southern states entirely in the hands of whites. They rejected the Fourteenth Amendment primarily because it made blacks legally equal to whites. They watched with utter disbelief as Congress passed the 1867 Military Reconstruction Act, for they simply could not imagine that the freedmen were to vote. Stunned, they saw army officers supervise voter registration—a process that excluded many prominent whites who had participated in the Confederate government but included more than 700,000 blacks, who formed a majority of the eligible voters in South Carolina, Florida, Alabama, Mississippi, and Louisiana. Knowing that these black voters were well organized by the Union League, often with the assistance of agents of the Freedmen's Bureau, whites were more apathetic than surprised when the fall elections showed heavy majorities in favor of convening new constitutional conventions.*

With hostile and unbelieving eyes, most Southern whites observed the work of these conventions, which between November 1867 and May 1868 drafted new

---

*The Texas election was not held until February 1868. Tennessee had no election, because it had already been readmitted to the Union.

Blacks Voting
*Under the congressional plan
of Reconstruction, Southern
states were required to give
blacks suffrage. This drawing
from* Harper's Weekly *shows
how both old and young
flocked to the polls to exercise their new right. Notable
is one young black who is
still wearing his US Army
uniform.*

constitutions for the former Confederate states. To Southern whites unac-
customed to seeing blacks in any positions of public prominence, the presence of
freedmen in these conventions meant that they were black-dominated. In fact,
except in the South Carolina convention, in which blacks did form a majority,
only between one-fourth and one-ninth of the delegates were blacks. Whites
ridiculed the black members' ignorance of parliamentary procedures, and they
laughed sarcastically when they read about how the "coal black" temporary
chairman of the Louisiana convention put a question by asking those who favored
a motion "to rise an stan on der feet" and then directing "all you contrairy men to
rise."

Racial prejudice also determined Southern whites' reactions to the constitutions produced by these conventions. Generally the whites denounced these new
charters as "totally incompatible with the prosperity and liberty of the people."
In reality the constitutions, often copied from Northern models, were generally
improvements over the ones they replaced. Besides giving blacks the right to vote
(as Congress had directed), they promised all citizens of the state equality before
the law. They reformed financial and revenue systems, reorganized the judiciary,
improved the organization of local government, and, most important of all,
instituted a state-supported system of public education, hitherto notably lacking
in most Southern states.

The Reconstruction Governments in the South

Because these constitutions guaranteed racial equality, Southern whites tried, without great success, to block their ratification. In Alabama whites boycotted the ratification election; in Mississippi they cast a majority of votes against the new constitution. In Virginia ratification was delayed because the conservative army commander of that district discovered that there was no money to hold an election, and in Texas all moves toward the creation of a new government lagged several months behind those in the eastern states. But despite all the foot dragging, new governments were set up, and in June 1868 Congress readmitted representatives and senators from Alabama, Arkansas, Florida, Georgia, Louisiana, North Carolina, and South Carolina. Two years later the Reconstruction of Virginia, Mississippi, and Texas was completed, and in early 1870 these states were also readmitted. Meanwhile Georgia experienced one further reorganization after its state legislature attempted to exclude blacks who had been elected to it. But by 1871, when the Georgia senators and representatives again took their seats in Congress, all the states of the former Confederacy had undergone Reconstruction and had been readmitted to the Union.

Most Southern whites were bitterly hostile to this reorganization of their state governments. The name "Black Reconstruction," as they called the ensuing period of Republican domination in the South, reveals the racial bias behind their opposition. In fact, these Southern state governments were not dominated by blacks, and blacks held a smaller proportion of offices than their percentage of the population. Blacks dominated the state legislature only in South Carolina. No black was elected governor, although there were black lieutenant governors in South Carolina, Louisiana, and Mississippi. Only in South Carolina was there a black supreme court justice. During the entire Reconstruction period only two blacks served in the United States Senate—Hiram R. Revels and Blanche K. Bruce, both from Mississippi and both men of exceptional ability and integrity. Only fifteen blacks were elected to the House of Representatives.

Even to the most racist Southern whites, it was obvious that most of the leaders of the Republican party in the South, and a large part of the Republican following as well, were white. Racists called the Northern-born white Republicans carpetbaggers because they allegedly came South with no more worldly possessions than could be packed into a carpetbag (a small suitcase), ready to live on and exploit the conquered region. The term, with its implication of corruption, was applied indiscriminately to men of Northern birth who had lived in the South long before the war, as well as to newly arrived fortune hunters, many of them recently discharged Union army officers.

Southern-born white Republicans were called scalawags, a term that cattle drivers applied to "the mean, lousy and filthy kine [cattle] that are not fit for butchers or dogs." Again the term was used indiscriminately. Southern racists applied it to poor hill-country whites, who had long been at odds with the plantation owners in states like North Carolina and Alabama and now joined the Republican party as a way of getting back at their old enemies. But other scalawags were members of the plantation-owning, mercantile, and industrial classes of the South. Many were former Whigs who distrusted the Democrats, and they felt at home in a Republican party that favored protective tariffs, subsidies for railroads, and appropriations for rebuilding the levees along the Mississippi River. A surprising number of Southern-born white Republicans were former high-ranking officers in the Confederate army, like General P. G. T. Beauregard and General James Longstreet, who knew at first hand the extent of the damage caused by the war and were willing to accept the victors' terms promptly.

Bitterly as they attacked these white Republicans, Southern Democrats reserved their worst abuse for blacks. They saw in every measure adopted by the new state governments evidence of black incompetence, extravagance, or even barbarism. In truth, much that these state governments did supplied the Democrats with ammunition. The postwar period was one of widespread political corruption, and there was no reason to expect that newly enfranchised blacks would prove any less attracted by the profits of politics than anybody else. Petty corruption prevailed in all the Southern state governments. Louisiana legislators voted themselves an allowance for stationery—which covered purchases of hams and bottles of champagne. The South Carolina legislature ran up a bill of more than $50,000 in refurbishing the statehouse with such costly items as a $750 mirror, $480 clocks, and two hundred porcelain spittoons at $8 apiece. The same legislature voted $1,000 to the speaker of the House of Representatives to repay his losses on a horse race.

But these excesses angered Southern Democrats less than the legitimate work performed by the new state governments. Unwilling to recognize that blacks were now equal citizens, they objected to expenditures for hospitals, jails, orphanages, and asylums to care for blacks. Most of all they objected to the creation of a public school system. There was considerable hostility throughout the South to the idea of educating any children at the cost of the taxpayer, and the thought of paying taxes in order to teach black children seemed a wild and foolish extravagance. The fact that black schools were mostly conducted by Northern whites, usually women, who came south with a reforming mission, did nothing to increase popular support. Too many of the teachers stated plainly and publicly their intention to use "every endeavor to throw a ray of light here and there, among this benighted race of ruffians, rebels by nature." Adding to all these hostilities was a fear that a system of public education might someday lead to a racially integrated system of education. These apprehensions had little basis in reality, for during the entire period of Reconstruction in the whole South there were significant numbers of children in racially mixed schools only in New Orleans between 1870 and 1874.

The Ku Klux Klan   Not content with criticizing Republican rule, Southern Democrats organized to put an end to it. They made a two-pronged attack. On the one hand, they sought to intimidate or to drive from the South whites who cooperated politically with the Republican regimes. On the other hand, they tried to terrorize and silence blacks, especially those active in

Ku Klux Klan Broadside
*A terrorist organization, the Ku Klux
Klan pictured itself as a defender not
merely of white supremacy but of the
nation itself against incendiary blacks.*

politics. Much of this pressure was informal and occasional, but much was the
work of racist organizations that sprang up all over the South during the postwar
years. The most famous of these was the Ku Klux Klan, which originated in 1866
as a social club for young white men in Pulaski, Tennessee. As the Military
Reconstruction Act went into effect and the possibility of black participation in
Southern political life became increasingly real, racists saw new potential in this
secret organization with its mysterious name and its bizarre uniforms of long
flowing robes, high conical hats that made the wearers seem unnaturally tall, and
white face masks.

In 1867 the Klan was reorganized under a new constitution that provided for
local dens, each headed by a Grand Cyclops. The dens were linked together into
provinces (counties), each under a Grand Titan, and in turn into realms (states),
each under a Grand Dragon. At the head of the whole organization was the
Grand Wizard—who, according to most reports, was former Confederate General Nathan Bedford Forrest. Probably this elaborate organizational structure
was never completely filled out, and certainly there was an almost total lack of
central control of the Klan's activities. Indeed, at some point in early 1869 the
Klan was officially disbanded. But even without central direction its members,
like those of the Order of the White Camellia and other racist vigilante groups,
continued in their plan of disrupting the new Republican regimes in the South
and terrorizing the blacks who supported these administrations.

Along with other vigilante organizations, the Klan expressed traditional
Southern white racism. White Southerners were willing to accept the defeat of

the Confederacy and were prepared to admit that slavery was dead. But they could not bring themselves to contemplate a society that would treat blacks and whites as equals. As a group of South Carolina whites protested to Congress in 1868: "The white people of our State will never quietly submit to negro rule.... We will keep up this contest until we have regained the heritage of political control handed down to us by honored ancestry. That is a duty we owe to the land that is ours, to the graves that it contains, and to the race of which you and we alike are members—the proud Caucasian race, whose sovereignty on earth God has ordained."

The appeal was shrewdly pitched, for the Southern racist knew how to reach his Northern counterpart. Joined together, their fears of men with darker skins helped to undercut the Reconstruction regimes in the South and to halt any congressional efforts at further innovative Reconstruction legislation.

CHRONOLOGY

1865 Lincoln assassinated; Andrew Johnson becomes president.
Johnson moves for speedy, lenient restoration of Southern states to Union.
Congress creates Joint Committee of Fifteen to supervise Reconstruction process.
Thirteenth Amendment ratified.

1866 Johnson breaks with Republican majority in Congress by vetoing Freedmen's Bureau bill and Civil Rights bill. Latter is passed over his veto.
Congress approves Fourteenth Amendment and submits it to states for ratification.
Johnson and Republicans quarrel. Republicans win fall congressional elections.
Ku Klux Klan formed.

1867 Congress passes Military Reconstruction Act over Johnson's veto. (Two supplementary acts in 1867 and a third in 1868 passed to put this measure into effect.)
Congress passes Tenure of Office Act and Command of Army Act to reduce Johnson's power.

1868 Former Confederate states hold constitutional conventions, in which freedmen are allowed to vote, and adopt new constitutions guaranteeing universal male suffrage.
Alabama, Arkansas, Florida, Georgia, Louisiana, North Carolina, and South Carolina readmitted to representation in Congress. Because of discrimination against black officeholders, Georgia representatives are expelled. (State is again admitted in 1870.)
President Johnson impeached. Escapes conviction by one vote.
Republicans nominate Ulysses S. Grant for president; Democrats select Governor Horatio Seymour of New York. Grant elected president.

1869 Congress passes Fifteenth Amendment and submits it to states for ratification.

SUGGESTED READINGS

Reconstruction: America's Unfinished Revolution (1988), by Eric Foner, is a full, eloquent account. Three shorter interpretations are John H. Franklin, *Reconstruction After the Civil War* (1961); Kenneth M. Stampp, *The Era of Reconstruction* (1965); and Rembert W. Patrick, *The Reconstruction of the Nation* (1967).

The best account of steps taken during the Civil War to reorganize the Southern states is Herman Belz, *Reconstructing the Union* (1969). William B. Hesseltine, *Lincoln's Plan of Reconstruction* (1960), argues that Lincoln had not one but many approaches to Reconstruction, all of them unsuccessful. LaWanda Cox, *Lincoln and Black Freedom* (1981), is an important study. Peyton McCrary, *Abraham Lincoln and Reconstruction* (1978), is the authoritative account of developments in Louisiana, where Lincoln's approach to Reconstruction was most fully tested.

The Presidency of Andrew Johnson (1979), by Albert Castel, is a balanced account, and Hans L. Trefousse's *Andrew Johnson* (1989) is the best biography of that president. Favorable versions of Johnson's Reconstruction program include George F. Milton, *The Age of Hate* (1930), and Howard K. Beale, *The Critical Year* (1930). The following accounts are critical: Eric L. McKitrick, *Andrew Johnson and Reconstruction* (1960); LaWanda Cox and John H. Cox, *Politics, Principle, and Prejudice* (1963); and W. R. Brock, *An American Crisis* (1963).

On constitutional changes in the postwar period, see Harold M. Hyman, *A More Perfect Union* (1973); Hyman and William M. Wiecek, *Equal Justice Under Law* (1982); Stanley I. Kutler, *Judicial Power and Reconstruction Politics* (1968); and Charles Fairman, *Reconstruction and the Union* (1971).

George R. Bentley, *A History of the Freedmen's Bureau* (1955), is a standard work, but it should be supplemented by William S. McFeely, *Yankee Stepfather: General O. O. Howard and the Freedmen* (1968). Claude F. Oubre, *Forty Acres and a Mule* (1978), discusses the abortive efforts of the bureau in land distribution.

Leon Litwack, *Been in the Storm So Long* (1979), is a masterful account of the transition from slavery to freedom. See also Peter Kolchin, *After Freedom* (1972), on Alabama; Willie Lee Rose, *Rehearsal for Reconstruction* (1964), and Joel Williamson, *After Slavery* (1965), on South Carolina; and Vernon L. Wharton, *The Negro in Mississippi* (1947).

Fred A. Shannon, *The Farmer's Last Frontier* (1945), and E. Merton Coulter, *The South During Reconstruction* (1972), give good general accounts of economic changes in the postwar South. Recently historians and economists using sophisticated quantitative methods have reexamined these changes: Stephen J. DeCanio, *Agriculture in the Postbellum South* (1974); Robert Higgs, *Competition and Coercion: Blacks in the American Economy* (1977); Roger Ransom and Richard L. Sutch, *One Kind of Freedom: The Economic Consequences of Emancipation* (1977); and Gavin Wright, *Old South, New South* (1986). On the alleged breakup of the plantation system, see Roger W. Shugg, *Origins of Class Struggle in Louisiana* (1939), and on the continuing dominance of the planter class, see Jonathan M. Wiener, *Social Origins of the New South* (1978).

On Radical Reconstruction, see Michael L. Benedict, *A Compromise of Principle* (1974); David Donald, *The Politics of Reconstruction* (1965); and Hans L. Trefousse, *The Radical Republicans* (1969). The best account of Grant's Southern policy is William Gillette, *Retreat from Reconstruction* (1980). Among the fullest biographies of Reconstruction politicians are Fawn M. Brodie, *Thaddeus Stevens* (1959); David Donald, *Charles Sumner and the Rights of Man* (1970); William S. McFeely, *Grant* (1981); and Benjamin P. Thomas and Harold M. Hyman, *Stanton* (1962).

David M. DeWitt, *Impeachment and Trial of Andrew Johnson* (1903), remains the standard account, but it should be supplemented with Michael L. Benedict's book of the same name (1973) and with Hans L. Trefousse, *Impeachment of a President* (1975).

On American racial attitudes, George M. Fredrickson, *The Black Image in the White Mind* (1971), is excellent. On Northern racism, see V. Jacque Voegeli, *Free But Not Equal* (1967), and Forrest G. Wood, *Black Scare* (1967).

Dan T. Carter, *When the War Was Over* (1985), ably traces the failure of presidential reconstruction in the South. For a favorable view of the Reconstruction governments in the South, see W.E.B. DuBois, *Black Reconstruction* (1935). Some excellent accounts of Reconstruction in individual states are Francis B. Simkins and Robert H. Woody, *South Carolina During Reconstruction* (1932); Jerrell H. Shofner, *Nor Is It Over Yet: Florida in the Era of Reconstruction* (1974); James W. Garner, *Reconstruction in Mississippi* (1901); and Joe G. Taylor, *Louisiana Reconstructed* (1974).

On the education of blacks after the war, see Henry A. Bullock, *A History of Negro Education in the South* (1967); William P. Vaughn, *Schools for All* (1974); and Roger A. Fischer, *The Segregation Struggle in Louisiana* (1974). Two useful accounts of the educational work of the Freedmen's Bureau are Ronald E. Butchart, *Northern Schools, Southern Blacks, and Reconstruction* (1980), and Robert C. Morris, *Reading, 'Riting, and Reconstruction* (1981).

Southern white resistance to the Reconstruction process is the theme of Michael Perman, *Reunion Without Compromise* (1973). Allen W. Trelease, *White Terror* (1971), is a harrowing recital of white vigilantism. *The Road to Redemption* (1984), by Michael Perman, traces southern politics from 1869 to 1879.

10

Compromises

1869–1877

*A*N EXCLUSIVE focus on the Southern states during the postwar years
obscures the fact that Reconstruction was a national, not just a sectional, process. In the North as well as the South the impulses unleashed by the
Civil War portended revolutionary consequences. With nationalism at high tide,
many Northerners favored an expansionist foreign policy. Just as some Radical
Republicans wished to overturn the entire Southern social system, so other
postwar leaders hoped to change the North. Some reformers wanted to expand
the role of the federal government in the economy. Civil service reformers sought
the end of the spoils system and the professionalization of governmental
bureaucracy. Other advocates of change wanted to improve the lot of labor, of
women, and of native Americans. But many—perhaps most—Northerners
objected to all these changes. To them the reforms proposed for their section
were almost as objectionable as Radical Reconstruction was to most white
Southerners.

This tension between those who opposed change and those who favored it
became a central theme of American history in the decades following the Civil
War. When the advocates of change were politically powerful and vigorously led,
supporters of the status quo found it necessary to accept compromises. Thus by
the 1880s a series of loose, informal, and frequently tacit understandings had
evolved, between Democrats and Republicans, between supporters and opponents of expansion, between friends and enemies of the high tariff and "sound"
currency. But where the innovators were politically inexperienced, like the
leaders of the women's movement in the 1860s, or poorly organized, like the
members of the early national labor unions, the powerful conservative majority
found it possible to ignore or overrule their wishes.

Compromises Between Equal Forces

Nationalism   In the years after the Civil War one major compromise reconciled divergent views as to the nature and direction of America as a nation. The war strongly encouraged nationalist sentiments among Northerners. The primary Northern war aim was not to guarantee equal rights to all men nor even to end slavery; it was to preserve the Union. By that often repeated phrase, men and women of the war years meant something more than merely maintaining the country as a territorial unit. The idea of union implied an almost mystical sense of the wholeness of the American people. Americans viewed themselves as a chosen people, selected to conduct an experiment in self-government, to be a test case of the viability of democratic institutions. As Lincoln declared, the United States was nothing less than "the last, best hope of earth."

That faith in the special destiny of the United States gave courage and hope to Northerners during the darkest hours of the war. Defeats on the battlefield, properly understood, seemed to them the fire that burned away the impurities in American life. As the Reverend Marvin R. Vincent of Troy, New York, announced: "God has been striking, and trying to make us strike at elements unfavorable to the growth of a pure democracy; and . . . he is at work, preparing in this broad land a fit stage for a last act of the mighty drama, the consummation of human civilization." A similar inspiration moved Julia Ward Howe to draw on the imagery of the Book of Revelation in composing the most powerful and popular battle hymn ever written:

> *Mine eyes have seen the glory of the coming of the Lord:*
> *He is trampling out the vintage where the grapes of wrath are stored;*
> *He hath loosed the fateful lightning of His terrible swift sword:*
> *His truth is marching on.*

Northerners believed that the Union would emerge from the war more powerful, more firmly united, than ever before. They expected that the United States would no longer be a confederation, or union of states, but rather a nation in the fullest sense. A small shift in grammar tells the whole story. Before the Civil War many politicians and writers referred to the United States in the plural— "the United States *are*"—but after 1865 only a pedant or the most unreconstructed Southerner would have dreamed of saying anything but "the United States *is.*"

The word *nation* now came easily to American lips. Unlike his predecessors, who generally avoided the term, Lincoln regularly referred to the United States as a nation. For example, he used the word no fewer than five times in his brief Gettysburg Address, most eloquently in the concluding pledge: " . . . that this nation, under God, shall have a new birth of freedom." In 1865, when Republicans agreed to establish a weekly journal that would reflect their views, they called it, as a matter of course, *The Nation,* and it became, as it has remained, one of the most influential periodicals in the country. When Charles Sumner, in 1867, took to the lecture circuit to supplement his senatorial salary, he chose for his topic, "Are We a Nation?" The answer, he believed, was obvious. Americans were "one people, throbbing with a common life, occupying a common territory, rejoicing in a common history, sharing in common trials." Never again should any "local claim of self-government" be permitted "for a moment [to] interfere with the supremacy of the Nation." He concluded: "Such centralization is the highest civilization, for it approaches the nearest to the heavenly example."

Political theorists as well as public men in the postwar generation exalted American nationalism. In 1865 Orestes Brownson, once a spokesman for Jacksonian ideals, published the first book-length contribution to the bibliography of American nationalism, *The American Republic: Its Constitution, Tendencies, and Destiny.* "Nations are only individuals on a larger scale," Brownson argued. His book was designed to resolve the identity crisis of the Civil War by persuading the American nation to "reflect on its own constitution, its own separate existence, individuality, tendencies, and end." Even more soaring were the claims of the Reverend Elisha Mulford's *The Nation: The Foundations of Civil Order and Political Life in the United States* (1870). Mulford's argument derived from the views of the early-nineteenth-century German philosopher Hegel: the nation was a mystic body, endowed with a spirit and a majesty of its own. "The Nation," he concluded, "is a work of God in history.... Its vocation is from God, and its obligation is only to God."

It would be easy to conclude from such statements that Americans of the post–Civil War generation, rejoicing in the newly restored unity of their country, were swept into an ultranationalistic frenzy comparable to that of the Germans, who almost simultaneously achieved national unity under Bismarck, or of the Italians, who were being reunited under Cavour. But a moment's reflection shows the weakness of these historical parallels. After all, the federal structure of the American government survived the Civil War. The government in Washington continued to coexist with the governments of the several states. If there was no further talk of secession, there was frequent invocation of states' rights, and regionalism and localism remained strong forces in American life.

American political theorists sought a formula to express the proper relationship between the nation and its constituent sections and groups. The most influential of these attempts was that of Professor Francis Lieber of Columbia University, whose book *On Civil Liberty and Self-Government,* published before the war, became a bible for statesmen of the postwar era. Lieber understood the power of nationalistic feeling; as a youth in Prussia he had wept when the armies of Napoleon overran his native land, and he had fought against the French at Waterloo. But he also was acquainted with the dangers of excessive nationalism, for the Prussian government had arrested him for harboring dangerous, liberal ideas and he had been obliged to flee to the United States. In this country he realized that nationalism was essential for "the diffusion of the same life-blood through a system of arteries, throughout a body politic." But he sought to check excessive centralization through organically related institutions—the family, the churches, the scientific community, the business community, and the like—which could provide "the negation of absolutism" by supporting "a union of harmonizing systems of laws instinct with self-government." Thus Lieber's theory simultaneously exalted American nationalism and encouraged autonomy for local and particularistic interests. It upheld the Union but sought to prevent its powers from becoming despotic. Lieber's political theory was, in short, typical of the compromises of the postwar period. His formulation allowed Americans to eat their cake and have it too.

American Foreign Policy

American diplomacy during the post–Civil War generation fell into a pattern that Lieber heartily approved. On the one hand, it was vigorously nationalistic, even at times bellicose; on the other, it drew back from conflict with foreign powers, and it refrained from pursuing goals strongly opposed by influential interest groups.

In the decade after the Civil War hardly a year passed without some significant American diplomatic move, either to assert the dominance of the United States in the Western Hemisphere or to annex new territory. These foreign policy

"The Stride of a Century"
Buoyed with nationalist sentiment, the United States celebrated at the Centennial Exposition at Philadelphia of 1876. This Currier and Ives print shows a boastful Uncle Sam bestriding the Western Hemisphere.

initiatives received considerable popular support. After Appomattox there was a general feeling that the United States, with a million seasoned veterans under arms, was in a position to humiliate the French emperor Napoleon III, to have a showdown with Great Britain, and to pick up any adjacent territory that it pleased. The expansionist spirit of Manifest Destiny, which had flourished in the 1840s but had languished during the war, sprang to life again. Even those who feared expansionism expected its triumph. The more optimistic rejoiced in the prospect. Advocating the annexation of both Haiti and the Dominican Republic, and hoping for the future acquisition of the Kingdom of Hawaii, President Johnson concluded in his 1868 annual message to Congress: "The conviction is rapidly gaining ground in the American mind that with the increased facilities for intercommunication between all portions of the earth the principles of free government, as embraced in our Constitution, if faithfully maintained and carried out, would prove of sufficient strength and breadth to comprehend within their sphere and influence the civilized nations of the world."

Even if the accomplishments of American foreign policy did not live up to Johnson's predictions, they were, nevertheless, considerable. From the point of view of national security, the most important feat was Seward's success in getting French troops out of Mexico. Introduced into Mexico during the Civil War, ostensibly to compel the bankrupt Mexican government of President Benito Juarez to pay its debts, French troops in 1864 provided the support for installing Archduke Maximilian of Austria as emperor of Mexico. While the war was going on, Seward could do no more than protest against this violation of the Monroe Doctrine's principle that European powers must not extend their "system" to the New World. But he adopted a more vigorous tone after Appomattox. Yet, knowing that the French emperor was a proud and volatile man, Seward refrained from direct threats and allowed Napoleon to discover for himself how expensive, unpopular, and unsuccessful his Mexican adventure was proving. By 1867 Napoleon finally decided to cut off further financial support for Maximilian's shaky regime and, under steady American pressure, withdrew his troops. Captured by Juarez's forces, Maximilian was shot by a firing squad on June 19, 1867.

A second diplomatic achievement of the Reconstruction years was the settlement of the *Alabama* claims—claims of American shippers against the British government for damages that British-built Confederate raiders had inflicted during the war. Immediately after the war it probably would have been possible to clear up this controversy speedily and inexpensively, had not the British government haughtily denied that it had violated international law by permitting Confederate raiders to be built in its shipyards. American grievances deepened with delay. Sumner, the powerful chairman of the Senate Committee on Foreign Relations, began to argue that the British not only owed repayment for actual damages done by the *Alabama* and other vessels; they also were responsible, he said, for prolonging the war—for the "immense and infinite" cost of the entire last two years of the conflict. Americans were further embittered by the failure of Reverdy Johnson, Seward's special envoy to Great Britain, to secure an apology or an expression of regret from the stubborn British government. A settlement was worked out only when Grant put Hamilton Fish in charge of the American State Department and a new cabinet came to power in Great Britain.

In the Treaty of Washington of 1871, Great Britain admitted negligence in permitting the Confederate cruisers to escape and expressed regret for the damages they had caused; and the United States quietly abandoned the extravagant claims put forward by Sumner and agreed that the amount of damages should be assessed by an arbitration commission representing five nations. Ultimately, damages to American shipping were estimated at $15.5 million, and the British government paid this amount. However, the precedent of settling international disputes by arbitration was more important than any monetary settlement, and the Treaty of Washington paved the way for an improvement in relations between the two greatest English-speaking nations. Not until the two world wars of the twentieth century would the full consequences of this development emerge.

Apart from the almost unnoticed American occupation of the Midway Islands in August 1867, the United States' sole territorial acquisition during the Reconstruction era was the purchase of Alaska. Seward's 1867 treaty to buy Russian America for $7.2 million brought under the American flag new territory one-fifth as large as the entire continental United States, a land of obvious strategic importance for the future of the United States in the Pacific. Nevertheless there was little popular enthusiasm for the purchase. Newspapers called Alaska "a national icehouse" consisting of nothing but "walrus-covered icebergs." Congressmen were equally unenthusiastic. Yet after much grumbling the Senate finally ratified the treaty and the House reluctantly appropriated the money for the purchase. Seward's success in part reflected his ability to convince senators that Alaska had vast hidden natural resources. It was also in part the result of the judicious payment of money to American congressmen by the Russian minister in Washington. The most important factor, however, was the general feeling that rejecting the treaty would alienate Tsar Alexander II, who alone of the leading European rulers had been sympathetic to the Union cause during the Civil War.*

Nothing came of other postwar plans for expansion. Each of them ran into snags that made American diplomats draw back. For example, the desire of many United States politicians, including Grant, Fish, and Sumner, to annex Canada had to be abandoned when it became clear that the British would not withdraw without a fight. Grant's plan to acquire the Dominican Republic aroused the

---

*The tsar's pro-Union policy resulted in part from unrest in the Russian-ruled Polish territories, which revolted in 1863 and were reconquered by military force. Like the Union, Russia feared European intervention in what both regarded as internal matters. After the Civil War, the tsar concluded that Alaska was vulnerable to seizure by the British in the event of a future conflict and that it would be better to sell the territory to the United States.

opposition of Sumner, who considered himself the blacks' senatorial voice and wanted the island to become not an American possession, but the center of "a free confederacy [of the West Indies], in which the black race should predominate." Seward's proposal for the purchase of the Danish West Indies (now the Virgin Islands) was pigeonholed by the Senate when those unfortunate islands were visited by a hurricane, a tidal wave, and a series of earthquake shocks.

It would, however, be a mistake to put too much stress on these special factors that stopped American expansionism. Broader forces were also at work. The American people were exhausted by four years of fighting, and they were not prepared to support a vigorously nationalistic foreign policy if it threatened another war. Northern businessmen felt that it was more important to reduce taxes and to return to a sound monetary policy than to engage in foreign adventures. The difficulties of racial adjustment in the South made increasing numbers of politicians hesitate before agreeing to annex additional dark-skinned populations. During Johnson's administration many Republicans opposed all Seward's expansion plans because they might bring credit to the unpopular president. During Grant's tenure alienated Republicans had similar motives for blocking the president's diplomatic schemes; by 1872, these dissidents had joined the Liberal Republican party and were opposing Grant's reelection. Most important of all, the American people were generally aware that they had plenty of room for expansion closer to home, in the lands still occupied by the Indians.

American foreign policy during the Reconstruction generation, then, was the result of compromise. On issues that clearly touched the national security, such as the presence of French troops in Mexico, there was a consensus sufficiently strong to allow the national government to act. But where there was no clear, overriding national interest, objections to expansion prevailed. Although presidents and secretaries of state often fumed, local, sectional, racial, and class objections blocked expansion.

Politics of the Gilded Age A similar deadlock marked the politics of the Gilded Age—so called after the novel of that title by Mark Twain and Charles Dudley Warner, which depicted the boom-and-bust mentality of businessmen of the post–Civil War era and the willingness of politicians to serve the needs of these speculators. The two major parties were almost equally balanced during the entire era. Most of the presidents of the period barely squeaked into office. Grant's success in 1868 was a tribute to a great military leader, not an endorsement of the Republican party that nominated him. Even so, he received only 53 percent of the popular vote. Grant's reelection by a huge popular margin in 1872 was due chiefly to his opponents' willingness to commit political suicide. Dissatisfied members of Grant's own party joined the Liberal Republican movement, which agitated for lower tariffs and for reconciliation with the South—and then proceeded to nominate for president the erratic *New York Tribune* editor Horace Greeley, famed as a protectionist and hated for his prewar denunciation of slaveholders. Holding its nose, the Democratic party also endorsed Greeley, but thousands of Democrats and Liberal Republicans stayed away from the polls. In 1876 Republican Rutherford B. Hayes received a minority of the popular vote and was inaugurated only after a prolonged controversy.

Even had these presidents been elected by overwhelming majorities, they would have been frustrated in attempting to implement any programs because their political opponents usually controlled Congress. To be sure, Grant started with safely Republican majorities in both houses of Congress, but Carl Schurz, Charles Sumner, and other leading Republicans soon defected to the Liberal Republican movement, voted with the Democrats, and blocked the administration's favorite measures. In the congressional elections of 1874 the Democrats for the first time since the Civil War won a majority in the House of Representatives which, except for two years, they continued to control until 1889. Given these conditions, it is easy to understand that the few measures enacted by the politicians of the Gilded Age had to be compromises.

Economic Issues of the Gilded Age
For the most part the national government had little to do with the basic economic problems of the Gilded Age. In dealing with economic issues, just as in dealing with those relating to the South and the freedmen, Americans were constrained by the doctrines of constitutionalism—by the belief that the government had only the fixed powers set forth in the Constitution. In the area of economics, only the tariff and the currency seemed to be clearly under the control of the national government. Therefore during the postwar years disagreements over economic issues were usually voiced in connection with these two endlessly troublesome, highly technical questions, so complex that only a handful of congressmen fully understood them.

The Tariff Problem
Debates on the tariff involved basic questions as to whether the industrial sector of the economy should be favored at the expense of the exporting agricultural sector and whether the factories of the Northeast should benefit at the expense of the farmers of the South and West. But these questions did not surface clearly, and during the debates in Congress the issue was rarely put in terms of free trade versus protection. Almost everybody during the Gilded Age recognized that some tariff barrier was needed to protect American industries from cheap foreign imports. The debates in Congress revolved around which industries and how much protection.

By 1865 most informed Americans recognized the need to modify the high tariffs that had been enacted during the Civil War to protect heavily taxed American industry from untaxed foreign competition. A bill intended to make a reasonable adjustment was drafted by the New England economist David A. Wells, who was appointed Special Commissioner of the Revenue in 1866. Wells's bill proposed to reduce duties on imported materials such as scrap iron, coal, and lumber; eliminated arbitrary and unnecessary duties on items like chemicals and spices; and made slight reductions in duties on most manufactured articles. Most lawmakers admitted the theoretical excellence of Wells's bill—and most opposed the provisions that lessened or removed protection from their own constituents' businesses. Consequently, Congress rejected Wells's bill, and during the next fifteen years there was no general revision of the tariff legislation.

The absence of general tariff acts did not mean that discussion of tariff rates had ended. To the contrary, throughout the period there was constant pulling and hauling between economic interests that stood to gain or lose from changes in duties on specific imported items. For example, during the war Boston and Baltimore had developed a considerable copper industry that smelted and refined Chilean ore, which paid a very low tariff duty. But in the late 1860s the great copper mines around Lake Superior began to be worked on a large scale, and their owners asked Congress to protect their product by raising duties on imported ore. After sharp disagreement, in which President Johnson supported the refiners and most congressional Republicans sided with the ore producers, the tariff on copper ore was increased in 1869 to a point at which most of the eastern smelting firms had to go out of business.

Other tariff changes were the consequence of combined efforts by the producers and processors of raw materials. An 1867 act revising the duties on raw wool and on woolen cloth was drafted at a convention of wool producers and manufacturers at Syracuse, and it was lobbied through Congress by the tireless and effective secretary of the Wool Manufacturers' Association, John L. Hayes.

Some of the minor adjustments made in the tariff during the postwar years reflected political pressures. In a general way Republicans, with some notable exceptions, tended to favor high protective tariffs, and Democrats, especially those in the South who needed foreign markets for their cotton, wanted to reduce duties. But the issue was rarely clear-cut, for Democrats in manufacturing states like Pennsylvania were high-tariff men. Moreover, both parties tinkered with the tariff issue at election time. In 1872, for instance, the Republican party faced a split. Many tariff reformers in the Liberal Republican movement were preparing to join the Democrats. Attempting to check the bolt, the Republican-dominated Congress rushed through a bill reducing all duties by 10 percent.

The complex history of tariff legislation during the Gilded Age demonstrates the continuing strength of the highly nationalistic impulse toward protectionism that had manifested itself during the war. At the same time it shows that powerful regional and economic interests adversely affected by high duties were able to secure relief without overturning the general protective framework.

Debates over Currency

The controversies over currency during the post–Civil War generation were more complex, but in general they illustrate the same tension between the needs of a national economy and the desires of local and special economic interests.

Unless a historian is prepared to write a book about these monetary issues, perhaps he ought to confine his account to two sentences: During the generation after the Civil War there was constant controversy between those who wished to continue, or even to expand, the inflated wartime money supply and those who wanted to contract the currency. Most debtors favored inflation because it would allow them to pay debts in money that was less valuable than when they had borrowed it; and creditors favored contraction, so that the money they received in payment of debts would be more valuable than it had been when they lent it.

But these two sentences, accurate enough in a general way, fail to convey the full dimensions of the controversy. They make the whole issue seem a purely economic question of profit and loss. In fact, for many people the resumption of specie payment—that is, the redemption in gold, at face value, of the paper money that had been issued by the United States government—involved the sanctity of contracts, the reliability of the government's pledges, and the rights of private property. Indeed, the return to the gold standard seemed to have an almost religious significance. Probably most economists of the period shared the conviction of Hugh McCulloch, Johnson's secretary of the treasury, that "gold and silver are the only true measures of value. . . . I have myself no more doubt that these metals were prepared by the Almighty for this very purpose, than I have that iron and coal were prepared for the purposes for which they are being used." On the other hand, the advocates of so-called soft, or paper, money argued that it was downright un-American to drive greenbacks out of circulation and return to the gold standard. "Why," asked the promoter Jay Cooke, "should this Grand and Glorious Country be stunted and dwarfed—its activities chilled and its very life blood curdled—by these miserable 'hard coin' theories, the musty theories of a bygone age?"

That two-sentence summary also ignores the fact that the currency controversy involved economic interests falling into categories more sophisticated than debtors and creditors. Merchants in foreign trade were ardent supporters of resumption because fluctuations in the gold value of United States paper money made the business of these importers and exporters a game of chance. On the other hand, many American manufacturers, especially iron makers, staunchly resisted resumption because they needed an inflated currency to keep their national markets expanding.

Finally, that two-sentence summary does not indicate that attitudes toward these monetary policies changed over time. Throughout the postwar period farmers were mostly debtors, but they were primarily concerned with such issues as railroad regulation and until 1870 showed little interest in the currency. Creditor interests of the Northeast were indeed mostly supporters of resumption, but when a depression began in 1873 they unsuccessfully urged President Grant to sign the so-called Inflation Bill of 1874, which would have slightly increased the amount of paper money in circulation. In other words, they preferred mild inflation to economic collapse. Moreover, by the late 1870s, inflationists were no longer calling for additional greenbacks; instead they joined forces with western mining interests to demand that the government expand the currency by coining silver dollars. When they discovered that, partly by oversight and partly by plan, the Coinage Act of 1873 had discontinued the minting of silver, they were outraged. Protesting the "Crime of '73," they demanded a return to bimetallism (both gold and silver being accepted in lawful payment of all debts) and the free and unlimited coinage of silver dollars.

With so many opposing forces at work, it is scarcely surprising that the history of currency policy and financial legislation in the postwar years is one of sudden fits and starts. Right after the war, Secretary McCulloch assumed that everybody wanted to return to specie payments promptly, and, in order to raise the value of the paper currency, he quietly held back greenbacks paid into the United States treasury for taxes and for public lands. His mild contraction of the currency restricted business expansion, and Congress forced him to stop. Subsequently, the greenbacks that had been taken out of circulation were reissued, and they remained in circulation for the next decade in the total amount of $382 million.

Indirectly the currency became an issue in the presidential election of 1868. During the previous year, what became known as the Ohio Idea gained popularity in the Middle West. Critics of hard money objected to the government's practice of paying interest on the national debt in gold—which was, of course, much more valuable than greenbacks. The critics argued that since the bonds had been purchased with greenbacks, it would be entirely legal and proper to pay their interest in the same depreciated currency. In this way the crushing burden of the national debt on the taxpayer would be reduced. This argument was so attractive that the Democratic national convention incorporated a version of the Ohio Idea in its 1868 platform. However, the party negated the move by nominating Governor Horatio Seymour of New York, an earnest hard-money man, for president. The Republican national convention sternly rejected the Ohio Idea—against the wishes of many western delegates—and nominated Grant with a pledge to reject "all forms of repudiation as a national crime."

Despite this commitment, Grant's administration witnessed the completion of a series of compromises on currency. The new president announced that he favored a return to the gold standard; but at the same time he warned: "Immediate resumption, if practicable, would not be desirable. It would compel the debtor class to pay, beyond their contracts, the premium on gold . . . and would bring bankruptcy and ruin to thousands." But lest anyone think that this last statement meant that he desired further issues of paper money, Grant vetoed the Inflation Bill of 1874, against the wishes of many of his advisers.

It was within this broad policy of affirmation checked by negation that John Sherman, the Senate expert on finance, persuaded Congress in 1875 to pass the Resumption Act. This law announced the United States government's intention to redeem its paper money at face value in gold on or after January 1, 1879. On the surface this legislation was a victory for hard-money interests, but in fact it was a brilliant compromise. It did commit the United States to resumption—but only after four years' delay. Sherman sweetened this pill for the silver-mining interests by providing that "as rapidly as practicable" silver coins would be minted to replace the "fractional currency"—notes of postage-stamp size in 3-, 5-, 10-, 15-,

25-, and 50-cent denominations—issued during the war. To placate the green-back interests in the South and West, Sherman's measure made it easier to incorporate national banks in those regions and thus increased their supply of treasury notes.

Although efforts were made after 1875 to repeal the Resumption Act, it was such a carefully constructed compromise that all these attempts failed. Sherman, who became secretary of the treasury in President Hayes's cabinet, skillfully managed the transition in 1879 so that resumption took place without fanfare and without economic disturbance. The whole controversy over currency during the Gilded Age thus illustrates the kind of compromises that Americans of this generation hammered out. The national policy of resumption, desired by most businessmen and needed if the United States was to play a part in world trade, was sustained; but local business interests were able to delay and modify imple-mentation of the policy so that it did not impose too sudden or heavy a burden on groups adversely affected by hard money.

Scandals and Corruption During the Gilded Age neither the Democrats nor the Republicans were able to take a decisive stand, whether on issues relating to the South or those connected with the national economy, and the principal means of cementing party loyalty became patronage and favoritism. As a result the Gilded Age was a period of low political morality in the United States, and many public officials were stained by charges of fraud, bribery, and subservience to special interests. During the 1870s reformers and crusading newspaper editors started to expose shocking scandals. The earliest revelations concerned New York City, which had fallen under the control of "Boss" William Marcy Tweed, who proceeded joyfully to loot the taxpayers. Tweed's ring began construction of a new county courthouse, on which $11 million was spent. Nearly $3 million went to a man named Garvey for plastering; after the amount of his fees leaked out, he became known as the "Prince of Plasterers." Tweed approved the purchase of so many chairs, at $5 each, that if placed in a line they would have extended seventeen miles. In 1871, when the *New York Times* began to expose the ring's padded bills, faked leases, false vouchers, and other frauds, the entire nation's attention was attracted, and when *Harper's Weekly* started carrying Thomas Nast's devastating caricatures of the Boss, Tweed's face became more familiar to Americans than that of any other man except Grant.

Soon revelations about the national government began to make equally fascinating reading. Shortly before the 1872 election, the *New York Sun,* a Democratic paper, exposed the workings of the Crédit Mobilier, the construction company that the Union Pacific Railroad Company paid to build its transconti-nental route. Investigation proved that members of the Crédit Mobilier were also members of the board of directors of the Union Pacific, who were thus paying themselves huge profits. Even more damaging was the revelation that, in order to prevent public inquiry, the Crédit Mobilier offered stock to Vice-President

Schuyler Colfax, Representative (and future President) James A. Garfield, and other prominent politicians. They were allowed to "purchase" the stock on credit, the down payment being "earned" by the high dividends that the stock began to pay.

Although Republicans found it advisable to drop Colfax from their ticket in 1872, scandal did not seriously touch the Grant administration until after the election. Then, in short order, stories of fraud began to appear about practically every branch of the executive offices. In the Treasury Department unscrupulous customhouse officers, especially in New York, preyed on importers. Merchants who failed to pay off the thieves had their shipments delayed; their imported goods subjected to minute, time-consuming inspection; and their crates and boxes that were not immediately removed from the docks stored at exorbitant rates. Corruption was rampant in the Navy Department, where political favoritism dictated everything from the employment of workers in the shipyards to the contracts for the construction of new vessels. Secretary of War William W. Belknap was proved to have accepted bribes from Indian traders, who had the exclusive and well-paying franchise to sell goods to Indians and soldiers at frontier posts. He resigned to avoid impeachment.

Of all these scandals, the closest to the White House was the Whiskey Ring. In order to avoid heavy excise taxes, first levied during the war, whiskey distillers, especially those at St. Louis, had for years been conspiring with officials of the Internal Revenue Service. During Grant's administration the dealers secured the cooperation of none other than Orville E. Babcock, the president's private secretary, who warned the swindlers whenever an inspection team was sent out from Washington. In return for his assistance, Babcock received such favors as a $2,400 diamond shirt stud—which he found defective and asked to have replaced with another, more expensive one—and from time to time the services of a prostitute. When Grant first learned of the scandal, he urged, "Let no guilty man escape." But as it became clear that his close friends and his personal staff were involved, he did everything he could to block further investigation. When Babcock went on trial, the president of the United States offered a deposition expressing "great confidence in his integrity and efficiency." Babcock was acquitted, and Grant retained him on the White House staff.

Civil Service Reform   The desire to reduce political corruption led to the emergence of the civil service reform movement during the Gilded Age. Although the spoils system had been criticized long before the Civil War, an organized reform drive did not appear until after Appomattox. Knowledge of widespread corruption among government officials, fear that President Johnson might convert the government bureaucracy into a tool to promote his renomination, and the example of the British system of appointing civil servants after competitive examinations gave strength to the movement. Early efforts to require federal appointees to pass competitive examinations failed in Congress, but the reformers, led by the politically ambitious George

William Curtis, editor of *Harper's Weekly,* and by E. L. Godkin of *The Nation,* hoped for success under Grant's administration.

The reformers were doomed to disappointment, for on this, as on all other controversial topics, Grant perfectly understood that compromise was the mood of the age, and he straddled. He made no mention of civil service reform in his first message to Congress. The future historian Henry Adams—the son of Lincoln's minister to Great Britain and the grandson and great-grandson of presidents—remarked in his snobbish way that Grant was inaugurating "a reign of western mediocrity." But when angry civil service reformers began to talk loudly about joining the Liberal Republican movement, Grant moved swiftly to head them off. In 1871 he pressured Congress into creating the Civil Service Reform Commission, and he neatly co-opted his chief critic by naming Curtis its chairman. Although the commission had little power and achieved less success, the move kept Curtis and a sizable number of reformers as supporters of Grant's reelection. Once the election was over, Grant lost interest in the commission and so blatantly violated its rules that Curtis had to resign.

Strengthened by news of the scandals that rocked Grant's second administration, civil service reformers claimed some of the credit for the nomination of Rutherford B. Hayes in 1876. But they found him as difficult to manage as Grant had been. On the one hand, the new president did take on the powerful political machine of New York's Senator Roscoe Conkling, and he succeeded in ousting some of Conkling's supporters—a group called Stalwarts, which included the future president Chester A. Arthur—from the New York customhouse. On the other hand, at election time the president wanted his own appointees to contribute to Republican campaign funds and to help organize Republican state conventions, much as their predecessors had done. "I have little or no patience with Mr. Hayes," exclaimed the reforming editor of the *New York Times.* "He is a victim of ... good intentions and his contributions to the pavement of the road to the infernal regions are vast and various."

Hayes's successor, James A. Garfield, gave civil service reformers little more satisfaction. With cruel accuracy one Massachusetts reformer characterized the new president as a "grand, noble fellow, but fickle, unstable, ... timid and hesitating." Civil service reform advocates noted suspiciously that Garfield's vice-president was Arthur, named by the Republican national convention in a vain attempt to placate Conkling. Consequently, reformers felt no special sense of victory when Garfield began to remove more of Conkling's Stalwarts from the New York customhouse. Conceited and arrogant, Conkling resigned from the Senate in a huff and rushed to Albany seeking vindication through reelection. To his surprise, the removal of his friends from federal office undercut his support, and the New York legislature failed to send him back to the Senate. Shortly afterward, a crazed office seeker named Charles Guiteau assassinated Garfield, shouting that he was a Stalwart and rejoicing that Arthur was now president. Shocked by Garfield's assassination, Congress in 1883 passed the Pendleton Act, which required competitive examinations of applicants for many federal jobs.

The measure was typical of the compromises of the period. It was a genuine measure of civil service reform and encouraged the emergence of a professional government bureaucracy, but it covered only a fraction of all government employees and permitted the spoils system to continue in the distribution of most federal patronage.

Where Compromise Did Not Work

Thus compromise was usually the outcome of struggles in the post–Civil War era when the rivals for the control of policy and power were relatively evenly balanced. But when the rival forces were unevenly matched, the outcome was very different, as the story of labor, women, and Indians reveals.

Labor Organization in the Gilded Age Industrial laborers in the United States were slow to organize. Factory workers came from many national backgrounds and spoke many languages. In the decade after the Civil War, more than 3.25 million immigrants, mostly from northern Europe, poured into the United States, and from these the labor force was largely recruited. By 1880, 87 percent of the inhabitants of Chicago, 84 percent of those in Detroit and Milwaukee, and 80 percent of those in New York and Cleveland were immigrants or the children of immigrants. Divided along ethnic and religious lines, they had little sense of workers' solidarity. Many members of the work force, moreover, regarded their status as transient. They hoped, unrealistically, to move west as homesteaders or, having made their fortunes, to return to their European homelands.

It was almost impossible for a meaningful national labor movement to emerge from such a fractured work force. One of the earliest efforts was the eight-hour movement, led by Ira Stewart, a Boston machinist who sought legislation to limit the workday to eight hours without reduction of wages. Under this pressure the United States established an eight-hour day for its employees in 1868, and legislatures in six states passed acts to make eight hours a legal day's work. In private industry these laws proved ineffectual because they instituted the eight-hour restriction only "where there is no special contract or agreement to the contrary." Consequently, most businessmen required employees to agree to work longer hours as a condition of employment.

The National Labor Union, created in 1866 at a Baltimore conference of delegates from various unions, proved little more effective. It was headed by William H. Sylvis, a dedicated propagandist and a superb speaker, whose interests, however, were not in conventional labor issues like hours and wages, but rather in cooperatives and currency reform. Sylvis recruited many members for the National Labor Union—it claimed 640,000 in 1868—but whether these were actual workingmen is questionable. A scornful observer remarked that the National Labor Union was made up of "labor leaders without organizations, politicians without parties, women without husbands, and cranks, visionaries, and agitators without jobs." After Sylvis's death in 1869, the organization began to decline, and it disappeared during the depression of 1873.

An ultimately more successful labor movement was the Knights of Labor, founded in 1869 by Uriah Stephens and other garment workers of Philadelphia. It grew slowly at first and, like the National Labor Union, received a serious setback in the depression. By the 1880s, however, its membership increased spectacularly as it attempted to create a broad union of all workingmen, skilled and unskilled.*

Neither the National Labor Union nor the Knights of Labor organized a large segment of the nation's industrial labor forces, and the tactics of both organizations did little to relieve the day-to-day problems of working men and women. Hours were long, wages were miserably low, regular employment was uncertain, health or accident insurance was absent, and there were no pension or retirement programs. Child labor was exploited, and employees who dared to speak out against such abuses found themselves blacklisted by employers.

The Panic of 1873 These labor organizations were even less able to help in the severe depression that followed the Panic of 1873, precipitated by the failure of the financial firm of the Civil War financier Jay Cooke, who had subsequently become deeply involved in speculative ventures. Between 1873 and 1879 business activity in the United States declined by about one-third, and bankruptcies doubled. Thousands of workers lost their jobs. During the winter of 1873–74 about one-fourth of all laborers in New York City were unemployed, and during the following winter the number increased to one-third. In this time of crisis, the National Labor Union virtually collapsed, and many local unions disappeared as well. In New York City, for example, membership in all unions dropped from 45,000 in 1873 to 5,000 in 1877.

Private charities did what they could to relieve distress. But nobody seemed to know how to end the depression. Experts tended to view the panic and the subsequent unemployment and suffering as part of the natural workings of the national economic order, necessary to purge unsound businesses and speculative practices. Economists warned that "coddling" laborers would only retard this inevitable and necessary process. Blaming the depression on the wartime habit of looking to the federal government for leadership, Democratic Governor Samuel J. Tilden of New York called for a return to "government institutions, simple, frugal, meddling little with the private concerns of individuals . . . and trusting to the people to work out their own prosperity and happiness."

Those labor leaders who remained active were little more helpful. Many sought panaceas for the economic crisis. A writer in the *Radical Review* found the cause of the depression in private landownership which, in his words, "begets . . . ground rent, an inexorable, perpetual claim for the use of land, which, like air and light, is the gift of Nature." Later, in 1879, Henry George made that idea the basis for the economic system proposed in his book *Progress and Poverty.*

---

*For the Knights of Labor in the 1880s, see chapter 22, p. 121.

Baltimore and Ohio Railroad Strike
The 1877 strike on the Baltimore and Ohio Railroad led to the worst labor violence the United States had experienced. President Hayes called upon federal troops to break the strike and to restore order.

Other labor voices supported the Socialist Labor movement, founded in 1874, which foresaw the ultimate overthrow of the capitalist system through a socialist revolution. As interim measures to combat the depression, the movement advocated federal aid for education, industrial accident compensation, and women's suffrage. It attracted only a tiny following.

Some labor spokesmen sought the way out of the depression by supporting independent political parties pledged to protect labor's position in the national economy. There was considerable labor support for the Greenback, or National Independent, party, which was organized in 1874 at Indianapolis. The party's national program opposed the resumption of specie payments and advocated further issues of paper money to relieve the country's depressed industries. But the Greenback party was not exclusively a labor movement: its presidential candidate in 1876 was the eighty-five-year-old New York iron manufacturer Peter Cooper. The 80,000 votes Cooper received came mostly from middle western farm states. In the congressional elections two years later, however, more laborers supported the National Independent party because it campaigned for governmental regulation of the hours of labor and for the exclusion of Chinese immigrants. Like other advocates of inflation, the party by this time had moved beyond favoring greenbacks and urged expansion of the currency through silver coinage. Candidates endorsed by the National Independent party received more than a million votes in the 1878 congressional elections.

With the collapse of the trade union movement, other laborers during the depression rejected politics in favor of strikes and terrorism.* In July 1877, the worst year of the long depression, labor unrest reached its peak in the Great Railroad Strike, a spontaneous and violent outburst that spread throughout the East and to some of the roads beyond the Mississippi and into Canada. Local and State governments proved unable or unwilling to cope with the crisis. To protect the national system of transportation so essential to the United States economy, President Hayes sent in regular army troops. This action marked the first time in American history that the army had been used on any extensive scale to crush a labor disturbance. The army promptly restored order, and the strike collapsed. Deeply disturbed members of the business community took steps to prevent any recurrence of such labor violence. State legislatures began passing conspiracy laws directed against labor organizations, and the courts began to invoke the doctrine of malicious conspiracy to break strikes and boycotts. Throughout the North the state militia, which had so often proved untrustworthy during the 1877 crisis, was reorganized and given stricter training. The inventor and manufacturer Cyrus Hall McCormick personally purchased equipment for the Second Regiment of Illinois militia because it had, he said, "won great credit for its action during... [labor] disturbances and can be equally relied on in the future."

The Women's Movement

The fate of the women's rights movement during the postwar era offers another illustration of how the conservative forces in society dealt with advocates of change who lacked political power and effective leadership. During the Civil War years the central concern of most women was to house and clothe their families after the men had gone into the army. Great numbers of women entered the teaching profession, and for the first time the number of women workers in the federal bureaucracy—mostly on lower, clerical levels—became significant. Others found new fields of usefulness by becoming army nurses. Dorothea Dix, famed as an advocate of reform of prisons and insane asylums, began a new career as head of the nursing service in the Union hospitals, and Clara Barton, who worked closely behind the lines of the Union armies, distributing medical supplies and nursing the wounded, gained the experience that later led her to found the American Red Cross.

During the war the leaders of the women's suffrage movement reluctantly put aside their crusade in order to give their wholehearted support to the Union cause. Critical of the Lincoln administration for its slowness in moving toward emancipation, both Susan B. Anthony and Elizabeth Cady Stanton sought to rally loyal women in support of a constitutional amendment abolishing slavery. With the motto "Let none stand idle spectators now," they organized the National Woman's Loyal League to secure signatures on a gigantic petition to Congress.

---

*Labor unrest in the 1870s is discussed in detail in volume 2, chapter 22, pp. 121–123.

Ultimately, nearly 400,000 women and men signed the document, which contributed to the adoption of the Thirteenth Amendment.

Quite reasonably, the leaders of the women's rights movement expected their services be recognized when the war was over. They were appalled to discover that in the proposed Fourteenth Amendment to the Constitution, which Congress began debating in the summer of 1866, only males were to be guaranteed the right to vote. Furious, Anthony pledged, "I will cut off this right arm of mine before I will ever work for or demand the ballot for the Negro and not the woman." Women were further outraged when the Fifteenth Amendment prohibited discrimination against voters "on account or race, color, or previous condition of servitude"—but not sex.

They looked for support from their former allies in the antislavery movement, only to be rebuffed. Horace Greeley's reformist *New York Tribune* had no good word for their complaints, and Charles Sumner, while admitting that women's suffrage was "obviously the great question for the future," refused to have the Reconstruction amendments "clogged, burdened, or embarrassed" by provisions for women's suffrage.

Angry, Stanton and Anthony in 1869 formed the National American Woman's Suffrage Association, to promote a proposed Sixteenth Amendment to the Constitution that would provide for women's suffrage, but their movement had little chance against the powerful conservative interests in society. Senator George Williams of Oregon announced that the proponents of women's suffrage were displaying "a spirit which would, if able, convert all the now harmonious elements of society into a state of war, and make every home a hell on earth," while Senator Theodore Freylinghuysen of New Jersey unctuously pronounced that women possessed "a milder, gentler nature, which not only makes them shrink from, but disqualifies them for the turmoil and battle of public life." By invoking women's higher and holier mission of domesticity, conservatives ended hopes for women's suffrage for the next fifty years.

Indian Problems   Equally unsuccessful in bargaining with the dominant forces of society were the Native Americans. Whites called all these diverse peoples Indians—meaning, really, "wild Indians." President Lincoln voiced the general paleface view of the redskin. To leaders of several western Native American nations who visited the White House in March 1863, just after the bloody battle of Fredericksburg, the president announced, with no intentional irony: "We are not, as a race, so much disposed to fight and kill one another as our red brethren."

Union leaders took advantage of the opportunities presented during the Civil War to limit the rights of native Americans and to restrict their territories. The loyalties of the Five Civilized Nations were divided between the Union and the Confederacy, and after the Union victory the treaties governing the Indian Territory were renegotiated. As a result the native Americans were forced to give up huge tracts of land and to grant a right of way to railroads crossing the territory.

**Westward Expansion and Indian Wars
1864-1876**

The first date indicates the establishment of the territory with the boundaries shown. In several instances earlier territories were formed with the same names but with different boundaries.

Far to the north, wartime inefficiency and delay, along with the endemic corruption of the federal Indian Bureau, which regulated white–Indian relations, kept promised supplies from reaching the Santee Sioux. In desperation, the Indians took to the warpath and threatened white settlements in Minnesota. Lincoln appointed John Pope, fresh from his defeat at the second battle of Bull Run, to command the armed forces in the Northwest, and the general announced that he would deal with the Sioux "as maniacs or wild beasts, and by no means as people with whom treaties or compromises can be made." When the Sioux surrendered in September 1862, about 1,800 were taken prisoner and 303 were condemned to death. Against the strong objections of local authorities, Lincoln commuted the sentences of most, but he authorized the hanging of 38—the largest mass execution in American history.

In 1864 warfare spread to the Central Plains after the discovery of gold in Colorado and the opening of the Pike's Peak trail led to an influx of whites. Because the regular army was fighting the Confederacy, maintaining the peace was the job of the poorly trained Colorado territorial militia. On November 29, 1864, a group of Colorado volunteers, under the command of a former minister, Colonel John M. Chivington, fell on Chief Black Kettle's unsuspecting band of Cheyennes at Sand Creek in eastern Colorado, where they had gathered under the protection of the governor. "As an act of duty to ourselves and civilization," the militia slaughtered about 150 native Americans, mostly women and children.*

The Restoration of "Home Rule" in the South

The final adjustment of the relationship between the triumphant Union and the conquered South provides yet one more illustration of the process of compromise in the Gilded Age. In this case there were three parties to the compromise: the victorious Northerners, eager to restore the Union but uncertain what constraints to impose on the South; the Southern whites, who had been conquered but not stripped of their economic power; and the Southern blacks, who had been emancipated and enfranchised but not given land.

Within eighteen months after Appomattox, Northern interest in Southern problems began to wane. In the fall elections of 1867, when many Northern states chose governors and legislators and filled vacancies in the House of Representatives, the Democrats made impressive gains. Responding to the popular mood of conservatism, the Republican party in 1868 passed over Radical presidential candidates like Benjamin F. Wade and nominated Ulysses S. Grant, who had only recently affiliated with the Republicans but whose broad popular appeal as a military hero was unrivaled. Shrewdly sizing up the country's changing attitude toward Reconstruction, Grant used his inaugural address to announce his policy: "Let us have peace."

Just what he meant was not immediately clear. Some thought the new president was appealing to the white Ku Kluxers who were trying to overthrow the Reconstruction governments in the South; others believed that he was speaking to Northern Radicals who wanted to bring about further changes in Southern society. As it proved, Grant had both extremes in mind. On the one hand, the president warmly supported the immediate and unconditional readmission of Virginia to the Union, even though Radicals like Sumner warned that the Virginia legislature was "composed of recent Rebels still filled and seething with that old Rebel fire." On the other hand, Grant was outraged by the terrorism rampant in the South, and he insisted that Congress pass a series of Enforcement Acts (1870–71) enabling him to crush the Ku Klux Klan. Under this legislation the president proclaimed martial law in nine South Carolina counties in which white

---

*Further outrages against the native Americans are discussed in volume 2, chapter 22, pp. 103–107.

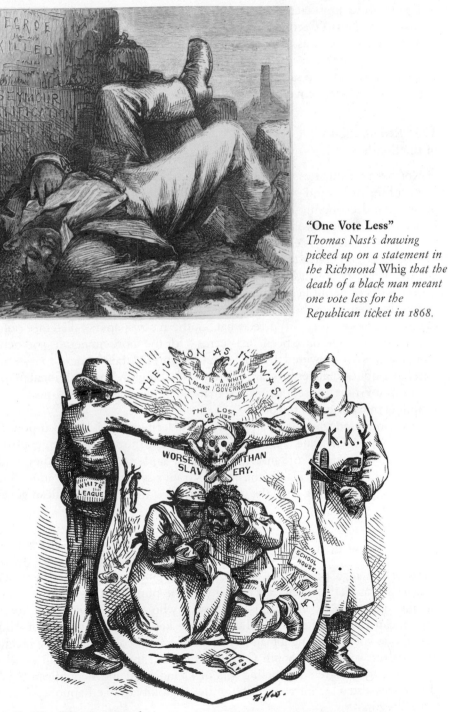

"One Vote Less"
Thomas Nast's drawing picked up on a statement in the Richmond Whig *that the death of a black man meant one vote less for the Republican ticket in 1868.*

Anti–Ku Klux Klan Propaganda
Thomas Nast, the celebrated Republican cartoonist, suggested that Democrats and the Ku Klux Klan wanted to return African Americans to a condition worse than slavery.

terrorists were most active, and federal marshals arrested many suspected Klansmen in North Carolina, Mississippi, and other Southern states. In brief, then, Grant's policy was to warn Southern whites that the national government would not tolerate open violence and organized military activity—but to let them understand that at the same time they would not be harassed if they regained control of their state governments through less revolutionary tactics.

The "Redemption" of the South Southern whites quickly accepted the hint. They promptly undertook the restoration of what they called home rule—the rule of native white Democrats. Aware of Northern sensitivities, they now downplayed, when possible, the more brutal forms of terrorism and outright violence. White Republicans had to face social pressure and economic boycott; many fled the South, and others joined the Redeemers (as the advocates of home rule and white supremacy liked to call themselves). Redeemers exerted economic pressure on blacks by threatening not to hire or extend credit to those who were politically active.

In several states whites organized rifle clubs that practiced marksmanship on the outskirts of Republican political rallies. Usually blacks were cowed by these tactics. In a few cases, however, they organized and tried to defend themselves. On such occasions there occurred what Southern newspapers called race riots— a better term would have been "massacres," for the more numerous and better-armed whites overpowered the blacks and slaughtered their leaders. In state after state, Republican governors appealed to Washington for additional federal troops, but Grant refused, convinced that the public was tired of "these annual autumnal outbreaks" in the South.

In consequence of Grant's policy, the Redeemers quickly seized power in Virginia, North Carolina, Tennessee, and Georgia. In 1875 they won control of Alabama, Mississippi, Arkansas, and Texas, and early in 1877 they ended Republican rule in Florida. By the end of Grant's second administration, South Carolina and Louisiana were the only Southern states with Republican governments.

The Election of 1876 The fate of these two remaining Republican regimes in the South became intricately connected with the outcome of the 1876 presidential election. The Democratic nominee, Samuel J. Tilden, undoubtedly received a majority of the popular votes cast—although, equally undoubtedly, thousands of blacks who would have voted for his Republican rival, Rutherford B. Hayes, were kept from the polls. But Tilden lacked one vote of having a majority in the electoral college unless he received some of the votes from South Carolina, Florida, and Louisiana, all of which submitted to Congress competing sets of Democratic and Republican ballots. (There was also a technical question of the eligibility of one Republican elector from Oregon.)

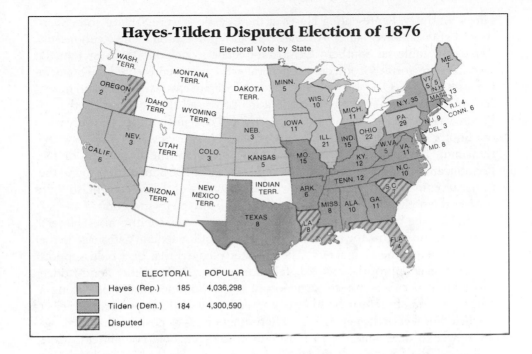

Hayes-Tilden Disputed Election of 1876

Electoral Vote by State

	ELECTORAL	POPULAR
Hayes (Rep.)	185	4,036,298
Tilden (Dem.)	184	4,300,590
Disputed		

Congress therefore confronted a crisis when it assembled in December 1876. If it decided to accept the disputed Democratic electoral votes, Republican control of the White House would be broken for the first time in a quarter of a century and the Reconstruction of the South would be ended. If Congress accepted the Republican electoral votes, that decision would run contrary to the will of a majority of the voters in the country.

Thus to resolve the impasse a compromise was needed—and not just a single compromise, but a complicated, interlocking set of bargains. After elaborate and secret negotiations, several agreements were reached. First, Congress decided that the disputed electoral votes should be referred to a special electoral commission, which should consist of five members from the House of Representatives, five members from the Senate, and five associate justices of the Supreme Court. This body was composed of eight Republicans and seven Democrats, and on every disputed ballot the commission ruled in favor of Hayes by the same 8-to-7 vote. In consequence of these decisions, Tilden's electoral vote remained at 184, while Hayes's slowly mounted to 185. In March 1877, for the fifth time in succession, a Republican president was inaugurated.

Democrats reluctantly accepted Hayes's election because of some other bargaining that took place while the electoral votes were being counted. One set of compromises came to be known as the Wormley agreement because it was negotiated in the luxurious Washington hotel owned by the black restaurateur

James Wormley. Representing Hayes at these sessions were Senator John Sherman, Representative James A. Garfield, and other prominent Republicans. Across the table sat Southern Democratic leaders, including Senator John B. Gordon, the former Confederate general who now represented Georgia in Congress, and L. Q. C. Lamar, once the Confederate envoy to Russia and now a senator from Mississippi. The Republicans promised the Southerners that, if Hayes was allowed to be inaugurated, he "would deal justly and generously with the South." Translated, this statement meant that Hayes would withdraw the remaining federal troops from the South and allow the overthrow of the Republican regimes in South Carolina and Louisiana. The Southerners found the terms acceptable, and they promptly leaked the news of the agreement, so as to protect themselves from charges that they had betrayed their section.

Behind the Wormley agreement lay other, less formal, compromises. Hayes's backers promised that the new president would not use federal patronage in the South to defeat the Democrats. They further pledged that he would support congressional appropriations for rebuilding levees along the flood-ridden Mississippi River and for construction of a transcontinental railroad along a Southern route. In return, Southerners agreed to allow the Republicans to elect Garfield Speaker of the new House of Representatives—a position that gave him the power to determine the membership of congressional committees. More important, the Southerners promised to protect the basic rights of blacks, as guaranteed in the Thirteenth, Fourteenth, and Fifteenth amendments to the Constitution.

Virtually all these informal agreements were ignored by both sides once Hayes was inaugurated. For his part, Hayes did order the removal of federal troops from the South and appointed a Southerner and former Confederate colonel, David M. Key, to his cabinet as postmaster general. But two-thirds of the federal officeholders in the South remained Republicans. Hayes changed his mind about supporting a Southern transcontinental railroad, alleging that federal funding would lead to corruption.

Southern Democrats likewise went back on their promise to support Garfield for Speaker. They eagerly joined in an investigation of alleged fraud in Hayes's election once the House was organized under Democratic leadership. Only a very few Southern Democratic politicians, among them Governor Wade Hampton of South Carolina, remembered their promise to respect the rights of blacks. Instead almost all took the final withdrawal of federal troops from the South as a signal that blacks, already put in a position of economic inferiority, could also be excluded from Southern political life.

Disfranchisement of Blacks Southern whites moved steadily and successfully to reduce black voting, although they had to act cautiously, so as not to offend public opinion in the North or to invite renewed federal intervention. One of the simplest devices was the poll

A Southern Chain Gang
Unwilling to spend much of their revenues to build penitentiaries, state governments instead turned black convicts over to railroads and other businesses, who leased the prisoners for cheap manual labor under brutal and degrading conditions.

tax, adopted in Georgia in 1877 and quickly copied by other Southern states. To Northerners the requirement that a voter pay $1 or $2 a year did not seem unreasonable. Yet because three-fourths of the entire Southern population had an average income of only $55.16 in 1880, the poll tax was a considerable financial drain, especially to poverty-stricken blacks. More imaginative was the "eight box" law adopted by South Carolina in 1882 and imitated by North Carolina and Florida. Under this system ballots for each contested race had to be deposited in separate boxes—one for governor, one for sheriff, and so forth. The system frustrated the illiterate black voter, who could no longer bring to the polls a single ballot, marked for him in advance by a Republican friend. To make the task of semiliterate voters more difficult, election officials periodically rearranged the order of the boxes. Still another device, which did not become popular until the late 1880s, was the secret ballot, also called the Australian ballot. The secret ballot was supposedly introduced in the South, as in the North, to prevent fraud. But actually it discriminated heavily against blacks, for as late as 1900 the number of illiterate black males ranged from 39 percent in Florida to 61 percent in Louisiana.

Despite all these obstacles, Southern blacks continued to vote in surprising numbers. In the 1880 presidential election, for example, more than 70 percent of the eligible blacks voted in Arkansas, Florida, North Carolina, Tennessee, and Virginia, and between 50 percent and 70 percent voted in Alabama, Louisiana, South Carolina, and Texas. These black voters posed a double threat to the Redeemers. Black voters were numerous enough that ambitious Northern Republicans, hoping to break the now solidly Democratic South, might be tempted again to try federal intervention in state elections. Even more dangerous was the possibility that Southern poor whites, whose needs for public education and welfare were consistently neglected by the business-oriented Redeemers, might find common cause with the poor blacks.

The Redeemers saw both these dangers materialize after 1890. Shortly after the Republicans gained control of the House of Representatives in 1889, Representative Henry Cabot Lodge of Massachusetts introduced a strong bill for federal control of elections, which promptly became known as the Force Bill. Although Democrats in the Senate defeated Lodge's bill in January 1891, Redeemers saw in it a threat to renew "all the horrors of reconstruction days." Their fear was doubtless greater because the almost simultaneous rise of the Populist movement threatened, as never before, to split the white voters of the region.* The Populist party appealed to farmers and to small planters and was the enemy of lawyers, bankers, and the rising commercial and industrial spokesmen of the so-called New South. Some of the Populist leaders, like Thomas Watson of Georgia, openly criticized the Redeemers' policy of repressing the blacks and seemed to be flirting with the black voters.

Faced with this double threat, Southern states moved swiftly to exclude the blacks completely and permanently from politics. Mississippi led the way with a constitutional convention in 1890 that required voters to be able to read and interpret the Constitution to the satisfaction of white registration officials. It is not hard to imagine how difficult even a graduate of the Howard University Law School would have found this task. In 1898 a Louisiana constitutional convention improved on the Mississippi example by requiring that a literacy test be passed by all voters except the sons and grandsons of persons who had voted in state elections before 1867. Because no Louisiana blacks had been permitted to vote before that date, this provision allowed illiterate whites to vote, while the literacy test excluded most black voters.

State after state across the South followed, or elaborated on, these requirements. South Carolina held a disfranchising convention in 1895. North Carolina amended its constitution to limit voting in 1900. Alabama and Virginia acted in 1901–02, and Georgia adopted a restrictive constitutional amendment in 1908. The remaining Southern states continued to rely on the poll tax and other varieties of legislative disfranchisement. When opponents of these measures accused their advocates of discriminating against blacks, Senator Carter Glass of

---

*For the rise of the Populist movement, see volume 2, chapter 22.

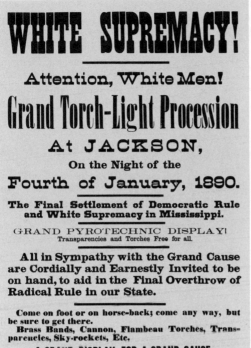

WHITE SUPREMACY!

Attention, White Men!

Grand Torch-Light Procession

At JACKSON,

On the Night of the

Fourth of January, 1890.

The Final Settlement of Democratic Rule and White Supremacy in Mississippi.

GRAND PYROTECHNIC DISPLAY!
Transparencies and Torches Free for all.

All in Sympathy with the Grand Cause are Cordially and Earnestly Invited to be on hand, to aid in the Final Overthrow of Radical Rule in our State.

Come on foot or on horse-back; come any way, but be sure to get there.
Brass Bands, Cannon, Flambeau Torches, Transparencies, Sky-rockets, Etc.

A GRAND DISPLAY FOR A GRAND CAUSE.

"White Supremacy!"
In 1890, when the Mississippi constitutional convention devised a way to disfranchise virtually all blacks, whites held a "grand pyrotechnic display" to celebrate.

Virginia replied for his entire generation: "Discrimination! Why that is precisely what we propose; that exactly is what this convention was elected for."

It took time, then, for the complete working out of the political compromises of the Reconstruction era. Not until the end of the nineteenth century did white Southerners receive the full price they had demanded in permitting the election of Rutherford B. Hayes. But by 1900 that payment had been made in full. The black man was no longer a political force in the South, and the Republican party was no longer the defender of black rights.

CHRONOLOGY

1866   National Labor Union formed.

1867   Maximilian's empire in Mexico falls. Purchase of Alaska.

1868   Ulysses S. Grant elected president in contest with Democrat Horatio Seymour.

1869   Knights of Labor organized.

1871   Treaty of Washington, settling differences between United States and Great Britain, signed. Tweed Ring scandals in New York City exposed.

1872   Crédit Mobilier scandals revealed.
Grant names G. W. Curtis to head
Civil Service Commission.
Grant reelected over Horace
Greeley, candidate of Liberal
Republicans and Democrats.

1873   Coinage Act demonetizes silver in
so-called Crime of '73.
Panic of 1873 begins long depression.

1874   Grant vetoes Inflation Bill.

1875   Specie Resumption Act provides
for return to gold standard by
1879.

1876   Exposure of Whiskey Ring reveals
further corruption in Republican
administration.
Republicans nominate Rutherford
B. Hayes for president; Democrats nominate Samuel J.
Tilden. Disputed returns leave
outcome in doubt.

1877   Congress creates electoral commission, which rules that all
disputed ballots belong to
Hayes, who is inaugurated
president.
Nationwide railroad strike and
ensuing violence lead to first
significant use of federal troops
to suppress labor disorders.

SUGGESTED READINGS

The best general treatment of social and economic change during the post–Civil War period is Allan Nevins, *The Emergence of Modern America, 1865–1878* (1927). Ellis P. Oberholtzer, *History of the United States Since the Civil War,* vols. 1–4 (1929–31), contains an enormous amount of unassimilated data.

Foreign affairs during the Reconstruction era are treated in Glyndon G. Van Deusen, *William Henry Seward* (1967); Allan Nevins, *Hamilton Fish* (1936); and David Donald, *Charles Sumner and the Coming of the Civil War* (1970). Adrian Cook, *The Alabama Claims* (1975), is authoritative. Thomas D. Schoonover, *Dollars over Dominion* (1978), examines Mexican-American relations. On expansionism the standard work is A. K. Weinberg, *Manifest Destiny* (1935).

For a spirited, irreverent, and not entirely accurate account of the politics of the Gilded Age, read Matthew Josephson, *The Politicos, 1865–1896* (1938). Morton Keller, *Affairs of State: Public Life in Late Nineteenth Century America* (1977), is much more judicious and analytical. For balanced studies of three Republican presidents, see William S. McFeely, *Grant* (1981); Harry Barnard, *Rutherford B. Hayes and His America* (1954); and Allan Peskin, *Garfield* (1978). Two full studies of corruption in New York City are Alexander B. Callow, *The Tweed Ring* (1966), and Seymour Mandelbaum, *Boss Tweed's New York* (1965). Ari A. Hoogenboom, *Outlawing the Spoils* (1961), is a model history of the civil service reform movement.

Three modern, sophisticated analyses of the currency controversy are Robert P. Sharkey, *Money, Class, and Party* (1959); Irwin Unger, *The Greenback Era* (1964); and Walter T. K. Nugent, *The Money Question During Reconstruction* (1967).

Wilcomb E. Washburn, *The Indian in America* (1975), and Robert F. Berkhofer, Jr., *The White Man's Indian* (1978), are superior works. On governmental policy toward the Native Americans, see David A. Nichols, *Lincoln and the Indians* (1978); Francis P. Prucha, *American Indian Policy in Crisis* (1975); and Loring B. Priest, *Uncle Sam's Stepchildren* (1942).

Labor organization and unrest are treated in depth in John R. Commons et al., *History of Labor in the United States,* vol. 2 (1918). Norman J. Ware, *The Labor Movement in the United*

States (1929), is especially valuable on the National Labor Union. On the changing character of work and laborers' responses to industrialism, see Herbert G. Gutman, *Work, Culture and Society in Industrializing America* (1976), and Daniel T. Rogers, *The Work Ethic in Industrial America* (1978).

Eleanor Flexner, *Century of Struggle* (1975), is the standard account of the woman's suffrage movement. For two excellent general accounts of the role of women, see Mary P. Ryan, *Womanhood in America* (1979), and Carl Degler, *At Odds: Women and the Family in America* (1980).

Many of the works cited in the previous chapter are also helpful in understanding the restoration of "home rule" in the South. C. Vann Woodward, *Reunion and Reaction* (1951), is an original reexamination of the compromise of 1876–77. Keith I. Polakoff, *The Politics of Inertia* (1973), is a more recent interpretation. For an analysis of the Redeemer regimes, see Woodward's *Origins of the New South* (1951). The best study of the disfranchisement of blacks is J. Morgan Kousser, *The Shaping of Southern Politics* (1974).

PART THREE

Nationalizing the Republic
1877–1920

John L. Thomas

$\mathcal{A}$S THE American people completed their industrial revolution in the half-century following the Civil War, they continued to celebrate unprecedented growth even as they were driven to experiment with new ways of regulating it. In 1900 as in 1850, most Americans saw a reason for national self-congratulation in the numerous signs of prosperity all around them. The standard of living was improving, the population was growing rapidly, great cities were rising, and the stock of consumer goods was steadily increasing. More thoughtful observers, however, noted that a high social price had been paid for all these achievements. A rural people had been suddenly uprooted and their communities disrupted, new masses of underprivileged persons had been forced into mobility, too many Americans worked under deplorable conditions, and a conspicuously unequal distribution of wealth persisted. Still, for most people caught up in America's industrial transformation, the benefits of rapid material growth clearly outweighed its costs.

Economic growth continued to verify earlier predictions of unlimited betterment, and most Americans continued to believe in the cherished ideal of progress. Freedom from external restraints on individual ambitions was the key concept in the doctrine of progress, and this concept had survived the Civil War—if not unscathed, at least largely intact. In 1900 a majority of Americans continued to maintain a simple faith in the individual, just as it had a generation earlier.

Yet despite the country's optimistic mood, by 1880 reform-minded citizens in all walks of life were beginning to note the signs of mounting social disorder. Industrialization, modernization, and urbanization forced a growing number of leaders in all parts of the national community to recognize the need for controls and systems in order to make American society efficient and stable. To improve their operations and increase their profits, businessmen sought consolidated power within their firms. Farmers quickly discovered an urgent need for better credit facilities and marketing mechanisms. Social theorists and urban reformers began to adjust their vision to the requirements of systematic planning. By 1890 the American way of life, which had once seemed a self-regulating device for producing happiness automatically, had come to be seen as a machine badly in need of repair, if not of a complete overhaul.

These would-be reformers of American society after 1890 did not always agree on priorities and means. But the thrust of their ideas and programs pointed unmistakably toward the construction of a new national order. In historical terms this new vision seemed to reject the libertarian philosophy of Thomas Jefferson and to revive the nationalist model of Alexander Hamilton. In the fields of law and constitutional theory, formal definitions of rights and duties were replaced by more flexible concepts of social utility, requiring new roles for lawyers and legislators alike. In social reform there was a new emphasis on training, expertise, and the predictive functions of science. In politics an organizational revolution brought new styles of leadership and new approaches to the workings of government.

The distance the nation had traveled by 1920 could be measured in two widely different assessments of American politics and society. The first assessment was that of the individualist prophet Ralph Waldo Emerson at the height of moral reform before the Civil War. Emerson located the essence of the American spirit in the "wise man" with whose appearance "the state expires." "The tendencies of the times," Emerson predicted, "favor the idea of self-government, and leave the individual . . . to the rewards and penalties of his own constitution which works with more energy than we believe whilst we depend on artificial restraints." But three-quarters of a century later, the progressive sociologist Charles Horton Cooley dismissed Emerson's self-enclosed individual as a moral abstraction unknown to history. "In a truly organic life the individual is self-conscious and devoted to his work, but feels himself and that work as part of a large joyous whole. He is self-assertive, just because he is conscious of being a thread in the great web of events." The story of the years separating Emerson, the sage of Concord, from the progressive social scientist Cooley is the account of the American discovery of the great social web and the multitude of connecting threads that composed it.

11

Stabilizing the
American Economy

⌒

*I*N THE first years of the Republic, Alexander Hamilton predicted that industry and agriculture would advance together in the American march toward abundance. Hamilton's promise was echoed a few years later by Henry Clay in his prophecy of the eventual triumph of his American System, and it was repeated again and again in the years before the Civil War by businessmen and promoters eager to exploit the country's resources. While in power, Hamilton, and later Clay and John Quincy Adams, had tried to build a framework for industrial growth. But not until the last decades of the nineteenth century did the American people make good on Hamilton's initial promise. At the end of the Civil War, the United States still stood on the threshold of the modern industrial world—as did France, Germany, Japan, and Russia. Thus in 1865 the United States continued to be a hungry importer of capital, labor, and most of its technology. Thirty years later the nation had transformed itself into a major exporter of foodstuffs and the producer of a mammoth stockpile of industrial and consumer goods. Within a generation it had joined Great Britain and Germany as one of the world's leading industrial powers.

Statistics, with which Americans were beginning to measure their success, told a story of unprecedented economic growth. The value of American manufactured products soared from $3 billion in 1869 to more than $13 billion at the turn of the century. Between the Civil War and 1900 industrial output tripled. The national labor force rose sharply too, from 13 million to 19 million, and the percentage of the national income that went to pay wages increased from 37 percent to 47 percent.

Figures like these led Charles E. Perkins, president of the Chicago, Burlington, and Quincy Railroad, to ask his fellow citizens: "Have not great merchants, great manufacturers, great inventors, done more for the world than preachers and philanthropists? . . . Can there be any doubts that cheapening the cost of necessities and conveniences of life is the most powerful agent of civilization and progress?" Some Americans had little love for great merchants and great manufacturers, whom they tended to blame for the period's economic disruptions and recurrent hard times. But most of them probably also agreed that material progress came first because the intellectual and cultural achievements of their civilization depended on such progress. In turn, material progress resulted from an industrial revolution that had changed the face of American society in less than a generation. What was this revolution? How did it happen? What forces accounted for it? How did it affect the nation's various regions—the Northeast and Midwest, the South and West—and the farming and industrial labor populations? And behind it was there any guiding plan? Did it have any goal?

The Foundations of the American Industrial Revolution

The search for an answer to these questions begins with the rapid settlement of the new lands across the Mississippi River—the Great Plains stretching westward from the tier of states along the river across the hundredth meridian to the foothills of the Rockies. Only a generation earlier this huge area had been marked the "Great American Desert" on the most up-to-date map, but now it was being billed by land speculators and railroad promoters as the "Great Breadbasket of the World." On the eve of the Civil War, settlement hugged the banks of the Missouri River where fifteen years earlier the historian Francis Parkman had stood scanning "level plains, too wide for the eye to measure, green undulations, like motionless swells of the ocean" before jumping off to follow the Oregon Trail westward toward "those barren wastes, the haunts of the buffalo and the Indian, where the very shadow of civilization lies a hundred leagues behind." In 1860 only the centuries-old Spanish town of Santa Fe and the new Mormon communities in Utah broke the emptiness of the High Plains. Yet by the time Parkman died in 1893, hordes of new settlers from the East and recent arrivals from California across the mountains formed clusters of settlement in an almost unbroken chain. In 1890 the superintendent of the United States census announced—a bit prematurely—the closing of the frontier. "Up to and including 1880 the country had a frontier settlement," he reported, "but at present the unsettled area has been so broken into by isolated bodies of settlement that there can hardly be said to be a frontier line."

A phenomenal growth of the national population kept pace with increasing western settlement. In the years between Appomattox and the centennial celebration in 1876, the population of the United States rose by 30 percent from 35.7 million to 46.1 million on a wave of immigrants, mostly from Europe, who flooded the nation. Their numbers were matched by massive increases in production in all sections of the economy. In these same years the American corn harvest increased by 100 percent. Railroad mileage grew by 111 percent; the production of bituminous coal, by a whopping 163 percent.

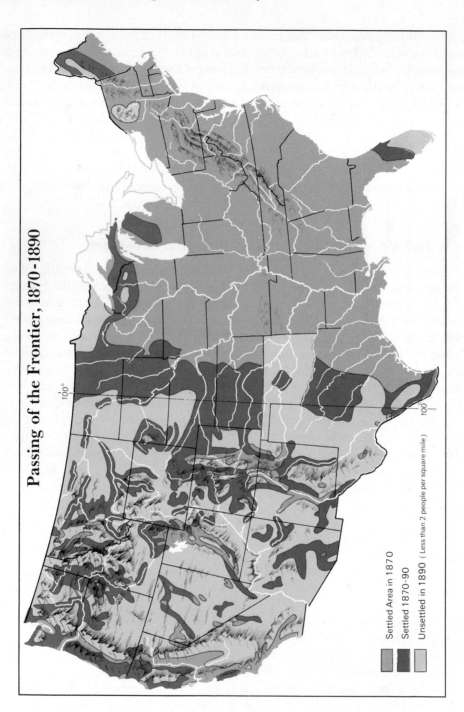

Passing of the Frontier, 1870-1890

Settled Area in 1870
Settled 1870-90
Unsettled in 1890 (Less than 2 people per square mile)

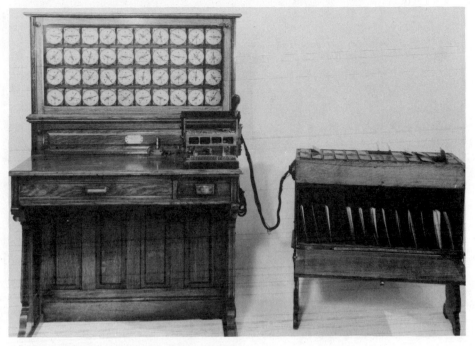

Herman Hollerith Census Tabulating Machine
New inventions made tabulating and storing needed statistics easier and more efficient.

Origins of National Economic Consolidation

The Gilded Age, as the immensely productive period following the Civil War was called, witnessed the rise to wealth and prominence of new industrial and financial leaders who began to apply the lessons learned from their wartime experience in developing and perfecting innovative technology and systems of large-scale management. For example, Andrew Carnegie, who arrived from Scotland as a poor but ambitious young immigrant, trained himself to become a skilled telegraph operator and served as an aide to Thomas Scott, the assistant secretary of war in charge of government railroads and transportation lines. From his vantage point at the managerial center of the Union war effort, Carnegie saw clearly the coming of a postwar expansion and reorganization of the nation's railroads, and he invested his savings in the company that owned the patents for Pullman sleeping cars. Soon these sleeping cars became standard equipment on the railroads, and Carnegie had acquired the necessary investment funds with which to build his steelmaking empire.

Another sharp-eyed entrepreneur who seized the opportunities provided by the Civil War was John D. Rockefeller, a pious young Baptist from Cleveland, Ohio, who got his start handling wartime contracts for hay, grain, meat, and other commodities. Rockefeller, like Carnegie, recognized the advantages of order and

Pioneer Run, 1865
The discovery of petroleum in western Pennsylvania led to its rapid and wasteful exploitation. Not more than one well out of twenty was properly sunk and carefully managed.

system as the means to increased efficiency with which to drive competitors from the field. In the early 1860s he began to apply these principles with a vengeance to the petroleum industry in western Pennsylvania, concentrating on gaining control of the refining process, and by 1863 he owned the largest refinery in Cleveland, which he used as a base to seize control of an oil industry that once had been openly competitive but also inefficient and wasteful. Within a decade Standard Oil of Ohio, as his company was called, made its own barrels for shipping oil, built and maintained its own warehouses, and owned an entire fleet of tankers.

Rockefeller's methods, although highly effective, violated the accepted norms of small-scale competition. With his suddenly increased volume of business, he succeeded first in convincing the railroads to give him lower shipping rates, and then in forcing on the carriers secret agreements for "drawbacks," or a percentage of the payments made by his competitors. By 1880, using more sophisticated variations of such methods, Standard Oil controlled 95 percent of the oil refining business in the country and nearly all of the transporting of oil, whether by railroad or pipeline. Casting up Standard Oil's accounts for the 1870s in his *Wealth Against Commonwealth* (1894), the muckraking journalist Henry Demarest Lloyd pronounced judgment on Rockefeller as an ignorant and irresponsible *arriviste:*

> Our barbarians come from above. Our great moneymakers have sprung in one generation into seats of power kings do not know. The forces and the wealth are

new and have been the opportunity of new men. Without restraints of culture, experience, the pride, or even the inherited caution of class or rank, these men, intoxicated, think they are the wave instead of the float, and that they have created the business which created them.

Lloyd's indictment of the new "American Pasha" was also directed to the predatory Jay Gould, the "greatest mouse-catcher in America" and the original model for the Gilded Age robber baron. To those observers like Lloyd, schooled in the ways of financial probity, Jay Gould seemed a demonic Horatio Alger, the sharp-eyed trickster who teaches costly lessons in wariness to Americans by bilking the stockholders of the Erie Railroad, bribing judges, cornering the Gold Market on Black Friday in 1869, draining the treasury of New York City's elevated railroad companies, arranging a hostile takeover of Western Union, and finally gaining control of the Texas and Pacific Railroad and breaking the Knights of Labor strike in 1886 with wholesale discharges, blacklists, scabs, and spies. The prince of financial pirates who learned his buccaneering in the war years, Gould died in 1892 in his Fifth Avenue mansion encased in tapestries, huge frescoes, and gilt ceilings, probably the most hated public figure in the country. "Ten thousand ruined men will curse the dead man's memory," declared the *New York World* in its obituary.

Growth of Cities

Cities—Rockefeller's Cleveland, Carnegie's Pittsburgh, Jay Gould's New York—furnished the stage on which the industrial transformation of late-nineteenth-century America was played out. The nation's big cities acted as magnets drawing native-born Americans and newly arrived immigrants off worn-out agricultural lands into new urban cores packed with factories and offices, stores and warehouses, tenements and apartments. The novelist Theodore Dreiser gave to his character Sister Carrie, as her train nears Chicago, the emotions experienced by millions of real-life new arrivals in the Gilded Age city. As Carrie sits gazing in wonder out of the window, other trains flash by and telegraph poles suddenly appear nearby to point the way to big smokestacks thrusting high into the air. Soon two-story frame houses in the suburbs give way to giant office buildings and warehouses until at last, Carrie realizes, "they were under a great shadowy train shed, where the lamps were already beginning to shine out."

> To the child [Dreiser comments], the genius with imagination, or the wholly untravelled the approach to a great city for the first time is a wonderful thing. Particularly if it be evening—that mystic period between the glare and gloom of the world when life is changing from one sphere or condition to another.... Though all humanity be still enclosed in the shops, the thrill runs abroad. It is in the air. The dullest feel something they may not always express or describe. It is the lifting of the burden of toil.

In the half-century after 1860 the number of people living in cities of more than 8,000 rose tenfold. By 1880 over a quarter of the American people lived in urban areas. In the remaining years of the century, the urban population grew at the phenomenal rate of 6 percent per decade, until by 1900 a full 40 percent of the people lived in cities. This huge demographic shift had actually begun in the years before the Civil War as the forces of commercial development began to alter the appearance of the older walking cities, filling up downtown residential zones with new financial and retailing establishments, sweatshops, and wholesale houses, and pushing middle-class residents out to the streetcar suburbs along the metropolitan periphery. By mid-century, canals, railroads, and the steam engine had already built the basic structure of the modern industrial city, segregating zones of work from wealthy residential neighborhoods and connecting them with rudimentary transit systems. After the Civil War this push-pull movement quickened, centripetal forces collecting large pools of willing workers—new ethnic groups from Europe, rural whites, and African Americans from the South—in the center of cities while centrifugal forces propelled older inhabitants out to the margins. The reciprocal "flow" of people and goods in, out, and through metropolitan centers quickly became a distinguishing characteristic of Gilded Age American life.

The largest cities were to be found in the Northeast and the Midwest where urban concentration proceeded most rapidly. Here in the new metropolis industrialization was already well advanced, and financial resources, transportation and communications links, and an army of eager workers were readily available. Big cities were increasingly segregated by wealth and work into zones of affluence and abject poverty, walled off but still within walking distance of each other. In the 1870s, in the depths of a severe depression, New York City's Fifth Avenue north of Twenty-sixth Street sported recently built monuments to conspicuous consumption in Renaissance palaces and French chateaus while immigrant families in the noisome Five Points neighborhood converted dark twelve-by-ten living rooms into sweatshops where they sewed precut garments or rolled cigars.

Here too in the industrial city were millions of anonymous consumers who furnished vast markets for a bewildering variety of new products—basic necessities like food, clothing, and furniture, and newly developed products like sewing machines, typewriters, and cigarettes. Inhabitants of the city quickly became dependent on a steady supply of consumer goods provided by manufacturers, processors, and distributors. "We cannot all live in cities," Horace Greeley, the aging editor of the *New York Tribune,* complained to a younger generation headed toward the metropolis, "yet nearly all seem determined to do so.... 'Hot and cold water,' baker's bread, the theater, and the streetcars... indicate the tendency of modern taste."

As these burgeoning cities expanded the boundaries of old commercial centers after the Civil War, they too became giant municipal consumers of the heavy industrial goods with which to modernize—electrical dynamos, telephone wire, lead piping and copper tubing, streetcars and the motors to run them.

Whether they subsidized huge public constructions like John and Washington Roebling's Brooklyn Bridge or encouraged massive private ventures like Henry Hobson Richardson's Marshall Field Warehouse in Chicago, big cities provided an insatiable appetite for all the products of the American industrial machine.

The railroad lines that tied cities together in an interurban corridor in the Northeast were joined at midwestern terminals by new roads that ran straight across the Great Plains and over the Rocky Mountains to the Pacific Coast, collecting on their several strands clusters of central-place cities and towns like beads on a string. The growth of western cities matched those east of the Mississippi: nationwide, the number of cities with populations of over 100,000 in the closing decades of the nineteenth century increased from 9 to 50, while the number of those cities with populations from 25,000 to 100,000 jumped from 26 to 178 and that of smaller cities with populations under 25,000 skyrocketed from 58 to 369. Major western cities straddled the transcontinental railroad lines that crossed the Great Plains and the Rockies, the northern tier stretching from Minneapolis to Spokane and on to Tacoma, Seattle, and Portland; a central urban band running from Chicago and St. Louis through Kansas City, Omaha, Cheyenne, to San Francisco; and a southern route sprouting cities, many of them new. All these instant cities served as distributing centers for surrounding regions and as producing centers for specialized regional products like beer, flour, meat products, and cotton oil. Already by 1880 the fabled West of the covered wagon and the cowboy was receding into history before the advance of mechanization and modernization.

The Civil War had devastated a number of major southern cities, among them Columbia and Charleston, South Carolina; Atlanta, Georgia; and Richmond and Petersburg, Virginia, all of which undertook rebuilding programs during Reconstruction. As in the trans-Mississippi West, railroads throughout the South opened up new inland cities like Houston and Dallas and rehabilitated old river ports like Memphis and Natchez for commercial and industrial development. The pattern of urban growth in the New South differed in scale and pace from metropolitan expansion in the Northeast and Midwest. Most southern cities continued to depend on the marketing of regional staple-crop agricultural products until late in the century, when commercial activity began to give way to industrial development.

The cityscape in the New South presented a lower profile than its urban counterparts in New York or Chicago, where tall office buildings with steel frames and curtain walls were beginning to create steep city canyons at the bottom of which pedestrians and vehicles of all kinds crawled and knotted. Nashville and Montgomery boasted two- and three-story commercial blocks fronting on miles of wide thoroughfares, a marked contrast to Chicago's Loop with its compact mix of banks, retail houses, business offices, city hall, library, museum, and opera house.

The emergence of new southern industrial cities like Birmingham was accompanied by the mushroom growth of smaller market towns that sprang up everywhere in the postwar years. Before the Civil War planters had invested in slaves at the expense of land and commercial development. Now, as Reconstruction drew to a close, new money, much of it initially from the North but increasingly local, began to flow into town-building, improved roads, and urban development all across the South. Urbanization in the South depended more and more heavily after 1880 on local enterprise and crash programs for building new markets in interior towns and financing cotton and lumber mills. Mill-building and town-building combined to connect outlying rural districts with regional cities and to extend the effects of rapid urbanization into the farthest reaches of the South.

Railroads Provide an Organizational Model

Railroads played a crucial role in America's industrial revolution by helping to develop a powerful national economy and dominating the American technological imagination for a generation. Railroads were giant consumers that fed heavy industry with ever-larger orders for steel rails, machines, and equipment. Railroading was the nation's first big business, and it provided the model for Gilded Age big businessmen—raising large amounts of capital, integrating operations, building distribution systems, and managing the movement of goods and people with regular timetables and systematic purpose.

Plans for a transcontinental railroad, which date from the 1840s, had been repeatedly shelved because of mounting sectional controversy, but in 1862 Congress lent its support to railroad promoters by incorporating the Union Pacific Railroad Company and financing it together with the Central Pacific with grants and huge tracts of public lands. Construction work began in earnest in 1865 with the Union Pacific pushing rapidly west across a thousand miles of Great Plains through Evans Pass in Wyoming to link up with the Central Pacific tunneling eastward through the Donner Pass. A reporter from the East described in amazement the construction of the Union Pacific: "Five men to the 500-pound rail, 28 to 30 spikes to the rail, three blows to the spike, two pair of rails to the minute, 400 rails to the mile, and half a continent to go...." On the western end, reaching 700 miles eastward, the Central Pacific sent some 10,000 Chinese "coolies" swarming over the canyons of the Sierras, boring through 1695 feet of solid rock, and blasting their way with a new untested explosive, nitroglycerine. Charles Crocker, one of California's Big Four merchant investors and the hard-driving construction boss of the Central Pacific, accepted a $10,000 bet that his men could not lay ten miles of track in a single day. On April 18, 1869, Crocker won his bet, and his colleague Leland P. Stanford drove the golden spike uniting the two lines at Promontory Point, Utah, as news flashed by telegraph to an awaiting nation.

The transcontinental railroads' achievements in conquering space and standardizing and compacting time caught the American imagination and quickly changed the image of the West from the Great American Desert with unknown

Promontory Point, Utah Territory, 1869
Joining the tracks of the Union Pacific and Central Pacific railroads.

Dining in Splendor While Heading West
By the 1870s dining cars were a regular feature on express trains to the West Coast.

potential into a scrambling economic region marked by large-scale industrialization and urbanization. All too quickly, the 160-acre homestead gave ground before the forces of corporate development. Railroads also altered the visual landscape of the West by imposing new rectilinear grids on once-open country and by fostering farm-supply towns and building huge grain elevators all along their lines.

Less dramatic than the accomplishments of the transcontinental lines but of greater immediate economic significance was the coordinating and consolidating of railroads east of the Mississippi. Before the Civil War there had been eleven different rail gauges in use on northern roads. President Lincoln's selection of the 4-foot 8½-inch gauge for the Union Pacific soon established that width as standard for all lines. Then came standardization of time with the mandating of time zones and successful experiments in cooperation between competing lines with bills of lading that facilitated easy transfer of goods. Before the Civil War passenger travel from New York to Chicago involved using eight to ten independent, hastily constructed lines and repeated time-consuming transfers. In 1869 Commodore Vanderbilt consolidated the New York Central and Hudson River railroads to provide continuous service from New York to Buffalo and five years later was able to provide through service to Chicago. At the same time the Pennsylvania Railroad, the Erie Railroad, and the Baltimore and Ohio Railroad completed connections and were offering competing service.

The completion of a modern communications network kept pace with the construction of railroads. As early as 1861 it was possible to send a telegram from San Francisco to Washington, D.C., even though the service was sporadic. But by 1866 the Western Union Telegraph Company, thanks to its wartime contracts with the military, had driven out its competitors and secured a virtual monopoly. Western Union made it possible for the first time for people in virtually every part of the country to communicate almost instantaneously with people in any other part of the nation. Then came the telephone, invented by Alexander Graham Bell and successfully demonstrated at the Centennial Exhibition in Philadelphia in 1876, which provided a second communications network. By the 1880s most doctors in major cities had telephones, and during President Hayes's administration an instrument was installed in the White House. The telephone was still such a novelty that, when it rang, the president himself was likely to answer it.

In the last three decades of the nineteenth century, railroads, supplied with instant communications, a uniform gauge, standard time zones, and improved bridge designs, managed to link the cities and their surrounding regions together, first in a loose network and then in a tighter web that composed a national design. Financiers and construction chiefs seldom looked beyond the problems involved in laying the next mile of track. As one investor explained, "We must get a cheap line and a safe road, but at the outset we must in grades and curves try to *save*— and trust to the future for higher finish." Time was money, and railroading an expensive business.

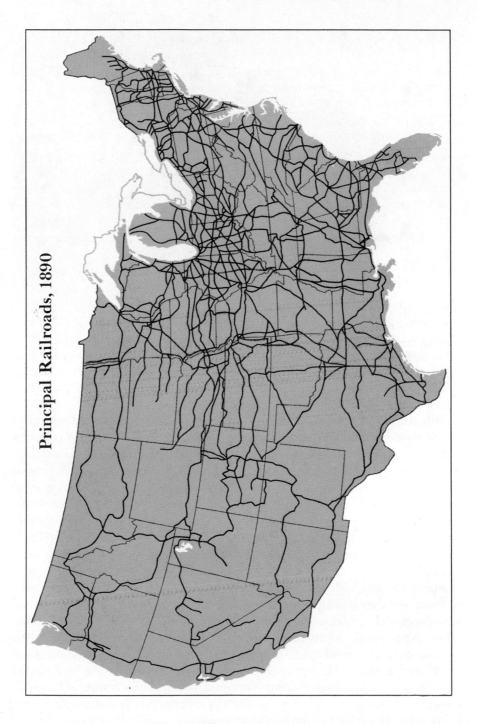

Principal Railroads, 1890

Wreck on the New York Central at Batavia, New York, 1885
Passenger safety was not always a top priority for the nation's railroads.

Still, statistics again told Americans what they wanted to hear: 35,000 miles of track in 1865 had become 242,000 by 1897. At the end of the Civil War railroads reached the end of the line just across the Mississippi in Iowa and Missouri. By century's close there were no fewer than five transcontinental lines. East of the river by 1890 railroad transportation had come to be dominated by a small group of integrated systems like the New York Central and the Pennsylvania roads. In the Midwest the Burlington line dominated as did the Union Pacific, Northern Pacific, and Great Northern with their routes to the West Coast. Here was a lesson in system-building that all American business would seek to learn and apply.

Financing and building the railroads involved massive financial chicanery and fraud, and they quickly acquired unsavory reputations, initially well deserved and subsequently difficult to overcome. "We . . . do not claim to be immaculate, beyond expediency," admitted one railroad executive, "[but] are content with right intentions and good results obtained on the whole." An investigation of the Crédit Mobilier scandal in 1872 caught the directors of the Union Pacific Railroad in the act of diverting huge sums to their own construction company of which they were the managers. When public inquiry threatened the continued success of this scam, the construction company sought to quash the investigation by offering stock on credit to Vice-President Schuyler Colfax and future President James A. Garfield. When he was discovered distributing railroad shares among

**Commodore Vanderbilt
Riding One of His Trains**
*A cartoonist's version of "The
public be damned."*

his fellow congressmen, Representative Oakes Ames brashly defended his actions: "I think a member of Congress has a right to own property in anything he chooses to invest in." His colleagues in the House disagreed and voted to "absolutely condemn" him. For the next twenty years the railroads continued to be accused (frequently with ample proof) of disregarding the safety and comfort of their passengers, watering their stock, jerry-building their roads as purely speculative ventures, and rigging rates that discriminated against farmers, merchants, and small shippers. When Commodore Vanderbilt consolidated the New York Central and Hudson River lines with a stunning increase in unsecured stock, Wall Street brokers paid him a backhanded compliment by unveiling a statue of him holding a gigantic watering can. "It is the use of water," a spokesman quipped, "not as a beverage but as an element of public wealth, which has been the distinguishing characteristic of Commodore Vanderbilt's later years." Charles Francis Adams, Jr.'s, verdict on the behavior of railroaders was more severe: "They exact success and do not cultivate political morality."

To their critics the railroad managers replied that as private enterprises they were accountable first and foremost to their stockholders, who demanded profits above all else. They also admitted to running their roads as *regional* systems that escaped regulation by crossing state boundaries—large operational units in which individual farmers and shippers were only cogs in their wheels. Rather than being forced to meet particular demands for rate regulation and warehousing rules, railroad spokesmen insisted, they should be left free to manage their own enterprises with an eye to eliminating competition and increasing efficiency. If, then, it cost twice as much to ship wheat from Fargo, North Dakota, to Duluth, Minnesota, where there was no competition, than it did to ship the same wheat from Minneapolis to Chicago, where competition was intense, this discrepancy could be explained as the workings of a free-market system.

Despite their growing unpopularity with farmers, shippers, and small merchants, railroads continued to compile an impressive record in establishing new traffic patterns. In 1865 the railroads were a collection of local systems without standard gauge or equipment and lacking even a common timetable. Twenty-five years later, railroad magnates, who gave less thought to acceptable public policy than to their own needs, had nevertheless supplied the country with an immense transportation system composed of regional units. In their attempt to keep their cars full, railroads necessarily gave rate preferences to large producers, and they both encouraged and took advantage of regional specialization. Along their tracks moved wheat, corn, and hogs from the Midwest, cotton and sugar from the Mississippi Delta, lumber from the Lakes states, oil products from Pennsylvania to seaboard terminals, and coal from West Virginia to Pittsburgh's steel mills. With improvements in refrigeration came meat from Chicago, Kansas City, and Omaha, and fruit and vegetables from California and Florida. In the pioneer achievements of these carriers, American business could recognize a national model of ever-larger firms practicing economies made possible by huge volume—economies of scale—and passing these savings along to consumers in a nation-wide market in the form of lower prices. As both an organizational ideal and a promise of abundance, railroads dominated the growth of the American economy for a generation and seized the American public's technological fancy.

Technology   Another powerful stimulant to late-nineteenth-century economic growth was swiftly developing technology. Even before the Civil War, the modern science of metallurgy had been born with the discovery in the 1850s first of the Bessemer process and then of the open-hearth method, which together made possible the production of high-grade steel in large amounts. Like many industrial improvements in the nineteenth century, these breakthroughs in steel technology originated in Europe but were quickly adapted to American conditions. Thus by the mid-1870s Bessemer mills in this country were producing 50 percent more steel than their British counterparts—and the margin widened every year as homegrown technological geniuses like Carnegie Steel's Captain "Bill" Jones designed more efficient layouts and found better ways of moving hot steel through them.

The American public could see for itself the countless new uses of steel when it visited Machinery Hall at the Philadelphia Centennial Exhibition in 1876 and examined firsthand all the productions deemed worthy of a Centennial Medal by the judges. Among the many American award-winning technological exhibits were Sharps rifles and Gatling guns; Midvale Steel's axles and shafts; Yale locks and Otis elevators; the Westinghouse air brake; Roebling's steel suspension bridge; Fitts road steam engines; and Pullman sleeping cars. Scattered in between these major exhibits were displays of hundreds of machine tools manufactured by Pratt and Whitney of Hartford, Connecticut, and Brown and Sharpe of Providence, Rhode Island.

In the center of the gigantic hall, dominating the other displays as both active presence and potent symbol stood the majestic Corliss engine designed by George Corliss of Providence—a double-acting, duplex vertical high-pressure steam engine standing on a platform fifty-six feet in diameter and supplying the power for all the machinery throughout the cavernous building. Visitors to the fair likened the Corliss engine to the human heart as a way of comprehending it as a system for generating power and sending it to its destination through metal arteries and leather capillaries. The massive engine rose forty feet in the air, weighed 680 tons, was powered by twenty boilers and equipped with cylinders forty-four inches in diameter with ten-foot strokes. The engine's massive flywheel—some thirty feet in diameter—made thirty-six revolutions per minute meshing with cogs on a pinion that turned an underground line geared to eight secondary shafts running along the ceiling the full length of the hall. All the machines beneath ran from belts attached to the 650-foot-long shaft that transmitted 180 horsepower. Here made visible for millions of onlookers stood the meaning and the promise of system for a dawning industrial age.

The number of inventions in post–Civil War America mounted steadily until the annual total of patent applications reached 25,000 in 1891. Thus the Hoe printing press and the Ingersoll air drill were invented in 1871; three years later came the third rail for subways and elevated lines. In the centennial year Alexander Graham Bell demonstrated the telephone at the Exposition in Philadelphia, and the next year the phonograph appeared. The year 1878 saw the installation of the first switchboard in New Haven, Connecticut, and in 1886 George Westinghouse perfected his system for transmitting alternating current over long distances. In every branch of industry and manufacturing, new inventions raised productivity, reduced man-hours of labor, and by competitive processes forced down the cost of finished goods.

American technology proved remarkably flexible in borrowing and improving foreign designs. Sometimes it provided lighter and faster machinery, as in the textile industry; at other times it developed bigger and more powerful equipment, like the mammoth steam shovels needed for heavy construction. In the oil industry the "cracking" process, which was developed in the 1870s, allowed refiners to control various yields by altering the molecular structure of the petroleum.

In the beginning inventors tended to work alone or in small unsubsidized groups, and frequently stumbled on their inventions by trial and error. The discovery of the Bessemer converter is an example. Only after some clever guesswork and haphazard experimenting did Sir Henry Bessemer in England and (working independently in the United States) William Kelly learn to force blasts of air into molten pig iron to burn out the carbon.

Soon after the Civil War, however, inventors like Thomas A. Edison came to understand the necessity of *system* rather than trial and error. An inveterate self-promoter, Edison always billed himself as a lone independent who required freedom from interference by combination or confederacy. "If you make the coalition," he warned the organizers of General Electric consolidation, "my usefulness as an inventor is gone. My services wouldn't be worth a penny. I can invent only under powerful incentive. No competition means no invention." Yet no one understood better than Edison the advantages of organization and order in the experimental process itself. His new approach to technological development and improvement took the forms of systematic organization of research in large independent or corporate-funded laboratories like his consortium at Menlo Park, New Jersey, and of the systematic application of a series of inventions—a process today called *innovation*—to a productive or extractive process conceived as a whole. Often invention and innovation combined to break a technological bottleneck that had blocked an entire process, as in the case of George Westinghouse's system for transmitting alternating current over long distances. In the same way, the rapid perfection of measurement devices, cutting tools, and lathes in the machine tool industry triggered a chain reaction of development of machine tools to make other machine tools to make tools.

This multiplier effect could be seen most clearly in the development of the combine harvester, patented before the Civil War but brought to Minnesota's wheat fields during and after the war. The combined reaper-thresher, to which was added a twine-binder by 1880, sold like the hotcakes it made possible throughout the 1880s, and together with the disc harrower and the wheeled gangplow quickly revolutionized wheat farming on the Great Plains, as mechanization spread from Minnesota's Red River Valley to California's interior valley bonanza farms. Mechanization on a rapidly expanding scale tripled American agricultural output between 1860 and 1920 and drastically reduced the farmer's labor costs. This new system of large-scale production and distribution of foodstuffs—which the twentieth century would call "agribusiness"—was being put firmly in place in the 1890s in a geographically segmented set of specialized farming regions extending in huge horizontal bands across the nation: a northern strip of hay and dairying land stretching from New England to Minnesota; spring wheat country pushing out through the Dakotas into eastern Montana; an expanding zone of "breadbasket" agriculture of wheat, corn, and hogs from Illinois out into the High Plains; a cotton belt running from South Carolina to the Texas and Oklahoma panhandles; and a Gulf Coast fringe of market-garden agriculture, by the turn of the century reaching up into California and the Pacific Northwest.

Equally impressive was the effect of technological system on American industry in fostering vertical integration—that is, the building of huge industrial firms that connected and controlled all the successive stages of manufacturing from the marshaling of natural resources to the marketing of the finished product. A good example of the accomplishments of vertical integration was provided by Judge Elbert H. Gary in his testimony before a congressional investigating committee. Gary, who was president of the Federal Steel Company and Andrew Carnegie's chief competitor, vehemently denied that he presided over any sort of "trust" or that he sought "monopoly." The key to Federal Steel's success, he explained, was vertical integration. "It takes the ore from the ground, transports it, manufactures it into pig iron, manufactures pig iron into steel, and the steel into finished products, and delivers these products." With its control of supplies of ore and the management of its own railroads, together with an efficient plant for making vast amounts of steel, Gary's company by the 1890s produced 30 percent of the steel rails in the country.

In the Mountain West, innovation in the extractive industries—logging and mining—made a similar impact with new systems devised to meet enormously expanding demands for lumber and metals of all kinds. In the silver, lead, copper, and iron mines across the country, the introduction of dynamite and then nitroglycerine led to more efficient, if highly dangerous, methods of getting out the ore. The depths of mine shafts sank from 3,000 feet to double that figure. Mining engineers employed by large syndicates found ways to straighten mine shafts to accommodate mechanized lifts and hoists. Air pumps and mining lamps to replace candles, arc lights and automatic drills, steam-driven regrinders and concentrators—all operated in concert within a new integrated system of production, altering the face of the American landscape and the lives of those who worked in that system.

A final example of rapid innovation and industrial system-building is the heavy construction industry in the cities, where giant steam shovels and steam-driven piledrivers, pneumatic drills, and electric cranes built the tall office buildings designed by newly integrated architectural firms in New York and Chicago.

Technology and a new science of management worked together to train the labor force in new skills and work patterns that were needed for industrialization. In celebrating the centenary of the Patent Office in 1891, one participant in the ceremonies listed the necessary ingredients for a successful policy of invention: individual enterprise; schools and universities; learned societies and professional organizations; and government aid. "To the modern investigator," he concluded, "leisure and opportunities are necessary . . . apparatus and laboratories are indispensable; and few men working alone can command either the needful time or the bare material necessities. During this century nine-tenths of the great discoveries have been made by men with institutions back of them." A huge pool of unskilled labor was still considered essential to American economic expansion, but the long-term trend pointed toward mechanization and, in the end, automation. Despite the willingness of native-born boys fresh from the farm, and young immigrants just off the boat, to feed the furnaces and work the lathes, it was machinery that sent American productivity soaring and consumption with it.

Capital Investment   Technology bred great expectations and a mounting hunger for capital. In the early years of the oil business just after the Civil War, John D. Rockefeller was able to acquire a small refinery for $10,000 and a large one for $50,000. By 1910 the market value of Rockefeller's Standard Oil was $600 million. Technology promised greater productivity and increased efficiency but also required ever-larger amounts of investment capital, which was readily forthcoming in the last three decades of the century. In 1860 a total of $1 billion was invested in the nation's manufacturing plants, which turned out a collective product worth $41.8 billion and employed 4.3 million workers. By 1900 the size of the work force had grown fivefold, and the total value of products nearly tenfold; at the same time, the amount of invested capital had multiplied twelvefold.

The sudden availability of large amounts of capital represented one of the most striking features of the American industrial revolution. The rate of savings, which had hovered around the 15 percent mark before the Civil War, suddenly shot up to 24 percent in the 1870s and 28 percent in the 1880s (compared, for example, to the present rate of savings by Americans, which is approximately 5 percent). Americans with money were turning to investment of their savings in the workings of the great industrial machine. The last half of the nineteenth century was a period of what economists call "capital deepening." Standard Oil and the Carnegie Steel Company regularly plowed back sizable portions of their mounting profits into the business; and individual investors, who in the Jacksonian years tended to buy land and mortgages, had been taught by the financial entrepreneur Jay Cooke during the Civil War to switch to government bonds as "the ready, *present* and *required* means to strike the death blow at rebellion," a preference for stocks and bonds they retained after the war.

The positive results of this process of accumulating savings could be seen in plant modernization, growing research and development programs, expanding product lines, and more efficient systems of distribution. The debit side of the ledger could be read in the growing disparity in income dividing well-to-do Americans from their less fortunate fellow citizens—a result in part of regressive federal tax policies (a small wartime income tax had been jettisoned after the war) that allowed wealthy people to keep their money for investment purposes. The earnings of the less wealthy—recent immigrants, unskilled workers, growing numbers of working women—increased over the last three decades of the nineteenth century, but not enough to close the gap in income and economic power.

To put this new money to work a host of new financial institutions appeared: commercial banks, savings banks, life insurance companies, and investment houses. These new institutions served as intermediaries between the eager investor and the needy business firm. By 1900 the stock market, now over a hundred years old, had established itself as the main mechanism for exchanging securities and mobilizing the vast funds required by new industrial firms. By the time of World War I, Wall Street had succeeded in creating a genuine national market for investment capital.

The pace of the American Industrial Revolution was unregulated and hence uneven. Boom-and-bust has historically been a flaw in free-market economies together with marked disparities in the distribution of income, and the economy of the Gilded Age was no exception. For the first time in American history a combination of potent forces was at work—a huge urban market, an efficient distribution system, a highly motivated work force, and vast amounts of capital. All that was lacking was a public policy that recognized the need for regulation and direction. Without such a program the transformation of the American economy was destined to be disorganized and at times chaotic.

Economic Instability The gains made by the American Industrial Revolution were real. Per capita income grew by 2 percent a year; between 1870 and 1910 it tripled. The workweek declined from sixty hours to fifty in these same years. A declining death rate outstripped a falling birthrate, and an improved diet and better health care raised the life expectancy for white males from thirty-seven to forty-six years in this period. (The average life span of black males, however, was sixteen years shorter.) Most important for American businessmen and consumers was a steady drop in prices of food and manufactures and the increasing availability of both to consumers. Recalling for a congressional investigating committee in 1883 his early years in the Manchester, New Hampshire, mills, the former governor of the state attributed his greatly improved standard of living to his frugality as a young man:

> I got $125 [a year]. . . . Now, how did I get my clothes? I clothed myself. I mended my own stockings; my employer used to give me a pair of socks sometimes. We had no new clothes as boys have nowadays. During the whole year that I was first in this place I never paid one dollar for a carriage; spent no money for cigars; no money for rum; we had no amusements, no holidays. I never heard of such a thing as a vacation for ten years. This is the way we grew up here—by constant labor. Labor is the foundation of prosperity.

If these long-term improvements in the standard of living were real, so too in the short term were the severe deprivations stemming from economic instability, particularly the decline in status among formerly independent artisans and mechanics. Testifying before the same congressional committee, a textile worker and union organizer from Fall River, Massachusetts, described working conditions in the city's mills:

> The condition of operatives in our city is a very unenviable one. The work there is very hard and the wages are very low—low in proportion to what they used to be some ten years ago, before the financial depression [of 1873–78] set in. Our females in particular are overworked; their strength is entirely overtaxed by the labors they have to perform. I have often argued myself that if our manufacturers would give over preaching so much about temperance and other things and try

to bring about a reform in the condition of their operatives, it would be better than all the many thousand temperance lectures and temperance tales.

The American economy after the Civil War swung like a pendulum between good times and hard times, and back again. The Panic of 1873 plunged the country into six years of depression, with massive unemployment, wage cuts, and price declines. Following a short season of recovery, a second recession buffeted the economy in 1884, and again sent prices skidding and workers into the ranks of the unemployed. Once more after a brief respite, the Panic of 1893 brought four more years of economic paralysis from which the country recovered only at the end of the century.

Satisfactory explanations of the causes of depressions were hard to come by. American observers compared depressions to a swing of the pendulum, the breaking of a wave, or the onset of a fever, but the experts despaired of controlling business cycles or erasing the effects of periodic slumps. Despite the recent lessons in the need for economic planning that the Civil War had suggested, the great majority of middle-class Americans still believed devoutly in the self-regulating market. And conventional wisdom declared that government should never interfere with this market. "Money-getters," the great showman P. T. Barnum warned the politicians, "are the benefactors of our race." Stand aside and let them do their work!

The result of this popular belief in unlimited business opportunity and citizen autonomy was a national government that frequently subsidized business but seldom regulated it. Politicians, professionals, and educators alike predicted marvelous achievements for a new industrial statesmanship left to its own devices. Big corporations, the wealthy ironmaster and mayor of New York City, Abram S. Hewitt, advised the Chicago Board of Trade, were the "best friends" the American people had. Far-seeing industrialists, having dispensed with the strictures of the Founders, were now busy "doing the work which was done by Jefferson and Madison in the early days of the Republic." William Graham Sumner, Yale's crusty sociologist and the great defender of American rugged individualism and self-help, amended this judgment only slightly: "The great leaders in the development of the industrial organization need those talents of executive and administrative skill, and fortitude, which were formerly called for in military affairs and scarcely anywhere else." Academicians and professionals chimed in. "I believe in general that that government is best which governs least," Francis A. Walker, president of the Massachusetts Institute of Technology, warned Congress, "and that interference with trade or manufactures is very undesirable."

As Gilded Age politicians deferred to business leadership and praised business values, the directive force of government tended to disappear in misty hopes for automatic prosperity. The great steel manufacturer and self-made man Andrew Carnegie explained the terms of this new social contract in a language that a business civilization instinctively understood. It would be a serious mistake

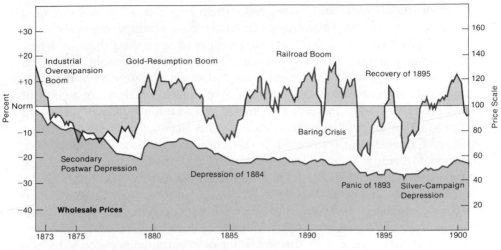

The U.S. Economy, 1873–1900

he joked, for the American community to shoot its millionaires because, after all, they were the "bees" that made the most honey: "Under our present conditions the millionaire who toils on is the cheapest article which the community secures at the price it pays for him, namely, his shelter, clothing, and food." Carnegie need not have worried: there would never be an open season on American millionaires.

Business Fills a Vacuum

Because the federal government was reluctant to assert its control over the economy—and because state governments responded only gradually with piece-meal and often ineffective legislation—the job of providing a measure of economic stability fell to American businessmen themselves. Only the application of system could manage the national economy efficiently and fairly, assuring all Americans a measure of financial security and personal well-being. Blessed with organizational talent and boundless energy, American businessmen were the first to respond to the challenge of disorder, even though they tended to concentrate on the specific problems confronting their own businesses rather than on the creation of an equitable national market system. In most businessmen's views, their needs did not require public policy; rather, they could be met by a series of limited private strategies designed to protect their own firms. Slowly a general pattern of self-regulation of business and industry emerged in response to threats to continued prosperity.

What were those threats? First of all, businessmen knew that their costs of production were rising as they took advantage of new technologies and expensive machinery to meet a mounting consumer demand. Throughout the last quarter of the century these capital costs, as they called them, kept increasing. To compound their problem, the same machinery that made mass production possible also attracted new investors and entrepreneurs eager to seize their share of a new national mass market. This competition drove prices inexorably downward toward cost: the wholesale price index sank from 100 in 1880 to 82 in 1890.

Thus the businessman faced the problem of how to break out of a circle of rising production costs, increasing competition, and tumbling prices. He could cut production, lay off his workers, and close his factory, but as the steelmaker Andrew Carnegie soon discovered, it was cheaper and more efficient for big business to "run full," even at a short-term loss, than to close down. The manufacturer could meet competition by slashing his prices, but not below the long-run break-even point. Faced with recurrent slowdowns and slumps, menaced by competitors, and confronted with shrinking profits, the nation's businessmen began to experiment with various ways of gaining greater control over their enterprises. The day of the small businessman attempting to solve the problem all by himself was over. "We live in an atmosphere of organization," one keen observer commented. "Men are learning the disadvantages of isolated action. Whether we approve of trusts and trades-unions and similar combinations, and whatever their motives, they rest on a foundation which is sound alike from the business and religious standpoint; namely, the principle of union and cooperation."

The first experiments in securing industrial order through the imposition of a system were improvised attempts made by a business community that was suddenly faced with severe problems but left to its own devices to find solutions. In deciding to demolish a small-business economy with its unregulated market forces and to replace it with new combinations, American business leaders played—often without realizing it—a genuinely revolutionary role.

Cartels and Trusts   The earliest forms of consolidation—those requiring the least amount of change—were *cartels.* These were loose trade associations, or *pools,* of independent business firms voluntarily joined together to dominate and hopefully direct an industry. With disarming candor, the organizer of the Wire Nail Association explained his case for forming a pool:

> There is nail machinery enough in this country to produce four times as many nails as can be sold. When there is no pool the makers simply cut each other's throats. Some people think there is something wicked about pools. When we were trying to get up the nail pool, I talked with directors of companies who held up their hands against going into any sort of combination. I said to them, "How much did you make last year?" "Not a cent." "Are you making anything now?" "No." "Well, what do you propose to do? Sit here and lose what capital you have got in the business? . . . " There is only one way to make any money in a business like the nail business, and that is to have a pool.

Pools attempted to meet the problem of overproduction and falling prices through gentlemen's agreements: competitors, while maintaining their independence, agreed among themselves to accept production quotas and refrain from price cutting. For example, the whiskey distillers agreed that "only 28 per cent of the full capacity shall be operated, and no stocking up beyond this amount under any circumstances." To tighten sagging steel prices, the steel rail manufacturers in 1887 formed a pool, the Steel Rail Association, which established a strict quota system and provided for a series of stiff fines for uncooperative members. Although the Steel Rail Association continually denied charges of price fixing, it nevertheless enjoyed a period of remarkable price stability thereafter.

Yet cartels had their drawbacks. They flourished in good times but collapsed under the pressure of recessions. Their agreements could not be enforced in the courts, and American consumers regarded them as an undue restraint of trade. Recognizing these limitations and sensitive to an aroused public opposition to secret agreements, pioneer organizers, among them John D. Rockefeller, turned to "horizontal" combinations, or *trusts*. The trust was the brainchild of a member of Standard Oil's legal staff, the affable and shrewd Samuel C. T. Dodd, who patiently explained its advantages to hesitant colleagues. Because state laws prohibited a company's outright ownership of another company's stock, there was no foolproof way of consolidating, holding, and managing a string of separate companies, Dodd admitted.

> But you could have a common name, a common office, and a common management by means of a common executive committee. . . . If the Directors of one of the companies and their successors shall be made Trustees of all such stock, you thus procure a practical unification of all the companies.

The idea worked. In 1882 forty-one stockholders in the Standard Oil Company of Ohio signed an agreement creating a board of nine trustees to whom they transferred all the properties and assets of their companies in exchange for trust certificates. The visible signs of this financial feat were 700,000 hundred-dollar certificates, the price of consolidated control over the American oil industry. The corporate spirit had worked its first miracle.

Once they acquired formal control over production and prices, many trusts and *holding companies* (similarly integrated firms that were allowed to hold stock in other corporations) were content to operate as loose cartels, simply parceling out shares of the market without trying to impose a centralized system or authority. The hoped-for efficiency and economies were not always forthcoming in such cases of partial consolidation, and soon the largest and most powerful businesses began to follow the examples of Carnegie Steel and Federal Steel by achieving "vertical" integration of their industries through control of the entire industrial process from raw materials to sales. In his annual report to stockholders in 1901 the president of a vertically integrated concern explained why his company looked inward for success rather than buying out the competition:

We turned our attention and bent our energies to improving the internal management of our business, to getting the full benefit from purchasing our raw materials in large quantities, to economizing the expense of manufacture, to systematizing and rendering more effective our selling department, and above all things and before all things to improve the quality of our goods and the condition in which they should reach the customer.

More and more frequently after 1890, big business tried to secure control "backward" to resources and transportation, as well as "forward" to control of the market through research departments and central business offices. From the last years of the nineteenth century through World War I, even more intensive consolidation would finish the demolition of Gilded Age capitalism and clear the ground for new twentieth-century giants.

The business drive toward a national economy in the Gilded Age did not go unopposed. For every gain there was a corresponding loss: for every winner, a disgruntled loser. Not all business in the Northeast, for example, welcomed every change made by integration. If New York City flourished as the new center of the nation's financial and transportation networks, its growth was at the expense of such former rivals as Boston and Philadelphia. If Standard Oil profited hand-somely from Rockefeller's nationalizing of the oil business, a large part of the cost was ultimately borne by hundreds of small independents driven from the field. Andrew Carnegie's J. Edgar Thompson steel mill mass-produced nails, which made building cheaper and more efficient, but it also cost blacksmiths, iron-mongers, and older artisans their livelihood.

And for what ends was the American financial and industrial order being transformed? The builders of the new corporate America, like their many admirers, were never entirely clear about their ultimate aims. Heavy investment capital, rapid plant expansion, increased production and reduced overhead, economies of scale and mass distribution systems—all to what greater good? For huge profits, surely, and for rising quantities of consumer goods for more and more people. But beyond that? What did mass advertising and the constant manipulation of consumer demand mean for individual freedom of choice? How were Americans to balance rising standards of living with loss of control over the workplace? Could big business be made to deliver on its promise of economic security for all citizens? Were huge industrial and financial combinations com-patible with political democracy and social responsibility? In short, was big really better? Neither the corporate revolutionists nor their uneasy admirers could quite answer these questions, which posed a dilemma that would persist throughout the twentieth century.

The Counter-revolution Fails These same questions troubled the opponents of big business, who called themselves "antimonopolists" and whose numbers and influence swelled in the late nine-teenth century, beginning with the farmers' and workingmen's fight against the railroads and culminating in the Populist movement in the 1890s. If these critics of monopoly and enemies of the Money Power finally failed to prevent economic concentration or to check its political influence, it was not for lack of numbers. The antimonopoly army in the last quarter of the century recruited at one time or another farmers and artisans with strong beliefs in equality and community; small businessmen with limited capital but limitless faith in individual initiative; and liberal publicists, country lawyers, clergymen, and educators determined to protect the claims of the "little people" against the incursions of monopoly. Stronger and fiercer than the party loyalties of Republicans and Democrats, the faith of the antimonopolists exhibited all the fervor of a civic religion promising spiritual renewal as well as economic restoration and political purity.

Many of the antimonopolists' complaints were pointed and direct. Monopolies, some charged, were the source of a prodigious waste of natural resources. In planning only for increased profits, big business misdirected investment, misallocated manpower, and thus kept the total output of American goods lower than it should have been. Others argued that the trusts behaved unfairly, tying the people's hands and then picking their pockets. If pools and trusts and all the other instruments of business collusion did not immediately raise prices, they had the power to do so and would soon invoke it. And that power, all the antimonopolists agreed, had been acquired by driving out honest competitors and seizing the citadels of power. The harshest indictment of monopolies was directed at their *political* influence. This was the charge leveled against Standard Oil by Henry Demarest Lloyd in his famous exposé *Wealth Against Commonwealth* (1894):

> Monopoly cannot be content with controlling its own business. . . . Its destiny is to rule or ruin, and rule is but a slower ruin. Hence we find it in America creeping higher every year up into the seats of control. Its lobbyists force the nomination of judges who will construe the laws as Power desires, and of senators who will get passed such laws as it wants for its judges to construe.

At the heart of the antimonopoly appeal lay a belief in a law of "natural development," which, left to operate as divine providence intended, would ensure steady, measured economic growth. Natural growth, critics like Henry Demarest Lloyd and Henry George insisted, would be accompanied by full employment, fair wages, and widespread abundance. In this alternative reading of American prospects, the United States had enjoyed a "normal" pace of economic development until monopolies played havoc by unduly accelerating the growth rate and encouraging speculation. If trusts, pools, and holding companies could simply be dismantled and their special privileges annulled, the country would return to a healthy state of "real growth" and a fairer distribution of wealth to all its citizens. The social reformer and antimonopolist Henry George described this future America for his fellow opponents of economic concentration. Without massive engrossment of land by railroads and absentee owners, and without the forced migration of the nation's yeomen to city slums where they became the new proletarians, the national future would bring utopia:

There would be no necessity for building costly railroads to connect settlers with a market. The market would accompany settlement. No one would have to go out into the wilderness to brave all the hardships and discomforts of the solitary life; but with the foremost line of settlement would go the church and the school-house and lecture room. The ill-paid mechanic of the city would not have to abandon the comforts of civilization, but where there would be society enough to make life attractive, and where the wants of his neighbors would give a product for his surplus labor. . . .

Behind such a vision stood a set of democratic-republican convictions whose history ran back to the middle of the eighteenth century and the American colonists' "country party" opposition to the commercial revolution and the British Empire. First of all, there was the view of history as an unending struggle between the virtue of the people and the dark forces of corruption lurking in the halls of state. Only the unsleeping vigilance of all citizens could stem the onslaught of predatory wealth and power bent on their destruction. Next came the distinction, still a vital one for the antimonopolists after the Civil War, between the true producers of the world—farmers, workingmen and -women, small businessmen—and the parasites who lived off their honest labor—bankers, lawyers, gamblers, and speculators. Finally, the opponents of big business held firm to the belief in the whole people organized in their communities and practicing a moral economy based on cooperation as well as competition. All these assumptions had survived the American Revolution to help direct the Jeffersonian opposition to the Federalists, and later, to inform the Jacksonians' attack on the Bank and to shape the abolitionist indictment of slavery. Now it was the turn of the Gilded Age antimonopoly forces to invoke them in their fight against economic concentration. Now, however, they had to learn the uses as well as the abuses of government: their ideal community of true producers and participatory democracy could be saved only by actions of the federal government to which they would have to appeal.

Public opposition to monopoly accomplished little in terms of legislation before 1890. In the 1870s the national farmers' organization, the Grange, and its allies among local businessmen pressured various midwestern state legislatures into passing laws regulating the rates that railroads charged for hauling freight and storing grain.* Although the Supreme Court originally upheld these so-called Granger Laws in *Munn* v. *Illinois* (1877), nine years later in *Wabash, St. Louis & Pacific Railway Co.* v. *Illinois* a more conservative minded majority declared that individual states could not regulate rates for interstate carriers.

On the federal level the Interstate Commerce Act (1887) was not much more successful in bringing the railroads to heel. The act prohibited pools, rebates, and rate discrimination, and it set up a commission to investigate and report viola-

---

*For the Granger movement as an expression of rural discontent, see pp. 111–112.

tions. But the commission's findings could be enforced only by the courts, a costly and cumbersome procedure. The Interstate Commerce Act marked the beginning of the American public's acceptance of the principle of government intervention, but it did not provide effective regulation. For that the country had to await Theodore Roosevelt's Square Deal.

By the time Congress responded to the public clamor to "do something about the trusts" by passing the Sherman Antitrust Act in 1890, more than a dozen states had already attempted some kind of antitrust legislation aimed at making restraint of trade illegal. Big business, however, deftly countered these attempts at control by moving into more permissive states like New Jersey, where they quickly secured favorable laws. Henry Demarest Lloyd, perhaps the severest critic of monopoly, complained that Standard Oil, in its bid for special favors, had done everything to the legislature of Pennsylvania except refine it.

The Sherman Act was designed to address concerns like Lloyd's, but it failed to destroy monopolies. The bill that Ohio senator John Sherman introduced in the Senate was quickly rewritten by the Judiciary Committee before the full Senate passed it by a vote of 52 to 1. The House in turn passed the measure unanimously. The result was an honest, although confused, attempt to regulate the trusts. But the long list of unanswered questions involving enforcement of the act showed that big business still had ample leeway. The act declared illegal "unreasonable restraint" of trade—but what did "unreasonable" mean? What was "trade"? What constituted a monopoly? How much power over an industry spelled "control"? How, in short, was the federal government to proceed with the job of breaking up the trusts?

The Sherman Act left these questions to government attorneys and judges, who, at least during the administrations of Grover Cleveland (1885–89, 1893–97) and William McKinley (1897–1901), were not disposed to stop the merger movement. Labor unions, on the other hand, seemed to capitalists and their subservient allies in the government thoroughly objectionable conspiracies against trade. When Eugene Debs's American Railway Union, in its momentous battle with the Pullman Company in Chicago in 1894, refused to move the trains with Pullman cars, President Grover Cleveland's attorney general Richard Olney drew up an injunction declaring the union in restraint of trade and successfully prosecuted Debs for contempt of court in violating the injunction. On appeal, the Supreme Court upheld the application of the Sherman Act to labor unions.

During the first ten years following its passage in 1890, only eighteen cases were initiated under the Sherman Act. It was successfully applied in only two railroad cases, in 1897 and 1898. But in the crucial *E. C. Knight* case of 1895, a poorly drafted government brief allowed a conservative majority on the Supreme Court to declare the American Sugar Refining Company—a trust controlling 98 percent of the sugar industry—not technically in restraint of trade. On this occasion the waspish Olney spoke for big businessmen everywhere when he declared: "You will observe that the government has been defeated in the

Supreme Court on the trust question. I always supposed it would be, and have taken the responsibility of not prosecuting under a law I believed to be no good."

The early twentieth century would see some apparent improvement in antimonopolists' fortunes. Presidents Theodore Roosevelt, William Howard Taft, and Woodrow Wilson, together with Congress, would all pursue trustbusting with varying degrees of enthusiasm. In 1904, in the *Northern Securities* case, the Supreme Court would apply the Sherman Act to end J. P. Morgan's dream of merging the Northern Pacific, Union Pacific, and Burlington railroads. Yet presidential, congressional, and judicial efforts to curb monopoly coincided with an unprecedented surge in business consolidation.* On balance, the counterattack against big business failed.

Rural Structure

Although individual American farmers, confronting a hostile nature and declining prices, were slow to acknowledge the change, their world too was being revolutionized by the forces of new technology, financial consolidation, and the corporate system. These new forces left their imprint on the nation's agriculture just as clearly as on its industry. Mechanical reapers, harrowers, spreaders and harvesters, steam plows, scientific agriculture—all these inventions and innovations spelled massive increases in productivity. And with increased production of staple crops—corn, wheat, sugar, cotton—came new systems of financing, organizing, and regulating farm work. A new arrangement of farm space, for example, began to alter the landscape of the Great Plains with rectilinear fencing, huge octagonal or circular barns, and towering grain elevators, symbols of the corporate revolution transforming the provinces just as skyscrapers and elevated trains marked its triumph in the metropolis. Huge twenty-five-ton steam engines crisscrossed the prairies of the trans-Mississippi West, dragging heavy disk plows, harrows, and harvesters. The largest of these steam-driven contraptions, encased in steel frames, could pull thirty plows and till a hundred acres in a single day. As early as 1880 some 80 percent of American wheat was being harvested by machine.

Soon new ideas for making farm work more systematic and scientific were being extended and applied to other aspects of farm management, such as improved storage facilities, double-entry bookkeeping, and better roads. By the opening of the new century American agriculture was already beginning to look like agribusiness. The rural equivalent of the industrial trust was the bonanza wheat farm, like the 55,000-acre spread owned by the California wheat baron Hugh J. Glenn, who employed an army of migratory Mexican and Chinese workers to plant and harvest his crop. Better known was the famous Dalyrumple operation in Cass County, North Dakota, incorporated by directors of the Northern Pacific Railroad and equipped with professional managers, 200 harrows, 125 seeders, 25 steam threshers, and 600 men to harvest the hundreds of

---

*See chapters 24 and 25.

thousands of bushels of wheat grown each year. Although there were increasing numbers of such large enterprises in the wheat belt by 1890, the bonanza farm was more a portent of the future than an immediate reality for hundreds of thousands of small and medium-sized farmers struggling, often blindly, within this new impersonal system to make a crop and turn a profit.

Indian Defeat on the Last Frontier   The key to agricultural surplus was the new land across the Mississippi River—the Great Plains stretching westward to the Rockies. In the 1870s and 1880s the Great Plains furnished a gigantic stage for the clash of four different civilizations, each with its own frontier, which was receding before the advance of corporate capitalism. First to be invaded and decimated were the native American tribes who formed the family of Plains Indians. In 1850 an estimated 250,000 Indians roamed the Great Plains, together with millions of buffalo that provided them with food, shelter, and clothing. The native American frontier on which an expanding capitalism imposed its system was first a killing ground and then a holding pen for those survivors deemed ready for assimilation. By 1885 the Indians' defeat and the destruction of the buffalo herds were virtually complete. Indian resistance was determined, fierce, and ultimately futile. The story of their defeat at the hands of mechanized white predation is a sordid one of broken promises, governmental corruption, and senseless massacre, already presaged by the slaughter at Sand Creek, Colorado, in 1864.*

With the end of the Civil War the whole of the Great Plains became a battlefield. For nearly two decades scarcely a year passed without significant clashes between United States soldiers, recently released from action in the South, and Indian warriors. With their hit-and-run tactics the native Americans were frequently victors in sharp skirmishes, for the United States army, dragging heavy supply trains, was unused to the ways of guerrilla war. For example, in 1866, when the army attempted to build and maintain a string of forts along the Bozeman Trail, which linked the North Platte with the recently opened mines in Montana, the Sioux fought them every step of the way, and in December wiped out a contingent of eighty soldiers.

More familiar is the legendary fate, ten years later, of George Armstrong Custer, the golden-haired boy-general of the Civil War, who had won several victories over the Southern Plains Indians. The discovery of gold in the Black Hills and the survey of the route of the recently chartered Northern Pacific Railroad brought whites swarming into ancestral lands that the Sioux considered the sacred dwelling place of their gods, and they fiercely resisted the advance of the white man. General Philip H. Sheridan, now the commander of the United States army in the West and Custer's superior officer, planned to force concessions of land from the Sioux by seizing the large Indian encampment on the Little Bighorn River (which the native Americans called Greasy Grass). Custer's

*See chapter 21.

column was part of a three-pronged attack, but when he reached the Indian encampment first, he ordered his men to charge without waiting to coordinate his attack with those of the other commanders. As Custer's soldiers advanced, Chief Low Dog called out to his warriors: "This is a good day to die; follow me." They did and within an hour on June 25, 1876, Custer and every one of his men had been killed.

But such short-lived Indian victories scarcely slowed the march of white settlers following in the tracks of the United States Army. Soon the Sioux were forced to give up their grazing lands to the horde of gold-seekers who rushed into the Black Hills in search of instant fortune. Farther west in Idaho, Chief Joseph of the peaceful Nez Percés, refusing to cede the tribal lands along the Salmon River, was forced to fight for them and, having lost, to undertake a heroic 1,500-mile retreat northeastward toward Canada. Chief Joseph and his depleted band of warriors were finally captured thirty miles from the border and confined to a reservation. In the Southwest it was much the same story with the last stand of Geronimo, a leader of the Chiricahua Apaches, who after a fifteen-year running war with white America was finally defeated and disarmed in 1886. Soon thereafter the Apache, Hopi, and Comanche were forced onto reservations in the Southwest; in the North the same fate befell the Sioux, Blackfeet, and Cheyenne.

In part the defeat of the Indians was the result of superior white force and fire power. The twenty-year war, it was estimated, cost $1 million and the lives of twenty-five soldiers for each native American warrior killed. In the long run, however, it was the completion of two transcontinental railroads—the Union Pacific and the Northern Pacific—that did more to defeat the Indians and destroy their way of life than all the military campaigns. The railroads and the towns strung along them disrupted traditional patterns of migration, and the slaughter of hundreds of thousands of buffalo intentionally stripped a nomadic people of their means of subsistence. Professional hunters boasted of killing two hundred animals a day, some for sport but many more for their hides, worth an average 25 cents apiece. Once more technology in the form of the railroad and repeating rifles made a design on the land described by one of the professional hunters:

> I have seen their bodies so thick after being skinned, that they would look like logs where a hurricane had passed through a forrest [sic]. . . . The buffalo would lie in this way until warm weather, drying up, and I have seen them piled fifty or sixty in a pile where a hunter had made his stand. As the skinner commenced on the edge, he would have to roll it out of the way to have room to skin the next, and when he finished they would be rolled up as thick as logs around a sawmill.

The final act in this saga of annihilation was played out at Wounded Knee in South Dakota on December 29, 1890. Two years earlier the Ghost-dance religion, promising a return to sacred ways and the recovery of ancestral lands, had spread rapidly among the remnants of the Sioux, but there had been no Indian raids on

A Buffalo Hunter and Skinner at Work
This scene of a buffalo hunt in Taylor County, Texas, in the 1870s shows how the Indians'
means of subsistence was eliminated.

white settlements when the Seventh Cavalry—George Custer's old unit—fell upon the village at Wounded Knee and methodically slaughtered men, women, and children, some of whom they pursued for miles outside the village. American Horse, one of the surviving chiefs who returned to Wounded Knee following the massacre, reconstructed for the Commissioner of Indian Affairs the act of butchery by identifying the spots where bodies had lain from the track of blood:

> There was a woman with an infant in her arms who was killed as she almost touched the flag of truce, and the women and children of course were strewn all along the circular village until they were dispatched. Right near the flag of truce a mother was shot down with her infant; the child not knowing that its mother was dead was still nursing.

As the proud nations that had once dominated the West were defeated by white technology, driven from their lands by rapid settlement, and degraded by the white man's alcohol, reformers and humanitarians across the United States began to realize that they were witnessing what Helen Hunt Jackson called *A Century of Dishonor*. This was the title of her book, published in 1881, which

End of the Ghost Dance, January 1, 1891
Burying the victims of the Wounded Knee Massacre.

reviewed the history of the government's underhanded and brutal treatment of the native American. But how could this record of inhumanity be reversed? What should well-meaning Americans propose as a measure of justice? Most Americans, it was clear, were prepared to go on confining the Indians to smaller and smaller reservations on poorer and poorer lands. The only alternative that humanitarian reformers could suggest was to transform the Indians through assimilation into, they hoped, independent citizens by breaking up the tribes and teaching the individual native American to fend for himself in a world made over. This process of incorporation was accomplished in the Dawes Severalty Act of 1887, which provided for nominal citizenship at the cost of native customs, language, and religion; an inferior vocational training; dissolution of tribal units and division of Indian lands into individual 160-acre plots that could not be sold for twenty-five years. Of the 187 million acres constituting the original reservations, only a third of them went to settled Indian families; the remainder—usually the best land—fell to land-hungry white settlers and speculators.

Even well-intentioned humanitarians and supporters of Indian rights viewed assimilation or extermination as the only options. Thus President Merrill E. Gates of Amherst College in 1887 told the Lake Mohonk Conference of the

Friends of the Indians that the answer to the native American's plight was incorporation as rapidly as possible into the capitalist market system:

> To bring him out of savagery into citizenship we must make the Indian more intelligently selfish before we can make him unselfishly intelligent. We need to awaken in him wants. . . . Discontent with the teepee and the starving rations of the Indian camp in winter is needed to get the Indian out of the blanket and into trousers—and trousers with a pocket in them, and with a pocket that aches to be filled with dollars.

As Indian resistance collapsed, miners, cattlemen, and farmers poured into the West, vying for mastery of this new frontier of capitalism.

The Indians' Successors Miners were the first white Americans since the antebellum fur trappers to exploit the West's natural wealth. In the years following the Civil War the miners' frontier moved rapidly eastward as nomadic California "placer" miners from the gold fields armed with pick, shovel, and sluicebox scrambled over the mountains into Colorado to work "the poor man's mines" as loners or partners. But with the discovery of rich deposits of lead, copper, and iron to compete with silver, the mining frontier spread rapidly northward into Idaho and Montana and southward as far as Arizona. In mining as in farming, technological improvements and innovative practices accelerated the growth of the industry: the use of mercury to separate the gold in huge retorts; steam-driven "stamp" mills to crush the ore; heavy machinery to sink deeper shafts; and the development of hydraulic mining with flumes and sluices, high-pressure hoses, and cannonlike nozzles that could skin a whole hillside in a day. Mining became more elaborate and expensive. "Quartz" mining, as it was called to distinguish it from surface "placer" mining, required ever-greater amounts of capital, which was readily forthcoming, first from regional investors like the "Comstock Millionaires" in San Francisco who cashed in and reinvested in the "Big Bonanza" at Comstock in the 1870s, and increasingly from eager eastern investors. Work grew specialized, and the new mining syndicates began to hire trained engineers to devise ways of getting the ore out more cheaply, accounting departments to balance the books and manage the payroll, and lawyers to keep an eye on compliant courts and legislatures. The more expensive mining technology became, the greater its destructive powers. Typical practices involved skimming the best and leaving the rest, moving out, and leaving behind open mine shafts and piles of tailings to pollute ground and surface water for over a century. By the mid-1880s the "Wild West" mining frontier with its boomtowns and vigilance committees, saloons, and brothels celebrated by Mark Twain in *Roughing It*, was disappearing into myth before the advance of mechanization and corporate managers.

The cattlemen's frontier had opened in the 1840s and 1850s when American settlers began drifting into Texas and the New Mexico territory, where they found a hardy breed of cattle, descendants of Mexican longhorns, that grazed on the open ranges. The early settlers promptly began to breed these cows for sale, branding the calves at yearly roundups and selecting the strongest steers for the long drive to the market. One of these pioneers, Richard King, owner of the famed King Ranch on the Gulf Coast south of Corpus Christi, built an empire that by 1870 consisted of 15,000 acres and employed 300 Mexican cowboys to handle 65,000 head of cattle, 10,000 horses, 7,000 sheep, and 8,000 goats. The early Texas cattle barons shipped their steers by cattle boat to regional markets in Galveston, New Orleans, and Mobile until the opening of the Great Plains by the railroads after the Civil War provided access to larger markets with links to eastern cities. In the beginning the huge herds were driven northward to Sedalia, Missouri, but when the Kansas Pacific Railroad reached Abilene, Kansas, in 1867, cattlemen discovered a shorter and better route to market. This was the Goodnight-Loving Trail, the first of a series of legendary cattle trails to new railhead towns—first Abilene, then Ellsworth, Wichita, Dodge City, and Cheyenne. Rough, primitive, and dirty, these railhead towns nevertheless served a basic economic function by connecting the cattle industry to the growing national economy.

Between 1866 and 1884 more than 5 million head of cattle were driven north from Texas, but by this time the entire cattle industry was heading northward on a sweeping arc of semiarid land a thousand miles long paralleling the mining frontier. Already by 1882, 7.5 million cattle grazed on the High Plains, and the cattle industry was valued at $187 million, a big enough sum to entice greenhorns like the young Theodore Roosevelt to the Dakota hills and corporate investors from across the Atlantic. The Swan Land and Cattle Company, incorporated in Edinburgh, Scotland, claimed control of a strip of grazing land in Wyoming 130 miles long and 42 miles wide. Like manufacturing, farming, and mining, the cattle business soon declared itself big business even as ex-rancher Roosevelt nostalgically described a lost way of life for eastern tenderfeet:

> The great free ranches, with their barbarous, picturesque, and curiously fascinating surroundings, mark a primitive stage of existence as surely as do the great tracts of primeval forests, and like the latter must pass away before the onward march of our people. . . .

In the absence of effective federal law, the management of the cattle kingdom fell to local groups of the cattle barons themselves. The most powerful of these was the Wyoming Stock Growers Association, widely acknowledged as the "unchallenged sovereign" of its vast grazing domain. While they struggled to maintain high beef prices and discourage rustling, the stock growers associations did little to prevent overgrazing or to check the ensuing soil erosion. Beef prices peaked in 1882 and plunged soon thereafter. Then nature took revenge on a wasteful industry, imposing many of the same conditions that unchecked competition brought to industrialists in the East and forcing ranchers to make man-

Wagon Train Resting in a Western Town
A common sight on the High Plains in the 1870s and 1880s.

agerial adjustments that emphasized greater capital investment and further consolidation. A severe winter in 1885 was followed the next year by a brutal blizzard that wiped out nearly 75 percent of the herds. The infamous Blizzard of '88 signaled the end of open-range grazing as the cattle business turned to raising smaller herds, improving stocks, sinking wells, building windmills, and settling down to the practice of scientific management.

The farmers' frontier was the last to close. Development of the Great Plains reached its peak in the 1880s and 1890s, when the total amount of improved land in the United States more than doubled from 189 million to 414 million acres. Railroad agents, boasting of bonanza farms and abundant crops, and local chambers of commerce, promising everything from a cure-all for the sickly to husbands for young women, seized developmental control of the Great Plains through a land policy tailored to mythical yeoman farmers and a homestead law written for an earlier generation.

Settlers lured across the ninety-eighth meridian with the promise of bountiful crops found an environment different from any they had ever experienced. John Wesley Powell, the geologist and explorer of the High Plains, spent much of his career after the Civil War trying to tell Americans what it was like to farm land where fewer than twenty inches of rain fell annually. The choice, he explained, was between organizing what he called "this new industry of agriculture by irrigation" in the Arid Regions as a voluntary cooperative community of small

John Wesley Powell's "Arid Regions and Invaders"
Wagon train crossing the High Plains in the 1870s.

landholders, on the one hand, or by an outside monopoly of "a few great capitalists" on the other. Few of Powell's contemporaries, least of all the individualistic farmers and their representatives in Washington, heeded his predictions of an emerging exploitative agribusiness.

The peopling of the trans-Mississippi West began in earnest with the passage in 1862 of the Homestead Act, which granted 160 acres of public lands free to any citizen over twenty-one or the head of a family who agreed to reside on his land for five uninterrupted years. Or, alternatively, a homesteader could buy his land outright from the government for $1.25 an acre after living on it for six months. Between 1862 and the turn of the century about 400,000 families took up homesteads under this act, although the old Jacksonian dream of free land as a safety valve for industrial discontent never materialized. Not many urban artisans and mechanics possessed the money or the skills to move west and make a go of farming. The vast majority of the new settlers were men and women who were already living on the land but hoped to improve their lot by relocating. But even experience could not ensure success: fully two-thirds of all homesteaders before 1900 failed at the venture.

Nor did all settlers in the New West take up their lands under the Homestead Act. Most of them either purchased land directly from the government or bought it from the railroads, which had received handsome grants from state and national governments with which to finance their construction. Congress, for example, gave the Union Pacific and the Central Pacific ten square miles of public land for every mile of track laid in the states, and twice that amount for each mile built in the territories.

Rural Discontents The farmers soon became part of the national market system emerging from the Civil War. For a few years immediately after the war they enjoyed flush times as a mounting demand for grain in eastern cities and the growing dependence of Great Britain on American harvests provided a booming market for staple crops.

Encouraged by rapidly rising prices, farmers in the Midwest and Plains states began to expand their operations to keep pace. Reaping machines and new and bigger plows were expensive, and small farmers, who were chronically short of funds, could not afford them. The future belonged to large producers who were willing and able to go into debt in order to buy the needed machinery. Now success depended not simply on the land and weather but on the workings of an international economic system. But the new national economy created severe problems for farmers, who suspected, often with good reason, that they were not getting their fair share of the growing national abundance.

Even in the prosperous years after the war, life on the Great Plains could be lonely and bleak. "I shall never forget the black prairie as I saw it in 1872, just after a prairie fire had swept over it," recalled one woman of her arrival at her new home in Adams County, Nebraska:

> To me, coming from southern Michigan with her clover fields, large houses and larger barns, trees, hills, and running streams, the vast stretches of black prairie never ending—no north, south, east, or west—dotted over with tiny unpainted houses—no I can't say barns—but shacks for a cow, and perhaps a yoke of oxen—that picture struck such a homesick feeling in my soul it took years to efface.

The Norwegian-born novelist Ole Rölvaag, drawing from immigrant accounts for his famous novel *Giants in the Earth* (1929), sketched the classic figure of the suffering pioneer woman in Beret, wife of Per Hansa, the vigorous and congenitally optimistic Norwegian immigrant who triumphs over droughts, blizzards, and plagues of grasshoppers in building a profitable farm. But Beret is driven mad by the solitude and the emptiness of life on a land without trees and neighbors. She falls victim to an overmastering fear: *"Something was about to go wrong."* Staring out across the flat plains that seem to have no horizon, she thinks: "Why, there isn't even a thing that one can *hide behind!*" Beret regains her sanity but at the price of religious fanaticism: she sends her hapless husband out into a blizzard to fetch the minister for a dying neighbor. He never returns, and his body is discovered the following spring in the shelter of a haystack, "his eyes set towards the west."

In an attempt to overcome the problems of loneliness and rural isolation, Oliver Hudson Kelley, who had lived in Massachusetts, Iowa, and Minnesota and traveled widely in the postwar South, founded the Patrons of Husbandry in 1867. In the beginning the Grange, as each local unit in Kelley's society was called, was primarily a social organization with a secret ritual, an educational program, and

Nothing to Hide Behind
The Sod House Frontier, Miller, Dakota Territory, 1885.

high hopes for communal solidarity. By the mid-1870s there were some 800,000 members of the Grange, most of them living in the Middle West and the South. The constitution of the Patrons of Husbandry prohibited members from engaging in politics under its name, but discussion of issues and candidates grew more heated as the economy cooled following the Panic of 1873.

Agrarian grievances were numerous and increasingly widespread. Farmers in Iowa, Nebraska, and Kansas complained bitterly that it took one bushel of corn to pay the shipping charges on another, a complaint echoed by wheat farmers in Minnesota and Dakota. Midwestern farmers, in particular, were incensed by the practices of the owners of the grain elevators who intentionally misgraded their grain, offering them only the lowest-grade price for superior produce. And everywhere in the West and South farmers complained about limited and expensive bank credit and the shortage of national banks in rural areas. Farmers in the Midwest were joined in their indictments of the railroads and grain elevator operators by shippers and businessmen who also objected to discriminatory rates and high-handed storage practices. Out of this shared discontent came state legislation, somewhat misleadingly called Granger laws because lawyers in Illinois, Wisconsin, Iowa, and Minnesota drafted legislation at the behest of businessmen, setting maximum charges for grain elevators and railroads and establishing state regulatory commissions with broad powers of enforcement. Farmers enthusiastically supported such laws even though they did not always initiate them. The Granger laws, however, were quickly challenged in the courts by the railroads and grain elevator companies, and soon were declared unconstitutional and modified or repealed. By 1880 it was clear that state regulation of interstate carriers and their facilities would not work.

After 1870 agricultural surpluses mounted steadily. Both a cause and a result of these surpluses were increasing crop specialization and the rise of single-crop agriculture—corn and wheat in the Midwest; wheat on the Plains; dairy products in the Old Northwest; and cotton in the South and Southwest. A rising demand for staples acted much like the growing demand for industrial goods in the nation's cities. In fact, the two developments were related. As American staples flooded Europe, prices for foodstuffs fell sharply there and land prices collapsed. The agricultural depression in Europe, beginning in the 1870s, drove millions of peasants and small farmers out of the countryside and into seaports, the first stopping point en route to American cities. In both Europe and America, cheaper food hastened industrial transformation. In the United States, however, farmers paid a large part of the price for this transformation by ensuring the nation a favorable balance of trade with mass exports of staple crops at declining prices. Nor could the individual farmer effectively cut production but, instead, was driven to produce even more in an already glutted market simply to get his share. Overproduction posed a conundrum the average farmer could not solve.

On the one hand the American farmer could consider the move from subsistence farming to specialized commercial farming as progress toward a higher standard of living. But this advantage was soon offset by the staple-crop farmer's suspicions that he had become the prisoner of the market, locked into a price structure from which there was no ready means of escape. With the onset of world agricultural depression in the 1870s, the price curve for staple crops plummeted, and the farmer's income slid with it. Wheat fell from $1.19 a bushel in 1881 to a low of 49 cents in 1894. Corn slipped in these same depression years from 63 cents a bushel to 18 cents. Buying in a market that was protected by tariffs, and selling in an unprotected market, the staple-crop farmer saw himself as the victim of an absurd situation: he was forced to grow more and more in order to earn less and less. Why, he asked himself, as the producer of the largest share of the nation's abundance, should he sink deeper into the mire each year? A Kansas farmer in 1891 summed up these feelings of betrayal:

> At the age of 52 years, after a long life of toil, economy, and self-denial, I find myself and family paupers. With hundreds of hogs, scores of good horses, and a farm that rewarded the toil of our hands with 16,000 bushels of golden corn we are poorer by many dollars than we were years ago. What once seemed like a neat little fortune and a house of refuge for our declining years, by a few turns of the monopolistic crank has been rendered valueless.

Conditions for staple-crop farmers were worst in the South, where a cotton monoculture fastened on the region an exploitative system of tenancy and sharecropping as a replacement for the antebellum plantation. Southern planters emerged from the Civil War with their landholdings intact but confronting an acute shortage of capital and credit. The freedmen, for their part, refused to work under the old gang system and preferred the promise of economic independence, however illusory. In agreeing to provide credit and "furnishings" at necessarily high but sometimes exorbitant rates, planters and country merchants were simply taking the advice of a veteran planter who urged: "Let each family work by itself, in separate fields or farms. This is much easier and I think far better than the old plantation style of all working together."

Sharecropping, tenancy, and crop liens (mortgages) formed interlocking parts of yet another system, this one constructed like an economic ladder with each of the rungs supporting a victim of exploitation. On the bottom rung stood the landless wage laborer with neither mule nor harness but standing ready to sell his labor for the subsistence wage paid him once he had made the owner's crop. Ranged on the intermediate rungs were the "croppers" working for varying shares of the cotton crop, usually from a third to a half depending on the ownership of a mule. A step higher on the ascending ladder came the full-fledged tenant, who rented the land outright for a sizable part of his crop. On the top rungs stood the planter and the furnishing merchant (often the same person), who supplied land, tools, seed, and furnishing at prohibitive rates of interest sometimes exceeding 40 percent.

Designed originally for the freedmen, sharecropping spread quickly across racial barriers so that by 1900 two-thirds of the share tenant farmers in the South were white. The system, which survived until World War II, devastated lives as well as the land by confining the exploited cropper—as it were—in a debtor's prison from which there was no escape. His debts mounted from one year to the next. He lacked all incentive to care for land that was not his own. Thrift was impossible; frequently he could not even read the contract that bound him. As one observer explained in describing how the malevolent system worked: "The debts of the people...have been no small factor in bringing about the overproduction of the great staple crop. Men in debt want money. Farmers know that cotton is the only crop that will bring in money...cotton brings money, and money pays debts. This will deliver the man from his trouble. Thus reasons the average farmer."

The Alliance and Populism

Independent farmers in the Midwest and Great Plains suddenly realized that, like their city cousins, they too were businessmen but that their business was always unpredictable and sometimes hazardous. To increase their output and cut their costs many staple-crop farmers borrowed heavily to buy more land, improve their farms, and purchase machinery—only to find themselves saddled with a crushing load of mortgage payments made all the heavier by falling prices and high interest rates. When the farmer hunted for money to renew his loan or make a payment, he was told by local bankers that credit was scarce because the pipeline of capital from the East had been turned off. Farmers reasoned that tight money lay at the root of their troubles: the rising value of the dollar could be traced directly to the decline in the actual number of dollars in circulation after the Civil War. The dollar, like the farmer himself, was being overworked. Bankers and eastern creditors could assure him that his problem was overproduction, but he knew it was "underconsumption" and cursed the restrictionist "gold bugs" and their minions on Wall Street.

Then, in 1887, a series of drought years and poor harvests tumbled the farmers into a deep agricultural depression. Local mortgage companies folded; interest rates soared; foreclosures mushroomed. The targets of the farmers' resentment were local bankers and the railroads, but increasingly they blamed a distant "price-fixing plutocracy"—which, they were sure, had rigged the system against them. "There are three great crops raised in Nebraska," a disgruntled small-town editor complained in 1889. "One is a crop of corn, one a crop of freight rates, and one a crop of interest. One is produced by farmers who by their sweat and toil farm the land. The other two are produced by men who sit in their offices and behind their bank counters and farm the farmers." Then there were the greedy trusts—the barbed wire trust and the plow trust in the West, the cottonseed oil trust and the jutebagging trust in the South—all of them gouging the small independent farmer. And behind all these oppressors stood state and federal governments that appeared to do their bidding. At the height of the agrarian distress in 1889, the still-unknown but aspiring writer Hamlin Garland found his neighbors caught up in a social crisis and engaged "in a sullen rebellion against government and against God":

> Every house I visited had its individual message of sordid struggle and half-hidden despair.... All the gilding of farm life melted away. The hard and bitter realities came back upon me in a flood. Nature was as bountiful as ever ... but no splendor of cloud, no grace of sunset, could conceal the poverty of these people; on the contrary, they brought out, with a more intolerable poignancy, the gracelessness of these homes, and the sordid quality of the mechanical routine of these lives. I perceived bountiful youth becoming bowed and bent.

The only answer, farmers and their advocates like Garland realized, was to organize to fight the bankers, the railroads, and the trusts—to wrest control of government away from the plutocracy and return it to the people. The 1880s saw the rapid growth of farm organizations in both the South and the West. The most powerful of them was the National Farmers Alliance and Industrial Union, or the Southern Alliance as it came to be called, which was originally formed in Texas in the late 1870s but which, during a decade of recruitment, education, and experimentation, had been fashioned into a mass democratic movement made more broadly reformist than the faltering Grange largely because of the vision and organizational genius of Dr. Charles W. Macune. By 1889 Macune had succeeded in uniting a group of regional societies into a cooperative crusade consisting of 3 million white farmers in the South and another 1.2 million black members organized separately as the National Colored Farmers Alliance. Meanwhile, in the West, hard-pressed farmers in Kansas, Iowa, and Nebraska also began to seek safety in numbers as early as 1880, but a six-year spell of good weather and bountiful crops dampened their organizational ardor until 1887, when another cycle of drought slashed yields and tipped the entire trans-Mississippi West into a prolonged depression. Two years later, in 1889, the Northern Alliance, as the federated state groups were called, merged with the larger and more adventurous Southern Alliance as farmers in both regions prepared to enter the political arena and challenge an unresponsive two-party system in the midterm elections of 1890. Here was the beginning of the Populist revolt that swept across agrarian America in the next six years.

In joining the Alliance movement and the People's party that grew out of it, farmers were responding to the same need for order and system that was driving American business toward consolidation and cooperation. But unlike their counterparts in business and industry the farmers professed a deep faith in the folk—the common people living in rural and small-town America and organizing in their several communities to build a program of mutuality and cooperation. American farmers' basic insight throughout the nineteenth century was the moral primacy of agriculture over all other ways of life. This enduring view was stated most eloquently by William Jennings Bryan in his famous "Cross of Gold" speech at the Democratic party convention in 1896. "You come to us and tell us that the great cities are in favor of the gold standard," Bryan thundered. "We reply that the great cities rest upon our broad and fertile prairies. Burn down your cities and leave our farms and your cities will spring up again as if by magic; but destroy our farms and grass will grow in the streets of every city in the country." Bryan confirmed the average farmer's deep-seated belief, borne out by the record, that the yeoman farmer had indeed built America—clearing and cultivating the land, pioneering in lonely isolation, raising the foodstuffs, feeding his own people and other people throughout the world, and laying the material base on which a modern industrial society now rested. Despite the damage methodically done to it, the land remained foremost in the American moral imagination. "On the land we are born, from it we live, to it we return again—children of the soil as truly as is the blade of grass or the flower of the field," Henry George wrote. And his message reached millions of already converted farmers who now sought government endorsement of their faith.

The farmers' fervent belief in an agrarian way of life was matched by an acute sense of their immediate practical needs and the role of the federal government in meeting them. Farmers were following the same route to effective organization taken by their business and industrial counterparts. As a first step they established member-financed Alliance stores and cooperatives, which offered discounts and provided affordable credit. In acknowledging their need for cooperatives farmers were responding to the impulse that was also driving businessmen to experiment in risk-pooling and to design new marketing and bargaining instruments. The pioneer Alliance cooperatives, however, were weakened by inadequate financing and falling staple-crop prices. It quickly became clear to farmers in both the South and the West that voluntary cooperatives, which lacked federal funding, were not enough; they needed federal support for a concerted plan for limiting risk and ensuring price stability. That plan, designed by Macune, was the "subtreasury system" in which the federal government would provide warehouses and elevators to hold the farmers' crops for the best price, meanwhile issuing them certificates of credit worth up to 80 percent of the crop. For a very modest rate of interest the average farmer would obtain cheap credit for fertilizer, machinery, and furnishings, together with government help in marketing his crop. The subtreasury system, quickly accepted by the Populists, was designed to eliminate the middleman in his various roles as furnishing merchant, local banker, mortgage company manager, and eastern investment-house promoter, all of whom joined forces to defeat the plan.

Out of this Alliance proposal for government-subsidized cooperation came the grassroots politics of Populism. Populism was the last stand of the republican producerist army against advancing corporate capitalism. The Populist creed consisted of the time-honored values and principles that marked workingmen's societies and land-reform leagues in the Age of Jackson. These made a blend of secular prescriptions and Christian ethics that defined a moral economy and a system of justice by making the distinction between the many who lived by the sweat of their brows and the selfish few who knew not the dignity of labor. The real workers of the world, in the view of the farmers and urban workingmen who voted the Populist ticket, were those men and women who, whether in the field or in the factory, actually built the nation, while the nonproducers "with no knowledge of frugality and without legitimate skill achieve a fortune in a day" and then look on in idleness and luxury. The true producers, Populists insisted, were responding to the universal instinct of workmanship with its spiritual as well as material rewards. Every citizen had a God-given right to a job, and held a just claim on society to provide one. Meaningful work, in the Populist creed, meant an entitlement to a birthright stake in a system that guaranteed the individual "the fruits of his toil." Labor came first in the providential scheme of things, and capital, if earned in reasonable amounts, constituted the proper reward for hard work. In a just economic system the natural and proper workings of the market ensured a balance between energy expended and wealth acquired. It was only when this equilibrium was upset by greed or privilege that the natural system broke down and producers suffered. Then it fell to the "plain people" of the country to enter politics and set matters right. "I believe that it is not God's fault that we are in this bad condition," the Populist leader Leonidas Polk told his listeners. "Congress could give us a bill in forty-eight hours that would relieve us, but Wall Street says nay." The task, then, was to rescue Congress from the "bold and aggressive plutocracy" that had usurped power and used it as a policeman "to enforce its insolent decrees."

Populists wanted the federal government to stand sponsor to their producerist way of life by encouraging invention, stimulating industry and cooperation, guaranteeing private property, and only occasionally stepping in to help the little man by redressing the political and economic balance in his favor. They explained their second-class status under the rule of the Money Power by resorting to a highly charged moral language as old as the American Revolution. Government, they asserted, had fallen prey to the "plutocracy" that filled public offices with "corrupt rulers" whose chief business was "robbing the honest yeomanry." These "money Kings" monopolized the "bounties of nature" once reserved by "Divine Providence" for the "sons of toil." Thus, while the "idle rich" continued to hoard their "blood money," the poor people in field and factory were being reduced to "servitude." Soon all American society would stand fatally divided between "masters and slaves."

When the cheering delegates of the People's party put forward their presidential candidate in the election of 1892, they were determined to save not simply the country's farmers but industrial workers and the whole nation from impending moral as well as material ruin. Populism declared itself a redemptive grassroots movement of the American folk, resolved to take their fellow citizens along an alternative route to the just society across the roadblocks put in their path by a selfish minority of plutocrats. "A vast conspiracy against mankind has been organized on two continents and is taking possession of the world," the Populist platform of 1892 declared. "If not met and overthrown at once, it forebodes terrible social convulsions, the destruction of civilization, or the establishment of an absolute despotism." With the coming of Populism in the 1890s, the American farmers' crusade organized by the Grangers twenty years earlier became a political war.

Workers and the Challenge of Organization

Of all the groups caught up in the late-nineteenth-century American economic revolution, industrial workers depended least on statistics to confirm what they already knew: that their rewards for tending the national industrial machine hardly matched their services. Real wages rose 25 percent in the 1880s, but in 1882 male Fall River textile workers could not support their families unless their wives also worked. As late as the turn of the century the workweek for the average worker was a little less than sixty hours, and the average wage for skilled workers was 20 cents an hour—and only half that amount for unskilled workers. Annual wages for most factory workers in 1900 came to an average of $400 to $500, from which a working family saved an average $30 per year. Nearly half the remainder went for food, another quarter for rent, and the balance for fuel, light, and clothing. There was not much left for luxuries.

Earnings for industrial workers continued to go up 37 percent between 1890 and 1914, but between 1897 and 1914 the cost of living climbed 39 percent. Despite growing national wealth, most American workers managed on the slimmest of margins. Their share of the pie, although larger than it had been a half-century earlier, was still comparatively small. The richest tenth of the population received 33.9 percent of the nation's income; the poorest tenth collected 3.4 percent. The rich were certainly getting richer, while American workers, if not absolutely poorer, were still not enjoying much of the wealth they were busy creating.

But despite these growing disparities in wealth between the well-to-do and the workers, the paramount considerations for industrial laborers were the conditions under which they were forced to work and the routines that the new impersonal system was pressing on them. At best, factory work was exhausting, repetitious, and boring—ten hours a day, for example, standing before a noisy mechanical loom in the half-light of an ill-ventilated factory. A mule spinner in one of New England's many cotton mills estimated that tending the four "stretches" made by his four "long mules" each minute meant walking some thirty miles a day. Children provided a pool of cheap, if inefficient, labor for the region's cotton and woolen mills, tying broken threads and scrambling in and out of the machinery despite state child labor laws. "Poor, puny, weak little children," complained a female spinner in one of Rhode Island's mills, "are kept at work the entire year without intermission of even a month for schooling. The overseers are to them not over kind and sometimes do not hesitate to make them perform more work than the miserable little wretched beings possibly can." The effect of the 1885 Rhode Island ten-hour law in giving her more free time was explained with unintentional irony by an "Irish widow" to a state factory inspector:

> Why, the extra quarter hour at noon gives me time to mix my bread; an' then when I comes home at night at six o'clock, it is ready to be put in the pans, an' I can do that while Katie sets the table; an' after supper, an' the dishes are washed, I can bake; an' then I am through an' ready to go to bed, mebbe, afore it's quite nine o'clock. Oh, it's splendid, the best thing as ever 'appened.

Making Steel
Work in the steel mills was hot, dirty, and dangerous.

Industrial labor was harsh, closely supervised, and often punitive in its sanctions: fines, docked pay, time clocks, bullying bosses and distant superintendents, blacklists and yellow-dog contracts forbidding workers to join a union— all combined to make mills and factories seem like prisons from which tired men and women contrived to escape at the end of the day. For the common unskilled laborer on the docks, a construction site, or a steel mill, work was not only backbreaking but extremely dangerous. The steel plant at Homestead shut down just twice a year, running "straight out" around the clock the rest of the time with steelworkers taking the swing shift—an uninterrupted twenty-four hours—every other week. Hamlin Garland, visiting Homestead, saw "pits gaping like the mouth of hell and ovens emitting a terrible heat, with grimy men filling and lining them. One man jumps down, and works desperately for a few minutes, and is then pulled up exhausted. Another immediately takes his place...." Under such conditions accidents were common and frequently fatal. In a single year in Pittsburgh's iron and steel mills there were 195 fatalities—22 from hot metal explosions, 10 from rolling accidents, and 5 from asphyxiation.

Workers Organize   For a number of reasons workers were slower to organize than businessmen or farmers. In the first place, most business leaders were implacably opposed to unions and spared no efforts to prevent their formation or break them up. With the help of lobbyists and their trade associations, industrialists were able to prevail on governors of states to send in troops nearly five hundred times between 1875 and 1910 to quell what middle-class Americans persisted in calling "labor unrest." Often direct recourse to state or federal courts was enough to prevent or break strikes. Then there was the huge diversity of the work force and the barriers of ethnicity and race that militated against feelings of labor solidarity. In the decade after the Civil War some 3.5 million immigrants, most of them from northern Europe, poured into this country and formed a vast labor pool in the industrial cities. By 1880, 87 percent of the inhabitants of Chicago, 84 percent of those in Detroit and Milwaukee, and 80 percent of those in New York and Cleveland were immigrants or the children of immigrants. Organizing such a diverse population speaking dozens of different languages and possessing a wide variety of skills proved a formidable task. Native-born Americans tended to hold the skilled jobs; immigrants found themselves relegated to the growing ranks of unskilled or semi-skilled workers. Craft unions—the "aristocracy" of labor—were apt to be exclusive, shutting out women, blacks, and menial workers from their organizations. Then too the workplace in industrial America was growing in size and impersonality. Machines replaced hand tools. Older artisans and master craftsmen saw their jobs disappear.

Despite these mounting odds against them, workers attempted in increasing numbers to unionize on a national scale. One early effort was William Sylvis's National Labor Union, which lasted only from 1866 to the Panic of 1873.* Only

---

*See chapter 21, p. 54.

slightly more successful in the immediate postwar years was the Knights of Labor, founded in 1869. Its ranks were also decimated by the depression of the 1870s, and not until 1879, with the election of Terence V. Powderly as General Master Workman, did the union acquire a truly national spokesman. Powderly, mercurial, dictatorial, and an ineffectual organizer, was a teetotaling labor evangelist who saw himself first and foremost as a teacher of the toiling masses in the ways of respectability and cooperation with employers. "Our order," he explained again and again to restive members of local assemblies of the Knights, "is above politics." The national leadership also opposed strikes. "Not once," he recalled proudly, "during my fourteen years in office of Grand Master Workman did I order a strike." It was the decisions of hundreds of local assemblies in the Great Upheaval of the mid-1880s to strike, even without the support of the national leadership, that accounted for the meteoric rise of the Knights of Labor, whose membership in 1886 topped three-quarters of a million.

Still, only a tiny fraction of the nation's work force belonged to any union before 1880. Some workers turned instinctively to politics and attempted to organize an independent political party pledged to support its demands for paper money and the free coinage of silver, an eight-hour day, and the exclusion of Chinese immigrants. This was the Greenback, or National Independent, party, organized in 1874, which fielded a presidential candidate in 1876 and whose congressional candidates two years later won more than a million votes. Greenbackers, however, enjoyed little success in achieving their goal of economic security.

Other workers in the throes of hard times in the 1870s turned to direct action—terrorism and the strike. In the anthracite coal fields of western Pennsylvania the so-called Molly Maguires, a secret cabal that controlled the Irish fraternal society, the Ancient Order of Hibernians, were accused and on flimsy evidence convicted of launching a crime wave against the coal bosses and their superintendents. Twenty-four Mollies were swiftly convicted and hanged, the last of them in 1878, and violence in the coal field subsided.

Even more frightening to middle-class Americans was the Great Railroad Strike of 1877, a spontaneous labor protest in the depths of a punishing economic depression. The Panic of 1873, triggered by the collapse of the financial firm of Jay Cooke, tipped the country into a six-year depression. Between 1873 and 1879 the national economy shrank by one-third. Thousands of workers lost their jobs, and unemployment in cities like New York ran as high as 33 percent. Caught in an unprecedented economic squeeze and faced with unresponsive politicians, industrial workers abandoned their newly formed unions in droves. In New York City, for example, union membership plummeted from 45,000 in 1873 to 5,000 in 1877.

The massive railroad strike that paralyzed business and struck terror into the hearts of American businessmen began in the small railhead town of Martinsburg, West Virginia, where workers learned of sharp wage cuts ordered by management and in retaliation stopped all trains and shut down the yards. When the local police failed to get the trains rolling again, troops were called in. Then a switchman attempting to derail a cattle train was shot and killed by the militia, and a crowd that had gathered to protest was dispersed with force. The incident at Martinsburg was just the beginning of a week of violence that spread from one major city to another, as wage cuts and layoffs were met by angry workers bent on sabotage and looting. In Baltimore, a regiment dispatched to protect Baltimore and Ohio Railroad property retreated before a hail of rocks, while the rest of the militia took refuge in a local armory, then broke out, panicked, and fired into the crowd, killing ten onlookers. In Pittsburgh the militia proved wholly unreliable until reinforcements from Philadelphia managed to clear a railroad crossing by killing twenty workers. Fighting back, strikers burned railroad yards, overturned cars, looted storehouses, and penned up the soldiers in a roundhouse into which they continued to pour rifle fire until they were finally driven off. In Buffalo, another mob, infuriated by the wanton killing of eleven of its members, tore up track and broke into an arsenal for the guns with which to defend themselves. In Chicago, striking switchmen roamed through the shops calling out their comrades and moving on to the stockyards and the packinghouses for support. Suddenly the city came to a standstill, and for the first time in American history middle-class citizens all over the country understood the power of workers to disrupt their lives.

American businessmen and industrialists quickly responded to these perceived threats to their welfare in what they continued to call the "labor problem" by resorting to corrective and punitive action, which only made relations with their workers worse. State legislatures, prodded by the business community, passed conspiracy laws designed to break up unions and prevent strikes. The courts, both state and federal, could be relied on to narrow the rights of workers to protest and organize in their own defense. State militias, which had proved unreliable in the Great Railroad Strike, were reorganized and given training in riot control. Thus, when another economic recession in the mid-1880s drove industrial workers in all sections of the country to strike in an attempt to recoup lost wages and regain control of working conditions, their attempts were met with the determined resistance of management backed now by a resentful middle-class public increasingly disposed to identify labor protest with the presence of "foreigners" and to denounce both as unpatriotic. The secretary of the Southern Industrial Convention, a trade association representing heavy industry in the South, spoke for an aroused consuming public in denouncing labor unions as "the greatest menace to this government that exists. . . . [A] law should be passed that would make it justifiable homicide for any killing that occurred in defense of any lawful occupation." Thus, when the Haymarket Square Riot occurred in May 1886, there were millions of Americans prepared to agree with the advocates of severe repression.

A few minutes after ten o'clock on the night of May 4, 1886, in Chicago's Haymarket Square, a crowd of some 2,000 workingmen, many of them members of a small German-speaking anarchist contingent, were listening to a denunciation of police brutality in dispersing a demonstration the day before at the

McCormick Harvester Company, when 180 uniformed policemen came rushing out of a nearby police station intent on breaking up the protest. Suddenly from out of nowhere a dynamite bomb came spiraling; it exploded, killing one policeman instantly and wounding sixty others, eight of whom subsequently died along with another eight onlookers. Three weeks later eight of the anarchists— the presumed ringleaders of a "conspiracy"—were charged with sixty-nine counts as accessories before the fact and with general conspiracy to murder. The verdict at the trial, presided over by the bitterly prejudiced Judge Joseph E. Gary, was a foregone conclusion: all eight defenders were found guilty, and within eighteen months four of them had been hanged, a fifth had committed suicide in his jail cell, and the remaining three were serving long sentences in the penitentiary (until they were pardoned in 1893 by Governor John P. Altgeld).

Overnight the shock waves of the Haymarket bombing went rolling across the country as an outraged middle-class public denounced the anarchist workers as "vipers" and "curs," "hyenas" and "serpents." "The only good anarchist is a dead anarchist," a Cincinnati newspaper declared. Haymarket broke the force of direct labor resistance to the new industrial order for nearly a decade. "A single bomb," wrote Samuel Gompers, the organizer of the fledgling American Federation of Labor, "had demolished the eight-hour movement."

Native-born Americans in the so-called comfortable classes, although they were quite wrong in attributing working-class agitation to recently arrived immigrants, nevertheless correctly noted the predominance of the new arrivals in the ranks of the nation's unskilled labor force. Throughout the post–Civil War decades the proportion of immigrants tending machines and performing unskilled tasks in the heavy industries mounted steadily. Where only one in three workers immediately after the Civil War was foreign-born, by the first decade of the new century four out of five steelworkers in Pittsburgh had come from southern or eastern Europe and were entering the work force at the bottom. Wages dipped from $22 a week for native-born white skilled workers to just half that for unskilled "Slavs," a broad category that covered Magyars and Italians, as well as such actual Slavic peoples as Slovaks, Croats, and Russians. Separation by ethnic origin, race, religion, or color divided workers and their families into tight urban enclaves and neighborhoods, each with its own churches, schools, and saloons—French Canadians on the floodplains of New England's mill cities, Slovaks on the cinder piles of Pennsylvania steel towns, African-Americans south of Chicago's teeming stockyards. The urban reformer Jacob Riis (himself Danish-born) described the social surface of New York's Lower East Side as having "more stripes than the skin of a zebra, and more colors than any rainbow." Ethnic neighborhoods were little cities within cities, havens from the impersonality and animosity of the outside world.

Work was being rapidly deskilled by the new forces of technology and new systems of industrial management as machine labor replaced skilled hand work and operatives found themselves at the mercy of the machines they tended. An older artisanal culture of skilled craftsmen who once considered themselves the backbone of America was being shattered by the systematic destruction of their skills and the division of their work routines by efficiency-minded managers. Still, friendship on the shop floor sometimes made work bearable and communication across language barriers possible, as a native-born "greenhorn" from the mid-western countryside learned on his first day on the floor of a steel mill:

> When I started in I figured I'd keep going as long as I could and loaf after I was played out. First the little Italian boy tapped me on the shoulder and advised, "Lotsa time! Take easy!" I slowed down a notch or two. A little later the Russian, wiping off the sweat as he sat for a moment on a pile of bricks, cautioned: "You keel yourself. Twelve hours long time." Finally, after every one had remonstrated, I got down to a proper gait—so you'd have to sight by a post to see if I was moving. But at that I guess they knew better than I—I'm certainly tired enough as it is.

With the huge increase in industrial scale that accompanied the shift from village workshop to urban factory came a new system of organization similar to that being applied to staple-crop agriculture and business and finance by the forces of consolidation and concentration. This new industrial system—impersonal, bureaucratic, mechanized—was designed to run according to the principles of *hierarchy*, which capitalists were beginning to recognize as the key to stable and efficient large-scale industrial operations. Hierarchy built a huge pyramid of productive forces with management at the apex and descending layers of middle managers and superintendents, shop-floor supervisors, foremen, and section bosses, all of them resting on a wide base of unskilled workers. Here, first in the imagination of planners and increasingly in actual fact, was an industrial army whose workings Edward Bellamy described in his utopian novel *Looking Backward* (1888): a gigantic national work force organized along military lines for increased productivity and efficiency with orders passed down the chain of command from the general staff at the top to the lowliest industrial recruit. More a goal than a reality until the twentieth century, this regimen recommended by pioneer scientific managers like Frederick Winslow Taylor promised to make American workers more efficient by fixing "scientifically" what managers considered "an honest day's work" performed by a "first-class man." Scientific management offered business leaders the hope of making the worker over into a human machine whose efficiency could be measured with a stopwatch, and Taylor himself described the ideal industrialist as a supervisor who insists on and gets from his workers discipline, obedience, proper motivation, and hard work. "If a man won't do right, *make* him," he urged.

Here was the view, still on the distant horizon in 1900, of the factory as a moral gymnasium complete with a "military system" to encourage what Taylor called "actual hard work" performed "under careful and constant supervision." In spelling out its logic for the new managers of the industrial work routine, Taylor insisted:

It is only through *enforced* standardization of methods, *enforced* adoption of the best implements and working conditions, and *enforced* cooperation that this faster work can be assured. And the duty of enforcing the adoption of standards and enforcing this cooperation rests with *management* alone.

Even partial implementation of scientific efficiency awaited the twentieth century and the further consolidation of big business, and in the meantime the battle between management and their workers for control of the shop floor continued to rage.

Many businessmen's attitude toward their "labor supply" before 1900 was likely to be that of the steelmaker who admitted to a congressional committee that "if I wanted boiler iron I would go out on the market and buy where I could get it the cheapest, and if I wanted to employ men I would do the same thing." The views of independent shop owners were often more pronounced. "While you are in my workshop," one manufacturer told his workers, "you must conform to my rules. . . . You must not attempt to take the control of the workshop out of my hands." As for American workers' well-known preference for "lager and leisure," Joseph Medill, publisher of the Chicago *Tribune,* warned his readers that the indulgence of the workers must be stopped by teaching them that their "impecunious condition" was the direct result of their "improvidence and misdirected efforts. . . . The wage-classes cannot support in idleness a quarter of a million saloon keepers . . . and at the same time hope to prosper themselves."

To correct such benighted attitudes Terence V. Powderly, who was elected president of the Knights of Labor in 1879, proposed a mass educational campaign to hasten the arrival of the "cooperative commonwealth" when American work-ingmen and women and their bosses would arbitrate their differences and securely establish the "nobility of toil." The Knights inherited their artisanal faith and consensual politics from the original workingmen's parties in Jacksonian America: a solid grounding in republican institutions; firm belief in the centrality of the local community; the cultivation of a hearty "manliness"; and the sustain-ing powers of home and hearth. These time-honored values of skilled craftsmen were now being threatened by the impersonality and the exploitation of the new industrial system, and the Knights were determined to organize in self-defense. Their organizational strategies in many cases looked forward rather than back-ward—to internal coordination among different groups of workers, common presentation of demands, shop committees of representatives from all trades in a mill or plant, and executive boards to handle grievances. Far from seeking to overthrow capitalism, as various groups of American socialists hoped to do after 1880, the Knights of Labor wanted simply to prevent "wage slavery" and to secure "personal dignity" within a more equitably arranged capitalist system. Theirs was a program of mass organization of all workers, education, voluntary cooperation, arbitration with employers, and, only as a last resort, moderate economic sanc-tions. The Knights shared with the Farmers Alliance and the Populists, with whom they made common cause and fashioned a movement culture, a moral economy that rewarded hard work and honest intentions. At the center of this collective dream stood the "new commonwealth" in which mere wealth would give way to standards of honorable work. In appealing to solidarity across class and occupational lines and in assigning government a limited mediational role, the Knights called for moderate production and equitable distribution of wealth, and an ultimate reliance on the community in which so many of its members lived, worked, and organized their local assemblies for fellowship as well as protection.

Matching the Knights of Labor in their sudden rise to prominence in the 1880s and 1890s were the Working Girls Clubs, which managed to outlive their male counterparts. In 1881 the first clubs were organized when women were inducted into the Knights as members. Women workers in the carpet, box, jute, and cigarette factories in the Northeast provided most of the original membership of the clubs, whose organization and growth were encouraged by wealthy philanthropists like Grace Dodge and Josephine Shaw Lowell. Like the local assemblies of the Knights of Labor, the Working Girls Clubs were social as well as labor organizations, and they offered their members classes in dressmaking, sewing, typing, and physical culture, and held evening discussions at which, as one participant explained, "we learn to speak quickly and think readily." The "master workman" who headed Chicago's 50,000-member District 24 was Elizabeth Rodgers, wife of an iron molder and mother of ten children. Like their brother Knights, too, these women sought "cooperation, self-government, self-support" and celebrated a "womanliness" that complemented the Knights' invocation of manly virtue. An anonymous poem in their *Journal of United Labor* put the case for all women who worked:

> We ask not your pity, we charity scorn,
> We ask but the rights to which we were born,
> For the flag of freedom has waved o'er the land,
> We justice and equality claim and demand.
> Then strive for your rights, O sisters dear,
> And ever remember in your own sphere,
> You may aid the cause of all mankind
> And be the true woman that God designed.

The Knights of Labor's educational campaign was aimed at converting employers to acceptance of arbitration and voluntary cooperation and at convincing their membership of the "folly of strikes." But education convinced neither businessmen, who considered union leaders as bad as Civil War secessionists, nor the local assemblies across the country, which began to retaliate against industrial management's attempt to wrest control of hours and wages away from them. With or without union help, workers began to turn to the strike in the mid-1880s as their chief defensive weapon against their employers. There were 477 work stoppages in 1881, nearly 2,000 a decade later, and more than 1,800 at the turn of the century. Strikes were usually responses to sharp wage cuts. The

Great Railroad Strike of 1877, the so-called Great Upheaval on Jay Gould's Southwestern system in 1886, and the rash of railroad strikes culminating in the Pullman Strike of 1894 were all triggered by management's determination to slash wages. The pattern was the same in nearly every industry: strikes followed employers' attempts to increase hours by "grinding" or "driving" workers beyond agreed-on limits or, more frequently, to cut wages during recessions. It was the policy of retaliatory strikes undertaken by local assemblies that broke the power of the Knights of Labor in their disastrous contest with Jay Gould's Texas Pacific Railroad in 1886. Soon thereafter the Knights entered a period of sharp decline—victims of mounting business antagonism, craft-union fears of industrial unionism, and their own decentralized organizational structure.

The American Federation of Labor (AFL), a flexible but conservative organization of craft unions formed in 1886, represented a new generation's coming to terms with the corporate revolution. Workers too could learn the lessons of consolidation. Samuel Gompers, the founder and longtime president of AFL, and his lieutenant, Adolph Strasser, readily confessed that their sole concern was for the skilled trades—carpenters, iron-molders, railroad engineers, and other affiliates—that they represented and for the immediate welfare of their members. When Strasser was asked to define the "ultimate ends" of his organization's "pure and simple unionism," he replied at once that the two terms were contradictory. "We have no ultimate ends. We are going on from day to day. We are fighting for immediate objects—objects that can be realized in a few years."

The new union leaders reminded businessmen that they too were "practical men"—not closet theorists or soft-headed dreamers, but pragmatists and opportunists. Like their employers, the new union leaders were tough-minded organizers with their eyes on the main chance. The distance the AFL had come from the cooperative industrial unionism and the republican hopes of the Knights of Labor could be measured in Gompers's reply to Socialist Morris Hillquit. Bent on discrediting his rival, Hillquit demanded to know whether Gompers really believed that American workers received the "full product" of their labor. Gompers brushed aside the question as meaningless. "I will say," he replied, "that it is impossible for anyone to definitely say what proportion the workers receive as a result of their labor, but it is the fact that due to the organized labor movement they have received and are receiving a larger share of the product of their labor than they ever did in the history of modern society." Irate socialists and labor radicals, many of them friends and mentors from the 1870s and early 1880s, could accuse Gompers of having sold out the movement by refusing to implement a genuine social philosophy. But Gompers had weighed the prospects of a socialist future as well as the promises of a united labor party and found both wanting. Now he and his fellow craft-unionists cheerfully admitted to a chastened belief in half a loaf and a willingness to follow "the lines of least resistance."

"Least resistance" for organized labor as the twentieth century opened meant accepting industrial consolidation and financial concentration, holding government at arm's length, calling for immigration restriction, and bargaining closely with big business—altogether a conservative strategy worthy of the most stalwart corporation head. The trusts, Gompers conceded, "are our employers, and the employer who is fair to us, whether an individual, or a collection of individuals in the form of a corporation or a trust, matters little to us so long as we obtain fair wages." Little, he felt, could now be gained by quarreling with the wage system on which an integrated capitalism rested or by dreaming up pie-in-the-sky substitutes. "The hope for a perfect millennium," Gompers told the United States Industrial Commission, "well, it don't come every night."

Working-Class Life   Workers, packed in slums and ghettos of center cities, knew precisely how far they stood from the margins of the millennium. The quality of life in the working-class districts of most American cities was appalling. For new arrivals from Europe and the American countryside, urban housing—whether three-story wooden firetraps in South Boston or dumb-bell tenements on New York's Lower East Side or dilapidated single-family shanties in Cincinnati, St. Louis, or Chicago—was generally deplorable and, worse still, expensive. Gas, water, electricity, sanitation, and transportation—all the services that were needed to make the life of city workers and their families tolerable—were in short supply and of poor quality as late as 1914. Jacob Riis's *How the Other Half Lives* (1890), an exposé of tenement life on the Lower East Side, described the onset of summer and hot weather along Mulberry Street Bend as the "time of greatest suffering among the poor":

> It is in hot weather, when life indoors is well-nigh unbearable with cooking, sleeping, and working all crowded into the small rooms together, that the tenement expands, reckless of all restraint. Then a strange and picturesque life moves up on the flat roofs. . . . In the stifling July nights, when the big barracks are like fiery furnaces, their very walls giving out absorbed heat, men and women lie in restless, sweltering rows, panting for air and sleep.

The main surge in urban rehabilitation began with the new century, and within a decade municipal services improved, giving cities a public face-lift and a new vitality. But housing and personal standards of living improved much more slowly. The public life of American cities responded to the work of urban reformers with their vision of revived democratic purpose; yet blighted neighborhoods, fractured communities, crumbling apartments, and stunted lives continued as a stark reality for too many American workers.

Recently arrived immigrants who endured these conditions and made up by far the largest portion of the industrial labor force by 1900 faced still another and more subtle kind of exploitation: the cultural drive to "Americanize" them as quickly and thoroughly as possible. All the ethnic groups arriving in such great numbers after 1880—Italians, Greeks, Poles, Russian Jews—were viewed at one time or another as potential bomb throwers who required the saving word and the restraining hand from "100 Percent Americans." Earlier generations had

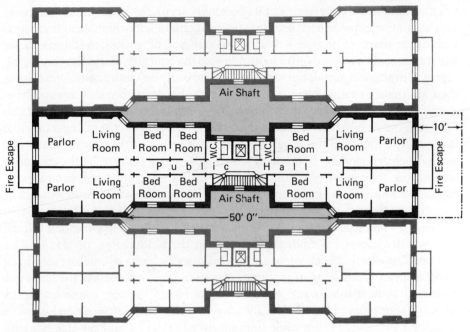

Dumbbell Tenement

In New York City's teeming Lower East Side, most families were crowded into the notorious "dumbell" tenements, seven or eight stories high. Only one room in any apartment in these wooden firetraps received direct sun or air. All the families on each floor shared a toilet in the hall, while in the oppressive heat of July and August people fled to fire escapes and roofs to sleep.

singled out the political party as the chief agent of cultural adjustment; reformers after 1880 emphasized the school as the chief agency of assimilation. As one observer explained to the readers of *World's Work* in 1903, "There are many things in which, as a rule, the public consider that the public schools fail, but one thing that cannot be denied—and it is the greatest—is that these boys and girls of foreign parentage catch readily the simple American ideas of independence and individual work and, with them, social progress." "Social progress" in the half-century after 1880 meant vigorous Americanization: widespread literacy, technological education, elimination of child labor, cultural conformity, and, last but not least, stimulating an aspiring working class's appetite for all the consumer goods produced by the huge American industrial machine.

Just as American businessmen after 1900 continued to form monopolies and oligopolies, and farmers launched their own organizational revolution, so the nation's industrial workers began to adjust their roles to the demands of corporate capitalism. By 1900 a majority of American workers had seemingly come to accept their assignments—and thus they added their weight to the impression of inevitability that the production statistics had created.

But were these impressions of inexorability accurate? Were American workers—both those inside and outside unions—content with their lot and satisfied with their share of the pie? The rising number of strikes, walkouts, work stoppages, and slowdowns after 1900 indicated the contrary, as did the continuing repressive tactics against labor employed by the business community. Were there, then, alternative routes open to the good society that American workers sought— roads not taken or paths only provisionally explored which, had they been followed, might have carried them there? One option was organizing a national labor party much like those being formed in Europe in these same years. For some American workers hopes for a united labor party persisted—the challenge of building their own platform of equity, lifting up committed comrades as candidates from the rank and file, and going to the people to capture control of the political as well as the industrial machinery of the nation. And in fact such partisans of labor politics—alone or in concert with other like-minded reform groups—did succeed periodically throughout the Gilded Age, on the local or state level, in electing a mayor, winning a majority on a city council, or sending a spokesman to a state legislature. But all too often labor's success at the polls was measured in near misses and second-best, as Henry George learned with his United Labor party in New York City's mayoral election of 1886, when he lost to Democrat Abram S. Hewitt while running ahead of the Republican silk-stocking candidate, young Theodore Roosevelt. Local hopes for a genuine national labor contender waxed and waned throughout the Gilded Age, but the road to Washington and the White House seemed a long one.

A second alternative to Gompers's course of least resistance was socialism with its calls for political action or trade-union agitation. These hopes would burn brightest for a minority of American industrial workers after the turn of the century when a loosely organized Socialist party led by Eugene Debs succeeded in winning an increasing number of votes and garnering new recruits. But those achievements lay in the future in 1900 when the obstacles in the road to socialist unity still seemed formidable. First there was the intransigence of an American business community that continued to identify socialism with dangerous "foreigners" and to tell the "reds" to go back where they came from if they didn't like it here. An equally strong set of constraints lay within the American labor movement itself, both native-born workers in whom republican radicalism and Protestant evangelicalism ran deep, and the new immigrant working class— divided by race, ethnicity, and religion and united chiefly in the hope of individual advancement. A majority in both groups in 1900 still shared the promise of achieving success inside a reformed, humanized, and more equitable capitalist system.

The American dream of 1900 remained what it had been a half-century earlier: a vision of a chosen people uniquely equipped to create and enjoy abundance. Economic integration and hugely increased production themselves seemed convincing proof of the near approach of what the journalist Herbert Croly called "the promise of American life." A national market had been built and the nation's shelves stocked with an incredible variety of goods. In this sense the economic well-being of the United States appeared to be exactly what the new corporation heads pronounced it—a single bountiful system binding producers and consumers, citizen and nation, together in a network of mutual obligations and benefits.

But beneath the surface, as the new century began, lay not unity, but multiplicity; not a single all-encompassing national purpose, but competing and even warring interests; not pressures unifying American society, but social forces threatening to fling it apart; not the conservation of national energies, but their diffusion in politically volatile forms. Americans in 1900 thus confronted a paradox capping a half-century of growth: the rapid integration that had seemingly saved them from the waste of competition and economic disorder had set in motion cultural and political counterforces that now threatened fragmentation and isolation. To cope with these threats to national order, Americans would need new and more sophisticated concepts of social change and political organization, and the capacity somehow to use them.

CHRONOLOGY

1873	Panic of 1873 begins six years of depression.	**1886**	AFL (American Federation of Labor) founded. The "Great Upheaval" stops work on Jay Gould's Texas Pacific Railroad. George Westinghouse founds Westinghouse Electric Co. and subsequently perfects use of alternating current.
1876	Alexander Graham Bell invents the telephone.		
1877	Great Railroad Strike.		
1879	Henry George's *Progress and Poverty* published. Thomas Alva Edison perfects the electric light bulb.	**1887**	Interstate Commerce Act passed to control railroads.
1880	Farmers' Agricultural Wheel and National Farmers' Alliance join together to form Southern Alliance.	**1888**	Edward Bellamy's *Looking Backward* published.
		1890	Sherman Antitrust Act passed in attempt to regulate monopolies in restraint of trade. Sherman Silver Purchase Act passed, resulting in depleted gold reserves. At "Battle" of Wounded Knee, South Dakota, federal troops massacre 200 Indians.
1882	John D. Rockefeller's Standard Oil of Ohio consolidates American oil industry under Standard Oil Trust.		
1883	Chicago builds first elevated electric railway. Brooklyn Bridge completed.		
1884	Recession and unemployment jar the economy.	**1891**	Hamlin Garland's *Main-Travelled Roads* describes hardships of

midwestern farmers' lives.
Louis Sullivan's Wainwright
Building completed in St. Louis.

1892 Populists organize; nominate
General James B. Weaver for
president at a national
convention in Omaha.
Grover Cleveland elected
president.
Homestead Strike in Carnegie steel
mills.

1893 Financial panic sends U.S.
economy into four years of
depression.
Repeal of Sherman Silver Purchase
Act.
Historian Frederick Jackson
Turner, in "The Significance of
the American Frontier,"
announces closing of the
frontier.

1894 Pullman Strike broken by federal
troops; Eugene V. Debs jailed.
Henry Demarest Lloyd's *Wealth
Against Commonwealth,* exposé
of Standard Oil Company,
published.

1895 In *U.S. v. E. C. Knight Co,*
government defeated in antitrust
suit against sugar monopoly.

1896 William McKinley elected
president, defeating William

Jennings Bryan and "Free
Silver."

1900 McKinley reelected president,
defeating Bryan once again.
National Civic Federation
established by labor leaders and
industrialists.
Theodore Dreiser's *Sister Carrie,*
naturalistic novel, causes literary
stir.

1901 Theodore Roosevelt becomes
president after McKinley
assassinated.
United States Steel Corporation
formed.

1903 Wright brothers make their first
flight.
National Association of
Manufacturers (NAM) formed.
Citizens Industrial Association
formed to secure open shop in
American industry.

1904 Case of *Northern Securities Co.* v.
U.S. upholds government's case
against railroad mergers.

1911 Triangle Shirtwaist Factory fire in
New York City's East Side kills
146 women; investigation and
revision of state factory codes
follow.

Suggested Readings

There are two outstanding general interpretations of the organizational revolution in American society in the half-century following 1870. A succinct account that remains the model for more recent interpretations is Samuel P. Hays, *The Response to Industrialism* (1957). Robert Wiebe, *The Search for Order* (1968), traces the shift from small-town America to modern mass society in terms of changing political outlooks and social values. Ray Ginger, *The Age of Excess* (1965), is a lively and impressionistic survey, and Howard Mumford Jones, *The Age of Energy: Varieties of American Experience, 1865–1915* (1970), explores Gilded Age manners and morals with sympathy and gusto.

Rodman Paul, *Mining Frontiers of the Far West* (1963), traces the opening of the Mountain West to modern mechanized mining, and Harry Sinclair Drago, *The Great Range Wars* (1985), recounts the stormy history of the early cattle industry. Sandra L. Myres, *Westering Women and the Frontier Experience* (1982), describes the activities of a variety of pioneer women. The literature on native Americans of the trans-Mississippi West is voluminous. Good overviews are Wilcomb E. Washburn, *The Indian in America* (1975), and Robert F. Berkhofer, *The White Man's Indian* (1978). Francis Paul Prucha, *The Great Father: The United States Government and the American Indians* (1984), is an informative and critical analysis of Indian policy.

The best recent overview of the American economy in these years is Stuart Bruchey's brief but perceptive essay, *Growth of the Modern Economy* (1975). The early chapters in Alfred D. Chandler, Jr., *Strategy and Structure: Chapters in the History of American Industrial Enterprise* (1966), provide a compact summary of the first phase of business concentration. Ralph L. Nelson, *Merger Movements in American Industry* (1959), gives a good account of the great merger movement at the end of the nineteenth century, and Hans B. Thorelli, *Federal Antitrust Policy: The Origination of an American Tradition* (1955), traces the course of the countermovement against monopoly. The industrial transformation of the United States is described as a success story in Edward C. Kirkland's survey, *Industry Comes of Age: Business, Labor, and Public Policy, 1860–1897* (1961), which can be read along with Thomas Cochran, *The Inner Revolution* (1965).

For a corrective account of the strategies of large corporations in the late nineteenth century, see Alfred D. Chandler, Jr., *The Visible Hand: The Managerial Revolution in American Business* (1977), and David Montgomery, *The Fall of the House of Labor: The Workplace, the State, and American Labor Activism, 1865–1925* (1987), which follows the attempts of organized labor to cope with the effects of rapid industrialization and new technology on the nation's labor force. For a highly informative account of women in the labor force, see Alice Kessler-Harris, *Out to Work: A History of Wage-Earning Women in the United States* (1982). Thomas P. Hughes, *American Genesis: A Century of Invention and Technological Enthusiasm* (1989), argues the centrality of technological innovation in the modernizing of the United States.

The connections between economic theory and public policy are explored in Sidney Fine, *Laissez-Faire and the General Welfare State* (1956). Richard Hofstadter, *Social Darwinism in American Thought* (1945), and Robert McCloskey, *Conservatism in the Age of Enterprise* (1951), are highly readable accounts of conservative thinking in the Gilded Age. Irvin G. Wyllie, *The Self-Made Man in America* (1954), scrutinizes a venerable American myth, and Edward C. Kirkland's lively essays in *Dream and Thought in the Business Community, 1860–1900* (1956) describe the musings of businessmen on the American social order. For an account of the careers of three notable critics of Gilded Age business practices, see John L. Thomas, *Alternative America: Henry George, Edward Bellamy, Henry Demarest Lloyd and the Adversary Tradition* (1983).

Urban growth and its accompanying problems are admirably summarized in Howard Chudacoff, *Evolution of American Urban Society* (1975), and Zane Miller, *Urbanization of America* (1973). The story of the mounting difficulties of the American farmer is well told in Fred Shannon, *The Farmer's Last Frontier* (1963). For an illuminating study of agrarian politics in the South in this period, see Theodore Saloutos, *Farmer Movements of the South, 1865–1933*. Grant McConnell, *The Decline of Agrarian Democracy* (1953), describes the rise of commercial farming. On American labor there are two useful surveys: Joseph G. Rayback, *A History of American Labor* (1959), and Henry Pelling, *American Labor* (1959). Herbert G. Gutman, *Work, Culture and Society in Industrializing America* (1976), points toward a new synthesis of cultural and labor history, and Daniel T. Rogers, *The Work Ethic in Industrial America, 1850–1920* (1975), examines shifting attitudes toward work that accompanied the industrial transformation of the United States. Daniel Walkowitz, *Worker City, Company Town: Iron and Cotton*

Worker Protest in Troy and Cohoes, New York, 1855–1884 (1978), compares two different social and cultural settings as they determine the responses of industrial workers.

Biographies of leaders in the American industrial revolution are many. Among the best are monumental works: Joseph Wall, *Andrew Carnegie* (1970); Alan Nevins, *Study in Power: John D. Rockefeller, Industrialist and Philanthropist* (2 vols., 1953); Matthew Josephson, *Edison* (1940); and Maury Klein, *The Life and Legend of Jay Gould* (1986).

12

The Politics
of Reform

~

*I*N THE quarter-century after the Civil War, politics appeared to give
Americans a sense of permanence and stability that their economic system
lacked. The Jacksonian generation had first discovered in the political party the
means of containing the disruptive forces of modern democracy until the moral
issue of slavery upset their developmental plans, broke both Whig and Democratic parties wide open, and precipitated a bloody civil war. Now the Jacksonian
generation's sons—the professionals who ruled the Republican and Democratic
parties after 1870—repaired the political system, which they attempted to run
with efficiency and assurance.

Their fragile creation—a new political equilibrium—depended, first of all,
on restoring a regional balance of power. Throughout the Gilded Age the
Republicans sought to include both northeastern workers and midwestern farmers in their plans for rapid business development, and until the 1890s they
continued to dream of competing with the Democrats in the South for the votes
with which to become for the first time a truly national party. The Democrats, for
their part, were busy repairing the broad Jacksonian coalition of southern
planters and northern city bosses, which had been badly shaken by the war. The
calm that seemingly descended on both contestants with the close of Reconstruction was nevertheless deceptive. Both parties remained caught between agendas:
the slavery issue, which had dominated the antebellum political scene, had
disappeared but left in its place the vexing questions of political rights and social
equality for black citizens that neither party was committed to solving. And it
would be another quarter of a century before a younger generation of progressives in both parties acknowledged the need for a program to correct the ills
resulting from rapid and uncontrolled industrialization. In the meantime both
parties struggled with dissidents in their ranks—moral reformers and prohibitionists, women, farmers, industrial workers—whose loyalty they failed to hold
and who periodically broke away to form splinter parties of their own. None of
these third parties, however, proved broad or durable enough to permanently

challenge the rule of the two major parties. It was the resilience and tenacity of Republican and Democratic managers that made both parties seem to their members more stable than they actually were.

Before the Populist revolt in the 1890s, the most serious challenges to the two major parties often came at the local level in municipal elections. In New York City in 1886, for example, the Knights of Labor and the city's trade union assemblies convinced the single-taxer Henry George to enter the mayoralty race against Democratic party stalwart Abram S. Hewitt and the Republican silk-stocking candidate, newcomer Theodore Roosevelt. Underfinanced and beset with severe organizational problems, George and his United Labor party conducted a "tailgate" campaign throughout New York. From early morning until late at night he dashed about the city in his horsecart, haranguing crowds of workers and passersby in neighborhood markets from his movable podium. On a typical day George addressed a group of Franco-Americans on the Lower East Side, met another ethnic gathering in Abingdon Square, spoke to a crowd of railway workers under the El, and closed the day with a huge rally at Sulzer's Harlem River Park at midnight. Told by Republican and Democratic party professionals that he would be "counted out," George proceeded to administer a lesson in popular campaigning by running a respectable second to Democrat Hewitt and garnering nearly 70,000 votes to Roosevelt's 60,000. Yet a year later the United Labor party disintegrated in a factional dispute between socialists and trade unionists, and in a second campaign for secretary of state of New York, George went down to ignominious defeat. Still, major party bosses could be taught a lesson when they ignored the interests of disaffected elements in their parties.

The smooth operation of American politics in the Gilded Age also depended on the mastery of a few basic rules. Chief among them was the principle, accepted by politicians in both parties, that their organizations did not differ in class or economic interests, which were often quite similar, or even in general policies, which were frequently fuzzy. Both Republicans and Democrats were now financed by wealthy citizens whose opinions party leaders carefully acknowledged while maintaining an egalitarian posture before the rest of the country. Party leaders realized that voters seldom approached political questions like the tariff and the currency as clear issues to be decided in reasoned terms. Instead the professionals considered these questions symbols and rallying cries with which to mobilize support for the party and its candidates. The skilled practitioners of Gilded Age politics had learned from the stormy debates of the Civil War years that most American voters' electoral behavior was ultimately determined by images and impressions, prejudices and preferences. Voters might consider themselves both rational and informed, but no office seeker could afford to ignore these vague but deeper forces at work in the political population.

Politicians at various levels of government seeking to instruct the American voter spoke in a variety of tongues and accents in explaining their purposes and setting their agendas. If Gilded Age politics was a search for a national political

Unveiling a Statue
Patriotism and purity combined readily in the Gilded Age imagination.

culture, the actual discovery awaited the arrival of a progressive generation at century's end. Meanwhile the American political language remained polyglot, a babble of competing voices defining the practice of politics in a variety of vocabularies and dialects according to particular interests and needs. Aging Boston Brahmins invoked a lost tradition in calling for the return to a pristine New England political community "during the first years of the century, before the coming of Jacksonian democracy and the invasion of the Irish." The now-triumphant Irish, secure in the fastness of Tammany Hall, listened to the practical advice dispensed by political boss George Washington Plunkitt from his rostrum at the New York County Courthouse bootblack stand concerning the indispensability of patronage. "Men ain't in politics for nothin'," Plunkitt reminded his admirers. "They want to get somethin' out of it. . . . Me and the Republicans are enemies just one day in the year—election day. Then we fight tooth and nail. The rest of the time it's live and let live with us."

> You see, we differ on tariffs and currencies and all them things, but we agree on the main proposition that when a man works in politics, he should get something

out of it. The politicians have got to stand together this way or there wouldn't be any political parties in a short time.

Many big businessmen approached politics and its professional practitioners in much the same spirit of candor with which the railroad buccaneer Collis P. Huntington instructed his lobbyist in Congress: "If you have to pay money to have the right thing done, it is only just and fair to do it. . . . If a man has the power to do great evil and won't do right unless he is bribed to do it, I think the time well spent when it is a man's duty to go up and bribe the judge."

It was the seemingly cozy partnership between businessmen and the politicians that outraged reformers who were determined to dry up the pools of patronage by passing a strong civil service law. Beginning with the Liberal Republican enemies of the Grant administration, who denounced its many scandals as "offensive to every right-thinking man," to the lamentations a decade later of the Mugwumps, those Republican bolters who could not stomach the presidential candidacy of James G. Blaine, "The Continental Liar from the State of Maine," reformers called for the return of the moral law, right reason, probity, and responsibility to the halls of state. Increasingly, as the century neared a close, the reform community invoked the language of medical science and public health in calling voters' attention to the "festering centers" of "urban corruption," the "moral contagions" and "plague spots" of city politics and statehouse rings.

The professionals in both parties responded to the reformers' complaints with open repugnance. Who were these namby-pambys and do-gooders, pursuing their "iridescent dream" of moral purity? demanded Senator John J. Ingalls of Kansas, his words dripping with vitriol. "Man-milliners," "carpet-knights," "dillettanti"—all of them eunuchs, "effeminate without being either masculine or feminine; unable to beget or bear; possessing neither fecundity nor virility, endowed with the contempt of men and the derision of women, and doomed to sterility, isolation, and extinction."

Both Republican and Democratic parties, in fact, were broad-based, non-ideological coalitions that appealed to businessmen, farmers, professionals, and workers. Wealth, political convictions, and social status did not separate Republicans and Democrats as much as did differing clusters of religious, racial, ethnic, and cultural values, which were often tied to older regional outlooks that ran deep into the American past. One way of describing these differences is to examine their roots in the antebellum party system. The Democratic party that Andrew Jackson and his political lieutenants assembled in the second quarter of the nineteenth century marched under the banner of states' rights, limited government, and laissez-faire in cultural as well as economic matters. From its beginnings, Jacksonian orators had preached what Gilded Age Democrats still honored as "the master-wisdom of governing little and leaving as much as possible to localities and individuals," a principle particularly appealing to the South, which was intent on protecting white supremacy against incursions from the North. Local autonomy also proved attractive to religious minorities like

Roman Catholics and Lutherans, as well as newly arrived immigrants intent on preserving their inherited customs and rituals. Throughout the Gilded Age most recent immigrants could be counted on to vote Democratic, a fact of political life wryly acknowledged by Mark Twain in his apocryphal account of an immigrant's first day in the United States. "When he first landed in New York," Twain joked, "he had only halted at Castle Garden for a few minutes to receive and exhibit papers showing that he had resided in this country two years—and then he voted the democratic ticket and went up town to hunt a house."

Democrats in Congress, which they dominated for most of the postwar period, generally followed the advice of one of the party's national spokesmen, Senator William L. Wilson of West Virginia, who insisted that "it is better for some things to be done imperfectly and clumsily than to set up a paternal and bureaucratic government to do them." Democrats generally favored lower tariffs and cheap money, limited government and the avoidance of "the unwholesome progeny of paternalism," by which they meant their Republican opponents. Democratic success in Congress and in the various states in the last thirty years of the century, their spokesmen boasted, was hardly accidental: "It can have no other rational explanation than that the party has been, from the beginning, the guardian and defender of some fundamental principle, or principles, of free government, in whose truth and permanence it has found its life and its growth."

Republicans also traced their antebellum ancestry across the Civil War, which had strengthened the party's nationalist proclivities. Like their Whig forebears, Republicans believed in energetic government charged with promoting growth and well-being, which they nurtured by admitting new states to the union in order to strengthen their political grip, underwriting a national railroad system, distributing public lands freely, enacting protective tariffs to favor a developing American industry, and regularly denouncing their do-nothing Democratic opposition (just as their Whig fathers had reviled the Jacksonians) as a "standing menace to the prosperity of the country." Before the Civil War, governmental activism had combined with a strong middle-class morality to give the Republican party a reformist thrust directed at the evils of slavery, intemperance, and personal immorality. Whig and Republican party members were primarily Protestant, predominantly of native stock or Anglo-Saxon descent, aggressively reform-minded, and eager to use government at all levels to impose their promotional schemes and behavioral standards on the rest of the community. George F. Hoar, the venerable Republican senator from Massachusetts, drew on all these moral resources after the war when he described his party as still composed of "the men who do the work of piety and charity in our churches, the men who administer our school systems, the men who own and till their own farms, the men who perform the skilled labor in the shops." The bitterly partisan Republican campaigner Robert Ingersoll was less charitable in naming the sins of the Democrats for an audience of midwestern farmers: "I believe in a party that believes in good crops.... The Democratic Party is a party of famine; it is a friend of the early frost; it believes in the Colorado beetle and the weevil."

Women's Temperance Movement
A local demonstration in Ohio by women against the saloon.

Business and financial interests steadily infiltrated the Republican party after 1880, but it continued to attract a broad range of social moralists—prohibitionists, sabbatarians, blue-law advocates, and moral reformers of every sort. Only at the end of the century had these evangelical types become marginal enough in the party as a whole for the managers to cast them aside as political liabilities in a new age of fund-raising and full campaign coffers.

Lacking the Republican concern with the mote in its neighbor's eye, the more permissive Democratic party seemed very different from its rival. It embraced Catholics as well as Protestants, and it claimed a tolerance of immigrants who lacked the compulsive morality of the native-born. Democrats continued to preach a "personal liberty" that was thought safest when government was kept minimal and local. The New York party organization expressed this viewpoint clearly when in 1881, harking back to the pronouncements of Andrew Jackson, it declared itself "unalterably opposed to centralization of power in either state or federal governments." While Republicans expected all government to be generous and active, Democrats hoped to keep it grudging and stingy, if only to check the Anglo-Saxon Republicans' "cultural imperialism" toward immigrants, as well as to curb the Republicans' appetite for patronage. Thus the differences between the two parties in 1880 were real, but they derived as much from ethnic origins, religious backgrounds, and cultural outlook as from strict class or economic interest.

This pattern of politics survived until the last decade of the century, when suddenly the very idea of party rule came under attack by a younger generation of political reformers. By 1890 rural Populists and urban progressives were challenging the code of business as usual and forcing the professionals in both parties to respond to new pressures. Out of their revolt came a transformation of politics that paralleled the revolution in the national economy and created new forms in the American political process, along with new ways of ordering it.

The Politics of Equilibrium

The Civil War shaped the thinking and molded the political behavior of Americans for a generation. Gilded Age politicians succeeded in tapping the emotions that had been aroused by the war in both sections of the country. They were able, first of all, to inspire remarkably high levels of voting. In the six presidential elections between 1876 and 1896, an average of 78.5 percent of the country's eligible voters actually voted, and an equally impressive 62.8 percent turned out for off-year elections. (In the late twentieth century, even presidential elections bring slightly less than half the eligible voters to the polls.) If political democracy is measured by a high rate of voter participation, then the Gilded Age remained flamboyantly, defiantly democratic despite its glaring social and economic inequalities.

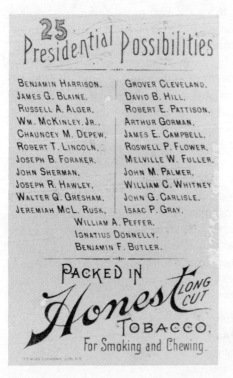

Advertising the Product
An advertising card inside a package of chewing tobacco listed nearly all of the available candidates from three parties in the presidential election of 1892.

The voting patterns remained strikingly consistent. Whether they marched to the polls behind candidates waving the "bloody shirt"—the Radical Republicans' vengeful rhetoric aimed at preserving northern hostilities toward the South—or stirred to memories of the Confederacy's Lost Cause, voters across the nation kept alive the Civil War even after the constitutional and ideological struggles of Reconstruction had ended. Joining enthusiastically in campaigns that came complete with mounted military troopers and fancy drill teams, they made national elections extremely close. Sixteen states could always be counted on to go Republican; fourteen just as regularly voted Democratic. Presidential elections were usually decided by the voters in five key states— Connecticut, New York, Indiana, Nevada, and California. Between 1872 and 1912 the Republicans held a grip on the presidency that was broken only by Grover Cleveland's two victories in 1884 and 1892. They appeared to be a well-established majority party. But in fact the Democrats controlled the House of Representatives with sizable majorities in seven out of ten congressional elections. In key states the margins of victory were perilously thin, particularly in New York and Indiana. With such intense competition and close contests, winners were not only lucky but often surprised. In the three presidential elections in the 1880s, the victor edged out his closest opponent by less than 1 percent. In the election of James A. Garfield in 1880 and of Cleveland in 1884, fewer than 25,000 votes separated the candidates. In 1888 the winner in electoral votes, the Republican Benjamin Harrison, received fewer popular votes than did Cleveland, the loser.

Party Lines Drawn   Throughout the 1880s the two parties remained drawn up against each other like two equally matched armies, their skirmishes resembling the engagements of the still-familiar Civil War. Political rhetoric featured famous military figures well into the decade—in songs, war whoops, and speeches by bewhiskered colonels "late of the Confederate Army" or beribboned commissary generals of the Grand Army of the Republic. The presidential election of 1880 pitted two former Union generals against each other—forty-eight-year-old James A. Garfield, Republican from Ohio, matched against General Winfield Scott Hancock, hero of Gettysburg and able military governor of Texas and Louisiana under congressional Reconstruction. Hancock's superb war record did not save him from sustained Republican attacks on his family as former Rebel sympathizers or canards on his supposed battlefield cowardice despite glowing tributes to his heroism from former President Grant. Then the Republicans shifted from slander to scare tactics, warning of the rise of a "Solid South" and the danger of a Democratic administration that would reimburse all Confederates for property damage done during the war and vote huge pensions for Confederate veterans. A Garfield campaign song singled out for ridicule black disfranchisement in the New South:

> *Sing a song of shotguns,*
> *Pocket full of knives,*
> *Four-and-twenty black men*

Republicans Celebrate Patriotism
*The Republican national convention at Chicago, June 2, 1880 invoked "Independent
America—The home of the freeman, where the humblest citizen can attain the highest honors
in the gift of her people."*

> *Running for their lives,*
> *When the polls are open*
> *Shut the nigger's mouth,*
> *Isn't that a bully way*
> *To make a solid South?*

Democrats countered with time-worn charges of corruption and the $329 bribe
presumably tendered Garfield in the Crédit Mobilier scandal in 1868, and by
exposing the misdeeds of Garfield's running mate, the notorious New York
custom house spoilsman Chester A. Arthur. A campaign long on personal
vituperation but short on issues still turned out the voters—three-quarters of all
those eligible—who provided "Boatman Jim" Garfield with a 10,000 popular
majority out of 9 million votes cast.

The median age of voters in the Gilded Age was thirty-seven, and so generally
they had arrived at political maturity under the guidance of fathers who had
fought to preserve the "glorious Union" or to rescue a "prostrate nation." Ticket
splitting suggested a lack of patriotism, and the voter who switched parties was
regarded as little better than a bounty jumper. Novelist Brand Whitlock remembered that in his youth being a Republican was "a fundamental and self-evident
thing....It was merely a synonym for patriotism, another name for the

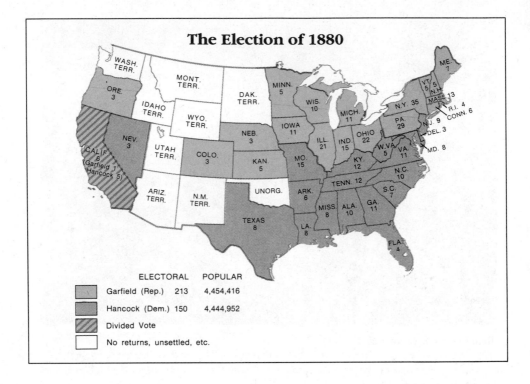

The Election of 1880

ELECTORAL   POPULAR
Garfield (Rep.)   213   4,454,416
Hancock (Dem.)   150   4,444,952
Divided Vote
No returns, unsettled, etc.

nation. . . . It was inconceivable that any self-respecting person should be a Democrat." Nor was it likely that in the South, increasingly solid in its support of the Democracy, a true gentlemen would require any greater comfort than the assurance given by Bourbon conservatives that "the nation as a nation, will have nothing more to do with the Negro."

Yet for all its apparent stability, politics in this era was in the process of transformation—the same stage of transformation that small-scale entrepreneurial capitalism was undergoing. Newly arrived immigrants were urban consumers in need of jobs, favors, and services. The political boss of Boston's South End, Martin Lomasney, once lectured the journalist Lincoln Steffens on the indispensability of the boss and his political machine: "There's got to be in every ward somebody that any bloke can come to—no matter what he's done—and get help. Help, you understand, none of your law and justice, but help." Here in crowded neighborhoods was a vast human market in which a wise investment of political capital could pay off handsomely. The new business of politics, unlike more established concerns, was open at the bottom to fresh talent and offered unlimited opportunity for making good and getting ahead. As an organizer and go-getter, the professional politician—ward heeler, precinct captain, county chairman, state assemblyman, or senatorial aspirant—was a salesman who had to know the buying habits of every prospective customer in his territory.

George Washington Plunkitt, one of the leaders of New York City's Democratic organization Tammany Hall, described the political district in terms familiar to every salesman out of New York or Chicago with a territory to cover, concluding: "If he holds his district and Tammany is in power, he is amply rewarded by a good office and the opportunities that go with it." The Gilded Age boss was the Horatio Alger rags-to-riches hero, in ward heeler's attire, sporting a campaign button. "Yes, many of our men have grown rich in politics," Plunkitt confided. "I have myself. I've made a big fortune out of the game, and I'm gettin' richer every day." The shortest route to success in the business of politics lay through the upstairs room at party headquarters, where the sign over the door read "Never closed."

The Urban Political Boss
From the city to the Senate, politics in the Gilded Age constituted a revitalized patronage society that in some ways resembled its eighteenth-century ancestor. Under the guiding hand and sharp eye of the boss, political power was organized vertically within the machine in a hierarchical system of patrons and clients. The style of the Gilded Age boss was new and coarse, more personalized and direct than that of his gentleman predecessor. To reform critics, among them Moisei Ostrogorski, whose *Democracy and the Organization of Political Parties* summed up the reformers' indictment of machine politics, the political boss was an all-powerful leader, unsleeping, devious, and ruthless, who commanded solely through "his strength of will, his cleverness, his audacity and his luck." In short, he was Niccolò Machiavelli's Renaissance prince come to life. As Ostrogorski described the political boss:

> To this one he lends a dollar; for another he obtains a railroad ticket without payment; he has coal distributed in the depth of winter; he makes gifts of other kinds; he sometimes sends poultry at Christmas time; he buys medicine for a sick person; he helps bury the dead by procuring a coffin on credit or half-price. He has a kind heart in virtue of his position and his position gives him the means of satisfying his need for kindness: the money which he distributes comes from the chest of the Machine; the latter has obtained it by the most reprehensible methods...but no matter. With this money he can also dispense an ample hospitality in the drinking saloons. As soon as he comes in, friends known and unknown gather round him, and he treats everybody, he orders one drink after another for the company; he is the only one who does not drink; he is on duty.

The urban machine's stock in trade was jobs and appointments, transit franchises, paving contracts, public construction bids, licenses, permits, and a hundred other salable items needed to conduct the business of the nation's cities. These were the methods perfected by Tammany boss Richard Croker in New York City after 1880. Croker maintained firm control over all municipal purchases by granting favors to friendly businessmen in whose concerns he took both a public interest and a handsome slice of honest graft for himself. Reformers forced Croker's resignation in the early 1890s following an investigation of police corruption, but soon he was back as head of Tammany, holding court at the Democratic Club on Fifth Avenue to thirty-five district leaders from whom he continued to exact tribute before being ousted by the reform forces of Mayor Seth Low in 1901.

In Philadelphia, Republican boss "King" James McManes ruled unopposed for two decades by controlling the city's finances through his adroit management of the board in charge of the municipal gas utility, which he used as a base for extending his power to the rest of the bureaucracy, collecting payoffs from contractors and kickbacks from city employees. Like many of the bosses, McManes grew rich on the spoils of office as he proceeded to increase the municipal debt by 350 percent. In Chicago, which lacked a strong boss with centralized authority, machine politics was more casual and confused with each ward the fiefdom of a highly visible ward boss: in the Nineteenth Ward, Johnny Powers came to be known as "The Chief Mourner" because of his unblemished record in attending the funerals of friends and supporters. Michael "Hinky Dink" Kenna and his colleague "Bathhouse" John Coughlin presided over the famous First Ward from his saloon, where he dispensed favors and a free lunch. "King" Michael McDonald's power in his bailiwick rested on a string of gambling houses, while the West Side belonged to the "Blond Boss" William Lorimer, the only Republican chieftain in the city.

Virtually every major city in the country experienced some form of boss rule—Democratic or Republican—in the half-century following the Civil War: Abe Ruef in San Francisco; Martin Behrman in New Orleans; Christopher Magee in Pittsburgh; the Pendergast brothers in Kansas City; and Edward Crump in Jersey City. The explanation for such concentrations of power is quite simple: city bosses with their machines were attempting to impose the same kind of order and system over their sprawling empires that businessmen sought in industrial and financial consolidation. The impulse motivating the city boss was essentially conservative: the need to bring a semblance of method and predictability in the running of his city. "Politics ain't bean bag," observed the Chicago Irish saloonkeeper Mr. Dooley, the fictional creation of the humorist Finley Peter Dunne. "'Tis a man's game; an' women, childher, an' prohybitionists do well to keep out iv it." The reformer, bosses knew, always suffered from innocence and amateurism. "He hasn't been brought up in the difficult business of politics," Plunkitt of Tammany Hall complained, "and he makes a mess of it every time." Bosses in all the metropolitan centers of the nation watched the aimless spreading of their cities and understood the problem of managing them. Their domains, they realized, were fragmented like giant jigsaw puzzles. Only a professional could provide the liberal application of patronage to glue them together, even though his workmanship might be both slipshod and expensive. All the boss's accomplishments—from new courthouses to public parks, transit systems to street lighting—came at the price of widespread corruption, waste, and an astronomical increase in the city's bonded debt.

Yet bosses seldom achieved the efficiency they sought. At best they built oligarchies and presided over loose federations of wards and precincts. In the 1890s the bosses' failings in efficiency and accountability would give progressive reformers much ammunition in attacking the urban machines. Meanwhile, in the absence of a genuine science of administration and of a corps of professional managers to apply it, the bosses at least provided a minimum of order and services—however lavishly and corruptly they improvised with the materials at hand.

Patronage Politics in the States   In the years immediately following the Civil War state bosses like Roscoe Conkling in New York and James G. Blaine, the "plumed knight" from Maine, were highly visible and colorful figures who organized their state parties while cultivating the arts of demagoguery and personal invective in Congress. Both these leaders were practiced congressional showmen and consummate haters with long memories. In fact, Conkling, head of the "Stalwart" faction of the Republican party, and Blaine, chief of the "Half-Breeds," were bitter rivals for control of federal patronage and cordially hated each other. Throughout the 1870s members of the House witnessed a series of verbal skirmishes. When, for example, Blaine learned from colleagues that the domineering and conceited Conkling had announced that the mantle of the famed Civil War orator Henry Winter Davis had fallen on himself, Blaine rose to demolish the "Turkey Gobbler" from New York with masterful sarcasm:

> The resemblance is striking. Hyperion to a satyr, Thersites to Hercules, mud to marble, dunghill to diamond, a singed cat to a Bengal tiger, a whining puppy to a roaring lion. Shade of the mighty Davis, forgive the almost profanation of that jocose satire.

By the 1880s, however, a younger generation of political leaders was taking over and quietly seizing control in many states by recruiting loyal followers and building efficient organizations. In New York, Thomas C. Platt, known to his friends as the "Easy Boss" and to his Democratic opponents as "Mousy," replaced the flamboyant Roscoe Conkling. Platt conducted party business on the sabbath at his "Sunday School" at the Amen Corner of the Fifth Avenue Hotel in New York City, where, it was said, vigorous "amens" from the assembled congregation of the faithful ratified his various nominations for governor, state senator, supreme court judge, or member of Congress. Platt's specialty was the "arrangement" with eager business interests whose spokesmen in turn regarded him as eminently "safe" and "sound." He was also a master of careful preparation for elections—what he called his "subsoil" work—and dispensed campaign funds with an unerring sense of the political odds. The New York State Assembly regularly did Platt's undemonstrative bidding, bottling up unwanted bills in committee and tailoring requested legislation to the Easy Boss's specifications. Friends and foes alike widely recognized Platt as the model of the new party leader whom one of his protégés, Elihu Root, described as the supreme power broker, "elected by no one, accountable to no one, bound by no oath of office, removable by no one."

Next door in Pennsylvania the Republican state boss was the sad-eyed, cynical calculator of his own strengths and other people's weaknesses, Matthew Quay, a veteran party man who had worked his way to the top of the political heap after twenty-five years' service. Matt Quay ran his statehouse ring out of his office in Harrisburg, which held his voluminous card-index files—"Quay's coffins"—containing useful information on every political figure in the state. The secret of Quay's success, like that of Platt in New York, was the quiet accommodation reached with the Pennsylvania Railroad, the directors of the Iron and Steel Association, and public-utility company executives whose needs he tended carefully and who were the principal beneficiaries of his silent rule.

The key device for harmonizing party interests at the state level was the caucus, where local bosses, county chairmen, and state legislators gathered to consult friendly business interests and stamp approval on the state boss's choice of candidates. But the real work was often done in advance and on the sly. Michigan boss James McMillan explained to his followers how his rise to the Senate only proved "what quiet work and an active continuance of party organization can accomplish.... When party organization is perfect, campaigns are more easily conducted and victory more certain."

Democratic party bosses won control over their states more slowly than Republicans, and, particularly in the one-party South, kept a looser grip on the party reins. Yet southern Democratic, or "Bourbon," conservatism soon became the model for longtime Democrats who continued to invoke the name of Jefferson in deploring the "spirit of centralization" while silently employing just that principle in staffing and strengthening their county cliques and statehouse operations. In both parties, as in the business world after 1880, concentration was the order of the day.

A New Breed of Professionals　　As late as 1880, however, much remained to be done. Democrats in that election year were entering the third decade of their prolonged period as the opposition party, and they still suffered from unimaginative leadership, a negative program, and a philosophy of "go slow." The Republican party had also fallen on evil days. Republicans had spent the 1870s watching their share of the popular vote dwindle and their hopes for holding the South dim and then disappear. In 1880 the party was still torn by contending factions—Conkling's "Stalwarts" and Blaine's "Half-Breeds." These factional squabbles concerned patronage rather than matters of policy, but they were serious enough to deadlock the Republican convention in 1880 and send delegates scurrying for a compromise candidate, James A. Garfield. Having gone down to defeat with three civilian contenders since the Civil War, Democrats decided to follow their Republican rival's example and try their luck with the military by nominating General Hancock, the hero of Gettysburg. From now on a new note of caution and calculation could be heard in the deliberations of the two major parties, both of which recognized the need for prudence and forethought in the tending of their political gardens.

Nevertheless the veteran professionals of the Civil War era stood firm against innovation and reform, inveighing against the nefarious plots of would-be reformers who sought to put them out of business with a federal bureaucracy free from political influence and the taint of corruption. For the old professionals in both parties, politics could not be cut and trimmed by moral shears or patched together with the principles of reform. Dismissing reform as contrary to human nature, and ridiculing its champions as long-haired men and short-haired women, the bosses snarled their defiance in crude and unambiguous language. Let the civil service reformers remain in their well-furnished parlors, exchanging rumors of political misbehavior while sipping their lemonade, declared Kansas Senator John J. Ingalls. The real world, the Ingallses and Blaines and Conklings insisted, was their own world of full whiskey tumblers and cigar smoke, fifteen-dollar votes, rolling logs, and brimming pork barrels.

But the day of the spoilsmen was ending, a political fact acknowledged even by the once-irreconcilable Ingalls himself, who likened the new political age to the long-extinct pterodactyl—the winged reptile with feathers on its paws and plumes on its tail. A political system in the chain of evolution that accommodated both the party loyalist and the reformer, Ingalls scoffed, "can properly be regarded as in the transition epoch and characterized as the pterodactyl of politics. It is, like that animal, equally adapted to waddling and dabbling in the slime and mud of partisan politics, and soaring aloft with discordant cries into the glittering and opalescent empyrean of civil service reform." In any event politics as usual was doomed to extinction.

Thus as the presidential election of 1880 approached and neither party appeared to have a decided edge, the professionals' confidence in the robust style and principle-be-damned began to evaporate. In subsequent presidential contests down to the turn of the century the new cautionary political style and prudential approach to policy was unmistakable, and nowhere was it more evident than among a new breed of presidential contenders.

The Lost Decade

The twentieth-century novelist Thomas Wolfe once observed that for most Americans the Gilded Age presidents from Hayes to Harrison have become irretrievably lost:

> their gravely vacant and bewhiskered faces mixed, melted . . . together in the sea-depths of a past, intangible, immeasurable, and unknowable. . . . For who was Garfield, martyred man, and who had seen him in the streets of life? . . . Who had heard the casual and familiar tones of Chester Arthur? and where was Harrison? Where was Hayes? Which had the whiskers, which the burnsides; which was which?

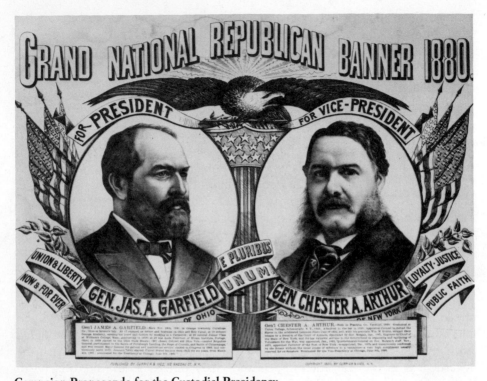

Campaign Propaganda for the Custodial Presidency
The "Grand National Republican Banner" provides the answer to Thomas Wolfe's question: "Which had the whiskers, which the burnsides; which was which?"

The limited concept of the presidential office in the Gilded Age, and the equally limited political imaginations of the men who filled it, consigned these shadowy figures to oblivion.

The Shadow Presidents   The principal task assigned to these presidents by party managers in Congress was to get themselves elected without compromising their reputations by saying anything provocative, and then to dispense patronage dutifully to the party worthies. Winning the presidency was not easy, especially when no clear-cut issues of public policy divided the two parties. James Bryce, the British minister in Washington who observed his first presidential election in 1884 in the heated contest between Blaine and Cleveland, was amazed to find that neither party had a distinctive platform: "Neither party has any principles, any distinctive tenets. Both have traditions. Both claim to have tendencies. . . . All has been lost, except office or the hope of it."

Once elected, the new president found that the first order of business was handing out jobs, a process that was complicated, time-consuming, and personally demeaning. Immediately following his nomination in the summer of 1880,

Garfield received his orders from Stephen Dorsey, field marshal of the Republican National Committee, who insisted imperiously on a hurried conference with Roscoe Conkling and the other eastern bosses as "an absolute essential to success in this campaign."

> They want to know whether the Republicans of the State of New York are to be recognized...or whether the "Scratchers" and Independents and "featherheads" are to ride over the Republican party of this state as they have for the last four years. They...can only be satisfied by a personal conference with you.

Garfield later claimed that he hadn't given out any "mortgages" at the conference. "No trades, no shackles," he noted in his diary, but wondered whether the New Yorkers had been properly mollified. "My letters indicate that the New York trip did no harm and much good." In his brief time in office, Garfield was exhausted by job hunters, although he had been chosen by Republican bosses precisely for his sensitivity to the patronage demands of the party's warring factions. Soon after his inauguration in March 1881, Garfield's mutterings about party office seekers swelled to a sustained wail: "My God! What is there in this place that a man should ever want to get into it?" He was not to remain in it long. In July 1881, as Garfield was boarding a train in Washington for a well-earned vacation, a crazed government clerk who had recently been dismissed shot him in the back. Garfield lingered through the summer and died in September. "I am a Stalwart," Charles Guiteau had shouted as he fired at Garfield, "and Arthur is President now."

"My God! Chet Arthur!" was the response of liberal Republicans and Democrats alike at the prospect of four years of boss rule by a veteran spoilsman. Chester A. Arthur, former head of the corrupt New York customhouse and loyal lieutenant of Roscoe Conkling, had been given second place on the ticket chiefly to placate New York's Stalwart faction, as Garfield was widely recognized as a protégé of Blaine and his Half-Breeds. Arthur was jovial, suave, accommodating, and thoroughly hardened to the work of dispensing patronage. He once explained his political philosophy to a fellow Republican as the honest brokerage of competing interests. Elections, he warned, are won only *"when all the men in politics* are pleased and satisfied and set to work with enthusiasm for the ticket. They bring out the votes, and if you trusted these elections to business men and *merely respectable influences,* the Democratic Party would get in every time." The new president genially oversaw the staffing of the federal bureaucracy with party hacks even as he signed the Pendleton Act (1883), which established the independent Civil Service Commission charged with classifying federal jobs and with administering examinations. In two notable respects Arthur surprised his critics: he urged the prosecution of those involved in the fraudulent Star Route postal contracts, and he vetoed an unprecedented $18 million rivers and harbors bill. The fact that the Star Route prosecutions failed and that Congress passed the pork-barrel appropriation over his veto in no way lessened the surprise and

appreciation of liberals and reformers in both parties who agreed, on his retirement, that Chet Arthur "had done well...by not doing anything bad."

In 1885 it was Grover Cleveland's turn to suffer the demands both of
Democratic bosses clamoring for jobs and of civil service hopefuls bent on
cleaning up the spoils system. Cleveland, like Garfield before him, endured a
"nightmare" and complained constantly about "this dreadful, damnable office
seeking." Cleveland's discomfort was the sharper because he had made his
political fortune out of reform, first as the so-called Veto Mayor of Buffalo, New
York, where he got rid of corrupt street-cleaning and sewer contracts, and then in
the governorship of New York, where he quickly became known as the "Great
Obstructionist" of the special interests. The "Big One," as the young
assemblyman Theodore Roosevelt called him, looked the part of the reform-
minded man of integrity—a massive three hundred pounds of jut-jawed, rocklike
imperturbability—who called for "the application of business principles to
public affairs" and perfected the veto as his chief weapon.

The Republicans had chosen as their 1884 standard-bearer the perennial
public favorite and scourge of the Democracy James G. Blaine. This move had
made Cleveland the obvious "reform" preference of the Democrats along with
those disaffected Republicans (called variously "Mugwumps," "Holy Willies,"
"Dudes," and "Goody-Goodies" by the party regulars) who could not stomach
the unsavory Blaine and bolted their party in the hope of destroying both the
"Plumed Knight" and the spoils system. Still, genuine issues dividing the two
contenders were difficult to discern. Blaine concentrated on the tariff, a recently
discovered bone of contention, and Cleveland stressed his leadership of a "far-
reaching moral movement," which left the two candidates much like Tweedledee
and Tweedledum. Both men, Lord Bryce noted with amusement, openly declared
their unyielding enmity to monopolies, their love of the flag, and their determination to defend the rights of Americans around the globe. Neither was willing to
venture beyond these patriotic pronouncements to the uncertain ground of
policy, and it was only a question of time before the issues became highly
personalized and cheapened into a contest, as one observer commented, between
"the copulative habits of one and the prevaricative habits of the other."

The presidential campaign of 1884 was a comedy of errors that dramatized
the poverty of ideas besetting both parties. Republican and Democratic national
organizations were equally matched. With firm control over the South, the
Democracy contended on even terms with its opponents in all the key northern
states by avoiding discussion of the tariff issue wherever possible. For their part,
Republicans had only recently discovered the tariff as a campaign issue with
which they were nervously testing the political waters. With no genuine policy
differences at stake, professional managers on both sides resorted to slander and
character assassination. The Republicans led off with a report of Cleveland's early
departure from the paths of righteousness in fathering a child out of wedlock
with a young widow who seemingly had "loved too well." Partisan press and
pulpit denounced Cleveland as a "moral leper," "a gross and licentious man,"

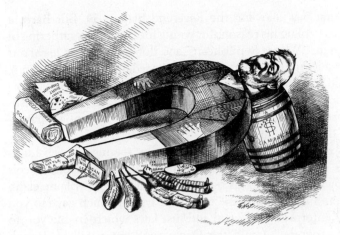

"Magnetic" Blaine
This Democratic party cartoon ridicules James G. Blaine as a magnet for corruption and chicanery in the presidential election of 1884.

and "a man stained with disgusting infamy." Stunned Democratic managers who brought the news to Cleveland were further astounded by the candidate's admission that the story, if exaggerated, was nevertheless true. "Above all," Cleveland instructed his lieutenants, "tell the truth."

Democrats, who needed something stronger than the truth with which to fend off Republican attacks, found their weapon in another batch of the Mulligan letters published by the Boston press and further implicating Blaine in the railroad scandals of the late 1860s. Among the telltale letters was one that Blaine himself had written, exonerating him from all charges of misconduct, which he had sent to Warren Fisher, a railroad attorney, to sign. "The letter is strictly true," Blaine explained, "is honorable to you and me, and will stop the mouths of slanderers at once. Regard this letter as strictly confidential." Blaine closed his instructions with the reminder that in signing the letter Fisher would be doing him "a favor I shall never forget" and a final command to "burn this letter." Here was the ready means of defending "Grover the Good," which Democrats so badly needed. Soon came a spate of songs, rallying cries, and chants:

> *Ma, Ma!*
> *Where's my pa?*
> *Gone to the White House*
> *Ha! ha! ha!*

and

> *Blaine! Blaine!*
> *The Continental Liar*
> *From the State of Maine!*
> *Burn this letter!*

By election eve it was clear that victory would hinge on New York's 36 electoral votes, and at the last moment Republican managers made two fatal miscalculations. The first was allowing the Reverend Samuel D. Burchard, a Presbyterian minister, to explain his reasons for voting for Blaine to a gathering of New York City clergymen: "We are Republicans, and don't propose to leave our party and identify ourselves with a party whose antecedents have been Rum, Romanism, and Rebellion." When Blaine neglected to disavow Burchard's unfortunate remark, Democrats seized the opportunity to secure the city's Irish-American vote by spreading thousands of handbills with the inflammatory statement throughout the city.

Blaine's managers only compounded his troubles by staging a lavish fundraiser for New York's millionaires in the glittering ballroom of Delmonico's restaurant where, following a sumptuous banquet, they listened to Blaine claim credit for "organizing and maintaining the industrial system which gave to you and your associates in enterprise the equal and just laws which enable you to make this marvellous progress." Again the Democratic press, led by Joseph Pulitzer's *New York World,* exploited the Republicans' mistake in bold headlines. Above a cartoon showing fat capitalists in diamond-studded boiled shirts gathered around the groaning board blazed the headline:

THE ROYAL FEAST OF BELSHAZZAR BLAINE AND
THE MONEY KINGS
BLAINE HOBNOBBING WITH THE MIGHTY MONEY KINGS
MILLIONAIRES AND MONOPOLISTS SEAL THEIR ALLEGIANCE
AN OCCASION FOR THE COLLECTION OF A REPUBLICAN
CORRUPTION FUND

Blaine lost New York by 1,149 votes out of more than a million cast, enough to give Cleveland the election in a national count, which provided the Democrats with a margin of 23,000 votes out of more than 9 million cast. Blaine explained his defeat as the result of an "intolerant and utterly improper remark," and added ruefully: "I should have carried New York by 10,000 if the weather had been clear on election day, and Dr. Burchard had been doing missionary work in Asia Minor or Cochin China."

As president, Cleveland attempted to play the role of the realistic reformer. He admitted, however, that the "boss system" survived in American politics, and because it did, it was a necessity—"a disagreeable necessity, I assure you"—for him to recognize it. Approached by a prominent Democratic senator with a complaint about his strict policy regarding appointments, Cleveland asked what he wanted the president to do. "Why, Mr. President, I should like to see you move more expeditiously in advancing the principles of the Democracy." "Ah," Cleveland shot back, "I suppose you mean that I should appoint two horse-thieves a day, instead of one." Cleveland managed to double the number of jobs covered under civil service from 14,000 to 28,000, at the same time appointing his own people to all the jobs left untouched by the Pendleton Act. He had not been elected "merely for the purpose of civil service," he reminded his reform critics, and asked to be saved from "the misguided zeal of impracticable friends." No one could accuse Grover Cleveland of pandering to reform!

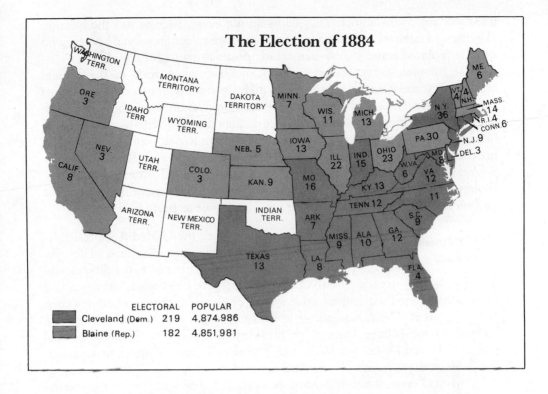

The Election of 1884

	ELECTORAL	POPULAR
Cleveland (Dem.)	219	4,874,986
Blaine (Rep.)	182	4,851,981

Cleveland had greater success in checking the abuses in awarding veterans' pensions. "We are dealing with pensions, not with gratuities," he reminded Congress, but many of the pension claims were as specious as the one presented by a man who had hurt his ankle while *intending* to enlist. In 1866 there were 126,722 pensioners paid a total of $15.5 million. In 1885 there were 345,125 recipients of $65,171,937. Cleveland personally inspected each and every pension bill passed by Congress, and then resorted to his favorite weapon—the presidential veto. In his first administration he vetoed over one hundred such bills.

Benjamin Harrison, a prosperous railroad lawyer from Indiana and grandson of "Old Tippecanoe," President William Henry Harrison, narrowly defeated Cleveland in his bid for reelection in what was probably the most corrupt presidential election in American history. He then announced that "providence" had awarded his party a great victory. "He ought to know," snorted Matt Quay, the Republican boss of Pennsylvania, "that Providence hadn't a damn thing to do with it." Harrison, he added, would never know "how close a number of men were compelled to approach the gates of the penitentiary to make him President." The new president—whose personality, one observer noted, had all the warmth of a "dripping cave"—was scarcely the man to meddle in patronage matters. "When I came into power," he recalled for a group of Republican leaders, "I found that the party managers had taken it all to themselves. I could not name my own Cabinet. They had sold out every place to pay the election expenses." Harrison continued to leave patronage to congressional bosses, who quickly replaced some 30,000 Democratic postmasters with Republicans.

Yet by 1890 the civil service principle had taken root in the federal bureaucracy, and it continued to grow until by 1900 there were 100,000 positions subject to rules enforced by the Civil Service Commission. The gradual triumph of civil service affected the president's work quite directly. With fewer and fewer officeholders who could be dunned for contributions to party coffers, it fell to the president as party leader to seek out wealthy donors—for Republicans the Rockefellers and the Jay Goulds, for Democrats the Levi Mortons and Henry B. Paynes—who now contributed the lion's share to the party treasury. In this sense civil service reform strengthened the president's role as party leader.

The Custodial Presidency   In other respects, however, the Gilded Age presidents were content with their custodial role. The real power—to make budgets, authorize expenditures, and draft legislation—remained with Congress, which in the 1880s was just beginning to modernize itself with an effective system of chairmanships and committees. With the great political questions of Reconstruction now dead letters, there seemed no compelling demand for presidential leadership. To congressional Republicans and Democrats alike, their president seemed simply a first-among-equals in constant need of advice and direction.

Grover Cleveland clearly defined the custodial presidency by insisting on the "entire independence" of the executive power from the legislative branch. Cleveland's power lay in the veto, with which he sought to make Congress accountable and the federal government honest, impartial, frugal, and not very energetic. He used the veto sweepingly: in his first term (1885–89) he vetoed three times as many bills as had all his predecessors combined. His veto messages embodied a social as well as a legal conservatism. In the aftermath of a series of devastating crop failures in the Texas Panhandle, Congress passed the Texas Seed Bill, appropriating the modest sum of $10,000 for seed grain for needy farmers. But the assumption that in times of distress the federal government could lend a helping hand aroused Cleveland's ire:

> I do not believe that the power and duty of the General Government ought to be extended to the relief of individual suffering which is in no manner properly related to the public service or benefit. A prevalent tendency to disregard the limited mission of this power and duty should, I think, be steadfastly resisted, to the end that the lesson should constantly be enforced that though the people support the Government, the Government should not support the people.

Republican presidents tended to be less inflexible, but they agreed that drafting policies and programs was no part of their duties. None of the major pieces of Republican legislation that were passed during Harrison's administration (1889–93)—the Sherman Silver Purchase, the Sherman Antitrust Act, and the McKinley Tariff—bore the stamp of his design or the mark of his favor. Presidents of both parties were generally content with the narrow functions that had been assigned them by an antebellum tradition of legislative dominance.

Thus Congress was the most visibly active branch of the federal government, even though its pace, accelerating slightly, was still leisurely, and its sense of itself as a national lawmaking body was limited. The volume of congressional business had doubled from an average 37,000 public and private bills per session in the 1870s to 74,000 by the mid-1880s. Gradually both houses of Congress were organizing themselves, modifying an older deliberative style and adapting it to the routine of new and stronger committees like the House's powerful Ways and Means Committee. By 1890 an informal but highly organized clique of a half-dozen senators who controlled all committee appointments were managing a Republican-dominated Senate. In the House both parties reluctantly were beginning to agree on the need for tightening rules and procedures. The average length of congressional tenure increased. In the 1870s more than half the membership in each session was new. During the 1880s only one member in three was newly elected, and a decade later only one in four. By the end of the century Congress was filled with seasoned professionals.

Still, Congress was slow to break with its past. Senators and representatives still used the congressional floor as the forum for debate among elected agents whose connections with their local constituencies were all-important. Lawmaking under these circumstances tended to become an involved exercise in horse trading by representatives of competing interests. Nowhere was this process more in evidence than in the making of the tariff.

Tariff Making The difficult and seemingly insoluble problem for Congress after the Civil War was not raising revenue but spending it. There was a surplus of federal revenue every year between 1866 and 1893, and the average annual surplus in the 1880s was $100 million, with more than half this amount coming from customs duties. To spend this enormous sum, legislators had only pork-barrel legislation and the patronage system that sluiced off some of the reserve into federal jobs (although for the latter the passage of the Pendleton Act restricted the use of federal funds). The tariff had become an embarrassment, and complaints multiplied against the principle of protection that took from the poor consumer and gave to the already-rich corporations. Republicans, suddenly in need of a strong defense of the tariff, took up James G. Blaine's cry that all the "wonders" of the previous twenty years were the result of high tariff schedules. Democrats gradually came to agree with Grover Cleveland that tariffs were "vicious, inequitable and illogical," in dire need of downward revision.

By the mid-1880s the tariff question had come to serve as a distinguishing symbol for Republicans and Democrats in much the same way that the race issue had functioned during Reconstruction and that the free-silver cause would operate in the 1890s. The tariff had a political as well as an economic significance. Combined imports and exports accounted for less than 10 percent of the gross national product. What kept the economy going, it was clear, was a burgeoning domestic market. The tariff, to be sure, was important for particular economic interests—wool growers, steel manufacturers, sugar refiners—who stood to gain directly from high import barriers. It was also true that as the decade of the 1880s opened, none of these interest groups had irrevocably tied itself to either the Republican or the Democratic party. Yet five years later "protection" had become the watchword of the Republican party, which increasingly catered to business and industry, and "a tariff for revenue only" was the war cry of the Democratic party, identified with farmers and urban consumers.

Tariff making defied science, reason, and all but the most tireless lobbyists. Enacting a new tariff—raising rates with Republicans or lowering them with Democrats—was an elaborate three-act drama. The opening act was filled with speeches concerning the dangers to civilization lurking behind higher or lower schedules—the babble of the innocents. Act Two was set in the legendary smoke-filled room where the lobbyists held court and the amendments were drafted. The final act contrasted the embarrassment of the bill's original sponsors with the quiet satisfaction of the special-interest groups who had rewritten it. This ritual began in 1882 when President Arthur appointed a blue-ribbon Tariff Commission and charged it with finding a way to lower the schedules for those American industries long past infancy and no longer in need of the paternal care provided by the tariff. The commission promptly obliged by drawing up a model bill that lowered the rates by an average 20 percent. When it was submitted to Congress, however, the carefully drafted bill lost whatever symmetry and harmony its draftees had originally claimed for it. The hammerings of the lobbyists and their representatives quickly reduced it to rubble. Still dissatisfied with their demolition work, both House and Senate wrote separate bills and then joined forces to pass a "compromise" that raised the schedules on almost every product.

In all the tariff contests between 1880 and 1900 the Republicans consistently frustrated the Democrats' attempts to lower schedules. Both the McKinley Tariff (1890) and the Dingley Tariff (1897) legislated sizable increases in protection, and the Democrats could not prevent their enactment. From 1880 until Woodrow Wilson's first administration more than thirty years later, Democrats failed to achieve a meaningful downward revision of the tariff schedules.

The real significance of the tariff debate lay in the rudimentary education in national policy planning it provided. In invoking Hamilton in support of an active government prepared to intervene in the economy, or in citing Jefferson in defense of limited government action, congressional debates slowly brought the outlines of national policy into focus across the country.

Toward a National Policy

The same recognition of the need for new national controls lay behind the Interstate Commerce Act (1887). In 1886 the Supreme Court in the *Wabash* case invalidated a state attempt to regulate rates for interstate railroads. In response the Senate appointed the Cullom Committee to investigate complaints against the railroads and to report on the feasibility of establishing a federal regulatory commission. Conservatives from both parties dominated the Cullom Committee, and the Interstate Commerce Act was a conservative law, even though anguished reactionaries like Senator Nelson B. Aldrich cried out that any regulation amounted to revolution. The Interstate Commerce Commission, which the law established, was empowered to forbid collusive manipulation by the railroads in the form of rebates, rate discrimination, and railroad pools. But its supervisory powers were narrowly defined, and its decisions were subject to review by the courts. The Interstate Commerce Act was intended as a means of establishing national railroad policy, but the commission itself never achieved that goal.

Gilded Age politics produced the semblance rather than the substance of national policy. Neither the president nor Congress had a clear understanding of the powers needed by government to function effectively in national affairs. The concepts of a comprehensive national policy and executive leadership capable of carrying it out did not emerge until the twentieth century. Meanwhile rapid industrialization was producing severe economic and social disruption. Farmers were caught in a downward spiral of prices and credit. Industrial workers were locked in combat with management over wages, hours, and the right to organize. And small-town America, uneasy with the new political order, felt the stirrings of still another crusade for a Christian society. Ever since the Civil War, farmers, laborers, and moral reformers had been involved in third-party politics, but with scant success. Their main efforts—the Greenback Labor party and the Prohibition party—had never won more than 3.5 percent of the vote in a national election. Watching the repeated failures of these would-be reformers, the Republican and Democratic party bosses felt sure that the political stability they had achieved was permanent.

But there were deeper stirrings by 1890. In agrarian revolts in the countryside and civic campaigns in the cities, reformers were beginning to draw on the resources of two deep-lying traditions in American politics. The Populist movement in the trans-Mississippi West and in the South revived a spirit of social reform with strong ethical and religious overtones that had erupted repeatedly in the past in moments of crisis. And by 1895, in the nation's cities, progressive reformers were challenging boss politics by drawing on the fears of the established elite groups, on business notions of efficiency and economy, and on the scientific ideas of a new generation of professionals and academics. In the midst of industrial strife and rural discontent, these two sets of reformers—Populists and urban progressives—shattered the professional politicians' confidence by confronting them with new interpretations and promises of American life.

Conditions Without Precedent: The Populist Revolt

The first reform effort to challenge the late-nineteenth-century political establishment was the Populist movement. The Populists had both political and social aims: they sought, first of all, to win elections and to send to Washington representatives who would repair the economic system, clean up political corruption, and return to "the plain people" the management of the social order. It was this combination of ambitions and aims that gave Populists the sense of being part of a great moral awakening rising from the "intellectual ferment" eagerly described by an early participant:

> People commenced to think who had never thought before, and people talked who had seldom spoken. On mild days they gathered on street corners, on cold days they congregated in shops and offices. Everyone was talking and everyone was thinking.... Little by little they commenced to theorize upon their condition. Despite the poverty of the country, the books of Henry George, Bellamy, and other economic writers were bought as fast as the dealers could supply them. They were bought to be read greedily; and nourished by the fascination of novelty and the zeal of enthusiasm, thoughts and theories sprouted like weeds after a May shower.... They discussed income tax and single tax; they talked of government ownership and the abolition of private property; fiat money, and the unity of labor;... and a thousand conflicting theories.

The great awakening that pointed the Populists toward a political course also raised two basic problems—defining ultimate economic ends and finding the necessary political means. They were going to have to organize quickly if they hoped to effect reforms. The preamble to the Omaha platform of July 1892 announced their grievances in the apocalyptic terms of an impending social crisis: "Corruption dominates the ballot box.... The people are demoralized.... The newspapers are largely subsidized or muzzled...our homes covered with mortgages; labor impoverished.... The fruits of the toil of millions are boldly stolen to build up colossal fortunes for the few...." After excoriating the two major parties for neglecting these problems and indulging in a sham battle over the tariff, the Populists announced their own intentions. At first glance the economic program of Populism seemed to bear all the marks of an earlier small-scale entrepreneurial capitalism, with its hopes for the independent producer, steady growth rate, and voluntary cooperation. These hopes had once sustained the North and Lincoln's Republican party in their war against slavery. But instead of the promised millennium of small producers, the war had brought rapid business and financial consolidation and the rule of the spoilsmen. The original yeoman vision had dimmed until it guided only such marginal political groups as the prohibitionists and the Greenbackers. Thus the calls for a "new politics" of purification and participation came from the political margins—from Henry George's legion of "single taxers," and from the recruits to Edward Bellamy's "industrial army" and the converts to what was beginning to be called the Social Gospel who preached Christian cooperation. All the grievances stated in the Populist platform at Omaha were issues with social and cultural as well as political and economic meaning. The Populists saw the demonetization of silver and constricted bank credit as the handiwork of the "gold bugs"—parasites and plutocrats from the East—"to fatten usurers, bankrupt enterprise, and enslave industry." Monopolists and their hirelings in the halls of justice "despised the

Salvation Army Meeting
"Soldiers" of the Salvation Army preach the gospel of social service and salvation.

republic" and trampled on the people. These grievances underscored feelings of isolation and the insignificance of the beleaguered little man in an increasingly impersonal society. The social seedbed of Populism lay in the convictions of farmers and their neighbors in town that they were being dispossessed and in their fierce determination to reverse the course of history by returning power to the people.

Regional Populism   The Populist grievances were real enough, and so were their proposals. In the trans-Mississippi West their problems were the result of the hectic pace of unregulated economic development; in the South they were the product of a new feudal order complete with tenancy, a crop-lien system, and a large submerged class of dirt-poor farmers, both black and white. In the South and the Midwest alike, Populist leaders strove to overcome the sectional hatreds and racial prejudices that survived from the Civil War era and to unite farmers in both sections of the country in defense of their common interests. In both regions after 1887, exorbitant shipping charges, greedy middlemen, and extortionate mortgage rates were compounded by a series of crop failures that sent land prices and farm income skidding. Years of retrenchment and retreat followed, and destitute farmers trekked back eastward from the sod-house frontier, leaving behind ghost towns with gilded opera houses and empty stores.

In the trans-Mississippi West, western Kansas lost half its population between 1882 and 1892, and South Dakota's population shrank by some 30,000. In 1891 an estimated 18,000 prairie wagons lumbered back to Iowa from the Nebraska frontier. A sign on an abandoned farmhouse in Blanco County, Texas, in the drought year 1886 read: "200 miles to the nearest post office; 100 miles to wood; 20 miles to water, 6 inches to hell. God bless our home! Gone to live with the wife's folks." Populist Mary E. Lease put it this way:

> We were told two years ago to go to work and raise a big crop, that was all we needed. We went to work and plowed and planted; the rains fell, the sun shone, nature smiled, and we raised the big crop they told us to; and what came of it? Eight-cent corn, ten-cent oats, two-cent beef, and no price at all for butter and eggs—that's what came of it. Then the politicians said that we suffered from overproduction.

Populism in the South, while plagued by many of the same problems, showed distinctive features. Tenancy and crop liens exploited an underclass of black and white farmers, whose keen sense of their plight was limited by their fears of challenging an elite based on white supremacy. Western farmers risked little more than failure in organizing a third party. But in attacking their political establishment in Dixie, southern farmers put their personal security and sometimes their lives on the line. In some parts of the South, Populists made genuine attempts to appeal to both black and white farmers and to organize them, albeit separately.

In both regions Populism emerged rapidly from a nonpartisan background in 1890 and drew into politics groups that had previously been politically inarticulate and inert. Some of these new recruits were women: Mary Lease, who gave impassioned speeches on the power of monopolies; Annie L. Diggs, who was bent on saving the West from alcohol as well as Wall Street; Sarah Emery, whose tract *Seven Financial Conspiracies* traced the national decline along a descending curve of democratic participation. For every seasoned veteran of third-party politics such as Ignatius Donnelly, "the Sage of Nininger," there were three new converts, including Georgia's Tom Watson, fired by Populist speeches for campaigns "hot as Nebuchadnezzar's furnace."

The atmosphere at Populist meetings was heavy with the spirit of revivalism—"a pentecost of politics," according to one participant, "in which a tongue of flame sat upon every man." In South Dakota in 1892 the Populists staged a convention that was the largest ever held in the state. "It lasted one week, and partook of the good old-fashioned camp-meeting order," an observer commented. "I never saw men so filled with zeal and inspired by a cause." "From Forge and Farm; from Shop and Counter; from Highways and Firesides," ran an Ignatius Donnelly campaign broadside, "come and hear the 'Great Commoner' on the mighty issues which are moving mankind to the ballot box in the great struggle for their rights." Recruits, like converts, came from everywhere: farmers, hard-pressed local merchants, cattlemen, miners, small-town editors; men with

Women Voting in Wyoming, 1888
Long before the Nineteenth Amendment enfranchising them (1920), women were voting in state elections, particularly in the West.

chin whiskers, broad-brimmed hats, and muddy boots, accompanied by wives "with skin tanned to parchment by the hot winds, with bony hands of toil, and clad in faded calico." Quickly they became stereotypes to the rest of the world—comic hayseeds to the political opposition, heroic figures in the folklore of Populism with nicknames to match: "The Kansas Pythoness," "Bloody Bridles," "Sockless Socrates." Behind the mask appeared the original type, frequently a biblical figure like William A. Peffer, a Topeka editor elected to the United States Senate, who, with his full beard, steel-rimmed glasses, frock coat, and "habitual expression" of gravity on an otherwise inscrutable face, reminded Hamlin Garland of the Old Testament prophet Isaiah. "He made a peculiar impression on me, something Hebraic," Garland recalled, "something intense, fanatical."

The Populists, or People's party, drew a great variety of contrasting types into their reform movement. Southern Populists listened to the saving word not only from "Stump" Ashby, the Texas cowpuncher, and "Cyclone" Davis, toting his volumes of Jefferson, but also from the shrewd and hard-hitting country editor C. W. Macune, the professional North Carolina organizer Leonidas L. Polk, and Virginia patricians bearing the names of Page, Beverly, and Harrison. In the Midwest, Ignatius Donnelly's fiery campaign in Minnesota was offset by the sober advice of Charles H. Van Wyck, the party's candidate for governor in Nebraska, who singled out solid issues like railroad regulation for his campaign. For the most part, however, Populist rank and file were political newcomers, and they considered inexperience in the dubious practices of politicking a virtue. To eastern professionals in the two major parties, the Populists, gathered under banners urging the steadfast to vote as they prayed, presented the strange spectacle of an embattled interest group talking in tongues much like the early Christians. In fact, the Populists were followers of a social vision that had once guided the abolitionists before the Civil War—the dream of a redeemed society, honest, just, open, and equitable as the corrupt world of the moneybags and their political henchmen clearly was not.

Building a National Party

The Populists were new to the work of organizing a national political party and encountered formidable obstacles in building a platform designed to appeal to farmers, attract urban workers, and detach Republicans and Democrats from their former loyalties. They discovered that appeals for votes could be made in two distinct ways. First, they could explain their problems as staple-crop farmers and call on the federal government for help. Or they could transcend interest-group appeals and call on the "people"—all those who lived by the sweat of their brow—to join the crusade of "true producers" against the Money Power. Populism undertook both of these assignments at the same time. The Omaha platform, for example, called on "all men" to "move forward until every wrong is remedied, and equal rights and equal privileges [are] securely established for all the men and women of this country," and then proceeded to "demand a national currency, safe, sound, and flexible."

The interest-group program of the Populists grew out of the reasoning of political leaders who urged the federal government to respond to the specific needs of rural America—in effect, to come to the rescue. They demanded a graduated income tax to lift the financial burden from farmers and workers. They called for nationalizing the railroads, a postal savings bank system, and the free and unlimited coinage of silver. And they advocated a subtreasury plan for storing surplus crops and issuing loans that would circulate like money. The Populists could justify all these demands as protective measures for producers who lacked the security and the privileges that had been made available to the more favored industrial interests. Some of the Populist leaders who formulated these demands had a sophisticated grasp of what should be done to relieve the farmers' economic plight. And many of these demands would eventually be enacted into law in the twentieth century—an income tax, a paper currency freed from the gold standard and pegged to the strength of the national economy, and government price-support programs. Although the late-nineteenth-century Populists would have no role in carrying out these reforms, larger American society would ultimately recognize the logic of their demands.

Another set of Populist demands represented an attempt to reach out to urban workers by calling for reform of state and local taxation, the eight-hour day, limitation on the use of injunctions in labor disputes, immigration restriction, punitive legislation against monopolies, and farmer-labor cooperation in building a brotherhood of true producers. In defining the American land as "the heritage of all the people" and denying that the public domain could be monopolized "for speculative purposes," Populists anticipated the pioneer conservation efforts of President Theodore Roosevelt's administration. And in insisting on such basic changes in the political machinery as the direct election of senators, the Australian ballot, referendum and recall, Populism antedated many of the demands progressives would make twenty years later. Looking back in 1914 over her long career as a reform agitator, Mary E. Lease expressed satisfaction "that my work in the good old Populist days was not in vain":

> The Progressive party has adopted our platform clause by clause, plank by plank....Direct election of senators is assured. Public utilities are gradually being removed from the hands of the few and placed under the control of the people who use them. Woman suffrage is now almost a national issue....The seed we sowed out in Kansas did not fall on barren ground.

But Populism above all was an act of political rebellion and a promise of spiritual renewal—a new Declaration of Independence from alien rule. The Omaha platform called on all the people to seize power for themselves as their ancestors had in founding the nation: "Assembled on the anniversary of the birthday of the nation, and filled with the spirit of the grand general chieftain who established our independence, we seek to restore the government of the Republic to the hands of the plain people with whose class it originated....We declare we must be in fact, as we are in name, one united brotherhood of freemen." In the ideal society that the Populists envisioned, honesty and integrity would infuse God's chosen people with high purpose and fierce determination. In the recesses of the Populist imagination lay dreams of a realm of harmony transcending partisan strife and economic exploitation—a haven where virtue and probity reigned supreme over a vast empire of rejuvenated yeomen. The triumph of American justice would finally come when the people had purified national life at the source. Only part of such a gigantic task involved the passage of "wise and reasonable legislation." A larger part involved a moral awakening "to bring the power of the social mass to bear upon the rebellious individuals who thus menace the peace and safety of the state."

Populism went beyond conventional politics in declaring itself "not a passing cloud on the political sky" nor a "transient gust of political discontent," but rather "the hope of realizing and incarnating in the lives of common people the fulness of the divinity of humanity." And with this shift in political perception came glimpses of social catastrophe should the people's courage fail—the swift approach of the "last days" before the final upheaval, nightmare visions of "men made beastlike by want, and women shorn of the nobility of their sex" pouring through the streets of Sodom past plutocrats who stand "grabbing and grinning" as the mob rushes to its destruction. Measured in the terms of a moral economy, the crisis facing the nation could be reduced to simple choices between justice and injustice, liberty and slavery. "The very fact of widespread suffering," a Nebraska Populist insisted, "is sufficient evidence that the whole system under which they have lived is a lie and an imposture." Once the people destroyed the Money Power, the old politics of individual greed and the selfish pursuit of wealth and power would die out. Like the abolitionists before the Civil War, the Populists emphasized issues that had symbolic resonance as well as practical import—above all the money question and, later, free silver.

It was unlikely that as political upstarts the Populists could immediately unseat the two major parties. Populists lacked the necessary funds with which to launch a national campaign, and, even more urgently they needed credible and attractive candidates. Populists sought to meet the first requirement with meager contributions from the faithful by passing the hat at midwestern whistle-stops. Even with the goodwill and support of local editors and the rural press, People's party candidates found it hard going against the organized and well-heeled major parties whose own editors scoffed at them as hayseeds and cranks, ne'er-do-wells and nincompoops:

> Why should the farmer delve and ditch?
> Why should the farmer's wife darn and stitch?
> The government can make 'em rich,
> And the People's Party knows it.
> So hurrah, hurrah for the great P.P.!
> 1 = 7, and 0 = 3
> A is B, and X is Z
> And the People's Party knows it!

More serious as a liability was the lack of candidates with a national reputation and more than regional appeal. When their first choice as a contender, Leonidas Polk, died in the summer of 1892, his mantle fell on the veteran campaigner and former Greenbacker General James B. Weaver. Party leaders balanced the ticket with "General" James G. Field of Virginia, who was actually a former Confederate major. Field's southern credentials did not protect him from rough handling by Democratic party thugs who broke up Populist rallies throughout the South with rotten eggs, heckling, and physical intimidation. Southern voters, fearful of black suffrage and a possible Republican resurgence, held fast to the Democratic party, while Democrats in the West undermined the People's party campaign by offering fusion and promising future political considerations.

Cleveland won the election of 1892 with 267 electoral and 5,500,000 popular votes to 145 electoral and 5,180,000 for Harrison. The Populists polled over a million popular votes and 22 electoral votes for Weaver while carrying Kansas, Idaho, Nevada, and Colorado and sending a dozen congressmen to Washington. But the party had made few inroads in the South against an entrenched Democracy, and owed its support in the Mountain States chiefly to the appeal of free silver. Already fusion with the Democrats held increasing appeal for many Populist leaders. The year 1892, in fact, represented the high-water mark of Populist achievement. As the Panic of 1893 tipped the country into the deepest depression it had ever known, the Populists tried to reach into the industrial cities for support. But their party was still short of funds and attractive candidates, beset with organizational problems, and confronted with voter intransigence, particularly in the South, where Democratic regulars stuffed ballot boxes and threw out Populist votes. "We had to do it!" one Democratic party organizer later explained. "Those damned Populists would have ruined the country."

Although the People's party increased its total popular vote by nearly 50 percent in the elections of 1894, it lost control of several of the western states it had won two years earlier, and after 1894 there was not a state in either the South or the West that could be considered safe for Populism. The meaning of these disturbing statistics was clear: the third party would have to seek a formal alliance—"fusion"—with the Democrats. In addressing the thorny question of the best strategy for survival if not success, the Populists confronted the same problem that had plagued the Liberty party and the Free Soil party before the Civil War—whether to seek short-term gains in winning elections with a single issue at the expense of larger principles or, on the contrary, to cling to long-term reform objectives at the cost of continuing electoral defeat. Translated into the terms of future political campaigning, the question was a stark one: Should Populists unite with their former Democratic enemies on a "fusion" ticket of free silver even though they would be forced to relinquish much of the platform and many of their reform aims? Or, conversely, should the party retain its independence and steer an uncompromising course in "the middle of the road"?

The issue of fusion with the Democrats split the Populists into two warring camps. Henry Demarest Lloyd, a delegate to the Populist convention in St. Louis in the summer of 1896, most forcefully stated the case against uniting with the Democrats: "The Free Silver movement is a fake. Free Silver is the cow-bird of the Reform movement. It waited until the nest had been built by the sacrifices and labour of others, and then it laid its eggs in it.... The People's party has been betrayed.... No party that does not lead its leaders will ever succeed." Resistance to fusion was headed by diehard reformers like Lloyd and Ignatius Donnelly, who insisted that whereas the Democratic party had learned a few of its lessons, Populists ought not to "abandon the post of teacher and turn it over to [a] slow and stupid scholar." The diehards realized that the Democrats were not interested in any of the People's party reforms except the free coinage of silver in addition to gold—and that the free-silver movement largely reflected the interests of a powerful silver lobby mounted by wealthy mine owners. For southern Populists, moreover, fusion seemed suicidal, because it meant joining the Bourbon conservatives whose ranks they had so recently deserted—and whose response to the Populist challenge had often been intimidation, ballot-box stuffing, and appeals to white supremacy. But for a majority of the delegates at St. Louis, following the advice of silverite leadership, a "Demopop" ticket headed by

William Jennings Bryan seemed to offer the only sure route out of the political wilderness. As one of the "practical" fusionists explained:

> I do not want [my constituents] to say to me that the Populists have been advocates of reforms, when they could not be accomplished, but when the first ray of light appeared and the people were looking with expectancy and anxiety for relief, the party was not equal to the occasion; that it was stupid; it was blind; it "kept in the middle of the road" and missed the golden opportunity.

Following an angry debate in which it was charged by the losers that the People's party had become "more boss-ridden, gang-ruled, gang-gangrened than the two old parties of monopoly," the delegates agreed to unite with their former rivals under the banner of free silver.

The Great Reversal: The Election of 1896

By 1896 the Democratic party was bitterly divided between agrarians and eastern business interests, and needed all the help it could get. Grover Cleveland's return to office four years earlier had been marked by the onset of a depression and a series of industrial strikes that seemed to many Americans the opening shots in a class war. In 1892 the first of these labor upheavals came outside Pittsburgh at Homestead, Pennsylvania, when Andrew Carnegie sailed for Scotland and left Henry Clay Frick, his hard-driving manager and an implacable enemy of labor unions, in charge of his steel company.

Frick took advantage of his chief's absence by attempting to break the Amalgamated Association of Iron and Steel Workers, whose eight hundred members at the Homestead plant were firmly supported by their unskilled comrades. The union's chief grievances were the reduction of a sliding scale, which amounted to a 20 percent cut in pay, and a matching reduction in tonnage rates at the steelworks, where new more efficient machinery had been installed. Frick countered the Amalgamated's demands by ordering a lockout, hiring strikebreakers, and erecting three miles of barbed-wire fence around Homestead. When his original plans for assembling a sheriff's posse of one hundred deputies yielded only twenty-three men, two of them on crutches and nineteen bearing doctors' certificates declaring them unfit to serve, Frick turned to the Pinkerton National Detective Agency, which supplied him with three hundred "watchmen" at $5 a day. The union retaliated by calling a strike, and prepared to repel the Pinkerton guards, who had been sent by barge up the Monongahela River with orders to seize the plant. A hail of bullets from the workers lining the shore met the invaders. In the pitched battle that followed, the Pinkertons were routed and their barges burned to the waterline. But final victory, as Frick and Carnegie had foreseen, lay with the company, which prevailed on the governor of Pennsylvania to send in the militia to open the plant. In July 1893 some 1,000 new workers entered the Homestead mill under military protection, and two months later a grand jury, following Frick's orders, indicted the union leaders on charges of murder, riot, and conspiracy. But when no jury could be found that would convict the defendants, charges were summarily dropped. Frick's unionbusting nearly cost him his life: in the course of the strike a young anarchist, Alexander Berkman, attempted to assassinate him but bungled the job. One of the soldiers stationed at Homestead was overheard to shout, after Berkman's failed attempt, "Three cheers for the assassin!" for which opinion his commanding officer had him strung up by his thumbs, ordered his head shaved and the miscreant drummed out of camp. The steel union fared little better. After five months out on strike, the Homestead workers were forced to accept the harsh new terms of the settlement, suffering a defeat that ended effective organizing in the steel industry for nearly half a century. Andrew Carnegie, who had kept in close touch with Frick throughout the strike from his sumptuous Skibo Castle in Scotland, cabled congratulations to his manager on a job well done.

The Pullman Strike   Cleveland threw his considerable weight on the side of management against the forces of organized labor in the Pullman Strike of 1894. The Pullman Strike, like the Homestead Strike, was a desperate response to the antiquated ideas of a big businessman whose sense of duty to his employees involved building them a model company town but did not extend to allowing them the right to negotiate their wages. The town of Pullman south of Chicago was widely hailed as a model workers' community with its substantial brick houses fronting on well-kept lawns and tree-lined streets, its library, meetinghouse, and public park. Living conditions at Pullman were vastly superior to housing available elsewhere in the region, but rents and taxes were high, and George Pullman's rules for property maintenance and personal behavior were arbitrary and irksome. Pullman's company town provided many of the amenities made possible by the new science of urban planning, but it also displayed all the unlovely features of industrial feudalism.

Worker protest stemmed from George Pullman's personal decision in the bitter depression winter of 1894 to reduce wages in his shops while at the same time keeping rents pegged at their current high level. Approached by a grievance committee of workers, Pullman announced that there was no connection between his two roles of town landlord and president of the Pullman Palace Car Company. He refused to hear the committee's complaints and instead summarily fired three of the delegates. When all requests for arbitration had failed, workers struck and Pullman closed his shops. As tensions mounted in the early summer of 1894, Pullman's workers appealed for help to the fledgling American Railway Union and its charismatic president, Eugene V. Debs. George Pullman turned to the General Managers Association, a tight-knit group composed of the chief executives of the twenty-four railroads entering Chicago. The General Managers promptly instructed their members to fire all workers who participated in the rapidly spreading strike. Debs's "one big union," flushed with its recent victory over James J. Hill's Great Northern Railroad, boasted 150,000 members in 465 locals. Although Debs was reluctant to commit his new union to an unequal contest with railroad management, the intransigence of the General Managers, whose members were spoiling for a fight, forced his hand. On the eve of the national boycott, the chairman of the General Managers Association was heard to admit that "we can handle the various brotherhoods, but we cannot handle Debs. We have got to wipe him out too." In his address "To the Railway Employees of America," Debs defined the issue squarely: "The struggle with the Pullman Company has developed into a contest between the producing classes and the money power."

When the Pullman Company, backed by the General Managers Association, rejected a final appeal for arbitration, Debs had no choice but to declare a boycott against all Pullman cars, even those carrying the mails. The company and the managers, turning this decision to their own advantage, sought an injunction from the federal courts and appealed directly to President Cleveland for the immediate dispatch of federal troops. Cleveland quickly obliged. Faced with a choice between the rights of labor and the rights of property, the president unhesitatingly sided with the men of property. The arrival of federal troops in Chicago triggered widespread protest and flaring violence as crowds of workers attacked a regiment that retaliated by firing at point-blank range, killing several participants and onlookers. By midsummer there were 14,000 troops in the city. Defeated and demoralized, workers were sullenly returning to work by the end of the summer, but George Pullman and the General Managers were still bent on revenge and punishment. A federal grand jury's indictment of Debs for conspiracy was dropped, but despite an able defense by his lawyer, Clarence Darrow, Debs was convicted of contempt in ignoring the injunction and sentenced to six months in jail.

The Depression of 1893

The American economy hit bottom in 1894. Five hundred banks closed their doors, 16,000 business firms collapsed, and unemployment reached nearly 20 percent. New issues on the New York Stock Exchange plummeted from $100 million to $37 million, and 2.5 million jobless workers tramped winter streets looking for work. Municipal governments and private charity organizations could not cope with the large numbers of destitute men who wandered aimlessly from city to city, finding factory gates closed everywhere and long lines at soup kitchens. Not since the dark days of the Civil War had the country seemed so threatened.

Workers met the depression and the savage wage cuts it brought with the only weapon they possessed—the strike. In 1894 alone there were more than 1,300 strikes. The mining industry was hit by a wave of strikes that rolled across the country from the coal fields of the East to Coeur d'Alene in Idaho, where besieged miners fought with sticks of dynamite, and Cripple Creek, Colorado, where armed deputies broke up demonstrations. For such acute economic suffering President Cleveland prescribed the heroic remedies of self-denial and sacrifice.

The specter of masses of starving men marching on the nation's cities to plunder and pillage in an uprising of the dispossessed turned into farce in the spring of 1894 with the arrival in Washington of Coxey's Army, a "petition in boots" that had come to the capital to ask for work. The leader of the few hundred jobless men who finally straggled into the city was the self-appointed "General" Jacob Coxey from Massillon, Ohio. Coxey simply wanted to present his plan for solving unemployment with a "good roads bill," which would finance public improvements with $500 million worth of government bonds. The Cleveland administration's reaction to this living petition was a measure of its fear of mass upheaval: Coxey's followers were dispersed and their leader jailed on a technicality, while rumors of revolution swept through the city.

Cleveland blamed the free-silver forces for the depression. In 1890 Congress had responded to the clamor of the silver interests and had passed the Sherman Silver Purchase Act, which required the government to buy 4.5 million ounces of silver each month and to pay for it with treasury notes redeemable in gold or silver. The Sherman Silver Purchase Act brought a sudden rush on the gold reserves of the United States by investors frightened by high imports and falling crop prices. The gold reserves plunged from $190 million to $100 million in just three years. As the depression deepened, Cleveland persuaded Congress to repeal the Silver Purchase Act. The purpose of repeal, he insisted, was to make the nation's currency "so safe . . . that those who have money will spend and invest it in business and enterprise instead of holding it." After a heated debate Congress complied in 1893, but the repeal seriously weakened Cleveland's control over his own party. He had succeeded in limiting the flow of silver from the mines at the behest of eastern bankers, but in so doing he had also lost support of the agrarian half of the Democratic party, as well as the senators representing western silver-mining interests. By 1895 the president was complaining that there was "not a man in the Senate with whom I can be on terms of absolute confidence."

The Gold Standard: "A Crown of Thorns"? To stop the drain on American gold, Cleveland issued government bonds at a generous rate of interest to attract European investors. In calling on the banking syndicates of J. P. Morgan and August Belmont to market the bonds, the president only compounded his political difficulties. Working together, the administration and the bankers arranged the sale of government bonds for gold on terms that allowed the banking houses to manipulate exchange rates in their own favor. To the Populists and to irate Democrats in the South and West, Cleveland's deal with the bankers was powerful proof of a Wall Street conspiracy to rig the economy against them. Even Joseph Pulitzer's *New York World,* again serving as the watchdog of the little man's interests, denounced the "Bond Scandals" in boldface headlines:

SMASH THE BOND RING
GO TO THE PEOPLE
SAVE THE COUNTRY FROM THE MISCHIEF, THE WRONG,
THE SCANDAL OF THE PENDING BOND DEAL WITH THE
MORGAN SYNDICATE

The silverites proceeded to make the presidential election of 1896 a one-issue campaign. Silver and gold quickly became organizing symbols for diametrically opposed (and, to modern economists, equally misguided) strategies for economic recovery. Financial policy was treated as sacred truth, and the opposing view was inevitably denounced as utterly sinful. According to its defenders silver was the "people's" money—abundant, cheap, and flexible. To businessmen and bankers gold was sacrosanct and the sole "honest currency"—solid and time-tested. Cleveland chose "sound money," the gold standard, and currency restriction as the only ethical course, while William Jennings Bryan described gold as "a crown of thorns" for bankrupt farmers and western debtors, pressed on the brow of the honest laborer who was being crucified by the moneylenders. In fact Cleveland's monetary policy did worsen the effects of the depression. But more important, it gave farmers a highly visible target for their grievances. Addressing his backcountry constituents, South Carolina demagogue Ben Tillman denounced the president as a Judas who had thrice betrayed the Democracy: "He is an old bag of beef, and I am going to Washington with a pitchfork and prod him in his fat ribs."

With similar intentions Democrats gathered in Chicago for the convention of 1896. Southern and western Democrats quickly realized that by rejecting Cleveland's restrictionist policies and advocating the free and unlimited coinage of silver, they had an opportunity to upstage the Populists. The thirty-six-year-old Bryan, "strong-limbed, strong-lunged," immediately emerged as the choice of the agrarian wing of the party, "the wild crowd" ready to be stampeded for the Nebraskan. "Ear-splitting noises were heard; waves of scarlet fans danced in the galleries." The westerners ran roughshod over the "sound money" wing of the Democratic party and drove them out of the convention to form their own splinter organization. Bryan spoke the mood of his followers in sounding a new note of resistance:

> We have petitioned, and our petitions have been scorned; we have entreated, and our entreaties have been disregarded; we have begged and they have mocked when our calamity came. We beg no longer; we entreat no more; we petition no more. We defy them!

The eastern press, both Republican and Gold Democratic, replied with charges of anarchy and treason. "The Jacobins are in full control at Chicago," one editor announced, comparing Bryan and his supporters to the radicals of the French Revolution. "No large political movement in America has ever before spawned such hideous and repulsive vipers." Both the promise and the danger of a Democratic victory seemed greater after the Populists' convention in St. Louis also endorsed Bryan for president. Not since 1860 had the fate of the nation appeared to hang in the balance of a single election. In 1896, as in 1860, the differences were sectional and economic, but they were also social and cultural, as two fundamentally opposed views of politics competed for the American voter's allegiance. There were those Republicans, Bryan told the assembled delegates, "who believe that, if you only legislate to make the well-to-do prosperous, their prosperity will leak through on those below." The Democratic party's idea, on the contrary, "has been that if you legislate to make the masses prosperous, their prosperity will find its way up through every class which rests upon them."

Bryan and his Republican opponent, William McKinley, between them gave more than nine hundred speeches in the campaign of 1896, the Republican from his front porch in Canton, Ohio, to throngs of admiring visitors shipped in by party managers, and the "Boy Orator of the Platte" at every whistle-stop in the West where local leaders could collect a crowd. Bryan traveled some 18,000 miles in the pioneer presidential railroad campaign, the last of which would be President Harry Truman's half a century later. Behind his picket fence in Canton, McKinley sounded the old Republican refrains of the "dignity of labor" and the danger of "cheap money" while appealing to American patriotism. "In America," he told his listeners, "we scorn all class distinctions. We are all equal citizens and equal in privilege and opportunity." The candidates' speeches riveted national attention on the money question, which quickly brought into focus cultural and social disagreements between urban and rural America. When a hostile eastern press accused Bryan of a lack of dignity in playing the demagogue, he replied that he would rather have people say "that I lacked dignity than . . . that I lacked backbone to meet the enemies of the Government who work against its welfare in Wall Street." To the delegations of war veterans, temperance leaders, ministers, loyal editors, and local notables who made the paid-for pilgrimage to his front porch in Canton, McKinley prophesied that the coming year would be "a year of patriotism and devotion to the country":

> I am glad to know that the people in every part of the country mean to be devoted to one flag, and that the glorious Stars and Stripes (great applause); that the people of the country this year mean to maintain the financial honor of the country as sacredly as they maintain the honor of the flag.

Bryan soon expanded his economic indictment of the Money Power to a plea for a national moral revival. Republicans, capitalizing on the gradual upturn in the economy late in the summer, continued to denounce Bryan's platform as "revolutionary and anarchistic . . . subversive of the national honor and threatening to the very life of the Republic."

Bryan: A Crusading Prophet A powerful orator and an appealing political figure, Bryan was new to the business of presidential campaigning. In casting his party adrift from its eastern financial moorings, he was forced to improvise. The professional politicians in the Democratic party withheld their support, sensitive to the sound-money opinions of their business backers and appalled by the prospect of an inflationary free silver. Bryan rejected the limited offers of the few party leaders who remained loyal to him. Sensing the need for new rules and definitions, he cast himself in the role of a crusading prophet who could purify his party and his country—by eliminating corruption, paring campaign budgets, purging the party of hacks, and preaching principles rather than praising men and cutting deals.

As the new mass leader, Bryan appeared an avenging angel of outraged American yeomanry, the people's savior stopping his campaign train for just one more sermon to his flock. He invariably apologized to his listeners, confessing that "a large portion of my voice has been left along the line of travel, where it is still calling sinners to repentance." Bryan's speeches drew on a fund of stock religious images as he mixed indictments of the Money Power, the tariff, and the gold standard with allusions to the Old Testament. His message was always the same: the people must arise in their majesty to smite the moneylenders and destroy their temple. Audiences came to know his arguments by heart and gathered to hear confirmation of their beliefs in the Protestant ethic of hard work and a just reward. When their leader assured them that "every great economic question is in reality a great moral question," they understood instinctively and they cheered. As Bryan preached the saving word of free silver, his audiences saw the stone suddenly rolled away and "the door... opened for a progress which would carry civilization up to higher ground."

"Live and Let Live" with McKinley   Republicans, following the orders of their new managers, chief among them Mark Hanna of Ohio, willingly exchanged places with their Democratic rivals. Tossing aside their moralistic reform heritage as a burden, they embarked on a pragmatic course toward a coalition of business and labor in the nation's major cities, where most of the votes lay. Their chosen candidate was the veteran Ohio politician William McKinley, who was a born compromiser and astute legislator, with no strikingly original ideas but presumably with plenty of political horse sense.

Behind McKinley in the shadows stood Ohio's Mark Hanna, a new breed of political boss—the wealthy businessman with an urge to play kingmaker. Hanna had made a fortune in the street railway business, and by 1896 was president of a large midwestern bank and a rich merchant prince whose fleet of ore boats on the Great Lakes brought coal and iron to the region's steel mills. A rival businessman once observed that "life meant war to Mark Hanna.... And he made war, not to bend men but to break them." Building on an interest in municipal politics to protect his franchises, Hanna turned to state politics and pioneered in forming Republican businessmen's associations in the Midwest. He was heard to say that in defining economic issues as primarily moral questions Bryan was quite wrong—"all questions of government in a democracy [are] questions of money." Money was just what he so successfully raised for his protégé McKinley. Hanna's career as Republican party manager represented a shift in the locus of power—from regional party professional to national businessman boss, and from the Northeast to the Midwest. Both these displacements were in evidence in a campaign confrontation in 1896 between Massachusetts Republican Senator Henry Cabot Lodge, the imperious "scholar in politics" and McKinley's burly,

Campaign Styles: Old and New
Bryan (above) barnstormed the country in the time-honored political fashion, while Republicans advertised McKinley (left) with an icon of prosperity.

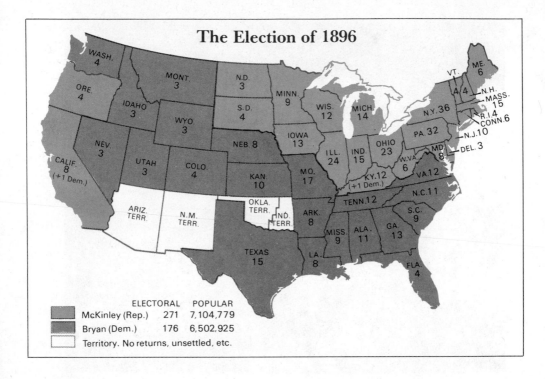

The Election of 1896

	ELECTORAL	POPULAR
McKinley (Rep.)	271	7,104,779
Bryan (Dem.)	176	6,502,925
Territory. No returns, unsettled, etc.		

rough-hewn campaign manager. Lodge presented Hanna with an ultimatum: he would follow Lodge's orders and put a gold plank in the platform for eastern banking interests or "we'll rip you up the back."

> "Who in hell are you?"
> "Senator Henry Cabot Lodge, of Massachusetts."
> "Well, Henry Cabot Lodge, of Massachusetts, you can go plumb to hell! You have nothing to say about it."

McKinley's image was the clever contrivance of Hanna and his Republican managers, who recognized the liabilities of moralism and a legacy of reform in an age of secular industrial organization, and the need for full-time professional organizers, effective propaganda, and a full treasury. From his front porch McKinley dispensed sage advice in the form of nostalgia and political truisms: "What we want, no matter to what political organization we may have belonged in the past, is a return to the good times of years ago. We want good prices and good wages, and when we have them we want them to be paid in good money...in dollars worth one hundred cents each." Meanwhile Republican workers released an unprecedented flood of pamphlets, posters, printed speeches, and editorials that reached into every corner of the country. All their efforts were carefully orchestrated to new themes of cultural and ethnic toleration and were arranged to appeal to farmers and workers, small businessmen and big bankers, shippers and consumers, Catholics as well as Protestants, and a variety of ethnic groups to whom the gold standard was offered as the last best hope of democracy. McKinley himself summed up the new Republican message: "We have always practiced the Golden Rule. The best policy is to 'live and let live.'" With the blessings of their candidate, the Republicans turned their backs on their moralist past and squared to the task of engineering a broad social consensus.

The Republicans won a decisive victory in the election. With 7 million popular and 271 electoral votes, McKinley swept the entire East and Midwest, carried California and Oregon, and held on to Minnesota, North Dakota, and Iowa. Bryan, with 6.5 million popular and 176 electoral votes, won the Solid South together with the Plains and Mountain States. Beneath the regional features of the election of 1896 lay the deeper meaning of the political turnabout. With their votes a majority of Americans declared their preference for toleration and accommodation.

The meaning of the Democrats' defeat was clear. The American electorate had rejected the producerist countercrusade against corporatism, modernism, and secularism. There would undoubtedly be new reforms as the twentieth century opened, but they would be tailored to the mounting demands of economic and political consumers. From now on, political parties would have to consider and cater to the wishes of a multitude of social interests, welcoming newcomers from a wide variety of ethnic, cultural, and religious groups, meeting their needs, listening to their complaints, and serving their interests.

The election of 1896 also made it clear that the organizational revolution that was transforming business and finance had now invaded politics. Just as both houses of Congress were beginning to modernize their procedures for doing the nation's business, so the two principal political parties had learned the importance of efficient organization, continuing communications, flexible and politically sophisticated candidates, and, above all, money with which to run their political machinery.

The Party System Realigned

Finally, and most significant for the immediate future, the election of 1896 broke the grip of party discipline and loyalty that throughout the Gilded Age had been considered a permanent feature of American politics. The election freed the American party system for a long-term realignment of voting patterns that would reveal the average voter as considerably more independent than the professionals had once assumed.

Bryan had uncovered a latent American suspicion of machine politics, a set of misgivings that had been buried in the rubble of the Civil War. In his unsuccessful campaign he had located this skepticism in the agrarian mind, had attempted to exploit it, and had failed. But by 1896 young urban reformers were already experiencing a similar distrust of entrenched political power and were beginning to experiment with still another form of politics. The political program of these emerging reformers, while it promised to end machine politics and return power to the people, envisioned not the rule of righteousness but the triumph of middle-class professionals. The vision of social reformers organizing American cities after 1890 centered on an efficient, accountable, economically run "organic city" that was man-made rather than God-given. With the stirring of these reform hopes came a second, more potent challenge to the old Gilded Age politics—the challenge of progressivism.

CHRONOLOGY

1880	James A. Garfield elected president.		McKinley Tariff raises duties to average 49.5 percent.
1881	Garfield assassinated; Chester A. Arthur becomes president.	1892	Populists organize, nominate General James B. Weaver for president.
1883	Pendleton Act establishes independent Civil Service Commission.		Grover Cleveland elected president.
			Homestead Strike in Carnegie steel mills.
1884	Grover Cleveland elected president, defeating Republican James G. Blaine.	1893	Financial panic sends U.S. economy into four years of depression.
1887	Interstate Commerce Act attempts to control railroads.		Congress repeals Silver Purchase Act.
1888	Benjamin Harrison narrowly defeats Cleveland and is elected president.	1894	Pullman Strike broken by federal troops; Eugene V. Debs jailed.
			"Coxey's Army" of unemployed marches on Washington.
1890	Sherman Silver Purchase Act passed, resulting in depleted gold reserves.	1896	William McKinley elected president, defeating William Jennings Bryan and "free silver."
	Sherman Antitrust Act passed in attempt to regulate monopolies in restraint of trade.	1897	Dingley Tariff raises duties to a new high of 57 percent.

SUGGESTED READINGS

The end of Reconstruction is chronicled in Eric Foner, *Reconstruction: America's Unfinished Revolution* (1988), and William Gillette, *Retreat from Reconstruction, 1869–1879* (1979). Michael Perman, *The Road to Redemption: Southern Politics 1869–1879* (1984), analyzes the return to power of the Democrats in the South after the Civil War, and Joel Williamson, *The Crucible of*

Race: Black-White Relations in the American South Since Emancipation (1984), traces the course of race relations in the South since the Civil War.

An invaluable introduction to American politics and society from the end of the Civil War to 1900 is Morton Keller, *Affairs of State: Public Life in Nineteenth Century America* (1977). There are several useful guides to politics in the Gilded Age. David Rothman, *Politics and Power: The United States Senate, 1869–1901* (1966), traces the emergence of the modern Senate as it is organized in the 1890s by new wealthy representatives of big business. H. Wayne Morgan, *From Hayes to McKinley: National Party Politics, 1877–1896* (1969), concentrates on the organizational problems of the two major parties. Robert D. Marcus, *Grand Old Party: Political Structure in the Gilded Age, 1880–1896* (1971), analyzes the workings of the Republican party, and Samuel Merrill, *Bourbon Democracy of the Middle West, 1865–1896,* gives a good regional account of the Democrats for the same period. Southern politics is perceptively treated in four important works: C. Vann Woodward, *The Origins of the New South, 1877–1913* (1951); Dewey Grantham, Jr., *The Democratic South* (1963); Albert D. Kirwan, *Revolt of the Rednecks: Mississippi Politics: 1876–1925* (1951); and Morgan Kousser, *The Shaping of Southern Politics: Suffrage Restriction and the Establishment of the One-Party South, 1880–1910* (1974). Lawrence Goodwyn, *Democratic Promise: The Populist Movement in America* (1976), rehabilitates the image of southern Populists. Stanley P. Hirshon, *Farewell to the Bloody Shirt: Northern Republicans and the Southern Negro, 1877–1893,* considers the race issue as it affected party politics. Mary R. Dearing, *Veterans in Politics* (1952), covers the activities of Civil War veterans, and Marc Karson, *American Labor Unions and Politics, 1900–1918* (1958), discusses unions and politics in the opening years of the twentieth century.

On agrarian political protest in the Gilded Age, see Steven Hahn, *The Roots of Southern Populism: Yeoman Farmers and the Transformation of the Georgia Upcountry, 1850–1890* (1983); Peter H. Argersinger, *Populism and Politics: William Alfred Peffer and the People's Party* (1974); and Martin Ridge, *Ignatius Donnelly: Portrait of a Politician* (1962). On African-American political participation in the New South, consult Howard N. Rabinowitz, *Race Relations in the Urban South* (1978); J. Morgan Kousser, *The Shaping of Southern Politics: Suffrage Restriction and the Establishment of the One-Party South* (1974); C. Vann Woodward, *The Strange Career of Jim Crow* (3d ed., 1966); and Louis R. Harlan, *Booker T. Washington: The Making of a Black Leader, 1865–1901* (1972).

There are a number of good studies of crucial elections in the 1880s and 1890s. Among the best are Paul W. Glad, *McKinley, Bryan, and the People* (1964); Stanley Jones, *The Presidential Election of 1896* (1964); and J. Rogers Hollingsworth, *The Whirligig of Politics: The Democracy of Cleveland and Bryan* (1963). Two challenging studies, Paul Kleppner, *The Cross of Culture: A Social Analysis of Midwestern Politics, 1840–1900* (1970), and Richard J. Jensen, *The Winning of the Midwest* (1971), explore cultural factors as determinants of voting behavior in the Midwest during the Gilded Age.

There are several excellent biographies of major political figures. Three of the best studies of Bryan are Paolo E. Coletta, *William Jennings Bryan: Political Evangelist, 1860–1908* (1964); Paul W. Glad, *The Trumpet Soundeth: William Jennings Bryan and His Democracy, 1896–1912* (1964); and Louis W. Koenig, *Bryan: A Political Biography of William Jennings Bryan* (1971). For McKinley see H. Wayne Morgan, *William McKinley and His America* (1963), and the very readable study of McKinley's life and times, Margaret Leech, *In the Days of McKinley* (1959), as well as the more recent, fuller account of the McKinley years, Lewis L. Gould, *The Presidency of William McKinley* (1980). Biographies of other major figures include Horace Samuel Merrill, *Bourbon Leader: Grover Cleveland and the Democratic Party* (1957); Kenton J. Clymer, *John Hay: The Gentleman as Diplomat* (1975); and a brilliant recent biography of Eugene V. Debs by Nick Salvatore, *Eugene V. Debs: Citizen and Socialist* (1982).

On the troubled 1890s a good overview is Harold U. Faulkner, *Politics, Reform and Expansion, 1890–1900* (1959).

13

The Progressive Impulse

⌒

IN 1915, as the progressive movement neared its peak, a young professor of government at New York University, Benjamin Parke DeWitt, published a book entitled *The Progressive Movement,* in which he catalogued the political and social reforms in the United States in the previous two decades. DeWitt, an active progressive and ardent admirer of Theodore Roosevelt, looked behind the campaigns and the elections and discovered three interlocking reform tendencies:

> *The first of these tendencies is found in the insistence by the best men in all political parties that special, minority, and corrupt influence in government—national, state, and city—be removed; the second tendency is found in the demand that the structure or machinery of government . . . be so changed and modified that it will be more difficult for the few, and easier for the many, to control; and finally, the third tendency is found in the rapidly growing conviction that the functions of government are too restricted and that they must be increased and extended to relieve social and economic distress.*

DeWitt's analysis was accurate. The progressives believed that government at all levels was both inefficient and corrupt. Because it was corrupt, it ignored the needs of the people. Therefore, the people themselves had to seize the initiative in repairing the whole system. According to progressive logic, the first job was to remove unworthy and inept politicians and to replace them with reliable public servants drawn from the popular ranks and equipped with the needed expertise. These new leaders would then see to it that government—city, state, and national—performed an expanding range of tasks efficiently and responsibly. Progressives, in short, found in the idea of scientific government the materials for building a national reform movement.

A variety of forces shaped the progressive movement. There was no single progressive type among the leaders or the rank and file; there was no typical age, status, background, religion, or education. The progressives were drawn from the mainstream of the native-born middle class that dominated American politics in the first two decades of the twentieth century. Educated, articulate, and eager to apply their ideas for reforming society and politics, they held no monopoly on political gentility and could be found in equal numbers in the reform wings of both the Republican and the Democratic parties.

The progressives had no uniform platform. They offered a wide array of reform proposals: initiative, referendum, recall, corporate regulation, child-labor laws, tariff reform, city-manager plans, zoning regulations, immigration restriction—even prohibition. Their priorities differed according to region and immediate interest. Farmers fought hard for regulation of railroad rates but ignored the problem of industrial accidents. Southern progressives pushed hard for tariff and banking reform but disfranchised the blacks. Settlement-house workers grappled with the bosses for control of their cities but neglected the problems of the small-town businessman.

With this great variety in progressivism from 1890 to 1914, it seems useful to analyze it not as a movement at all, but rather as a patchwork of the efforts of different interest groups that occasionally agreed on specific measures but were unable to combine behind a unified and coherent program. The progressives thought otherwise. They realized that the United States was entering a new era of economic and political consolidation, one that required new techniques for managing what all of them agreed was a flourishing national enterprise. Even though they admitted that there was much wrong with America, they saw little that could not be mended by using governmental authority and scientific efficiency. In the spirit of the Founders, whose nationalism they so admired, progressive reformers, despite their differences, thought of themselves as the architects of a stable social order based on many of the principles that had guided their Federalist ancestors.

With their experiments in new political techniques, the progressives were innovators, but at a deeper level they were conservatives and restorationists. They picked up the promise of American life where their eighteenth-century forebears had dropped it—with the creation of a strong national government capable of harnessing and directing the energies of all its citizens. Part of the progressives' call for the people to take power back from their corrupt rulers seemed to invoke the spirit of Jefferson. But the heart of their program was the Hamiltonian demand for a new national leadership using the power of government to set priorities and provide direction. The ghosts of Hamilton and Jefferson fought over the progressive terrain just as the two statesmen had bitterly contested each other's principles a century earlier. To the delight of his many progressive admirers, Hamilton won the victory that had been denied him during his lifetime. For in effect, if not in intent, progressivism marked the rebirth of original Federalist hopes for a managed republic in which men of talent and training guided the affairs of a prosperous people.

Consolidation Sweeps Forward:
The Building of Corporate America

The Merger Movement

As the twentieth century opened, prosperity seemingly depended on ever-greater economic concentration. By 1900 the integration of the American economy was entering a second phase of "horizontal consolidation" as a sudden surge of industrial and financial mergers demolished the old entrepreneurial order of Gilded Age capitalism and cleared the ground for new twentieth-century corporate giants. From one angle the great merger movement at century's end appeared to be a towering peak of corporate consolidations. The annual number of mergers of American industrial firms traced a sharp trajectory: 69 in 1897, 303 in 1898, and 1208 in 1899, leveling off in the next three years at between 350 and 425. In 1900 there were 73 so-called trusts, each with a total capital investment of more than $10 million. Two-thirds of them had been established in the previous three years.

Viewed negatively, the merger movement simply looked like a gigantic black hole into which some 300 businesses tumbled each year, swallowed by huge new combinations like United States Steel and General Electric. United States Steel absorbed more than 200 manufacturing and transportation companies and soon controlled almost two-thirds of the steel market. American Tobacco combined 162 independent companies and ruled all but 10 percent of the tobacco market. By 1904 the approximately 2,000 largest firms in the United States composed less than 1 percent of the total number of the nation's business firms yet produced 40 percent of the annual value of the country's industrial goods. By 1910 monopoly (entire control of an industry by a single firm) and oligopoly (control of an industry by a few large firms) had secured the commanding positions from which to dominate twentieth-century American life.

The merger movement, which climaxed a half-century's search for industrial system and economic order, was both a logical outgrowth of rapid industrial development and an unsettling departure from remembered ways. It was natural for the newly emerging generation of promoters and industrial bankers to see in combination, if not the hand of God, at least an unchanging law of nature at work ordering the business affairs of the world. Samuel C. T. Dodd, Rockefeller's counsel, warned of the futility of tinkering with the celestial machinery: "You might as well endeavor to stay the formation of the clouds, the falling of the rains, or the flowing of the streams as to attempt by any means or in any manner to prevent organization of industry, associations of persons, and the aggregation of capital to any extent that the ever-growing trade of the world may demand." And indeed, the seeming success of mergers seemed hard to deny.

By 1895 the remarkable growth and sizable profits of Standard Oil, American Sugar Refining, and American Tobacco marked what appeared to be a sure route to salvation through combination and system. The Federal Steel Corporation's president, Judge Elbert Gary, boasted that his integrated firm "takes the ore from the ground, transports it, manufactures it into pig iron, manufactures pig iron into steel, and steel into finished products, and delivers those products." Even more impressive was the formation in 1901 of United States Steel, into which went not only some 200 manufacturing plants and transportation companies, but also 1,000 miles of railroad, 112 blast furnaces, and 78 ore boats. Soon United States Steel was employing 170,000 workers as it gathered control over 60 percent of the country's steel. Its initial capital investment at $1.4 billion was three times the annual expenditure of the federal government.

Increased efficiency, elimination of waste, bigger shares of the market, anticipated but often elusive economies of scale, and, above all, mounting profits—all these convinced adventurous big businessmen of the need to pursue mergers. By 1910 mergers had spread to all the principal sectors of the economy. When the great wave of mergers receded in 1903, it left in its wake a new corporate capitalism—a system of mammoth integrated enterprises with interlocking structures, selling their increasing variety of products in shared markets at prices jointly agreed on by the dominant firms. The great merger movement declared the bankruptcy of old-fashioned small-scale competition and announced the arrival of a modern corporate society that needed new definitions and values to replace the outworn Horatio Alger pieties of pluck and luck. In place of a host of small and medium-sized businesses scrambling for a share of the market, there now stood huge unified structures. The corporate revolution was by no means over by 1914, and the nation throughout this period—known as the Progressive Era—continued to support a dual economy of big and little businesses. But the central message of the merger movement was clear to most Americans: bigger was better.

Organizing the mergers and raising the capital to launch them became the specialty of investment bankers like J. P. Morgan and Jacob Schiff. Their role was critical, and they dominated the American economy at the turn of the twentieth century as they never would again. While taking a handsome slice of stock in the new consolidations for themselves, these bankers became powerful middlemen between a public eager to invest and an expansive business community. The investment bankers arranged mergers and floated (sold) stock; they dictated terms and dominated the workings of their new creations; they even manufactured the favorable publicity needed to popularize them. Their success could be read most clearly in the achievements of the House of Morgan, which by 1912, together with the Morgan-controlled First National Bank of New York and the Rockefeller-managed National City Bank, held 341 directorships in 112 corporations worth $22.2 billion.

To the public the investment banker personified the whole merger movement, its promise as well as its awesome concentration of power. The banker was part savior of a threatened economy, part devil in disguise. As though to conceal embarrassing questions of right and wrong, an air of conspiracy or an atmosphere of inevitability characterized even the fictional portraits of the big businessmen of the day—Van Harrington in Robert Herrick's *Memoirs of an American Citizen,* S.

J.P. Morgan Poses for Photographers
Next to President Theodore Roosevelt, Morgan was perhaps the most powerful man in America in the first decades of the twentieth century.

Behrman in Frank Norris's *The Octopus,* and Frank Cowperwood in Theodore Dreiser's portrait of a Progressive Era big businessman. For their everyday heroes Americans might have preferred the homely inventor and the unassuming engineer—Thomas Edison, Alexander Graham Bell, George Westinghouse—but they also admired, feared, envied, and puzzled over the giant captains of industry and the financial wizards who mysteriously ran the country: the predatory J. P. Morgan, the cautious Jacob Schiff, and their clients and lesser breeds of big businessmen.

The builders of the new corporate America, like their many admirers, were never entirely clear about their ultimate aims. Heavy capital investment, rapid plant expansion, increased production and reduced overhead, economies of scale, and systems of mass distribution—all to what greater good? For huge profits, surely, and for rising quantities of consumer goods for more and more people. But beyond that? What did the discovery of new needs and essentials and the constant manipulation of consumer demand through mass advertising signify for individual freedom of choice? How were Americans to balance rising standards of living with loss of control over the workplace? Could big business be made to deliver on its promise of economic security for all citizens? Were huge industrial and financial combinations compatible with political democracy and social responsibility? In short, was big really better? Neither the corporate revolutionists nor their uneasy admirers could quite answer these questions, which posed a dilemma that would persist throughout the century.

Agricultural Cooperatives

By 1900 the Populists' prediction of social and spiritual ruin had failed to materialize and their original political hopes had flickered and died. The twentieth century opened with a sharp economic upturn, and in this rapid recovery the American farmers abandoned their demands for massive change. In return they accepted the more immediate gains furnished by rising farm incomes as domestic consumption and world demand suddenly mounted. The advantages of organization, consolidation, and integration, which were the same lessons being taught by big business, had now become too obvious for farmers to ignore. They too— whether New England dairy farmers, midwestern corn and wheat farmers, or cotton farmers in the South—could learn to read the statistics that told them what to do. The encouraging figures on production and prices that farmers began to consult were being compiled by the Division of Statistics of the Department of Agriculture, whose other busy departmental divisions—soils, chemistry, and animal husbandry—were proof of the continuing bureaucratic revolution of American agriculture.

These figures, whether for rising staple prices, declining shipping costs, or estimates of increasing production, assured farmers down to World War I that their sudden prosperity was real. Between 1900 and 1910 the price of corn shot up from 35 cents to 52 cents a bushel; wheat jumped from 62 cents to 91 cents. The wholesale farm price index rose 50 percent, and the average price of farmland doubled from $20 to $40 an acre. At last the economy seemed to be responding to farmers' needs and demands. Just as American businessmen were applying the lessons of consolidation, so American farmers were learning to follow the seemingly simple rules for finding safety in system and prosperity in new organization. The Country Life Commission itself was proof of the growth of the farmers' political influence. Appointed by President Theodore Roosevelt in 1908, the commission was charged with the task of improving rural life in the United States. After taking the pulse of rural America in all the nation's regions and listening to a recital of its ailments, the commissioners concluded that farmers needed to catch up with their city cousins, to "even up" the amenities between city and country. The recovery of the patient, according to the commissioners' diagnosis, required more agricultural credits, improved technology, a highway program, rural free delivery of mail, and better schools. By 1910 Hamlin Garland's Populist cry for justice "for the toiling poor wherever found" in rural America had become a faint echo as American farmers entered their golden age.

The most efficient of the early twentieth-century farm organizations were producers' cooperatives, adapted from the earlier experiments of the Farmers'

Alliance, which concentrated on solving the problems of pricing and marketing. Except for their official nonprofit status and their democratic voting procedures, cooperatives were really modern corporations—as streamlined and efficient as their counterparts in business. Like corporations, cooperatives came to rely on experts and specialists, trained managers and accountants, legal advisers, lobbyists, and public relations men. And like integrated industrial firms, they achieved forward integration by building their own facilities at railroad terminals and by writing ironclad contracts with their members, compelling them to hold their crops off the market until the price was right. By 1910 the antimonopoly scruples of big farmers were fast disappearing.

The new farm cooperatives advertised no grandiose social aims nor did they demand radical political change. Rather, they were content, with the return of prosperous times, to perfect the means that the organizational revolution had assigned them. Their members were essentially agricultural trade unionists who thought and behaved like cotton planters, corn-hog producers, apple-growers, and dairy farmers. Why, they asked themselves, replace an economic system capable of producing abundance that, however belatedly, was now being showered on them?

Soon the cooperative marketing movement was in full swing, and dozens of livestock unions, dairymen's leagues, grain exchanges, cotton cooperatives, and tobacco pools were being founded each year. Cooperatives in turn spawned hundreds of new pressure groups—the Farmers' Equity Union, the Farmers' Mutual Benefit Association, the Farmers' Social and Economic Union, the Farmers' Relief Association. All these groups proclaimed as their own the slogan of the American Society of Equity: "What the farmer wants to produce is not crops, but money." In 1912 cooperatives secured the blessing of the Department of Agriculture, which provided them with their own fact-finding agency, the Bureau of Markets. Eight years later the formation of the American Farm Bureau Federation announced the imminent appearance of modern agribusiness as a national force. If the arrival of progressivism signaled an attempt at discovering a national order, farmers as well as businessmen joined enthusiastically in the search.

Workers Respond to the Challenge of Organization

As the twentieth century opened, big business and organized labor entered a new age of wary alliance and cautious cooperation, both sides beginning to count the costs of industrial strife. But American labor won grudging recognition only slowly. The American Federation of Labor (AFL), modest in its aims, indifferent to unskilled workers, overcame the determined resistance of small and medium-sized employers only with great difficulty. Although AFL membership grew from 140,000 at its founding in 1886 to more than 2 million in 1914, less than one-third of the country's skilled workers could be found in its ranks in 1900. When World War I broke out in Europe in 1914, only 15 percent of the nonagricultural workers in the United States were members of any union.

American workers faced formidable obstacles to organization placed in their path by a stubborn small-business community abetted by a conservative Supreme Court. Two antilabor Court decisions in the first decade of the twentieth century severely limited the AFL's right to protest. In the *Danbury Hatters* case (1908) the Court upheld a lower court decision outlawing a boycott of a Connecticut hatmaker and awarding the company damages while holding the union leaders fully accountable for them. A year earlier, in the *Bucks Stove and Range Co.* case, the Court upheld an injunction against Gompers and the executive committee of the AFL while removing the jail sentences imposed on the leadership for ignoring the injunction. In 1903 the National Association of Manufacturers (founded in the 1890s to advance the interests of small businessmen) organized the ultraconservative Citizens Industrial Association to spread the gospel of the nonunion "open shop" under the name of "The American Plan," which touted businessmen as freedom-loving individualists, made heroes of strikebreakers, and damned union leaders as anarchist agitators and dangerous socialists. The success of their American Plan, reactionary businessmen promised, would spell the doom of "un-American" unions. Confronted with the "iron fist" of employer resistance, labor leaders like Gompers turned to the Democratic party and more receptive big businessmen in hopes of escaping judicial harassment and business animosity.

More enlightened big-business leaders for their part hoped to control labor through the concept of guided democracy. They stressed a paternal concern for the American worker, along with arbitration schemes and appeals to "responsible leadership" on both sides of the bargaining table: "A man who won't meet his men half-way is a God-damn fool!" Mark Hanna, one of the new business leaders, announced in deriding the obstinacy of George Pullman and similarly old-fashioned businessmen. The new corporate leaders recognized that many of labor's grievances were real and its demands for better treatment legitimate—a belated acknowledgment that American workers' needs for security and stability were not so very different from the goals of management. In 1900 progressive financiers like George E. Perkins and J. P. Morgan, together with industrialists like Mark Hanna, struck a bargain with the beleaguered Gompers and founded the National Civic Federation. The federation's basic principle was that labor, like business, must be encouraged to organize its interests responsibly and rally its forces for full participation as junior partners in the new corporate society.

Any strategy for improving industrial relations required, first of all, vastly improved working conditions. Well into the twentieth century factory work remained alarmingly dangerous. A survey of industrial accidents for the year 1913 showed that some 25,000 workers had been killed on the job and another 750,000 seriously injured. Then there were problems of incentive, alienation, and the loss of worker solidarity resulting from increased scale and the impersonality of the plant. These conditions contrasted with earlier ones within the memory of aging workers, one of whom, a veteran shoe worker, described the old routines for the Industrial Commission in 1899. "In these old shops," he told the commissioners, "one man owned the shop; and he and three, four, five or six others, neighbors, came in there and sat down and made shoes, and there was no machinery. Everybody was at liberty to talk." The present rule for survival in a large factory was a guarded silence: "Keep your mouth shut and don't tell any man, woman, or child on the face of the earth what wages you get, unless you don't get what you are worth, in which case go to the office *alone* and fix it at once. Remember that."

Could a long-vanished shop-floor comradeship be recovered or re-created? "We do not want to go back to the time when we could do without the sewing machine or the machinery for manufacturing purposes, or the large aggregations of capital," the shoemaker told the congressmen, "but we want capital controlled in such a way that it will not result in the displacement of three-fourths of the population for the increased wealth of one-fourth of the population." In grudging admissions like this and plaintive calls for equity lay the secret of big business's success.

Cities in Revolt: The Rise of Urban Progressivism

The progressive search for order in a disordered world began in the city. Wherever urban reformers looked in the closing years of the nineteenth century, they saw disorganization and fragmentation. Wealthy neighborhoods with million-dollar mansions were set apart by parks and boulevards from teeming ghettos with dilapidated tenements and filthy streets. These conditions presented all-too-visible proof of the immense distances—social and psychological as well as economic and geographical—that separated the rich from the poor.

It was to close the distance between urban affluence and sprawling poverty that in 1889 Jane Addams, the pioneer settlement-house worker, moved into Hull House, a battered mansion on the corner of Polk and South Halstead streets in the heart of Chicago's Nineteenth Ward.

> The streets are inexpressibly dirty [she reported], the number of schools inadequate, factory legislation unenforced, the street-lighting bad, the paving miserable and altogether lacking in alleys and smaller streets, and the stables defy all laws of sanitation.... Hundreds of houses are unconnected with the street sewer.... Back tenements flourish; many houses have no water supply save the faucet in the back yard; there are no fire escapes; the garbage and ashes are placed in wooden boxes which are fastened to the street pavements.... Our ward contains two hundred and fifty-five saloons; our own precinct boasts of eight.... There are seven churches and two missions in the ward.

In listing the Nineteenth Ward's needs, Jane Addams summarized the main points in the urban progressive indictment of boss politics. Progressivism began as a spontaneous revolt of city dwellers who were convinced that they had been short-changed in their share of the American social fund.

Mulberry Street in the Lower East Side of New York City
By 1910 the Lower East Side was one of the most densely populated spots on earth.

A pragmatic assessment of urban blight was the first phase in the drive to clean up the nation's cities. Broad coalitions of voters demanded immediate solutions to a wide range of problems: they sought tax reforms, more effective health regulations, lower streetcar fares, better utility services, and efficient city governments free of corrupt bosses and greedy special interests. The depression of the 1890s, by placing new burdens on consumers, created a sense of urgency and focused public attention on the shortcomings of rule by the political machines.

The progressive attack centered on "invisible government," the alliance between municipal authorities and business interests. The connection between "corrupt government" and "corporate arrogance," which the progressives fought to destroy, was a simple one of mutual need. In attempting to modernize their cities, machine politicians had discovered that secret agreements with transit, utility, and construction interests were a handy device for providing minimal service while lining their own pockets. At the same time, the new and unstable industries that were involved with urban development were undergoing rapid reorganization and were always short of funds. These industries saw in monopoly franchises, wholesale bribery, and kickbacks a measure of certainty in an otherwise unpredictable world. By 1890 such bargains had been sealed in most of the country's major cities. The only real loser in this arrangement was the public.

Thus progressivism began as a "people's movement" aimed at eliminating corruption and inefficiency. Cutting across class lines and focusing on specific issues like dangerous railway crossings, poor sanitation, and high streetcar fares, the progressive movement in its early years developed a style that was both democratic and moralistic. The twin devils in the reformers' morality plays were the businessman and the boss. Lincoln Steffens, the dean of reform journalists, pronounced the American businessman "a self-righteous fraud": "I found him buying boodlers in St. Louis, defending grafters in Minneapolis, originating corruption in Pittsburgh, sharing with the bosses in Philadelphia, deploring reform in Chicago, and beating good government with corruption funds in New York." From the beginning the progressives developed an antibusiness rhetoric that continued to obscure the real contributions of businessmen to urban reform.

Progressive Mayors   The bosses offered even more enticing targets. Urban reformer Frederick C. Howe reported that Boss Cox of Cincinnati ruled his city "as a medieval baron did his serfs." The only remedy for boss rule lay in building citizens' coalitions to unite a fragmented community. "The very nature of city life," one progressive commentator pointed out, "compels manifold cooperation. The individual cannot 'go it alone'; he cannot do as he pleases; he must conform his acts in an ever increasing degree to the will and welfare of [his] community. . . . "This concept of the organic city fitted neatly with the interests and ambitions of a new group of reform mayors in the 1890s who launched individual campaigns to overhaul their cities.

The first of these progressive mayors was Hazen Pingree, mayor of Detroit from 1889 to 1896, when he was elected governor of Michigan. Pingree, a shoe manufacturer turned "reform boss," campaigned vigorously in all the wards of the city. He steered clear of controversial moral and religious questions like prohibition and parochial schools, concentrating instead on the hard economic issues that would win him the broadest support. Pingree exposed bribery in a local electric company's dealings with his predecessors and embarked on an extensive program of school and park construction. After a long battle with the transit and utility interests, he succeeded in reducing streetcar fares and gas rates while building the city's municipal lighting plant. During the depression of the 1890s, he started work-relief programs for Detroit's unemployed and extended a variety of social service programs. Pingree set a pattern for his successors by attacking Detroit's "invisible government" and replacing it with an efficient, responsive administration.

It remained for Tom Johnson, the mercurial mayor of Cleveland from 1901 to 1909, to exploit most fully a whole new range of possibilities for leadership. Johnson had made his fortune by reorganizing transit systems, and he had been converted to reform after reading Henry George's *Social Problems.* After two successful terms in Congress as a reform Democrat, he returned to Cleveland to build a political coalition to fight Republican boss Mark Hanna and the transit interests. Energetic, tough-minded, and the ultimate politician, down to the unlit cigar he waved while speaking from the nearest soapbox, Johnson borrowed the techniques of the machine politicians and improved on them. He inaugurated his reform program by arranging for a regulated system of prostitution free from police graft. Like Hazen Pingree, he threatened the transit interests with regulation; his most widely acclaimed achievement was the 3-cent fare. Johnson provided his city with free public bathhouses, recreational facilities, and effective sanitary inspection, and he continued to agitate for municipal ownership of utilities.

Progressive mayors who launched their careers from a platform of pragmatic opposition to the "interests" were frequently driven to face broader questions of social welfare. Some mayors—like Pingree, Johnson, and later Brand Whitlock in Toledo, Ohio, and Mark Fagan in Jersey City, New Jersey—were forced to adjust to shifting economic interests within their reform coalitions and to support welfare measures that went far beyond the political and structural reforms they originally had called for. The "social justice" mayors, as they have been called, also came to question the value of strict party identification. Increasingly they relied on the advice and services of new nonpartisan experts in municipal management who were concerned with finding more efficient ways of running American cities.

Social Experimentation

"Streetcar politics" was only the most visible sign of the urban revival in the 1890s. City churches were keenly aware of their declining membership among the working class and responded to the crisis by developing the "institutional church" in lower-class neighborhoods. By providing services like lodging houses, reading rooms, recreational halls, and day nurseries, church progressives hoped to spread the "social gospel" of Christianity. Then too, by 1890 groups of earnest young college graduates, many of them women, were moving into slums to live in settlement houses modeled on London's famed Toynbee Hall. By 1895 there were more than fifty such settlements in major cities around the country, each with a staff of idealistic college graduates and seminarians.

Settlement-house workers were invariably young (most were under thirty), religious (predominantly Congregationalists and Presbyterians), college-educated, and single, and overwhelmingly they came from middle-class families. For these young intellectuals and professionals, some of them with advanced training in the new social sciences taught in German universities, the city settlement offered an escape from gentility and from feelings of uselessness, and provided the chance to practice new skills. Settlements freed them from what Jane Addams called "the snare of preparation" for unknown careers. More important, they developed a new and deeper understanding of the complex social and cultural relations that made up the modern city. Teachers, housing reformers, charity

How the Other Half Lived
Reform journalist and photographer Jacob Riis documented his exposé of life in New York City's slums with startling photographs of tenement interiors.

organizers, child-labor opponents, health inspectors, and visiting nurses found a congenial home in the reform settlements, which seemed to them miniature models of the good society.

The reform achievements of the settlement-house workers were limited but real. Their biggest gains were won in securing public health and safety regulations for their cities, ensuring improved working conditions for urban industrial workers, and extending the reach of progressive education out from the metropolis. They enjoyed only modest and frequently ephemeral success in checking the abuses of machine politics, and—like most middle-class Americans in the progressive period—they failed to note the ravages of racial inequality or prevent the growth of ghettos. Yet if they hesitated to acknowledge the deeper structural problems generated by a maturing corporate capitalism, settlement-house people brought with them from the countryside, where most of them had been born, reassuring notions of the neighborhood and extended households that helped make the city with its collisive ethnic cultures seem not just manageable but challenging and exciting. And women, whose numbers dominated the movement in the United States from the beginning, found not simply new careers and satisfactions in their communal homes but a sudden sense of equality with men as organizers, directors, and publicists of a new message of social solidarity.

The progressive movement was not only a major effort in social engineering. It involved also a profound intellectual revolution. The reformers came to understand the complexity and the interconnectedness of modern life. They experienced firsthand the difficulty of isolating the underlying causes of the problems they dealt with, and the futility of proposing simple solutions. Whether they were lawyers, engineers, clinicians, historians, sociologists, or economists, the progressives found themselves working with a new approach to knowledge that the philosopher John Dewey, one of their teachers, called "creative intelligence," and another powerful intellectual, William James, called "pragmatism." James taught these young reformers to seek truth not in abstractions, but in action. "How will truth be realized? What, in short, is truth's cash-value in experiential terms?" Truth was not a "stagnant property" inherent in an idea, as Emerson and the Transcendentalists had believed. Truth *worked,* James insisted. *"True ideas are those we can assimilate, validate, corroborate, and verify. False ideas are those we cannot."*

John Dewey, whose interest in social reform was as strong as James's, saw the origins of this so-called instrumentalist logic in Charles Darwin's evolutionary biology and in the scientific thinking that did away with the old search for "absolutes and finalities." This new logic, Dewey told his progressive students, brought new intellectual responsibilities. Philosophy would hereafter have to deal with "the more serious of the conflicts that occur in life" and develop a method of "moral and political diagnosis and prognosis." Oliver Wendell Holmes, Jr., judge and legal instrumentalist, was even more specific. He taught the progressives that the true function of law was the expression not of abstract principles, but of "accurately measured social desires."

By 1900 the settlement house had become an indispensable laboratory of social experimentation. In devising urban programs and services, the progressives relied heavily on new methods of research and fact gathering as essential to the work of reordering urban society. One of Jane Addams's first assignments was to collect and collate the raw data on the surrounding neighborhood; in 1895 *Hull House Maps and Papers* appeared as the first detailed account of an immigrant community published in the United States. In 1903 Lawrence Veiller and Robert W. DeForest published their two-volume *Tenement House Problems,* an attempt to relate housing to the larger setting through statistics and firsthand observation. Perhaps the most ambitious project for studying the city in its entirety was the six-volume *Pittsburgh Survey* (1909–14), which treated politics, crime, prostitution, the family, housing, and working conditions as aspects of a functioning social organism.

Social surveys underscored the need for trained personnel and scientific management. The independent commission, staffed by trained professionals and given the power to revamp tax structures, regulate transit and utility rates, and provide efficient city services, quickly became an essential agency of effective urban reform. The multiplication of commissions increased the demand for trained personnel. University education in key fields spread throughout the nation, and a new range of professions, each with its own organization, arose. By 1910 economists, political scientists, sociologists, tax reformers, charity organizers, settlement-house workers, and dozens of other specialized professionals had formed national societies, each with its own publications and communications network. These national organizations both strengthened the sense of professional community among progressives and cemented an alliance with newly founded universities that provided the training and facilities for investigating urban problems. In Chicago the residents of Hull House soon established close connections with the new University of Chicago through reform-minded academics like John Dewey, sociologists Albion Small and William I. Thomas, and political scientist Charles Merriam. In New York economists and sociologists from Columbia University joined freelance writers and publicists in analyzing city problems and working out solutions. Settlement houses proved vital for young professors by providing laboratories for testing their new concepts of behavior and by drawing them into the exciting world of business and politics beyond university walls.

Businessmen and professors often disagreed, however, on the question of how to apply the new critical spirit of reform. University scholars—historians, economists, and social theorists—now had sharp analytical tools for dissecting old conservative myths and challenging entrenched institutions. Historian Charles A. Beard was the best known of the young professors who were beginning to question the narrow interpretations of American law and the Constitution as well as the ancestor worship they encouraged. Beard's own Columbia University typified the new tradition-breaking spirit. There, economist Edwin Seligman, James Harvey Robinson, an earnest advocate of the "New History" as a reform tool, and pioneer students of administrative law such as Frank Goodnow were busy probing the economic roots of political behavior. At the same time, political scientist Arthur F. Bentley, in the *The Process of Government* (1908), approached political decision making as a complex process that was subject to the shifting forces of interest groups. At the University of Washington radical historian J. Allen Smith, in a book entitled *The Spirit of American Government* (1907), dismissed the Constitution as a "reactionary document" designed to restrict the forces of democracy. After 1900 the alliance between highly critical academics and their corporate financial supporters grew increasingly strained as the professors began to question the very business civilization on which their universities had come to depend.

Scientific Reform   The universities also supplied a more conservative product. With the appearance of concepts of "social control" and "scientific efficiency," progressive reformers made contact with another reform tradition. This tradition was alien to the open tolerance of reform politicians and to the democratic and humanitarian hopes of social workers, and concentrated instead on efforts to impose strict efficiency and economy. For many progressives the modern corporation embodied these business values and procedures. The picture of the efficient, impersonal corporation was not drawn by businessmen alone. It was a widely accepted model of organization that appealed to intellectuals and professionals as well as to industrialists and financiers who recognized its uses in rebuilding American politics. The progressives criticized the trust largely because unscrupulous promoters had misused it, not because of its seemingly rational structure. "The trust is the educator of us all," Jane Addams announced in explaining the need for new kinds of collective action. Seen in this light, the corporation appeared as a corrective of the waste and inefficiencies of an earlier age, an actual model of social and political reform that, like the utopian communities before the Civil War, could be extended to American society as a whole.

The "scientific" urban reformers believed, however, that they could manage the city simply by tightening expenditures, consolidating power in the hands of experts, and revising the political system without particular regard to human needs. Good government, they reasoned, would be rigorously honest, determinedly efficient, unfailingly frugal, and strictly accountable. But such scientific reform restricted democratic participation. It limited the influence of "uninformed" voters—workers and immigrants—whose numbers it sought to reduce through literacy tests and tighter political registration laws. Such restrictions were comparable in spirit to the disfranchisement of blacks then under way in the South.

These scientific reformers considered the city a challenge that was not very different from the challenges met by industrialists and financiers. Efficiency and economy came to be equated with business practices of budget paring, cost cutting, tax trimming, and service chopping according to the ledger-book ethics of corporation accountants. "Municipal government is business, not politics," was the slogan of the scientific reformers. The modern corporation's shaping power in determining these reformers' outlook was reflected in their vocabulary, which developed a set of useful analogies. The mayor served as *chairman of the board* of an urban *corporation* composed of big and little *stockholders,* who were expected to vote their *proxies* at *annual meetings* and to accept their *dividends* without constantly interfering with the *managers* of the *enterprise.*

It was hardly a coincidence that the last years of the century, which saw the triumph of the corporation and the advent of scientific municipal reform, also witnessed the opening assault on the concept of a rational "public opinion," once considered the cornerstone of democratic politics. In dismissing ordinary public opinion as frivolous or perverse, scientific reformers demonstrated a distrust of democracy. The first order of reform business, insisted Frank Goodnow, an expert in administrative law and spokesman for the scientific reformers, was to recruit loyal and politically unambitious civil servants whose efficiencies would allow "the business and professional class of the community to assume care of the public business without making too great personal sacrifice." For the good-government advocates and business-dominated mayors who tried to clean up the cities after 1900, urban reform meant a chance for middle- and upper-class

Americans, armed with new technical skills, to regain control of urban politics that an earlier generation had abandoned to the bosses.

The progressive businessmen and professionals shared a new set of values that reshaped their aims into concepts of system, control, stability, and predictability. Charity organizers now realized the need for accurate data in drafting workable solutions to social disorganization. A giant lumber company like Weyerhaeuser came to appreciate the importance of planning and cooperation with the new experts in the United States Forestry Service. College professors and high school teachers recognized the need for professional solidarity to protect their rights. Public-service lawyers, among them Louis Brandeis, acknowledged the complexities of new legal relations and began to play the role of "counsel to the situation" in experimenting with new techniques of arbitration.

The social perceptions of these middle-class leaders in the bureaucratic revolution stemmed from their sense of American society as a national collectivity in need of a new set of operating procedures. To implement their bureaucratic values, progressive reformers centralized authority in a hierarchical order, concentrated decision-making power in an energetic executive, established impersonal relations in restructuring their organizations, and above all planned for maximum efficiency.

The urban reform movement was therefore split between those who sought to extend popular influences in government and those whose programs limited popular participation. Reformers faced a choice between two widely different estimates of democracy and human nature. Some of them, like sociologist Edward A. Ross, frankly rejected the idea of democratic participation in favor of open elitism. Politically, Ross argued, democracy meant not the sovereignty of the average citizen, "who is a rather narrow, shortsighted, muddleheaded creature," but the "mature public opinion" of an educated elite. The case for democracy was most forcefully explained by Brand Whitlock, novelist, social welfare reformer, and mayor of Toledo from 1905 to 1913, who defined the "city sense" as democracy and as "the spirit of goodwill in humanity." Whitlock predicted that cities would arise that would "express the ideals of the people and work wonderful ameliorations in the human soul."

The conservative bias of many progressive reformers could be clearly seen in their attacks on the boss and the machine, but their real intentions were often obscured, even to themselves, by their seemingly democratic enthusiasm. "The people are finding a way," exclaimed progressive publicist William Allen White, who pointed in astonishment to the rapid growth of "fundamental democracy" throughout the country. A whole roster of progressive proposals for open government was billed as a democratic device for ensuring popular control at the grass roots. Thus the direct primary and direct election of senators would release the bosses' stranglehold on the electoral process. Referendum would send important questions of policy to the people, over the heads of unresponsive legislators. Recall would return the power to remove officeholders to the voters, with whom it belonged.

Urban progressives were not hypocrites in advertising their reforms as democratic, but they did not always make it clear that by "the people" they meant not the huddled masses in center cities, but solid citizens with sensible views and sober habits. Below the blaring trumpets of democracy could be heard, subdued but distinct, the progressive call for the politically vanquished middle class to return to the struggle armed with new weapons.

By 1900 a dual tradition had emerged, polarized around conflicting values of social efficiency and democratic liberation. These contrasting principles, which had combined briefly in the 1890s to challenge the politics of the bosses, would continue to diverge in the twentieth century, creating tensions within progressivism that would make it a confused yet creative movement.

The nerve center for urban progressivism after 1900 consisted of municipal leagues, civic federations, citizens' lobbies, commercial clubs, and bureaus of municipal research. These civic groups provided forums for the lively exchange of ideas between academics and businessmen eager to try out new concepts of efficiency and economy. From organizations like the National Municipal League and the National Civic Federation poured a flood of proposals and plans for repairing city government: home rule and charter revision; ballot reform and literacy tests; citywide election schemes and city-manager plans, all of them aimed at the bosses' power base.

At first the reformers concentrated on improving procedures. They proposed segregated budgets for economy. They introduced time clocks, work sheets, job descriptions, and standardized salaries. They developed systematic ways of giving out contracts to replace the old patronage system. But the heart of their reform program was the commission and city-manager plans, modeled on the corporation. Combining executive and legislative functions in a single board, the commission plan spread rapidly until by 1913 more than three hundred cities in the United States had adopted it. The city-manager plan, a refinement of the original commission idea, further consolidated decision making in municipal government, and by the 1920s it too had been widely adopted.

Urban progressives never succeeded in putting the political boss out of business. Nevertheless progressivism successfully challenged boss politics by confronting it with another way of doing the business of the city. The machine's power lay in the center city, with its immigrants and working classes. Middle-class reformers generally operated from power bases along the suburban periphery. Boss politics, for all its sins, was marked by a high degree of accountability and popular participation in the wards and precincts. Progressives tried to reduce direct popular involvement at both the voting and the officeholding level. Bosses were wasteful but democratic; progressives were economical and bureaucratic.

Progressive success was limited. All too often, procedures changed but official policy did not. Still, if the boss and his clients proved adept at smashing the electoral hopes of reform candidates, they could no longer ignore the cries for more effective city government. The progressives' dream of a shiny, streamlined administrative model never materialized. Yet the modernizing of American cities proceeded with or without the politicians' approval. In their partial overhaul of the nation's cities, the progressives scored important gains for the new bureaucratic order.

The Man with the Muckrake

Many of these contradictions could be seen in the work of the muckrakers who supplied progressivism with an agenda. The name *muckrakers* was given to a new brand of reform journalists by President Theodore Roosevelt, who complained that their relentless exposure of corruption in high places hindered rather than helped him in his work of improving American society. Roosevelt compared this group of headstrong publicists to the gloomy figure who, in the seventeenth-century English Puritan John Bunyan's *Pilgrim's Progress,* refused a celestial crown and kept a muckrake. The president denounced these muckrakers' "crude and sweeping generalizations" and their delight in pointing the finger of civic shame. For their part the muckrakers—Lincoln Steffens, Ida Tarbell, Ray Stannard Baker, David Graham Phillips, and many less famous colleagues—accepted the label and wore it defiantly as proof of their devotion to the Jeffersonian principle of a free and vigilant press.

Muckraking was the product of two forces that had combined by the end of the nineteenth century: major advances in the technology of printing, which made it possible to produce inexpensive, illustrated popular magazines; and the simultaneous arrival on the metropolitan scene of reform reporters sensitive to the new social concerns of the middle-class reader and eager to exploit them. S. S. McClure, founder of *McClure's,* was one of the pioneer explorers of the lucrative field of reform journalism, and he was quickly joined by dozens of competitors who were drawn to social criticism by their keen sense of the market and the prospect of sizable profits. From the outset muckraking proved that reform could be a paying proposition. Gathering a staff of trained, well-paid newspapermen, McClure and other editors launched an attack on the underside of American life with articles on sweatshops, tainted meat, the white slave traffic, insurance company scandals, labor racketeering, city bosses, and high finance. Muckrakers happily compiled a list of all the social wrongs that their enlightened readers would presumably set right.

Muckraking offered both a new kind of factual reporting and an old form of moral publicity. Always extravagant and frequently sensational, the muckrakers perfected the uses of contrast and contradiction in pointing to the gap between venerable American ideals and startling social facts. In an article for *Cosmopolitan* on child labor in southern cotton mills, for example, poet Edwin Markham depicted "The Hoe Man in the Making" in the faces of "ill-fed, unkempt, unwashed, half-dressed" children penned in the narrow lanes of the mills, little victims whose dreary lives mocked the "bright courtesy of the cultured classes." Social gospelist Ernest Crosby contrasted the appearance of a majestic United States Senate with the reality of a "House of Dollars," a political

"U.S. $enate 'House of Dollars'"
Collier's, *one of the leading Muckraking journals, featured this cartoon on the cover of an issue denouncing the political power of trusts and monopolies.*

monopoly modeled on an industrial trust. Samuel Hopkins Adams explained the national failure to regulate the food and drug industries as the result of "private interests in public murder" when "everybody's health is nobody's business."

Muckraking thus presented a publicity technique rather than a philosophy, a popular journalistic style rather than a searching analysis. As social critics, journalists like Lincoln Steffens and David Graham Phillips were tough-minded and factual but also romantic, moralistic, and sentimental. Like their millions of readers, they were the beneficiaries of a fundamental change in the idea of publicity, which they conceived of as an open-ended process of fact gathering that reflected the shifting nature of social reality. Read in this subdued light, their articles could be considered wholesome remedies and useful correctives. Their work, the muckrakers insisted, was never done, since an unfolding social process required constant adaptation of old theories to new facts—of accepted values to changing conditions.

Muckraking also tapped traditional morality while exploiting the time-honored role of the disinterested observer—the clear-eyed, hard-nosed investigator with a fierce desire to get all the facts and expose them to the sanitizing rays of publicity. Muckrakers liked to think of themselves as brave detectives, dashing from one hidden clue to another, looking for the fragments of information that, once collected and arranged, would tell reformers what to do next. There was a strong bias against party government in the muckrakers' view of American politics, as well as a weakness for conspiratorial interpretations. They believed that the masses of American voters, once given the facts, would demand reform. Tell the people the truth, they said, and they would correct injustice forthwith. Conscience, duty, character, virtue—these were the muckrakers' watchwords, and also a measure of their limited understanding of the problems confronting progressive America. Muckrakers identified the symptoms of disorder, but they could not isolate its causes or prescribe effective remedies. For these tasks a clearer understanding of the workings of modern industrial society was needed.

Progressivism Invades the States

After 1900 the progressives, building on urban achievements, set out to reform state politics. Beginning in 1900 with the first administration of Wisconsin governor Robert M. La Follette, reform swept across the nation in the next decade and transformed the conduct of state politics.

Although progressivism varied widely in the different sections of the country, there were enough similarities to give political reform at the state level the appearance of a national movement. In the South progressives who had inherited a number of Populist grievances often wore the trappings of a redneck revolt against the business-minded Bourbons. By the opening years of the twentieth century, one governorship after another was falling to economy-minded agrarians from upcountry or downstate. The southern rebellion against the alliance of big business and Democratic politicians drew on popular sympathies and produced railroad and corporate regulation, antimonopoly laws, insurance company controls, and improved public education and child-labor laws—but all with mounting racist demagoguery and the continuing disfranchisement of the black population.

Progressivism in the Midwest and on the Pacific Coast also grew out of a revolt, usually within the Republican party, which was perceived to be too generous to railroads and corporations. Midwestern progressives drew more heavily from the arsenal of democratic political reforms—the initiative and referendum, for example—than did their counterparts in the East, who tended to rely more on administrative reforms. But everywhere big business's control of state legislatures made an inviting target. Corporate dominance of New Jersey state politics, for example, was all but complete by 1900. "We've got everything in the state worth having," a spokesman for corporate interests boasted. The legislature regularly elected two senators who represented the utility interests and the insurance companies; and the executive branch of the state government was staffed by former employees of the Pennsylvania Railroad.

Massachusetts Machine Shop, 1895–96
Working on lathes lacking proper safety guards and powered by uncased belts was highly dangerous.

The governors who organized the revolts against these statehouse rings headed the cast of new progressive folk heroes. The most popular of the reform governors cast themselves as western heroes, riding into office with a mandate to clean up the state, setting about their task with grim determination, and moving on to bigger things when the job was done. Typically the reform governor, denied office by state party leaders, collected his small band of rebels and tried, unsuccessfully at first, to take over the party. To help in subsequent efforts, he enlisted other mavericks and began to explore such electoral reforms as the primary system of party nomination and the direct election of senators. Fixing his sights on the "interests," he eventually defeated the party regulars.

Once elected, the progressive governor moved quickly to neutralize his opposition by absorbing some of its members into his reform coalition. He learned to wield patronage with a surprising ruthlessness, and with secure majorities in the legislature he went to work on his reform program. This generally included strict regulation of railroads and public-service corporations, a revamped tax structure, and major pieces of social legislation to improve working and living conditions in the state. After a hectic term or two in which he managed to complete at least part of this reform program, the progressive governor moved on to the United States Senate, where he was joined by other like-minded rebels from similar backgrounds who had the same hopes of imposing their reform designs on national politics. The career of one such progressive hero, Robert M. La Follette, illustrates the main features of this legend of progressive reform.

"Battling Bob" La Follette, an intense, unsmiling, self-made man, was a small-town lawyer who struggled to the top of the political heap in Wisconsin. In his three terms as governor after 1900, he enacted a reform program that became the envy of progressives across the country. Young La Follette was a walking example of the Protestant ethic. Born in Primrose, Wisconsin, in meager circumstances, he put himself through the state university at Madison by teaching school, and he prepared himself for a career in politics by studying for the bar. At the University of Wisconsin he came under the reform influence of its president, John Bascom, who was just beginning to build a public-service institution, a task that La Follette himself would complete a quarter of a century later.

Short and wiry, with a shock of bristly iron-gray hair, La Follette combined a rock-hard moralism with a fanatical combativeness. He won his first office as district attorney without the endorsement of the Republican machine by barnstorming the county and haranguing rural voters on the need for integrity and independence. In 1884, again without the support of party regulars, he was elected to the first of three terms in Congress, where he was the youngest member of the House. He was defeated for reelection in the Democratic landslide of 1890 and came home to a lucrative law practice.

In Wisconsin as in a number of other states, the Republican party had been the effective instrument of the railroad and lumber companies. Faced with a lawsuit against their corrupt state treasurers, the party bosses tried to bribe La Follette to secure his influence with a judge, who happened to be his brother-in-law. La Follette promptly cried havoc and later reckoned the attempted bribe as the turning point of his career: "Nothing else ever came into my life that exerted such a powerful influence upon me as that affair." In exposing the machine's crime to the voters, he effectively isolated himself from the party leaders and spent nearly a decade trying to collect enough votes from Scandinavian farmers and industrial workers in Milwaukee to overthrow the machine. By 1900 he had succeeded.

La Follette's victory won him instant national acclaim. After destroying the power of the old machine by winning over some of its leaders to his own cause, he set out to modernize Wisconsin. The "Wisconsin Idea," as it came to be known, depended on a progressive majority in the state legislature, which the new governor secured by campaigning personally for his supporters and then holding them strictly accountable. Soon his enemies were complaining that he had made himself the boss of a ruthlessly efficient machine of his own. The substance of the

Wisconsin Idea was a set of related reforms: a direct primary law, an improved civil service, a railroad rate commission, a fair tax program, state banking controls, conservation measures, a water power franchise act, and protective labor legislation. At the center of La Follette's reform movement stood the independent regulatory commission, staffed by experts from the state university and given wide administrative latitude.

To his many admirers across the country, La Follette seemed a political anomaly, a popular leader with his feet firmly planted in the grass roots but at the same time an enthusiastic convert to scientific government. Exacting, fiercely partisan, and a powerful hater, he often viewed the world as a gigantic conspiracy against "Battling Bob." He kept ready for display at a moment's notice the image of the sea-green incorruptible who preached the virtues of direct democracy and constantly urged his followers to "go back to the people." "Selfish interests," he declared, "may resist every inch of ground, may threaten, malign and corrupt, [but] they cannot escape the final issues. That which is so plain, so simple, and so just will surely triumph."

The other half of La Follette's reform equation, however, was filled with the facts and figures that his investigatory commissions collected. His own interminable speeches came loaded with statistics and percentages provided by a corps of tax experts, labor consultants, industrial commissioners, and social workers. He hammered these facts at the voters of Wisconsin in the belief that the people, once they learned their meaning, would hardly fail him. The conflicting principles

Senator Robert M. La Follette Discusses His Campaign Plans with His Son and Namesake
"Battling Bob" founded a reform tradition that he passed on to his two sons who carried it into the New Deal.

of popular democracy and government by an expert elite hardly bothered La Follette. The expert commission, secure above the battle of parties and interests—the key agency of the Wisconsin Idea—seemingly embodied the detachment and patriotism it was designed to foster in the people. La Follette's growing national reputation, in fact, rested on the belief he inspired that direct democracy and scientific government were not simply compatible, but complementary.

State Progressive Reform

An important feature of progressive reform programs in the states was a package of new laws, drawn up by civic groups, women's organizations, and consumer interests, that humanized working conditions. As late as 1900, more than half the states had no laws that established a minimum age for workers. By 1914 every state but one had an age limit on the employment of children. In most states new laws for the protection of women in industry paralleled the drive to abolish child labor. Illinois led the way in 1892 by limiting hours for women. New York and Massachusetts followed, and then the movement spread rapidly westward. When the Supreme Court upheld the principle of state regulation of hours for women in the celebrated case of *Muller* v. *Oregon* in 1908, barriers collapsed. By the time America entered World War I in 1917, thirty-nine states had written new laws protecting women or had significantly strengthened old laws, while eight states had gone even further by passing minimum wage laws for women. Another feature of the progressive social reform program was the campaign for employers' liability laws and industrial accident insurance, which did away with the worst abuses of the older legal rules that governed workplace safety and contributory negligence. By 1916 nearly two-thirds of the states, reacting to mounting pressures from a progressive public, had established insurance programs.

Progressivism, taking different forms in different states, marked a shift in power within the American political system. Cumbersome, interest-dominated legislatures gave way to a new public authority lodged in the executive branch and in its supporting administrative agencies that were charged with discovering and then serving the public interest. To justify their roles as custodians of the public interest, progressives unearthed a national-interest theory of politics as old as the Founders. "I would not be a dredger congressman, or a farm congressman, or a fresh-egg congressman," a typical progressive told his constituents in summoning up the spirit of Edmund Burke and virtual representation.* "I would like to be an American congressman, recognizing the union and the nation." If warring economic and class interests were chiefly responsible for the lack of direction and the low tone of American politics, progressives reasoned, then it was wise to ignore them and appeal instead to a potential public virtue in the concept of citizenship. "Progressivism," another reformer added, "believes in nationalism . . . opposes class government by either business, the laboring class, or any other class." This tendency to reject interest-group government (govern-

---

*For Burke and virtual representation in the eighteenth century, see volume 1, chapter 7, pp. 240–42.

ment as a bargaining process between blocs of big business, big labor, and big agriculture) drove progressives to embrace the idea of leadership from above—from those "good men" in whom idealism presumably ran deeper than self-ishness. "While the inspiration has always come from below in the advance of human rights," the California progressive William Kent insisted, the real accomplishments in improving American society must always be "the disinterested work of men who, having abundant means, have ranged themselves on the side of those most needing help." In the progressive interpretation of American politics, underdogs announced their needs, but topdogs filled them.

Draped with the mantle of disinterested benevolence, state progressivism resembled, more than anything else, a rebuilt model of Federalism, suitably modernized to fit an industrial society. Like their Federalist ancestors, progressives feared the idea of party government and class division, and they sought to take the politics out of American life in the name of scientific management. In place of eighteenth-century rule by republican notables, they substituted leadership by experts whose skills were to command the instant allegiance of all enlightened citizens. Most progressive political reforms aimed at securing stability and control. And in the same fashion, the progressive social justice programs initiated by the states were designed to strengthen corporate capitalism by empowering the government to reassign responsibilities and lessen the harshness of the American industrial environment. To carry out their policies at the national level, the progressives looked to the figure of the new statesman, and in Theodore Roosevelt they found their hero.

Theodore Roosevelt: The Progressive as Hero

In September 1901 President William McKinley died in Buffalo of an assassin's bullet, and Theodore Roosevelt—"this crazy man," as Republican managers thought him—was catapulted from the vice-presidency into the post of national leader. Blueblood, historian, student of the classics, amateur naturalist, cowpuncher, and Rough Rider, Roosevelt at forty-two appeared to millions of admirers as the last of the universal men, but to uneasy Republican bosses like Mark Hanna as "that damned cowboy."

With an audible sigh of relief, Old Guard Republicans heard the new president announce his intentions "to continue, absolutely unbroken, the policy of President McKinley." McKinley had stood for high tariffs, the gold standard, a not-too-vigorous prosecution of the trusts, and just the right amount of imperial ambition.* The prospect of a continuing custodial presidency reassured those congressional conservatives who feared above all a rambunctious executive. Yet within the year, Roosevelt had begun to challenge congressional authority, and, by the time he retired from his second term in March 1909, he had succeeded in

---

*For American expansionism under McKinley, see chapter 26, pp. 260–70.

creating a national progressive movement, reinvigorating American foreign policy, and laying the foundations of the twentieth-century welfare state.

A Patrician Cowboy   Roosevelt was the product of New York society, the son of a banker-philanthropist who had dabbled in genteel reforms and organized the city's upper-class contribution to the Union cause during the Civil War. A graduate of Harvard, where he had amused his classmates with his odd earnestness and vibrancy, young Roosevelt immediately settled on a life of politics among the "kittle-kattle" of spoilsmen and mugwumps. He held the comfortable classes chiefly to blame for the moral chaos of Gilded Age politics, and with a highly developed sense of the upper class's social responsibility he entered the New York State Assembly as a representative from one of the city's wealthy Republican districts.

In the assembly, where he served a single term from 1882 to 1884, he displayed the unique mixture of social conservatism, pugnacity, and political shrewdness that was to become his distinguishing mark. In 1886 he accepted the Republican nomination in the three-way mayoralty race in New York City and ran a respectable third behind Democratic winner Abram S. Hewitt and single-taxer Henry George. The 1880s also saw the growth of a sizable body of Roosevelt's historical writing—*The Winning of the West,* a biography of Gouverneur Morris, and another of Thomas Hart Benton—in which Roosevelt proclaimed his unqualified approval of the nationalist designs of the Federalists, denounced Jefferson as a humbug and a hypocrite, and hymned the glories of westward expansion and the fulfillment of America's continental destiny.

When his first wife died in 1884, Roosevelt retired to the frontier he had described so eloquently, finding solace in Dakota ranch life filled with cowboys, frontier justice, and manly virtues. As a steadfast but unpredictable young Republican, he was appointed to the United States Civil Service Commission by President Benjamin Harrison in 1889 and served in Washington in a blaze of publicity until 1895, when he returned to New York to head the Board of Police Commissioners. Here he made another name for himself as a result of late-night prowls with his friend, journalist Jacob Riis, in futile efforts to enforce the city's blue laws. McKinley rewarded such energy by appointing him assistant secretary of the navy, despite Roosevelt's outspoken views on behalf of American military power.

The Spanish-American War in 1898 drew Roosevelt out of the shadows of appointive office and into the limelight of electoral politics. As self-appointed leader of the Rough Riders, the First Regiment of the United States Cavalry Volunteers, he caught the fancy of a jingoistic public that followed with keen interest his dramatic, if somewhat excessive, exploits in charging up San Juan Hill, pausing now and then to exult over all "those damned Spanish dead" as he rallied his own disorderly troops.

Disembarking to the tune of "There'll Be a Hot Time in the Old Town Tonight," Roosevelt was promptly elected governor of New York and just as quickly upset party bosses by taking a firm progressive stand on a state factory inspection law and on another law regulating the hours of state employees. "If there is going to be any solution of the big social problems of the day," he warned his supporters, "it will come, not through a sentimental parlor socialism, but through actually taking hold of what is to be done, working right in the mire." Republican leaders in New York responded by lifting their governor out of the mire of reform politics and into the clean and safe office of the vice-presidency. Their hopes for squelching the exuberant progressive were curtailed when McKinley's assassination put Roosevelt in the White House.

Roosevelt as President   Americans soon learned what kind of president they had acquired, for Roosevelt had strong opinions on every conceivable subject and delighted in publishing them in pungent and readable phrases. The objects of his interest ranged from the novels of the French writer Emile Zola (which he generally disliked) to the "full baby carriage" (which he heartily endorsed); and his advice ranged from conduct becoming football players and would-be reformers ("Don't flinch, don't foul, hit the line hard!") to what one observer called an "unflagging approval of the Ten Commandments." A vigorous intellectual, interested in birds and political bosses, trusts and big game, divorce and "practical idealism," Roosevelt collected facts and ideas that he regularly assembled in print—not writing with a pen, as one reader put it, so much as charging with it.

Roosevelt's forceful and sometimes contradictory opinions revealed two distinct personalities. The first was described by a New York politician as "the most indiscreet guy I ever met," the keeper of the national conscience always ready to speak his mind. This public Roosevelt served as the confident spokesman of an aggressive American nationalism—prophet of a coming Anglo-Saxon supremacy, celebrant of military valor, unblushing advocate of power politics, and a true believer in the American mission to order the affairs of the rest of the world. The national hero, "Teddy"—a name he disliked—looked the part. With pince-nez adorning a bulbous nose, toothy grin stretched in a near grimace, a full square face with its several chins resting on heavyset shoulders, a reedy voice, and pump-handle gestures, he was a cartoonist's dream.

In the role of the mad American of his generation, as he has been called, Roosevelt could and frequently did talk great nonsense. He lashed out with equal contempt at "radical fanatics" and the "lunatic fringe" of soft-headed reformers. "Sentimental humanitarians" he denounced as "a most pernicious body, with an influence for bad hardly surpassed by that of the professional criminal classes." He stressed the importance of "good blood" flowing through the veins of well-bred, self-denying gentlemen. He predicted race suicide for any of the world's people who preferred "effeminacy of character" to the "rougher and manlier virtues." For handling mobs he recommended "taking ten or a dozen of their leaders out, standing...them against a wall, and shooting them dead." For anarchists and socialist agitators he had a similar prescription—troops supplied

**Theodore Roosevelt
Campaigning in Wyoming, 1903**
*Against a backdrop of patriotic
bunting and antler horns,
Roosevelt demonstrates his
Square Deal.*

with real bullets and "the most wholesome desire to do them harm." Americans, whether delighted or appalled by such balderdash, recognized in Roosevelt the authentic American hero, the compulsive man of action who shot from the hip and whose motto read: "Get action; do things; be sane."

The other Roosevelt, unlike the trigger-happy dispenser of justice, was a thoughtful if highly partisan student of American history with a keen appreciation of the original work of the Founders. Young progressives entering the political arena after 1900 with credentials from the new universities brought with them training in such new disciplines as economics and sociology. But for the slightly older progressive leaders, the study of history was still the primary tool for examining American society. Despite the rapid growth of the "scientific" monograph, much of the popular history written after 1880 continued to be the work of gentlemen amateurs like Roosevelt and his friends Henry Adams and retired industrialist James Ford Rhodes, who measured the achievements and noted the shortcomings of nineteenth-century American democracy. The thrust of much of this popular history was toward political nationalism and social conservatism, whether in John Fiske's admiring account of the Founders, in Henry Adams's search for the principles of scientific government in his magnificent nine-volume history of the administrations of Jefferson and Madison, or in Roosevelt's own hymns to national valor in *The Naval War of 1812* and *The Winning of the West*.

Roosevelt's Political Philosophy

This reflective, history-minded Roosevelt was the first president after Lincoln and the last of the moderns with an understanding of the eighteenth century. Beneath his dramatic account of America's rise to greatness lay a clear grasp of the original Federalist design and the men who fashioned it. National greatness, it seemed to Roosevelt, was based, just as it had been in the past, on the "power to attain a high degree of social efficiency." By this he meant "love of order" and the "capacity to subordinate the interests of the individual to the interests of the community." The Federalists, he believed, led by such farseeing nationalists as Hamilton and Gouverneur Morris, had tried to teach the first Americans the same lesson that his own generation had just learned—that "the sphere of the State's action may be vastly increased without in any way diminishing the happiness of either the many or the few."

Roosevelt was convinced that the American people had been given the wrong directions by a demagogic Jefferson and had drifted steadily toward the Civil War even as they had expanded and enriched their domain. From Jefferson and his Jacksonian heirs they had acquired the illusions that little government was needed and that the moral order was self-regulating. Despite their magnificent material accomplishments in filling out a continent and building an industrial empire, the American people had failed to devise the political means of managing it. Only briefly during Lincoln's wartime administration had Americans caught a glimpse of true national unity. With the onset of the Gilded Age, the original stateman's question "Will it work?" had been replaced by the huckster's demand "Does it pay?" and the national energy had been squandered in money grubbing. One fact was clear at last—Americans had to "abandon definitely the *laissez-faire* theory of political economy, and fearlessly champion a system of increased Governmental control."

The opening years of the twentieth century, Roosevelt believed, represented "an era of federation and combination" that had been foreshadowed by the age of the Founders. The president, like his Federalist teachers, deplored class politics and called for the rule of enlightened men of integrity, whom he always identified with the better half of the Republican party. But wherever found, the disinterested patriot, Roosevelt was convinced, held the key to the future. By the time Roosevelt took over the presidency in 1901, he had acquired a clear definition of his role as general manager of the United States, even though the details of his plan for its "orderly development" emerged only gradually from the recesses of his conservative mind.

"Wise Radicalism and Wise Conservatism": The Square Deal

As president, Roosevelt firmly established the regulatory principle as the foundation of administrative government. What he and the country came to call the Square Deal as he campaigned for reelection in 1904 began as a loose collection of proposals for directing national economic development. Roosevelt had inherited from Gilded Age Republicanism an Old Guard of conservatives. They had built their stronghold in the Senate, where they kept firm control over the lawmaking process and saw to it that presidents followed their dictates. Roosevelt was immediately forced to bargain with their leader, Senator Nelson W. Aldrich of Rhode Island, and to agree to keep his hands off the tariff question in exchange for a limited freedom to pursue his plans for intervention elsewhere. These concerns, like those of his progressive followers, first centered on the trusts.

Trustbusting When Roosevelt took office in 1901, the fortunes of the opponents of monopoly appeared to improve. The Sherman Act, besides breaking up the Northern Securities Company in 1903, was applied successfully under Roosevelt's handpicked successor, William Howard Taft, against the Standard Oil and American Tobacco companies (1911). Yet by the end of Roosevelt's second administration in 1909 it was already clear that the act, far from achieving the results its framers had intended twenty years earlier, was strengthening rather than stopping the forces behind industrial and financial mergers. By admitting that not every restraint of trade was unreasonable, and by ruling cartel behavior unacceptable but full-blown mergers legitimate, the courts, first in Roosevelt's and then in Taft's administration, simply invited big business to abandon looser forms of organization for tighter and more effective ones.

Roosevelt shared the progressives' ambivalence toward big business. "Nothing of importance is gained," he admitted, "by breaking up a huge interstate and international organization which has not offended otherwise than by its size.... Those who would seek to restore the days of unlimited and uncontrolled competition ... are attempting not only the impossible, but what, if possible, would be undesirable." He believed that the trusts' behavior, not their size, constituted the test of their utility, and he declared it the government's duty to operate "in the interest of the general public." To prevent the trusts from fixing prices and manipulating the market, he proposed a watchdog agency modeled on the Interstate Commerce Commission, a body appointed by him and staffed with "trained administrators, well known to hold the scales exactly even in all matters." After a sharp skirmish with big business and its defenders in Congress, he succeeded in 1903 in establishing the Bureau of Corporations within the new Department of Labor and Commerce to police business practices and report its findings to the public.

Publicity formed the keystone of Roosevelt's regulatory program, and he quickly perfected the art of disclosure in launching a series of actions under the Sherman Antitrust Act. He advised the beef trust of his strictly honorable intentions to "Destroy the Evils in Trusts, But Not the Prosperity," and he insisted publicly on settling "the absolutely vital question" of federal power to regulate the trusts with the Northern Securities Company, the United States Steel Company, and the American Tobacco Company. It was essential, he announced, for the president and his administrators to maintain "strict supervision" of big business and see that it did not go wrong.

To make good his promise, in 1902 Roosevelt gave the signal to the Department of Justice to move against J. P. Morgan's railroad combine, the Northern Securities Company. Morgan, he recalled with relish, "could not help regarding me as a big rival operator who intended to ruin all his interests." But it was power that interested the president, who considered the clash with Morgan a dynastic one of rival sovereignties. In upholding the government's case against the railroad merger in *Northern Securities Co. v. United States* in 1904, the Supreme Court gave Roosevelt his precedent. In the *E. C. Knight* case (1895), he announced with obvious satisfaction, the Court had erroneously decided that the federal government lacked the power to break up dangerous combinations: "This decision I caused to be annulled." He did not add what soon became obvious—that he had not at the same time suppressed the merger movement.

Roosevelt's views on organized labor mirrored his convictions on big business: the ultimate test for both sides was a willingness to provide order and stability of their own volition. If trusts threatened the balance of economic power with irresponsible behavior, Roosevelt reasoned, labor could prove disruptive and greedy. If there were "good" and "bad" trusts, there were also dependable labor leaders like Samuel Gompers, and dangerous visionaries like Eugene Debs. In either case it was the president who had to distinguish legitimate demands from crackpot notions. The only standard he could finally invoke was conduct: "Where in either one or the other, there develops corruption or mere brutal indifference to the rights of others, and short-sighted refusal to look beyond the moment's gain, then the offender, whether union or corporation, must be fought."

The test of Roosevelt's opinion of unions, strikes, and injunctions came early in the first administration, when the United Mine Workers struck against the anthracite coal operators. The confrontation alarmed the whole country and gave Roosevelt welcome public support. Led by the canny John Mitchell, the miners demanded a pay increase and an eight-hour day along with acknowledgment of their right to organize the coal industry. George Baer, president of the Reading Railroad, bungled the case for the coal operators from the outset. Baer proclaimed it his "religious duty" to defeat the strikers, insisting that "the rights and interests of the laboring men will be protected and cared for—not by labor agitators, but by Christian men to whom God in his infinite wisdom has given control of the property interests of the country."

Roosevelt, his hand strengthened by the operators' obstinacy, quickly called for an investigation by his labor commissioner and used the findings to try to force the coal companies to compromise. When they refused, he ordered both parties to a conference in Washington, where the operators, under a presidential threat to send in troops, finally agreed to an arbitration panel. The Anthracite Coal Strike Commission awarded a 10 percent pay increase and a reduction of hours to the miners, while refusing their demand for a closed shop. Once again, as in regulating the trusts, it was principle and procedure—the orderly disposition of grievances by disinterested men—that most concerned the president.

New Consumer Legislation

Roosevelt's theory of expanded executive power developed from his belief that only "a great exertion of federal authority" could meet the needs of all the people. The most vulnerable members of a largely unregulated commercial society were American consumers. In consumer legislation, as in his dealings with big business and labor, Roosevelt assumed the leadership of forces that had already begun to organize by 1900. The Pure Food and Drug Law, passed in 1906, was the result of a carefully orchestrated public outcry and shrewd presidential direction. Although limited, the law capped a strenuous campaign for effective legislation by Harvey Wiley, chief chemist of the Department of Agriculture, who twice had seen his recommendations accepted in the House only to languish in the Senate, where the food and drug interests dominated. Aided by a series of lurid exposés furnished by the muckrakers, Roosevelt finally collected the votes he needed to prohibit the manufacture and sale of misbranded or adulterated foods and drugs, a limited power that has been wielded cautiously ever since.

Support for the Meat Packing Act (1906) also came from consumers, many of whom learned of the appalling conditions in the industry from Upton Sinclair's sensational novel *The Jungle.* In attacking the packers, Sinclair traced the shipment, from prairie to slaughterhouse, of cows "that developed lumpy jaw, or fell sick, or dried up of old age," carcasses "covered with boils that were full of matter." Although Roosevelt was annoyed by Sinclair's fictionalized account, the president promised him action. An investigation verified most of Sinclair's charges in a fact-studded report that Roosevelt, in a calculated piece of blackmail, threatened to release unless the packers accepted minimum regulation. Like most of the Square Deal legislation, the final bill represented a series of compromises—increased appropriations for inspection in exchange for the removal of inconvenient requirements for enforcement. The legislation left the matter of appeal to the courts in what Roosevelt called "purposeful ambiguity." Once the industry had accepted the principle of federal regulation, the big packers welcomed those requirements that could be expected to drive out their smaller competitors. For his part the president was perfectly willing to compromise on details in order to gain the principle of federal control.

In his willingness to sacrifice specifics for the precedent, Roosevelt frequently disappointed his more determined progressive supporters, who complained that he gave in too easily on points that might have been won. His critics appear to have won their case in the tug of war over the Hepburn Act (1906), which regulated railroad rates. In 1903 the railroad senators who refused to grant the government effective control over rate making had drafted the Elkins Act, a piece of legislation supposedly prohibiting discriminatory rebates to favored shippers. But Roosevelt was determined to acquire this authority. An administration measure passed by the House was designed to strengthen the Interstate Commerce Commission by giving it genuine power to fix rates and make them stick. In the Senate, however, Roosevelt's plan met the stubborn opposition of Nelson Aldrich and the railroad senators, who had decided to teach the president a

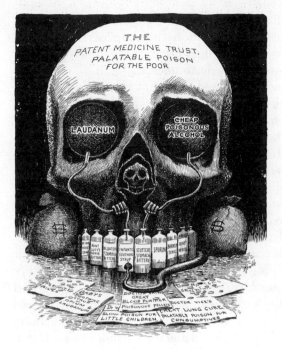

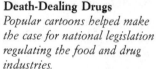

Death-Dealing Drugs
Popular cartoons helped make the case for national legislation regulating the food and drug industries.

lesson. Aldrich and his conservatives quickly bottled up the bill in committee, where they conducted interminable hearings for the benefit of its enemies.

Roosevelt tried a second time with another bill, this one sponsored by Representative William P. Hepburn of Ohio. This even more moderate measure would empower the ICC to set reasonable rates after hearing complaints from shippers. Once again Aldrich stepped in, sent the bill to the Senate floor without endorsement, and looked on with detachment as one amendment after another stripped the bill of its original intent. In the end Roosevelt failed to rally a successful coalition of faithful Republicans and disgruntled Democrats, but he did manage to win over enough moderate Republicans to force Aldrich to compromise. The final version of the Hepburn bill increased the powers of the ICC but left intact the provision against enforcing new rates in cases that were under court appeal. At best, Roosevelt had won a very limited victory.

A Formula for Conservation

In the case of conservation, the last main item on the Square Deal agenda, compromise again weakened principle. Although Roosevelt himself was a nature lover and preservationist by inclination, he abandoned the tradition of the naturalists Henry David Thoreau and John Muir for a developmentalist strategy designed for multiple use of the nation's natural resources. He called on citizens to look ahead to "the days of our children" and warned against the waste and destruction that would "result in undermining . . . the very prosperity" that ought to be passed on to them "amplified and developed." Yet his formula for conservation remained the same as that for other national needs: expert advice from scientists committed to development rather than preservation, much publicity, and permissive governmental oversight of private interests.

These long-term limitations were obscured for the moment in the flurry of executive actions during Roosevelt's second term as he added 43 million acres to the national forests, withdrew from entry more than 2,500 water power sites and 65 million acres of coal lands, and established 16 national monuments and 53 wildlife refuges. The issue of conservation assumed a crucial symbolic significance in Roosevelt's mind as he found himself blocked by Congress from pursuing other social justice goals. He turned to the management of natural resources as "the fundamental problem which underlies almost every other problem in national life," the acid test of federal power. He flouted the congressional will with a "midnight proclamation" that set aside twenty-three new forest reserves and then threw down his challenge: "If Congress differs from me . . . it will have full opportunity in the future to take such positions as it may desire anent the discontinuance of the reserves." While Congress fumed, he moved rapidly ahead with plans for building a conservation empire consisting of bureaus and commissions filled with geologists, hydrologists, foresters, and engineers taking their orders from Gifford Pinchot, his volatile but capable chief forester. In 1908, sensing widespread public interest, Roosevelt called a National Conservation Congress, which was attended by forty-four governors and over five hundred conservation experts.

Yet despite its appearance as a popular crusade, Roosevelt's conservation program was less a grass-roots movement to save the environment than an executive scheme for national resource management imposed from above. The president envisioned a grand design in which irrigation, flood control, forestry, and reclamation would be "interdependent parts of the same problem" of regional development. He had to settle for much less. Government experts and lumber company executives shared a strong distaste for the preservationists' ideas. The new federal agencies were understaffed and underfinanced, and they soon found themselves dependent on the goodwill of the same private interests they were supposed to police. Small operators, whose reputation for gouging the landscape was well earned, were sometimes driven out, but the large companies continued their policies of exploiting national resources under a government seal of approval. From the perspective of three-quarters of a century, Roosevelt's national conservation program, like the original Federalist partnership between wealth and government, appears to have identified with the welfare of powerful private interests.

The Limits of Neofederalism

Having retired from the presidency after two terms in office, Roosevelt embarked for Africa on a hunting trip in the spring of 1909, leaving in the White House his handpicked successor, the ponderous William Howard Taft, to "carry on the work substantially as I have carried it on." In many ways the conservation issue symbolized both the partial success and the ultimate limitations of Roosevelt's attempt to forge a new national purpose. The key to his plan was teaching the American electorate the meaning of national unity and strong government, an educational task he performed admirably for seven years.

The conservation campaign, which slowly moved to the center of the progressive consciousness, meant a fight against sectionalism, states' rights, business interests, and a Congress that gave them all voice. To halt these divisive forces and hold the allegiance of his reform followers, Roosevelt had revitalized the presidential office and buttressed it with new concepts of civic duty and loyalty. "I believe in a strong executive; I believe in power," he announced, and he proceeded to use his power in ways that no president since Lincoln had contemplated. To aid him in his work of executive renovation, he drew heavily from the ranks of progressive experts and professionals, whose cause of scientific government he championed enthusiastically. His reform program, for all its timid approach to the regulatory principle and its deference to vested interests, marked at least a step toward the orderly republic he envisioned.

If Roosevelt's utopia lay well over the horizon in 1909, it was because he intentionally set conservative limits to the application of governmental power and in the last analysis believed firmly in a guided democratic process. Although he chafed under the restraints placed on him by his party and a laggard Congress, he managed both of them with consummate skill, alternately bullying and cajoling both, but breaking with neither. In negotiating for his limited reforms, he was willing more often than not to take the shell and leave the kernel, concerned as he was with winning a principle. Yet his presidency was no mere exercise in educational politics. Roosevelt wanted results that the country would accept, and to get them he willingly used traditional and even conservative political methods. When he left office, the results were clear. He had raised the presidency to its twentieth-century position of dominance. He had laid the foundation for a governmental bureaucracy and had collected the presumably disinterested professionals to run it. And finally, he had preached with unflagging zeal the virtues of high-mindedness, integrity, and service as indispensable to the new citizenship.

Further than this neither Roosevelt nor the nationalist-minded progressives could go. Roosevelt spoke for progressives across the country in demanding the return to service of "the man of business and the man of science, the doctor of divinity and the doctor of law, the architect, the engineer, and the writer," all of whom owed a "positive duty to the community, the neglect of which they cannot excuse on any plea of their private affairs." An organized army of political hacks had long since defeated the ordinary citizen, "to whom participation in politics is a disagreeable duty." Now, Roosevelt and the progressives believed, it was time to try the extraordinary citizen wherever he could be found. Neither Roosevelt nor the progressives would have been surprised to learn that the average citizen was taking less rather than greater interest in politics. Voter turnout, which in the Gilded Age had averaged nearly 80 percent in presidential years and 60 percent in off-years, fell a full 15 percent after 1900. Possibly because they were disenchanted with the prospects of a managed republic that the progressives promised them, or perhaps simply because they were discovering more pressing concerns outside the political arena, fewer Americans were troubling themselves with the duty of taking what Roosevelt called "their full part in our life."

Here indeed lay the outermost reaches of Roosevelt's political domain. If Jefferson's political formula had long since proved hopelessly inadequate for managing an industrial republic, his original estimate of the diverse sources of American energy had not. Jefferson had counted the advantages as well as the dangers of sectional division, religious variety, ethnic diversity, and even class disagreement. With Roosevelt's retirement in 1909, these forces of social and political pluralism began to take revenge on his promise of national unity, first shaking the party structure and then disrupting the national social consensus that Roosevelt and his followers had attempted to construct. In a suddenly revived Democratic party the American people would find a different variety of progressive reform, and in Woodrow Wilson a very different kind of leader.

CHRONOLOGY

1889	Jane Addams founds Hull House; beginning of settlement-house movement. Hazen Pingree elected mayor of Detroit; first progressive mayor.	**1901**	Theodore Roosevelt becomes president after McKinley assassinated. Tom Johnson elected mayor of Cleveland.
1890	Muckraking photo-journalist Jacob Riis publishes *How the Other Half Lives,* depicting life in New York's slums.	**1902**	Roosevelt launches antitrust action against Northern Securities Company. Roosevelt settles anthracite coal strike through arbitration.
1893	First issue of *McClure's* magazine. Conference for Good City Government inaugurates urban progressive reform movement.	**1903**	Bureau of Corporations established within new Department of Labor and Commerce.
1899	John Dewey's *School and Society,* pioneer progressive education tract.	**1904**	Roosevelt elected president, defeating Democrat Alton B. Parker and Socialist Eugene V. Debs. Case of *Northern Securities Co.* v. *U.S.* upholds government's case against railroad mergers. Lincoln Steffens's *The Shame of the Cities* published.
1900	Robert La Follette elected to his first of three terms as progressive governor of Wisconsin. William McKinley reelected president, defeating William Jennings Bryan.	**1906**	Upton Sinclair's novel *The Jungle* published.

1906 Meat Packing Act passed.
Pure Food and Drug Act passed.
Hepburn Act passed,
strengthening powers of
Interstate Commerce
Commission.
John Spargo's *The Bitter Cry of
Children,* exposé of child labor,
published.

1907 Financial panic; Roosevelt turns to
J. P. Morgan and the bankers for
help.
William James's *Pragmatism*
published.

1908 Supreme Court upholds state
regulation of working hours for
women in *Muller* v. *Oregon.*
Roosevelt convenes National
Conservation Congress.
William Howard Taft elected
president, defeating Bryan and
Debs.

1911 Frederick Winslow Taylor's
*Principles of Scientific
Management,* pioneer work in
industrial efficiency.
"Dissolution" of Standard Oil and
American Tobacco trusts.

SUGGESTED READINGS

George E. Mowry, *The Era of Theodore Roosevelt, 1900–1912* (1958), and Arthur S. Link, *Woodrow Wilson and the Progressive Era, 1900–1917* (1954), provide an excellent survey of the politics of the progressive period. Recent interpretive essays include William L. O'Neill, *The Progressive Years: America Comes of Age* (1975); David M. Kennedy, ed., *Progressivism: The Critical Issues* (1971); Lewis L. Gould, *The Progressive Era* (1973); and John D. Buenker, *Urban Liberalism and Progressive Reform* (1973). Two recent overviews of progressivism are John D. Buenker, John C. Burnham, and Robert M. Crunden, *Progressivism* (1977); and Arthur S. Link and Richard L. McCormick, *Progressivism* (1983). Dewey W. Grantham, *Southern Progressivism: The Reconciliation of Progress and Tradition* (1983) provides a regional survey of the movement, and Jack Temple Kirby, *Darkness at Dawning: Race and Reform in the Progressive South* counts the cost of progressive racism.

The literature on bosses and machines in the progressive period is impressive. Among the best accounts are Lloyd Wendt and Herman Kogan, *Bosses in Lusty Chicago: The Story of Bathhouse John and Hinky Dink* (1943); Zane L. Miller, *Boss Cox's Cincinnati* (1968); Lyle Dorsett, *The Pendergast Machine* (1968); and Walton E. Bean, *Boss Ruef's San Francisco* (1952).

Two autobiographical accounts provide the best introduction to muckraking: Lincoln Steffens, *The Autobiography of Lincoln Steffens* (1931), and Ida M. Tarbell, *All in the Day's Work* (1939). Harold S. Williamson, *McClure's Magazine and the Muckrakers* (1970), is a good account of the career of the pioneer muckraking editor. Arthur Weinberg and Lila Weinberg, eds., *The Muckrakers* (1961), and Harvey Swados, ed., *Years of Conscience: The Muckrakers* (1962), offer a wide range of muckraking reporting.

Robert La Follette's career in Wisconsin and in the United States Senate is chronicled in David Thelen, *Robert La Follette and the Insurgent Spirit* (1976); Robert S. Maxwell, *La Follette and the Rise of Progressivism in Wisconsin* (1956); and Herbert Margulies, *The Decline of the Progressive Movement in Wisconsin, 1890–1920* (1968). For a portrait of another progressive political leader who was the temperamental opposite of La Follette, see Robert F. Wesser, *Charles Evans Hughes: Politics and Reform in New York State, 1905–1910* (1967).

There are many good biographies of major political figures on the national scene during the Progressive Era. John Milton Cooper, Jr., *The Warrior and the Priest: Theodore Roosevelt and Woodrow Wilson* (1983) is a deft comparison of presidential styles and philosophies. For Roosevelt they include William H. Harbaugh, *The Life and Times of Theodore Roosevelt* (1961); the brief but perceptive John Morton Blum, *The Republican Roosevelt* (1954); G. Wallace Chessman, *Theodore Roosevelt and the Politics of Power* (1969); and Edmund Morris, *The Rise of Theodore Roosevelt* (1979), a highly readable account of Roosevelt's prepresidential years. A useful study of Taft is Donald E. Anderson, *William Howard Taft* (1973). Biographies of other important progressives include Alpheus T. Mason, *Brandeis: A Free Man's Life* (1946); Melvin I. Urofsky, *Louis D. Brandeis and the Progressive Tradition* (1981); Dexter Perkins, *Charles Evans Hughes and American Democratic Statesmanship* (1956); Richard Lowitt, *George W. Norris: The Making of a Progressive* (1963); John A. Garraty, *Right-Hand Man: The Life of George W. Perkins* (1960); Richard Leopold, *Elihu Root and the Conservative Tradition* (1954); and M. Nelson McGeary, *Gifford Pinchot: Forester-Politician* (1960).

Progressive social issues have been discussed in several important works. John W. Chambers II, *The Tyranny of Change: America in the Progressive Era, 1900–1917* (1988) traces the course of progressive reformers' intervention in the economy and society at large. James H. Timberlake, *Prohibition and the Progressive Crusade* (1963), examines the connections between progressive politics and moral reform. Jack Holl, *Juvenile Reform in the Progressive Era* (1971), explores another important aspect of progressive reform. The progressive concern with eugenics and birth control is described in Donald K. Pickens, *Eugenics and the Progressive Era* (1971), and David Kennedy, *Birth Control in America: The Career of Margaret Sanger* (1970). Changing patterns of morality emerge clearly from William L. O'Neill, *Divorce in the Progressive Era* (1967), and crucial developments in progressive education from Lawrence Cremin, *The Transformation of the School: Progressivism in American Education, 1876–1956* (1961). Samuel P. Hays, *Conservation and the Gospel of Efficiency* (1959), provides a close look at the less democratic features of that reform movement. Walter I. Trattner, *Crusade for Children* (1970) is a good account of child labor reform. John F. McClymer, *War and Welfare: Social Engineering in America, 1890–1925* (1970) explains the impact of war on progressive social engineering.

The intellectual climate of progressivism has been discussed in several excellent studies. Charles Forcey, *The Crossroads of Liberalism: Croly, Weyl, Lippmann and the Progressive Era, 1900–1925* (1961), gives a lively account of three leading progressive publicists. Robert W. Schneider, *Five Novelists of the Progressive Era* (1965), traces reform ideas through popular fiction. Roy Lubov, *The Progressives and the Slums* (1962), shows the concerns of leading reformers with cleaning up the cities. The best introduction to the writing of progressive history is Richard Hofstadter, *The Progressive Historians* (1968). Samuel J. Konefsky, *The Legacy of Holmes and Brandeis* (1956), explains the legacy of the two great progressive jurists. Samuel Haber, *Efficiency and Uplift: Scientific Management in the Progressive Era, 1890–1920* (1964), shows the effect of the ideas of Frederick Winslow Taylor in shaping progressive values. For sharply etched portraits of three key intellectuals in the Progressive Era, see David Riesman, *Thorstein Veblen: A Critical Introduction* (1963); Ralph Barton Perry, *The Thought and Character of William James* (2 vols., 1935); and Sidney Hook, *John Dewey: An Intellectual Portrait* (1939).

Personal reflections—sometimes illuminating, always entertaining—on the meaning of progressivism by two active progressives are collected in William Allen White, *The Autobiography of William Allen White* (1946), and Frederic C. Howe, *The Confessions of a Reformer* (1925).

14

Progressives and the Challenge of Pluralism

∽

*I*N 1910 Theodore Roosevelt, after a year's trek through Africa and the capitals of Europe, returned home to a rebellion in his own party. Once he learned of the widening rift between President William Howard Taft's supporters and his own leaderless progressive followers, Roosevelt moved quickly to return the Republican party to his original vision of a unified national purpose. In an incisive speech in 1910 dedicating a state park in Osawatomie, Kansas, where John Brown had fought with Missouri ruffians a half-century earlier, Roosevelt gave his program a name—the "New Nationalism." In part, Roosevelt's speech owed its clarity to his recent reading of Herbert Croly's *The Promise of American Life,* a progressive's indictment of American political drift with which the former president fully agreed. But in a broader sense both Croly's lengthy analysis and Roosevelt's call to action at Osawatomie summed up the arguments for an organized national society that Roosevelt had formulated years earlier.

Roosevelt was not calling for "overcentralization," he assured his Kansas audience, but for "a spirit of broad and far-reaching nationalism" to guide the American people as a whole. His New Nationalism, which put national needs ahead of sectional interests and private advantage, would bring an end to "the utter confusion that results from local legislatures attempting to treat national issues as local issues." After listing the many unfinished tasks awaiting federal action, Roosevelt drove home his point with a comparison that he hoped would have meaning for the few aging veterans of the Civil War in the crowd. "You could not have won simply as a disorderly mob," the Rough Rider reminded them. "You needed generals; you needed careful administration of the most advanced type.... You had to have the administration in Washington good, just as you had to have the administration in the field.... So it is in our civil life."

Unfortunately for Roosevelt, administration of the most advanced type was not yet a fact, as the man who was to be his chief rival in the election of 1912 already sensed. Woodrow Wilson, a Southerner and a Democrat, drew on both these traditions in sounding the principal countertheme of progressivism. As a former professor of political science and president of Princeton, currently the reform governor of New Jersey, Wilson was fully Roosevelt's match as a historian and intellectual. In examining the American political and social system in 1910, he came closer to understanding the complex play of social forces at work in the country than both of his Republican rivals, Taft and Roosevelt.

Roosevelt's New Nationalism called for the reordering of American priorities and the acquiring of new habits and duties. The "New Freedom"—as Wilson came to call his vision—offered another view of progressivism as a liberation movement. Wilson pictured an open, complex society, composed of immigrants and women as well as native-born white males, Catholics and Jews as well as Protestants, reformers as well as professional politicians, and visionaries of all sorts as well as political realists. In the election year of 1912, these broader strokes of Wilson's New Freedom seemed to present a truer picture of the complexity of early-twentieth-century American life than did the views of Roosevelt and the New Nationalists. But it remained to be seen whether the Democratic party, emerging from sixteen years of enforced retirement, could succeed in turning these various energies into a political program.

Changing the Progressive Guard

By 1910 it seemed that reform had slowed. Congress, with a bipartisan faction of conservatives in both houses, was in no mood to finish the work of building a national banking system or designing a program of business regulation. And a watchful conservative Supreme Court stood ready to stop any further advances toward the social service state.

Of all the branches of the federal government, the Supreme Court was the least responsive to the problems confronting industrial society and the most alert to the dangers of curtailing corporate privilege. Although it had agreed to Roosevelt's breaking up of the Northern Securities trust and the oil and tobacco monopolies, the Court was much less enthusiastic about the new progressive forms of administrative regulation and the use of commissions to make and enforce rulings. The struggle for administrative effectiveness after 1890 often seemed to be waged between a handful of conservative justices clinging tenaciously to the right of judicial review and a circle of frustrated congressional reformers hoping to strengthen the administrative arm of the federal government. To these reformers the Supreme Court's stubborn defense of its prerogatives seemed a usurpation—taking away from the Interstate Commerce Commission and other federal agencies the power to do their job. Progressives remembered, too, that the Supreme Court had recently declared a federal income tax unconstitutional and had set severe limits on the powers of the states to enact social legislation.

Justice Holmes and the Court

The spirit of progressivism invaded the Supreme Court with the appointment of Oliver Wendell Holmes, Jr. He was chosen by Roosevelt in the hope that he would reeducate his senior colleagues in the uses of judicial restraint and bring a more enlightened view of regulatory power to the Court. Holmes considered the Constitution not a yardstick for measuring the shortcomings of imperfect laws, but rather a flexible instrument for providing for the "felt necessities" of the modern age. The life of the law, he was convinced, was inherent in its utility and function. Holmes dismissed those of his colleagues on the Court who still claimed to believe in higher law as willing captives of "that naïve state of mind that accepts what has been familiar and accepted by them and their neighbors as something that must be accepted everywhere." As for himself, the outspoken newcomer admitted, "I . . . define truth as the system of my limitations and leave absolute truth for those who are better equipped."

Holmes explained his belief in the necessity of social experimentation in the famous *Lochner* case of 1905, a decision overturning a New York law that reduced the workweek for bakers to sixty hours. In a five-to-four decision the majority of the Court declared that the law was another "meddlesome interference with the rights of individuals" and thus unconstitutional. In his dissent Holmes lectured his fellow justices on the danger of intruding their laissez-faire views into the law. The Constitution, he declared, had not been intended "to embody a particular economic theory, whether of paternalism and the organic relation of the citizen to the state or of laissez-faire." Instead it was made for people who frankly differed, and "the accident of our finding certain opinions natural and familiar, or novel and even shocking, ought not to conclude our judgment upon the question whether statutes embodying them conflict with the Constitution of the United States." In a series of similar dissents during the next two decades, Holmes— together with Justice Louis Brandeis, who joined the liberal side of the Court in 1916—argued for restraint on the judicial activism of a conservative majority that was concerned with slowing the progressive drift toward a managed society.

Political Conflicts Under Taft

Congress was frequently divided within itself after 1909 and could make little headway against the Supreme Court's certainty of conservative purpose. Both the House and the Senate witnessed a series of sharp clashes between aggressively reform-minded Insurgents and stubborn conservatives over tariffs, conservation, and governmental reorganization. With no leadership from President Taft, who backed the majority of conservative Republican regulars, reformers lost heart.

Meanwhile Taft's political lethargy and his ineptitude made an inviting target for the barbs of Republican reformers, including La Follette. Although Roosevelt had recommended Taft as a thorough-going reformer, the new president lacked Roosevelt's concern with strengthening the federal government, as well as the former president's skill in managing his party. Taft was graceless, stubborn,

William Howard Taft
*Taft preferred conservative
Republicans to crusading
Insurgents.*

unschooled in the arts of political persuasion, and wholly lacking in Roosevelt's popular appeal—and he quickly made it clear that he was no crusader.

Taft's administration accordingly was punctuated by a series of political explosions. The first was touched off by a struggle over conservation policy. Gifford Pinchot, chief of the United States Forest Service, "Sir Galahad of the Woods," as his numerous enemies called him, accused Taft's secretary of the interior, Richard Ballinger, of neglecting his duties. More specifically, Pinchot accused Ballinger of unsavory conduct in validating the Bering River coal claims that had mysteriously come into possession of the Morgan-Guggenheim syndicate. Although a congressional investigation cleared Ballinger of any hint of fraud, and although the feisty and self-righteous Pinchot overplayed his hand by appealing to the American public at large, Ballinger felt obliged to resign. Taft, who had supported Ballinger, lost face and with it the loyalty of a sizable group of Roosevelt progressives.

Taft only increased his problems in his handling of the tariff question. After promising downward revision of the schedules, he backed away from the ensuing congressional struggle and looked on as the protectionist forces of Nelson Aldrich and the Old Guard loaded the original bill with higher schedules. Then, to the amazement of the progressive Insurgents, the president hurried to their midwestern stronghold, where he proclaimed the now unrecognizable Payne-Aldrich Act the "best tariff ever passed by the Republican party."

Roosevelt: The Bull Moose Candidate Roosevelt watched Taft's mismanagement of his party with growing disdain. "A lawyer's administration," he snorted, was proving itself "totally unfit" to lead the country. For like-minded progressives who had recently formed the Progressive Republican League, there were two choices. The first was to appeal to Roosevelt to intervene in party councils in their behalf and help them replace Taft with a candidate of their choosing; the second, and more desperate, strategy was to bolt the Republican party altogether and set up an independent reform party. By 1912 Republican progressives remained sharply divided on this question.

As the election year approached, Roosevelt himself was undecided about the best course. On the one hand, he was convinced that the Taft regime had paid little attention to the "needs of the country." On the other hand, he was dubious of the success of any movement on his own behalf, and he confessed to little enthusiasm for "staggering under a load on my shoulders through no fault of my own."

Whether he knew it or not, Roosevelt had practically declared his availability with his "New Nationalism" speech at Osawatomie. The New Nationalism, composed of schemes for the improved regulation of corporations, physical evaluation of railroads, a graduated income tax, a reformed banking system, labor legislation, a direct primary, and a corrupt practices act, seemed exhilarating to his progressive followers but nothing less than revolutionary to the Old Guard Republicans. Far from closing the breach between the two wings of the Republican party, the New Nationalism speech in effect was Roosevelt's challenge to Taft and his conservatives.

When Taft refused to step out of Roosevelt's way and Senator Robert La Follette entered a rival bid for the nomination, Roosevelt, who distrusted Taft and heartily disliked La Follette, decided to run. But Taft regulars put to good use the southern Republican delegates, whom they held securely. Roosevelt's hopes at the convention rested on some 252 contested seats, at least 100 of which he needed in order to win the nomination. With the credentials committee and the whole party apparatus in the hands of the regulars, he succeeded in winning only 14 of these contested seats. After hurried consultations with his financial backers, George W. Perkins and Frank Munsey, who promised to see him through, Roosevelt agreed to bolt and call his own convention to launch an independent Progressive party.

The loyal 10,000 who gathered in the Chicago Auditorium in August 1912 to hear their leader pronounce himself as fit as a "bull moose" and to sing with them the "Battle Hymn of the Republic" constituted a motley collection of mavericks and reformers, nationalists and big businessmen, social workers and intellectuals, all determined to stand with the "Colonel" at Armageddon and to "battle for the Lord." Conspicuously absent were most of the original liberal Insurgents, who declined to make a risky investment in third-party politics. Although the vibrant spirit of the old progressivism was evident at Chicago, Roosevelt and his advisers realized that winning the election would prove difficult. As Roosevelt intoned the Eighth Commandment and called down divine judgment on his Republican betrayers, he must have known that a Democratic victory was all but inevitable.

Wilson: The Shining Knight of Progressivism
Yet if fortune was about to shine its face on the Democrats in the election of 1912, it gave no sign. Democrats had their own liabilities, chief among them their titular head and perennial candidate, William Jennings Bryan, who had labored sixteen years to undo the damages of his ill-fated experiment in pietistic politics. In the center ring at the 1912 Democratic convention stood "Champ" Clark, speaker of the House and veteran southern leader of the party, who had the support of the rural wing; William Randolph Hearst, the demagogic newspaper publisher and pseudo-reformer; and Woodrow Wilson, the shining knight of New Jersey progressivism. Fresh from a series of legislative encounters that had seen the passage of a direct primary law, railroad legislation, workmen's compensation, and a corrupt practices act, Wilson represented the hopes of urban progressives in the East.

The Democratic convention in Baltimore was every bit as uproarious as the Republican convention. Clark, armed with preconvention pledges, jumped out to an early lead, which he maintained until the Wilson forces finally caught up. On the forty-sixth ballot, after endless maneuvering and a final agreement between southern agrarians and northern city bosses, the deadlock was broken and Wilson received the two-thirds vote necessary for nomination. Before they adjourned, the Democrats patched up their differences in a platform that roundly condemned Republican centralization—as Democratic platforms had unfailingly done since Reconstruction—and advertised its own brand of progressivism guaranteed to lower the tariff and break up the trusts, give the banks back to the people, and destroy all special privilege.

But the heart of the Democratic promise in 1912 lay in Wilson's call for liberation from the rule of big business and big government. Taft's official Republicanism, Wilson predicted, would spell continuing business domination, while Roosevelt's plan for monitoring the trusts simply added the powers of the government to those of the monopolists. Wilson pictured Democratic deliverance as "coming out of the stifling cellar into the open," where people could "breathe again and see the free spaces of the heavens." Remove the restrictions on private enterprise, Wilson urged, so that the younger generation would never

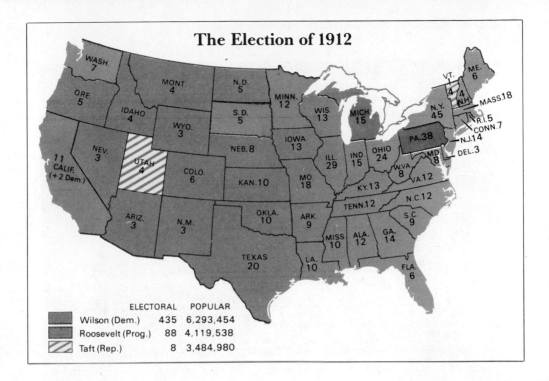

The Election of 1912

	ELECTORAL	POPULAR
Wilson (Dem.)	435	6,293,454
Roosevelt (Prog.)	88	4,119,538
Taft (Rep.)	8	3,484,980

become "the protégé of benevolent trusts" but rather would be free to go about making of their lives whatever they wished.

Wilson won the presidency with 6,286,214 popular votes—42 percent—and 435 electoral votes. Even with the split among the Republicans, who gave Taft some 3.5 million votes and Roosevelt's Progressive party more than 4 million, Wilson's victory was impressive. It remained to be seen whether the new president represented a new kind of leadership.

President Wilson: Schoolmaster to the Nation

If the intellectual sources of Roosevelt's New Nationalism lay in the eighteenth-century world of the Founders, the roots of Woodrow Wilson's New Freedom were firmly planted in nineteenth-century morality. Wilson, who was born in 1856 in Staunton, Virginia, grew up in the heart of the Confederacy, briefly attended Davidson College, and graduated from Princeton in 1879. After a year spent studying the law, for which he had no particular liking, he turned to his real interests, political science and history. He studied with the great historian of institutions Herbert Baxter Adams at Johns Hopkins University and earned a doctorate there in 1886. Then came several years of climbing the academic ladder, with appointments at Bryn Mawr, Wesleyan, and Princeton, where he taught for twelve years before becoming its president in 1902. Wilson's books, polished although not sparkling works of political science and history, made a varied collection: *Congressional Government* (1885); an extended essay, *The State* (1889); a history of the Civil War years, *Division and Reunion* (1893); the

Woodrow Wilson: Schoolmaster to the Nation
Wilson was a diligent campaigner and a highly effective speaker.

five-volume *History of the American People* (1902); and *Constitutional Government in the United States* (1908).

By temperament as well as training, Wilson was an academic, an educator-scholar who felt a calling to instruct a progressive generation in the science of good government. As schoolmaster to the nation, he looked the part—with a lean, angular face, a long nose adorned by a pince-nez, full pursed lips, and eyes that seemed to look through his visitors rather than at them. Distant, formal, somewhat severe in his relations with the public, he appeared correct but cold. He recognized this deep reserve in himself and thought it a weakness. "I have a sense of power in dealing with men collectively," he once confessed, "which I do not feel always in dealing with them singly." There was little familiarity in the man and no feeling of camaraderie. As president of Princeton, governor of New Jersey, and chief executive, Wilson was a man one worked *for* but not *with*. Both as a teacher and as an administrator, he had a problem not so much in disciplining his followers, at which he excelled with a frosty politeness, as in controlling his own high-voltage temper and his tendency to bristle when challenged. When opposition to his plans mounted, as it did in a serious struggle over the graduate school at Princeton, Wilson would cling to his position, personalize the conflict, and accuse his opponents of malice while avowing the purity of his own motives.

At his best, however, Wilson was a superb leader, directing the work of his subordinates with cool precision, holding their loyalty with ideals, and winning the American public over with his moral authority. On the few occasions when his self-confidence flagged in the face of enemy attack, he could be petty and vindictive. But at all times he lived the role of the statesman as educator, standing before and slightly above the American people, to whom he sought to teach effective government.

Some of the lessons Wilson taught were curiously old-fashioned and abstract—moral precepts rather than practical proposals. For him words like *liberty, justice,* and *progress* still retained their mid-nineteenth-century clarity. In his mind these words were connected with the Christian principles of "obligation," "service," and "righteousness" that his father, a Presbyterian minister, had preached. These moral abstractions were the skeletal truths around which Wilson packed such flesh-and-blood meaning as fitted his southern Democratic heritage. His intellectual origins led him to view American politics in terms of both individual rights and pluralistic values. In his vision of America, Wilson agreed with the English liberal philosopher John Stuart Mill's definition of liberty as the absence of external restraint. On the other hand, Wilson's southern upbringing had given him a generally unenlightened view of race and a quiet respect for the South's reasoning in discriminating against blacks.

Wilson sensed clearly that American life in the opening years of the twentieth century remained too disorganized, its forms too complex to be encased in a formula like the New Nationalism. "The life of the nation has grown infinitely varied," he reminded his fellow Democrats in pointing to a flourishing cultural and ethnic diversity. In his view the most urgent American reform task was releasing the creative impulses of a free people. Nations, he argued with strict Jeffersonian logic, are renewed from the bottom up, from "the great struggling unknown masses of men" at the base of society. The nation must preserve these Jeffersonian values even as it becomes industrialized and urbanized. Ultimately, Wilson hoped to reconcile modernization with the traditional values of small-town and rural America.

> If America discourages the locality, the community, the self-contained town, she will kill the nation. A nation is as rich as her free communities. . . . The welfare, the very existence of the nation rests at last upon the spirit in which they go about their work in the several communities throughout the broad land.

What the nation needed most, Wilson firmly believed, was to listen to the counsel of the working men and women of the country—and indeed Wilson sought and received labor backing in his campaigns, although he did not always give the labor movement what it asked.

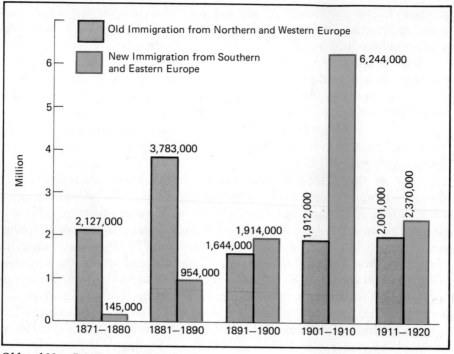

Old and New Immigration, 1871–1920

Americans—New and Old

Many of the men and women who did the nation's daily work were recent arrivals from Europe. The decade after 1900 saw the climax of a century-long European exodus in the cresting of a wave of new immigrants from new sources. Until roughly 1890 the great majority of immigrants had come from northern and western Europe. Although these early newcomers were the source of fears and of problems of cultural identity for native-born Americans, these anxieties paled beside those accompanying the arrival of the so-called new immigration. In the first place, the very number of new immigrants overwhelmed the nativists, who stood for the values and interests of old-stock Americans. The nativists' worst fears were confirmed in statistics. In the quarter-century before World War I, 18 million new arrivals walked down the gangplanks, 80 percent of them from southern and eastern Europe. In the first decade of the twentieth century alone, some 5.8 million people arrived from Austria-Hungary, Spain, Italy, and Russia.

Another set of figures reinforced the nativists' fears. In the peak year, 1882, when more than three-quarters of a million immigrants had disembarked at Atlantic ports, a third of their numbers had come from Germany, while Italy sent only 32,000 people and Russia not quite 17,000. The peak year in the progressive era, 1907, reversed this balance: Germany sent only 37,000, while Italy dispatched 285,000 citizens; the Austro-Hungarian empire, another 338,000; and Russia (including Russia's Baltic provinces), still another 250,000 people. For the entire period the Italians headed the list of European immigrants with 3 million. Next came the Jews, most of them from Russia, numbering about 2 million, followed by a million Poles by 1914. These three main groups, together with Hungarians, Greeks, Armenians, Syrians, and Turks, attested to the results of leaving the gates open.

A Bewildering Ethnic Variety   Four out of five of the new arrivals settled in industrial cities in the Northeast and the Midwest in areas where jobs could be found. Their collective impact on these cities became clear to progressives when they suddenly realized that 75 percent of the populations of New York, Chicago, Cleveland, and Boston were immigrants or children of immigrants. Like it or not, progressives faced a bewildering ethnic and religious variety in the unmistakable presence of many new people eager to get ahead in their new home.

The new immigrants, like the earlier ones, were attracted by economic opportunity, which drew them off worn-out lands and out of the ghettos of European port cities into an American setting of deprivation that at first seemed all too familiar. Once arrived, they started at the bottom of the occupational

Labor Agency on New York City's Lower West Side
Here recently arrived immigrants found the menial jobs allotted to them by labor contractors.

ladder doing the nation's dirty work—construction, mining, smelting, factory work, and domestic service. They usually settled in tight ethnic communities near their work, finding security in an enforced segregation. This pattern of inner-city concentration fed old-stock American fears even as it made the "foreigners" invisible to suburbanites. Frequently, too, the newcomers elbowed their predecessors out of the neighborhoods, sending them further out along the city's extremities.

Old-stock Americans tended to assign the new arrivals a national identity that most of them did not possess. For example, nativists were inclined to stereotype these new immigrants as Poles, Italians, or Russians, but in fact the vast majority did not conform to the stereotypes. Most had come from provincial cultures whose outlook had long been restricted to the locale, the region, or the village. Although the immigrant enclaves in American cities appeared compact and uniform to outsiders, in fact they were splintered ethnic and religious clusters: each neighborhood boasted its own churches and patron saints, feast days, and civic associations.

Packed into slums, exploited by native-born employers and their own contractors alike, harassed by nativist groups and earlier arrivals, fighting among themselves for a foot on the economic ladder, millions of the new immigrants at first lived marginal lives close to the edges of defeat. The going rate for piecework in New York's garment industry was 8 cents an hour. Steelworkers in Pittsburgh sweated a sixty-hour week for $12.50. A husband-and-wife team on Tenth Street in New York's Lower East Side in 1900 could expect $3.75 for every thousand cigars they wrapped. By working fifteen hours a day, the two of them could turn out 3,000 cigars. Leisure for educational and cultural pursuits was a scarce commodity in America's Little Italys and Little Warsaws.

Slowly these immigrant communities gained a measure of stability. Neighborhoods built lively subcultures through their churches, foreign-language newspapers, service organizations like the Sons of Italy and the Pan-Hellenic Union, and a variety of social agencies and immigrant-aid societies. Edward Corsi, who later became President Herbert Hoover's commissioner of immigration and naturalization, recalled the congested tenement-house life of New York's East Harlem, with "five thousand human beings in one city street, as many as fifteen to a four-room flat; two, three, and even four hundred to a tenement intended for fifty"—twenty-seven nationalities all told, including Chinese laundrymen, Syrian shopkeepers, and gypsy phrenologists. On the East River there were Italians; along Pleasant Avenue, Poles, Austrians, and Hungarians; over in West Harlem, Jewish shopkeepers besieged by Turks and Spaniards. And driving all before them, the blacks. Old-stock Americans lived in lonely social islands in this sea of immigrants, "like refugees in exile."

Corsi's East Harlem boasted a lusty popular culture—not the imposing facades of opera houses, theaters, and hotels, but Old World pageants in cafés, rathskellers, spaghetti houses, cabarets, and dance halls. "We have Yiddish theaters and Italian marionette shows," Corsi boasted, "not to mention movie

The Lower East Side

The Jewish Immigrant
District of New York City

1910

	Galician Jews
	(From Southeast Poland)
	Hungarian Jews
	Rumanian Jews
	Levantine Jews
	(From E. Mediterranean Seacoast)
	Russian Jews

The Lower East Side

New York City's Jewish community in 1910 was splintered into national neighborhoods.

and vaudeville houses. Our secondhand book shops are as good as those of Paris. So are our music stores."

The "New Immigration": Unassimilable?

Mystified and a little frightened by the variety of immigrant life, most progressive Americans took refuge in increasingly irrelevant schemes for "Americanizing" the new arrivals. At dockside, civic-aid societies handed out pamphlets, printed in English, warning the newcomers to be "honest and honorable, clean in your person, and decent in your talk"; but these instructions scattered in the swirl of numbers like so many pious hopes. Advocates of immigration restriction agreed with Theodore Roosevelt in deploring the "tangle of squabbling nationalities" as "the one certain way of bringing the nation to ruin," yet the fact remained that hyphenated Americanism—Italian-Americanism, Greek-Americanism, Polish-Americanism—was the only avenue to full citizenship. Even the hopeful immigrant Israel Zangwill, looking ahead to the day of total assimilation, described a dream rather than a reality. The composer-hero of Zangwill's popular play *The Melting Pot* hears the melodies for his "American symphony" in the "seething crucible—God's crucible," where a new amalgam, "the coming superman," is being forged over divine fires. Yet Zangwill told progressive audiences what they wanted to hear, not what they saw around them.

A clearer view of the forces of cultural pluralism came from the more reflective immigrants themselves, who exposed the progressive idea of complete Americanization as the myth it really was. "There is no such thing as an American," a Polish priest told the genteel social worker Emily Greene Balch. Poland, he explained, was a nation, but the United States was simply a country—in the beginning an empty land open to all comers in turn. Immigrants, according to the recently arrived Mary Antin, who later published a vivid account of the immigrants' hardships, were just people who had missed the *Mayflower* and taken the next available boat.

A growing number of young progressive intellectuals responded enthusiastically to this concept of cultural diversity and ethnic pluralism. In the excitement of cultural variety they found escape from stifling middle-class gentility. Randolph Bourne, a radical young student of John Dewey at Columbia University, found a title for this diversity—"Trans-National America"—and hailed the United States as the "intellectual battleground of the world . . . a cosmopolitan federation of national colonies, of foreign cultures, from whom the sting of devastating competition has been removed."

Bourne's concept of America as a world federation in miniature ran headlong into the barrier of national fears. The concept of the "new immigrants" took on a variety of ugly shapes. Immigrants, some said, were dangerously illiterate and culturally deprived; they brought with them either an unenlightened Catholicism or private visions of the destruction of free society; they were doomed to a permanently inferior place on the Darwinian scale of races and could never master the skills that democracy demanded. Amateur and professional sociologists consulted the numbers and predicted "race suicide." Sociologist Franklin Giddings announced hopefully, if somewhat ambiguously, that the traits of Americans—who were "preeminently an energetic, practical people"—would undergo "softening" as Mediterranean instincts crept into the national character. Eventually, he claimed, old-stock Americans with their original Baltic and Alpine ethnic heritage would be transformed into "a more versatile, a more plastic people," both gentler and more poetic. But Giddings's prophecy raised the inevitable question that a progressive reformer asked in an article in the magazine *Charities:* "Are we not, most of us, fairly well satisfied with the characteristics, mental and physical, of the old American stock? Do we not love American traits as they are?"

The Dillingham Commission, a joint House-Senate investigatory panel appointed by Theodore Roosevelt in 1907, underscored these progressive anxieties by making an official distinction between the already assimilated "old immigration" and the presumably unassimilable "new immigration." The commission took four years to complete its report, which filled forty-two volumes. Although it collected much useful information on the work patterns and living conditions of immigrants, the Dillingham Commission assumed from the beginning the need to limit the flow of new arrivals—if not through a literacy test, then through a quota system. When Congress obliged by passing a literacy test bill in 1913, the outgoing president Taft vetoed it in deference to Republican employers who still sought cheap labor. But the idea of a quota system survived, and it was made into law in the 1920s. The Dillingham Report marked a reversal in American attitudes toward cultural minorities: by 1910 the hopes of the immigration restrictionists soared as the more tolerant aims of the pluralists flickered and died.

Wholesale Discrimination Against Blacks

In the case of black Americans, white fears produced an even harsher reaction. The progressive generation had inherited from the late nineteenth century most of the ingredients of a racist myth, and progressives improved the formula of exclusion with new "scientific" evidence of the black race's biological inferiority. Not surprisingly, the opening years of the twentieth century saw the nearly total disfranchisement of black voters in the South.

This disfranchisement was hastened by the defeat of Populism everywhere in the South. Populism had pitted the poor white farmers against the region's white establishment and had sometimes appealed to black farmers as well. Thus the rise of the Populist movement had offered blacks an opportunity to gain political leverage by supporting the side that offered them the most. In some areas blacks quickly became politically active. After Populism went down to defeat, the white political establishment decided that such a danger would not recur and set about systematically denying blacks the right to vote. The techniques varied from state to state—poll taxes, grandfather clauses, literacy tests, white primaries—but all served effectively to bar the great majority of blacks from the polls throughout

Rural Virginian Family
In 1900 most African-American families, like this one, still lived in the rural South.

the South. Politically, the Solid South was now firmly in the grip of the Democratic party, which vowed to keep the blacks "in their place." Some former
Populists, among them Georgia's Tom Watson, who had once courted the black
vote, turned to bitter racist appeals in order to keep their political careers alive.
While deploring such crude demagoguery, southern liberals and progressives
often justified discrimination against the black man with a variant of the argument that northern reformers used to exclude the immigrant—that good government required the political removal of the untrained, the inferior, and the unfit.

Most northern liberals continued to regard blacks as a uniquely southern
problem, despite mounting evidence to the contrary. But it was South Carolina's
racist demagogue Ben Tillman who probed the softest spot in the progressives'
plan for political improvement—the lack of moral certainty. "Your slogans of the
past—brotherhood of man and fatherhood of God—have gone glimmering
down the ages," he chortled. A progressive age, lacking the moral absolutes that
once guided the abolitionists, readily accepted the racist conclusions presumably
proved by up-to-date science.

In the opening decade of the twentieth century, however, statistics obscured
the long-term effects of the industrial revolution on southern blacks, most of
whom were tied to the land by tenancy and sharecropping. In 1900 there were

fewer than 1 million blacks north of the Mason-Dixon line, and thirty years later a full 80 percent of the black community still lived in the South. Nevertheless, the intervening years saw a net gain to northern cities of 1.4 million black migrants from the South, drawn northward by the often illusory lure of economic opportunity and personal freedom. Herded into big-city ghettos—New York's black community numbered 70,000 by the turn of the century—they encountered wholesale discrimination. As lynchings in the South slowly declined, their northern counterpart, race riots, increased—in the small Indiana town of Greensburg in 1906; in Springfield, Illinois, two years later; and in explosive racial tensions in New York, Chicago, Philadelphia, and most of the major industrial cities of the North. Blacks paid a high price for their escape from sharecropping and the Jim Crow laws.

Booker T. Washington and W.E.B. Du Bois Black American leaders attempted to counter discrimination and economic exploitation with two strategies, neither of them very successful in overturning white progressive prejudices. The official black spokesman, the "office broker for the race," as admiring white officials called him, was Booker T. Washington. The son of a slave, Washington learned the gospel of self-help at Hampton Institute in Virginia and put it into practice at Tuskegee, Alabama, where he founded the Normal and Industrial Institute for Negroes. There he trained thousands of young men and women in the industrial and domestic arts. Washington explained his philosophy in a famous address at the Atlanta Exposition in 1895: he urged his black listeners to strike their roots in southern soil by "making friends in every manly way of the people of all races by whom we are surrounded." To whites he offered the same suggestion, urging them to cast down their buckets among a race "whose habits you know, whose fidelity and love you have tested." Publicly, Washington continued to disclaim the vote for southern blacks, explaining in his autobiography *Up from Slavery* (1901) that "the opportunity to freely exercise such political rights will not come in any large degree through outside or artificial forcing, but will be accorded to the Negro by the Southern white people themselves." Privately and often secretly, however, Washington supported many of those blacks calling for stronger measures.

Most white liberals took Booker T. Washington to their hearts as a "credit to his race," although not all of them approved of Theodore Roosevelt's inviting him to lunch at the White House. Washington became the symbol of the "good Negro" who knew his place and aspired only to keep it—the man of sorrows who accepted the fact of racial prejudice while rejecting all its assumptions and who labored patiently to lift his people the few notches that a dominant white society allowed. The question Washington's program did not address, however, was the one that muckraker Ray Stannard Baker asked in his pessimistic commentary on American race relations, *Following the Color Line* (1908): "Does democracy really include Negroes as well as white men?"

W.E.B. DuBois
The famous black progressive reformer is shown in this 1919 photograph.

By 1900 the black progressive William E. B. Du Bois, together with several northern liberals of both races, had concluded that until blacks gained full political rights, democracy would never be theirs. The northern black leadership in the big cities appealed to a constituency different from Booker T. Washington's, and it presented another approach to black advancement. Du Bois, a New Englander and a graduate of Harvard, had followed the typical progressive route to professionalism by studying in Berlin before returning to an academic career at Atlanta University in 1897. Like his counterparts among white liberals, he recognized the pressing need for accurate data on the actual living conditions of blacks, particularly in urban America. To provide some of the evidence, Du Bois pioneered with a sociological study of the Philadelphia blacks, in which he gave a clear picture of life in the ghetto. In *The Souls of Black Folk* (1903), he appealed to potential black solidarity by criticizing Booker T. Washington's "gospel of work and money." Washington's doctrine, complained Du Bois, "has tended to make the whites, North and South, shift the burden of the Negro problem to the Negro's shoulders and stand aside as critical and rather pessimistic spectators; when in fact the burden belongs to the nation." In place of accommodation and outmoded programs for industrial arts, Du Bois suggested the cultivation of a black intellectual and cultural elite—the "Talented Tenth"—and called for immediate plans to mobilize a black political vanguard. In this early and optimistic phase of his career before World War I, Du Bois developed an unmistakably progressive program aimed at substituting "man-training" for moneymaking, and at fostering "intelligence, broad sympathy, knowledge of the world" in a new elite.

Although Washington's accommodationist tactics and Du Bois's elitist strategies complemented each other in theory, a bitter rivalry for the limited support available developed between the Tuskegee machine and the Niagara Movement of northern radicals agitating for full political and social equality for blacks. By the time the National Association for the Advancement of Colored People was founded in 1909 through the joint efforts of white neo-abolitionists Mary Ovington and Oswald Garrison Villard and the black followers of Du Bois, neither a moderate nor a militant approach to the "race problem" had succeeded in denting the prejudices of most white Americans. Actively or passively, whites continued to support strict segregation and the fiction of "separate but equal"— a formula endorsed by the United States Supreme Court in its 1896 decision in *Plessy* v. *Ferguson,* which upheld the practice of racial segregation.

The Jeffersonian tradition of decentralization and localism worked to the distinct disadvantage of black Americans throughout the progressive period. It perpetuated sectional patterns of discrimination and fostered a national disregard for what was quickly becoming the fundamental challenge of the twentieth century. The progressive compromise with bigotry and prejudice blocked any real hopes for a federal program to give blacks their political rights or to open the door of economic opportunity. For all its liberating idealism, progressivism rested on unspoken racist assumptions and condoned discrimination that had changed little since the Civil War.

Women's Organizations

One of the outlets for women's growing social concerns was the Women's Club movement, which provided a useful, if somewhat limited, perspective on the problems of industrial society. In 1904 the recently elected president of the General Federation of Women's Clubs, Sarah Platt Decker, announced to her membership that "Dante is dead. He has been dead for several centuries, and I think it is time that we dropped the study of his *Inferno* and turned our attention to our own." A commanding presence and effective organizer, Mrs. Decker restructured the federation and recruited new talent like the progressive journalist Rheta Childe Dorr, whom she appointed chair of the Committee on the Industrial Conditions of Women and Children. Dorr, in turn, drew on her numerous settlement-house contacts for the statistics and information with which to lobby Congress for federal legislation on the working conditions of women and children. Although the federation avoided political partisanship, individual branches took up controversial issues like factory inspection and child labor, agitated for criminal justice reforms, and experimented with tenement-house improvements. In a variety of "study groups" its middle-class members discovered an expanding range of problems: the poor quality of municipal services, urban political graft, the need for pure food and drug laws, conservation, and, ultimately, the crucial importance of the vote for women.

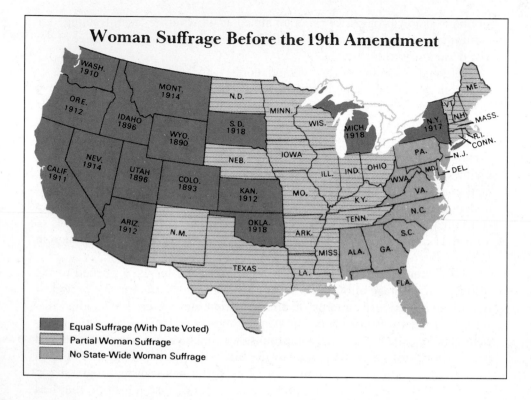

Women's clubs generally popularized and supported rather than initiated progressive reforms. Their most important contribution lay in their support, however cautious, for women's suffrage as the campaign for the vote gained momentum after 1910. In the meantime they succeeded in gradually shifting the interests of well-to-do women from the home to national social concerns.

A second and more sharply focused women's organization, which gave a practical point to the humanitarian concerns of the women's clubs, was the National Consumers' League (NCL). Modeled on English precedents, the NCL grew out of the early work of the upper-class charity organizer Josephine Shaw Lowell, who had taken up the cause of New York City's working girls late in her career. Out of her efforts in the 1890s came a small group of well-to-do women who decided to use their buying power to enforce an enlightened labor policy on the city's employers. As the consumer movement spread to other cities, a national league arose in 1899, headed by a remarkable administrator, Florence Kelley. An abolitionist congressman's daughter, trained at Cornell University and later in Zurich, a socialist, a superb lobbyist, and Illinois's first factory inspector, Florence Kelley brought impressive credentials and skills to her job. Under her firm guidance the National Consumers' League grew rapidly until it numbered sixty local branches in twenty states, all applying the league's White Label to approved products.

The league specialized in protective legislation for women and children, lobbying successfully for the Ten-Hour Law in Oregon and retaining Louis Brandeis to argue this law's constitutionality before the United States Supreme Court. The league also joined the campaign for establishing the Children's Bureau within the Department of Labor; and it helped its sister organization, the National Child Labor Committee, to press Congress for a child-labor law. Working together in a new spirit of professionalism, the social feminists recruited such dedicated administrators as Frances Perkins (later to be Franklin D. Roosevelt's secretary of labor) and Pauline and Josephine Goldmark, who would carry their crusade against child labor and social abuse into the 1920s. These women reformers, skilled in bureaucratic methods but free from the profit motive, were experimenting with an alternative to what Rheta Childe Dorr called the "commercial ideal" of American business.

Working-class feminism arrived with the formation in 1903 of the National Women's Trade Union League (NWTUL), modeled on its counterpart in England. At first women workers, most of them young, unskilled, and underpaid, proved difficult to organize, and the league received scant encouragement from trade unionist Samuel Gompers and his AFL. In these early years the NWTUL's chief accomplishment was winning the support of middle-class women like Mary Dreier and her sister, Margaret Dreier Robins, who provided money and leadership. Gradually, however, recruitment reached down into the ranks of the workers and included effective organizers like Pauline Newman, Leonora O'Reilly, and Rose Schneiderman, who provided a new activism. Their greatest success came among the women in the garment trades in New York City—a majority of them Jewish, many of them socialist. In major strikes in the garment industry—in New York in 1909, Chicago a year later, and Lawrence, Massachusetts, in 1912—the league provided invaluable support, publicizing the workers' grievances, raising substantial amounts of money, and distributing much-needed relief supplies. Such activities as these united working-class and middle-class women, muting class consciousness in favor of moral publicity that called the nation's attention to the horrific conditions in urban factory lofts and calculated for American consumers the human costs of exploitative business practices.

Settlements   The same distaste for the business world also characterized the settlement-house movement. In contrast to its British counterpart, in which young men from Oxford and Cambridge universities took the lead in founding settlements in the slums of London's East End, the American wing of the movement was dominated by women from the outset. The settlements themselves stood in the middle of sprawling slums and quickly became focal points for the public activities of their inhabitants. To the busy complex at Hull House, for example, or to New York's Henry Street Settlement or Boston's South End House came neighborhood children to nurseries and playgrounds, their mothers for classes in hygiene and domestic economy, and, in the evenings, men for lessons in English and discussions of politics.

The impulse behind settlements was religious, although not sectarian, and Christian ethics dominated the atmosphere of all of them—Graham Taylor's Chicago Commons, New York's University Settlement, Kingsley House in Pittsburgh. Inevitably the earnestness of young college women, bent on lifting the tone of immigrant neighborhoods with lectures on the English art critic John Ruskin and with displays of reproductions of pre-Raphaelite paintings, drew sneers. Economist and social critic Thorstein Veblen dismissed the settlements as "consistently directed to the incubation, by precept and example, of certain punctilios of upper-class propriety." But it was not long before the settlement-house workers learned to estimate the needs of their neighbors more accurately, and cultural uplift gave way to hard practicality.

The restless energies of residents, combined with their vagueness about political means, gave the settlement houses all the features of a full-fledged alternative to progressive bureaucracy. Turnover remained high in the settlement houses, which were often mere collecting points for members whose jobs as teachers, social workers, visiting nurses, architects, and planners kept them out in city streets. For both men and women reformers, settlements provided halfway houses between the closed intellectual communities of the college or university and the specialization of a professional career. Settlement houses made possible flexible arrangements of work and leisure based on shared commitments to solving social problems.

Education formed the core of settlement-house work. Initially settlement workers conceived of the educational process as a one-way street of instruction and learning that would lead immigrants toward citizenship. But education was quickly redefined as a mutual learning experience, one that involved genuine exchange and not simply the bestowal of education. As Jane Addams explained to an increasingly receptive public, "A settlement is a protest against a restricted view of education." The settlement-house workers' guide was the educational theory of John Dewey, which defined learning as a social experience and suggested ways of unifying settlements and the life of the community.

When women first founded their settlements, they carefully avoided clashes with the city bosses on the theory that urban politics was hopelessly corrupt. Soon, however, they came to agree with Jane Addams that "to keep aloof from it [politics] must be to lose one opportunity of sharing the life of the community." Still, they found it difficult and often impossible to work with the unsympathetic ward bosses, who distrusted them as do-gooders and rivals for the affections of their clients. Cooperation turned to confrontation over matters of garbage removal, street lighting, police protection, and the location of a neighborhood park. The boldest of the settlement-house workers opposed the bosses, but the contest was unequal, as Jane Addams learned in trying to unseat Alderman Johnny Powers in Chicago's Nineteenth Ward. She attacked Powers with every argument she could muster and capped her indictment with the charge that, although he dispensed free turkeys at Christmastime, he gave poor service on the other 364 days of the year. But turkeys continued to turn the political trick, and

the likes of Johnny Powers generally succeeded in maintaining political control in
their districts.

Struggling to resist the politicians' counterattacks, the settlement-house
women deliberately turned their institutions into public forums where social and
political opinions of every kind could be aired. Chicago Commons, for example,
featured a weekly "Free Floor Discussion" billed as "self-conscious democracy,"
in which a labor leader, a college professor, an anarchist, and a businessman
discussed the future of capitalist society. From these discussions the women
themselves learned valuable political lessons as the logical thread connecting
reform to the vote became too obvious to ignore: women needed the vote to make
good their promise to improve American life. Without the franchise they could
do little more than advance moral arguments, while their enemies—the crooked
contractors and sweatshop owners—used their votes to intimidate the politicians. By 1910 mounting frustrations were beginning to lead many settlement-
house women to join the drive for women's suffrage.

**The Suffragists
Divided**
The two main groups in the suffrage movement after
1912 were the staid and cautious National American
Woman Suffrage Association, headed by Carrie Chap-
man Catt, and its more militant offshoot, the National Women's Party, organized
by the formidable Quaker agitator Alice Paul. Suffragists presented two basically

Suffragist Rally
*A suffragette addresses a middle-class crowd from the backseat of an automobile in a new
version of tailgate campaigning*

different and even contradictory arguments. The first was well suited to the progressive political temper and was summed up by Mary Putnam Jacobi, a veteran suffragist and leading woman doctor:

> No matter how well born, how intelligent, how highly educated, how virtuous, how refined, the women of today constitute a political class below that of every man, no matter how base born, how stupid, how ignorant, how vicious, how poverty-stricken, how brutal.

The second suffragist argument singled out women's special interests and capabilities that were in need of recognition. According to this reasoning, women were uniquely endowed with humanizing qualities and, given the vote, could soften the rigors of industrial society and nurse the United States back to health. Such was Jane Addams's explanation for the feminine political role: "If women have in any sense been responsible for the gentler side of life which softens and blurs some of its harsher conditions, may not they have a duty to perform in our American cities?" In justifying their claim to the vote, middle-class women could take their choice between a demand for simple justice and the promises of a healing creed.

Idealistic or purely practical, the case for women's suffrage was strengthened by the more glaring absurdities of its male opponents. One of them, a worried military officer, warned against the "dilution with the qualities of the cow, of the qualities of the bull upon which the herd's safety must depend."

The suffrage movement gathered momentum at the state level. In 1910 the state of Washington gave the vote to women, and the next year California succumbed to a high-pressure campaign and also awarded women the vote. In 1912 Arizona, Kansas, and Oregon followed suit as Theodore Roosevelt's Bull Moose party, despite its leader's initial reservation, adopted a plank calling for national women's suffrage.

In the presidential election campaign of 1912, a more militant strategy emerged, which concentrated on congressional and presidential candidates— few of whom were particularly sympathetic to the suffragist cause. Alice Paul, the leader of a small band of radical suffragists working at the national level, began to take direct action. She was a grimly determined feminist who had earned a doctorate at the University of Pennsylvania and had spent five years in England studying suffragist Emmeline Pankhurst's disruptive tactics before returning home to try them out for herself. Intense, untiring, a stickler for principle, and an able tactician, Alice Paul promptly singled out Woodrow Wilson and the occasion of his inauguration for a giant protest parade, involving 5,000 women, which ended in a near riot. Then, applying the idea of the English suffragists, she organized an aggressive and highly verbal lobby, which soon became the National Women's Party, dedicated to direct action. The National American Woman Suffrage Association, stung by the success of its more militant rival, began to revive under Mrs. Catt's leadership, and a reorganized board of directors redoubled its efforts to reach women at the state and local levels.

Charlotte Perkins Gilman
*The well-known feminist author
and reformer.*

By 1917, as the country prepared to enter World War I, Wilson's administration faced two groups of political feminists with distinctly different views of the world conflict: a small organization of militants who bitterly protested American participation in the war and demonstrated against "Kaiser Wilson" with marches and hunger strikes; and a much larger group of moderates who supported the war in the belief that peace would bring victory to women as well as to the cause of democracy. In June 1919 Congress rewarded the moderates' patience by passing the Nineteenth Amendment, which gave the vote to all adult Americans regardless of sex. Yet the cause of democracy and reform, American women would learn, was not to be advanced by their sudden invasion of the polls. Notwithstanding their arguments to the contrary, women did not compose an interest group with special needs and talents, nor did their demands for their share of political responsibility alter the course of progressivism. Proposals for a comprehensive recasting of industrial society and for the complete reordering of American priorities were put forward only by the socialists.

Paradise Lost: Socialism in America

American socialism in the years before World War I was a lively and varied critique of the capitalist system presented by an inventive but faction-ridden party, drifting steadily away from its nineteenth-century revolutionary moorings. Despite its official collectivist ideology, American socialism in action kept alive a Jeffersonian tradition that defied the wishes of progressive nationalists.

In its best days between 1900 and 1914, the socialist movement was a volatile combination of regional groups. Party members included industrial workers in the cities of the Northeast, members of older ethnic groups in the urban enclaves of the upper Midwest, agrarians with memories of Populism in the Plains states, hard-bitten miners and lumber stiffs from the Rocky Mountains and the Pacific Northwest, and a core of college-trained intellectuals preaching everything from Christian Socialism and gradualist doctrines derived from the British Fabians to revolution-for-the-hell-of-it. If socialists never quite lived up to their reputation as the chief American menace to law and order, they nevertheless presented a case against corporate capitalism that progressives found deeply disturbing.

Socialism as a political force dated from the turn of the twentieth century. In 1901 disgruntled members of the tiny Socialist Labor party, fed up with the dictatorial ways of their hard-lining Marxist leaders, bolted. Collecting other splinter groups, including Eugene V. Debs's Social Democratic party, they formed the Socialist Party of America. The 94,000 votes Debs won in the presidential election of 1900 marked the beginning of a shift among the majority of American socialists toward the moderate center. They also drifted toward a theory of nonviolent parliamentary socialism, a move that was not always clear to the embattled participants themselves.

The Two Faces of Socialism American socialism showed two faces. To progressive outsiders it was a menace to their capitalist system. According to the socialists, capitalism was traveling a historically determined road to oblivion, destroying small-scale enterprise, saturating international markets, and establishing spheres of influence and imperialist outposts along the way. Most progressives took comfort in the conviction that class war did not in fact appear likely. Yet to most Americans the very vehemence of socialist prophesying suggested a conspiracy of chronic grumblers and political madmen. The progressives prepared to deal with the enemy in the best way they knew—by intimidation and suppression.

To socialists themselves, American development seemed a baffling exception to the doctrines of economic determinism. Their list of unanswered questions lengthened as American capitalism continued to display surprising powers of accommodation. Did the immediate goals of shorter hours and improved working conditions strengthen class solidarity, or did they simply adjust workers to a wage system in which they had no power? Could socialists accomplish more through political action—by running candidates of their own—or did such politicking amount to betraying the interests of the working class? Was the overthrow of the capitalist system imminent, or would the socialist takeover come only gradually, following the education of the workers? The socialists' failure to reach agreement on these matters was seen by most progressives as proof of the absurdity of their ideas—but also as a warning to a society willing to tolerate them.

Gradually the center of the Socialist party was occupied by solid and sensible moderates—men like Milwaukee's shrewd tactician, Victor Berger; New York's scarred veteran of innumerable ideological campaigns, Morris Hillquit; and the "Pennsylvania Dutchman," James Hudson Maurer, who hoped for an alliance with the major trade unions. This moderate center hoped to educate the country away from its capitalistic habits with the lessons of evolutionary socialism. The moderates were bitterly attacked by the diehard members of the militant Socialist Labor party, and also by their own left wing, which had come to believe in industrial unionism and direct action. In the years after 1900, the Socialist party, far from solving its theoretical and organizational problems, kept on dividing into camps of pragmatists and hard-lining idealists, opportunists and "impossibilists."

The "Wobblies" Of all the dissident left-wing socialist groups, the most alarming to progressives was the Industrial Workers of the World (IWW), a faction of militant industrial unionists led by the charismatic "Big Bill" Haywood. The "Wobblies," as they were called by a derisive but apprehensive American public, rejected all forms of political action and recommended strikes and sabotage as the only way to make the world over. The IWW aroused fear and resentment far out of proportion to its membership, which was mostly made up of unskilled and migratory workers. The Wobblies saw their mission as the total destruction of capitalist exploitation and the forming of a new society "within the shell of the old." Progressives shuddered at the prospect.

Lawrence, Massachusetts, Strike, 1912
Soldiers confront striking factory workers organized and led by the IWW.

The Wobblies waged a desperate struggle for survival during their brief and stormy existence. Although they scored short-lived victories in strikes in the Pennsylvania steel town of McKees Rocks in 1907 and again in the Lawrence, Massachusetts, mills in 1912, they lacked the funds and the organization for sustained membership drives and strikes. Their myth of the "general strike" and the vision of "one big union" served chiefly to rally the spirits of marginal men who dreamed of participatory democracy among the downtrodden. At no time did the Wobblies threaten the American capitalist order.

Seen in perspective, the Wobblies represented another attempt of a nine-teenth-century producerist mentality to recover an imaginary world without politics, where abundance automatically rewarded the natural cooperation of free men. "Big Bill" Haywood could have been speaking for progressives when he confessed his hopes for the elimination of politics:

> I have had a dream that I have in the morning and at night and during the day, that there will be a new society sometime in which there will be no battle between capitalist and wage-earner . . . there will be no political govern-ment . . . but . . . experts will come together for the purpose of discussing the means by which machinery can be made the slave of the people instead of part of the people being made the slave of machinery.

Ironically, it was a progressive majority bent on finding another way of going beyond politics with the rule of experts that clubbed the Wobblies' dream to death.

Moderate socialists were burdened with many of the same liabilities that the radicals faced—a tradition of local self-government within the movement, fierce rivalries for leadership, and a host of competing views on the meaning of history. Somehow Eugene Debs retained the leadership of this splintered party. Tall, angular, with a shambling gait and an easygoing manner, Debs served the party faithfully as a national walking-delegate, captivating hundreds of thousands with homely speeches filled with allusions to America's past. His talents were the home-grown ones of the moral agitator; his heroes were the abolitionists Wendell Phillips and William Lloyd Garrison. A spellbinder with no large fund of useful ideas, Debs was nevertheless an able conciliator and a durable campaigner. In 1904 he won some 400,000 votes for his party, and four years later he duplicated the feat with a whirlwind rail tour across the country in his "Red Special," giving as many as twenty speeches a day. The big leap in Socialist party totals, however, came in 1912, when voters gave Debs nearly a million votes in his fourth try for the presidency.

Socialism as a Dissenting Party   The chief socialist contribution to the American plu-ralist tradition was the example it set of the open society it sought to create. The Socialist party remained a model of pluralism in action—a loosely organized, tactically divided community that was in general agreement on condemning capitalism but unable to unite on

Socialist Party Campaign Poster, 1904
In 1904 the tireless Socialist Party campaigner Eugene V. Debs headed the ticket in the second of his presidential campaigns.

the question of how to replace it. These disagreements crystallized in the lives of young academics, artists, and intellectuals who were drawn to socialism as much by its promise of cultural revolution as by its economic platform. Socialist intellectuals made it clear that they opposed both the moral pieties of progressivism and the bureaucratic collectivism of Socialist party centrists. They made their spiritual home in the Intercollegiate Socialist Society (ISS), the brainchild of the novelist Upton Sinclair, which was composed primarily of students and their teachers, artists, and intellectuals. The membership rolls of the ISS listed some of the most impressive and varied talent in the country and offered a range of criticism extending from the moderate Fabianism of John Spargo to the protocommunism of Louis Budenz; from the civil libertarianism of Roger Baldwin and Alexander Meiklejohn to the protest fiction of Ernest Poole and Zona Gale; from the progressivism of Walter Lippmann to the pacifism of A. J. Muste and Jessie Wallace Hughan. Connecting these diverse personalities were a strong distaste for the commercial spirit, an abiding fear of privilege, and not much more.

The striking variety of American socialism, its shifting assessment of ends and means, and its inventiveness in tapping the rich reserves of American dissent made it a lively, if not ultimately powerful, opponent of progressivism. Despite occasional successes at the local level, the Socialist party was never a major political force, even before World War I. Perhaps its greatest days were spent in vocal but isolated opposition to that war and to the destructive mindlessness of superpatriots.* Its most effective role, like the role of the Populist party before it, was largely educational. It taught, more by example than by design, the uses of a secular, imaginative, permissive society. In doing so it supplied useful correctives for a compulsive progressive order, from which Americans might have profited. Its disruption and decline with the coming of the war dealt a major setback to the Jeffersonian tradition that Woodrow Wilson was pledged to preserve.

The New Freedom

Woodrow Wilson, like Theodore Roosevelt before him, believed in a strong presidency. In the course of his scholarly career, Wilson had made an extensive examination of American institutions and political leadership. His training at Johns Hopkins had come at a time when political scientists were beginning to turn away from their preoccupation with constitutional questions and definitions of sovereignty, but before they had acquired the economic and sociological skills to examine the ways institutions actually function. "My purpose," Wilson announced in one of his books, "is to show…our constitutional system as it looks in operation." Yet the workaday reality of American politics was precisely what Wilson's analysis always lacked—the linking of larger social forces with political action. Despite repeated promises to "look below the surface" of American institutions, Wilson was at his best in expounding a philosophy of politics that his rival Theodore Roosevelt would have endorsed: "All the country needs is a new and sincere body of thought in politics, coherently, distinctly, and boldly uttered by men who are sure of their ground." Like Roosevelt, Wilson believed that the key to effective democratic government rested in the hands of a powerful and energetic president who offered "the best chance for leadership and mastery."

Wilson's Program   Wilson, then, favored strong executive leadership yet felt a contradictory urge to dismantle federal power and liberate the energies of a free people. These seeming contradictions—strong presidential authority and the reduction of regulatory power—were linked in his mind by the figure of the national leader, such as the great nineteenth-century British prime minister William Gladstone, who could sense the aspirations of the common people and give them voice as commands to the legislature. But more would be required than sensing the "generous energies" of citizens. The federal government, in particular the presidency, had its uses, as Wilson understood. The real question was whether it could be used to eliminate business coercion, break up clusters of privilege, restore competition, and rescue the little man from the grip of impersonal economic forces. For this work Wilson needed a man with a better understanding of social and economic forces than he himself possessed.

---

*For the home-front excesses of World War I and its aftermath, see chapter 27, pp. 300–05.

The chief architect of the New Freedom was Louis Brandeis, the nation's leading progressive lawyer, who had made a career of challenging big business. In the course of this combat, Brandeis had worked out a complete alternative to Roosevelt's New Nationalism. His program rested on the conviction—reached after watching corporate capitalists play loosely with other people's money—that the country was drifting toward oligarchy. Financial power, he warned, would soon become political despotism through the same process that had made Julius Caesar master of the ancient Roman Republic. In referring to the fate of Rome, Brandeis touched a sensitive Democratic nerve in Wilson, who also feared monopoly but had not yet devised an effective method of controlling it.

Brandeis supplied the guiding concepts for Wilson's first administration. The core of Brandeis's program was a dismantling operation that would ensure the survival of regulated business competition by shoring up small businesses, breaking up new conglomerates, returning the market to free enterprise, dispersing wealth more widely, and reaching out a helping hand to the workingman.

Out of the collaborative thinking of Wilson and Brandeis came the New Freedom's attack on monopoly and a distinction between acceptable and anti-social business behavior, which recalled Roosevelt's program. Big business, Wilson agreed, was natural and thus inevitable, but trusts were artificial and wholly undesirable. "A trust is an arrangement to get rid of competition, and a big business is a business that has survived competition by conquering in the field of intelligence and economy," the president announced in explaining how it was that he could support big business yet oppose monopoly. Wilson was also sure that Roosevelt's scheme of a regulatory commission to oversee the operations of big business was impractical: "As to the monopolies, which Mr. Roosevelt proposes to legalize and welcome, I know that they are so many cars of juggernaut, and I do not look forward with pleasure to the time when juggernauts are licensed and driven by commissioners of the United States." But could the New Freedom offer a better solution? Was the destruction of monopoly really feasible?

Before Wilson tackled the trusts, he decided to make good on the perennial Democratic party promise to lower the tariff. Calling Congress into special session and breaking precedent by appearing in person, he called for immediate tariff reduction. The Underwood Tariff rode through the House quickly, but in the Senate it ran into a barrier erected by Republicans and Democrats representing the sugar and wool interests. Wielding patronage skillfully, Wilson turned aside the protectionists' attacks. The Underwood Tariff lowered duties an average of 10 percent, placed the manufactured goods of the trusts on the free list, and added a small income tax to compensate for the loss of revenue.

Tariff reform tested Wilson's skills as an "honest broker," but banking reform strained them to the limit. Most Americans were primarily interested in obtaining more credit than the eastern banking establishment was currently providing. But there were also traces of Andrew Jackson's Bank War in the struggle between big bankers in the East, with their plans for a central banking system under their direct control, and smaller regional bankers, who sought freedom from Wall Street in a decentralized system. Ranged somewhere between these contenders was a third group of progressives in both parties who wanted a genuinely national system under government management that would ensure stability.

Federal Control of Currency   The Federal Reserve Act (1913) was another compromise between conflicting interest groups with diametrically opposed notions of what the country needed. Establishing twelve districts, each with a Federal Reserve branch bank owned and directed by the member banks, the act provided for a certain degree of decentralization and regional control. But the creation of a new national currency—Federal Reserve notes—and a supervisory seven-member board in Washington gave the federal government an effective instrument of monetary control.

Big bankers need not have fretted, however. Much depended on the willingness of the Federal Reserve Board to interpret its powers generously. Not for another two decades would the board feel a vigorous urge to regulate the nation's financial machinery. The immediate effect of the Federal Reserve Act was to strengthen rather than weaken the control of New York banks by consolidating their partnership with the government. As a stabilizing device for corporate capitalism involving a minimum amount of government interference and direction, the Federal Reserve System worked with reasonable efficiency. As a "democratic" reform designed to parcel out financial power to the people, it was an illusion. The gain for monetary efficiency was immediate, but the democratic social goals would be postponed for a later generation to achieve.

Wilson's experience with the trusts also ended in compromise. The spirit of the original antimonopoly crusade survived down to World War I. Trustbusting seemed to gather new economic coherence from the economic analysis and social ideas of Louis Brandeis and other of Wilson's advisers who supplied the impetus for the passage in 1914 of the Clayton Antitrust Act. The confusions of a quarter-century's attempted enforcement of the Sherman Act had made clarification essential. The question was how to proceed. What degree of monopolistic control of an industry was permissible, and what degree constituted undue restraint of trade? The Clayton Act, as originally drafted in 1914, had tried to answer this question with a long list of "thou shalt nots." The bill listed unfair trade practices in tedious and confusing detail. Continuing debate, however, and anguished cries from big business made it increasingly obvious that a complete list of forbidden practices was an impossibility. Yet if it was impossible to specify each and every example of wrong conduct, the only alternative lay in vesting a regulatory commission with the discretionary power to make concrete applications of a very general rule. Here was the course Roosevelt and the New Nationalists had advised all along—regulating rather than forbidding and dismantling.

In reluctantly agreeing to the commission proposal, Wilson endorsed administrative government, which he had earlier rejected. His intentions in securing passage of the supplemental Federal Trade Commission Act in 1914 closely

paralleled Roosevelt's aim of creating an objective body of experts whose judgments would rest on scientifically assembled evidence. In any case, the advantages of bigness now seemed undeniable, a fact that was attested to by the
incorporation of the giant General Motors soon after the Clayton Act was passed.
The counterattack against big business had failed.

As a regulatory agency with power to mediate conflicts between public needs
and private economic opportunity, the Federal Trade Commission (FTC) disappointed its progressive champions. During World War I its functions in preventing business concentration were drastically curtailed, and after the war even its
fact-finding powers brought down the wrath of big business and of Congress
itself. Congressional conservatives demanded an investigation of its methods. In a
series of adverse decisions, the courts stripped the FTC of its power to define
unfair practices. Business simply defied the FTC by denying it access to company
records and ignoring its rulings. Government by commission in the 1920s
provided no cure for a new rash of financial consolidations.

In other areas of national life as well, Wilson's dream of liberating the
energies of "the great struggling unknown masses of men" ended in perplexity
and defeat. Not the "people" of his earlier progressive imaginings, but highly
organized interest groups—exacting, clamorous, selfish—descended on Washington, seeking protection and advancement of their concerns. In some cases
Wilson's administration proved generous: for newly organized farmers there
were rural credit facilities; for labor, a federal employees' compensation act; for
consumer groups, the National Child Labor Act (promptly declared unconstitutional). But there were limits to Wilson's receptivity to interest-group politics. He
disapproved of women's suffrage, and he refused to lift the burden of antitrust
suits from the backs of labor organizations. He also tacitly supported the
secretary of the interior and the postmaster general in maintaining racial segregation in their departments and only reluctantly reversed himself when liberals
objected. Not all interests, it was clear, could command the attention of a broker
president.

**Wilson's Program:
More, Not Less,
Government**

By 1916, as Americans watched the war in Europe settle
into a protracted and bloody stalemate, the Wilson
administration had largely completed its progressive
program. The president's initial promise of reversal and
restoration had not been fulfilled. In each of his major attempts at reform—
lowering the tariff, building the Federal Reserve System, controlling the trusts—
the president had preferred to disperse power; but instead he had been driven in
exactly the opposite direction. He had created the Tariff Commission to sys-
tematize the nation's trade policies, the Federal Reserve Board to manage the
monetary affairs of the country, and the Federal Trade Commission to police big
business.

The meaning of these reforms was unmistakable: *more,* not *less,* government;
an increase rather than a decrease in governmental agencies; a greater rather than
a lesser reliance on experts and bureaucratic procedures; and a supportive

relationship rather than a supervisory one between government and the large organized interest groups it presumably sought to regulate in the name of the people. And presiding over this expanded system of government agencies and bureaus was a president who was fully as powerful as the most ambitious New Nationalist could ever have wished.

CHRONOLOGY

1896 Supreme Court in *Plessy* v. *Ferguson* establishes "separate but equal" doctrine, whereby separate facilities for blacks and whites are declared constitutional.

1899 National Consumers' League founded.

1901 Socialist Party of America organized.
Booker T. Washington's autobiography *Up from Slavery* published.

1902 Oliver Wendell Holmes appointed to Supreme Court by Roosevelt.

1903 W.E.B. Du Bois's *The Souls of Black Folk* published.

1904 Theodore Roosevelt elected president.
Anna Howard Shaw becomes head of National American Woman Suffrage Association.

1905 *Lochner* v. *New York;* Supreme Court declares unconstitutional a state law regulating work hours for bakers.
Niagara Movement formed to agitate for integration and civil rights for blacks.
Industrial Workers of the World (IWW) formed.

1907 Dillingham Commission investigates "new" immigration problem.

1908 William Howard Taft elected president, defeating William Jennings Bryan and Eugene Debs.

1909 Payne-Aldrich Tariff raising rates to protect eastern manufacturers provokes opposition of South and Midwest.
National Association for the Advancement of Colored People (NAACP) founded.

1910 Woodrow Wilson elected New Jersey governor.
Roosevelt's "New Nationalism" speech at Osawatomie, Kansas.
Women enfranchised in state of Washington.

1911 Triangle Shirtwaist Factory fire in New York City's East Side kills 146 women; investigation and revision of state factory codes follow.

1912 Woodrow Wilson elected president, defeating Republican regular Taft, Progressive "Bull Moose" Theodore Roosevelt, and Socialist Eugene Debs.

1912   Lawrence (Massachusetts) strike against American Woolen Company led by IWW.
Radical National Women's Party under Alice Paul formed.

1913   Federal Reserve System created. Underwood Tariff lowers duties.

1914   Clayton Antitrust Act passed. World War I begins in Europe.

Federal Trade Commission created to regulate business practices.

1916   Louis Brandeis appointed to Supreme Court.

1919   Congress passes Nineteenth Amendment, giving vote to women; ratified in following year.

SUGGESTED READINGS

A good introduction to the study of immigration and assimilation is Leonard Dinnerstein and David Reimers, *Ethnic Americans: A History of Immigration and Assimilation* (1975). Oscar Handlin, *The Uprooted* (2d ed., 1973), although challenged on many points by more recent studies, is nevertheless a classic, as is John Higham, *Strangers in the Land: Patterns of American Nativism* (1955), on the hostile reactions of native Americans. Philip Taylor, *The Distant Magnet* (1971), is particularly good on the European setting. Milton Gordon, *Assimilation in American Life: The Role of Race, Religion and National Origins* (1964), corrects old American myths of the melting pot and easy assimilation. For a good survey of immigrants and the industrial process, see John Bodnar, *Immigration and Industrialization* (1977); for an account of immigrant urban life, see Alan M. Kraut, *The Huddled Masses: The Immigrant in American Society, 1860–1921* (1982).

The literature on specific minorities is extensive. Among the best collective portraits are Moses Rischin, *The Promised City: New York's Jews, 1870–1914* (1970); Irving Howe, *World of Our Fathers: The Journey of the East European Jews to America and the Life They Found and Made* (1976); Humbert Nelli, *The Italians of Chicago, 1880–1920* (1970); Stanford M. Lyman, *Chinese Americans* (1974); and Stephan Thernstrom, *The Other Bostonians: Poverty and Progress in the American Metropolis, 1880–1970* (1973).

August Meier, *Negro Thought in America, 1880–1915* (1963), is the best assessment of black aspirations and programs during these years. Jack Temple Kirby, *Darkness at the Dawning: Race and Reform in the Progressive South* (1972), gives an accurate estimate of the social price of progressive reform in the region, while the story of Harlem is well told in Gilbert Osofsky, *Harlem, The Making of a Ghetto, 1890–1930* (1966). Louis R. Harlan, *Booker T. Washington* (1972), is a definitive account of that leader, and Elliot M. Rudwick, *W.E.B. Du Bois: Propagandist of the Negro Protest* (1969), analyzes the contributions of a mercurial black progressive. Charles F. Kellogg, *NAACP: The History of the National Association for the Advancement of Colored People, 1909–1920* (1967), is a solid survey of that pioneer organization.

Two readable surveys of women's rights and social feminism are Eleanor Flexner, *Century of Struggle: The Woman's Rights Movement in the United States* (1959), and Lois Banner, *Women in Modern America* (1974). Aileen Kraditor, *The Ideas of the Women's Suffrage Movement, 1890–1900* (1965), is an account of the ideology of suffragism, and Robert Smuts, *Women and Work in America* (1959), discusses the problem of work. Entrance of women into the work force is chronicled in Alice Kessler-Harris, *Out to Work: A History of Wage-Earning Women in the*

United States (1982), and Elyce J. Rotella, *From Home to Office: U.S. Women and Work, 1870–1930* (1981).

On socialism Howard Quint, *The Forging of American Socialism* (1953), and David Shannon, *The Socialist Party of America: A History* (1955), present helpful overviews. For more critical treatments of the subject, see James Weinstein, *The Decline of Socialism in America* (1967), and Daniel Bell, *Marxian Socialism in the United States* (1967). An excellent survey of the rest of the radical spectrum in the early twentieth century is contained in John P. Diggins, *The American Left in the Twentieth Century* (1973). Melvyn Dubofsky, *We Shall Be All: A History of the Industrial Workers of the World* (1969), is a full account of the Wobblies, and Christopher Lasch, *The New Radicalism in America, 1889–1963* (1965), presents an indictment of cultural radicalism in the Progressive Era. The best study of the nineteenth-century legacy to American socialism is Nick Salvatore, *Eugene V. Debs* (1982).

On the intellectual and cultural transformation of American society in the opening years of the century, Henry F. May, *The End of American Innocence* (1959), is still standard. Literary histories of the new Age of Realism abound. Among the best are Alfred Kazin, *On Native Grounds* (1942), and two volumes by Maxwell Geismar: *Rebels and Ancestors: The American Novel, 1890–1915* (1953), and *The Last of the Provincials: The American Novel, 1915–1925*. Kenneth S. Lynn, *William Dean Howells: An American Life* (1970), is a sensitive portrait of a fractured artistic sensibility in a rapidly modernizing age. A useful survey of progressive political ideas is John D. Buenker, *Urban Liberalism and Progressive Reform* (1973). For changing notions of marriage and the family, see Elaine Tyler May, *Great Expectations: Marriage and Divorce in Post-Victorian America* (1980). Robert Crunden, *Ministers of Reform: The Progressives' Achievement in American Civilization* (1982) presents a series of intellectual portraits of Progressive Era figures.

Indispensable for an understanding of Woodrow Wilson and the New Freedom is the magisterial Arthur S. Link, *Wilson* (5 vols., 1947–65), although the hostile John Blum, *Woodrow Wilson and the Politics of Morality* (1956), and the skeptical John Garraty, *Woodrow Wilson* (1956), offer critical insights unavailable to the sympathetic Link. Biographies of other important figures during the New Freedom years include Dorothy Rose Blumberg, *Florence Kelley: The Making of a Social Pioneer* (1966); Charles Larsen, *The Good Fight: The Life and Times of Ben Lindsey* (1972); Julius Weinberg, *Edward Alsworth Ross and the Sociology of Progressivism* (1972); Robert C. Bannister, *Ray Stannard Baker: The Mind and Thought of a Progressive* (1966); and H. C. Bailey, *Edgar Gardner Murphy* (1968). Melvin I. Urofsky, *Louis D. Brandeis and the Progressive Tradition* (1981), defines the great liberal justice's intellectual and political legacy.

15

The Path to Power: American Foreign Policy

1890–1917

$\mathcal{F}$OR MOST of the nineteenth century, Americans managed their affairs with no general foreign policy except that of George Washington's determination to avoid entangling alliances. The defeat of Napoleon in Europe, coupled with the brilliant success of the American peace commissioners in 1815 following the near disaster of the War of 1812, brought a strong conclusion to an era of diplomatic failure for the new nation, perched so precariously on the rim of the Atlantic world and subject to the buffetings of the two major European powers, Britain and France. After 1815 geographical isolation and ideological separation gave the American people an open continent to explore and exploit without interference. By the mid-nineteenth century, George Washington's prediction of a separate American destiny had seemingly come true. Secure on its own continent, its dominance of the Western Hemisphere guaranteed by British sea power, the United States turned inward to explore its interior and develop its resources.

A favorable international climate, together with unlimited opportunity at home, fostered extravagant versions of an American "Manifest Destiny," which at one time or another pointed to the annexation of Canada, the acquisition of Cuba, and the taking of "all Mexico." Expansionists such as the naval officer and oceanographer Matthew Fontaine Maury, who plotted to colonize Mexico with ex-Confederates, dreamed of the Caribbean as an American lake, or of the Mississippi Valley as the center of a vast heartland empire reaching eastward across the Atlantic and westward to China shores. But these flickering dreams of empire, like the extravagant reckonings of farmers, businessmen, and shippers who visualized huge profits to be found in untapped foreign markets, were hopeful predictions rather than policy directives. Despite occasional American interest in the fate of republican movements in Europe, Manifest Destiny remained primarily an article for home consumption—exuberant, aggressive, but not really intended for export. The slavery problem also curbed the American expansionist appetite after the Mexican War; the debate over the future of slavery in the newly opened territories monopolized national attention and absorbed the nation's political energies.

By the last quarter of the nineteenth century, however, a chain of circumstances abroad began to draw the United States into international power politics. The most important development was the sudden imperialist scramble by the major European powers—first Britain, then France, Germany, and Russia—to carve out generous colonies for themselves in Asia and Africa. American diplomats abroad and politicians in Washington watched with growing apprehension as the European powers, following the lead of business investments, rushed for possessions and spheres of influence in the undeveloped regions of the world.

Still, in his inaugural address in 1885, President Grover Cleveland offered only the briefest word on American foreign policy. The unique nature of American democratic institutions and the real needs of the people, Cleveland explained, required a "scrupulous avoidance of any departure from that foreign policy commended by the history, the traditions, and the prosperity of our Republic." In case his audience might have forgotten that traditional policy, he restated it clearly: "It is the policy of independence, favored by our position.... It is the policy of peace suitable to our interests. It is the policy of neutrality, rejecting any share in foreign broils and ambitions upon other continents and repelling their intrusion here."

This traditional passivity was reflected in the dilapidated foreign-policy establishment over which the president presided. A casual and still largely amateur operation, the diplomatic service had no effective fact-gathering apparatus; although it boasted a handful of able diplomats, it was saddled with a great many nobodies and friends of influential politicians. Most of the useful information trickling back to Washington from European capitals came from cosmopolitan private citizens personally concerned with the shifting scenes of international politics. Until 1890 Europe appeared willing to take this American claim of disinterest at face value and considered the United States a second-class power. The diplomatic corps residing in Washington was not on the whole a distinguished one, and more than once a European state simply neglected to fill a vacant post in this country that had come to seem unnecessary.

Yet at the very moment when Cleveland spoke the platitudes that had passed for foreign policy throughout the nineteenth century, new forces were beginning to collect around a different set of propositions, which were drawn directly from the study of European imperialist adventures. Lord Bryce, whose perceptive analysis of American government and society, *The American Commonwealth*, appeared in 1888, noted the difference between those who shaped foreign policy in England and their counterparts in the United States. In America, Bryce explained, "there are individual men corresponding to individuals in that English set, and probably quite as numerous." There were a sizable number of journalists of real ability, a handful of literary men, and not a few politicians who understood the mechanisms of international power politics. But these Americans remained isolated and disorganized for the most part, vulnerable constantly to public pressures and mass opinions, while the "first set" in England clearly was not. "In England the profession of opinion-making and leading is the work of specialists; in America...of amateurs." By the time Bryce published this observation, however, a small group of like-minded amateurs concerned with foreign affairs was already at work in Washington, building the intellectual foundations for a foreign-policy establishment and calling for a more vigorous pursuit of world power.

The Origins of American Expansionism

By the 1890s it began to dawn on the small number of Americans concerned with the conduct of foreign affairs that the United States was in danger of being left far behind in the race for territory and markets. Looking back on the last decade of the nineteenth century, the rabid expansionist Senator Albert J. Beveridge summed up the lessons taught the American people as trustees "under God" of world civilization: "He has made us the master organizers of the world to establish system where chaos reigns." Not all Americans in 1900 agreed with Beveridge that destiny had mapped an imperial course for the nation, but it had become clear that they could no longer view the international scene indifferently. Somehow the United States would have to catch up with its European rivals.

A second force pushing the United States into the imperialist competition— a concern with world markets—was not so easy to analyze. After 1875 American businessmen, bankers, industrialists, and shippers began to call for readier access to global markets. Their demands took on dramatic point with the erratic development of the domestic market—the repeated depressions and gluts—and growing doubts as to its capacity to absorb American manufactured and staple goods. But the American market in the undeveloped areas of the globe remained quite small as late as 1900, despite increasingly noisy demands for enlarging it. The state of overseas markets furnished a focus for popular debate around which both expansionists and antiexpansionists, interventionists and isolationists argued over the proper role for the United States. No one denied the importance of foreign markets in the American economy and their importance too in spreading the blessings of democracy. But did the search for markets necessarily mean intervention in the domestic affairs of undeveloped and politically unstable countries? Did it require outright annexation? Were markets for the investment of capital fundamentally different from markets for manufactured or staple goods? And, most troublesome of all, how could the spokesmen for new and bigger markets catch and hold the attention of an unresponsive federal government?

Conditions in the United States also helped focus attention on possibilities abroad. The 1890s saw severe economic disorder, rising class conflict, political instability, and intellectual discord. The combined effect of these tensions and struggles was a growing popular belief that the United States had reached maturity as a fully developed modern nation. Whether or not they read the historian Frederick Jackson Turner's famous warning in 1893 of the consequences of the closing of the frontier, many Americans were well aware of the passing of an era in which free land and geographical mobility had been all-important. Viewed as a fact or a symbol of America's vast, seemingly limitless possibilities, the frontier had dominated the American imagination for two centuries. The announcement of its closing reinforced a widely shared sense of irreversible change. For the generation of the 1890s, the extension of the frontier concept into territories overseas quickened the old sense of mission and enterprise, and it released pent-up feelings of humanitarianism as though the answer to a loss of certainty at home was the vigorous pursuit of democratic purpose abroad.

Pacifism or Power? In these shifting circumstances abroad and at home, a struggle developed for control of an emerging American foreign policy. The contestants played a variety of roles in the quarter-century before American entry into World War I. Some upheld international law or preached pacifism. Others advocated national power or defended American honor. Yet beneath the diversity lay two conflicting ideas about American power and responsibility.

The first view of the nature of power and of America's future was forcefully summarized by Captain Alfred Thayer Mahan, naval strategist and geopolitical theorist, in his *Interest of America in Sea Power, Present and Future* (1897). Mahan argued that since governments could not be expected to act on any ground except national interest, patriotism and the will to fight were indispensable human qualities.

> Not in universal harmony, nor in any fond dream of unbroken peace, rest now the best hopes of the world....Rather in the competition of interests, in that reviving sense of nationality...in the jealous determination of each people to provide first for its own...are to be heard the assurance that decay has not touched yet the majestic fabric erected by so many centuries of courageous battling.

The second and opposing view of the American mission was most effectively expressed by William Jennings Bryan, who limited the nation's role to that of providing a moral example. Nations, Bryan insisted, redeem only by force of example: "Example may be likened to the sun, whose genial rays constantly coax the buried seed into life, and clothe the earth, first with verdure, and afterward with ripened grain; while violence is the occasional tempest, which can ruin, but cannot give life."

Until 1900 Mahan's invitation to national greatness took precedence over Bryan's warnings of its eventual costs. Mahan had spent most of his career wandering about the world observing the patterns of European imperial politics.

Now his notice to Americans was direct and unmistakable. The United States, he announced, must pursue an aggressive expansionist foreign policy based on naval supremacy and undisputed control of the world's sea lanes, a vigorous development of foreign markets, and an energetic cultivation of all the domestic spiritual resources needed to promote the national mission overseas. In a Darwinian world of warring nations, he argued, the United States must organize itself into a spiritual and military garrison ready to defend its interests with power. Mahan did not deny the existence of a universal law of conscience, but he anchored it in the concept of the national state fully aware of its duty and prepared to perform it. In his view, the "evils of war" paled before the dangers of "moral compliance with wrong." In the last analysis all depended on Americans' willingness to take up their appointed tasks as the democratic saviors of civilization: "Whether they will or no, Americans must now begin to look outward."

Architects of Empire   Mahan's arguments, which won him enthusiastic support in Britain and Germany, were also warmly received by a small circle of influential Americans whose own examination of the international situation in the 1890s led them to conclude that the United States should take its place among the imperialist powers. "You are head and shoulders above us all," wrote Theodore Roosevelt in promising Mahan that he would do all he could "toward pressing your ideas into effect." Other important converts to the captain's expansionist doctrines joined in: John Hay, soon to become McKinley's secretary of state; the freewheeling romantic reactionaries Brooks and Henry Adams, and their protégé, Senator Henry Cabot Lodge; young, aggressive cosmopolitans like the diplomat Richard Olney, and staid conservatives like lawyer Joseph Choate; academic popularizer John Fiske, with his own version of Manifest Destiny; and social-gospeler Josiah Strong, whose best-selling *Our Country* (1885) argued the Christian evangelist's case for spiritual renewal through expansion. The views of these would-be architects of American empire were expressed with increasing frequency in metropolitan newspapers and liberal journals, which called for a higher appraisal of American capabilities. And when the test of strength came between imperialists and anti-imperialists over a "large policy" for the United States, these spokesmen for expansion would prove to be particularly effective.

In the meantime, American diplomacy continued to heat up. A series of minor crises early in the 1890s signaled America's intention to take a firmer hand in managing foreign policy by asserting national interest and defending national honor whenever the opportunity arose. In the South Pacific a German threat to impose a protectorate over the entire group of Samoan islands brought United States naval forces steaming into the Samoan harbor of Apia—in time to be destroyed by a typhoon. In Chile a barroom brawl involving American sailors ended in an American ultimatum to that country. And in 1895 a dispute between the unstable and financially irresponsible Venezuela and Great Britain over the boundary of British Guiana called forth a declaration of American power in the

Western Hemisphere. "Today," Richard Olney, Cleveland's secretary of state, boasted to the startled British, "the United States is practically sovereign on this continent, and its fiat is law upon the subjects to which it confines its interposition . . . its infinite resources combined with its isolated position renders it master of the situation and practically invulnerable against any or all other powers." By 1896 events like these, minor irritations evoking a disproportionate American belligerence, paved the way for a popular American crusade on behalf of Cuban independence.

President McKinley's "Wonderful Experience"

In 1895 the Cuban revolution against Spain, which had been smoldering for nearly a quarter of a century, flared up once again, and Spain sent 50,000 soldiers to extinguish it. American sympathies, a mixture of genuine outrage and "jingo" bluster, instinctively went to the underdogs, who were widely credited with wanting to establish a Yankee-style republic. The Cuban rebels responded to this encouragement by dispatching a high-powered lobby to New York City with orders to raise money and goodwill while supplying a steady stream of atrocity stories to the reporters of the sensationalist newspapers owned by William Randolph Hearst and Joseph Pulitzer. Soon the Cuban revolutionaries in New York began to receive help from unexpected quarters—from Latin American trading interests, promoters of a canal across Central America, a variety of patriotic groups, and even trade unions. Carefully orchestrated "spontaneous" rallies across the country whipped up enthusiasm for American intervention. Democrats and Populists vied with their Republican rivals in denouncing Spain and demanding a declaration in support of the Cuban rebels. It was obvious to the incoming McKinley administration that the president would have to move quickly to avoid being captured by a warlike public mood.

Annexation or "Cuba Libre"
As late as 1896, however, the exact meaning of this public clamor over Cuba's fate was not altogether clear. To the small group advocating the "large policy," intervention on the island seemed a foregone conclusion. Roosevelt, who admitted to being "a quietly rampant 'Cuba Libre' [Free Cuba] man," told Mahan that intervention was inevitable if the United States was to retain its self-respect. Many expansionists agreed: the Cuban affair would be a heaven-sent opportunity to annex Hawaii. As for Cuba's fate, no one could predict. Even Roosevelt, although he angrily dismissed "the craven fear and brutal selfishness of the mere money-getters" who opposed American intervention, doubted the wisdom of annexing Cuba "unless the Cubans wished it." "I don't want it to seem that we are engaged merely in a land-grabbing war," he explained. Until war was actually declared, there was little support for the idea of permanent United States involvement on the island, even among the most vocal interventionists.

In the fiercely contested presidential election of 1896, the issue of Cuba had given way to domestic problems of free silver and the tariff. It took the renewed campaigns of the Cuban revolutionaries in December 1896 and the murder of their leader, Maceo, to anger the American public once more. This time the response was different. Instead of planned demonstrations and organized rallies, there were loud outbursts of protest all over the country—genuinely spontaneous meetings in which businessmen joined patriots and humanitarians in demanding an end to Spanish rule. McKinley's administration now had to contend with a powerful popular indignation.

At this point Spain added fuel to the interventionist fire when its troops on the island began brutally herding Cubans into makeshift camps, where they died by the thousands. Meanwhile a wavering government in Madrid continued to agonize over the dwindling options left to it. The decaying Spanish monarchy, torn by rival factions of liberals and conservatives, unable to pacify the island but unwilling to give it up, temporized hopelessly. Confusion was nearly as great within the McKinley administration as the president found himself in an intense crossfire between Republican expansionists crying for justice at the point of an American sword and his conservative business backers fearful of the effects of a war on business recovery from the depression of the 1890s. As popular pressure for intervention rose alarmingly, McKinley was also driven to play for time. Publicly the president demanded promises of instant reform from Madrid, while privately he reined in the most radical members of his party with promises of his own.

War with Spain   By 1897 the horrors of Spain's reconcentration program in Cuba had forced the president to press for even firmer Spanish concessions. Then a series of incidents brought relations between the two countries to the breaking point. First came the release of an indiscreet letter from Depuy de Lôme, the Spanish minister in Washington, to his government, in which he ungenerously—but not inaccurately—described McKinley as "weak" and "a bidder for the admiration of the crowd." Then came the explosion in Havana harbor that destroyed the American battleship *Maine.* There were rumors everywhere that Spain had engineered the explosion—this "gigantic murder" of innocent American sailors, as Senator Lodge put it. At last the expansionist jingoes had an aroused American public crying for retaliation in the name of justice and democracy.

McKinley's dilemma grew more painful as conflicting reports of Spanish intentions came flooding into Washington. On the one hand there were accounts of the Spanish government's total unwillingness to compromise; on the other there were assurances that it was ready to comply with demands for full self-government for Cuba. Given the choice between waiting and taking immediate action, McKinley finally decided to act. Two days after Spain had agreed to his demands for an immediate armistice and an end to reconcentration—while still declining to grant Cuban independence—the president sent a message to Congress requesting authority to intervene and restore peace on the island. By the time word of Spain's partial compliance reached Washington, it was too late. Intervention, McKinley knew, meant war, and Congress made the decision official

The Cause and the Cure
The battleship Maine *on the morning after the explosion.*

The Spanish Brute
A magazine cover reflects the rising war fever.

The Spanish War in the Caribbean 1898

on April 19, 1898, by declaring that a state of war existed. McKinley had lacked a clearly defined set of goals and the means of achieving them, and he had been caught in a domestic political crossfire. He accepted the prospect of what Secretary of State John Hay called "a splendid little war" for no particularly compelling reasons of national interest.

In the brief war that followed, the United States made short work of Spain's broken-down navy and demoralized army. Commodore George Dewey's Asiatic Squadron quickly demolished the monarchy's Pacific fleet in the battle of Manila Bay, and the United States' Atlantic Squadron as easily penned up Admiral Cervera's ships in Santiago, Cuba, and systematically destroyed them. Spanish troops scarcely did any better when they fought the American land forces, although the Americans were poorly trained, badly equipped, and disorganized. After endless confusion General William R. Shafter finally succeeded in assembling some 18,000 troops for an invasion of Cuba and managed to land his army, complete with press corps, foreign dignitaries, and well-wishers, near Santiago. There Colonel Roosevelt and his Rough Riders, a flamboyant cavalry regiment recruited from the cattle ranges and mining camps of the West, seized the lion's share of the glory of what the colonel called a "bully fight," the capture of San Juan Hill. The battle of Santiago capped the successes of the navy, and American soldiers settled in on the jungle heights above San Juan, where more of them died from yellow fever than in actual combat. A small expeditionary force that was dispatched to nearby Puerto Rico encountered no real resistance. In August 1898, Spain's meager military resources were entirely spent, and its morale shattered. The Spanish had no choice but to give up and sign the peace protocol.

The Spanish War in the Philippines 1898

The Philippines: "Those Darned Islands"

The problem of disposing of the remnants of Spain's empire caught McKinley by surprise. In the case of Cuba, Congress in an unaccountable burst of self-denial had rushed through the Teller Amendment, declaring the island free and independent and disavowing any American intentions of annexing it. Not for conquest nor for empire had American soldiers fought so bravely, but, as one Republican senator put it, "for humanity's sake ... to aid a people who have suffered every form of tyranny and who have made a desperate struggle to be free." But within a year these expressions of high-mindedness had been cast to the winds.

The new question of the Philippines, together with the old problem of Hawaii, added to McKinley's worries. "If old Dewey had just sailed away when he smashed the Spanish fleet, what a lot of trouble he would have saved us," the president grumbled, confessing that he "could not have told where those darned islands were within 2,000 miles." But with Spain's collapse the barriers to American empire also began to fall, both within the administration and in the nation at large, as groups once hostile to the idea of acquiring new territory began to have second thoughts. Business leaders, banking and mercantile interests, church organizations, and even social reformers joined in calling for the retention of the Philippines, if not as a permanent possession, at least as a temporary way station on the route to Asian markets.

When the Senate came to debate the question of annexation, the opponents of the new imperialism argued strenuously that "political dominion" was not commercially necessary and that, in any case, both the Constitution and the

Declaration of Independence forbade it. Under the Declaration, Senator George F. Hoar told his colleagues, "you can not govern a foreign territory, a foreign people, another people than your own . . . you can not subjugate them and govern them against their will, because you think it is for their good. . . . " But the logic of expansion worked against the anti-imperialists. Annexationists argued that if, in order to secure commercial opportunity, the United States needed political stability in Hawaii and the Philippines, then why not go the whole way and at the same time lift untutored peoples to the level of democratic self-government? McKinley spoke the public mood in presenting a narrow range of choices. It would be "cowardly and pusillanimous," he insisted, for the United States "to turn the islands back to Spain, giving them power again to misrule the natives." Equally "despicable" was the notion of handing them over to Britain or allowing Japan to take them by default. "There is only one logical course to pursue," McKinley announced:

> Spain has shown herself unfit to rule her colonies, and those [that] have come into our possession as a result of war, must be held, if we are to fulfill our destinies as a nation . . . giving them the benefits of a christian civilization which has reached its highest development under our republican institutions.

The problem of ruling the Philippines admitted of no such simple solution as McKinley proposed. Before war with the United States broke out, Spain had finally suppressed an uprising of Filipino independence fighters by bribing their leader, General Emilio Aguinaldo, to leave the islands. Following his smashing naval victory, Admiral Dewey brought Aguinaldo back to Manila to help fight the Spanish in exchange for a vague promise of eventual independence. But when it became clear that the United States had no intention of giving up control of the Philippines, Aguinaldo and his followers took up arms again, this time against their former allies. In the course of a savage four-year guerrilla war, the Filipino patriots, suffering heavy military and civilian casualties at the hands of American "pacifiers," killed more than 4,000 American soldiers before surrendering and swearing allegiance to the American flag.

As the debate over the peace terms intensified, there emerged a small vocal group of "anti-imperialists," as they called themselves, hastily assembled and ranged along a broad spectrum of opinion. The nucleus of this anti-imperialist opposition consisted of venerable mid-nineteenth-century liberals whose distinguishing mark and chief liability was their advanced age and distrust of mass democratic politics. Veteran antislavery campaigner Carl Schurz was seventy-one; free trader Edward Atkinson, seventy-three; Republican maverick George F. Hoar, seventy-four; steelmaker Andrew Carnegie, sixty-five. Most of the anti-imperialists stood on the margins of their parties and the government, respected but minor figures who held long and honorable records in the cause of dissent against the Gilded Age. As imperial ambition swept up the majority of their countrymen, they found themselves severely handicapped by their caution and

McKinley's "Little Brown Brothers"
American troops pacify the Filipino followers of Aguinaldo.

self-denial. "Who will embarrass the government by sowing seeds of dissatisfaction among the brave men who stand ready to serve and die, if need be, for their country?" McKinley demanded of a cheering crowd in Omaha in the heartland of America. "Who will darken the counsels of the republic in this hour, requiring the united wisdom of all?" The anti-imperialists could not prevail against such expansionist ardor. Unskilled in the new arts of mass propaganda, advocating a negative program, often distrustful of the democratic forces supporting the president, the anti-imperialists were quickly outmanned and outmaneuvered by the expansionists.

Some anti-imperialist arguments expressed racist doubts about the wisdom of incorporating dark-skinned, unschooled peoples. Others appealed to the Constitution and the spirit of the Founders in denying Congress the power to govern other people against their wills. With social scientist William Graham Sumner, a loyal few railed against the prostitution of statesmanship to mere party interest. But the core of the anti-imperialists' case against expansionism was the charge that in betraying the cherished principles of the Declaration of Independence, their country had abandoned the moral law. Charles Eliot Norton, professor of the arts at Harvard, spoke to this point most eloquently:

> We believe that America had something better to offer to mankind than those aims she is now pursuing, and we mourn her desertion of her ideals which were

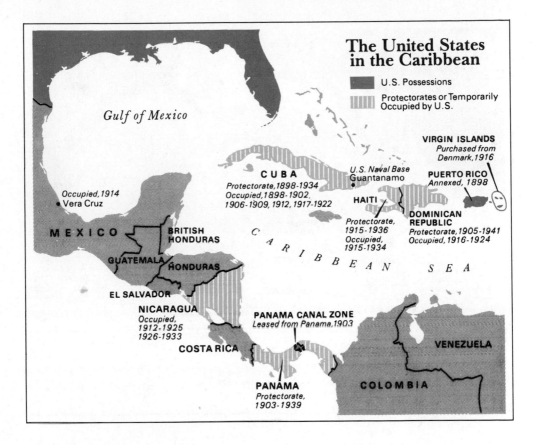

The United States in the Caribbean

U.S. Possessions

Protectorates or Temporarily Occupied by U.S.

Gulf of Mexico

VIRGIN ISLANDS
Purchased from Denmark, 1916

CUBA
Protectorate, 1898-1934
Occupied, 1898-1902.
1906-1909, 1912, 1917-1922

U.S. Naval Base Guantanamo

PUERTO RICO
Annexed, 1898

HAITI
Protectorate, 1915-1936
Occupied, 1915-1934

DOMINICAN REPUBLIC
Protectorate, 1905-1941
Occupied, 1916-1924

Occupied, 1914
• *Vera Cruz*

MEXICO

BRITISH HONDURAS

C A R I B B E A N   S E A

GUATEMALA

HONDURAS

EL SALVADOR

NICARAGUA
Occupied, 1912-1925 1926-1933

PANAMA CANAL ZONE
Leased from Panama, 1903

VENEZUELA

COSTA RICA

PANAMA
Protectorate, 1903-1939

COLOMBIA

not selfish nor limited in their application, but which are of universal worth and validity. She has lost her unique position as a potential leader in the program of civilization, and has taken up her place simply as one of the grasping and selfish nations of the present day.

A few of the older anti-imperialists looked back to a less complex world of a half-century earlier, when the United States, as one traditionalist put it, was "provincial, dominated by the New England idea." These venerable men, however, were joined by younger pragmatic critics of imperialism, among them William James, who skillfully probed the false "realism" of the expansionists and dissected their flabby arguments. As the bloody and inconclusive pacification program in the Philippines dragged on and the freedom fighter Emilio Aguinaldo gave American troops a lesson in jungle warfare, James centered his own attack on the American inclination to substitute "bald and hollow abstractions" for the "intensely living and concrete situation." An unrestrained appetite for power, he scoffed, had caused the country to "puke up its ancient soul . . . in five minutes without a wink of squeamishness."

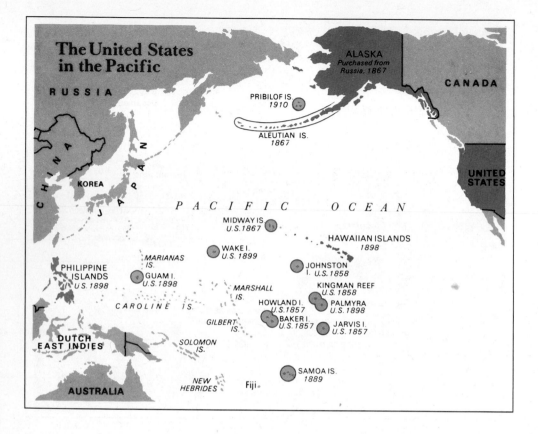

The United States
in the Pacific

Could there be a more damning indictment of that whole bloated idol termed "modern civilization" than this amounts to? Civilization is, then, the big, hollow, resounding, corrupting, sophisticating, confusing torrent of mere brutal momentum and irrationality that brings forth fruits like this?

Until the Philippine uprising revealed the shallowness of American expressions of benevolence, the opponents of expansion made very little headway against the winds of imperial destiny. McKinley, after wrestling with his conscience, announced that "without any desire or design on our part," the war had brought new duties to "a great nation." Accordingly, he instructed his peace commissioners to stand firm against any and all Spanish protests over the dismantling of Spain's empire. By the terms of the peace treaty signed late in 1898, Spain agreed to dismemberment, giving up Cuba, the Philippines, Puerto Rico, and Guam. In 1898 the United States also annexed Hawaii, which was dominated by American sugar planters who five years earlier had overthrown the native queen, Liliuokalani, and established a nominal republic.

**Colonial Fruits
of War**
In the Senate the treaty was taken in hand by the Republican faithfuls, including Lodge and Beveridge, who were aided in their work by Bryan's odd notion that the course of empire could be determined only in the presidential election of 1900. The majority of senators agreed with Beveridge in striking a balance between the immediate material rewards of expansion and long-term spiritual gains. "It is God's great purpose," Beveridge declared, "made manifest in the instincts of the race whose present phase is our personal profit, but whose far-off end is the redemption of the world and the Christianization of mankind." Despite the anti-imperialists' warnings that the nation was descending from the "ancient path" of republican righteousness into the "cesspool" of imperialism, the Senate voted 57 to 27 to accept the treaty. Hawaii became an incorporated territory under the Organic Act of 1900. Guam was acquired as a naval station administered by the Navy Department. And Puerto Rico, under the Foraker Act (1900), was attached as unincorporated territory with an elective legislature and a governor appointed by the president.

With the gathering of the colonial fruits of war with Spain and the arrival of Theodore Roosevelt in the White House, the initiative in formulating foreign policy fell to the activists who agreed with the new president that the aggressive pursuit of national interest provided the only sound base for a democratic foreign policy. "If we stand idly by," Roosevelt warned as the century opened, "if we seek merely swollen, slothful ease and ignoble peace, if we shrink from the hard contests where men must win at hazard of their lives and the risk of all they hold dear, then the bolder and stronger people will pass us by.... Let us therefore boldly face the life of strife." Strife marked and often marred Roosevelt's conduct of foreign policy from first to last—in Cuba and Panama and throughout Latin America, and in American dealings with China and Japan. In the Roosevelt years national interest came to mean national egotism.

In Cuba the occupation by American forces continued as the United States launched a program of administrative and public health reforms that culminated in a successful campaign against yellow fever. The Platt Amendment of 1901 drew even tighter the "ties of singular intimacy" between the United States and the island by providing for American intervention in case an unstable new government failed to protect life, liberty, and property. With the help of some heavy pressure on the Cuban leadership, this provision was written into the new republic's constitution in 1901 and was incorporated in the treaty between Cuba and the United States two years later. By 1903 the United States, despite earlier disavowals, had established a virtual protectorate on the island and reserved to itself the right to intervene in the internal affairs of its neighbor, a privilege it would regularly invoke in the next half-century.

In the Philippines the establishment of American control awaited the outcome of Aguinaldo's uprising, which dragged on until March 1901, when the Filipino leader was captured and his scattered forces surrendered. Under the terms of the Philippine Organic Act of 1902, the United States provided for a bicameral legislature and a governor with broad executive powers appointed by the president. Although there would be a gradual loosening of the governmental reins in the Philippines for the next three decades, full independence would not be achieved until 1946.

The turn of the century marked the final achievements of American expansion. Within a decade the dreams of a handful of "large policy" advocates had become a reality. The United States, without actually willing it, had acquired an imperial base for commercial and ideological expansion throughout the world.

Open and Closed Doors: Progressive Foreign Policy Under Roosevelt and Taft

If a "splendid little war" had suddenly thrust the United States into the ranks of the world's big powers, the war's aftermath taught corrective lessons on the limits of American influence. The United States proved a slow and often stubborn pupil in the school of international power politics, and as late as 1914, when war broke out in Europe, it still had much to learn about world affairs and a democracy's proper role in managing them.

An "Open Door" in China

American education in the limits of power began in China at the turn of the century. The dream of a rich and limitless China market was older than the nation itself; it had been a prime motive in original explorations and in the search for the fabled Northwest Passage. After the American Revolution the dream became a reality as the new nation began to open markets in the Far East to compensate for the loss of old ones. Success in these distant markets in the age of the clipper ships, the 1840s and 1850s, continued to feed American hopes for gaining untold riches in the Orient. Still, by the end of the nineteenth century, less than 2 percent of United States foreign trade involved China, and it was with expectations of increasing this slim total that commercial and banking interests, concession hunters, and investment seekers nervously watched European influence mount in the Far East. The fatal weakness of the Manchu dynasty, which ruled China, had become apparent in China's disastrous war with Japan in 1894–95. By 1900 Germany, France, Russia, and Japan had secured generous "spheres of influence" in China, together with exclusive economic "concessions" to develop these areas through long-term leases and special trading privileges. If the United States intended to establish its own foothold on the Chinese mainland, it would have to move quickly.

Once again, as in the case of the Monroe Doctrine seventy-five years earlier, American and British interests coincided on the point of equal trading rights and market opportunity for all nations. And once again the British Foreign Office proposed a joint statement, only to be told by the McKinley administration that the United States preferred to make its own unilateral pronouncement. The result of this decision was a series of notes dispatched to the European capitals and Tokyo by Secretary of State John Hay, announcing America's Open Door policy. This policy embodied three principles. Nations with spheres of influence in China (1) would promise to respect the "vested interests" of other nations within their own spheres; (2) would agree to allow Chinese customs officials to continue to collect duties in every sphere of interest "no matter to what nationality it may belong"; and (3) would pledge not to discriminate against competitor nations in levying port duties and railroad rates within their respective spheres of interest. At best Secretary Hay received ambiguous replies from all the governments to which he had sent the notes setting forth American policy. Nevertheless, he boldly announced the "final and definitive" acceptance of the principles of the Open Door.

Hay's optimism was soon severely tested by the Boxer Rebellion, a series of militant antiforeign riots in China that cut off the international community in Peking from the outside world. The European powers, Japan, and the United States retaliated by sending a rescue expedition (including 2,500 American soldiers fresh from the Philippines) to lift the siege and punish the Chinese nationalists. Once again the road lay open to further Chinese concessions that might lead to the dismantlement of the Chinese empire. Now Hay was forced to write a second note to the other powers, this one announcing simply that the United States intended to maintain the territorial integrity of the empire. Here was a sharp departure in American diplomacy—not simply a commitment to preserving equal economic opportunity on the mainland, but a pledge to uphold the sovereignty of China.

The Open Door, it was clear, would control imperialistic ambitions exactly to the extent that Britain and the United States wanted it to. Events soon disillusioned American policymakers. The Chinese empire lay in shambles, its days numbered before revolution toppled the dynasty in 1911. In the decade between the Boxer Rebellion and the outbreak of the Chinese Revolution, Britain accepted the inevitable by hastening to make overtures to Japan, acknowledging that country's predominant interests on the Chinese mainland. Meanwhile the rivalry between Russia and Japan over mining and railroad concessions in Manchuria led to the outbreak of war in 1904. In a series of smashing victories over the Russians, Japan played to perfection the part of "underdog" so appealing to Americans, and forced Russia to accept the mediation of President Roosevelt, who suddenly appeared in the unfamiliar role of peacemaker.

The Portsmouth Treaty   The Portsmouth (New Hampshire) Treaty of 1905, which Roosevelt forced on an unhappy but thoroughly beaten Russia, established Japan as the dominant power in the Far East. But the treaty did not advance the principles of the Open Door. In a secret agreement in 1907, Russia and Japan agreed to divide Manchuria, Mongolia, and Korea into spheres of influence with "special interests." Roosevelt reluctantly recognized Japan's special interests in Manchuria in the Root-Takahira Agreement (1908), thus presiding over the ceremonial closing of the Open

Door. Although the president admitted that the Open Door principle was "an excellent thing" so far as it could be upheld by general diplomatic agreement, he nevertheless confessed that the policy simply disappeared once a nation like Japan chose to disregard it. In this sense the Open Door ended in failure.

Intervention in North Africa

In the Moroccan crisis of 1905–06, Roosevelt managed to salvage at least some aspects of an Open Door policy while improving on his record as a peacemaker. The crisis grew out of conflicting French and German interests in North Africa, and a clash resulted in which the United States, according to Roosevelt's secretary of state, Elihu Root, was not justified in taking "a leading part." Nevertheless Roosevelt broke a tradition of nonintervention by actively directing the Algeciras Conference (1906). As he intended, the settlement halted German penetration of North Africa momentarily, united France and Great Britain in solid opposition to Kaiser Wilhelm II, and reaffirmed for the United States the principles of the Open Door. Roosevelt, who already distrusted German military power, boasted of having stood the Kaiser on his head "with great decision." Yet imperial Germany soon righted itself, and it was clear that Roosevelt's departure from a century-long tradition of nonentanglement in European affairs would not soon be repeated.

Intervention in the Caribbean

No such doubts about the American role of policeman inhibited progressive foreign policy in the Caribbean. Here economic interests and dominant American power combined in a shortsighted policy of constant intervention that would leave a legacy of ill will and distrust. American interference in the internal affairs of unstable Latin American governments quickly became a pattern. Behind this pattern lay rapidly expanding American economic interests—not just in trade, but in banking, investments, and the development of natural resources, all of which seemingly required a favorable political climate and the willingness of Caribbean governments to grant generous concessions to the United States.

Trouble began in that "infernal little Cuban republic," as Roosevelt called it, in admitting to a recurrent urge to "wipe its people off the face of the earth." Four years after the removal of American forces in 1902, the troops were back again for another attempt at restoring order. A policeman's lot, the president agreed, was not a happy one. "All that we wanted from them was that they would behave themselves and be prosperous and happy so that we would not have to interfere." Instead, the Cubans persisted in playing at revolution and "may get things into such a snarl that we have no alternative save to intervene—which will at once convince the suspicious idiots in South America that we do wish to interfere after all, and perhaps have some land hunger." The president neglected to add that it was not land hunger but the drive to establish economic dominance in Latin America that dictated his interventionist strategy.

A habit of constantly intervening in the domestic affairs of neighbors to the south required an explanation, and Roosevelt provided this in the famous "corollary" to the Monroe Doctrine in his annual message to Congress in 1905. Once again, as in Cleveland's administration ten years earlier, the occasion was a fiscal crisis in Venezuela, where a chronically unstable and corrupt dictatorship refused to honor its debts. In 1903 Germany tried to nudge the Venezuelan government toward a more conciliatory stance by bombarding Fort San Carlos, and only prompt American condemnation of the "outrage" dissuaded the Germans from taking further measures. To forestall similar European moves to protect their investments, Roosevelt offered his corollary. "Chronic wrongdoing," he admitted, would inevitably invite retaliation from the "civilized" nations determined to protect their investments in Latin America. Since the Monroe Doctrine effectively prevented the European powers from intervening directly, the United States, "however reluctantly," might be forced to step in "in flagrant cases of such wrongdoing or impotence." In short, Latin America properly belonged within the sphere of influence of the United States, which would undertake the work of an "international police power."

The meaning of the Roosevelt Corollary became clear in the Dominican Republic in 1905 when, after considerable urging from the United States, the Dominican government agreed to request American assistance in straightening out its finances. Despite congressional reservations, President Roosevelt was more than happy to provide such advice. With the control of the Dominican customhouse firmly in American hands, the United States succeeded in preventing German intervention once again, but at the cost of a policy that would continue to breed hemispheric ill will throughout the twentieth century.

The Panama Canal Affair The problem of Panama and of securing American rights to a canal across the Central American isthmus offered the clearest example of a foreign policy based on narrow and shortsighted national interest. High-powered lobbying by the new Panama Canal Company, the successor of a defunct French company that had tried and failed to build a Panamanian canal, caused the American government to abandon the Nicaraguan route, which had intrigued Americans for more than a century. A combination of French adventurers and American entrepreneurs succeeded in convincing Roosevelt, Mark Hanna, and other Republican leaders of the distinct advantages of the route through Panama, which was then a province of Colombia. With the help of a few carefully placed investments in the future of their party, they managed to win congressional support for their lucrative deal. By 1902 all that remained was to convince the inept Colombian government of the benefits that civilization was about to confer.

For a while negotiations proceeded smoothly. The Hay-Herran Treaty of 1903 gave the United States rights to a canal zone six miles wide for the price of $10 million plus an annual rental of $250,000. Then suddenly Colombian patriots,

"Teddy" Defends Civilization
Anti-imperialist cartoon lampoons Roosevelt's Latin American policy.

Digging the Panama Canal
Roosevelt poses at the controls of a giant steam shovel in Panama.

preparing to overthrow a corrupt dictator and realizing that they were being swindled, forced the Colombian senate to withdraw the treaty.

Roosevelt duly denounced his new opponents as "inefficient bandits" and "contemptible little creatures" who were willfully blocking the march of progress across the hemisphere. With his initial scheme now frustrated, the president agreed to an alternative plan for a pocket revolution in Panama, engineered by canal promoters and by a handful of native *insurrectos,* who proceeded to establish Panamanian independence from Colombia with the blessing of the United States and the help of its navy. After hasty recognition by the United States, the new state of Panama obliged its benefactor by granting the terms for the canal that Colombia had just refused. Roosevelt had his canal project, the Panamanian patriots had their revolution, and the promoters had their profits. Roosevelt never ceased defending his part in the affair: "If I had followed traditional conservative methods, I would have submitted a dignified state paper of probably two hundred pages to Congress and the debates on it would have been going on yet; but I took the Canal Zone and let Congress debate; and while the debate goes on the Canal does also."

Roosevelt's Style of Diplomacy

With this bald assertion of presidential and national power, Roosevelt drew together the strands of his diplomacy. In the first place, his diplomatic style was a highly personal one that assumed that most of the issues in foreign affairs were best handled, as he said, "by one man alone." Although on occasion he made effective use of his secretaries of state, John Hay and Elihu Root, just as often he bypassed them completely, and he seldom gave them credit for decisions that he rightly or wrongly considered his own. Roosevelt was determined to play the lone hand, and he fumed at the Senate's constant interference and its tampering with what he considered an executive prerogative. Deliberative bodies, he insisted, were virtually useless when there was "any efficient work" to be done. It was for the president alone to take charge of foreign policy in the same way that he took the lead in formulating domestic priorities of reform and reorganization. His aim in intervening in Latin American affairs, he later wrote, was to wake up the American people "so that they would back a reasonable and intelligent foreign policy which would have put a stop to the crying disorders at our very doors."

"Crying disorders"—here was the link between domestic progressive reform and foreign policy. Order and stability in Asia, Roosevelt was to learn, lay beyond the reach of American policy. In Europe, where his leverage was greater, he could mix balance-of-power diplomacy with hopes for a perpetual Anglo-American supremacy throughout the world. But it was in the Western Hemisphere that the benefits of order and system seemed to him the greatest, and he did not hesitate to seek these benefits for American business.

Although Roosevelt presided over the transformation of territorial imperialism into a policy of economic penetration, his language revealed his ignorance of his historical role. He spoke constantly of "honor, territorial integrity and vital interests" as the only basis for an American foreign policy. There were higher things in life, he kept insisting, than the enjoyment of material comforts or the pursuit of wealth: "It is through strife, or the readiness for strife, that a nation must win greatness." And greatness for Roosevelt was primarily spiritual. His speeches rang with the clichés of "righteousness" and "duty" as he combined moralism and nationalism in a blend of power politics that glossed over the hard economic motives he never clearly acknowledged.

The central theme running through Roosevelt's foreign policy pronouncements was the danger that American preoccupation with domestic prosperity would turn right-minded citizens into a mere "assemblage of well-to-do hucksters" who cared for nothing beyond their own borders. But to argue the case for an aggressive foreign policy purely in terms of high-mindedness was to ignore the economic forces that increasingly controlled the making of American foreign policy. These forces included investment opportunities, concessions, corporate resource development, and other forms of economic penetration—all requiring political and economic stability, which was essential to the effective exploitation of colonial economies. Roosevelt's rhetoric concealed the fact that as president he became, if not the captive, at least the ally of exactly the economic forces he presumably distrusted.

Taft's "Dollar Diplomacy" The Taft administration substituted dollars for bullets and displayed no such squeamishness in acknowledging the reality of economic imperialism. Taft's choice of secretary of state, corporation lawyer Philander C. Knox, was itself proof of the growing intimacy between the Wall Street investment community and the State Department. Knox, who was given a much freer hand in formulating policy than Roosevelt had allowed his secretaries of state, was the chief architect of Taft's program of "dollar diplomacy." Dollar diplomacy, a form of democratic state capitalism, used American export capital, together with dominant political and military power, to give force, as Taft himself put it, "alike to idealistic humanitarian sentiments, to the dictates of sound policy and strategy, and to legitimate commercial aims."

Dollar diplomacy extended the principles of domestic progressivism to the conduct of foreign policy. Investment capitalists were encouraged to proceed with the economic penetration of undeveloped areas under conditions of stability and profitability provided by the government. "In China," Taft told Congress in citing his favorite example, "the policy of encouraging financial investment to enable that country to help itself has had the result of giving new life and practical application to the open-door policy." Taft's administration was committed to encouraging the use of American capital in China to promote "those essential reforms" that China had pledged to the United States and to the other major powers. Taft offered for congressional approval a "new diplomacy," practiced by a foreign service "alert and equipped to cooperate with the businessmen of America" and dedicated to "improved governmental methods of protecting and stimulating it."

Taft's open avowal of the economic motive did not alter the pattern of American success and failure—conspicuous success in attracting investment to nearby Latin America, where the bankers were more than willing to go, and nearly total failure in the Far East, where the bankers were not willing to go. In attempting to open China once more to American capital, Taft met the determined resistance of British, French, and German bankers, who excluded the Americans from an international business group to finance and build the Hukuang Railway in China, an ill-considered project that was never completed. By placing heavy diplomatic pressure on the Chinese emperor, Knox succeeded in gaining admission to the railway consortium. But he needlessly made trouble for himself by another poorly conceived experiment in state capitalism in Manchuria. Like Hay's original plan, the Taft administration's attempt to pry open the door for American capital ended in failure.

No such difficulties were encountered in Latin America, where American capital continued to pour in. Here a combination of supersalesmanship and regular government intervention to protect American investments—in Nicaragua, Guatemala, Honduras, and Haiti—kept the gates open.

Taft's foreign policy concentrated on Latin America and the Far East and virtually neglected Europe. In warning against an exclusive concern with the Far East, progressive writer Herbert Croly (who had also presumed to advise Roosevelt in *The Promise of American Life*) predicted the early arrival of an international confrontation of major powers that might force the United States to interfere "in what may at first appear to be a purely European complication." When that time came, Croly hastened to add, American policymakers ought to meet it with "a sound, well-informed, and positive conception of American national interest rather than a negative and ignorant conception." Taft, however, preferred to keep his distance. The legal framework for dollar diplomacy was provided by a deep faith in arbitration: with arbitration Taft hoped to defuse international crises in much the same way that boards of mediators in domestic affairs depoliticized economic conflict. Twenty-five arbitration treaties had been signed in the last days of the outgoing Roosevelt administration, and Taft sought to apply the same principle to all "justiciable" issues. The Senate, however, eliminated the procedures for discussion and consultation in every case in which the United States might be presumed to have an interest. Nevertheless, the arbitration scheme lived on as a progressive panacea, drawing the attention of Woodrow Wilson and his secretary of state, the "Prince of Peace," William Jennings Bryan. There would be continuities as well as new departures in Wilson's missionary diplomacy.

"The Organized Force of Mankind": Wilsonian Diplomacy and World War

At first Woodrow Wilson appeared to represent a new constituency in American foreign policy. The years after 1900 saw peace groups, proponents of arbitration, and other idealists combine in a broad coalition behind the principles of missionary diplomacy, moral publicity, and open rather than secret international agreements. In rejecting both Roosevelt's role of big brother to the oppressed and Taft's dollar diplomacy, Wilson entered office with an appeal to national high-mindedness that warmed the hearts of moralists everywhere. "My dream is that as the years go on and the world knows more and more of America," the president told a Fourth of July audience in 1914, "it . . . will turn to America for those moral inspirations which lie at the basis of all freedoms . . . and that America will come into the full light of day when all shall know that she puts human rights above all other rights and that her flag is the flag not only of America but of humanity." Yet three months earlier Wilson had ordered the occupation of the Mexican port of Vera Cruz to vindicate American honor.

One of the ironies of American foreign relations in the early twentieth century was that both of the widely divergent formulations of policy—national egotism and national high-mindedness—led to similar involvements of the United States throughout the world and almost constantly to forcible intervention in the affairs of neighboring countries. Both the demands of national interest and the less precise requirements of moral mission ended in the application of raw power. By 1917 the United States had clearly arrived as a world power, but it remained to be seen how American power would be used in reordering a world at war. Americans entered World War I still seeking an answer to this question.

Like most Americans before 1914, Woodrow Wilson had given little serious attention to the specifics of American foreign policy. Diplomatic questions had not figured prominently in the campaign of 1912, and to solve such questions Wilson could offer only the conventional wisdom of an active peace movement in the United States concerning the exportability of the American democratic way. During his two terms Wilson often served as the mouthpiece of this movement and adopted many of its principles, fashioning them into an alternative to balance-of-power politics.

By 1914 there was a well-established faith among progressive intellectuals in the imminent arrival of an age of international harmony. Progressive reformers and professionals believed that improved worldwide communications, international technology, and arbitration would soon create a new moral order. The peace movement in the United States was made up of a variety of groups and interests: church-affiliated peace societies and new secular foundations (including Andrew Carnegie's Endowment for International Peace); students of international law intent on constructing new legal frameworks; preachers of disarmament; and prophets of a vast people-to-people crusade. Many of these peace advocates shared a uniquely American set of assumptions that defined peace as an adjunct to domestic progressive reform.

Arbitration: The Key to World Order   The first of these assumptions was the belief that the path to world order had been discovered by the United States as it progressed from a loose federation of sovereign states to a genuine union of all the people. From similar beginnings, the promoters of peace reasoned, one world of harmony and democratic striving might take shape. A second assumption that was associated with this golden vision of an Americanized world order was a stubborn faith in arbitration itself. Arbitration, many assumed, was a key mechanism for resolving tensions and potential conflicts. This mechanism could take various forms: the International Court at the Hague, the Netherlands, which had been created by international agreement in 1899; a body of international law; or bilateral "cooling off" treaties.

These progressive beliefs led Wilson to accept the views of the peace advocates. His language, like Roosevelt's, was consistently abstract. But whereas Roosevelt, a self-declared "realist," spoke of national duty, honor, and integrity, Wilson translated these terms into the language of idealism. He denounced narrowly understood national interest as "selfishness" and the rule of unbridled materialism. "Balance of power" to him meant unstable coalitions of aggressive interests. The outlook of "average" people the world over, on the other hand, was becoming "more and more unclouded" as national purposes fell more and more into the background and the "common purpose of enlightened mankind" took their place. Wilson spoke of the time, not far distant, when these "counsels of plain men" would come to replace the "counsels of sophisticated men of affairs" as the best means of securing world peace. Then the statesmen of the world would be forced to heed the "common clarified thought," or they would be broken.

These views constituted a preliminary version of Wilson's plan for an alternative system of world politics, which had begun to take shape in his mind even before war broke out in Europe. Wilson's schoolmasterish language was equal to his vision as he took on what his critics called his "papal role" in dispensing a humanitarian theology. "I do not know that there will ever be a declaration of independence or grievances for mankind," he told an audience at Independence Hall in Philadelphia in 1914, scarcely a week before the outbreak of war, "but I believe that if any such document is ever drawn it will be drawn in the spirit of the American Declaration of Independence, and that America has lifted high the light which will shine unto all generations and guide the feet of mankind to the goal of justice and liberty and peace." The president, noted the acid-tongued editors of *The New Republic* magazine, uttered nothing that might sound trivial at the Last Judgment.

The first fruits of this Wilsonian "missionary" spirit were bitter ones for the promoters of dollar diplomacy. Wilson quickly dashed the hopes of the outgoing Taft administration for continued investment in China by rejecting a scheme for railroad financing as a violation of Chinese sovereignty. In the delicate negotiations over the Panama Canal tolls, he argued that American exemption from payment showed a "dishonorable attitude," and at the risk of dividing his own party he secured a repeal. Then in October 1913, in an address in Mobile, Alabama, that became famous, he completed the reversal of dollar diplomacy by promising to emancipate Latin America from its "subordination" to "foreign enterprise."

Intervention in Mexico

Yet in Latin America, where United States business interests were real and compelling, Wilson found it impossible to reverse his predecessors' policy of intervention. His formal disavowal of American interference ended in bitter irony. In fact, under Wilson the United States intervened in the affairs of its neighbors more often than ever before. There was a military occupation of Haiti in 1915; financial supervision in the Dominican Republic in 1916; renewed controls in Cuba in 1917; and minor meddling in behalf of American investors throughout the Caribbean. Moralistic though he frequently was, Wilson was not blind to the operation of economic motives nor deaf to the appeals of American entrepreneurs. His difficulties in Latin America resulted in large part from his tendency to identify the beneficent workings of American capital with the welfare of "the submerged eighty-five per cent" of native populations, to whom he wanted to bring the blessings of parliamentary democracy.

Wilson's theories of moral diplomacy were tested by events in Mexico and were found inadequate. In 1911, following a long period of oppressive rule, Mexican dictator Porfirio Díaz was overthrown by moderate constitutionalists led by Francisco Madero. The new government received prompt recognition from the Taft administration. Then, less than two years later, Madero himself fell victim to a counterrevolutionary coup directed by one of his lieutenants, Victoriano Huerta, who murdered his former chief and seized the presidency. This was the situation confronting Wilson as he took office.

Outraged by Huerta's brutality, Wilson lost no time in denouncing him as a thug and a butcher, and refused to recognize his government. Wilson's refusal to grant recognition rested partly on genuine moral revulsion but also on the knowledge that Britain had recognized Huerta's dictatorship in the hope of gaining further economic concessions. Wilson meant to put an end to Britain's pretensions by toppling Huerta. Although economic and strategic concerns usually appeared on the fringes of Wilson's moral vision, they were never quite out of sight. He continued to insist that the United States must never abandon morality for expediency. But in Mexico, profits for American investors and parliamentary democracy for the Mexican people seemed to him wholly compatible.

Wilson was determined to replace Huerta with the moderate rule of Venustiano Carranza, another constitutionalist who had succeeded in rallying popular opposition to the dictator. Wilson seized the occasion for overthrowing Huerta when a boatload of American sailors was arrested and unlawfully detained in Tampico. The president demanded an immediate apology. When Huerta predictably refused to concede to a government that had refused to recognize him, Wilson ordered the occupation of Vera Cruz, an exercise that cost the lives of nineteen Americans and a great many more Mexicans. Under heavy pressure from the United States, and besieged by the forces of Carranza's constitutionalists, Huerta resigned and fled to Spain in 1914. Yet Carranza's liberal regime was no more willing to tolerate American intervention than the deposed dictator

Mexican-American Relations, 1916–17
Pancho Villa's (left) raid on a New Mexico town and his murder of American citizens called for a U.S. punitive expedition led by General John J. Pershing (below).

had been. Only a timely offer by the so-called ABC Powers (Argentina, Brazil, and Chile) to mediate the dispute allowed Wilson to withdraw American forces and save face.

The second act of the Mexican crisis opened with the attempt of Pancho Villa, a bandit leader and an unsavory associate of Carranza, to overthrow his chief and take power for himself by provoking war with the United States. Wilson very nearly obliged him. On January 10, 1916, Villa and his band stopped a train at Santa Ysabel in the northern provinces, took seventeen Americans off, and shot sixteen of them. Then in March, Villa raided the tiny New Mexico town of Columbus, burned it to the ground, and killed nineteen more American citizens. Wilson responded, as Villa had hoped he would, by dispatching General John J. Pershing and his troops on a punitive expedition. Pershing chased the bandit chief some three hundred miles back into Mexico without managing to catch him. Carranza demanded the immediate withdrawal of Pershing's expeditionary force. Faced with the near certainty of war with Germany, Wilson could only comply. In 1917, as Villa roamed the Mexican countryside and an unstable Carranza government lurched toward still another constitutional crisis, Wilson had nothing to show for his five-year labors. Now, however, his attention was fixed on Europe.

War in Europe   In the summer of 1914 World War I broke out in Europe. When Serbian nationalists assassinated the heir of the multinational Austro-Hungarian empire in June 1914, Austria-Hungary decided to crush its troublesome small neighbor, Serbia. Russia, as Serbia's protector, warned Austria-Hungary not to attack and began to mobilize its vast armies. Germany, which regarded Austria-Hungary as its sole dependable ally, demanded that Russia halt its mobilization; when the Russian tsar refused, Germany declared war on August 1. Germany then demanded that Russia's ally, France, give assurances that it would not come to Russia's aid; and when these assurances were not offered, Germany declared war on France on August 3. Germany promptly set its military plan in motion by striking a heavy blow in the west to knock out France before the slow-moving Russian armies could do serious harm in the east. The German plan involved an invasion of France through neutral Belgium. On August 4, when Germany attacked Belgium, Britain declared war on Germany. The German armies in the west drove deeply into northern France, but Paris was saved, and by the late fall of 1914 the war had settled down to a bloody stalemate on the Western Front. After a Russian offensive against Germany and Austria-Hungary failed, a similar stalemate developed in eastern Europe. Meanwhile Japan entered the war in order to seize Germany's Pacific islands and holdings in China. By 1915 Italy had joined the anti-German coalition, and Bulgaria and Turkey had taken Germany's side.

The outbreak of war caught the Wilson administration and the entire United States by surprise. At first the news that Austria was threatening tiny Serbia evoked little more than the traditional American sympathy for the underdog.

Because neither European nor American diplomats yet realized the scope of the coming catastrophe, it was not difficult for Wilson to declare American neutrality and to call on all citizens to remain "impartial in thought as well as in action." Behind the proclamation of neutrality lay the president's conviction that the war would be a short one that would end in a settlement that the United States, from its Olympian station above the battle, could help arrange. And behind this unwarranted assumption lay still another belief—that America could play an effective role in creating a new moral order.

As the war dragged into its second year, all of Wilson's hopes for remodeling the world of power politics came to hinge on a doctrine of neutrality that itself rested on two misconceptions. First, developments quickly showed that the United States was not and could not be unconcerned with the outcome of the war. As shrewd observers had noted before the war broke out, Britain had directly contributed to American growth and well-being by upholding the European balance of power throughout the entire nineteenth century. And Germany, at least since 1890, had consistently threatened American security with a belligerent new diplomacy, an arms buildup, and a frightening doctrine of militarism. An Anglo-German conflict was thus bound to affect the United States in crucial ways.

The first year of the war drove this lesson home. Britain increasingly monopolized direct access to information about the war and supplied the American press with a constant stream of accounts (most of them greatly exaggerated) of German "atrocities." Except for many German Americans and Irish Americans, ordinary people in the United States came to view the war in pro-Allied, anti-German terms, even if they did not favor actual American entry. The British skillfully manipulated their propaganda advantage until the president and his advisers came to argue, as one of them put it, that "Germany must not be permitted to win this war." By 1915 the administration began, not always consciously, to act on that assumption. The American economy was placed at the disposal of the Allies, who, despite the embarrassing presence on their side of Imperial Russia, were presumed to be fighting autocracy and militarism in the name of democracy and freedom. The government proclaimed trade with the Allies "legal and welcome." When Allied credit soon evaporated, American bankers rushed to the rescue with credits and loans that totaled $2.5 billion by the time the United States entered the war in 1917. On the other hand, there were virtually no American wartime investments in Germany. Wilson continued to press both Britain and Germany for a settlement of the war, but when neither side agreed he tended to excuse the former and blame the latter for the disastrous military stalemate.

The *Lusitania* Incident

The second misconception underlying Wilson's doctrine of neutrality stemmed from his failure to understand the logic of total war or to acknowledge the effect of modern technology. The submarine had made the traditional rights of neutrals obsolete. As they grappled for an economic stranglehold on each other, both

"He Kept Us Out of War"
Wilson campaigns for re-election in 1916.

combatants had to resort to novel practices that were clear violations of the established rules of war. Britain extended the right of naval search to new lengths and established a blockade that virtually extinguished the rights of neutrals. Yet American diplomatic exchange with Britain settled into a predictable pattern of violation, protest, discussion, and eventual resumption of the objectionable practice.

With Germany, on the other hand, the exchange grew brittle, and Wilson's language became increasingly blunt. The Germans' use of submarines, which struck without warning and made no provision for the safety of passengers and crew, touched a raw nerve in the American people. When in May 1915 a German U-boat torpedoed without warning the British liner *Lusitania* with the loss of 128 American lives, Wilson initiated an angry dialogue that grew more and more strident in the next year and a half. Germany quite correctly pointed out that the ship was carrying munitions, but that fact hardly weakened Wilson's determination to apply the old rules. For the president, the sinking of the *Lusitania* was proof of the practical impossibility of using submarines "without disregarding those rules of fairness, reason, justice, and humanity, which all modern opinion regards as imperative." In deciding to hold Germany "strictly accountable," Wilson put the United States on a collision course. Secretary of State Bryan, realizing that Wilson's policy was no longer truly neutral, resigned in protest.

In the meantime, following the *Lusitania* incident, Germany said it would comply with Wilson's terms. Then in 1916 the German attack on the unarmed French passenger ship *Sussex* in the English Channel resulted in injury to American citizens, and the meaning of "strict accountability" suddenly became clear to the president. Submarine warfare, he informed Germany, "of necessity, because of the very character of the vessels employed," was "incompatible" with the "sacred immunities of noncombatants." Unless the Kaiser's government agreed to abandon its methods forthwith, the United States would have no choice but to sever relations. Germany agreed to discontinue the practice, but only if the United States could force Britain to lift the blockade. Until then the German government reserved the right to take back its pledge. The president's options were dwindling fast.

Wilson's growing indignation reflected another, more personal, anxiety. For three years he had continued to pile a heavy load of moral principles onto the conventional concept of neutral rights. Now he was forced to admit that the United States might not be able to impose its will on warring Europe without joining the Allies. A nation that, as he had said, had been "too proud to fight" and that had reelected him on the slogan "He kept us out of war" now faced the prospect of securing a "peace without victory" only by becoming a participant. As he became aware of this, Wilson began to redefine America's mission as nothing less than the building of a system of collective security to replace the collapsed system of balance of power. If compelled to fight, the United States would fight for utopia.

A New World Order In January 1917, a week before Germany announced its decision to resume unrestricted submarine warfare, Wilson described his vision of a new world order to the Senate. The United States, prepared by "the very principles and purposes" of its humanitarian policy, must rebuild the machinery of diplomacy. Its terms for peace must "win the approval of mankind" and not merely "serve the several interests and immediate aims of the nations engaged." As an integral part of the peace settlement, Wilson proposed the establishment of a perpetual league of peaceful nations. This league should be a collective instrument that would be "so much greater than the force of any nation now engaged or any alliance hitherto projected" that governments and their leaders would instinctively bend to its dictates. The future of the world would thus come to depend not on a balance of power, but on a community of opinion; not on "organized rivalries," but on "organized peace." Wilson proposed, in short, to concentrate the moral force of peoples themselves who, with open covenants openly arrived at, would enforce their collective will for national self-determination, democratic government, and lasting peace. To skeptical senators, particularly those in the Republican ranks, Wilson explained that his were at once "American principles" and "the principles of all mankind."

A week later the German imperial government renewed its submarine attacks in a desperate gamble to win the war before the United States could enter. In March, German submarines without warning sank four unarmed American merchantmen, and on April 2, 1917, Wilson appeared before a joint session of Congress to request that it accept the war that had been "thrust" upon the United States. By a vote of 82 to 6 in the Senate and 373 to 50 in the House, Congress agreed to the presidential request.

United States citizens would learn from a year and a half of war and another year of peacemaking that their country had arrived at a position of world power that very few of them could have envisioned thirty years earlier. The nation had gone to war with Spain on the flimsiest of pretexts and had built an empire on its victory. But in the intervening years most Americans, far from embracing imperial responsibilities, had neglected the chores of maintaining an empire. Except in their own hemisphere, they had forgotten their regenerative mission. Now, as their president called on them to fight another and infinitely greater war, they turned to him for a sense of direction and for a definition of their moral commitment.

For his part the president, having determined that war was the only option left open to him, made a prophecy to the nation and a private confession in considering his course. "We are at the beginning of an age," he told the country, "in which it will be insisted that the same standards of conduct and responsibility for wrong done shall be observed among nations and their governments that are observed among individual citizens of civilized states." But privately, in the solitude of the White House on the eve of his appearance before Congress, he admitted to fears about the unintended and uncontrollable effects of going to war. "Once lead this people into war," he told Frank Cobb, the editor of the *New York World*, "and they'll forget there ever was such a thing as tolerance. To fight you must be brutal and ruthless, and the spirit of ruthless brutality will enter into the very fibre of our national life, infecting Congress, the courts, the policeman on the beat, the man in the streets." The meaning of Wilson's prophecy of a new international morality awaited the outcome of the war, but his prediction of the domestic dangers involved in fighting it soon proved all too accurate.

CHRONOLOGY

1895   United States intervenes in boundary dispute between Britain and Venezuela as Secretary of State Richard Olney declares nation "practically sovereign on this continent."
Spain sends troops to quell Cuban revolution.

1896   Cuban rebel leader Maceo murdered, resulting in American popular support for Cuba.
William McKinley elected president.

1897   A letter from Spanish minister

Depuy de Lôme, in which he calls McKinley "weak" and "a would-be politician," is intercepted, worsening American and Spanish relations.
U.S. battleship *Maine* explodes in Havana harbor.

1898   Spanish-American War; United States acquires Philippines, Puerto Rico, and Guam, and annexes Hawaii.

1899   Hay's "Open Door" notes to world powers, calling for "equal and impartial trade" in China and preservation of "Chinese territorial and administrative" integrity.

Senate ratifies peace treaty with Spain.

United States, Germany, and Great Britain partition Samoa.

1900 Foraker Act establishes civil government in Puerto Rico.

Organic Act incorporates Hawaii as a territory of the United States.

McKinley reelected president, defeating Bryan once again.

Boxer Rebellion in China.

1901 Platt Amendment authorizes U.S. intervention in Cuba.

Theodore Roosevelt becomes president after McKinley assassinated.

Hay-Pauncefote Treaty with Great Britain gives United States sole right to build, control, and maintain neutrality of an isthmian canal in Central America.

Philippine Organic Act passed, making Philippine islands an unorganized territory of the United States.

1902 United States returns civil government to Republic of Cuba.

1903 Hay-Herran Treaty with Republic of Colombia, giving United States ninety-nine-year lease on Canal Zone, is rejected by Colombia.

Roosevelt aids revolt in Panama.

Hay-Bunau-Varilla Treaty gives United States full sovereignty in Canal Zone.

United States–Cuba reciprocity treaty forms close economic ties between both countries.

1904 Roosevelt Corollary to Monroe Doctrine.

Roosevelt elected, defeating Democrat Alton B. Parker and Socialist Eugene V. Debs.

1905 Roosevelt mediates in Russo-Japanese War.

1906 American troops intervene in Cuba to restore order.

Algeciras Conference with Roosevelt's help settles French-German conflict in Morocco.

1908 William Howard Taft elected president, defeating Bryan and Debs.

Root-Takahira Agreement; United States recognizes Japan's interests in Manchuria.

1909 Taft inaugurates "Dollar Diplomacy" in China and Latin America.

United States intervenes in Haitian and Nicaraguan finances.

1911 Marines sent to Nicaragua.

1912 Woodrow Wilson elected president, defeating Republican regular William Howard Taft, progressive "Bull Moose" Theodore Roosevelt, and Socialist Eugene V. Debs.

1914 World War I begins; Wilson declares American neutrality.

Wilson orders occupation of Vera Cruz, Mexico.

Panama Canal opened.

1915 United States troops occupy Haiti.

United States recognizes Carranza government in Mexico.

Germans declare unrestricted submarine warfare and sink *Lusitania* with loss of American lives.

Preparedness movement.

1916	Wilson reelected, narrowly defeating Charles Evans Hughes. House-Grey Memorandum on United States' efforts for negotiated peace. American troops occupy Dominican Republic.		General John J. Pershing's expedition into Mexico.
		1917	Germans resume unrestricted submarine warfare and United States enters war. Purchase of Danish Virgin Islands.

Suggested Readings

The boundaries of post-1890 American foreign policy are established in two critical surveys. George F. Kennan, *American Diplomacy, 1900–1950* (1951), points to consistently unprofessional and uninformed leaders as the chief difficulty, while William Appleman Williams, *The Tragedy of American Diplomacy* (1959), cites economic expansion as the source of a peculiar kind of American imperialism. Robert E. Osgood, *Ideals and Self-Interest in America's Foreign Relations* (1953), evaluates the positions of both parties to the great debate over ends and means in the conduct of American diplomacy. Richard W. Leopold, *The Growth of American Foreign Policy* (1962), provides an excellent survey of the development of American interests in the rest of the world, as does Foster R. Dulles, *America's Rise to World Power, 1898–1954* (1955). For an extended review of American anti-imperialism before World War I, see E. Berkeley Tompkins, *Anti-Imperialism in the United States: The Great Debate, 1890–1920* (1970). For an analysis of expansionist fervor from the 1890s through World War II, consult Emily S. Rosenberg, *Spreading the American Dream: American Economic and Cultural Expansion, 1890–1945* (1982). Robert Seager II, *Alfred Thayer Mahan* (1977), is a good introduction to the most determined and articulate of American expansionists.

The origins of American expansionism are critically but carefully examined in Walter LaFeber, *The New Empire: An Interpretation of American Expansion, 1860–1898* (1963). The best account of the diplomatic crisis leading to the Spanish-American War is Ernest R. May, *Imperial Democracy: The Emergence of America as a Great Power* (1961). Robert L. Beisner, *The Anti-Imperialists, 1898–1900* (1968), assesses the arguments and the futile activities of the opponents of expansionism. Leon Wolff, *Little Brown Brother* (1961), gives an outraged account of the Philippine insurrection and the American pacification program. For a fuller and more balanced account of pacification and American colonial policy in the Philippines, see Stuart Creighton Miller, *"Benevolent Assimilation": The American Conquest of the Philippines, 1899–1903* (1982). Richard E. Welch, *Response to Imperialism: The United States and the Philippine-American War* (1979), concentrates on war in the islands, while David R. Trask, *The War with Spain in 1898* (1981), surveys the entire contest.

Areas of growing American interest and control in international affairs have been covered in a number of excellent monographs: Merze Tate, *The United States and the Hawaiian Kingdom* (1965); Charles Vevier, *The United States and China, 1906–1913* (1955); Paul A. Varg, *The Making of a Myth: The United States and China, 1899–1912;* Warren Cohen, *America's Response to China* (1971); Michael Hunt, *The Making of a Special Relationship: The United States and China to 1914* (1983); Charles E. Neu, *The Troubled Encounter: The United States and Japan* (1975); Howard F. Cline, *The United States and Mexico* (1953); Samuel F. Bemis, *The Latin American Policy of the United States* (1967).

On Theodore Roosevelt's foreign policy, see Howard K. Beale, *Theodore Roosevelt and the Rise of America to World Power* (1956), and the more recent Raymond A. Esthus, *Theodore Roosevelt and the International Rivalries* (1970). Dwight C. Miner, *Fight for the Panama Route* (1966), tells a complicated story well, and Robert A. Hart, *The Great White Fleet: Its Voyage Around the World* (1965), is a highly readable account of Roosevelt's colorful gesture. Walter V. Scholes and Marie V. Scholes, *The Foreign Policies of the Taft Administration* (1970), analyzes the workings of dollar diplomacy, and Dana G. Munroe, *Intervention and Dollar Diplomacy in the Caribbean, 1900–1921* (1964), examines its consequences in Latin America.

The fullest discussion of Woodrow Wilson's diplomacy from a presidential point of view is to be found in the volumes of Link's *Wilson.* P. Edward Haley, *Revolution and Intervention: The Diplomacy of Taft and Wilson with Mexico, 1910–1917* (1970), is an even-handed assessment of Mexican policy, as is Robert Freeman Smith, *The U.S. and Revolutionary Nationalism in Mexico* (1972), for the later period. Robert E. Quirk, *An Affair of Honor: Woodrow Wilson and the Occupation of Veracruz* (1962), criticizes the president for his misguided actions in that unfortunate affair. John M. Cooper, Jr., *The Warrior and the Priest* (1983), presents contrasting portraits of Roosevelt and Wilson with their differing views of the conduct of both domestic politics and foreign policy.

Neutrality and American intervention in World War I fascinated a depression generation reluctantly preparing for another war and produced a number of highly critical accounts of American intervention, the best of which is Walter Millis, *The Road to War* (1935). Among the best of more recent accounts are Ernest R. May, *The World War and American Isolation, 1914–1917* (1959); John M. Cooper, Jr., *The Vanity of Power: American Isolation and the First World War, 1914–1917* (1969); Ross Gregory, *The Origins of American Intervention in the First World War* (1971); and Daniel M. Smith, *The Great Departure: The United States in World War I, 1914–1920* (1965).

16

Progressivism and the Great War

⁓

By the time the United States entered the war in April 1917, the European powers were rapidly approaching exhaustion. After three years of stalemate, Germany was suffering from starvation as a result of Britain's naval blockade, as well as a collapse of civilian morale. Austria-Hungary managed to continue the war only by imposing martial law. Russia was crippled by astronomical losses that had led to the overthrow of the tsarist regime in March 1917, and now it stood on the brink of a second revolution that would bring Lenin's Bolsheviks to power by the end of the year. France, its national will shattered, faced widespread mutiny in its armies. Britain, having sacrificed an entire generation of young men to German machine guns since 1914, was beset with severe manpower shortages both at home and in the field.

Slaughter on the Western Front

The original prediction of both sides—Germany's hopes for a six-week war and the Allies' plans for rolling back the enemy on the vast Western and Eastern fronts—had long since been buried under mounds of casualties. Shared strategic obsessions with artillery barrages and with massed infantry assaults on entrenched positions had created a war of appalling senselessness and butchery. Two million casualties on the Western Front in 1916 had failed to move the line of advance for either side, and the war had descended once again into the trenches, which stretched in an unbroken line from the sea to the mountains. A week after President Wilson asked for a declaration of war in April 1917, the British launched still another frontal assault in Belgium on the Ypres sector of the front; in five days they gained only 7,000 yards, at the terrible cost of 160,000 dead and wounded.

"Over There"
American aviators prepare to take off in a French-built Caudron in France, 1918.

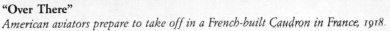

Saying Good-Bye...
War Department photograph, 1917.

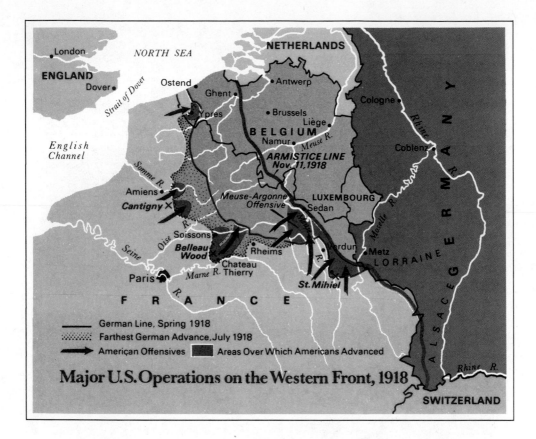

Major U.S. Operations on the Western Front, 1918

Although the United States entered the war late and suffered proportionately fewer losses, the meaning of the slaughter lingered in the American imagination for a generation. In a scene in F. Scott Fitzgerald's *Tender Is the Night,* one of the characters leads a party of sightseers across the Somme Valley after the war. "See that little stream," he says. "We could walk to it in two minutes. It took the British a whole month to walk to it—a whole empire walking very slowly, dying in front and pushing forward behind. And another empire walked very slowly backward a few inches a day, leaving the dead like a million bloody rugs." American soldiers in the last year of the war followed the footsteps of their British and French predecessors. In joining the Allies the United States committed its forces to a war in which the ultimate loser was the side that won the most battles. Woodrow Wilson's hopes for a just peace died along with more than 100,000 American soldiers on the Western Front.

It took eight months for American troops to join the fighting on the Western Front in effective numbers, and it was nearly a year before they were decisively engaged in helping to turn back the final German offensive. In the meantime the Allied cause hung in the balance. In November 1917 Lenin and the Bolsheviks overthrew the provisional revolutionary government of Russia, established a party dictatorship, and took Russia out of the war. Russia's withdrawal released badly needed German divisions for a last offensive on the Western Front. In the spring drive along the Somme beginning in March 1918, the Germans routed the British and penned up the French, but without making a decisive breakthrough.

In May and June the American Second Division was dispatched to the Marne River, where it bolstered sagging French defenses. In the first big American engagements of the war, United States forces halted a German advance at Chateau-Thierry and slowly drove the enemy out of Belleau Wood. These American actions were only preliminaries to the great Allied counteroffensive, which in late summer began to push the German army relentlessly back toward its frontier. By September the American commander, General John J. Pershing, who had stubbornly held out for an independent command, had over half a million men at his disposal, a number that would double by the end of the war two months later. In October, Pershing, in conjunction with British and French offensives elsewhere along the line, opened a massive American drive out of the Argonne Forest aimed at the railhead at Sedan—the last sustained American action of the war.

On November 3 Austria-Hungary collapsed, and on the same day the German navy mutinied at its main base, Kiel, raising the specter of another communist revolution. Six days later a general strike in Germany, led by the Independent Socialists, forced the Kaiser to abdicate, and a coalition of socialists and liberals proclaimed a republic. Forty-eight hours later the new German republic accepted as the basis for an armistice the peace proposals that Wilson had put forward in January 1918, the Fourteen Points.* The Great War was over.

It was immediately clear that the American entry had brought desperately needed troops and supplies to the Allies at a critical moment. American troops provided the decisive advantage of power needed to win the war. Equally important was the role of the United States in replenishing stockpiles of food and materiel with its "bridge of ships," replacing the merchantmen sunk by German submarines, and experimenting successfully with the convoy system of protecting Allied shipping, which in the last analysis saved the Allies. The American contribution was essential, and it came at a crucial time. Yet despite the provisional German acceptance of the Fourteen Points as the agenda for peacemaking, the American war effort had not wiped out national fears and hatreds embodied in wartime secret agreements and arrangements among the Allies, nor had it established the moral climate, either at home or in Europe, that Wilson knew was essential to lasting peace.

With the American entrance, a conflict that had already grown fiercely ideological became a crusade for democracy and national rebirth. All the powers had secured control over the actions and opinions of their civilian populations as they accepted the logic of total war. But the United States entry completed an

---

*For the Fourteen Points, see pp. 315–17.

American Soldiers in France
Elderly French couple welcomes American doughboys.

ideological shift for the Allies by defining the war in moral as well as political terms, as a struggle of the forces of peace and democracy against the dark powers of militarism. In announcing his Fourteen Points, and by explaining American war aims as "the right of those who submit to authority to have a voice in their own government" and "a universal dominion of right by...a concert of free peoples," Wilson unconsciously hardened the resolve of his allies to seek an unconditional surrender and a punishing peace. Perhaps the greatest irony of World War I lay in the president's determination to inject into it a democratic ideology that in the end would make his own role as the evenhanded peacemaker impossible.

Total war also imposed an organizational logic on the participants, all of whom were forced to adjust to the national need for centralization and control. Early in the war Germany recruited civilian administrators for its War Raw Materials Department, which established efficient mechanisms for allocating manpower, arms, and equipment. Britain organized its dwindling resources under the Defense of the Realm Act, which provided for full mobilization of all available manpower. France, which had lost its northern industrial provinces for

The Kaiser and His Victims
The American entrance into the war brought a surge of anti-German propaganda.

the duration, used the powers of government to relocate factories and regulate food production. Once in the war the United States followed the same pattern in building a war machine, enlisting civilians in the war effort, and improvising the bureaucratic controls demanded by the emergency. By the time the war ended in November 1918, Wilson's administration had completed an organizational revolution and had brought the power of government into nearly every phase of American life.

War and the Health of the State

For some progressives the coming of the war seemed a heaven-sent opportunity to realize the American promise. The war, they confidently predicted, would bring genuine national unity and an end to class and ethnic division. It would discredit dangerous radicalism by giving the nation's citizens a new spirit of patriotism. The demands of war would also destroy all selfish materialism and preoccupation with profits and replace both with the higher goals of service and sacrifice. National preparedness and mobilization, central features of the New Nationalism, would foster moral virtue and civic purity in soldiers and civilians alike. Those progressives who continued to define their basic purpose as creating a new American morality and citizenship saw in the impending war effort the outlines of what one of them called a "true national collectivism" based on efficiency, social control, high-mindedness, and revived moral purpose.

On a more practical plane many more progressives responded enthusiastically to the organizational and reform challenges that were furnished by the war. Those reformers who saw their work as a form of moral cleansing—of vice, alcoholism, and prostitution—viewed the war as a chance to purify democracy at home while saving it abroad.

World War I drew to the political surface darker currents of coercion and repression that had been part of progressive reform from the beginning— programs for checking unacceptable behavior and encouraging healthy attitudes in American citizens. Old progressives like Theodore Roosevelt who had been born during or soon after the Civil War carried into the twentieth century Victorian notions of propriety and righteousness, which they continued to define as "natural" and "normal." They were concerned with preserving "manliness" and fostering the "strenuous life," and they worried openly about the "feminization" of American life. Moral progressives had long targeted the saloon and the house of prostitution, and they sought remedies in a national prohibition campaign and federal laws like the Mann Act (1910). Some progressive believers in Americanization proposed strict limits on immigration and stringent literacy tests to exclude recently arrived immigrants and African Americans from the political process. Other reformers discovered in the science of eugenics and programs for sterilization a method for controlling breeding patterns of Americans and presumably eliminating the "unfit," however defined. A few progressives capitulated to the illogic of popularizers of racism like Madison Grant, whose *The Passing of the Great Race* (1916) predicted the decline of civilization as a result of the loss of "Nordic" purity. Many progressives also worried about the enervating effects of movies, vaudeville, amusement parks, and dance halls in seemingly weakening the fiber and sapping the vitality of the lower orders. All these prescriptions and programs stemmed from a progressive conviction of the need for more effective devices for securing what sociologists now began to call "social control." The coming of war simply opened the doors to such fears of cultural pluralism and political permissiveness, and strengthened the urge in moral progressives to direct their fellow citizens into the paths of civic righteousness.

The war advanced the progressives' hopes in a number of important ways. The preparedness campaign furthered the ideal of universal military service as a school for citizenship. Americanization programs aimed at controlling the immigrant took on new life. Prohibitionist hopes soared, and women's suffrage suddenly seemed possible. City planners, social-justice workers, child-labor reformers, and other progressive humanitarians warmed to the prospects of a domestic reformation in the midst of a foreign war.

The war seemed to hold the greatest promise for progressives in administration and public service—those reformers who sought to join Roosevelt's New Nationalist emphasis on efficiency, administrative centralization, and executive power with Wilson's New Freedom faith in fact finding, voluntary cooperation, and democratic participation. "We must speak, act, and serve together," Wilson reminded the nation. Efficiency quickly became the watchword for a new managerial elite that descended on Washington with proposals for a planned war effort. Wesley C. Mitchell, a professor-turned-bureaucrat who joined the Division of Planning and Statistics of the War Industries Board, explained why government service appealed to professionals and businessmen, many of whom signed up for the duration. "Indeed I am in a mood to demand excitement and make it up when it doesn't offer of itself. I am ready to concoct a new plan for running the universe at any minute." Efficiency as the dominant progressive ideal fixed itself to the image of the war machine turning out men and materiel automatically without the interference of politics and partisanship.

Regulations and Controls

American performance fell far short of the progressive ideal. The most urgent task for Wilson's war state was mobilizing industry. Even before war was declared, Congress established the Council of National Defense, an advisory body composed of cabinet members and industrial and labor leaders, which was charged with taking an inventory of national resources. Out of the council's preliminary survey came the War Industries Board, which attempted—at first unsuccessfully—to control production, arrange purchases, allocate scarce resources, and regulate labor relations. The War Industries Board failed to function effectively until Congress overhauled it, conferring near-dictatorial powers on the president. In turn Wilson brought Wall Street banker Bernard Baruch to Washington early in 1918 to head the agency and gave him sweeping powers to establish priorities and increase production. Baruch's agency, however, was hampered in its work by inadequate information. By the end of the war, the War Industries Board was just beginning to unsnarl the problems of production.

In addition to regulating industry, Wilson moved quickly to bring food, fuel, and transportation under control. To head the Food Administration he appointed Herbert Hoover, who used his powers under the Lever Act to extend government control over staples. Poor harvests complicated Hoover's problems, and he was forced to experiment with price fixing and a massive consumer-education campaign to limit consumption. His strategy succeeded, first doubling and then tripling the amount of food that could be exported to starving Europe. Hoover's efficient management of food production represented the chief accomplishment of wartime progressivism. The Fuel Administration, headed by progressive Harry A. Garfield, followed Hoover's lead in the Food Administration by seeking to increase coal production with price supports fixed to guarantee profits, and, less successfully, with schemes for systematizing production and distribution on a national scale.

Managing the nation's railroads proved even more difficult than increasing food production. At first Wilson experimented unsuccessfully with a voluntary system under the Railroads War Board. Attempts to increase the number of

Women on the Home Front
Women contributed significantly to the war effort with various kinds of work.

railroad cars and to equalize traffic broke down completely in December 1917. Congress demanded an investigation, out of which came a revised United States Railroad Administration with effective power. Gradually the Railroad Administration extricated itself from confusion, and by the end of the war it too, like the War Industries Board, was beginning to function effectively. Shipping presented Wilson's administration with its most severe problem. Here the challenge was deceptively simple—to build or commandeer ships faster than the German U-boats could sink them. The solution, the Emergency Fleet Corporation—originally an offshoot of the United States Shipping Board—failed. Divided leadership impeded effective planning, and the heads of the competing agencies spent half the war quarreling over priorities and programs. Wilson finally removed them and put the competing interests under a single director. By September 1918 the Emergency Fleet Corporation had built only 500,000 tons of new shipping, less than German submarines had sunk in an average month early in 1917.

The Wilson administration's labor policy was aimed at including the workingman in the wartime partnership with business and government—as a junior partner, but one entitled to a fair share of war prosperity. Yet here too success came slowly. Not until April 1918 did Wilson move to establish the National War Labor Board, with power to hear and settle disputes between labor and management. Under the direction of former President Taft and progressive lawyer Frank P. Walsh, the National War Labor Board heard over a thousand cases during the war involving three-quarters of a million workers. In general, Wilson's labor policy was a generous one that was designed to tolerate, if not encourage, unions; to establish an eight-hour workday; to avert strikes through the use of arbitration; and to sanction limited increases in wages.

Overall, the wartime effort in planning was hardly an unqualified success. Lacking an effectual bureaucracy at the outset, Wilson's administration necessarily fumbled and improvised, dispersing rather than centralizing power through a host of overlapping and competing agencies. Not surprisingly, confusion and inefficiency resulted as bureaucrats painfully groped their way toward centralization, learning slowly from their many mistakes. When the armistice came, the American war machine was just beginning to produce at a level approaching full capacity.

The most important consequence of the national war effort was the completion of the alliance between big business and the government. This collaboration was inevitable, because it was only from within the consolidated national industries that the government could recruit needed managerial talent. To Washington, accordingly, came the leaders of business and industry, primed with patriotism but also determined to advance the interests of their sector—which they quickly identified with the national good. Wilson's appointment of Bernard Baruch was only the most visible symbol of this new alliance. From the ranks of railroad management and from big steel, the machine tool industry, finance, and banking came the self-appointed leaders of national mobilization. Along with expertise all of them brought demands for stability and predictability in their industries, which could be furnished only by the government.

Corporate War Profits

Big business profited from the war directly and indirectly—directly, in the form of arrangements like the cost-plus contract, which guaranteed high levels of profit; indirectly, in the education that business leaders received in the uses of government power. Labor fared less well. The cost of living, soaring on the crest of wartime inflation, more than doubled between 1913 and 1920 and cut deeply into wage increases. Farmers benefited from a substantial rise in real income during the war, a gain that would quickly disappear with the return of peace. But corporate profits skyrocketed in the years between 1914 and 1919, increasing threefold by the time the United States entered the war and leveling off in the following years at an annual increase of 30 percent. Gains in the steel industry ranged from 30 percent to 300 percent. In the lumber industry they averaged 17 percent; in oil, 21 percent; in copper, 34 percent. Even with the moderate excess-profits tax and steeper levies on higher incomes, the war made an estimated 42,000 millionaires. If the progressive programs of Theodore Roosevelt and Woodrow Wilson had sought, at least in part, a fairer distribution of American wealth, the war tended to reverse the effects of their efforts by piling up profits in the upper reaches of the economy.

The progressive plans for constructing an effective system of bureaucratic management also came to little. American governmental bureaucracy in 1917 was still in its infancy. The handful of federal agencies at the policymaking level—the Federal Reserve Board, the Federal Trade Commission, and other fledgling agencies—had not yet fully asserted their powers. Inevitably, the wartime administrative apparatus creaked and strained under the pressures of mobilization. Ambitious reorganizational schemes were never carried out. Programs broke down. Authority almost always overlapped, and agencies collided over matters of precedence and priority. By a method marked by more trial and error than most progressives expected, the United States moved hesitantly from administrative chaos to at least some bureaucratic order at war's end.

Repression and Hysteria

If the gains for the federal bureaucracy brought by the war proved partial and in some cases temporary, the same was not true of the wartime campaign for loyalty and uniformity. Here the original progressive dream of an aroused and patriotic citizenry turned into a chauvinist nightmare, and the country experienced a crisis of civil liberties.

The American people responded to war with a spontaneous burst of nationalist fervor, which triggered a chain reaction of repression and hysteria. In the first few months of the war, hundreds of thousands of self-styled patriots banded together in vigilantelike groups bearing impressive titles—the American Defense Society, the National Security League, the American Anti-Anarchy

JOIN THE NAVY
America's new prestige in world affairs will mean a greater Navy
BE A PART OF IT

Apply at Navy Recruiting Station: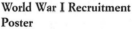
U. S. NAVY RECRUITING STATION
LAW BUILDING

U. S. NAVY RECRUITING S
LAW BUILDING
9TH & MARKET ST
WILMINGTON, DE

World War I Recruitment Poster

Association, even the Boy Spies of America—and dedicated to rooting out heresy wherever they found it. The directors of these grassroots purges were usually leaders in local communities—businessmen, professionals, and merchants—who combined more useful service for the Red Cross and YMCA with the witch-hunting escapades common to superpatriots in any age. Wilson's administration, unable or unwilling to stop these popular excesses, joined in purging dissent. The result was a fevered public uprising against nonconformity of all kinds, and the ruthless suppression of American liberties.

The war hysteria fed a progressive appetite for national unity that had not been offset by a tradition of civil liberties. The central weakness of the progressive program had been the absence of a libertarian concern with protecting basic freedoms, and this absence made a domestic war on liberalism wholly predictable. Patriots and vigilantes, equipped with ropes, whips, and tar and feathers, enjoyed a ritualistic field day complete with flag-kissing ceremonies and forced declarations of loyalty. German Americans, including some prominent persons, were often the targets of this reign of terror. But the victims were mainly marginal people, uneducated or alienated, isolated and without power. In Bisbee, Arizona, the "best" people rounded up some 1,200 striking miners led by the Industrial Workers of the World ("Wobblies"), piled them into freight cars, and hauled them across the state line into the desert, where they were left stranded. In Montana a mob dragged the IWW organizer Frank Little out of his boardinghouse and hanged him from a railroad trestle. Soon the federal government itself joined in the campaign to crush radical dissent: in September 1917 Justice Department agents rounded up 113 officers and organizers of the IWW and impounded five tons of books and pamphlets with which to arraign and convict them.

Out of these acts of suppression came loose national organizations and federations, perversions of the original progressive consumer and reform leagues, dedicated to rooting out subversion and punishing disloyalty. With support from local and state law enforcement agencies, the National Security League and the Council of Defense fixed on new targets—the Non-Partisan League in North Dakota, which aimed at nothing more seditious than interest-group politics, and the People's Council of America for Peace and Democracy, a group of pacifists widely condemned as "traitors and fools." Within six months of Wilson's declaration of war, a rigid censorship, combined with political repression, had reached into the American press, schools and universities, the churches, and even the new movie industry.

A Pyramid of Repression
This mass popular reaction formed the base of a pyramid of repression supporting a middle range of official and semiofficial bodies, from citizens' councils to state administrative agencies such as the Minnesota Commission on Public Safety, which became a model for the rest of the country. Other states passed criminal syndicalism laws that were aimed primarily at left-wing dissenters but were also designed as dragnets for a variety of nonconformists. Soon the traditional American distinction between public and private had dissolved in a welter of competing patriotic agencies.

The federal government itself completed the apex of this national system of extralegalism through a number of agencies and activities. The chief agency was the Committee on Public Information, headed by progressive journalist George Creel and charged with mobilizing public opinion behind the war. Creel perfected the progressive technique of moral publicity and encouraged a voluntary censorship program. And he turned to the new public relations industry for a national core of opinion shapers, who launched a propaganda campaign of frightening proportions.

Another weapon in the government's domestic arsenal was an administrative technique inherited from prewar progressivism—deportation of undesirable aliens and radicals. The deportation procedure was a simple administrative process. Not courts but magistrates made the decision to deport undesirable aliens. As a result, maximum freedom was provided for administrators and minimum safeguards for the rights of the accused. This original procedure for the

The New York Stock Exchange at the Turn of the Century
"Wall Street" became the hated symbol of those leftwing opponents of the war and war profiteers.

swift removal of undesirables had been created by the Immigration Act of 1903, and the war simply gave widened scope for these summary actions.

The federal government's main contributions to the repression of basic liberties were the Espionage Act of 1917 and the Sedition Act of 1918. Like the Federalists' Alien and Sedition Acts of the 1790s,* these laws were twin declarations of bankruptcy by a society that had reached the limits of toleration. The Espionage Act dictated fines of up to $10,000 and twenty years in prison for anyone convicted of causing insubordination, mutiny, or disloyalty in the armed forces by "false reports or false statements." The law also empowered the postmaster general to withhold mailing privileges to newspapers and periodicals that were considered subversive. Wilson's postmaster general, Albert S. Burleson, turned this authority into a formidable weapon against dissent. With Wilson's knowledge, if not always with his approval, Burleson wielded discretionary power with a vengeance in banning socialist periodicals such as *The Masses* and Victor Berger's *Milwaukee Leader;* he even banned a single-tax journal for suggesting that more revenue be raised through taxation.

---

*For the Alien and Sedition Acts, see chapter 10, pp. 329–30.

The Sedition Act of 1918 was designed to close the few loopholes in the Espionage Act through which thousands of "spies" and "traitors" were presumed to have escaped. The new law provided punishment for anyone who should "utter, print, write or publish any disloyal, profane, scurrilous, or abusive language about the form of government in the United States, or the uniform of the Army or Navy" or any sentiments intended to bring the government or the military "into contempt, scorn, contumely, or disrepute."

More than 1,500 Americans were tried and more than 1,000 convicted under these laws. Senator Hiram Johnson pointed out that the government was simply warning, "You shall not criticize anything or anybody in the Government any longer or you shall go to jail." For example, Eugene Debs was convicted and sentenced to ten years in prison under the Sedition Act for telling a socialist audience that the master class causes wars while the subject class fights them. But most of the victims of this heresy hunting were ordinary people guilty of nothing worse than saying that John D. Rockefeller was a son of a bitch who helped start a capitalist war.

Administrative Agencies   In part, the war hysteria of the years 1917–19 was simply a deviation, a brief departure from good sense, and a betrayal of progressive ideals. But at a deeper level the excesses were growths—malignant, to be sure—of progressivism itself. Discretionary power vested in administrative agencies—a progressive innovation—provided flexibility and promptness but at the expense of more deliberate regular processes amenable to judicial oversight. The progressive device of administrative government, whose aim was to free policymakers and administrators from constant interference by the legislature, had its merits. But when it was applied to citizens' ideas and opinions rather than to administrative procedures, the new process revealed the evils of government action cut adrift from accountability and control.

At times the war crisis lowered the principle of administrative autonomy to the level of license. In the case of Postmaster General Burleson, for example, even the president was unable to limit misguided enthusiasm and the personal conviction that no American should ever be allowed "to say that this Government got into the war wrong. . . . It is a false statement," Burleson fumed, "a lie, and it will not be permitted." Such arbitrary power lodged either in the federal bureaucracy or in the lower levels of state and local administrations inevitably fostered an alarming national irresponsibility by subjecting opinion and expression to the whims and caprices of petty officials who were freed entirely, as one of them boasted, from "exaggerated sentimentalism [or] a misapplied reverence for legal axioms."

It would have been difficult in any case for Wilson's administration to have curbed the patriotic passions of an American generation preoccupied with rescuing national unity from a vigorous cultural pluralism. But the wartime policy of the federal government amounted to issuing hunting licenses to superpatriots to track down and destroy dissent—in pacifists, liberal reformers, socialists, anarchists, and also in many cultural as well as political radicals opposed to war. These dissenters were not simply outside the mainstream of the war effort. They were part of a more general movement, growing quickly after 1900, of what might be called cultural radicalism—a movement running counter to progressivism with deep roots in America's prewar experience. By 1917 a major shift in the artistic and intellectual life of the country had long been evident in a series of clashes, some symbolic and others real, between an inherited system of truth and the powerful, diverse forces of cultural modernism.

The Little Rebellion: Progressivism and the Challenge of Culture

On February 17, 1913, the International Exhibition of Modern Painting opened in the cavernous Sixty-ninth Regiment Armory in New York City. To the music of a military band, beneath rafters festooned with huge banners and pine boughs, visitors strolled through a maze of 1,600 paintings, drawings, prints, and pieces of sculpture. The Armory Show, two years in the planning, took for its motto "The New Spirit," which was emblazoned on a mammoth replica of the Revolutionary-era Massachusetts Pine Tree flag—a message that many American viewers translated as "the harbinger of universal anarchy."

The exhibition had originally been conceived as a strictly American affair, and it was actually dominated numerically by American work, which made up three-quarters of the show. The initial plans, however, had been scrapped for the more ambitious idea of a vast international retrospective tracing the rise of modernism from its nineteenth-century sources in Goya, Ingres, and Delacroix, through the French realist Courbet, to impressionism and the bewildering canvases of post-impressionists, expressionists, and cubists. It was not the dark, looming shapes of the American painter Albert Pinkham Ryder that outraged patrons, or the realistic cityscapes of the "New York Eight," with their conventional images and brushwork, but rather what one critic called "the imported ideology" of the new European artists—Picasso, Matisse, Brancusi, Picabia, Léger, Rouault, Kandinsky, Duchamp, and Lehmbruck. Their collective impact carried the force of revolution. Staid art critic Kenyon Cox admitted to spending "an appalling morning" at the show, where he had witnessed the "total destruction of the art of painting.... To have looked at it is to have passed through a pathological museum where the layman has no right to go. One feels that one has seen not an exhibition, but an exposure."

The Armory Show collected into a single public image the disparate meaning of European modernism. In the bold thin colors of Matisse's *The Red Studio* or the splashes of one of Kandinsky's *Improvisations* or the frozen motion of Duchamp's *Nude Descending a Staircase,* Americans viewed the results of a perceptual revolution that had transformed the European intellectual and artistic world and had now arrived in the United States. Here were the visible effects of a general revolt—embodied in the work of such controversial European cultural

Henri Matisse, *The Red Studio*, 1911
This painting, first shown in the United States at the Armory Show, outraged viewers who were used to scenes of social realism.

figures as Nietzsche, Bergson, Sorel, Freud, Ibsen, and Strindberg—against nineteenth-century positivism, with its faith in scientific objectivity. The new art was the all-too-apparent result of recent explorations into the unseen, the unknown, the irrational, and the relative, yielding new definitions of time, space, energy, force, and will. For those progressives who chose to examine the work of the modernists, the Armory Show took on the dimensions of a social crisis.

An Artistic Revolution

The crisis rose directly out of the challenge to the comfortable realism and moralism of the average educated American, who firmly believed in the solidity of the objective social world and in the power of "good art," whether in print or on canvas, to represent that world. Socially useful art, most progressives believed, was the art of representation. Progressivism was nourished by a strong sense of social reality—the belief that the world, after all, consisted of commonplace and everyday occurrences strung in orderly and predictable sequences. Progressivism had been born in the country and had moved to the city, and it relied on the moral code of an earlier rural society to make otherwise bewildering problems manageable. There was also a lingering idealism in the progressive outlook—Theodore Roosevelt called it "practical idealism"—that combined easily with newly discovered techniques of social analysis. These two halves of the progressive outlook were held together by the belief that science and the scientific method, baffling as they might seem to the layman, would ultimately establish the unity of truth and the fact of progress.

These social opinions supported a set of aesthetic preferences. The progressives' favorite novelist was the reliable William Dean Howells, who once (like so many progressives) had been a young man from the provinces who had come to the metropolis to make his way. Howells built a career and a considerable fortune as a novelist and an editor with his cautious, sensitive probings of modern issues: divorce and the disintegration of the family; economic inequality and the insecurities of a commercial existence; the decline of an older business ethic in a new world of bigness. Howells weighed all these complexities in terms of the loss of certainty among small-town Americans and the hope that it might somehow be restored. In his portraits of the puzzled editor Basil March in *A Hazard of New Fortunes* and of the confused businessman in *The Rise of Silas Lapham,* Howells offered recognizable modern types, and progressive readers could find their own problems stated and finally solved in his fiction. And when realism paled, there was always fantasy and that favorite fictional hero, Owen Wister's "Virginian," the unassuming yet self-assured cowboy untainted by corrupting commercialism.

Tolerance of the excessive, the outsized, and the grotesque was strictly limited by a psychology that insisted on the rational, the measurable, the predictable. Whatever lay beyond these borders was ignored or rejected as unhealthy or unclean—Frank Norris's examination of regression and bestialism in *McTeague,* Henry James's subtle studies of corruption, Mark Twain's experiment in determinism in *The Mysterious Stranger,* Theodore Dreiser's frank exploration of sexuality in *Sister Carrie.*

In the visual arts informed opinion had reluctantly come to terms with the so-called Ashcan School of New York painters, among them John Sloan, George Luks, and George Bellows, whose realistic paintings of street scenes and city types drew from the same sources as those of progressive reformers and writers. The New York Eight, as members of this group were also called, sought to encompass the whole city scene with their illustrators' techniques and documentary style. Most progressives understood and accepted the social realism of the Eight, for it was directly involved with the pictorial aspects of twentieth-century urban life. "The tramp sits on the edge of the curb," the Eight's spokesman, Robert Henri, explained. "He is huddled up. His body is thick. His underlip hangs. His eyes look fierce.... He is not beautiful, but he could well be the motive for a great and beautiful work of art." Progressives who were engaged in similar explorations of city life agreed with Henri, for they shared his insistence on "fundamental law" and those axioms "controlling all existence." By 1910 realism had broken the Genteel Tradition's grip on the American imagination without, however, dissolving its view of objective reality.

It was just this sense of the manageability of their world that gave progressives the confidence to reform and improve it. Experimenting with the new tools of social analysis helped sharpen the progressive method, but it also strengthened the belief that the world was plastic after all and could be molded into a controlled environment. The recent knowledge explosion in American universities had shaken but not destroyed the progressive idea that the great facts in life were simple.

This conviction that art and politics amounted to the same thing made the Armory Show a troubling spectacle for most American viewers. It threatened not simply their aesthetic preferences, but also their belief in the possibilities of planning and social control. The "detestable things" created by Picasso, Matisse, and Duchamp—"degraded, indecent, and insane," they were called—disclosed the lurking presence of the unpredictable and the ungovernable, of flux and formlessness. A Matisse painting reminded humorist Gelett Burgess of the havoc a "sanguinary" girl of eight, "half-crazed with gin," might wreak on a blank wall with a box of crayons. In choosing a revolutionary theme for their exhibition, the organizers of the Armory Show were only following the path their European counterparts had taken for more than a century. But American viewers took the show's political challenge literally. As one hostile critic announced: "The exploitation of a theory of discords, puzzles, ugliness, and clinical details is to art what anarchy is to society and the practitioners need not so much a critic as an alienist [psychiatrist]." Artistic madness would certainly lead to barbarism.

Criticism flowed naturally from aesthetic into political channels. "The United States is invaded by aliens," warned the archconservative critic Royal Cortissoz, "thousands of whom constitute so many acute perils to the health of the body politic. Modernism is of precisely the same heterogeneous alien origin and is imperiling the republic of art in the same way." The Armory Show, Cortissoz warned, was dominated "by types not yet fitted for their first papers in aesthetic naturalization—the makers of true Ellis Island art."

Proletarian Art: The Paterson Pageant   Modernism in the Armory Show presented most viewers with a symbolic dilemma: how to ensure the improvement of American society without underwriting revolution. Once again, as in all other matters concerning America, Theodore Roosevelt had the last word. "It is vitally necessary," the retired president reminded his followers, "to move forward to shake off the dead hand of the reactionaries; and yet we have to face the fact that there is apt to be a lunatic fringe among votaries of any forward movement." Still, the problem remained— how to give support to the sane and deny it to the dangerous. The political evidence was obvious. In New York City on a June evening in 1913, less than four months after the Armory Show, 1,000 silk workers from Paterson, New Jersey, stepped off the ferry and marched in a solid phalanx up Broadway and into Madison Square Garden. There, before a crowd of 15,000, they proceeded to reenact the events of their prolonged strike against mill owners. Spectators witnessed a new form of proletarian art—social drama as participatory ritual.

The Paterson Pageant
Workers, many of them women, march up Broadway to Madison Square Garden to participate in John Reed's pageant.

The Paterson Pageant was the brainchild of young radical journalist John Reed and a handful of socialist intellectuals and artists who dreamed of fashioning a new mass art out of working-class grievances and the formal protest of the intellectuals. The Paterson strike had been triggered by the mill owners' decision to increase the work load for unskilled silk weavers and dyers already living on the edge of destitution. Most of the workers in the Paterson dye houses and mills, some 25,000 in all, were new immigrants from Italy, Russia, and eastern Europe, a large number of them young girls earning an average wage of $6 or $7 a week. The IWW entered the town in the winter of 1913 to help organize this unpromising material around the immediate issues of shorter hours and higher wages. "Big Bill" Haywood, fresh from his triumph in the Lawrence, Massachusetts, textile workers' strike, joined the young Wobbly agitator Elizabeth Gurley Flynn and the romantic syndicalist Carlo Tresca in teaching the Paterson workers that it was "far better to starve fighting than to starve working." By February 1913 they had succeeded in uniting the unskilled workers and shutting down the town.

In trying to break the strike with its skilled workers, the AFL fed the progressive tendency to identify the immigrant with radicalism. Yet throughout the spring the strikers' ranks held firm. The mill owners fought back, stirring up hatred of "outside agitators" and enlisting the police in their efforts to break the strike. "There's a war in Paterson," John Reed told his fellow artists and intellectuals in Greenwich Village. "But it's a curious kind of war. All the violence is the work of one side—the Mill Owners."

Reed had reason to know. Like many of the Village socialists and radicals, he had made the Sunday excursion to Paterson to see for himself the clash between the workers and the bosses. He had been jailed, and he later returned to New York to compose his indictment of the owners for Max Eastman's *The Masses.* A cultural radical as yet without any clear sense of ideological direction, Reed dreamed of rallying artists and intellectuals to the strikers' side as the beginning of a permanent alliance for the radical reconstruction of American life. This was the idea he brought back to socialite Mabel Dodge's salon, the gathering place of New York's radical writers and intellectuals. Out of the sessions at Dodge's came the plans for a gigantic pageant to raise money for the strike fund and to educate liberals on working-class solidarity. Reed threw himself headlong into the project, spending eighteen hours a day on the script, drilling a thousand amateur performers into a theatrical company, designing the massive sets with the artist John Sloan and stage designer Robert Edmond Jones. By June he was ready, Sloan's huge factory scenes and red curtains were in place, and the cast was primed for performance.

The pageant caught the spirit of solidarity that Reed had sensed in Paterson. As it opened, throngs of workers moved down the center aisle to linger in front of the huge gray mills before entering to the sound of whirring machinery. Suddenly the chant began—"Strike! Strike!"—growing louder and more insistent until the workers came pouring out of the factory doors, and life moved outside the empty, dark mills. In front of these dead industrial husks, the workers reenacted the scenes of the strike—mass picketing, police harassment, the clash between strikers and the scabs in which a worker was killed, and finally the climactic funeral procession.

The audience, many of them workers admitted at 25 cents a seat, joined in booing the police, chanting strike slogans, and lustily singing the socialist anthem, the "Internationale." For a brief moment it seemed that Reed and the radical cultural critics had succeeded in forging new weapons for social justice out of the materials of mass art.

But life did not imitate art, and the pageant brought a cresting of radical hopes that quickly receded. The spectacle had originally been intended to replenish the strike fund, but actually it yielded a check for only $150. The 24,000 strikers who had not participated began to question the dubious honors bestowed on them by the intellectuals. "Bread was the need of the hour," Elizabeth Gurley Flynn complained, "and bread was not forthcoming." The gulf between art and politics could not be bridged by mere ceremony. The skilled

"Loop the Loop," Coney Island
Commercialized leisure provided escape from the workaday world.

workers broke ranks during the summer and returned to the mills. Then the mill owners, in a series of shop-by-shop settlements that conceded nothing to the unskilled workers, shattered their morale and routed the IWW leadership. By summer's end the Paterson workers were back on the job on their employers' terms. John Reed's script for the oppressed laborers of America acting out "the wretchedness of their lives and the glory of their revolt" had failed to close the distance between the intellectual radicals and the workers.

Instead, the gap between industrial workers and their bosses in the Progressive Era was being bridged by a new mass consumer culture. This rising popular culture, while it did not erase organized labor's list of grievances, softened workers' convictions of being exploited. By 1917, when the United States entered the war, a culture of commercialized leisure was already at work ministering to a mass American public's hunger for all kinds of fantasy—for toylands and dream worlds, remembered play and recovered childhoods—made possible by what the novelist Henry James called "a willing suspension of disbelief." The new counterculture of longing and fulfillment offered a full-blown alternative to the workaday progressive world of efficiency, routine, and time clocks with seductive promises of never-ending amusement. At Coney Island's Luna Park, in New York City's huge Hippodrome (the largest commercial theater in the world), and hundreds of music halls and vaudeville houses across the country, in baseball parks and football stadiums, along the gaudy midways ringing a succession of world's fairs and international expositions, in 25-cent movie palaces—an adversary world of carnival for the masses flourished. Here for a paying public stood a gigantic playground complete with dazzling lights and exotic colors, fake oriental architecture and circus barkers, outsized dolls and marionettes, sports celebrities, cartoon characters, and matinee idols, all providing temporary escape from the world of the ten-hour day. This new consumer culture counseled self-indulgence rather than self-denial, urged spending rather than saving, and promised mounting abundance. Twentieth-century consumer culture, aided by technology, mass marketing, and the sales pitch, continued to adjust—though it never succeeded in completely reconciling—American workers to their lot in a corporate economy. Genuine abundance still eluded the great majority of American workers in 1917, but the prophecy together with its supportive cultural fantasies continued to stimulate the appetites of millions of consumers in all classes of society.

Artists and Scientists: Critics of Progressivism

Other critics of progressivism before World War I perceived different divisions in American society and suggested other ways of closing them. In 1914 Walter Lippmann published his *Drift and Mastery,* and a year later Van Wyck Brooks brought out his bitter essay *America's Coming of Age.* Both authors demanded a reassessment of progressives' aims and aspirations. Lippmann and Brooks represented a new intellectual type, the liberal publicist directing criticism toward the progressive elite. They were neither journalists in a traditional sense nor philosophers, but rather saw themselves as cultural and social commentators whose task it was to direct the flow of American life through channels of publicity and informed criticism toward new national goals. They sought to lift their roles as critics to the realm of public power through their analysis of American society.

Brooks's Critique   Van Wyck Brooks, a recent graduate of Harvard, where he had studied under philosophers William James and George Santayana, was the chief spokesman for the "little renaissance" in American art and culture that swept across the country after 1912. By the time Brooks issued his challenge to progressivism, the signs of cultural rebellion were everywhere. Brooks joined the expanding circle of artists and intellectuals in Greenwich Village after a brief teaching career at Stanford University and at the Worker's Educational Association in Cambridge, England. In the Village he met Walter Lippmann, who urged him to contribute to the literary renaissance by closely examining the "noble dream" of American democratic culture in the light of the "actual limitations of experience." Brooks promptly obliged with what he called an address to his own "homeless generation" of intellectuals and would-be critics.

Brooks perceived a basic American duality in the cultural split between "highbrow" and "lowbrow"—a fatal division, he said, that had paralyzed the creative will of the nation for more than a century. He argued that the American impasse stemmed from the conflict between high-flown theory and the "catchpenny realities" of a business civilization. Between these poles lay a cultural wasteland in which no true community could thrive. Brooks traced the roots of this American schizophrenia to the original sin of Puritanism, "the all-influential fact in the history of the American mind." He attributed to Puritanism both the "fastidious refinement" of current tastes and the "opportunism" of American moneymakers.

Like the progressive historian Vernon L. Parrington, who was already at work compiling the materials for his *Main Currents of American Thought* that would document this view, Brooks presented his authors in sets of paired opposites: Jonathan Edwards and Benjamin Franklin; Henry Wadsworth Longfellow and Mark Twain; James Russell Lowell and Walt Whitman—figures on opposite sides of a chasm between literate and illiterate America. Brooks argued that throughout the nineteenth century the divorce of the real from the ideal had resulted in an "orgy of lofty examples, moralized poems, national anthems and baccalaureate sermons" until the average citizen was now "charged with all manner of ideal purities, ideal honorabilities, ideal femininities, flagwavings and skyscrapings of every sort." In the meantime the American landscape had become a stamping ground for every greedy commercial impulse of every last businessman who held that "society is fair prey for what he can get out of it."

Brooks pointed to the shortcomings of the progressive approach to reform. Progressivism, for all its moral certainties and good-government ideals, had failed to solve the fundamental problem of modern industrial society—the "invisible government" of business and the profit motive. So far, well-meaning progressive reformers' efforts to change American priorities had added up to nothing. Progressivism simply consolidated the rule of "commercialized men." Of what use was it, Brooks demanded, to tinker with political mechanisms or "do any of the other easy popular contemporary things" unless the quality of American life could also be improved?

Here Brooks reached the core of his critique. Meaningful betterment of American society would require more than rationalizing a business system, more than the cheerful cooperation of business and government, whether in the name of the New Nationalism or the New Freedom. All that would suffice now would be the massive shift of American energies from business and politics to psychology and art. Otherwise progressivism would fail in its mission to give America new life. When World War I broke out, Brooks still hoped for the cultural rebellion for which he spoke. Three years later, American entrance into the war broke these hopes on the rocks of the war state.

Lippmann's Analysis Walter Lippmann also saw a split in twentieth-century American life that progressivism had failed to repair. But his definition centered on the conflict between Victorian silences—what he called the "sterile tyranny of taboo"—inherited from the nineteenth century, and his own generation's desire "to be awake during their own lifetime." "Drift" was the result of the rule of old bogeys. "Mastery" meant applying the scientific method to politics. Like Brooks, although for different reasons, Lippmann faulted the progressives for their lack of rigorous thought. Although the New Nationalism had examined some of the worst abuses of industrialism, it still spoke the language of the old moralists. The New Freedom continued to make false promises of a return to free competition. "You would think that competitive commercialism was really a generous, chivalrous, high-minded stage of human culture," Lippmann scoffed, instead of "an antiquated, feeble, mean, and unimaginative way of dealing with the possibilities of modern industry." Lippmann agreed with Brooks on the need for relocating American energies outside politics, but he differed dramatically on the means. Unlike Brooks and the cultural radicals, he championed the cause of business consolidation and the rule of industrial statesmen who would go beyond politics by lifting decision making out of the marketplace to the level of scientific management. Whereas the cultural radicals hoped to destroy the rule of big business, Lippmann sought to rationalize and reform it. His aim was to create a truly cooperative society, neither strictly capitalistic nor wholly collectivist, but a new commonwealth composed of managers, workers, and consumers, each applying the instruments of measurement and control provided by modern science.

The Seven Arts and The New Republic   American entry into World War I threatened Van Wyck Brooks's plans for reconstructing American culture. But it brought a welcome test for Lippmann's pragmatic liberalism and his design for a businessmen's government. Brooks deplored the war as a betrayal of his dreams; Lippmann embraced it as a challenge. By 1917 these two critiques of progressivism had been institutionalized in two very different magazines: *The Seven Arts,* which Brooks and his cultural radical friends Randolph Bourne and James Oppenheim founded in 1916 and nursed through a year of shaky existence; and *The New Republic,* which Lippmann together with liberal nationalists Herbert Croly and Walter Weyl had launched in 1914. The war records of these two magazines testified to the divergent fates of cultural radicalism and liberal nationalism under emergency conditions.

The Seven Arts lasted just a year before the fervor of the patriots killed it. Brooks's mantle fell on the diminutive frame of Randolph Bourne, who more clearly than any of the other opponents of the war saw the coming defeat of "that America of youth and aspiration" standing below the battle. In "War and the Intellectuals," the most scathing of his attacks on Lippmann and the prowar liberals, Bourne ridiculed the "war technique" of liberal reform that had led the intellectuals to the illusion that they had willed the war "through sheer force of ideas." Bourne charged that in welcoming the war *The New Republic* editors had allied themselves with the least democratic forces in American society, those primitive interests that still were trumpeting notions of the national state and the doctrines of economic privilege. The war, Bourne concluded, provided an escape for progressives who had become prisoners of their own fantasies of the ordered society. The collapse of *The Seven Arts* after a year of lonely opposition to the war, along with Bourne's untimely death, marked the end of the cultural radical attempt to reconstruct progressivism by supplying it with higher values.

Lippmann and the other editors of *The New Republic* continued to cling to the belief that they could help direct a democratic war and write a liberal peace. The American entrance, Lippmann explained soon after Wilson's declaration of war, would prove "decisive in the history of the world": the United States could now proceed to "crystallize and make real the whole league of peace propaganda." Nor did he fear the effects of a war psychology on the prospects of liberalism. In October 1917 he offered his services to the administration and was appointed secretary of The Inquiry, Wilson's handpicked body of experts charged with preparing the American agenda for the peace table. Herbert Croly, who remained in his editorial post at *The New Republic,* quickly grew disillusioned as he realized the nature of the liberal impasse both at home and abroad. Lippmann's hopes for a liberal peace remained high. But eighteen months later, discouraged by the president's failure at the Paris Peace Conference and dubious now about the uses of war as a means of social reconstruction, Lippmann joined those "tired radicals" seeking to defeat the treaty.

The Ordeal of Woodrow Wilson

In his address to Congress on January 8, 1918—at the low point in the American war effort—Woodrow Wilson outlined the steps the United States and the Allies would have to take to ensure a postwar world "made fit to live in." Wilson presented his Fourteen Points as a blueprint for peacemaking drawn to his own progressive specifications. The central element in his thinking was the principle of "open covenants openly arrived at"—the extension of the New Freedom idea of moral publicity to international politics. A counterweight to this first point in Wilson's moral scales was the fourteenth, calling for "a general association of nations . . . formed under specific covenants for the purpose of affording mutual guarantees of political independence and territorial integrity to great and small states alike." The main substantive points in Wilson's utopian scheme included a general disarmament, complete freedom of the seas, fair adjustment of colonial claims in the interests of the peoples involved, and a series of specific provisions for drawing national boundaries in Europe on the basis of the language spoken in each region ("linguistic nationalism"). These were the lofty terms that Wilson, in the face of mounting opposition from his war partners, intended to impose at the peace table.

Problems with the Fourteen Points

In attempting to achieve his aims, Wilson was driven by circumstance, as well as by his own intensely moral nature, to make several costly miscalculations. Part of his trouble lay in the Fourteen Points themselves. What, for example, did his principle of national self-determination mean, and by what general formula could it be applied? What adjustments might be needed when linguistic nationalism failed to coincide with economic viability or military aims? Then, how could the new Soviet regime with an exportable totalitarian ideology, which had been established two months before, be given "an unhampered and unembarrassed opportunity" for political development? How, in short, could Wilson, as the representative of the only impartial power at the peace table, establish in each and every instance his claim to be the enlightened conscience of mankind?

A related set of problems concerned Wilson's political position at home. Who but himself—the president—he asked, could convert the Allies to his program and ensure the triumph of collective security? Determined to play the dominant role at the Paris conference, he insisted on making his peace program a partisan issue in the fall elections of 1918 by warning that a Republican victory would be a rejection of his leadership and vision. Republicans, who had already grown restive under the nonpartisan war policy, now retaliated by accusing Wilson himself of partisan dealings. In 1918 the Republicans regained control of both houses of Congress. If their victory did not quite mean a vote of no confidence, it did serve to warn Wilson that the spirit of party politics had been revived and would be decisive in settling the fate of his peace program.

Even more serious was Wilson's refusal to include Republican leaders among his advisers at the peace conference. Former President Taft, the 1916 Republican presidential nominee Charles Evans Hughes, and a number of other leading Republicans had expressed cautious interest in the idea of a League of Nations. But Wilson's calculated exclusion of these men from the American delegation to Paris isolated him from the moderate Republican internationalism he so desperately needed. On the eve of his departure for Europe in December 1918, there were already ominous signs of a growing presidential detachment from the realities of domestic politics, as Wilson began to retreat into the recesses of his moralistic nature. "Tell me what is right," he urged his advisers as he prepared for the conference, "and I'll fight for it." Wilson fought tenaciously, even heroically, for his Fourteen Points against overwhelming odds. But in forgetting the first rule of politics and ignoring the domestic disarray he had left behind, he fatally compromised his position.

Problems in Paris   In Paris the president confronted other national leaders who, as he came to realize with chagrin, spoke for their countrymen as he could not: David Lloyd George of Great Britain, Georges Clemenceau of France, and Vittorio Orlando of Italy. The Allies had suffered grievously during the war, and their leaders could count on unwavering support at home for a peace that would punish Germany—one that would assign all the war guilt to Germany, completely strip it of its colonial possessions, extract enormous reparations, and provide all the necessary safeguards against future aggression. To counter these narrow nationalistic aims, Wilson brought with him to Paris only the Fourteen Points and his vision of a new concert of power. Despite his initial popularity with the peoples of Europe, his lone voice became

The Council of Four
From left to right: Vittorio Orlando of Italy, David Lloyd George of England, Georges Clemenceau of France, Woodrow Wilson.

lost in the clamor of competing nationalisms. The American story of the peace deliberations was one of mounting frustration and a forced retreat from idealism.

The first of the Fourteen Points to be abandoned was the utopian concept of "open covenants." Soon after the conference began, the plenary sessions (open meetings of all delegations) gave way first to a Council of Ten, dominated by the heads of state and their foreign ministers, and then to a Council of Four, composed of Wilson, Lloyd George, Clemenceau, and Orlando, meeting behind closed doors. The press was barred from working sessions and became almost wholly dependent on news releases that were handed out after each plenary session. Wilson added to his problems of communication by withdrawing coldly from his colleagues on the council and ignoring most of his advisers, who complained of his aloofness. Removed from presidential oversight, the American staff floundered in confusion. Wilson announced that he had no desire "to have lawyers drafting the treaty of peace" and played a lone hand at Paris. He quickly exhausted his reserves of moral capital.

On a few of the specific issues of the peace settlement, Wilson was partially successful in moderating the extortionate demands of his partners. After an epic battle of wills with the cynical Clemenceau, who likened his adversary to Jesus

Christ and Moses bearing the Ten Commandments, Wilson forced France to agree to a multinational defense pact. But he gained this victory at the cost of the immediate return to France of Alsace-Lorraine,* French occupation of Germany's Rhineland, and huge reparations to be paid by Germany. On the question of the former German colonies, he abandoned the principle of "impartial adjustment" but salvaged his plan for a mandate system under League auspices. For Poland he secured a corridor to the sea at the expense of linguistic nationalism.† In constructing a new Austria out of the Austro-Hungarian empire, which had disintegrated at the end of the war, he presided over the transfer of some 200,000 German-speaking people to Italy in order to assure the latter of a militarily defensible frontier. When he refused to agree to a similar transfer to Italy of a strip of the Dalmatian coast—territory inhabited overwhelmingly by Yugoslavs—he brought on a major crisis by appealing for self-restraint directly to the Italian people over the heads of their representatives. This blunder only hardened Italian resolves and further discredited Wilson with his colleagues at the peace table. Self-determination of peoples speaking the same language—a legacy of nineteenth-century romantic nationalism—was violated at Paris as often as it was successfully applied.

But the president suffered his sharpest defeat on the question of reparations. France originally suggested the preposterous figure of $200 billion, and Britain seemed unwilling to settle for much less. Clemenceau and Lloyd George, bowing to heavy pressure from their respective publics, overrode Wilson's objections to their crippling demands and forced him to accept the inclusion of civilian damages and military pensions in the final assessment on Germany. The president, pushed beyond the limits of endurance, had become ill and confused. He agreed to the principle of massive repayments and allowed the fixing of specific amounts to be postponed. The Council of Four provided for a reparations commission, which in 1921 set the indemnity at $56 billion without regard for Germany's ability to pay or for the political consequences for the struggling new German republic.

The League of Nations   Throughout the agony of daily defeat, Wilson was sustained by his hopes for the League of Nations and the work of drafting the League Covenant. The League, he told himself, would correct the mistakes and make good the deficiencies of the peace settlement, to which it must be firmly tied. By tying the League closely to

---

*Alsace-Lorraine was a largely German-speaking region in eastern France that Germany had annexed in 1871, against the wishes of most of its inhabitants. The recovery of Alsace-Lorraine had been a primary French aim in World War I. Wilson would have preferred settling the issue by a plebiscite.

†The so-called Polish Corridor, a strip of territory assuring Poland access to the Baltic Sea, contained a large German minority unwilling to come under Polish rule. The corridor also cut the province of East Prussia off from the rest of Germany. The German-speaking port of Danzig (now Gdansk) was transformed into a free city under League of Nations auspices. In 1939 Hitler's demand for the return of Danzig and the Polish Corridor led to the outbreak of World War II.

the treaty,* the president hoped to get around his congressional opponents by presenting them with a complete package that they would have to accept or reject as a whole. He never seriously considered that they might succeed in destroying his great work.

Article X of the League Covenant became the great symbolic issue that eventually wrecked his dream. Article X provided that

> the members of the League undertake to respect and preserve as against external aggression the territorial integrity and existing political independence of all the Members of the League. In case of any such aggression or in case of any threat or danger of such aggression the Council shall advise upon the means by which this obligation shall be fulfilled.

For Wilson, Article X represented the triumph of moral force. The details of applying sanctions against future aggressors concerned him less than did the simple recognition by the nations of the world of his principle of collective security. This principle, at least, he had managed to rescue from the ruins of the treaty, and he meant to defend it at all costs.

The League of Nations, on which Wilson ultimately pinned all his hopes, in part represented the progressive idea of commission government applied to international politics. Like a federal commission designed to free policymaking from the whims of politicians, the League, together with its various branches and agencies, would provide the means of defusing international crises and resolving conflicts through arbitration. But in another and more profound sense, Wilson's League was simply the application of inherited nineteenth-century liberal principles and a doctrine of progress.

In the president's mind the League embodied old truths and moral principles. The most important of these was the belief that as American institutions and ideas reformed the rest of the world, and as the beneficent workings of trade and commerce gathered peoples together in harmony and abundance, the old selfish national interests would die out. Ultimately a worldwide legal community would arise in place of the discredited system of balance of power. Wilson had witnessed four years of international slaughter and had seen embittered nationalists at Versailles impose a savage, punishing peace on Germany, and he was convinced that the time had finally come for building such an international moral order. Although he was willing to concede much—and in fact had conspicuously failed to control the peace conference—he was not prepared to compromise on the League of Nations or on the role his country would have to play in its creation.

Wilson's utopian commitment led him to overlook two fundamental problems. The first resulted from attaching the League to the peace treaty. A second problem was that of intent. Was the League intended simply to enforce a victor's

---

*Actually, not one peace treaty was drawn up, but five. The Treaty of Versailles, which included the League Covenant, applied only to Germany; separate treaties were imposed on each of Germany's allies: Austria, Hungary, Bulgaria, and Turkey.

"When Johnny Comes Marching Home"
Fifteenth New York Regiment marching up Fifth Avenue, 1919.

peace, or would it work to adjust shifting balances of national power, incorporate new members including the defeated nations, and underwrite orderly change and development? No amount of Wilsonian rhetoric about "the general moral judgment of mankind" could obscure the basic uncertainty of purpose in the president's attempt to replace power relations with moral force.

The Red Scare Wilson returned to the United States in the summer of 1919 and found a nation already in the throes of reaction. The shadow of the Russian Revolution, which had fallen over the peace table, now lengthened across the Atlantic. The threat of revolution strengthened the forces of reaction everywhere in Europe as conservatives rushed to defend their states from the Bolshevik menace. The Soviet challenge seemed particularly frightening to Americans because it threatened their own revolutionary tradition. Russia was undergoing no mere political rebellion and rearrangement, sensibly completed and solicitous of property rights and personal liberties, but instead a vast social upheaval with a collectivist ideology that was the antithesis of Western capitalist democracy.

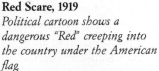

Red Scare, 1919
*Political cartoon shows a
dangerous "Red" creeping into
the country under the American
flag*

The American response to the new Soviet regime was twofold. First, the
Wilson administration undertook an abortive attempt to strengthen the counterrevolutionary forces in Russia by landing American troops (soon withdrawn) at
Murmansk in North Russia and Vladivostok in the Far East. These operations
were undertaken in conjunction with larger (but equally unsuccessful) British,
French, and Japanese interventions. Second, there was a tendency at home to see
"Reds" everywhere. By the summer of 1919, the so-called Red Scare had taken full
possession of the national imagination as a wartime fear of subversion was
suddenly turned into a dread of imminent revolution. In fact, two rival American
Communist parties were established in September 1919. (They united only in 1921
under pressure from Lenin.) One was led by left-wing defectors from the Socialist
party and the other by John Reed, recently returned from witnessing the Russian
Revolution, which he described dramatically in his book *Ten Days That Shook the
World.* Neither group attracted an important following, and Reed soon returned
to Russia, where he died in an epidemic and was buried in Red Square. Much
more significant was the widespread fear of radicalism. This fear branded as
subversive not only the tiny communist and IWW movements and the larger,
moderate Socialist party, but also liberal ideas in general, whether in art or
politics. All were met with strident protests against nonconformity and demands
for unconditional loyalty.

**Republicans Oppose
Wilson**
Wilson also felt the force of a congressional reaction
that had been building since the armistice. Mobilization for war had concentrated power in the executive
branch of the government, thus completing the political cycle that had begun
with Theodore Roosevelt's presidency. But now, with reconversion and demobi-

lization, the political pendulum began to swing the other way, as Congress moved firmly to reassert its control over foreign affairs as well as domestic policy.

Congressional resurgence had already become a highly partisan matter with the revival in the 1918 elections of the Republican party, which with forty-nine seats in the Senate now enjoyed a two-vote margin over the Democrats. Republicans could scarcely resist an opportunity to limit Wilson's power by modifying the terms of American participation in the new League of Nations. Republican leaders were also prepared to roll back wartime controls and curb the regulatory power of federal agencies, whose activities they now tended to equate with socialism. The League was only the most obvious issue with which the Republican party aimed to establish itself in the majority once again.

Yet the Republican members of the Senate remained divided on the question of accepting Wilson's treaty and American participation in the League. On the right of the party stood some dozen or fifteen "irreconcilables"—isolationists opposed to nearly any continued international involvement. At the other end of the spectrum were the "mild reservationists," who supported the League in principle but were concerned with the extent of Wilson's commitment to collective security and were anxious to limit it. Ranged between these two ideological poles were the "strong reservationists," making up the majority faction and led by Senator Henry Cabot Lodge. Lodge combined a cordial hatred of the president with a narrow nationalism that had not changed since the Spanish-American War. The "strong reservationists" were willing to consider United States participation in the League only on their own terms, and they were fully prepared to force on Wilson significant reservations limiting American commitments and making Congress rather than the president the final judge of their applicability.

Within his own party Wilson could count on solid internationalist support, but it was clear at the outset of the struggle that he would have to win a sizable majority of moderates away from Lodge in order to gain acceptance of his League of Nations. By July 1919 Wilson faced a formidable but not an impossible task, one that would require great patience and even greater flexibility.

For his part Lodge followed a clever strategy contrived to exploit every advantage over his opponent. He packed the Senate Foreign Relations Committee with his followers; he conducted lengthy hearings that gave voice to every conceivable opponent of the League; he courted right-wing businessmen like Henry Clay Frick and Andrew Mellon; and he loaded the treaty down with amendments. By fall his original forty-five amendments had been reduced to fourteen reservations—one for each of Wilson's initial Fourteen Points. The first reserved to the United States the sole right to decide whether it had fulfilled its obligations under the covenant, and it gave Congress the power to withdraw the United States from the League. The second, directed at the controversial Article X, was also aimed at Wilson's greatest weakness. It provided that the United States would accept no obligation to enforce the collective-security provisions of the covenant without the consent of Congress in each and every case. Other reservations rejected any mandates assignable to the United States, reserved the right to determine which questions involving American interests might be submitted to the League, and stipulated that the Monroe Doctrine was not to be subjected to international debate. Taken together, Lodge's reservations were significant but not crippling modifications, as the subsequent history of the League would show.

Yet, as Lodge hoped, Wilson believed otherwise. He consistently refused to make a realistic assessment of the situation. He was unwilling to discuss the specific circumstances under which the United States might be called on to apply sanctions—either economic or military—against other nations because he was convinced that full discussion in the forum of the League would make sanctions unnecessary. For him the real questions were simple: Was the United States prepared to make the significant moral gesture toward peace and international security? Would the American people see to it that the Senate carried out its obligation? Although the actual fight in the Senate grew complicated with proposals and counterproposals, amendments, reservations, and interpretations, the president's position remained essentially the one he had taken in presenting the treaty to the Senate: "The stage is set, the destiny disclosed.... We cannot turn back. We can only go forward, with lifted eyes and freshened spirit, to follow the vision."

Wilson's own vision led him away from Washington on an 8,000-mile tour of the nation, during which he gave forty speeches explaining to the American people the League's importance to their future security and welfare. In taking his case to the country, Wilson was violating one of his own rules. "The Senate," he once wrote, "is not...immediately sensitive to [public] opinion and is apt to grow, if anything, more stiff if pressure of that kind is brought to bear upon it." Now President Wilson ignored Professor Wilson's advice. His tour of the nation carried him farther and farther away from political reality and the problem of securing the Senate's consent. Although he referred frequently to specific issues and explained the limited nature of the American commitment, he returned to the theme of moral principle:

> You have no choice, my fellow citizens.... You cannot give a false gift.... Men are not going to stand it. There is nothing for any nation to lose whose purposes are right and whose cause is just.... The whole freedom of the world not only, but the whole peace of mind of the world, depends upon the choice of America.... I can testify to that.... The world will be absolutely in despair if America deserts it.

Worn out and distraught, collapsing under the weight of his moral mission, Wilson suffered a stroke in Pueblo, Colorado, on September 26, 1919, and was rushed back to Washington. A week later a second stroke left him paralyzed. Wilson in effect had spoken his last word on the treaty. Desperately ill, physically isolated from his followers and advisers, he was locked in a private moral world. Loyal Democrats received their presidential orders: vote to reject the treaty with the Lodge reservations. On November 19, 1919, by a vote of 39 for and 55 against, the Senate rejected the Treaty of Versailles with the reservations; the Democrats had dutifully joined with the irreconcilables to defeat it. Wilson still hoped to make the presidential election of 1920 the occasion of a giant referendum on the League. But his advisers, along with more objective observers, knew the fight was over. The president's dream was dead.

Domestic discord in the year 1919 mirrored the collapse of Wilson's moral world. A calendar of violence marked the decline of original progressive hopes:

> In January shipyard workers in Seattle struck for higher wages, organized a general strike, and paralyzed the city. At the mayor's request the federal government sent in the Marines.

> In May four hundred soldiers and sailors sacked the offices of a socialist newspaper, the New York *Call,* and beat up the staff.

> In the summer race riots erupted in twenty-five cities across the country; the most serious outbreak was in Chicago, where thirty-eight were killed and more than five hundred injured.

> In September the Boston police force struck for the right to unionize, and the city experienced a wave of looting and theft until leading businessmen and Harvard students restored order.

> In September 350,000 steelworkers struck for the right to unionize and for an eight-hour day.

> In November a mob in Centralia, Washington, dragged IWW agitator Wesley Everett from jail and castrated him before hanging him.

> In December agents of the Labor Department rounded up 249 Russian-born American communists and deported them to Finland.

There were Americans in 1919 who recalled Wilson's definition of the progressive task six years earlier as "the high enterprise of the new day.... Our duty is to cleanse, to reconsider, to correct the evil without impairing the good, to purify and humanize every process of our common life without weakening or sentimentalizing it." For those who remembered, there could be little doubt that the new day had ended.

CHRONOLOGY

1913	Armory Show in New York City. Paterson strike.
1914	World War I begins; Wilson declares American neutrality. "Ludlow Massacre"; National Guard attacks tent colony of strikers in Ludlow, Colorado, killing eleven women and two children.
1915	Germans declare unrestricted submarine warfare and sink *Lusitania* with loss of American lives.
1916	Wilson reelected, narrowly defeating Charles Evans Hughes. House-Grey Memorandum on United States efforts for negotiated peace.
1917	Germans resume unrestricted submarine warfare and United States enters war. Russian Revolution; "February Revolution," establishing provisional government; "October Revolution," engineered by Bolsheviks. Draft Act. Espionage Act. Purchase of Danish Virgin Islands. Creation of War Industries Board. First Pulitzer prizes awarded.
1918	Wilson's Fourteen Points, outlining administration's peace aims. United States troops at Belleau Wood. Saint Mihiel salient, first United States offensive. Meuse-Argonne offensive. Sedition Act, providing severe penalties for expressing "disloyal" opinions. Armistice; Germany defeated.
1919	*Schenck* v. *U.S.,* upholding Espionage Act and government curtailment of free speech during wartime. *Abrams* v. *U.S.,* upholding Sedition Act. Eighteenth Amendment (Volstead Act), prohibiting sale or manufacture of alcoholic beverages. Steel strike. Race riots in Chicago, East St. Louis, and Washington.
1920	Great Red Scare. Defeat of Versailles Treaty by Senate. Nineteenth Amendment gives vote to women. Warren G. Harding elected president, defeating James M. Cox and Eugene Debs.

SUGGESTED READINGS

There are two good surveys of American military conduct of the war: Edward M. Coffman, *The War to End Wars: The American Military Experience in World War I* (1968), and Russell F. Weigley, *The American Way of War* (1973). Ellis W. Hawley, *The Great War and the Search for a Modern Order: A History of the American People and Their Institutions, 1917–1933* (1979) traces the effects of the war on American social policy. Robert D. Cuff, *The War Industries Board* (1973) recounts the activities of a major administrative agency, and Maurine W. Greenwald, *Women, War and Work* (1980) surveys working women's war participation.

The years since World War II have seen a growing number of studies of American civil liberties during and after World War I. Beginning with Zechariah Chafee, *Free Speech in the*

United States (1941), the list includes Harry N. Scheiber, *The Wilson Administration and Civil Liberties, 1917–1921* (1960); Donald M. Johnson, *The Challenge to American Freedoms* (1963); H. C. Peterson and Gilbert Fite, *Opponents of the War, 1917–1918* (1957); William Preston, Jr., *Aliens and Dissenters: Federal Suppression of Radicals, 1903–1933* (1963); and Paul L. Murphy, *Red Scare: A Study of National Hysteria, 1919–1920* (1955). For accounts of wartime management of public opinion see Alfred E. Cornebise, *War as Advertised: The Four Minute Men and America's Crusade, 1917–1918* (1984); Carol S. Gruber, *Mars and Minerva: World War I and the Uses of Higher Learning in America* (1975); Stephen Vaughn, *Holding Fast the Inner Lines: Democracy, Nationalism, and the Committee on Public Information* (1980). David M. Kennedy, *Over Here: The First World War and American Society* (1980) is a highly readable account of the domestic war effort.

The immediate shock of war as experienced by artists and intellectuals is described in Stanley Cooperman, *World War I and the American Novel* (1967), and its lingering effects in Malcolm Cowley, *Exiles Return: A Literary Odyssey of the 1920's* (1951). Sam Hunter, *American Painting and Sculpture* (1959), and Barbara Rose, *American Art Since 1900: A Critical History* (1967), are good accounts of American art in the early twentieth century. For the Armory Show see Milton Brown, *The Story of the Armory Show* (1963); the best brief discussion of its revolutionary impact is Meyer Schapiro, "Rebellion in Art," in Daniel Aaron, ed., *America in Crisis* (1952).

The best approach to the intellectual history of the progressive years is through the writers themselves. Major works of social and political analysis, now considered classics, include Jane Addams, *Twenty Years at Hull House* (1910); Randolph Bourne, *Youth and Life* (1913), and a collection of Bourne's war pieces, *War and the Intellectuals* (1964), edited by Carl Resek; Louis Brandeis, *Other People's Money* (1914); Van Wyck Brooks, *America's Coming of Age* (1915); Charles H. Cooley, *Human Nature and the Social Order* (1922); Herbert Croly, *The Promise of American Life* (1909); John Dewey, *School and Society* (1899); W.E.B. Du Bois, *Souls of the Black Folk* (1903); Charlotte Perkins Gilman, *Women and Economics* (1898); Walter Lippmann, *Drift and Mastery* (1914); John Reed, *Insurgent Mexico* (1914), and *Ten Days That Shook the World* (1919); and Walter Weyl, *The New Democracy* (1912).

On the diplomacy of war and peacemaking, Arno J. Mayer, *Political Origins of the New Diplomacy, 1917–1918* (1959), and *Politics and Diplomacy of Peacemaking: Containment and Counterrevolution at Versailles, 1918–1919* (1967), are both ponderous and provocative. N. Gordon Levin, *Woodrow Wilson and World Politics: America's Response to War and Revolution* (1968), focuses on the presidential strategies, as does Warren Kuehl, *Seeking World Order: The United States and World Organization to 1920* (1969). Two older works by Thomas A. Bailey, *Woodrow Wilson and the Lost Peace* (1944) and *Woodrow Wilson and the Great Betrayal* (1945), detail Wilson's tragic postwar course. On the opposition to the League of Nations, Ralph A. Stone, *The Irreconcilables: The Fight Against the League of Nations* (1970), is admirable. John Garraty, *Henry Cabot Lodge* (1953), offers a sympathetic but not uncritical appraisal of Wilson's archenemy. Two recent accounts of Wilson and his chief adversary are Robert H. Ferrell, *Woodrow Wilson and World War I, 1917–1921* (1985) and William C. Widenor, *Henry Cabot Lodge and the Search for an American Foreign Policy* (1980). On Soviet-American relations, see George F. Kennan, *Russia Leaves the War* (1956), and *The Decision to Intervene: Prelude to Allied Intervention in the Bolshevik Revolution* (1958). Peter G. Filene, *Americans and the Soviet Experiment* (1967), and Christopher Lasch, *The American Liberals and the Russian Revolution* (1962), consider the varied American reactions to the Revolution. Betty M. Unterberger, *America's Siberian Expedition* (1956), explains the failure of that misguided action. Lawrence E. Gelfand, *The Inquiry: American Preparations for Peace, 1917–1919* (1963), is an account of the role of the president's advisers at Versailles. Paul Birdsall, *Versailles: Twenty Years After* (1973), assesses the peacemaking from the perspective of a later crisis.

APPENDIX

Declaration of Independence

IN CONGRESS, JULY 4, 1776

THE UNANIMOUS DECLARATION OF THE THIRTEEN UNITED STATES OF AMERICA

When, in the course of human events, it becomes necessary for one people to dissolve the political bands which have connected them with another, and to assume, among the powers of the earth, the separate and equal station to which the laws of nature and of nature's God entitle them, a decent respect to the opinions of mankind requires that they should declare the causes which impel them to the separation.

We hold these truths to be self-evident: That all men are created equal; that they are endowed by their Creator with certain unalienable rights; that among these are life, liberty, and the pursuit of happiness; that, to secure these rights, governments are instituted among men, deriving their just powers from the consent of the governed; that whenever any form of government becomes destructive of these ends, it is the right of the people to alter or to abolish it, and to institute new government, laying its foundation on such principles, and organizing its powers in such form, as to them shall seem most likely to effect their safety and happiness. Prudence, indeed, will dictate that governments long established should not be changed for light and transient causes; and accordingly all experience hath shown that mankind are more disposed to suffer, while evils are sufferable, than to right themselves by abolishing the forms to which they are accustomed. But when a long train of abuses and usurpations, pursuing invariably the same object, evinces a design to reduce them under absolute despotism, it is their right, it is their duty, to throw off such government, and to provide new guards for their future security. Such has been the patient sufferance of these colonies; and such is now the necessity which constrains them to alter their former systems of government. The history of the present King of Great Britain is a history of repeated injuries and usurpations, all having in direct object the establishment of an absolute tyranny over these states. To prove this, let facts be submitted to a candid world.

He has refused his assent to laws, the most wholesome and necessary for the public good.

He has forbidden his governors to pass laws of immediate and pressing importance, unless suspended in their operation till his assent should be obtained; and, when so suspended, he has utterly neglected to attend to them.

He has refused to pass other laws for the accommodation of large districts of people, unless those people would relinquish the right of representation in the legislature, a right inestimable to them, and formidable to tyrants only.

He has called together legislative bodies at places unusual, uncomfortable, and distant from the depository of their public records, for the sole purpose of fatiguing them into compliance with his measures.

i

He has dissolved representative houses repeatedly, for opposing, with manly firmness, his invasions on the rights of the people.

He has refused for a long time, after such dissolutions, to cause others to be elected; whereby the legislative powers, incapable of annihilation, have returned to the people at large for their exercise; the state remaining, in the mean time, exposed to all the dangers of invasions from without and convulsions within.

He has endeavored to prevent the population of these states; for that purpose obstructing the laws for naturalization of foreigners; refusing to pass others to encourage their migration hither, and raising the conditions of new appropriations of lands.

He has obstructed the administration of justice, by refusing his assent to laws for establishing judiciary powers.

He has made judges dependent on his will alone, for the tenure of their offices, and the amount and payment of their salaries.

He has erected a multitude of new offices, and sent hither swarms of officers to harass our people and eat out their substance.

He has kept among us, in times of peace, standing armies, without the consent of our legislatures.

He has affected to render the military independent of, and superior to, the civil power.

He has combined with others to subject us to a jurisdiction foreign to our constitution, and unacknowledged by our laws, giving his assent to their acts of pretended legislation:

For quartering large bodies of armed troops among us;

For protecting them, by a mock trial, from punishment for any murders which they should commit on the inhabitants of these states;

For cutting off our trade with all parts of the world;

For imposing taxes on us without our consent;

For depriving us, in many cases, of the benefits of trial by jury;

For transporting us beyond seas, to be tried for pretended offenses;

For abolishing the free system of English laws in a neighboring province, establishing therein an arbitrary government, and enlarging its boundaries, so as to render it at once an example and fit instrument for introducing the same absolute rule into these colonies;

For taking away our charters, abolishing our most valuable laws, and altering fundamentally the forms of our governments;

For suspending our own legislatures, and declaring themselves invested with power to legislate for us in all cases whatsoever.

He has abdicated government here, by declaring us out of his protection and waging war against us.

He has plundered our seas, ravaged our coasts, burned our towns, and destroyed the lives of our people.

He is at this time transporting large armies of foreign mercenaries to complete the works of death, desolation, and tyranny already begun with circumstances of cruelty and perfidy scarcely paralleled in the most barbarous ages, and totally unworthy the head of a civilized nation.

He has constrained our fellow-citizens, taken captive on the high seas, to bear arms against their country, to become the executioners of their friends and brethren, or to fall themselves by their hands.

He has excited domestic insurrection among us, and has endeavored to bring on the inhabitants of our frontiers the merciless Indian savages, whose known rule of warfare is an undistinguished destruction of all ages, sexes, and conditions.

In every stage of these oppressions we have petitioned for redress in the most humble terms; our repeated petitions have been answered only by repeated injury. A prince, whose character is thus marked by every act which may define a tyrant, is unfit to be the ruler of a free people.

Nor have we been wanting in our attentions to our British brethren. We have warned them, from time to time, of attempts by their legislature to extend an unwarrantable jurisdiction over us. We have reminded them of the circumstances of our emigration and settlement here. We have appealed to their native justice and magnanimity; and we have conjured them, by the ties of our common kindred, to disavow these usurpations, which would inevitably interrupt our connections and correspondence. They, too, have been deaf to the voice of justice and of consanguinity. We must, therefore, acquiesce in the necessity which denounces our separation, and hold them, as we hold the rest of mankind, enemies in war, in peace friends.

We, therefore, the representatives of the United States of America, in General Congress assembled, appealing to the Supreme Judge of the world for the rectitude of our intentions, do, in the name and by the authority of the good people of these colonies, solemnly publish and declare, that these United Colonies are, and of right ought to be, FREE AND INDEPENDENT STATES; that they are absolved from all allegiance to the British crown, and that all political connection between them and the state of Great Britain is, and ought to be, totally dissolved; and that, as free and independent states, they have full power to levy war, conclude peace, contract alliances, establish commerce, and do all other acts and things which independent states may of right do. And for the support of this declaration, with a firm reliance on the protection of Divine Providence, we mutually pledge to each other our lives, our fortunes, and our sacred honor.

JOHN HANCOCK [*President*]
[*and fifty-five others*]

Constitution of the United States of America

PREAMBLE

We the people of the United States, in order to form a more perfect union, establish justice, insure domestic tranquillity, provide for the common defense, promote the general welfare, and secure the blessings of liberty to ourselves and our posterity, do ordain and establish this Constitution for the United States of America.

Article I

Section 1. All legislative powers herein granted shall be vested in a Congress of the United States, which shall consist of a Senate and a House of Representatives.

Section 2. The House of Representatives shall be composed of members chosen every second year by the people of the several States, and the electors in each State shall have the qualifications requisite for electors of the most numerous branch of the State Legislature.

No person shall be a Representative who shall not have attained to the age of twenty-five years, and been seven years a citizen of the United States, and who shall not, when elected, be an inhabitant of that State in which he shall be chosen.

Representatives and direct taxes shall be apportioned among the several States which may be included within this Union, according to their respective numbers, *which shall be determined by adding to the whole number of free persons, including those bound to service for a term of years, and excluding Indians not taxed, three-fifths of all other persons.* The actual enumeration shall be made within three years after the first meeting of the Congress of the United States, and within every subsequent term of ten years, in such manner as they shall by law direct. The number of Representatives shall not exceed one for every thirty thousand, but each State shall have at least one Representative; *and until such enumeration shall be made, the State of New Hampshire shall be entitled to choose three, Massachusetts eight, Rhode Island and Providence Plantations one, Connecticut five, New York six, New Jersey four, Pennsylvania eight, Delaware one, Maryland six, Virginia ten, North Carolina five, South Carolina five, and Georgia three.*

When vacancies happen in the representation from any State, the Executive authority thereof shall issue writs of election to fill such vacancies.

The House of Representatives shall choose their Speaker and other officers; and shall have the sole power of impeachment.

NOTE: Passages that are no longer in effect are printed in italic type.

Section 3.   The Senate of the United States shall be composed of two Senators from each State, *chosen by the legislature thereof,* for six years; and each Senator shall have one vote.

Immediately after they shall be assembled in consequence of the first election, they shall be divided as equally as may be into three classes. The seats of the Senators of the first class shall be vacated at the expiration of the second year, of the second class at the expiration of the fourth year, and of the third class at the expiration of the sixth year, so that one-third may be chosen every second year; *and if vacancies happen by resignation or otherwise, during the recess of the legislature of any State, the Executive thereof may make temporary appointments until the next meeting of the legislature, which shall then fill such vacancies.*

No person shall be a Senator who shall not have attained to the age of thirty years, and been nine years a citizen of the United States, and who shall not, when elected, be an inhabitant of that State for which he shall be chosen.

The Vice President of the United States shall be President of the Senate, but shall have no vote, unless they be equally divided.

The Senate shall choose their other officers, and also a President *pro tempore,* in the absence of the Vice President, or when he shall exercise the office of President of the United States.

The Senate shall have the sole power to try all impeachments. When sitting for that purpose, they shall be on oath or affirmation. When the President of the United States is tried, the Chief Justice shall preside: and no person shall be convicted without the concurrence of two-thirds of the members present.

Judgment in cases of impeachment shall not extend further than to removal from office, and disqualification to hold and enjoy any office of honor, trust or profit under the United States; but the party convicted shall nevertheless be liable and subject to indictment, trial, judgment and punishment, according to law.

Section 4.   The times, places and manner of holding elections for Senators and Representatives shall be prescribed in each State by the legislature thereof; but the Congress may at any time by law make or alter such regulations, except as to the places of choosing Senators.

The Congress shall assemble at least once in every year, and such meeting *shall be on the first Monday in December, unless they shall by law appoint a different day.*

Section 5.   Each house shall be the judge of the elections, returns and qualifications of its own members, and a majority of each shall constitute a quorum to do business; but a smaller number may adjourn from day to day, and may be authorized to compel the attendance of absent members, in such manner, and under such penalties as each house may provide.

Each house may determine the rules of its proceedings, punish its members for disorderly behavior, and with the concurrence of two thirds, expel a member.

Each house shall keep a journal of its proceedings, and from time to time publish the same, excepting such parts as may in their judgment require secrecy; and the yeas and nays of the members of either house on any question shall, at the desire of one-fifth of those present, be entered on the journal.

Neither house, during the session of Congress, shall, without the consent of the other, adjourn for more than three days, nor to any other place than that in which the two houses shall be sitting.

Section 6.   The Senators and Representatives shall receive a compensation for their services, to be ascertained by law and paid out of the treasury of the United States. They shall in all cases except treason, felony and breach of the peace, be privileged from arrest during their attendance at the session of their respective houses, and in going to and returning from the same; and for any speech or debate in either house, they shall not be questioned in any other place.

No Senator or Representative shall, during the time for which he was elected, be appointed to any civil office under the authority of the United States, which shall have been created, or the emoluments whereof shall have been increased during such time; and no person holding any office under the United States shall be a member of either house during his continuance in office.

Section 7.   All bills for raising revenue shall originate in the House of Representatives; but the Senate may propose or concur with amendments as on other bills.

Every bill which shall have passed the House of Representatives and the Senate, shall, before it become a law, be presented to the President of the United States; if he approve he shall sign it, but if not he shall return it with objections to that house in which it originated, who shall enter the objections at large on their journal, and proceed to reconsider it. If after such reconsideration two-thirds of that house shall agree to pass the bill, it shall be sent, together with the objections, to the other house, by which it shall likewise be reconsidered, and, if approved by two-thirds of that house, it shall become a law. But in all such cases the votes of both houses shall be determined by yeas and nays, and the names of the persons voting for and against the bill shall be entered on the journal of each house respectively. If any bill shall not be returned by the President within ten days (Sundays excepted) after it shall have been presented to him, the same shall be a law, in like manner as if he had signed it, unless the Congress by their adjournment prevent its return, in which case it shall not be a law.

Every order, resolution, or vote to which the concurrence of the Senate and House of Representatives may be necessary (except on a question of adjournment) shall be presented to the President of the United States; and before the same shall take effect, shall be approved by him, or being disapproved by him, shall be repassed by two-thirds of the Senate and House of Representatives, according to the rules and limitations prescribed in the case of a bill.

Section 8.   The Congress shall have power

To lay and collect taxes, duties, imposts and excises, to pay the debts and provide for the common defense and general welfare of the United States; but all duties, imposts and excises shall be uniform throughout the United States;

To borrow money on the credit of the United States;

To regulate commerce with foreign nations, and among the several States, and with the Indian tribes;

To establish an uniform rule of naturalization, and uniform laws on the subject of bankruptcies throughout the United States;

To coin money, regulate the value thereof, and of foreign coin, and fix the standard of weights and measures;

To provide for the punishment of counterfeiting the securities and current coin of the United States;

To establish post offices and post roads;

To promote the progress of science and useful arts by securing for limited times to authors and inventors the exclusive right to their respective writings and discoveries;

To constitute tribunals inferior to the Supreme Court;

To define and punish piracies and felonies committed on the high seas and offenses against the law of nations;

To declare war, grant letters of marque and reprisal, and make rules concerning captures on land and water;

To raise and support armies, but no appropriation of money to that use shall be for a longer term than two years;

To provide and maintain a Navy;

To make rules for the government and regulation of the land and naval forces;

To provide for calling forth the militia to execute the laws of the Union, suppress insurrections, and repel invasions;

To provide for organizing, arming, and disciplining the militia, and for governing such part of them as may be employed in the service of the United States, reserving to the States respectively the appointment of the officers, and the authority of training the militia according to the discipline prescribed by Congress;

To exercise exclusive legislation in all cases whatsoever, over such district (not exceeding ten miles square) as may, by cession of particular States, and the acceptance of Congress, become the seat of government of the United States, and to exercise like authority over all places purchased by the consent of the legislature of the State, in which the same shall be, for erection of forts, magazines, arsenals, dock-yards, and other needful buildings;—and

To make all laws which shall be necessary and proper for carrying into execution the foregoing powers, and all other powers vested by this Constitution in the government of the United States, or in any department or officer thereof.

Section 9. *The migration or importation of such persons as any of the States now existing shall think proper to admit shall not be prohibited by the Congress prior to the year 1808; but a tax or duty may be imposed on such importation, not exceeding $10 for each person.*

The privilege of the writ of habeas corpus shall not be suspended, unless when in cases of rebellion or invasion the public safety may require it.

No bill of attainder or ex post facto law shall be passed.

No capitation, or other direct, tax shall be laid, unless in proportion to the census or enumeration herein before directed to be taken.

No tax or duty shall be laid on articles exported from any State.

No preference shall be given by any regulation of commerce or revenue to the ports of one State over those of another; nor shall vessels bound to, or from, one State, be obliged to enter, clear, or pay duties in another.

No money shall be drawn from the treasury, but in consequence of appropriations made by law; and a regular statement and account of the receipts and expenditures of all public money shall be published from time to time.

No title of nobility shall be granted by the United States: and no person holding any office of profit or trust under them, shall, without the consent of the Congress, accept of any present, emolument, office, or title, of any kind whatever, from any king, prince or foreign state.

Section 10. No State shall enter into any treaty, alliance, or confederation; grant letters of marque and reprisal; coin money; emit bills of credit; make anything but gold and silver coin a tender in payment of debts; pass any bill of attainder, ex post facto law, or law impairing the obligation of contracts, or grant any title of nobility.

No State shall, without the consent of Congress, lay any imposts or duties on imports or exports, except what may be absolutely necessary for executing its inspection laws: and the net produce of all duties and imposts, laid by any State on imports or exports, shall be for the use of the treasury of the United States; and all such laws shall be subject to the revision and control of the Congress.

No State shall, without the consent of Congress, lay any duty of tonnage, keep troops or ships of war in time of peace, enter into any agreement or compact with another State, or with a foreign power, or engage in war, unless actually invaded, or in such imminent danger as will not admit of delay.

Article II

Section 1. The executive power shall be vested in a President of the United States of America. He shall hold his office during the term of four years, and, together with the Vice-President, chosen for the same term, be elected as follows:

Each state shall appoint, in such manner as the legislature thereof may direct, a number of electors, equal to the whole number of Senators and Representatives to which the State may be entitled in the Congress; but no Senator or Representative, or person holding an office of trust or profit under the United States, shall be appointed an elector.

The electors shall meet in their respective States, and vote by ballot for two persons, of whom one at least shall not be an inhabitant of the same State with themselves. And they shall make a list of all the persons voted for, and of the number of votes for each; which list they shall sign and certify, and transmit sealed to the seat of government of the United States, directed to the President of the Senate. The President of the Senate shall, in the presence of the Senate and House of Representatives, open all the certificates, and the votes shall then be counted. The person having the greatest number of votes shall be the President, if such number be a majority of the whole number of electors appointed; and if there be more than one who have such majority, and have an equal number of votes, then the House of Representatives shall immediately choose by ballot one of them for President; and if no person have a majority, then from the five highest on the list said House shall in like manner choose the President. But in choosing the President, the votes shall be taken by States, the representation from each State having one vote; a quorum for this purpose shall consist of a member or members from two-thirds of the States, and a majority of all the States shall be necessary to a choice. In every case, after the choice of the President, the person having the greatest number of votes of the electors shall be the Vice-President. But if there should remain two or more who have equal votes, the Senate shall choose from them by ballot the Vice-President.

The Congress may determine the time of choosing the electors and the day on which they shall give their votes; which day shall be the same throughout the United States.

No person except a natural born citizen, *or a citizen of the United States at the time of the adoption of this Constitution,* shall be eligible to the office of President; neither shall any person be eligible to that office who shall not have attained to the age of thirty-five years, and been fourteen years a resident within the United States.

In case of the removal of the President from office or of his death, resignation, or inability to discharge the powers and duties of the said office, the same shall devolve on the

Vice-President, and the Congress may by law provide for the case of removal, death, resignation or inability, both of the President and Vice-President, declaring what officer shall then act as President, and such officer shall act accordingly, until the disability be removed, or a President shall be elected.

The President shall, at stated times, receive for his services a compensation, which shall neither be increased nor diminished during the period for which he shall have been elected, and he shall not receive within that period any other emolument from the United States, or any of them.

Before he enter on the execution of his office, he shall take the following oath or affirmation:—"I do solemnly swear (or affirm) that I will faithfully execute the office of the President of the United States, and will to the best of my ability preserve, protect and defend the Constitution of the United States."

Section 2.   The President shall be commander in chief of the army and navy of the United States, and of the militia of the several States, when called into the actual service of the United States; he may require the opinion, in writing, of the principal officer in each of the executive departments, upon any subject relating to the duties of their respective offices, and he shall have power to grant reprieves and pardons for offenses against the United States, except in cases of impeachment.

He shall have power, by and with the advice and consent of the Senate, to make treaties, provided two-thirds of the Senators present concur; and he shall nominate, and by and with the advice and consent of the Senate, shall appoint ambassadors, other public ministers and consuls, judges of the Supreme Court, and all other officers of the United States, whose appointments are not herein otherwise provided for, and which shall be established by law; but Congress may by law vest the appointment of such inferior officers, as they think proper, in the President alone, in the courts of law, or in the heads of departments.

The President shall have power to fill up all vacancies that may happen during the recess of the Senate, by granting commissions which shall expire at the end of their next session.

Section 3.   He shall from time to time give to the Congress information of the state of the Union, and recommend to their consideration such measures as he shall judge necessary and expedient; he may, on extraordinary occasions, convene both houses, or either of them, and in case of disagreement between them, with respect to the time of adjournment, he may adjourn them to such time as he shall think proper; he shall receive ambassadors and other public ministers; he shall take care that the laws be faithfully executed, and shall commission all the officers of the United States.

Section 4.   The President, Vice-President and all civil officers of the United States shall be removed from office on impeachment for, and on conviction of, treason, bribery, or other high crimes and misdemeanors.

Article III

Section 1.   The judicial power of the United States shall be vested in one Supreme Court, and in such inferior courts as the Congress may from time to time ordain and establish.

The judges, both of the Supreme and inferior courts, shall hold their offices during good behavior, and shall, at stated times, receive for their services a compensation which shall not be diminished during their continuance in office.

Section 2.   The judicial power shall extend to all cases, in law and equity, arising under this Constitution, the laws of the United States, and treaties made, or which shall be made, under their authority;—to all cases affecting ambassadors, other public ministers and consuls;—to all cases of admiralty and maritime jurisdiction;—to controversies to which the United States shall be a party;—to controversies between two or more States;— *between a State and citizens of another State;*—between citizens of different States;— between citizens of the same State claiming lands under grants of different States, and between a State, or the citizens thereof, and foreign states, citizens or subjects.

In all cases affecting ambassadors, other public ministers and consuls, and those in which a State shall be party, the Supreme Court shall have original jurisdiction. In all the other cases before mentioned, the Supreme Court shall have appellate jurisdiction, both as to law and fact, with such exceptions, and under such regulations, as the Congress shall make.

The trial of all crimes, except in cases of impeachment, shall be by jury; and such trial shall be held in the State where said crimes shall have been committed; but when not committed within any State, the trial shall be at such place or places as the Congress may by law have directed.

Section 3.   Treason against the United States shall consist only in levying war against them, or in adhering to their enemies, giving them aid and comfort. No person shall be convicted of treason unless on the testimony of two witnesses to the same overt act, or on confession in open court.

The Congress shall have power to declare the punishment of treason, but no attainder of treason shall work corruption of blood, or forfeiture except during the life of the person attainted.

Article IV

Section 1.   Full faith and credit shall be given in each State to the public acts, records, and judicial proceedings of every other State. And the Congress may by general laws prescribe the manner in which such acts, records, and proceedings shall be proved, and the effect thereof.

Section 2.   The citizens of each State shall be entitled to all privileges and immunities of citizens in the several States.

A person charged in any State with treason, felony, or other crime, who shall flee from justice, and be found in another State, shall on demand of the executive authority of the State from which he fled, be delivered up, to be removed to the State having jurisdiction of the crime.

No person held to service or labor in one State, under the laws thereof, escaping into another, shall, in consequence of any law or regulation therein, be discharged from such service or labor, but shall be delivered up on claim of the party to whom such service or labor may be due.

Section 3.   New States may be admitted by the Congress into this Union; but no new State shall be formed or erected within the jurisdiction of any other State; nor any State be formed by the junction of two or more States, or parts of States, without the consent of the legislatures of the States concerned as well as of the Congress.

The Congress shall have power to dispose of and make all needful rules and regulations respecting the territory or other property belonging to the United States; and nothing in this Constitution shall be so construed as to prejudice any claims of the United States, or of any particular State.

Section 4.   The United States shall guarantee to every State in this Union a republican form of government, and shall protect each of them against invasion; and on application of the legislature, or of the executive (when the legislature cannot be convened), against domestic violence.

Article V

The Congress, whenever two-thirds of both houses shall deem it necessary, shall propose amendments to this Constitution, or, on the application of the legislatures of two-thirds of the several States, shall call a convention for proposing amendments, which, in either case, shall be valid to all intents and purposes, as part of this Constitution, when ratified by the legislatures of three-fourths of the several States, or by conventions in three-fourths thereof, as the one or the other mode of ratification may be proposed by the Congress; provided *that no amendents which may be made prior to the year one thousand eight hundred and eight shall in any manner affect the first and fourth clauses in the ninth section of the first article;* and that no State, without its consent, shall be deprived of its equal suffrage in the Senate.

Article VI

All debts contracted and engagements entered into, before the adoption of this Constitution, shall be as valid against the United States under this Constitution, as under the Confederation.

This Constitution, and all the laws of the United States which shall be made in pursuance thereof; and all treaties made, or which shall be made, under the authority of the United States, shall be the supreme law of the land; and the judges in every State shall be bound thereby, anything in the Constitution or laws of any State to the contrary notwithstanding.

The Senators and Representatives before mentioned, and the members of the several State legislatures, and all executive and judicial officers, both of the United States and of the several States, shall be bound by oath or affirmation to support this Constitution; but no religious test shall ever be required as a qualification to any office or public trust under the United States.

Article VII

The ratification of the conventions of nine States shall be sufficient for the establishment of this Constitution between the States so ratifying the same.

Done in convention by the unanimous consent of the States present, the seventeenth day of September in the year of our Lord one thousand seven hundred and eighty-seven and of the Independence of the United States of America the twelfth. In witness whereof we have hereunto subscribed our names.

[Signed by]
G° WASHINGTON
Presidt and Deputy from Virginia
[*and thirty-eight others*]

Amendments to the Constitution

Article I*

Congress shall make no law respecting an establishment of religion, or prohibiting the free exercise thereof; or abridging the freedom of speech, or of the press; or the right of the people peaceably to assemble, and to petition the government for a redress of grievances.

Article II

A well-regulated militia being necessary to the security of a free State, the right of the people to keep and bear arms shall not be infringed.

Article III

No soldier shall, in time of peace, be quartered in any house without the consent of the owner, nor in time of war, but in a manner to be prescribed by law.

Article IV

The right of the people to be secure in their persons, houses, papers, and effects, against unreasonable searches and seizures, shall not be violated, and no warrants shall issue but upon probable cause, supported by oath or affirmation, and particularly describing the place to be searched, and the persons or things to be seized.

Article V

No person shall be held to answer for a capital, or otherwise infamous crime, unless on a presentment or indictment of a grand jury, except in cases arising in the land or naval forces, or in the militia, when in actual service in time of war or public danger; nor shall any person be subject for the same offence to be twice put in jeopardy of life or limb; nor shall be compelled in any criminal case to be a witness against himself, nor be deprived of

---

*The first ten Amendments (Bill of Rights) were adopted in 1791.

life, liberty, or property, without due process of law; nor shall private property be taken for public use without just compensation.

Article VI

In all criminal prosecutions, the accused shall enjoy the right to a speedy and public trial, by an impartial jury of the State and district wherein the crime shall have been committed, which district shall have been previously ascertained by law, and to be informed of the nature and cause of the accusation; to be confronted with the witnesses against him; to have compulsory process for obtaining witnesses in his favor, and to have the assistance of counsel for his defence.

Article VII

In suits at common law, where the value in controversy shall exceed twenty dollars, the right of trial by jury shall be preserved, and no fact tried by a jury shall be otherwise re-examined in any court of the United States, than according to the rules of the common law.

Article VIII

Excessive bail shall not be required, nor excessive fines imposed, nor cruel and unusual punishments inflicted.

Article IX

The enumeration in the Constitution, of certain rights, shall not be construed to deny or disparage others retained by the people.

Article X

The powers not delegated to the United States by the Constitution, nor prohibited by it to the States, are reserved to the States respectively, or to the people.

Article XI
[Adopted 1798]

The judicial power of the United States shall not be construed to extend to any suit in law or equity, commenced or prosecuted against one of the United States by citizens of another State, or by citizens or subjects of any foreign state.

Article XII
[Adopted 1804]

The electors shall meet in their respective States, and vote by ballot for President and Vice-President, one of whom, at least, shall not be an inhabitant of the same State with themselves; they shall name in their ballots the person voted for as President, and in distinct ballots the person voted for as Vice-President, and they shall make distinct lists of all persons voted for as President, and of all persons voted for as Vice-President, and of the number of votes for each, which lists they shall sign and certify, and transmit to the seat of government of the United States, directed to the President of the Senate;—The President of the Senate shall, in the presence of the Senate and House of Representatives, open all the certificates and the votes shall then be counted;—the person having the greatest number of votes for President shall be the President, if such number be a majority of the whole number of electors appointed; and if no person have such majority, then from the persons having the highest numbers not exceeding three on the list of those voted for as President, the House of Representatives shall choose immediately, by ballot, the President. But in choosing the President, the votes shall be taken by States, the representation from each State having one vote; a quorum for this purpose shall consist of a member or members from two-thirds of the States, and a majority of all the States shall be necessary to a choice. And if the House of Representatives shall not choose a President whenever the right of choice shall devolve upon them, before *the fourth day of March* next following, then the Vice-President shall act as President, as in the case of the death or other constitutional disability of the President.

The person having the greatest number of votes as Vice-President shall be the Vice-President, if such a number be a majority of the whole number of electors appointed; and if no person have a majority, then from the two highest numbers on the list the Senate shall choose the Vice-President; a quorum for the purpose shall consist of two-thirds of the whole number of Senators, and a majority of the whole number shall be necessary to a choice. But no person constitutionally ineligible to the office of President shall be eligible to that of Vice-President of the United States.

Article XIII
[*Adopted 1865*]

Section 1.   Neither slavery nor involuntary servitude, except as a punishment for crime whereof the party shall have been duly convicted, shall exist within the United States, or any place subject to their jurisdiction.

Section 2.   Congress shall have power to enforce this article by appropriate legislation.

Article XIV
[*Adopted 1868*]

Section 1.   All persons born or naturalized in the United States, and subject to the jurisdiction thereof, are citizens of the United States and of the State wherein they reside. No State shall make or enforce any law which shall abridge the privileges or immunities of citizens of the United States; nor shall any State deprive any person of life, liberty, or property, without due process of law; nor deny to any person within its jurisdiction the equal protection of the laws.

Section 2.   Representatives shall be apportioned among the several States according to their respective numbers, counting the whole number of persons in each State, excluding Indians not taxed. But when the right to vote at any election for the choice of Electors for President and Vice-President of the United States, Representatives in Congress, the executive and judicial officers of a State, or the members of the legislature thereof, is denied to any of the male inhabitants of such State, being twenty-one years of age and citizens of the United States, or in any way abridged, except for participation in rebellion, or other crime, the basis of representation therein shall be reduced in the proportion which the number of such male citizens shall bear to the whole number of male citizens twenty-one years of age in such State.

Section 3.   No person shall be a Senator or Representative in Congress, or Elector of President and Vice-President, or hold any office, civil or military, under the United States, or under any State, who, having previously taken an oath, as a member of Congress, or as an officer of the United States, or as a member of any State legislature, or as an executive or judicial officer of any State, to support the Constitution of the United States, shall have engaged in insurrection or rebellion against the same, or given aid or comfort to the enemies thereof. Congress may, by a vote of two-thirds of each house, remove such disability.

Section 4.   The validity of the public debt of the United States, authorized by law, including debts incurred for payment of pensions and bounties for services in suppressing insurrection or rebellion, shall not be questioned. But neither the United States nor any State shall assume or pay any debt or obligation incurred in aid of insurrection or rebellion against the United States, or any claim for the loss of emancipation, of any slave; but all such debts, obligations, and claims shall be held illegal and void.

Section 5.   The Congress shall have the power to enforce, by appropriate legislation, the provisions of this article.

Article XV
[Adopted 1870]

Section 1.   The right of citizens of the United States to vote shall not be denied or abridged by the United States or by any State on account of race, color, or previous condition of servitude.

Section 2.   The Congress shall have power to enforce this article by appropriate legislation.

Article XVI
[Adopted 1913]

The Congress shall have power to lay and collect taxes on incomes, from whatever source derived, without apportionment among the several States, and without regard to any census or enumeration.

Article XVII
[Adopted 1913]

Section 1.   The Senate of the United States shall be composed of two Senators from each State, elected by the people thereof, for six years; and each Senator shall have one vote. The electors in each State shall have the qualifications requisite for electors of [voters for] the most numerous branch of the State legislatures.

Section 2. When vacancies happen in the representation of any State in the Senate, the executive authority of such State shall issue writs of election to fill such vacancies: Provided, that the Legislature of any State may empower the executive thereof to make temporary appointments until the people fill the vacancies by election as the Legislature may direct.

Section 3. This amendment shall not be so construed as to affect the election or term of any Senator chosen before it becomes valid as part of the Constitution.

Article XVIII
[Adopted 1919; Repealed 1933]

Section 1. *After one year from the ratification of this article the manufacture, sale, or transportation of intoxicating liquors within, the importation thereof into, or the exportation thereof from the United States and all territory subject to the jurisdiction thereof, for beverage purposes, is hereby prohibited.*

Section 2. *The Congress and the several States shall have concurrent power to enforce this article by appropriate legislation.*

Section 3. *This article shall be inoperative unless it shall have been ratified as an amendment to the Constitution by the legislatures of the several States, as provided by the Constitution, within seven years from the date of the submission thereof to the States by the Congress.*

Article XIX
[Adopted 1920]

Section 1. The right of citizens of the United States to vote shall not be denied or abridged by the United States or by any State on account of sex.

Section 2. The Congress shall have the power to enforce this article by appropriate legislation.

Article XX
[Adopted 1933]

Section 1. The terms of the President and Vice-President shall end at noon on the 20th day of January, and the terms of Senators and Representatives at noon on the 3d day of January, of the years in which such terms would have ended if this article had not been ratified; and the terms of their succesors shall then begin.

Section 2. The Congress shall assemble at least once in every year, and such meeting shall begin at noon on the 3d day of January, unless they shall by law appoint a different day.

Section 3. If, at the time fixed for the beginning of the term of the President, the President-elect shall have died, the Vice-President-elect shall become President. If a

President shall not have been chosen before the time fixed for the beginning of his term, or if the President-elect shall have failed to qualify, then the Vice-President-elect shall act as President until a President shall have qualified; and the Congress may by law provide for the case wherein neither a President-elect nor a Vice-President-elect shall have qualified, declaring who shall then act as President, or the manner in which one who is to act shall be selected, and such persons shall act accordingly until a President or Vice-President shall have qualified.

Section 4. The Congress may by law provide for the case of the death of any of the persons from whom the House of Representatives may choose a President whenever the right of choice shall have devolved upon them, and for the case of the death of any persons from whom the Senate may choose a Vice-President whenever the right of choice shall have devolved upon them.

Section 5. Sections 1 and 2 shall take effect on the 15th day of October following the ratification of this article.

Section 6. This article shall be inoperative unless it shall have been ratified as an amendment to the Constitution by the Legislatures of three-fourths of the several States within seven years from the date of its submission.

Article XXI
[*Adopted 1933*]

Section 1. The eighteenth article of amendment to the Constitution of the United States is hereby repealed.

Section 2. The transportation or importation into any State, Territory, or Possession of the United States for delivery or use therein of intoxicating liquors, in violation of the laws thereof, is hereby prohibited.

Section 3. This article shall be inoperative unless it shall have been ratified as an amendment to the Constitution by conventions in the several States, as provided in the Constitution, within seven years from the date of submission thereof to the States by the Congress.

Article XXII
[*Adopted 1951*]

Section 1. No person shall be elected to the office of President more than twice, and no person who has held the office of President, or acted as President, for more than two years of a term to which some other person was elected President shall be elected to the office of President more than once. But this article shall not apply to any person holding the office of President when this article was proposed by the Congress, and shall not prevent any person who may be holding the office of President, or acting as President, during the term within which this article becomes operative from holding the office of President or acting as President during the remainder of such term.

Section 2. This article shall be inoperative unless it shall have been ratified as an amendment to the Constitution by the legislatures of three-fourths of the several States within seven years from the date of its submission to the States by the Congress.

Article XXIII
[Adopted 1961]

Section 1. The District constituting the seat of Government of the United States shall appoint in such manner as the Congress may direct:

A number of electors of President and Vice-President equal to the whole number of Senators and Representatives in Congress to which the District would be entitled if it were a State, but in no event more than the least populous State; they shall be in addition to those appointed by the States, but they shall be considered for the purposes of the election of President and Vice-President, to be electors appointed by a State; and they shall meet in the District and perform such duties as provided by the twelfth article of amendment.

Section 2. The Congress shall have the power to enforce this article by appropriate legislation.

Article XXIV
[Adopted 1964]

Section 1. The right of citizens of the United States to vote in any primary or other election for President or Vice-President, for electors for President or Vice-President, or for Senator or Representative in Congress, shall not be denied or abridged by the United States or any State by reason of failure to pay any poll tax or other tax.

Section 2. The Congress shall have the power to enforce this article by appropriate legislation.

Article XXV
[Adopted 1967]

Section 1. In case of the removal of the President from office or of his death or resignation, the Vice-President shall become President.

Section 2. Whenever there is a vacancy in the office of the Vice-President, the President shall nominate a Vice-President who shall take office upon confirmation by a majority vote of both Houses of Congress.

Section 3. Whenever the President transmits to the President pro tempore of the Senate and the Speaker of the House of Representatives his written declaration that he is unable to discharge the powers and duties of his office, and until he transmits to them a written declaration to the contrary, such powers and duties shall be discharged by the Vice-President as Acting President.

Section 4. Whenever the Vice-President and a majority of either the principal officers of the executive departments or of such other body as Congress may by law provide, transmit to the President pro tempore of the Senate and the Speaker of the House of Representatives their written declaration that the President is unable to discharge the powers and duties of his office, the Vice-President shall immediately assume the powers and duties of the office as Acting President.

Thereafter, when the President transmits to the President pro tempore of the Senate and the Speaker of the House of Representatives his written declaration that no inability exists, he shall resume the powers and duties of his office unless the Vice-President and a majority of either the principal officers of the executive department[s] or of such other body as Congress may by law provide, transmit within four days to the President pro tempore of the Senate and the Speaker of the House of Representatives their written declaration that the President is unable to discharge the powers and duties of his office. Thereupon Congress shall decide the issue, assembling within forty-eight hours for that purpose if not in session. If the Congress, within twenty-one days after receipt of the latter written declaration, or, if Congress is not in session, within twenty-one days after Congress is required to assemble, determines by two-thirds vote of both Houses that the President is unable to discharge the powers and duties of his office, the Vice-President shall continue to discharge the same as Acting President; otherwise, the President shall resume the powers and duties of his office.

Article XXVI
[Adopted 1971]

Section 1. The right of citizens of the United States, who are 18 years of age or older, to vote shall not be denied or abridged by the United States or by any State on account of age.

Section 2. The Congress shall have power to enforce this article by appropriate legislation.

Presidential Elections*

Election	Candidates	Parties	Popular Vote	Electoral Vote
1789	**George Washington**	No party designations		69
	John Adams			34
	Minor Candidates			35
1792	**George Washington**	No party designations		132
	John Adams			77
	George Clinton			50
	Minor Candidates			5
1796	**John Adams**	Federalist		71
	Thomas Jefferson	Democratic-Republican		68
	Thomas Pinckney	Federalist		59
	Aaron Burr	Democratic-Republican		30
	Minor Candidates			48
1800	**Thomas Jefferson**	Democratic-Republican		73
	Aaron Burr	Democratic-Republican		73
	John Adams	Federalist		65
	Charles C. Pinckney	Federalist		64
	John Jay	Federalist		1
1804	**Thomas Jefferson**	Democratic-Republican		162
	Charles C. Pinckney	Federalist		14
1808	**James Madison**	Democratic-Republican		122
	Charles C. Pinckney	Federalist		47
	George Clinton	Democratic-Republican		6
1812	**James Madison**	Democratic-Republican		128
	DeWitt Clinton	Federalist		89
1816	**James Monroe**	Democratic-Republican		183
	Rufus King	Federalist		34
1820	**James Monroe**	Democratic-Republican		231
	John Q. Adams	Independent Republican		1

*Candidates receiving less than 1% of the popular vote are omitted. Before the Twelfth Amendment (1804) the Electoral College voted for two presidential candidates, and the runner-up became vice-president. Basic figures are taken primarily from *Historical Statistics of the United States, 1789–1945* (1949), pp. 288–90; *Historical Statistics of the United States, Colonial Times to 1957* (1960), pp. 682–83; and *Statistical Abstract of the United States, 1969* (1969), pp. 355–57.

Election	Candidates	Parties	Popular Vote	Electoral Vote
1824	**John Q. Adams** (Min.)*	Democratic-Republican	108,740	84
	Andrew Jackson	Democratic-Republican	153,544	99
	William H. Crawford	Democratic-Republican	46,618	41
	Henry Clay	Democratic-Republican	47,136	37
1828	**Andrew Jackson**	Democratic	647,286	178
	John Q. Adams	National Republican	508,064	83
1832	**Andrew Jackson**	Democratic	687,502	219
	Henry Clay	National Republican	530,189	49
	William Wirt	Anti-Masonic ⎫		7
	John Floyd	National Republican ⎬	33,108	11
1836	**Martin Van Buren**	Democratic	762,678	170
	William H. Harrison	Whig ⎫		73
	Hugh L. White	Whig ⎪		26
	Daniel Webster	Whig ⎬	736,656	14
	W. P. Mangum	Whig ⎭		11
1840	**William H. Harrison**	Whig	1,275,016	234
	Martin Van Buren	Democratic	1,129,102	60
1844	**James K. Polk** (Min.)*	Democratic	1,337,243	170
	Henry Clay	Whig	1,299,062	105
	James G. Birney	Liberty	62,300	
1848	**Zachary Taylor** (Min.)*	Whig	1,360,099	163
	Lewis Cass	Democratic	1,220,544	127
	Martin Van Buren	Free Soil	291,263	
1852	**Franklin Pierce**	Democratic	1,601,274	254
	Winfield Scott	Whig	1,386,580	42
	John P. Hale	Free Soil	155,825	
1856	**James Buchanan** (Min.)*	Democratic	1,838,169	174
	John C. Frémont	Republican	1,341,264	114
	Millard Fillmore	American	874,534	8
1860	**Abraham Lincoln** (Min.)*	Republican	1,866,452	180
	Stephen A. Douglas	Democratic	1,375,157	12
	John C. Breckinridge	Democratic	847,953	72
	John Bell	Constitutional Union	590,631	39
1864	**Abraham Lincoln**	Union	2,213,665	212
	George B. McClellan	Democratic	1,802,237	21
1868	**Ulysses S. Grant**	Republican	3,012,833	214
	Horatio Seymour	Democratic	2,703,249	80
1872	**Ulysses S. Grant**	Republican	3,597,132	286
	Horace Greeley	Democratic and Liberal Republican	2,834,125	66

*"Min." indicates minority president—one receiving less than 50% of all popular votes.

Election	Candidates	Parties	Popular Vote	Electoral Vote
1876	**Rutherford B. Hayes** (Min.)*	Republican	4,036,298	185
	Samuel J. Tilden	Democratic	4,300,590	184
1880	**James A. Garfield** (Min.)*	Republican	4,454,416	214
	Winfield S. Hancock	Democratic	4,444,952	155
	James B. Weaver	Greenback-Labor	308,578	
1884	**Grover Cleveland** (Min.)*	Democratic	4,874,986	219
	James G. Blaine	Republican	4,851,981	182
	Benjamin F. Butler	Greenback-Labor	175,370	
	John P. St. John	Prohibition	150,369	
1888	**Benjamin Harrison** (Min.)*	Republican	5,439,853	233
	Grover Cleveland	Democratic	5,540,309	168
	Clinton B. Fisk	Prohibition	249,506	
	Anson J. Streeter	Union Labor	146,935	
1892	**Grover Cleveland** (Min.)*	Democratic	5,556,918	277
	Benjamin Harrison	Republican	5,176,108	145
	James B. Weaver	People's	1,041,028	22
	John Bidwell	Prohibition	264,133	
1896	**William McKinley**	Republican	7,104,779	271
	William J. Bryan	Democratic	6,502,925	176
1900	**William McKinley**	Republican	7,207,923	292
	William J. Bryan	Democratic; Populist	6,358,133	155
	John C. Woolley	Prohibition	208,914	
1904	**Theodore Roosevelt**	Republican	7,623,486	336
	Alton B. Parker	Democratic	5,077,911	140
	Eugene V. Debs	Socialist	402,283	
	Silas C. Swallow	Prohibition	258,536	
1908	**William H. Taft**	Republican	7,678,908	321
	William J. Bryan	Democratic	6,409,104	162
	Eugene V. Debs	Socialist	420,793	
	Eugene W. Chafin	Prohibition	253,840	
1912	**Woodrow Wilson** (Min.)*	Democratic	6,293,454	435
	Theodore Roosevelt	Progressive	4,119,538	88
	William H. Taft	Republican	3,484,980	8
	Eugene V. Debs	Socialist	900,672	
	Eugene W. Chafin	Prohibition	206,275	
1916	**Woodrow Wilson** (Min.)*	Democratic	9,129,606	277
	Charles E. Hughes	Republican	8,538,221	254
	A. L. Benson	Socialist	585,113	
	J. F. Hanly	Prohibition	220,506	
1920	**Warren G. Harding**	Republican	16,152,200	404
	James M. Cox	Democratic	9,147,353	127
	Eugene V. Debs	Socialist	919,799	
	P. P. Christensen	Farmer-Labor	265,411	

*"Min." indicates minority president—one receiving less than 50% of all popular votes.

Election	Candidates	Parties	Popular Vote	Electoral Vote
1924	**Calvin Coolidge**	Republican	15,725,016	382
	John W. Davis	Democratic	8,386,503	136
	Robert M. La Follette	Progressive	4,822,856	13
1928	**Herbert C. Hoover**	Republican	21,391,381	444
	Alfred E. Smith	Democratic	15,016,443	87
1932	**Franklin D. Roosevelt**	Democratic	22,821,857	472
	Herbert C. Hoover	Republican	15,761,841	59
	Norman Thomas	Socialist	881,951	
1936	**Franklin D. Roosevelt**	Democratic	27,751,597	523
	Alfred M. Landon	Republican	16,679,583	8
	William Lemke	Union, etc.	882,479	
1940	**Franklin D. Roosevelt**	Democratic	27,244,160	449
	Wendell L. Willkie	Republican	22,305,198	82
1944	**Franklin D. Roosevelt**	Democratic	25,602,504	432
	Thomas E. Dewey	Republican	22,006,285	99
1948	**Harry S Truman** (Min.)*	Democratic	24,105,812	303
	Thomas E. Dewey	Republican	21,970,065	189
	J. Strom Thurmond	States' Rights Democratic	1,169,063	39
	Henry A. Wallace	Progressive	1,157,172	
1952	**Dwight D. Eisenhower**	Republican	33,936,234	442
	Adlai E. Stevenson	Democratic	27,314,992	89
1956	**Dwight D. Eisenhower**	Republican	35,590,472	457
	Adlai E. Stevenson	Democratic	26,022,752	73
1960	**John F. Kennedy** (Min.)*	Democratic	34,226,731	303
	Richard M. Nixon	Republican	34,108,157	219
1964	**Lyndon B. Johnson**	Democratic	43,129,484	486
	Barry M. Goldwater	Republican	27,178,188	52
1968	**Richard M. Nixon** (Min.)*	Republican	31,785,480	301
	Hubert H. Humphrey, Jr.	Democratic	31,275,166	191
	George C. Wallace	American Independent	9,906,473	46
1972	**Richard M. Nixon**	Republican	45,767,218	520
	George S. McGovern	Democratic	28,357,668	17
1976	**Jimmy Carter**	Democratic	40,276,040	297
	Gerald R. Ford	Republican	38,532,630	241
1980	**Ronald W. Reagan**	Republican	43,899,248	489
	Jimmy Carter	Democratic	35,481,435	49
1984	**Ronald W. Reagan**	Republican	54,451,521	525
	Walter F. Mondale	Democratic	37,565,334	13
1988	**George H. W. Bush**	Republican	47,946,422	426
	Michael S. Dukakis	Democratic	41,016,429	112

*"Min." indicates minority president—one receiving less than 50% of all popular votes.

Presidents and Vice-Presidents

Term	President	Vice-President
1789–1793	George Washington	John Adams
1793–1797	George Washington	John Adams
1797–1801	John Adams	Thomas Jefferson
1801–1805	Thomas Jefferson	Aaron Burr
1805–1809	Thomas Jefferson	George Clinton
1809–1813	James Madison	George Clinton (d. 1812)
1813–1817	James Madison	Elbridge Gerry (d. 1814)
1817–1821	James Monroe	Daniel D. Tompkins
1821–1825	James Monroe	Daniel D. Tompkins
1825–1829	John Quincy Adams	John C. Calhoun
1829–1833	Andrew Jackson	John C. Calhoun (resigned 1832)
1833–1837	Andrew Jackson	Martin Van Buren
1837–1841	Martin Van Buren	Richard M. Johnson
1841–1845	William H. Harrison (d. 1841) John Tyler	John Tyler
1845–1849	James K. Polk	George M. Dallas
1849–1853	Zachary Taylor (d. 1850) Millard Fillmore	Millard Fillmore
1853–1857	Franklin Pierce	William R. D. King (d. 1853)
1857–1861	James Buchanan	John C. Breckinridge
1861–1865	Abraham Lincoln	Hannibal Hamlin
1865–1869	Abraham Lincoln (d. 1865) Andrew Johnson	Andrew Johnson
1869–1873	Ulysses S. Grant	Schuyler Colfax
1873–1877	Ulysses S. Grant	Henry Wilson (d. 1875)
1877–1881	Rutherford B. Hayes	William A. Wheeler
1881–1885	James A. Garfield (d. 1881) Chester A. Arthur	Chester A. Arthur
1885–1889	Grover Cleveland	Thomas A. Hendricks (d. 1885)
1889–1893	Benjamin Harrison	Levi P. Morton
1893–1897	Grover Cleveland	Adlai E. Stevenson
1897–1901	William McKinley	Garret A. Hobart (d. 1899)
1901–1905	William McKinley (d. 1901) Theodore Roosevelt	Theodore Roosevelt

Term	President	Vice-President
1905–1909	Theodore Roosevelt	Charles W. Fairbanks
1909–1913	William H. Taft	James S. Sherman (d. 1912)
1913–1917	Woodrow Wilson	Thomas R. Marshall
1917–1921	Woodrow Wilson	Thomas R. Marshall
1921–1925	Warren G. Harding (d. 1923) Calvin Coolidge	Calvin Coolidge
1925–1929	Calvin Coolidge	Charles G. Dawes
1929–1933	Herbert C. Hoover	Charles Curtis
1933–1937	Franklin D. Roosevelt	John N. Garner
1937–1941	Franklin D. Roosevelt	John N. Garner
1941–1945	Franklin D. Roosevelt	Henry A. Wallace
1945–1949	Franklin D. Roosevelt (d. 1945) Harry S Truman	Harry S Truman
1949–1953	Harry S Truman	Alben W. Barkley
1953–1957	Dwight D. Eisenhower	Richard M. Nixon
1957–1961	Dwight D. Eisenhower	Richard M. Nixon
1961–1965	John F. Kennedy (d. 1963) Lyndon B. Johnson	Lyndon B. Johnson
1965–1969	Lyndon B. Johnson	Hubert H. Humphrey, Jr.
1969–1974	Richard M. Nixon (resigned 1974)	Spiro T. Agnew (resigned 1973); Gerald R. Ford
1974–1977	Gerald R. Ford	Nelson A. Rockefeller
1977–1981	Jimmy Carter	Walter F. Mondale
1981–1985	Ronald W. Reagan	George H. W. Bush
1985–1989	Ronald W. Reagan	George H. W. Bush
1989–	George H. W. Bush	J. Danforth Quayle

Growth of U.S. Population and Area

Census	Population	Percent of Increase over Preceding Census	Land Area, Square Miles	Population per Square Mile
1790	3,929,214		867,980	4.5
1800	5,308,483	35.1	867,980	6.1
1810	7,239,881	36.4	1,685,865	4.3
1820	9,638,453	33.1	1,753,588	5.5
1830	12,866,020	33.5	1,753,588	7.3
1840	17,069,453	32.7	1,753,588	9.7
1850	23,191,876	35.9	2,944,337	7.9
1860	31,443,321	35.6	2,973,965	10.6
1870	39,818,449	26.6	2,973,965	13.4
1880	50,155,783	26.0	2,973,965	16.9
1890	62,947,714	25.5	2,973,965	21.2
1900	75,994,575	20.7	2,974,159	25.6
1910	91,972,266	21.0	2,973,890	30.9
1920	105,710,620	14.9	2,973,776	35.5
1930	122,775,046	16.1	2,977,128	41.2
1940	131,669,275	7.2	2,977,128	44.2
1950	150,697,361	14.5	2,974,726*	50.7
†1960	178,464,236	18.4	2,974,726	59.9
1970	204,765,770	14.7	2,974,726	68.8
1980	226,504,825	10.6	2,974,726	76.1
1990	249,632,692††	10.2	2,974,726	83.9

*As remeasured in 1940.

†Not including Alaska (pop. 226,167) and Hawaii (632,772).

††As released by U.S. Census Bureau, December 26, 1990. Critics of the census count have estimated that this figure may have undercounted the U.S. population by as much as 5 million persons.

ILLUSTRATION CREDITS

The following abbreviations are used for some sources from which several illustrations were obtained:
AAS–American Antiquarian Society. BA–The Bettmann Archive. BB–Brown Brothers. CP–Culver Pictures. DPH/SI–Division of Political History, Smithsonian Institution. GC–Granger Collection, New York. LC–Library of Congress. NA–National Archives. NPG/SI–National Portrait Gallery, Smithsonian Institution. SI–Smithsonian Institution. UPI/BN–UPI Bettmann Newsphotos.

Part 1   p. 1, LC.

Chapter 1   p. 9, LC; p. 13, Bureau of Public Roads, Department of Commerce; p. 16, LC; p. 19, LC; p. 21, Museum of American Textile History; p. 23, Collection of Business Americana, SI; p. 28, National Life Insurance Company, Montpelier, Vermont; p. 33, Woolaroc Museum, Bartlesville, Oklahoma.

Chapter 2   p. 48, LC; p. 54, Francis A. Countway Library of Medicine, Harvard University; pp. 56, 59, LC; p. 69, Division of Graphic Arts, SI; pp. 71, 73, LC; p. 75, National Museum of American Art, Washington, D. C./Art Resource, New York; p. 76, Munson-Williams-Proctor Institute, Museum of Art, Utica, New York; p. 77, NPG/SI, gift of anonymous donor.

Chapter 3   p. 83, United States National Museum, Washington, D. C.; pp. 86, 88, 90, 92, LC; p. 94, DPH/SI; p. 95, LC; p. 97, Division of Domestic Life, SI; p. 103, Harvard College Library; pp. 106, 110, LC.

Chapter 4   p. 120, LC; p. 123, NPG/SI; p. 126, LC; p. 127, NPG/SI, Gift of J. William Middendorf II; p. 130, NA; p. 135, Division of Cultural History, SI; pp. 136, 138, LC; p. 143, DPH/SI.

Chapter 5   pp. 157, 158, LC; p. 161, U.S. Signal Corps Photo, NA; p. 167, LC; p. 169 (top), Boston Public Library; p. 169 (bottom), AAS.

Chapter 6   p. 177, AAS; pp. 179, 182, LC; p. 185, The Metropolitan Museum of Art, Gift of I. N. Phelps Stokes, Edward S. Hawes, Alice Mary Hawes, Marion Augusta Hawes, 1937; p. 191, DPH/SI; p. 198, Print Collection, Miriam & Ira D. Wallach Division of Art, Prints and Photographs, The New York Public Library, Astor, Lenox and Tilden Foundations; p. 204, Illinois State Historical Society; p. 205, NPG/SI; p. 207, Kansas Historical Society, Topeka, Kansas; p. 209, LC.

Part 2   p. 215, LC.

Chapter 7   pp. 219, 221, 228 (right), LC; p. 228 (left), Eleanor S. Brockenbrough Library, The Museum of the Confederacy, Richmond, Virginia; p. 229, Chicago Historical Society; p. 238, LC; p. 245, NA.

Chapter 8   pp. 250, 265, 266, 268, LC; p. 278, Valentine Museum, Richmond, Virginia; pp. 279, 281, LC.

Chapter 9   pp. 291, 293, 294, 308, 310, 314, 315, LC; p. 318, R. B. Hayes Presidential Center, Fremont, Ohio.

Chapter 10   pp. 325, 338, LC; p. 343 (top), DPH/SI; p. 343 (bottom), NW; p. 347, LC; p. 349, DPH/SI.

Part 3   p. 353, LC.

Chapter 11   p. 359, SI; p. 360, LC; p. 365 (top), NA; p. 365 (bottom), LC; p. 368, LC; p. 369, LC; p. 387, Texas State Archives; p. 388, Nebraska State Historical Society; p. 391, LC; p. 392, University of Washington; pp. 394, 401, LC.

Chapter 12   p. 419, Pennell Collection, University of Kansas; p. 423, DPH/SI; p. 425, LC; p. 432, DPH/SI; pp. 435, 443, NW; p. 445, DPH/SI; p. 457 (top), BB; p. 457 (bottom), DPH/SI.

Chapter 13   p. 466, UPI/BN; pp. 471, 474, LC; p. 481, CP; p. 483, BB; p. 485, UPI/BN; p. 490, LC; p. 495, *Colliers,* June, 1905.

Chapter 14   p. 504, LC; p. 508, BB; p. 511, Lewis W. Hine Collection, United States History, Local History and Genealogy Division, The New York Public Library, Astor, Lenox and Tilden Foundations; pp. 516, 518, LC; p. 523, CP; pp. 525, 527, 529, LC.

Chapter 15   p. 544 (top), LC; p. 544 (bottom), CP; p. 548, LC; p. 556 (top), GC; p. 556 (bottom), BA; pp. 563 (top and bottom), 566, LC.

Chapter 16   p. 573 (top), U. S. Air Force Photographic Collection, National Air and Space Museum, SI; p. 573 (bottom), NA; p. 576, NA; p. 577, CP; p. 580 (top), LC; p. 580 (bottom), NA; pp. 583, 585, LC; p. 588, The Museum of Modern Art, New York; p. 591, BA; p. 593, LC; p. 599, NA; p. 602, LC; p. 603, GC.

INDEX